The Jewish Bible *and the* Christian Bible

Julio Trebolle Barrera

The Jewish Bible
and the Christian Bible

AN INTRODUCTION TO THE
HISTORY OF THE BIBLE

Translated from the Spanish by
Wilfred G.E. Watson

BRILL   EERDMANS

1998   Leiden   Grand Rapids, Michigan
        New York   Cambridge, U.K.
        Köln

BS
445
.T6813
1998

This book has been translated with the financial assistance of the Dirección General del Libro y Bibliotecas of the Ministerio de Cultura, Madrid, Spain.

Original title: *La Biblia judía y la Biblia cristiana*, Copyright © 1993 by Editorial Trotta SA, Madrid, Spain.

English edition Copyright © 1998 by Koninklijke Brill NV, Leiden, The Netherlands.

Published jointly 1998 by Brill Academic Publishers
P.O. Box 9000, 2300 PA Leiden, The Netherlands, and
Wm. B. Eerdmans Publishing Company
255 Jefferson Ave. S.E., Grand Rapids, Michigan 49503.

All rights reserved. No part of this publication may be reproduced, translated, stored in a retrieval system, or transmitted in any form or by any means, electronic, mechanical, photocopying, recording or otherwise, without prior written permission from the publisher.

Authorization to photocopy items for internal or personal use is granted by Brill provided that the appropriate fees are paid directly to The Copyright Clearance Center, 222 Rosewood Drive, Suite 910, Danvers MA 01923, USA. Fees are subject to change.

Printed in the United States of America

Brill ISBN 90 04 10888 2 (cloth)
Brill ISBN 90 04 10889 0 (paperback)
Eerdmans ISBN 0 8028 3830 8 (cloth)
Eerdmans ISBN 0 8028 4473 1 (paperback)

Library of Congress Cataloging-in-Publication Data
Trebolle Barrera, Julio C.
[La Biblia judía y la Biblia cristiana. English]
The Jewish Bible and the Christian Bible: an introduction to the
history of the Bible / by Julio Trebolle Barrera; translated by
Wilfred G.E. Watson.
p.   cm.
Includes bibliographical references and index.
Brill ISBN 90 04 10888 2 (cloth : alk. paper)
Brill ISBN 90 04 10889 0 (pbk. : alk. paper)
Eerdmans ISBN 0 8028 3830 8 (cloth : alk. paper)
Eerdmans ISBN 0 8028 4473 1 (pbk. : alk. paper)
1. Bible—History. I. Title.
BS445.T6813 1997
220'.09—dc21   97-23769
                       CIP

Die Deutsche Bibliothek – CIP-Einheitsaufnahme
Trebolle Barrera, Julio:
The Jewish Bible and the Christian Bible : an introduction to the
history of the Bible / by Julio Trebolle Barrera. Transl. by Wilfred G.
E. Watson. – Leiden ; New York ; Köln : Brill, 1997
Einheitssacht.: La Biblia judía y la Biblia cristiana <span.>
ISBN 90–04–10888–2

Design: Bert Arts BNO

Contents

128947

Note
Each chapter in this book is preceded by its own detailed table of contents.

Note to the Revised English Edition

This translation includes a revised and updated version of the text for the sections with the headings «The Dead Sea Scrolls» and «Developments of the canon outside the canon: Parabiblical literature». I would like to thank Professor Florentino García Martínez (Groningen) for the text he made available to me earlier, now published as «Literatura exegética» and «Literatura parabíblica» in *Literatura judía intertestamentaria*, eds., G. Aranda Pérez – F. García Martínez – M. Pérez Fernández, Estella 1996, 87–192.

JULIO TREBOLLE BARRERA

Translator's Note

This project has taken two years to complete and includes a considerable amount of new and corrected material supplied by the author. I now wish to thank Brill for their friendly cooperation over this period and in particular, Professor Julio Trebolle, who invited me to Madrid for a week of intensive translation work, which was interpersed with more leisurely activities including a memorable visit to Toledo.

WILFRED G. E. WATSON

Foreword

After writing almost exclusively research studies with only a very restricted readership, I have felt the need and above all have had the great pleasure to write a book which attempts to be in the nature of a «textbook» or «reference book», and also in large measure a book with wide circulation, intended for a more general public. This work arises from that research which suggested many ramifications that are developed here.

I ignored the advice of a friend and colleague who warned me: «Don't write a book like this, least of all for students». In recent years, especially in the universities of the United States, university teaching and large circulation have been sacrificed on the altar of pure research, which gives the professor more prestige and allows him greater access to the funds required to secure academic work. From this perspective, writing books for students or for the general public is time wasted or at least time stolen from research.

The professor has often ceased to be a professor. He becomes a researcher who at most imparts to his doctoral students the methods and results of his research. If, at the behest of the administration, he is required to give more general courses, he focuses his attention on very specific topics, leaving the student to acquire for himself the general information to be found in current «Introductions» and in the monographs available. As a result this has gradually led to the basic formation of the university student at the intermediate level being abandoned. Some American universities have become aware of this mistake and now attempt to remedy it, reinstating the role of the teaching professor.

The view which the research scholar has of the Bible and of biblical texts can be extremely incomplete. Professor Goshen-Gottstein of the Hebrew University of Jerusalem, who died in 1991, has left in writing harsh criticism of the present situation of biblical studies, in what was his first public appearance, a few years after having survived a deep coma for several months. Goshen-Gottstein criticised *the current fragmentation of biblical studies*, separated into several disciplines or specialties, with no communication possible or foreseen among the specialists and among the associations or publications of each specialised field: Masoretic text, Greek version, ancient versions, apocryphal or pseudepigraphical books, texts from Qumran, Targumic texts, inscriptions, Ugaritic texts, etc.[1] Study of the biblical books, both OT and NT, also proceeds along very different and unconnected paths, depending on method and analytical approach: textual criticism, source criticism, tradition criticism, redaction criticism, comparative philology and literature, historical and sociological study, history of religion and of exegesis, biblical theology, etc. The very trends which claim to represent a global and «holistic» approach, focusing, for example, on stylistic and structural analysis of the biblical books or on study of the Bible in terms of the canon as a whole, end up creating new schools and specialisations under the guidance of new *authorities*. Teaching experience shows, however, that it is difficult for the student and reader to gain a *systematic and global vision* of the many aspects offered by study of biblical literature.

This book attempts to build bridges between fields of study which used to be connected at the beginning of modern criticism but which the demands of specialisation have increasingly separated. It will come as a great surprise that a single book discusses in the same breath the more practical matters of textual criticism and the approaches of highly theoretical hermeneutics. Study of the Bible requires the cooperation of epigraphers and palaeographers at one extreme and of historians of biblical religion and of Jewish and Christian thought at the other. Today there are many problems which need *interdisciplinary discussion*.

Throughout the whole of this book and for the sake of objectivity, all personal opinion concerning facts, arguments and conclusions of current research is avoided. However, the overall approach of the book and the choice of material presented as well as the opinions discussed, consistently match a personal vision of all the questions discussed and the serious intention of providing a new vision of the study of «Biblical Literature». This Foreword and the Introduction are suitable places for showing the author's preferences and the perspective for problems debated throughout the book.

1. In the *field of linguistics*, the trilingual Bible requires a new dialogue instead of the old remoteness among scholars of Hebrew, Greek and Latin. The Hebrew-Aramaic-Arabic trilingualism in which the Jewish masoretes, grammarians and exegetes of the Arabian East and of Muslim Spain operated should not forget the assistance of Arabic for understanding the grammatical and exegetical tradition accompanying the transmission of the biblical Hebrew text. The discovery in modern times of the Semitic languages of the ancient Near East has given rise to a new form of trilingualism made up of the language trio Hebrew/Aramaic-Ugaritic-Akkadian, which helps to explain many questions either badly posed or inaccurately resolved in the past with the sole aid of textual criticism or the witness of the versions. It

---

1. M. H. Goshen-Gottstein, «The Hebrew Bible in the Light of the Qumran Scrolls and the Hebrew University Bible», *Congress Volume-Jerusalem 1985*, Leiden 1988, 42-53.

also allows biblical literature and religion to be set in the cultural context from which it originated.

2. Within *literary studies*, the present book tries especially to connect two fields which modern biblical criticism has increasingly separated: the study of the *literary and redactional formation* of the biblical books and the study of the *transmission and interpretation of the text* of these books. Literary-historical criticism has reserved the first field for itself, by preference devoting attention to study of the «origins» of the traditions and of the biblical texts in terms of the archaeology, history, literatures and religions of the ancient Near East. The second field remained the province of sciences considered to be auxiliary, such as textual criticism or the history of Jewish and Christian interpretation of the Bible, with a special bias towards the history of theology.

This book gives particular importance to an area bordering on both those fields: the area represented by the history of the transmission of the text and the textual criticism of the OT and NT. The lengthy *process of the formation of the Bible and of the religion of Israel* crystallised in the different *texts of the OT*, which produced a *process of interpretation* This, in turn, crystallised into the *new texts of the Christian religion*, the NT, and *of the Jewish religion*, the Mishnah and the Talmud.

The first of these two processes, the literary formation of the Bible, remains outside the purview of this book. Study of the sources, traditions, redactions, literary forms, etc., of the various biblical books is the favourite subject considered in the many books with the title «Introduction to the Bible». They are also studied in the series of exegetical commentaries on the different biblical books. These matters will continue to determine the programme of «Biblical Literature» courses and will also continue to require a very considerable part of research on the Bible. This book, however, demands much more space for discussion of another set of problems, some virtually forgotten and others apparently marginal or clearly marginalised.

This requires giving a new focus on the course as a whole, a focus also required for a *new direction in biblical studies* in general. The view of the Bible provided in the standard «Introductions to the Bible», which come chiefly from Germany and are usually used for teaching in Faculties, is to a large extent incomplete. This is because it leaves out or treats very perfunctorily aspects which from every point of view are indispensable for understanding the Bible and cannot be considered as purely introductory matters or as mere post-biblical developments. This is the immense area of everything connected with the *canons*, *texts*, *versions* and *interpretations* or *hermeneutics* (all these terms are in the plural) both of the Hebrew Bible and of the Christian Bible, and both forming an integral part of the *social and intellectual context* in which Judaism was born in the Persian and Hellenistic periods, in which there then arose Christianity in the Roman period. The content of this book, therefore, becomes a *true history of the Bible*, from the period in which the collections of OT books were formed until the period when, both in Judaism and in Christianity, the canon, the text, the versions and the main lines of biblical interpretation became crystallised.

In this period, Jewish and Christian intellectuals had to complete three basic tasks which the *classical philology* of the Alexandrians had achieved only shortly before in respect of Greek literature: to establish a canon of works from the «classics», fix their text and interpret their content according to principles and methods suited to the literary form of each work. Using the work programme of Alexandrian philology as a model, this book is divided into three main sections devoted to literary, textual and hermeneutic tasks. Here, the «Alexandrian connection» serves at every moment as a reminder not to forget the need to maintain the *connection between classical and Semitic studies* which produced the «Trilingual Colleges» of the Renaissance and the fertile study of the Bible until 19th century philology.

3. In respect of *history*, particular attention is paid here to the *Persian, Hellenistic and Roman periods*, now better known thanks especially to the discoveries from the Dead Sea. This is when the various collections of the OT books took shape and the process of transmission, translation and interpretation of the OT began, until the time when on the one hand the Christian NT was formed, and on the other the *corpus* of rabbinic literature was formed.

The *origins of Christianity* should not be sought in the Hellenistic pagan world of mystery religions and Gnosticism so much as in its Jewish, Old Testament and intertestamental roots, without forgetting, however, that the Judaism of that period was already very Hellenised.

Judaism and Hellenism should not be perceived so much as two opposite poles: it is preferable to speak of a *«Hellenistic Judaism»*, which incorporated many elements from Greek culture into Jewish tradition, without necessarily giving in to pagan syncretism.

Nor should the Judaism of the Hellenistic period be seen through the prism of the *«normative» Judaism* of the Mishnaic and Talmudic period. Still less should it be seen with the prejudices which turned the Judaism of the Persian and Hellenistic period into a late, decadent and legalistic phenomenon compared with the earlier religion of the biblical prophets or later Christianity. On the contrary, the Judaism of the centuries before the destruction of Jerusalem is marked by a great variety of movements and social groups and the vitality of its ideas and beliefs. These cannot be lumped together under the adjective *«sectarian»*, for as yet there was no agreed norm and therefore no normative Judaism.

The Hellenistic period, which was post-classical and post-biblical, distinguished by the meeting of cultures from the East and the West, caused languages, literary traditions and religious beliefs to come into contact. This meeting occurred more often in countries of transit and in frontier zones like those of the geography of Israel. Hellenistic Judaism was a first attempt, fruitful and painful at the same time, at what shortly after was developed in Christianity: the *symbiosis between Greek culture and biblical tradition* by means of accepting some elements and rejecting others from each.

4. The *formation of canonical and non-canonical collections*. In the 18th and 19th centuries, classical works and periods were studied for preference, with the neglect of the ancient period, criticised as primitive, and of the post-classical period, disregarded like the Hellenistic, as syncretistic, baroque and decadent. Study of the Bible also has usually been reduced to study of the classical books of Judaism and Christianity, the respective collections of *canonical books*, ignoring or despising the remaining literature, especially apocryphal works. On the other hand, confessional study of the Bible as carried out both by Jews and by Christians did not cease to stress study of the canonical books, to the exclusion, in practice, of the apocryphal books. In Judaism and Christianity, study has largely been centred on their respective orthodoxies and central movements, represented by the rabbinism of the Synagogue and by the Great Church.

Study of the Hebrew Bible must be carried out, instead, within the wider context of Jewish literature of the Persian and Hellenistic period, with special attention to study of the *apocryphal literature* or pseudepigrapha, which imitates and develops canonical literature. Study of this kind complements and also stabilises the confessional direction of biblical studies, concentrated almost exclusively on the books of the canon.

Before considering the Bible from a theological perspective as a collection of canonical books to the exclusion of the apocrypha, it is necessary to consider the Bible from the literary and historical perspective, as a collection of books of different genres (legal, historical, prophetic, wisdom and apocalyptic). This was to give rise to a range of *imitative literature, mimicking* what was already considered to be classical, as well as a whole corpus of traditional interpretation collected together in rabbinic literature and, suitably Christianised, in the NT. In contrast to the various classifications possible for the apocryphal books - by genre, language, origin, background, content, theological authority, etc. - the present book classes the apocrypha and the pseudepigraphical books in terms of their relation to the canonical books in all the aspects just mentioned.

On the other hand, the textual and literary history of canonical and apocryphal literature, both Jewish and Christian, has to be considered in *relation to the social and intellectual history* of the period. The collection of canonical and apocryphal books, their text, and above all the interpretation of their contents, acquire very different perspectives depending on whether reference is made to Samaritans, Sadducees, Pharisees, Essenes, Hellenists, Jewish-Christians, ex-pagan Christians, Gnostic Jews, Gnostic Christians, etc.

It is not possible to continue speaking of the existence of an Alexandrian Greek canon, which was absorbed by Christianity, nor even of a *closure of the canon* at the synod of Yabneh towards the end of the 1st cent. CE. Some authors tend to suppose that the Hebrew canon of the OT was already virtually formed in the mid-2nd cent. BCE. It cannot be said, however, that this path leads to a satisfactory explanation of the origin of the Christian canon of the OT from its Jewish precursors among the Essenes or among the Jews of the Greek diaspora, which supposed the existence of a canon which was still open or, at least, not completely closed.

In this book, a *history of the canon of the Hebrew Bible* will be attempted which runs parallel with the history of the Temple. Defining the limits of the sacred area of the Temple and defining the limits of the textual area of the canonical Scriptures run in parallel and have a matching development. Four periods can be distinguished in the restoration and progressive expansion of the Temple and of the sacred Book: the canon of the Restoration after the Exile, the canon of the Maccabaean restoration after the Hellenistic crisis, the canon corresponding to the expansion of the Temple in the Herodian period (expansion of Scripture orally among the Pharisees or in writing among the Essenes and Hellenists), and, lastly, the canon of the Pharisee Restoration after the disaster of 70 CE.

Critical study of the Bible, guided by the spirit of the Enlightenment, has preferred to be concerned with the analysis of literary sources and of the historical origins of the biblical tradition and very little with the knowledge of later developments of actual biblical tradition. However, the Bible, the Book of Life, like the Tree of Life of paradise, demands to be known and explained *as much or more by its fruits as by its roots.*

Biblical scholars use editions of the Hebrew text of the OT books (BHS) and editions of the Greek text of the NT. However, the Hebrew Bible was never published or read as a separate and completely unrelated book in the way it is published and read by modern critics. The Hebrew Bible was never separated from other texts compiled and read together with the biblical text. It is enough to look at a rabbinic edition of the Bible to realise that the Jew does not have only the biblical text before his eyes. The text is printed centre page, as if it were a quotation or text reference, surrounded by other texts printed in parallel columns and in the upper and lower parts of the same page (the Aramaic versions or Targumim and rabbinic commentaries). A Jew reads the Bible *within the context of a complete tradition* which moulds Judaism; he reads the written Torah in the light of the oral Torah. In the same way, the Christian Bible ends with the books of the NT, so that a Christian reads the complete Bible in the perspective of its ending and of the books which gather together the tradition that gave rise to Christianity.

The type of study advocated here complements and balances the critical direction of biblical studies and tries to re-evaluate a field of study traditionally left in the hands of those studying rabbinism or the history of Christian theology. This field is the history of biblical interpretation which starts from the exegesis practised within the Bible itself up to the exegesis developed in Jewish and Christian, rabbinic and patristic literature, passing through the exegesis contained in all intertestamental and apocryphal literature. Study of Jewish and Christian exegesis also demands reflection on the kind of hermeneutics sustaining them both.

When the preparation of this book was well under way I had the satisfaction of reading an article by Professor J. L. Kugel of Harvard University with the title «The Bible in the University» (1990). First he criticises current teaching of the Bible, which mixes approaches derived from historical and literary discipline with certain positions of a confessional character, mostly Protestant. Then he notes that biblical studies have to have as their subject the history of how the Bible was formed and how it was transmitted, read and interpreted, from the formation of the biblical collections up to the periods when these collections became the *Miqraʾ* or *Tanak* of the Jews and the *Bible* of Christians.[2]

Critical exegesis, even what appears to be the most secular, has not ceased to be very influenced by the Protestant distinction between the Word of God contained in Scripture and the merely human words contained in later interpretations and in the dogmas of the Christian Church or the Jewish Synagogue respectively. In this perspective, critical exegesis grants more importance to the oracles attributed to the prophet Isaiah than to others which seem to have been added in the book bearing his name. However, exegesis has to forego giving preference to the before or after of biblical texts, especially if the criteria of choice are foreign to the texts and to biblical tradition. Kugel describes very clearly the intention which should direct study of the Bible as envisaged by this book: «to trace the growth of the Bible from its earliest origins in the life and thought-world of ancient Israel to its institutionalization in the life and thought-world of early Judaism and Christianity» (Kugel, 163).

Kugel prepares for the field of the Hebrew Bible and of Jewish exegesis. He does not explain the field of the history and criticism of the text, but from time to time can provide data for a history of exegesis. Biblical tradition, however, is primarily the transmission of the actual text of the Bible in material form: the *meaning of Scripture* is contained in the *letters of the script*.

5. The field of *textual criticism* is the preferred terrain of the spirit of the Renaissance and of the Enlightenment. To this is dedicated the central section of this book which is, no doubt, the most cautious. It relates the history of the biblical text by going back through history. Modern research had to recreate the textual history of the Bible starting from modern editions of the Bible and reaching back (through mediaeval manuscripts, recensions of the Byzantine period, Jewish versions and the newly discovered manuscripts from Qumran) to the stage of the most ancient texts preserved, and as far as possible, to reconstruct the text closest to the original of the biblical authors.

In principle, textual criticism of the canonical texts is no different from that of classical texts. The final aim is to try and reconstruct the text of the works of the biblical authors exactly as they came from their hands. The possible differences between textual criticism of classical texts and of the biblical Scriptures are due to the extreme complexity of the transmission of biblical texts, made worse especially by the existence of many versions and an-

2. J. L. Kugel, «The Bible in the University», *The Hebrew Bible and Its Interpreters*, eds. W.H. Propp-B. Halpern-D.N. Freedman, Winona Lake, IN 1990, 143-165 (160-161).

cient recensions. On the other hand, religious texts took on new value in each and every one of the stages of their long textual transmission nor are they only valid in the form which can be considered original or oldest. Biblical criticism has to decide between keeping to the original and ancient texts which may bring us closer to the times of Moses and of Jesus of Nazareth, and faithfulness, on the other hand, to later tradition which formed Judaism and Christianity. The first of these concerns, the return to the original word of the great *founders*, which is the basis of the *inspired* character of *Scripture* corresponds to the scientific concern to unearth the oldest text from the collection of texts preserved from antiquity. Strangely, this is a concern which, from different perspectives, «fundamentalists» and critics share. The second concern affects what is undeniable for a Jewish or Christian reader of the Bible: the preservation and appreciation of the *Tradition* of the Jewish 'abot (*Fathers*) and of the *Fathers* of the Church, for this Tradition determines the extent of the biblical canon and the *canonical* interpretation of Scripture. This concern is foreign to scientific criticism which places that tradition in parentheses or despises it, considering it to be a dogmatic development which detracts from the original texts.

In this field of textual criticism, so conspicuously positivistic, this book tries to provide not only the results of modern research but also to present as well the paths, sometimes unsuccessful and almost always tortuous, by which modern research has gone forward and goes forward. It provides the cooked dish and the kitchen recipe, so that the student and the reader can actually share the secrets of the brew which is modern research and know the ingredients used by researchers in their mixtures, and thus be initiated into the mysteries of investigative reason.

In previous studies on the text of the historical books of the OT I have drawn attention to an extreme example which, while not very common, comprises the best example of how the Bible is trilingual, not only in interpretation but also in text - and how this trilingual character allows a path to be traced of *approaching the ancient forms of the biblical text*. It is a matter of those cases in which the Old Latin text (the *Vetus Latina*) translates the Greek text of the LXX version which in turn translated a different Hebrew text from the traditional or masoretic text. These texts in Greek and Hebrew were lost, displaced by the official texts then current, and have only survived as variants in the Old Latin text. This can be expressed concisely as «From the Old Latin through the Old Greek to the Old Hebrew».[3]

To counter the surprise this could provoke, an important example can be remembered here of how similar events can happen in modern times as well. A few years ago, the text of the address which Albert Einstein would have given had he been present at the official session when he received the Nobel Prize for physics in Stockholm in 1921 was published in Germany. At that time Einstein was in the University of Kyoto where he gave an address in

---

3. J. Trebolle, «From the 'Old Latin' through the 'Old Greek' to the 'Old Hebrew' (2 Kgs 10,23-25)», *Textus* XI (Jerusalem, The Hebrew University, 1984), 17-36.

German of which he left no written record. One of Einstein's Japanese students translated it for those attending the conference and took very detailed notes, which he published two years later in Japanese. This text was translated into English in 1982 (*Physics Today* 8, 1982). A German translation was made of this English version, and published in 1983. One has to ask whether, after all these translations (from German to Japanese, then into English and then into German), Einstein would have recognised as his own the text now published in its original language. Evidently, the initial formulation has undergone many changes, but the content of the publication is important enough to merit the attention of scientists. In a similar way, readings of a lost Hebrew text can sometimes be reconstructed on the basis of a Latin text which faithfully translates the partially lost text of the LXX version, itself a faithful translation of that Hebrew text. The fact that some manuscripts from Qumran represent that lost textual tradition confirms the correctness of the hypothesis even in those cases where there is no evidence among the Qumran manuscripts.

Study of the manuscripts from Qumran Cave 4 has reassessed *the witness of the ancient versions* as a means of approaching lost forms of the Hebrew text now reappearing piecemeal among the fragments from Qumran. Accordingly, a special section is devoted to a new phenomenon with rich rewards: quite a few OT books underwent *successive editions* and were transmitted in *different textual forms* which circulated freely in the various geographic centres of Judaism and among the various Jewish groups of the pre-rabbinic and pre-Christian period. The biblical manuscripts from Qumran published most recently have brought new texts to light which must be described as «*borderline*», for they lie halfway between the biblical text, properly speaking and a paraphrase text, which can retain old elements or add new ones. The *literary and textual diversity* of the biblical books corresponds to the diversity of Jewish society in the Persian and Hellenistic periods, as mentioned already.

It will be stressed repeatedly that it is not possible to solve adequately the problems relating to the literary formation of the biblical books (source criticism, tradition criticism, redaction criticism) without at the same time taking into account the facts and criteria of the history and criticism of the text. Literary theory makes a crystal clear distinction between the process of the literary *formation* of a book and the *transmission* and *interpretation* of its text. In practice, analysis shows that these three fields constantly touch and overlap so that it is not possible to reach a satisfactory solution to the problems except through an *interdisciplinary dialogue among scholars studying literary criticism, textual criticism and the history of interpretation*. The principles and methods of textual criticism do not change, but their application varies depending on whether the history of the biblical text is viewed as a single straight line of transmission or as bundles of lines coming from very different sources and intersecting each other a great deal. The history of modern biblical criticism has known several movements and trends. Some are more favourable to literary criticism (sources, traditions, redactions) and others more unwilling to accept the need for it, tending to keep textual criticism and literary criticism well apart. Some are more inclined to the reconstruction of texts and «original» literary forms, others more sceptical in this regard with a greater tendency to stress the soundness of the textual and literary tradition; some more inclined to follow the Masoretic Hebrew text and others more prepared to correct its possible mistakes and accept the validity of alternative textual traditions. Some more convinced of the possibility of the critical use of the versions, even as a historical source, and others no less convinced of the targumic and exegetical nature of its variants, etc.

What is certain is that, at the time of reconstructing history, since they are books which present two different forms of the text which correspond to two different editions, it is not wise to rely on passages included in the text of the second edition of the book. This is the case of the longer version of the book of Jeremiah transmitted by the MT and to give one example, such is the case of Jer 39:4-13. Comparison between the short text (LXX) and the long text (MT) will show up the characteristics of the second «corrected and augmented» edition and at the same time make it possible to engage simultaneously in a holistic, horizontal and genetic exegesis on the two forms of text.

6. *Interpretation and hermeneutics.* Once the text is known in its various forms, times and places and also in the most original form possible, it is time to pay attention to the wide field of biblical interpretation. It is not the aim of this book or even of biblical studies as such to write a *history of the rabbinic and Christian exegesis* of the Bible. The words of Jaroslav Pelikan apply here even more than in his own classic work: «The history of biblical interpretation and the development of hermeneutics deserve study on their own merits and are not our direct concern here».[4] Study of biblical literature must always and above all be a reading and re-reading (Mishnah = «repetition») of the actual biblical texts. The aim of this book, however, cannot be to carry out exegesis or to present the conclusions of Jewish or Christian exegesis.

In the section dealing with Christian hermeneutics, attention is paid in a special way to the problem which *the twofold legacy, Jewish and pagan,* the OT and Greek philosophy, posed for Christianity. It is also a matter of finding the paths which the Great Church and other marginal or marginalised movements of Christianity followed with the aim of incorporating, purifying or rejecting different aspects of that double *praeparatio evangelica.* In the context of the dispute about the historical primacy of orthodoxy or heterodoxy and of the various Christian movements which started but stopped midway or veered away from the central movement, here special attention is paid to *Jewish-Christianity* as a catalyst in the shift from Jewish exegesis to Christian exegesis and to the peculiar exegesis of Old Testament and Jewish passages and motifs practised by *Gnosticism.*

4. J. Pelikan, *The Christian Tradition. A History of the Development of Doctrine, 1. The Emergence of the Catholic Tradition (100-600),* Chicago-London 1971, 6.

The way Jewish and Christian hermeneutic is presented here follow like *a guiding thread* the dichotomy between a literal and historical interpretation and an allegorical and spiritual interpretation (between *pᵉšaṭ* and *dᵉraš*). This *dialectic between letter and meaning* set in motion mediaeval exegesis, both Jewish and Christian. The same dialectic also drives modern hermeneutic, which oscillates between two poles. One is historical and philological analysis, more positivist and an heir to enlightenment hermeneutic. The other is the need to give meaning and relevance for our time to the great myths, legends, traditions and texts of the classics, according to the ideal of romantic and post-critical hermeneutic.

This amounts to no more than hinting at fundamental questions for the history and understanding of the Bible: the *hermeneutical assumptions* and the *methods of interpretation* developed within the biblical books and in the Jewish and Christian literature of that period or immediately after; the global but detailed vision which the *Tanak* and the whole of the OT and NT together acquired in Judaism and Christianity respectively; the main lines of Jewish and Christian interpretation; the inclusion or rejection of elements from the philosophy, religion and literature of the Persian world at first and then of the Greek and Roman world, etc.

The formation of the New Testament texts and their interpretation of the OT is only intelligible if the procedures and exegetical traditions of Jewish hermeneutic are known. However, Jewish exegesis should not be studied in terms of a better understanding of Christian sources. *Jewish hermeneutic*, both halakhic and haggadic, is a reality in its own right. It comprises the very heart of Judaism, defined as the religion of the double Torah, the written Torah, comprising the *Tanak* and the oral Torah, included in the corpus of authorised interpretations of the Tanak (the Mishnah and the Talmud).

Similarly, study of *Christian hermeneutic* consists in investigating thoroughly the very essence of Christianity as the religion of the «new» Covenant founded on the «old»: the Christian Bible is simultaneously «Old» and «New» Testament («Covenant/Testament», *diathēkē, foedus/testamentum*).

7. Jewish Bible and Christian Bible. This book maintains a basic thesis. There is a correspondence between the lines of formation and transmission of the books of Jews and Christians and the channels by which Judaism and Christianity were formed and spread. The first writings of the Christians gave the impression of being merely additional texts of Jewish literature. Christianity seemed to be one more «sect» or marginal group among those which existed in Judaism in the period before 70 CE. However, this affirmation alone is not enough to explain «the origin, being and existence» (to paraphrase the title of a book by Américo Castro) of Christians in terms of Jewish literature and the Judaism of the period. From the very first moment Christians accepted and passed on as their own books, texts and interpretations of the various Jewish groups. From the beginning, Christianity also assimilated followers from all these groups: Samaritans, Essenes, Hellenists and even Pharisees, Sadducees and others. The first Christians did not make up a new group of «separate ones» as the Pharisees were ($p^e ru\bar{s}im$=separate ones) or the Essenes who withdrew to the desert of Qumran. Peter's decision to remain in Jerusalem after the death of Jesus and later to take the road to the Mediterranean coast and finally, the mission among the gentiles is in contrast with the decision of the Teacher of Righteousness to lead his Essene community to the desert of Judah.[5]

Recent research continues to find parallels between the New Testament texts and the Essene writings and others, now known through the Dead Sea Scrolls. It has to be said that in the NT there is hardly one literary expression, institution, rite or ethical norm, or even one idea or theological symbol which does not have antecedents in the OT and Jewish «intertestamental» literature (however, for a complementary view, cf. pp. 32-35). It is symptomatic that there have been attempts to connect Jesus with the Essenes and to reduce Christianity to «an Essenism that succeeded», as Renan so aptly (but incorrectly) put it. Nowadays, however, research is equally aware of the weight of the differences, or more so. In the early years of study of the biblical manuscripts from Qumran, more attention was paid to the agreements of the new manuscripts with the MT or LXX. Today it is accepted that it is also necessary to notice the differences and the idiosyncrasies of each text. Similarly, in socio-religious study it is necessary to acknowledge the weight of the differences between the Christian group and the other Jewish groups. Ultimately, the figure of Jesus is closer to a Pharisee than to an Essene and originates principally in the figures of the biblical prophets and of the late biblical Hasidim.

Research into the parallels between the NT and Qumran have been focused on studying many matters of detail. However, if after looking at the trees it is a matter of seeing the wood, in other words, if libraries or collections of books are compared and not only isolated verses from one book or another, two contrasting scenes emerge. Pharisaic Judaism, although the most open and dynamic of the Jewish groups, was moving even before the period of Yabneh towards establishing a closed biblical canon, excluding works asserted to be «apocrypha» from other groups and even from the Pharisaic group itself. It was also moving towards the fixing of a single biblical text and of an authorised tradition of oral interpretation, to the exclusion or abandonment of other forms of the biblical text and of the interpretative traditions of other Jewish groups. On the other hand, Christianity appears as a marginal group of Judaism which, however, accepts from the first moment all the forms of the biblical text (Hebrew, Aramaic and Greek) and all the works and literary forms which circulated among the various Jewish groups, and takes on board Jews following all movements and origins. It can be said that before forming a symbiosis with the immense Greek and Roman world and achieving a full syncretism of Jewish and pagan elements, Christianity made a first but no less important meld of all the literary, social, reli-

5. W.H.C. Frend, *The Rise of Christianity*, Philadelphia PA 1984, 86.

gious and theological elements of the Judaism of the period.

The awareness that the first Christians had to be the «true Israel» coincides with what the Qumran community thought of themselves or the Pharisees could claim for themselves. However, the Christians claimed to represent «all Israel» and to be the heirs of all possible types of Judaism, especially those which soon ceased to be influential in the official Judaism of the rabbis. It is important that until the second Christian generation, the generation of Paul's disciples, elements from Essenism continued to enter Christianity. Also, this generation experienced a return to Old Testament ritual elements which came from the Sadducees.

In this book great importance is paid to the fact that the Christians accepted the Greek Bible of the LXX and a large part of the Jewish apocryphal works, which rabbinic Judaism rejected so soon. (The Christians also continued to pay attention to works typical of official Judaism, such as the versions of Aquila, Symmachus and Theodotion.) Those works came into Christianity from the hands of very different groups (Hellenists, Essenes, Samaritans, Sadducees, Pharisees, Zealots, etc.). These works brought into Christianity a wide range of trends and ideas: sapiential and philosophical, apocalyptic, messianic, zealot, etc. It is a mistake to contrast Jesus and «apocalyptic» Christians, close to the Essene group with «legalistic» Pharisees and «ritualistic» Sadducees. All these groups were equally affected by apocalyptic ideas and, at the same time, by legal and ritual concerns, and shared in one way or another in the Hellenistic environment. Christianity attempts a dialectic synthesis of these elements, overcoming them all (*Aufhebung*). It has to execute a triple surrender and a triple transformation. It abandons the Temple very soon (in a form very like that of Qumran Essenism), but transforms and absorbs many of the Old Testament and Zadokite ritual traditions (just as pharisaic rabbinism will be forced to as well, but in a different way). It abandons practising the Torah which it gradually transforms into an allegory of the New Covenant, and it also abandons apocalyptic hope in a «restoration of Israel» which it slowly exchanges for a «realised eschatology» inaugurated by the coming of Christ the Messiah.

So then, Judaism ended by closing ranks around the leaders of the pharisee movement, who set in train a series of actions to unite Judaism. From the multiplicity of books texts and interpretations and from the array of movements and socio-religious groups it became a unity and a monolith in terms of literature, social practice and religion (although this did not mean that differences ceased within rabbinism). The literary and textual history of the Jewish Bible is the history of the reduction from a multiplicity of books, texts and interpretations to one canon, one text and one authorised interpretation. The history of Judaism is also the history of the pharisaic movement, which unseated other groups and other forms of Judaism. Among these «failed forms of Judaism», Samaritanism was the only one develop to some extent, whereas Sadduceeism and Essenism, which had known great splendour,[6] remained completely forgotten. Sadducees, Essenes, Zealots and other

Jewish groups deserted history and a large part of their literature was preserved only through the Christian tradition.

With a broader and more open criterion than in pharisaic Judaism, the Christians collected many of the Jewish books banished by rabbinic Judaism, even some of pharisaic extraction although it must not be forgotten that Christianity discarded completely the rich and ancient halakhic literature which did not fit its vision of the Torah. The Christians included in their Bible the so-called deutero-canonical books and preserved many of the apocryphal books, some of which enjoyed great authority in various churches. They also absorbed all the forms of the text in circulation, with every kind of variant and in different text editions (e.g. the book of Job). They also used all the literary forms of Jewish literature, many of them abandoned in later rabbinic literature. In one sense it can be said that triumphant and normative Judaism, formed in the period of the Mishnah and the Talmud, was born somewhat later than Christianity. The latter preserved many elements from earlier Judaism and evolved in continuity with the Old Testament traditions and the Jewish traditions of the Persian and Hellenistic period, traditions which rabbinic Judaism itself declined or ceased to develop.

The inclusion of so many divergent Jewish elements within Christianity brought in its wake the germ of disagreements which together with the disagreement caused by the inclusion of very different sectors from the Greek and Roman world, could only spark off the continuous emergence of various «heresies». In many cases these were not real objections to an orthodoxy which had not yet been established. Rather, they were anticipations or unsuccessful approximations, which helped the central movement of Christianity define the main lines along which it had to move (cf. pp. 242-243).

8. *Jewish Religion and Christian Religion*. In terms of the history of religions, Judaism and Christianity appear to be *two religions derived from one and the same biblical religion*, but on diverging lines of development because of their different approach to interpreting biblical literature and religion. With the binomial «the Law and the Prophets», Judaism stresses the Law or Torah of Moses and Christianity stresses the Prophets who foretold Christ the Messiah. Judaism and Christianity are two blends and two different developments of «the Law and the Prophets». Judaism prefers to be inspired by Genesis and develops a religion of fulfilling the Law. Christianity is directed more towards an Apocalypse, and develops a religion of hope in apocalyptic salvation. Judaism develops the Law through an oral tradition comparable in worth to the written Law. The interpretation of the Law by the Wise men of Israel takes the place of the word of the Prophets who had

---

6. H. Stegemann expressed the opinion that Essenism represented the main movement of Judaism in the 2nd cent. BCE. H. Stegemann, «The Qumran Essenes - Local Members of the Main Jewish Union in Late Second Temple Times», *The Madrid Qumran Congress. Proceedings of the International Congress on the Dead Sea Scrolls. Madrid 18-21 March, 1991*, eds. J. Trebolle Barrera and L. Vegas Montaner, Vol. I, Leiden - Madrid 1992, 83-166.

ceased in Israel. In turn, Christianity writes a NT claiming to be the fulfilment of the biblical Prophecies and the culmination of the Law.

A Jew tends to equate Judaism with biblical religion. A Christian also tends to think of Judaism, in effect, as an extension of biblical religion, but maintains at the same time that the OT has its true culmination in Christianity and not in Judaism. On the other hand, modern criticism tends to isolate the OT from later tradition, Jewish and Christian, and to consider it as testimony to a religion of the ancient Near East.

The collection of texts which makes up the OT had an open structure, which allowed an oral or written development and at the same time required a continuous effort of interpretation, which gave rise to the oral Torah and the apocryphal literature. The Torah or Pentateuch displays an open promise with an unresolved ending. The *fulfilment of the Torah* is the essential condition for speeding up the *fulfilment of the Promise*. Therefore, Judaism developed a body of literature, focused on the observance and legal fulfilment of the Torah. Christianity developed another body of literature, directed instead to the fulfilment of the Promise in Christ. When Judaism and Christianity began to take shape in their respective «normative» forms, the differences between them began to deepen and become more obvious. The Jewish religion is focused on the knowledge and practice of a sacred Law and not on a historical person (Moses). Christianity, instead, focuses on the person of Jesus of Nazareth who takes on the prerogatives of prophet and Messiah and the position of «Son of God».

The Mishnah and the Talmud, the body of literature developed by rabbinic Judaism, can be considered as «new» in respect of Jewish literature of the preceding period. So is the «New Testament», though more from a prophetic and apocalyptic aspect. The Jewish groups most anchored in the ancient priestly Torah, as were the Samaritans and Sadducees, accused the Pharisees and Essenes of bringing in a new Law and new laws, in short, a new Bible. On the other hand, the NT seems to be more rooted in the literary forms and in the apocalyptic of the period before 70 CE than in the distinctive literature of Judaism, the Mishnah and the Talmud. The NT imitates the OT more in structure, genres, motifs, etc. The literature of rabbinic Judaism, later than the Christian NT, in fact breaks away from the genres, themes and motifs typical of intertestamental literature and becomes a sort of cento (a genre typical of the time) of interpretations of chapters and verses from Scripture.

It can be said that history has not known more than two actual Bibles: the rabbinic Bible, which includes the oral Torah, and the Christian Bible, which adds the NT. A third Bible could have been formed - the Gnostic Bible - but it did not amount to more than a failed attempt just like Gnostic religion. The «plain» Bible, i.e., the separate and independent OT as modern criticism now studies it in the *Biblia Hebraica*, never existed. True, before the formation of the rabbinic and Christian traditions there did exist a collection of sacred writings of the old religion of Israel. However, this collection began to be formed at the same time as it was being absorbed into a Jewish tradition which right from the first accompanied it, marking the limits of the collection, the text of each book and the channels of their interpretation.

Neither in Judaism and Christian can one speak of the existence of a «Bible» until the moment when a biblical canon began to be determined. This does not happen until the moment when a tradition of interpretation has also started to take shape and begins to have authoritative and canonical value. In Judaism, the process of closing the canon of the Scriptures and the parallel formation of oral tradition happened basically between the 2nd cent. BCE and the 2nd cent. CE. In Christianity, this process was practically completed towards the end of the 2nd cent., when the nucleus of the NT books already accompanied the OT as a unit. In Judaism, the Mishnah and the Talmud do not form part of the Scriptures, but they form the canon of their interpretation. In Christianity, instead, the NT ended up forming an integral part of the canon of Scriptures and forms both the canon and the interpretation of the OT.

Modern criticism studies biblical religion as a religion of the ancient Near Eastern world. It analyses biblical texts in the form that they had before they made up the Bible as a unit. In other words, when they were no more than isolated texts, put together at most in small collections of legal, narrative, prophetic or wisdom content. This critical approach desecrates the biblical texts and detaches them from later creeds, Jewish and Christian. Against this critical view, which decomposes the Bible into its original elements, voices are raised today which from confessional stances, sometimes decidedly conservative, reclaim a canonical view of the Bible («canonical criticism») and also from purely literary viewpoints advocate a «holistic» and structural view of the Bible.

Modern criticism of the OT which isolates its field of study from all later tradition of interpretation, Jewish or Christian, can think that the detached writings collected together in OT and the process which leads to its make-up, can be the object of literary or theological study, deprived even of Jewish or New Testament connotations. There are many attempts at a «Theology of the OT» which, however, still have a more or less Christian inspiration and attitude.

To consider the OT as *Biblia Hebraica*, independent and autonomous, comes chiefly from the Reformation and the Enlightenment more than from Judaism itself. Protestantism tends to consider the OT independently of the NT, as two opposite poles which represent Law and Grace. Biblical criticism, heir of the Enlightenment, tends to consider biblical literature in terms of the other literatures of the ancient Near East, isolating it from its later canonical developments at the hands of the rabbis and the Fathers. It is significant that in Protestantism a «Biblical Theology» of the OT could have developed more or less independent of the NT (Zimmerli, etc.). Catholicism has hardly known this development and Judaism definitely does not know a theology of the *Tanak*, independent of Jewish tradition.

So then, the problem of the relationships between the two historical *Bibles*, rabbinic and Christian, and of both to the *Tanak* or «Old Testament» comprises the central problem of biblical hermeneutics and at the same time the problem of the relationship among the three religions which phenomenologists and historians of religion distinguish: the religion of ancient Israel, Jewish religion and the Christian religion. A Jew tends to equate the religion of Israel and the Jewish religion. The Christian tends to forget the Jewish origins of biblical religion and to consider the Christian religion as its true heir. Modern criticism tends to establish differences and discontinuities, forgetting that religious tradition and biblical tradition especially is a *continuum* which, in spite of distances in time and space, runs from Abraham to Hillel and Jesus of Nazareth and continues in the Church and Synagogue.

The relationship between the OT and NT is not *one* of the problems of Christian theology but *the* theological problem par excellence. It demands the limits of what is Christian and what is not to be defined. From the 2nd cent. CE, Christianity conclusively accepted the OT as an integral part of the Christian Scriptures, but the question was posed, without any real answer, of how to interpret them in a way suiting a Christian viewpoint. Pietistic interpretation of the OT and the very acceptance of the OT in Christianity have been and continue to be the subject of discussion. Certain movements have taken up positions which can only revive the Marcionite rejection of the OT.

Since the 18th cent., modern biblical hermeneutics has wavered between an «enlightened» and a «devotional» consideration of the Bible. The first studies the Bible as one more book from the ancient world in a purely historical perspective (in the manner of Wrede), as 'decontextualised' as possible from the presuppositions of the interpreter and completely removed from any application or 'actualization' through a biblical theology for the present day. Devotional and romantic hermeneutics cannot conceive, instead, a decontextualised interpretation, immersed rather in tradition and intended for practical use. It is assumed that the first takes place in universities and the second in the pulpits of churches and synagogues. The Bible resists this division of labour. Its unceasing influence on the course of history (*Wirkungsgeschichte*) and its buried presence in every philosophy of history or in every ahistorical utopia, prevent it being turned into a museum piece and an object of archaeological study, or being enclosed in genizahs and sacristy back-rooms. Its textual, literary, historical and religious make-up resists rational criticism better than many of the fideistic approaches with which many attempt to defend it.

The critical and modern approach to the Bible only revives the first encounters of Judaism and Christianity and the first separation from the rational criticism of the Greeks in the Hellenistic period. The challenge of biblical hermeneutics continues to be to *introduce rational discourse into the course of biblical tradition*. Post-modern and post-critical hermeneutics (Heidegger, Gadamer, Ricoeur) strives for a balance between critical science and traditional con-science. This book ends with a short chapter on some aspects of contemporary hermeneutics, a knowledge of which is presumed necessary for every hermeneutic exercise of understanding texts, especially classical texts and ancient religious texts. Both the critical approach and the devotional approach of the believer to the world of the Bible presuppose an awareness of a whole set of assumptions. To those born after the Enlightenment and in the closing stages of modernity, such assumptions are our indispensable companion in our approach to the texts of the pre-modern world, to which the great classical and biblical texts belong, whose myths, symbols and allegories continue to hold meanings which, beyond any attempts at critical *explanation* demand an attempt at *understanding* its radical otherness. If the hermeneutics of enlightened modernity have developed critical judgment and methodological rigour in the analysis of the literal, philological, and historical meaning, far from the allegorical constructions which ancient and mediaeval exegesis built upon the biblical texts, it is necessary for post-critical and post-modern hermeneutics, so as to recover the meaning of the allegorical and symbolic interpretations as to be able to approach the understanding of the biblical texts in a way more suited to them. In my view, this «restoration of allegory» defended by Gadamer has still not been sufficiently developed in today's hermeneutic and biblical exegesis.

The readers of this book, in particular the specialists who only read what concerns their own specialised topic, will understand the mistakes and gaps they can find in it. In the discussion of many problems, no more has been attempted than to draw attention to their importance, emphasising aspects and examples which seem the most important. Perhaps a work of this nature should have been written by several authors in collaboration. However, I thought that an overall view, like the one provided here, of the problems and topics discussed could compensate for the many imperfections of detail which could be noticed. Works written in collaboration tend to be more precise and better documented, but discussion of problems is generally so diffuse and sometimes so full of inconsistencies among what each author says, that the reader ends up lost among so many trees and does not manage to enjoy seeing the wood. I have faced the risk of falling into «generalisation», reviled until recently but which can very soon become a new speciality and even a new profession, the «generalist», perhaps with better prospects than. many specialist topics so intensively studied now.

All that has been unfolded in this book has been slowly maturing in the preparation of a course on «The Literature of the Old Testament» given over the last few years in the Department of Hebrew and Aramaic of the Universidad Complutense of Madrid. It also includes material from work and discussion from other seminars, especially from various doctoral courses on «The Dead Sea Scrolls». The final form is a textbook with the features of an encyclopaedia on many occasions and of an academic essay on others. The writer of an encyclopaedia can never be exhaustive and the essayist and scholar can never be definitive. Many problems discussed today are simply noted, accompanied by the appropriate bibliography. The specialist will always miss other problems and other bibliographical references.

This book cannot avoid a degree of repetition which shows the relationships among the various problems and facilitates occasional reference or dipping into a chapter, without reading the rest. Frequent cross-references connect some passages with other, marking interrelated facts or approaches.

The bibliography for each section tries to provide the student and the reader with a spectrum of the more important sources, tools, monographs and research papers, sometimes stressing the most recent.

I wish to express my gratitude for the hospitality I received over many years in L'École Biblique et Archéologique Française of Jerusalem. In its magnificent library I was able to read and to gather the material needed for the preparation of this book. My thanks go to Professor Miguel Pérez Fernández, of the University of Granada, for his advice to me in editing the text on computer, although the pleasant conversations on the topics of this book are more present in my memory. My thanks also go to Professor Montserrat Abumalham, of the Universidad Complutense of Madrid, for reading successive versions of this book and as Reader's Champion, contributing to its final form. I also have to thank Miss Beatriz Moncó for her careful and precise preparation of the original and for her later correction of the proofs. The book has no dedication, but at every moment I have had in mind the students who followed and follow my courses in the Universidad Complutense, and many others who took part in courses or biblical seminars, such as those organised by the Spanish Biblical Institute in Jerusalem, which I remember in a special way.

Introduction 27-52

Topical Questions and Approaches 29-52

Introduction

Topical Questions and Approaches

The discovery of the Dead Sea Scrolls in the years following 1947 marked a *change of direction* in studies on ancient Judaism and the origins of Christianity and especially studies on the history of the Bible in the Persian (538-325 CE) and Hellenistic (325-135 CE) period.

To this change of direction many other *factors* of very different kinds also contributed. These range from the most tangible, such as the archaeological finds in biblical lands, to those of a more intellectual order, such as the various currents of thought which have guided studies in recent decades.

Among the *archaeological finds* must be listed the discovery of the Gnostic library of Nag Hammadi in Upper Egypt, the excavations of Jewish synagogues in Capernaum, Chorazin, Tiberias, Meron, Khirbet Sheman, etc., the excavations of the palaces and fortresses of Herod the Great (Jericho, Masada, Herodion, Maritime Caesarea, Sebastiyyeh), the archaeological remains found in the areas close to the precinct of the Temple of Jerusalem, etc.

Among the *factors of an intellectual order* must be mentioned the currents of thought prevailing in the West after the second World War, whose influence is still felt today. Some currents were very far from having a sensitivity to the Semitic world. For R. Bultmann, the Christian faith was born with the paschal exaltation of the *Kyrios,* and the historical and almost Old Testament figure of the Jewish Jesus could contribute little, let alone matter. Other movements were deeply anti-Hellenistic, perhaps in reaction to the superiority previously attributed to Greek in explaining the origins of Christianity. O. Cullmann's work on time and the resurrection presumed complete incompatibility between Greek thought, based as it was on a cyclical concept of time, and biblical thought, rooted in a linear vision of history.

The trend represented by the «New hermeneutics» and the *«return to the Historical Jesus»* movement, maintained by Bultmann's disciples, the «post-bultmannians» Käsemann, Fuchs and Ebeling, supposed a shift from the existential and eschatological towards the historical, and by the same token, towards the Semitic. Other trends in exegesis believed it was possible to discern in the Greek texts of the NT the Aramaic substratum of the language spoken by Jesus and his apostles, and even the «actual words» (*ipsissima verba*) uttered by Jesus (J. Jeremias) .This last trend has been encouraged by the discovery of new apocryphal writings of the OT and of Targum *Neophyti* enabling many elements of Jewish exegesis incorporated in the NT to be identified.

The most decisive fact is certainly the immense *quantity of data* of all kinds accumulated in the last few decades and posing new questions. They also pose afresh other questions which since ancient times have nourished the disputes between Jews and Christians, Protestants and Catholics, Hellenist and Hebraists, philologists and historians, «ancient» and «modern», etc. We focus attention on the new approaches and perspectives concerning the questions discussed in this book: (I) the pattern of relations among Hellenism, Judaism and Christianity, and (II) the history of the canon, of the text and of the interpretation of the Bible at the beginnings of Judaism and Christianity.

I.   HELLENISM, JUDAISM AND CHRISTIANITY

1.   *The Roots of Christianity: Greek or Jewish?*
Before the discovery of the Dead Sea Scrolls it was common to establish a *very marked contrast between Hellenism and Judaism*. The origins of Christianity and the literature of the NT were studied principally if not exclusively from the perspective of the Hellenistic world and only at a very secondary stage, in reference to Jewish history and literature and to the OT itself.

A.   THE HELLENISTIC APPROACH OF THE «THE HISTORY OF RELIGIONS SCHOOL»

Although Jesus of Nazareth, the twelve apostles, Paul of Tarsus and a large part of the first Christian generation were Jews by birth, for quite a long time the origins of Christianity were studied without paying much attention to their unquestionably Jewish roots. The classic work by Wilhelm Bousset, *Kyrios Christos*, set up a radical opposition between Hellenistic Christianity, which was greatly influenced by the pagan mystery religions, and the community of the early Christians of Palestine from Jewish roots. R. Bultmann developed this historical outline of the formation of Christianity in two stages, one Jewish and the other Greek. He contrasted the figure of the «historical Jesus» who lived in Palestine with the figure of the «Christ of faith» developed by Hellenistic Christianity. Bultmann also stressed the influence of syncretistic Gnosticism on this Hellenistic Christianity.

The «History of religion school» (*Religionsgeschichtliche Schule*) insisted that students of the NT had to know Seneca, Epictetus, Plutarch, Lucian, Musonius Rufus, Marcus Aurelius, Cicero and the Stoic texts (Weis). R. Bultmann wrote his doctoral thesis on the diatribe, H. Lietzmann drew attention to the Greek elements contained in the lists of virtues and vices of the NT and M. Dibelius suggested that the so-called household codes (*Haustafel*) were loans of Stoic origin. The origins of Christianity were studied preferably in relation to the *popular religion of the Hellenistic period* and to a lesser degree to the literature and thought of the Classical Greek period. Christian worship seemed to be closely related to the pagan cults of the «*Mystery religions*» (at Eleusis, of Dionysius, Osiris, Attis, Mithras, Isis and Serpais, etc.) The Greek terms *mystérion, sophía, Kýrios, Sōtér*, etc., used in the Pauline epistles, seemed to find a suitable explanation within Greek language and philosophy.

It also seemed easy to discover *Gnostic ideas and symbols* in passages from the NT, such as 1 Cor 2:8 and Gal 4:3.9: Adam's sin affected the whole of creation, which is found subjected by him to the demonic powers until such time as Good wishes to restore the original order. In other passages such as 1 Cor 2:14ff and 15:14, it is believed that dualistic concepts are found, alien to Jewish tradition, which oppose body and spirit: by means of «gnosis» or knowledge revealed by Christ, the Christian peels off the man of flesh to become a purely spiritual being; Christian *gnosis* leads to salvation.

B. AFTER QUMRAN, STUDIES FAVOUR THE SEMITIC APPROACH

The early enthusiasm for comparison of primitive Christianity with the mystery religions has cooled down a great deal with the passing of years and has given place to more complex approaches. These religions were not so widespread as had been thought, and did not have the missionary character attributed to them. And most important of all, they did not reach the peak of their development until the 2nd cent. CE, when Christianity had become independent and had already taken flight unaided. The Mystery religions, in fact, were a sort of «religious atmosphere» which prevailed at the time (Nilsson). Its success was due above all to the attraction of its religious language, a language which was in the air at that time and could only flourish in any religious writing. If the New Testament writings sometime imitate this language, this does not mean that they would have taken the writings directly from the mystery cults.

The analogies which Bultmann established between Christian baptism and the sacraments of initiation into the mysteries, between the «Lord's supper» and the banquets of the initiates, between Pauline Christology and various categories of gnostic myths, especially the alleged pre-Christian myth of a Redeemer (Yamauchi), etc., have been subjected to harsh criticism over time. So, for example, the opposition between the terms «life-death» and «light-darkness», so common in John's gospel (cf. Jn 1:10), and apparently indicating Gnostic influence, now appear in Essene writings from Qumran and in the actual title of the work *The War of the Sons of Light against the Sons of Darkness*. The gospel of John is no longer considered as the gospel of non- Jewish Hellenists. Bultmann himself was forced to acknowledge that the Gnostic characteristics noticed in the source of the «discourses of revelation» (*Offenbarungsreden*) of John's gospel do not correspond to a pagan substratum but to one that is Semitic and even Jewish.

So then, the balance of studies on the origins of Christianity has tilted towards *a more Semitic context, closer to Jewish tradition*. The point of comparison has shifted from the Hellenistic pagan world to the smaller world of Hellenistic Judaism. It was the first channel through which the first pagan influences entered Christianity.

The view of the origins of Christianity has been strongly conditioned by the typically Hegelian opposition, established by F. C. Baur in 1845, between two trends in the primitive Church, one «Pauline» and Hellenising, the other «Petrine» and Judaising. However, Paul and Judaism do not represent two opposing worlds. It has even been possible to state that Christianity, for Paul, is not a new religion but the culmination of Judaism: Christ is the «new Torah» (W.D. Davies). The OT is the source of Pauline theology (A. T. Hanson). Jewish eschatology occupies a central position in Pauline thought, even more decisive than the theology of justification which Protestantism has developed, perhaps, too one-sidedly (Munck, Schoeps, Sanders). A large part of the NT texts has been seen in a new light thanks to the study of sources and of the social context of the Judaism of the period (Daube, Derret, Gerhardsson). Not only isolated texts but the NT as a whole must be understood in the light of the Judaism of the Second Temple (Rowland).

The Greek gospels are based on a Palestinian Aramaic tradition (Black). Some approaches try to date the origin of this Aramaic tradition back to Jesus himself with the intention of supporting the historical credibility of the gospels in this way (J. Jeremias).

The figure of Jesus of Nazareth belongs incontrovertibly to the context of the Judaism of Galilee, in whatever form could be imagined: as a charismatic man, saint and exorcist, who performed cures and carried out miraculous actions (G. Vermes) or as an eschatological prophet who considered himself to be the last messenger of God before the coming of the Kingdom (E. P. Sanders) or like a Mediterranean peasant farmer who preached and practised a radical egalitarianism (Crossan), etc. Vermes pays one-sided attention to the ministry of Jesus, rather than the fundamental fact of his judgment and death. Certainly, Jesus' contemporaries saw him as a religious figure of great importance, though as yet without reference to the *kerygma* of death-resurrection. However, the NT focuses more on this message than on the very meagre biographical information concerning the figure of Jesus.

C.   GREEK AND JEWISH ELEMENTS IN THE NEW TESTAMENT

To emphasise the Jewish connection of early Christianity should cause the no less obvious Greek and Roman connection to be forgotten. It is enough to think of the geographical situation in which Christianity was born, the Palestine of the Ptolemies, Seleucids, Hasmonaeans and Herodians. Also the area through which Christianity spread was the Greek and Roman world, where cultural and religious syncretism ruled, in which both Judaism and early Christianity had to struggle to make their mark and gain the recognition of history or their entry into history. At the very start Christianity was a Jewish-Christianity and through contact with paganism it became a precipitate of Eastern and Western, Semitic and Greek and Roman, monotheistic and pagan elements. The decisive factor is to note here that Palestinian Judaism itself was thoroughly Hellenised (Hengel) so that Hellenism and Judaism cannot be opposed as has been done for so long. The Jewish element which the first Christians absorbed had been Hellenised for some time. And the Hellenistic element which the first Christians could absorb reached them more easily through Judaism (cf. p. 38).

Research has continued to bring to light new elements of contact between the NT and the world of the Greeks and Romans.

W. Jaeger was able to say that Greek philosophy exerted no influence at all on the NT but only on later Christianity. Today, the trend is to think that Paul knew at first hand and not only through Jewish sources the traditions in vogue among the philosophers of his age and that he even made use of them (cf. p. 537). Recent decades have known a renewed study of the relations between the NT writers and the philosophers of the Greek and Roman world, not only the Stoics, favoured as they were at the beginning of the century (Seneca, Musonius Rufinus, Epictetus) but the Platonists, Peripatetics, Cynics, Epicuraeans and Pythagoraeans within the philosophical *koiné* of this period. Nor is the syncretism typical of this philosophy seen yet as a homogenising process which caused the loss of cultural and religious differences, but as a phenomenon with its own authentically creative character. Therefore, recent studies on the character of the *theîos anér* or «divine man» are important (Georgi).

Study of the relationship between *Greek literary forms* has been particularly fruitful. Bultmann had already established a relationship between the genre of cynical-stoic diatribe and the style of Paul's preaching. The very genre of «gospel», generally considered as a literary creation peculiar to Christianity, has been related to Hellenistic aretologies (Hadas, M. Smith, Koester). All the literary forms of the NT have parallels and antecedents in Greek literature: the anecdote, the apothegm, the parable, the miracle account and the sayings (*logia*) of the source Q (*Quelle*) in the synoptic gospels.

The *anecdotes* (*khreîai*) of the synoptic gospels have their closest parallels in the Greek writings about philosophers and politicians (K. Berger). The presence of anecdotes in all the strata of the NT is an indication of the evolution of primitive Christianity, which moves from an apocalyptic vision to concern for the course of history as the sphere for the development of Christian life.

The *apothegm*, a maxim or short saying, is not a genre found in the Jewish sources of the Mishnah and of intertestamental literature. The rabbinic debates follow the model of consensus in which collective opinion counts for more. The biographies by Greek writers of philosophers, poets and politicians provide a more suitable background than that of Jewish literature to account for the interest in apothegms in the New Testament community (G.G. Porton).

To emphasise one-sidedly the Jewish background and the presumably pre-Paschal Aramaic context of Jesus' *parables* (J. Jeremias) is to ignore the dependence of the synoptic parables on *all* ancient parables, Jewish or Hellenistic, biblical or non-biblical in terms of style and structure. The parables of Jesus are not *sui generis* (against the view of J. Jeremias); instead, in narrative structure and in other characteristics, they belong completely to Mediterranean cultural tradition.

The *sayings of the Q source* show generic features of the collections of sayings of the Greek and Roman world (J.M. Robinson). Paul was influenced greatly by Hellenism and is responsible for Christianity in its present form (Maccoby).

The synoptic literature is a form of biography which fits the context of Hellenistic literature in the form of biographies of ancient philosophers. Written biographies in the Mediterranean world of that period are intended to nip in the bud misrepresentations of the life and teaching of very well known figures and to provide, instead, the true image of the philosopher in question: Socrates (*Memorabilia* of Xenophon), Pythagoras (Porphyry's *Life of Pythagoras*), Apollonius of Tiana (Philostrates' *Life of Apollonius*), Agricola (Tacitus' *Life of Agricola*), etc. At that time, biographies of the founders of prestigious philosophical schools enjoyed as much popularity as those of famous warriors or politicians.

To keep on looking for Aramaic originals behind the NT texts has ceased to be a promising approach in current research. These texts were composed in Greek, for a Greek public in a Greek style using Greek forms. The synoptics are not translations of Hebrew or Aramaic originals but basically compositions written in Greek. The Semitisms of the NT are best explained as Septuagintisms. The authors of the Greek NT could make use of Semitisms to confer authority and give a certain Palestinian Jewish character to their accounts, the style and structure of which do not cease to be completely Hellenistic. It is possible to suppose even that the pre-synoptic traditions in Greek are based on oral traditions, also transmitted in Greek (Guenther, but cf. pp. 405 and 414).

The attempts at connecting the NT with the forms of Greek and Roman literature seem to be fully justified. It could be objected that there was a deep contrast between the so-called Greek and Roman «belles lettres» and «popular literature» to which the NT writings would belong. Against this can be observed that between these two extremes there was a very wide literary and linguistic spectrum and that the stylistic conventions of the upper classes also reached the lowest strata, and could appear even in such forms of popular literature as the NT (D. E. Aune).

The supposition that an Aramaic tradition is hidden behind the Greek gospels is closely linked with the image that the Christian movement was rural in origin and character, only later developing into forms of urban life in the Hellenistic social world. According to Meeks, however, Jesus's movement was a complete failure as an attempt at renewal within Judaism. Christianity only succeeded in those cities to which it was linked from the start. On the other hand, to equate the Aramaic tradition of the NT with rural surroundings is to forget that there is a whole literary tradition written in Aramaic.

The Greek character of the NT is not as connected with the mystery religions as had been supposed in the history of religions school. It was connected more with Jewish-Hellenism and the Jewish Hellenists, who are quoted in the NT. Palestinian Judaism is a Hellenistic Judaism (Hengel, see the next chapter) and the Christian religion brings about a fusion of Jewish and Greek elements. If, to use Käsemann's apt expression, one can say that Jewish apocalyptic represents the maternal line of Christian theology, it should also be said that the thought and style of the Greeks comprise the paternal line of Christianity.

As an exception to what has been said above, a separate bibliography is provided concerning Christianity in relation to Judaism and Hellenism.

BIBLIOGRAPHY

Christianity and Judaism

BLACK, M., *An Aramaic Approach to the Gospels and Acts*, Oxford 1969.
BONSIRVEN, J., *Textes rabbiniques des deux premiers siècles chrétiens pour servir à l'intelligence du Nouveau Testament*, Rome 1955.
CROSSAN, J.D., *The Historical Jesus. The Life of a Mediterranean Jewish Peasant*, New York 1991.
DAVIES, W.D., *Paul and Rabbinic Judaism: Some Rabbinic Elements in Pauline Theology*, London 1948.
DAUBE, D., *The New Testament and Rabbinic Judaism*, London 1956.
DERRET, J.D.M., *Law and the New Testament*, London 1970.
GERHARDSSON, B., *Memory and Manuscripts: Oral Tradition and Written Transmission in Rabbinic Judaism and Early Christianity*, Lund 1961.
MURPHY O'CONNOR, J.-CHARLESWORTH, J.M. (eds.), *Paul and the Dead Sea Scrolls*, New York 1990.
ROWLAND, CH., *Christian Origins. An Account of the Setting and Character of the Most Important Messianic Sect of Judaism*, London 1985.
SANDERS, E.P., *Paul and Palestinian Judaism: A Comparison of Patterns of Religion*, Philadelphia PA 1977.
SANDERS, E.P., *Jesus and Judaism*, London-Philadelphia PA 1985.
SCHOEPS, H.J., *Paulus: Die Theologie des Apostels im Lichte der jüdischen Religionsgeschichte*, Tübingen 1959.
SCHWARTZ, D., *Studies in the Jewish Background of Christianity*, Tübingen 1992.
SHANKS, H. (ed.), *Christianity and Rabbinic Judaism. A Parallel History of Their Origins and Early Development*, London 1993.
STRACK, M.-BILLERBECK, P., *Kommentar zum neuen Testament aus Talmud und Midrasch*, 6 vols., Munich 1924-1928.
VERMES, G., *Jesus the Jew: A Historian's Reading of the Gospels*, London 1994.
VERMES, G., *The Religion of Jesus the Jew*, London 1993.

Christianity and Hellenism (cf. pp. 543-545)

AUNE, D.E., *The New Testament in Its Literary Environment*, Philadelphia PA 1987.
AUNE, D.E., (ed.), *Greco-Roman Literature and the New Testament*, Atlanta GA 1988.

BALCH, D.L.-FERGUSON, E.-MEEKS, W.A., *Greeks, Romans and Christians. Essays in Honor of A.J. Malherbe*, Minneapolis MN 1990.

BOUSSET, W., *Kyrios Christos. Geschichte des Christusglaubens von den Anfängen des Christentums bis Irenaeus*, Göttingen 1913.

BULTMANN, R., *Das Urchristentum im Rahmen der antiken Religionen*, Zurich 1949.

BULTMANN, R., *Das Evangelium des Johannes*, Göttingen 1950.

CULLMANN, O., *Christus und die Zeit. Die urchristliche Zeit- und Geschichtsauffassung*, Zurich 1962³.

DIBELIUS, M., *An die Kolosser, an die Epheser, an Philemon*, Tübingen 1913.

DROGE, M., *Homer or Moses? Early Christian Interpretations of the History of Culture*, Tübingen 1989.

GEORGI, D., *Die Gegner des Paulus im 2. Korintherbrief: Studien zur religiösen Propaganda in der Spätantike*, Neukirchen-Vluyn 1964.

GUENTHER, H.O., «Greek: Home of Primitive Christianity», *Toronto Journal of Theology* 5 (1989) 247-279.

GRANT, F.C., (ed.), *Ancient Roman Religion*, New York 1957.

GRANT, R.M., *Gods and One God*, Philadelphia PA 1986.

HADAS, M.-SMITH, M., *Heroes and Gods*, New York 1965.

HANSON, H.T., *Studies in Paul's Technique and Theology*, Grand Rapids MI 1974.

JAEGER, W., *Early Christianity and Greek Religion*, Cambridge MA 1961.

LIETZMANN, H., *An die Römer*, Tübingen 1906.

MACK, B.L., *Rhetoric and the New Testament*, Minneapolis MN 1990.

MAHLERBE, A.J., *Paul and the Popular Philosophers*, Minneapolis MN 1989.

MARTIN, F., *Narrative Parallels to the New Testament*, Atlanta GA 1988.

MOMIGLIANO, A., *On Pagans, Jews, and Christians*, Middletown 1989.

MUNCK, J., *Paulus und die Heilgeschichte*, Copenhagen 1954.

NILSSON, M.P., *Geschichte der griechischen Religion*, 2 vols., Munich 1941 and 1950, 3rd revised ed. 1967.

REITZENSTEIN, R., *Hellenistic Mystery-Religions: Their Basic Ideas and Significance*, Pittsburgh PA 1978.

ROBINSON, J.M., «Logoi Sophon: On the Gattung of Q», *The Future of Our Religious Past: Essays in Honour of R. Bultmann*, ed. J.M. Robinson, New York-Evanston-San Francisco 1971.

ROKEA, D., *Jews Pagans and Christians in Conflict*, Jerusalem-Leiden 1982.

SMITH, M., *Jesus the Magician*, New York 1978.

VAN DER HORDT, P.W., *Hellenism - Judaism - Christianity. Essays on Their Interaction*, Kampen 1994.

WILLIAMS, R., *The Making of Orthodoxy. Essays in Honour of H. Chadwick*, Cambridge 1989.

YAMAUCHI, E.M., *Pre-Christian Gnosticism: A Survey of the Proposed Evidences*, Grand Rapids MI 1973.

2. Judaism and Hellenism

A. THE HELLENISING OF JUDAISM

Rather than contrasting unduly Hellenism and Judaism, nowadays it is accepted that *the Semitic world* and *the Greek world had remained closely related from very ancient times*, perhaps even going back to prehistoric periods (Hadas). The discovery of Ugarit (on the Syrian coast of the Mediterranean) has highlighted the existence of many contacts between Greece and the Near East, from the beginning of the second half of the second millennium BCE. The flourishing trade by Phoenicians and Greeks throughout the whole Mediterranean basin favoured these contacts of which the most significant fruit was the adoption of the Phoenician alphabet by the Greeks (cf. pp. 85-86/85f).

These relations between East and West, between Phoenicia and Greece, between Palestine and the Hellenistic world acquired still *greater growth and significance in later periods* (Hengel). Only the intensity of these earlier relations can explain why it was possible that, after the rapid passage of Alexander through the East, the Semitic world of the East could assimilate Hellenism with such speed and so successfully. In the 5th and 4th centuries BCE, even before the arrival of Alexander, Palestine already formed part of the cultural area which included Greece, Asia and Egypt. All the populations from the Delta up to Cilicia lived immersed in a single culture of very eclectic character (Bickerman). Palestine, through which everything had to pass, received these cultural influences with greater intensity.

It must also be considered that, contrary to what has been thought, *there was no sudden historical gap between the Persian period and the Hellenistic period*. In general, history does not admit such fits and starts (Tcherikover). Alexander the Great's invasion and the resulting disappearance of the Persian empire did not imply the complete collapse of everything. The cultural centre was not shifted from one pole to the other, from East to West, from Persia and Mesopotamia to Macedonia and Greece. Rather, there arose at that time several cultural and political poles through the length and breadth of the Hellenistic world. The incorporation of Palestine into the Persian Empire had already supposed it to belong within a political and cultural whole which included large Greek territories in Asia Minor. Accordingly, Alexander's conquest did not suppose an absolute beginning in the relations between Jewish, Semitic and Iranian cultures on the one hand and Hellenic culture on the other. It was, instead, simply a strengthening of relations that already existed.

Nor did Alexander's conquest imply an end to the spread of Persian culture. It continued to influence biblical and apocryphal literature, especially in respect of the dualistic vision of the cosmos and of history and the development of angelology and demonology. Again, the approach represented by the history of religions school tends to stress the influence of a foreign element, in this case Iranian, on biblical religion and Judaism. Other approaches suppose, instead, that the biblical tradition evolved independently, co-inciding sometimes with the development of Iranian religion. Points of contact between Iranian religion and Biblical religion are monotheism, the figure of a prophet or reformer, eschatological hope based on a God who governs history, the regulation of religious life by means of a Law and the resulting conversion of religion into a Law or Torah, etc. (Hultgård). As for Iranian influences on Judaism (dualism, angelology, demonology, etc.), it has to be taken into account that Egyptian and Greek would also have an influence in the same areas, especially in the case of the roots of Gnosticism.

After the Persian period, relations between Judaism and Hellenism were not those of hostilities between two cultural and religious worlds, unable to avoid coming into in conflict. The invasion of the Jewish world by Greek culture was something inevitable and accepted by all Jews, something which did not need to be discussed. The differences of opinion, which instead were very hostile, concerned the extent to which Hellenic culture was to be accepted. It is symptomatic that the success of the uprising by the Maccabees against the Greeks did not prevent these champions of Jewish tradition from ultimately becoming kings in a Hellenistic monarchy like so many others, with all the appropriate attributes: a constitution written by Simon Maccabaeus, nobles and priests who adopted Greek names, an army of mercenaries which supported the king, etc. Far from ending during the reigns of the last Maccabees, Hellenic influence even increased from then onwards.

Lieberman and Bickerman, Jewish scholars and therefore perhaps less suspect when it comes to recognising similarities between Judaism and Hellenism, have noticed several *points of contact between very traditional institutions and ideas of Judaism and institutions and ideas of contemporary Hellenism*. The grand architectural lines used in the Herodian Temple of Jerusalem as well as some of the most trivial details of the Jerusalem cult reveal the influence of traditional models from the cultural and religious world of Hellenism. The education of the Jewish rabbis was carried out in accordance with guidelines of Greek *paideia*. The rabbinic rules for interpreting the OT, attributed to Hillel, correspond to the hermeneutics practised in Alexandria and in other centres of Hellenism (Lieberman, Daube, cf. pp. 460 and 479). Something as characteristically Jewish as the fact that an oral law accompanied the written Torah and the resultant insistence by Pharisees and rabbis on the importance of education are not features typical of or exclusive to Judaism but the common heritage of the Hellenistic world (Bickerman). Palestinian Judaism, particularly the Pharisee group, must be considered forms of the Hellenistic culture of the period (Neusner).

Permanent contact between Judaism and Hellenism was both cause and effect of a whole historical process. This process, begun before the 4th cent. BCE was subsequently set in motion and reached Syria and Palestine up to the time of Hadrian. (This happened later than in Greece, where the Hellenistic period ended with the battle of Actium in 31 BCE). The result was «*Hellenistic Judaism*», which has its most characteristic expression in the LXX version, in «Jewish-Hellenistic» literature and in the works of Philo of

Alexandria. The Hellenisation of Judaism is just one more element in a whole process of Hellenisation of the East. It comprises both the permeation of the East by Greek culture and the fusion of the Semitic and Greek cultures to give an eclectic precipitate made from both and yet different from either.

B.   SOCIAL AND RELIGIOUS DIVERSITY IN HELLENISTIC JUDAISM

The classic work *A History of the Jewish People in the Times of Jesus Christ* by E. Schürer, which was the manual for many generations of students until recent years, reveals in its very title that the perspective from which the history of Judaism has nearly always been studied is alien to Jewish history itself: the real interest always lies in knowledge of the origin and development of Christianity.

On the other hand, historians of so-called «*ancient Judaism*» or «*late Judaism*» (*Spätjudentum*) worked with a generally negative idea of this postbiblical Judaism. This applies to E. Schürer, J. Wellhausen and to many later authors between 1880 and 1930: Charles, Kautzsch, Bousset, Gressmann, Riessler, etc. Often, especially in the Protestant world, so sensitive to the Pauline opposition between Law and Grace, considered «ancient Judaism» to be religious legalism, more concerned with the external fulfilment of obsolete precepts than with the commitment to a message of grace. Not even the superb collection of rabbinic parallels to the NT completed by H. Strack and P. Billerbeck avoids this negative view of Judaism, even though the intention of this work was to emphasise the importance of rabbinic literature for study of the NT. The very label «late Judaism» used to describe the Judaism of the second Temple period (from the end of the 6th cent. to 70 CE) entailed the conception of it circulated by J. Wellhausen. According to him, after the period of splendour of biblical kings and prophets (8th-6th cents. BCE) and beginning with Ezra the scribe (5th cent. BCE), Judaism fell into a ritualistic and legalistic paralysis at the hands of the priests and lawyers governing the institutions of Jewish theocracy during the Persian and Greek periods.

Other labels used to refer to the Judaism of this period though apparently more neutral, also hint at a certain negative judgment on it. The term «*post-biblical Judaism*» tends to make Judaism seem like the successor to the classical biblical period. The label «*pre-rabbinic Judaism*» assumes a degree of subordination of the Judaism of the centuries prior to the later Mishnaic period. The labels «*Judaism between the Bible and the Mishnah*» and «*intertestamental Judaism*» transform the Judaism of this period into a transition between two periods of splendour and between two great sets of literature, the Bible and the Mishnah or the OT and the NT.

Starting from the period of Ezra and Nehemiah, one can begin to speak of the existence of «Judaism» as something new and different, although obviously continuous with «ancient Israel» of the pre-exilic period. On the other hand, the destruction of Jerusalem in 70 CE and the spread of Christianity in the same period mark a decisive historical change. Even though rabbinic Judaism is a continuation of the Judaism of the previous period, there is no doubt that both periods present very different characteristics (Neusner).

From a Christian perspective and for theological reasons, there is a tendency to mark a divide in 70 CE between what precedes and what follows this date: Judaism after the exile is considered as a continuation of biblical tradition. This does not apply to rabbinic Judaism which for a Christian is something very strange and deviant in respect of biblical tradition. For theological reasons also, Judaism too stresses the continuity between biblical and rabbinic traditions, passing rapidly over the intervening period of formation of Pharisee oral tradition. Historians of religion, though, tend to speak of two different religions, biblical religion and Jewish religion, with a period of transition between the two.

G.F. Moore came to the defence of the distortion of the history of the Jewish religion underlying the approaches of J. Wellhausen and E. Schürer. Moore, instead, presented rabbinic Judaism as *«normative» Judaism*, formed between the 2nd and 6th cents. CE in the huge collections of the Mishnah, the *Targumim* and the Babylonian and Jerusalem Talmuds. Moore contrasted normative Judaism with other forms of Judaism labelled «sectarian»: those represented by groups such as the Sadducees, Essenes, Zealots, therapeutae and others, which disappeared owing to the destruction of Jerusalem in 70 CE.

This opposition between normative Judaism, and sectarian and marginal Judaism also implied setting up a similar opposition between a *normative literature*, comprising the OT and the Mishnah and the Talmud and other *literature considered as «sectarian»* and quasi-heretical, collected in the pseudepigraphical books of the OT, differing widely in literary form and origin. On many occasions the world of ideas reflected in this literature was on the borderline of what was considered traditional and typical of Judaism. Suspicions were persistently aroused until to read it was ultimately forbidden. The movement for the reunification of Judaism, begun after the disaster of 70 CE, placed restrictions on the distribution of those books representing centrifugal trends of the Judaism of the previous period, which had brought in its wake such disastrous consequences for the Jewish people. These books could have continued encouraging dangerous movements of dispersal. This is why the books rescued from oblivion have survived only through copies transmitted through Christian channels. For very different reasons in each case, in these books some churches and Christian groups found theological ideas or information of a very different kind, and used them in their theology and in the interpretation of the OT and the NT.

Recent studies do not allow such a sharp distinction between official, normative Judaism and marginal, «sectarian» forms of Judaism to be established. In the centuries before the appearance of Christianity, Judaism was a mosaic of groups with quite varied trends. The documents of Qumran, apocryphal literature, Jewish-Hellenistic literature and archaeological finds provide a spectrum of the Judaism of this period which differs greatly from the monolithic and uniform picture provided by the rabbinic literature of the later period. Rabbinic Judaism itself even continued to allow some dissent within itself.

After the destruction of Jerusalem in 70 CE, Judaism united around the Pharisee movement and caused the disappearance of all the groups which in the earlier period formed part of Judaism with the same rights as the Pharisee group. The destruction of the Temple resulted in the disappearance of the Sadducees, close to the priestly families. The failure of the first Jewish revolt against the Romans in the years 68-70 followed by the new failure of Bar Kochba's revolt in 135 had as a consequence the partial disappearance of messianic hopes and, in a special way, the discrediting of the apocalyptic movements and groups which had fed the revolt against the Romans. The armed groups of Zealots and Sicarii, who had supported the revolt to the extent of despair and suicide, left no trace except in the historical memory of the people of Israel.

Therefore, the rabbinic Judaism of the Mishnah and the Talmud cannot be used as a rod to measure the degree of Judaism of the Jewish movements and groups of the previous period. At that time, the idea of a canonical and official Judaism which excluded the dissident sects and groups had not yet developed, nor had the idea of a closed and definitive canon of the biblical books. So-called official Judaism, represented by rabbinism, is very far from having developed a system of dogmatic truths, as did the Christian Church in the same period (forced by the centrifugal and separative movements nestling within it). And the Judaism of the Hellenistic period housed within it movements and groups united by common reference to the Torah and the Temple, but in opposition to each other because of the different meaning which Torah and Temple had for each, the history and messianic hope of Israel, the position of Israel among the nations, etc. In the words of L.H. Schiffmann, with Darwinian overtones: «After all, Second Temple Judaism was to a large extent a set of competing alternatives grappling with one another in what ultimately became a test of yhe survival of the fittest. In that struggle tannaitic Judaism prevailed»

To call the Essene community of Qumran a «sect» is inappropriate as is denouncing as «sectarian» the writings of that community or the «pseudepigraphical» books of the OT. Nor does the use of the term «apocryphal» presume a reduction in value of those books, as if they were less representative of Judaism than the books we call canonical. Recent decades have seen a renewal of the study of this pseudepigraphical literature, thanks chiefly to the discovery of manuscripts of books about which only the title or even nothing was known (cf. p. 184 and p. 200).

If in the eyes of official Judaism of the 2nd - 6th cents. CE, a negative judgment about other social and ideological sectors of Judaism before 70 CE cannot be given, from a Christian and NT perspective, equally negative perceptions of the whole of Judaism cannot be established either. The discoveries from the Dead Sea and recent studies have contributed to the rediscovery of the matrix in which Christianity gestated: Jewish apocalyptic messianism, and more generally, the whole range of traditions in Judaism (Collins).

BICKERMAN, E., *From Ezra to the Last of the Maccabees: The Historical Foundations of Post-Biblical Judaism*, New York 1962.

BOCCACCINI, G., *Middle Judaism. Jewish Thought, 300 B.C.E.-200 C.E.*, Minneapolis MN 1991.

BOUSSET, W., -GRESSMANN, H., *Die Religion des Judentums im späthellenistischen Zeitalter*, Tübingen 1926³.

CHARLES, R.H. (ed.), *The Apocrypha and Pseudepigrapha of the Old Testament*, 2 vols., Oxford 1913.

COLLINS, J.J., *Between Athens and Jerusalem. Jewish Identity in the Hellenistic Diaspora*, New York 1986.

DAVID, PH.R. - WHITE, R.T. (eds.), *A Tribute to Geza Vermes. Essays on Jewish and Christian Literature and History*, Sheffield 1991.

FELDMAN, L.H., *Jew and Gentile in the Ancient World. Attitudes and Interactions from Alexander to Justinian*, Princeton NJ 1993.

FISHBANE, M.-TOV, E., *«Sha'rei Talmon». Studies in the Bible, Qumran, and the Ancient Near East Presented to Shemaryahu Talmon*, Winona Lake, IN 1992.

HAASE, W., (ed.), *Hellenistisches Judentum in Römischer Zeit: Philon und Josephus*, Principat: Religion, ANWR II 21.1, Berlin-New York 1984.

HADAS, M., *Hellenistic Culture: Fusion and Diffusion*, New York 1972.

HENGEL, M., *Judaism and Hellenism. Studies in the Encounter in Palestine during the Early Hellenistic Period*, 2 vols. London 1974.

HENGEL, M., *The 'Hellenization' of Judaea in the First Century after Christ*, London 1990.

HULTGÅRD, A., «Das Judentum in der hellenistisch-römischen Zeit und die iranische Religion- ein religionsgeschichtliches Problem», *ANWR* II 19.1, 513-583.

KAUTZSCH, E. (ed.), *Die Apocryphen und Pseudepigraphen des Alten Testaments*, 2 vols., Tübingen 1900.

LIEBERMAN, S., *Hellenism in Jewish Palestine: Studies in the Literary Transmission of Beliefs and Manners of Palestine in the I Century B.C.E. – IV Century C.E.*, New York 1950.

MOORE, G.F., *Judaism in the First Centuries of the Christian Era: The Age of the Tannaim*, Cambridge MA, 1927-30.

NEUSNER, J., *From Politics to Piety: The Emergence of Pharisaic Judaism*, Englewood Cliffs NJ 1973.

RIESSLER, P., *Altjüdisches Schrifttum ausserhalb der Bibel*, Heidelberg 1928.

SCHIFFMAN, L.H., *The Dead Sea Scrolls and the Early History of Jewish Liturgy, The Synagogue in Late Antiquity*, ed. L.I. Levine, Philadelphia PA 1987, 33-48.

SCHÜRER, E., *Geschichte des jüdischen Volkes im Zeitalter Jesu Christi*, Lepizig 1901-7, 3ª ed., for English edition cf. Vermes, G.

SMITH, M., *Palestinian Parties and Politics that Shaped the Old Testament*, New York 1971.

TALMON, SH. (ed.), *Jewish Civilization in the Hellenistic-Roman Period*, Sheffield 1991.

TCHERIKOVER, V., *Hellenistic Civilization and the Jews*, Philadelphia PA 1959.

VERMES, G. - MILLAR, F. - BLACK, M. - M. GOODMAN, *The History of the Jewish People in the Age of Jesus Christ (175 B.C.–A.D. 135)*, 3 vols., Edinburgh 1979-1987.

WELLHAUSEN, J., *Die Pharisäer und die Sadducäer. Eine Untersuchung zur inneren jüdischen Geschichte*, Greifswald 1874.

II. THE BIBLE IN THE PERSIAN, GREEK AND ROMAN PERIODS

The history of the formation and transmission of the text of the biblical books runs in tandem with the development of Judaism in the Persian and Hellenistic period. The literary history and the social history of Judaism have to be studied together for both to be understood.

In the Persian and Hellenistic period, from the 5th cent. BCE until the beginning of the 2nd cent. CE, the most decisive steps in the history of the Bible were made. The collections of books were established which later came to make up the canon, and the process of transmission, distribution and translation of its text were started. Also, the of principles and methods of interpretation began to be established. In addition, a huge tradition of oral and written interpretation of the Scriptures was amassed.

It is important to know the approaches dominating research prior to the discoveries from the Dead Sea and also to know the new avenues which in recent years have opened up among research scholars. The books of introduction to the OT and NT are always very sparing in presenting and discussing the problem of the canon, the text and the versions. Older Introductions to the OT such as those by Eissfeldt, Weiser and Rost, provided if possible, more discussion of these questions than the many introductions published later on. The first of these three even provided a lengthy section on apocryphal and pseudepigraphical literature. The new material collected over the last decades and the new approaches which they entailed show that the themes of formation of the canon, apocryphal literature, history and criticism of the biblical text, history and criticism of the biblical translations and history, literary forms and processes of biblical interpretation can very well comprise at least a third of what could be a university course on «Biblical Literature: Old and New Testament(s)». The other two-thirds are made up of (a) a classical introduction to each of the canonical books and (b) comparison of biblical literature with ancient near Eastern and Greek and Roman literature. It is understandable that in the courses of a Faculty of Theology more space and importance is granted to introduction and exegesis of the canonical books. In Faculties of Philology and History, more importance will be given to placing biblical literature, the history of Israel and of Christianity within the general and literary history of the ancient world. The material discussed in this book is the subject of very differing yet closely related disciplines. They range from palaeography and textual criticism to the techniques of translation and interpretation and hermeneutic philosophy.

1. Canon or Canons. Canonical and Apocryphal

A. CANON OR CANONS IN THE OLD TESTAMENT

Research in recent decades has questioned positions held since ancient times about the history of the formation of the Hebrew and Christian canon and the existence of an Alexandrian canon.

Since the work by Ryle (1892) it was usual to divide the *history of the formation of the* OT *into three stages*, taking the Samaritan schism as a reference point. This schism, it was assumed, had taken place in the 5th cent. BCE. The first stage corresponded to that century when, prior to the Samaritan schism, canonical value was accorded the Torah or Pentateuch. The second stage, in the 3rd cent., corresponded to the canonisation of a collection of prophetic books, but rejected by the Samaritans who had by then already broken with Judaism. The *Ketubîm* or Writings came to form part of the canon in the last stage, dated to about 90 CE, on the occasion of the so-called Synod of Yabneh at which the canon of the Hebrew Bible was finally closed (Graetz 1871).

It was thought, on the other hand, that the Judaism of the diaspora in Alexandria had its own canon available, the «Alexandrian canon». This canon was represented by the collection of books included in the Greek Bible of the LXX and had been accepted by early Christianity before the Hebrew canon was finally closed around 90 CE.

The two canons, Palestinian and Alexandrian, were Jewish in origin, but when the Christians began to use the Greek version of the LXX and its (correspondingly) longer canon, the Jewish rabbis decided to establish a single recognised and authorised canon, the *Tanak* in Hebrew, as a completely fixed text and with a shorter canon of biblical books, which left «outside» those considered «outside» (*ḥîsonîm*) or apocryphal, some of which are found in the Greek Bible of the Christians.

In recent years, all the presuppositions upon which these theories were based have collapsed. Lewis and Leiman (cf. pp. 165 and 167) have demolished the hypothetical closure of the canon in Yabneh in the year 90 CE. (cf. p. 000). Sundberg has proved that an Alexandrian canon did not exist and Purvis has undermined the «Samaritan connection» (cf. pp. 211 and 216), dating the so-called Samaritan schism to the 2nd cent. CE, after the canonisation of the prophetical books and not before.

In fact, a trend seems to be developing which considers the Hebrew canon to have been formed in the Maccabaean period, towards the middle of the 2nd cent. BCE. As yet the problem concerning what later came to be the Christian canon of the OT has no real solution. If it can no longer be said that the Christians inherited from the Jews of the diaspora a longer list of books than in the Hebrew Bible, the fact that the Christians did not feel constrained by the strict Hebrew canon has yet to be explained. Rather, this fact seems to have precedents in Essene community of Qumran. While it cannot be said to have been aware of re-opening an already closed canon, it would seem to have granted some writings a sacred character comparable to that of other books included in the canon (the book of *Jubilees*, VanderKam, cf. pp. 196 and 228) and possibly it rejected, instead, certain books from the canon, such as Esther (cf. pp. 176-177).

On the other hand, even if the Hebrew canon was essentially the same for all the Jewish groups (Sadducees, Pharisees, Essenes and the Jews of the diaspora) from the mid-2nd cent. BCE, the way each group made use of this canon determined different movements and interpretations. This almost justifies speaking of different canons or of several canons within the canon.

B.   CANON AND CANONS IN THE NEW TESTAMENT

The question of the NT *canon* has been re-opened in recent decades. In theological studies discussion has centred on Käsemann's thesis, according to which the NT canon does not found the unity of the Church but testifies instead to the plurality and diversity of churches from the beginnings of Christianity (cf. p 254). On the other hand, in the case of both the NT and OT canons, the tendency today is to go beyond the limits of the canon, studying the canonical books in relation to all the literature of the period, particularly the Jewish and Christian apocryphal books.

Until the end of the 19th cent., *apocryphal literature* was still virtually unknown. The definitive edition of Schürer's work (between 1901 and 1909) comprised a synthesis of the material known at that time. In the period between the two world wars there were hardly any important discoveries in this field. But then the discovery of the Dead Sea Scrolls implied a true revolution. However, research and changes of attitude proceed very slowly. Even in 1974 it was possible to state, in the introduction to an important work, that there was no need to take these writings into account since «these, too, did not become part of the Jewish tradition» (*Compendia* 1974, editor's introduction). Ten years later, though, and at the other extreme, G. Vermes asks himself the question, which he himself qualified as «to express myself a little more rashly»,[1] whether it was justifiable to remove from NT studies the independence they enjoyed and consider them, together with other Jewish writings of the period, as belonging to the general history of Judaism (Vermes). If the attempt to sketch the profile of Jesus by omitting anything referring to his judgment and death remains one-sided, it would be even more one-sided to reduce the NT to mere parameters of the Judaism of that period.

The Introductions to the NT generally discuss only canonical literature, isolating it completely from the apocryphal literature of the OT and NT and also separating it from rabbinic literature and the Christian literature of the sub-apostolic and patristic period. Two recent and very important works, instead, declare themselves to be true histories of early Christian literature in its entirety. The work by P. Vielhauer, *History of early Christian literature*, however, does not allow a division between early Christian literature and patristic literature to be made, not only for historical and theological reasons, but also for reasons of a literary nature. The literary forms of the NT (letters, gospels, apocalypses and «acts») did not persist or develop in patristic literature. H. Köster's *Introduction to the NT* affects to go further and unfolds a history of early Christian literature, both canonical and non-canonical, in the context of the ancient literary, religious and cultural world. However, Köster does not explain clearly which are the criteria relating the different

1.   G. Vermes, «La littérature juive intertestamentaire à la lumière d'un siècle de recherches et de découvertes», *Études sur le judaïsme hellénistique*, 19-39 (29).

texts to each other and to that context. Nor does he explain the contribution made to the understanding of early Christian literature by inserting it in the Greek and Latin literature of the period. Texts and contexts are presented as juxtaposed entities without any very clear connection between. In this way, it is difficult for the reader to realise that Judaism effectively comprises the reference point for the study of early Christianity.

The Introductions to the OT and NT will continue to be centred on canonical literature as this comprises the required referent of all Bible study. This is not only because they are the sacred texts of Judaism and of Christianity but because the canonical Bible, as a book made up of a particular set of books and not of others, has had a decisive influence on the culture of East and West and continues to be a reference point for literary and theological creativity.

2.   *The Text of the Bible and Biblical Texts*

Before the discovery of the biblical manuscripts from Qumran it was possible to imagine that the transmission of the biblical text had occurred following a single straight line which began from the autographs of the biblical authors and reached as far as the mediaeval Hebrew manuscripts, and from them to our own printed editions. The biblical manuscripts from Qumran, however, have shown clearly that the history of the transmission of the biblical text in the Hellenistic period is very diverse and complex. The as yet incomplete history of the Qumran discoveries can be summarised by pointing out four successive surprises provided by study of the manuscripts.

1. The first surprise came from the lengthy manuscripts of Isaiah, studied in the fifties. These manuscripts confirmed the immense *fidelity* with which the Hebrew text was preserved throughout the one thousand years which come between the Qumran period and the 9th and 10th centuries, a period when the mediaeval manuscripts preserved until the present were copied (cf. p.254).

2. Years later, other manuscripts were studied, especially the books of Samuel and Jeremiah. These showed clear *differences* in respect of the masoretic Hebrew text, yet to a large extent they agreed with the form of text represented by the LXX version. This led to the idea that some books of the Bible underwent a sort of «second edition, corrected and enlarged». The text of this second edition is the one transmitted by the masoretic textual tradition, while the shorter and more original form of the text is the one which the translators of the LXX version knew already (cf. pp.393-396).

3. Study of the manuscripts came to show that the Samaritan Pentateuch does not, as was believed, comprise a *«sectarian» Samaritan text* (apart from slight additions of that kind) but reproduces a type of text known throughout Palestine in the 2nd cent. BCE, in a much later period than when the Samaritan schism was supposed to have occurred. Study of these «proto-Samaritan» texts has forced the history of the actual Samaritan schism to be re-opened (cf. pp. 211-216).

4. Finally, the biblical manuscripts, or rather perhaps the «para-biblical» manuscripts published recently (4QDeut^j, 4QDeut^n, 4QNum^m, and especially 4QRP, «Reworked Pentateuch», cf. p. ooo) have uncovered problems unsuspected until now. For example, the need to establish criteria for determining where the border lies between what is biblical and what is not. This is so that a new text can be classified among the biblical manuscripts or has to be assigned to a sort of no-man's land in which *borderline*, «anthological» or «paraphrase» texts are located (Tov, White, Duncan, cf. p. ooo). In some sectors of Judaism, the biblical text or some forms of it still allowed very considerable development, without this necessarily meaning loss of the biblical character of the text. Future research will undoubtedly focus on study of such texts on the «borderline» between biblical and non-biblical. All this must pose questions related to the problem of the biblical canon (Ulrich).

The theory of «local texts» (Babylonian, Egyptian and Palestinian) developed by F.M. Cross (cf. pp. 292-294) as a result of these discoveries, has been questioned in some of its aspects. The plurality of texts of the OT seems to be due, on the one hand to the duplication or multiplying of editions of some biblical books («double editions») and on the other hand to the «expansionist» tendencies of some streams of text transmission.

Study of the biblical manuscripts from Qumran has boosted the value of the masoretic Hebrew text, but it has also entailed a revaluation of the text of the versions, especially of the LXX translation (and of the Old Latin) which on many occasions faithfully reflects a Hebrew text different from and older than the masoretic text. All this has contributed to a renaissance of studies in the textual criticism of the OT, somewhat sluggish in the decades before the appearance of the new material. At the same time it has posed anew the problem of the relationship between textual criticism and literary criticism and between what is meant by a critically established text and an authorised or canonical text.

3.   *Biblical Hermeneutics: Interpretation and Interpretations*

In recent decades studies on hermeneutic theory, biblical hermeneutics and the interpretation of the OT and NT have flourished considerably.

Today it is accepted that the history of biblical exegesis is rooted in the origins of the Bible itself. Some biblical books interpret others, the more recent books interpret older ones. The interpolations or reworking of the texts are no longer considered as mere inferior products of a late and decadent period but as witness to Jewish exegesis, the forerunner of Christian exegesis.

Study of apocryphal literature has recovered immense importance. Its raison d'être is largely to comment on and interpret canonical literature and comprises, on the other hand, the immediate literary substratum in which the NT was born. The LXX version and Hellenistic Jewish literature, like the writings of the Qumran community, are also studied from the point of view of their relationship to the OT, a source of inspiration and fount of exegesis for them.

The exegesis by the NT writings of the OT books has been studied intensely, so that on many occasions the NT is called a kind of long midrash on the OT. Study of the targums, in particular of Targum *Neophyti*, has been particularly fruitful in this respect.

Special attention is paid to the study of the methods practised in Jewish exegesis, which were also developed much later in Christian exegesis.

The quotations and «intertextual» echoes of the OT in intertestamental literature and in the NT, and of the NT in later Christian literature, comprise an area of study which has grown considerably in recent decades and still offers unexplored avenues for research. It has been possible to define several of the NT books and many NT passages, not without a certain misuse of terms, as exegetical commentaries, *midrašîm* or *haggadôt* on OT texts.

The history of dogma is to a large extent a history of exegesis. Christian doctrine, as well as many elements of Christian organisation and worship, are based on very concrete interpretations of many passages from Scripture. Until the Middle Ages, Judaism and Christianity developed a whole corpus of exegesis of their respective Scriptures, the basic lines of which form part of the traditional doctrine of Jews and Christians.

In the 18th cent. the critique of the Enlightenment and in the 19th cent. romantic hermeneutics developed a theistic or completely secularised reading of the Bible. Historical criticism converted the Bible into one more book in the enormous library of ancient Near Eastern literature and of the Greek and Latin world, and biblical religion into one more religion among the many religions of Antiquity.

Following a trend typical of both the Enlightenment and of Romanticism, the interests of modern criticism have preferred to focus on the «original» form and meaning of the biblical texts, with the abandonment of if not contempt for the whole history of interpretation of the Bible carried out later in Judaism and Christianity. The hermeneutical presuppositions and the prejudices of historical criticism made themselves felt more in the usually negative view of later periods, and especially of the final stages of the redaction of the biblical books. This applies as well to the large number of interpolations which the critics have detected in them: in the eyes of many critics, the redactions and glosses are the expression of trends peculiar to decadent periods, Judaising in the case of the OT and catholicising in the case of the NT.

This immersion of the biblical texts in the ocean of ancient literature, their separation from the natural medium in which they developed (rabbinic tradition in the case of the *Tanak* and Christian tradition for the combination formed by the OT and NT) has not failed to provoke reactions which have tried to save above all what is specific to biblical religion and literature. On the other hand, the «suspicion» made systematic towards the biblical texts which modern criticism seems to spread, together with the provisional nature and uncertainty which surrounds many of the conclusions of that criticism, has aroused in other movements of present-day biblical studies a reaction of «suspicion» towards the methods and results of modern criticism. There are many voices raised against an archaeological reading of the Bible, which prefers to value the most primitive nucleus, very often hypothetical, of the prophetic texts or the gospels, without taking into account the mediating value of later biblical tradition and of the whole history of biblical interpretation (the hermeneutic space which covers the «temporal distance» between the text and contemporary interpretation, Gadamer, cf. pp. 554-555).

Contemporary hermeneutic has emphasised, however, the need to pay attention to the *Wirkungsgeschichte* (Gadamer) or «historical effectiveness» which is translated into a revaluation of the effective influence of the myths, symbols and ideas of the past on the history and social life of later periods. The biblical Scriptures, like all literature and more than any literature, are a continual rewriting of what is already written. The Bible comprises not only its texts but also the quotations, allusions and echoes of its books in other texts (intertextuality) which in their turn enable new aspects of the actual biblical texts to be discovered. If biblical literature was born from simple forms such as the song, the proverb, oracles, etc., post-biblical literature was born from the «quotation», and it is all an enormous quotation from the OT. The quotation is not mere reproduction of a text but the production of a new text. The shift of context changes the meaning of the quotation which claims to be more precise, giving new meaning to what is quoted.

After what more than a few consider to be over-attention to the study of sources, traditions and redactions of the biblical books, a large portion of current studies is directed towards other aspects. These include the analysis of the meaning of the texts in the global context of the canon («canonical criticism», Childs, cf. pp. 416-418), valuing the Bible as a work of literature which demands an unbroken and respectful reading of the actual literary structure of its texts (Alonso Schökel)[2], the study of the interpretation of the Bible in post-biblical literature, considering patristic literature as a large *corpus* of exegesis of the Bible, etc.

The importance assumed by interpretation of the Bible is evident since it was possible to say that the split between Jewish synagogue and Christian Church happened at the precise moment when Christians ceased to interpret the Law «to the letter» and as a result, ceased to practise it. In the time of Bar Kochba, the Jewish-Christians of Palestine still read the Torah in a «literal» way and carried it out to the letter. The other Christian groups had given up this practice long before, perhaps after the destruction of the Temple in 70 CE (L. H. Schiffman, cf. p. 234).

2. L. Alonso Schökel, «Poética hebrea. Historia y procedimientos», *Hermenéutica de la palabra. II. Interpretación literaria de textos bíblicos*, Madrid 1987

Introductions to the Old Testament

CHILDS, B.S., *Introduction to the Old Testament as Scripture*, Philadelphia PA 1989.
EISSFELDT, O., *The Old Testament. An Introduction*, Oxford 1966.
FOHRER, G., *Introduction to the Old Testament*, London 1970.
FRIEDMAN, R.E., *Who Wrote the Bible?*, London 1988.
GOTTWALD, N.K., *The Hebrew Bible. A Socio-Literary Introduction*, Philadelphia PA 1987.
HAYES, J.H., *An Introduction to Old Testament Study*, Nashville TN 1986.
HUMMEL, H.D., *The Word Becoming Flesh. An Introduction to the Origin, Purpose, and Meaning of the Old Testament*, St Louis 1979.
KAISER, O., *Introduction to the Old Testament: a presentation of its results and problems*, trans. by J. Sturdy, Oxford 1975.
LASOR, W.S.-HUBBARD, D.A.-BUSH, F.W., *Old Testament Survey. The Message, Form, and Background of the Old Testament*, Grand Rapids, MI 1987.
PFEIFFER, R.H., *Introduction to the Old Testament*, New York 1941³.
RENDTORFF, R., *The Old Testament: An Introduction*, Philadelphia PA 1986.
SANDMEL, S., *The Hebrew Scriptures. An Introduction to their Literature and Religious Ideas*, New York 1963.
SCHMIDT, W.H., *Einführung in das Alte Testament*, 5th revised ed., Berlin-New York 1995.
SOGGIN, J.A., *Introduction to the Old Testament, from Its Origins to the Closing of the Alexandrian Canon*, Westminster 1982.
WEISER, A., *An Introduction to the Old Testament*, London 1961.

Biblical theology

BOTTERWECK, G.J. - RINGGREN, H., *Theological Dictionary of the Old Testament*, Grand Rapids MI 1977-.
BULTMANN, R., *Theology of the New Testament*, 2 vols., London 1952-1955.
CONZELMANN, H., *An Outline of the Theology of the New Testament*, trans. by J. Bowden, London 1969.
KRAUS, H.-J., *Die biblische Theologie: Ihre Geschichte und Problematik*, Neukirchen-Vluyn 1970.
KÜMMEL, W.G., *The Theology of the New Testament According to its Major Witnesses: Jesus-Paul-John*, Philadelphia PA 1974.
SCHRAGE, W., *The Ethics of the New Testament*, Edinburgh 1988.

Introductions to the New Testament

CHILDS, B., *The New Testament as Canon: An Introduction*, Philadelphia PA 1985.
KÖSTER, H., *Introduction to the New Testament. History, Culture, and Religion of the Hellenistic Age*, 2 vols., New York-Berlin 1982.
KÜMMEL, W.G., *Introduction to the New Testament*, London 1975.
LOHSE, E., *The Formation of the New Testament*, Nashville 1981.
MARXSEN, W., *Introduction to the New Testament: an Approach to its Problems*, Philadelphia PA 1974.
PERRIN, N., *The New Testament. An Introduction*, New York 1974.

History

BARRETT, C.K., *The New Testament Background: Selected Documents*, Revised Edition, London-San Francisco 1989, 1st ed. 1956.

BRUCE, F.F., *New Testament History*, Garden City NY 1972.

GRABBE, L.L., *Judaism from Cyrus to Hadrian*, 2 vols., Minneapolis MN 1992.

HORSLEY, R.A.-HANSON, J.S., *Bandits, Prophets, and Messiahs. Popular Movements in the Time of Jesus*, Minneapolis MN 1985.

LAGERSMA, H., *A History of Israel to Bar Kochba*, London 1994.

LOHSE, E., *The New Testament Environment*, London 1976.

MALINA, B.J., *The New Testament World. Insights from Cultural Anthropology*, Atlanta GA 1985.

REICKE, B., *The New Testament Era: The World of the Bible from 500 B.C.. to A.D. 100*, Philadelphia-London 1968.

VERMES, G., *Jesus and the World of Judaism*, London 1983.

Dictionaries of the New Testament

KITTEL, G., (ed.), *Theological Dictionary of the New Testament* (trans. G.W. Bromiley), Grand Rapids MI-London 1964-76.

JENNI, F. - WESTERMANN, C., *Theologisches Handwörterbuch zum Alten Testament*, Munich 1971-76.

Introductions to Exegesis

COGGINS, R.J. - HOULDEN, J.L., *A Dictionary of Biblical Interpretation*, London 1990.

KOCH, K., *The Growth of the Biblical Tradition: The Form-Critical Method*, trans. by S.M. Cupitt, New York 1969.

MCKENZIE, S.L. - HAYNES, S.R., *To Each Its Own Meaning. An Introduction to Biblical Criticisms and their Application*, Louisville, KT 1993.

TUCKER, G.M., *Form Criticism of the Old Testament*, Philadelphia PA 1971.

Chapter I

Bible and Book in the Ancient World

Postea promiscue patuit usus rei qua constat immortalitas hominum.
(Pliny, *Natural History* XIII 70)

«and afterwards the employment of the material on which the immortality of human beings depends spread indiscriminately»
(Pliny, *Natural History*, vol. IV, trans. by H. Rackham, Cambridge MS - London 1968, 140-141).

Chapter I

Bible and Book in the Ancient World 53

I

The Languages of the Bible

Academic study of the Bible requires prior knowledge of the languages in which the biblical books were written: Hebrew and Aramaic, and the Greek of the LXX version and of the NT. For a certain type of study it is also necessary to know the languages into which the Bible was translated during the first centuries of Christianity (Latin, Syriac, Coptic, Armenian, etc.). On the other hand, modern discoveries have rescued from oblivion other Semitic languages to which Hebrew is related (Akkadian, Ugaritic, Phoenician, etc.) as well as non-Semitic languages which in one way or another influenced Hebrew and Aramaic.

The «biblical scholar» has in principle to be a polyglot. «Polyglots» were the Renaissance editions of the Bible as was also the famous hexaplar edition of Origen in the 3rd cent. CE. Ultimately, the OT itself is also polyglot since in the final centuries of the biblical period it could be read indiscriminately in Hebrew, Aramaic and Greek. The biblical scholar seems to be moving in the world of confused tongues created in the tower of Babel. For the Christian, the prophetic vision about the peoples assembled on Zion (Is 56:6-7) has its fulfilment on the day of Pentecost, when peoples from all the nations are assembled in Jerusalem and each hears the Christian *kerygma* in his own language (Acts 2:8).

In accordance with the ancient tradition of «tri-lingual biblical» philology, the biblical scholar has to be instructed in the classical languages, which from the Renaissance to the 18th cent. included Hebrew and Aramaic. The biblical scholar moves in a frontier zone between classical philology (Greek and Latin) and ancient Semitic philology. He belongs to two cultural worlds, whose origins are more connected than is commonly thought, and live together in a rich symbiosis during the Hellenistic and Byzantine periods. The wars of the Medes, the Punic and Parthian wars, the Islamic conquests and the Christian re-conquests and crusades, forms of colonialism and fundamentalism have alienated the world of the East from the West, to the point of making knowledge of each other very difficult and confrontation very easy.

Scholars of classical Greek and Latin on the one hand and Semitists on the other have separated into two camps in studying the ancient world, with mutual ignorance and even mutual disdain. A «polyglot vision» of the Bible helps prevent the serious mistakes which have beset biblical research at times. The old and acrimonious disputes between Hebraists and Classical scholars have persisted since the Renaissance and still lurk in very subtle guise in many discussions today.

The languages of the Bible (OT) are Hebrew, Aramaic and Greek. Hebrew and Aramaic belong to the family of Semitic languages. Superficially and largely from a geographical aspect, these can be divided into four groups: South, Northwest, North and South Semitic.

Northwest Semitic is Canaanite in its different forms: Hebrew, Moabite and Edomite on the one hand and Ugaritic, Phoenician and Punic on the other.

North Semitic is basically Aramaic, subdivided into two groups. The Western group includes Biblical Aramaic and Aramaic of the targums and of the Gemara of the Palestinian Talmud, as well as Samaritan and Nabataean. The Eastern group comprises the Aramaic of the Babylonian Talmud and the Syriac of the biblical translations and of Christian and Mandaean writings.

East Semitic comprises Akkadian and its daughter languages, Assyrian and Babylonian.

South Semitic includes Arabic and Ethiopic. In the past, Arabic was virtually the only way to approach to the study of ancient Semitic. Today it can be said that Akkadian has replaced Arabic in this role. However, present day commentaries on the biblical books ignore many useful references to Arabic which filled commentaries of the first half of this century.

Other classifications of the Semitic languages are possible, such as those which distinguish only two large groups of Semitic languages, one Northern and the other Southern, or three groups, Northwest, Northeast and Southwest (Sáenz Badillos).

I.   HEBREW. LANGUAGE, TEXT AND INTERPRETATION

Here we can run through some of the more outstanding features of the Hebrew *language*, focusing on the difficulties they entail for the faithful *transmission* and *interpretation* of the ancient Hebrew texts. The biblical scholar must have the knowledge of a linguist, a textual critic and an interpreter or exegete, and be sensitive to the various demands of each in these fields.

The Hebrew language is known in the Bible as the «language of Canaan» (Is 9:1) and more frequently as «Judaean» (Is 36:11; 2 Chr 32:18). The groups of Hebrews related to the *ḥapiru* who entered Canaan towards the end of the 13th cent. BCE, joined other tribes of the future Israel who had been there from of old. After their settlement in Canaan, the groups which had come from outside also began to speak Hebrew.

The Hebrew *alphabet* contains 22 characters, all of them consonants.

Some of these characters (*b, g, d, k, p, t*) can represent two different sounds, occlusive or fricative, depending on their relation to contiguous sounds. Some Hebrew consonants represent sounds unknown in English. Such is the case for *ʾalep* (ʾ), a voiceless glottal occlusive, for *ʿayin* (ʿ), a voiced glottal fricative and for some of the five sibilants known in Hebrew. In the Dead Sea Scrolls and in the masoretic tradition itself, there is frequent confusion between these gutturals (e.g., the interchange between *ʿl*, «upon», and *ʾl*, «towards»). The dialectal variants and the linguistic changes in the transition from one period to another often caused confusion. A typical example is that of the different pronunciations of the same word: *šibbolet* in the mountains of Ephraim, but *sibbolet* in Transjordan, which gave rise to the famous episode related in Jgs 12:5-6.

In an initial period, during 900-600 BCE, Hebrew *spelling*, as in Phoenician, tended to represent graphically only the consonants. Throughout the 9th cent. BCE, the Aramaeans developed a rudimentary system of vocalic notation by means of what are called *matres lectionis* («mothers of reading»). This system was also used by the Israelites from the beginning of the 9th cent. BCE. The consonants *h*, *w* and *y* could represent final vowels: $w = \bar{u}$, $y = \bar{\imath}$ and $h = \bar{a}$, $\bar{e}$ and $\bar{o}$. Sometimes, *w* and *y* could indicate the medial vowels $\bar{u}$ and $\bar{\imath}$ respectively (Cross). In the period between 600 and 300 BCE, they began to use the *matres lectionis* to indicate the presence of a long vowel, especially at the end of a word. In the Lachish ostraca, from the beginning of the 6th cent. BCE, long vowels within words are already indicated. With the passage of time the tendency developed of representing short vowels also. The Dead Sea Scrolls present a «fuller» spelling than in the MT, extending to the short vowels (e.g. *kol*, «all», written *kwl*; *lōʾot*, written *lwʾ*). The spelling of the Dead Sea Scrolls gives cause for several kinds of comparison with different traditions of Hebrew pronunciation, especially the Samaritan.

The variations in spelling can sometimes be very important. The name of the city of «Sodom» reflects the Greek transcription *Sódoma* as against the Hebrew form of the MT *Sᵉdōm*. The Qumran spelling *swdm* presumes the pronunciation *sodom*, possibly with even stress instead of an acute accent.

Until the 5th and 6th cents. CE, Hebrew did not have a writing system which included vowels. The gradual neglect of Hebrew in favour of Arabic caused the exact pronunciation of the biblical text to be more and more forgotten. To avoid this loss, it was necessary to supply the consonantal script with a system of vowels and accents. These are not indicated by means of letters as in Western languages but through dots and various dashes placed above or below the consonant after which they were pronounced. It is easy to imagine the difficulty which a manuscript copy without vocalisation presented for a correct transmission of the biblical text. One example is enough: according to the MT, 1 Kgs 5:32 mentions the «builders» (*bônê*) of Solomon whereas the Greek version assumes a text which refers to the «sons» (*benê*) of Solomon. In the translation of Hebrew terms the vocalisation gave rise to the search for homophonous terms and to interpretations of a midrashic character. This might be the case in the translation of the name «Eve» (*ḥawwâ*) by the Greek term *Zōē*, «life».

This consonantal structure of the Hebrew language, when playing with changes of vowel within the same fixed consonantal root, as well as the writing system, when using directly signs with consonantal value (cf. p. 83), allow and even enjoy phonetic and graphic changes which involve changes in meaning («significance», F. de Saussure). They allow double meanings in many legal or narrative texts, which required or at least gave rise to the exercise of *deraš* or of interpretation according to the methods of rabbinic hermeneutics (cf. 468). The inconsistencies in spelling with *matres lectionis*, for example in the spelling of the word *tôle̱dôt* («generations») in the Pentateuch, could correspond to an attempt at establishing the text and at the same time its particular interpretation. The same relationship between text and interpretation can explain the irregular use of the determinative *ha-* in front of *'ādām* in the accounts of Gen 1-5 (Barc).

The most striking characteristic of the linguistic structure of Hebrew and of the Semitic languages in general is the *triliteral formation of roots*, many of which were originally bi-consonantal. Verbs and nouns which refer to the same nucleus of meaning derive from the same root. So, for example, the three consonants *MLḴ* form the noun *MeLeḴ* («king») or the verbal form *MāLaḴ* («he was king»). To determine which of the two forms should be read in a particular passage, the reader, deprived of the support of the vocalic script, has no other course but to turn to the context. The forms indicating tense and person are produced by means of internal inflection and by prefixes, affixes or infixes: *MēLaḴ-TeM* («you [pl.] rule»), *HiMLîḴ* («he caused to rule»), etc. Nouns derived from a single root are formed in the same way: *MaLKâ* («queen»), *MaLKûṮ* («kingdom»), *MaMLāḴâ*, («sovereignty»), etc.

Any student of Hebrew knows the occasional difficulty in identifying the root of a verb form. It is not unusual for the Hebrew text itself to provide two variant readings due to identifying a different verbal root. Moses disobeyed a command of Yahweh at Meribah and so could not enter the Promised Land (Nm 20:2-13). Dt 1:37 attempts to clear Moses of the blame, laying it on the people as a whole. The same interpretation is found in Ps 106:32-33, as follows: «They (the people) angered (Yahweh) at the waters of Meribah..., for they embittered his spirit». The interesting thing to note here is that the consonantal Hebrew text allows two readings and, therefore, a double meaning: the MT reading *himrû*, «they rebelled» (from the root *mrh*) and another reading based on the root *mrr* with the change of meaning «they embittered» (cf. BHS). The homiletic interpretations of the rabbis frequently played on these double meanings.

The *tenses* of the verb, perfect and imperfect, do not really denote the time of action (past, present or future) but its character as complete (perfect) or incomplete (imperfect). The reader must determine from the context whether the verb refers to past, present or future time.

Hebrew poetry can use the perfect and imperfect indiscriminately, juxtaposing them for the pure pleasure of parallelism: *ya'āmōdû/'āmādû*, «they stood» (Ps 38:12; Watson). A Jew from the post-exilic period would be as surprised as a modern translator in seeing two verb forms of different aspects in the same verse: *šᵉʾû / wᵉhinnāśᵉʾû*, «Rise..., may they rise...» (Ps 24:7; cf. BHS). Such poetic patterns could give rise to textual variants. Much care has to be taken not to correct the poetic texts in accordance with the grammatical criteria of later periods.

The first Jewish scribes could have left indications of a grammatical nature in the text which should not be confused with the actual biblical text, so that the philologist must know the techniques used by the scribes in copying manuscripts. In the expression from Ps 68:8b «Grace and loyalty (+ *mn*) will protect him», the consonants *mn* do not appear in any witness of the text nor are they found in the similar passage Prov 20:28 so that the proposal to remove them from the text seems tempting (cf. BHS). It is certainly a note inserted by the scribe: *mn* is an abbreviation of *mālēʾ nûn* («*plene nun*»), which warns that the *nûn* of the verb in the future tense, which follows immediately, is not elided but has to be written even though it occurs in a closed non-stressed syllable. These two consonants should not be taken, therefore, as the Hebrew particle *min* («of, from») nor as the Aramaic interrogative pronoun *man* («who»).

Originally, Hebrew used certain endings to indicate the *cases of nouns*. However, as happened in the development of the Romance languages, starting with Latin, the cases ended up disappearing and subordination changed to being expressed by means of word order and by the use of particles. To express the genitive, Hebrew used the form known as the «construct». The loss of case in Hebrew forced the shift from a synthetic language to an analytical language. However, this shift is still incomplete, for Hebrew still retains the use of the construct state.

Hebrew is relatively poor in true *adjectives*. It also lacks specific forms to express the comparative and superlative. In their place it uses the construct form or another type of expression. So, for example, «the Holy of Holies» denotes the most sacred area of the Temple and «the Song of Songs» denotes the Song *par excellence*.

Hebrew *syntax* prefers parataxis to the complex subordination of clauses (hypotaxis) which is typical of Greek and Latin. This characteristic imparts a simple and popular style to Hebrew narrative, though it is nonetheless expressive and profound (cf. p. 133).

The poetic texts frequently preserve *archaic forms* of Hebrew. Such is the use of the imperfect *yiqtol* to express past time instead of the *qatal* or *waw* + *yiqtol* forms. Ps 78 has several examples of this poetic usage, typical of the poems of Ugarit. Similarly, archaising poems such as Ps 68 show a tendency to avoid the definite article *ha(n)-* which was introduced and became common after 1200 BCE.

As for Hebrew *lexicography*, noteworthy are the numerous loan-words which the Israelites took from the languages of those peoples with whom they came into contact throughout the 1st millennium BCE. Lexical variants can give rise to textual variants. The text of 1 Kgs 8:2 originally referred to the «month (= *yeraḥ*) of *ʾetānîm*», corresponding to the term used in the

Canaanite calendar. Later, an explanatory gloss was added, which converted it to the numerical system used in Israel to denote the months: «this is (*hû'*) the seventh month». The Hebrew text used by the translators of the LXX clearly no longer knew this explanatory gloss (cf. BHS; likewise, 1 Kg 6:38).

From ancient Egyptian, which is not a Semitic language, Hebrew absorbed terms such as *par'oh* («pharaoh» = «big house» in Egyptian). Importing Egyptian products such as ebony, linen, amethyst, marble, etc. brought with it the borrowing of the corresponding Egyptian terms. There are also loans from Hittite and Hurrian. The term *seren*, «prince», which is used exclusively to denote Philistine princes, is undoubtedly a loan from the language of the Philistines who reached the coasts of Canaan in one of the waves of the «Sea Peoples». This Philistine term, *seren*, corresponds to Greek *tyrannos*, «tyrant», which the Greeks probably adopted from a language of Asia Minor, perhaps Phrygian or Lydian. Similarly, the Hebrew term *lappîd*, «torch», is a Philistine loanword related to Greek *lampas/-ados*.

Hebrew borrowed many terms from East Semitic, especially those belonging to the semantic fields which refer to the administration of justice, to institutions of government and the army. In many cases it is impossible to prove that they really are loanwords. It is always possible that they are only terms belonging to the common stock of the Semitic languages.

Borrowings from non-Semitic languages are of particular interest. From Persian comes the term *pardès* which through the Greek of the LXX (*paradeisos*) and the Latin of the Vulgate (*paradisum*), gave rise to the words «paradise», «paradis», «paraíso», etc. of the Romance languages. The distance separating Hebrew from Persian could cause a borrowed term to be so mangled that sometimes it becomes very difficult to recognise what the Persian term was which gave rise to the Hebrew equivalent. The book of Esther mentions the Persian king «Ahasuerus», better and more commonly known as «Xerxes».

Comparative linguistics enables obscure terms or passages of the OT to be illuminated by reference to analogous words or expressions in other Semitic languages. Akkadian sources have always been dominant in studies of this kind. The discovery of the texts from Ugarit in 1929 directed studies towards the [geographic and cultural] Canaanite setting which comprises the natural habitat of biblical language and literature. From the Ugaritic texts we know, for example, that beside their meanings of «in» and «to», «for» respectively, the Hebrew particles *b^e-* and *l^e-* both mean «from». Accordingly, the expression in the Hebrew text of Isa 59:20 has to be translated «a redeemer will come *from* Zion», matching an interpretation found attested in Rom 11:26. Ugaritic texts which are parallel to biblical texts allow the reconstruction of the original form and meaning of Hebrew words badly copied or badly interpreted in the manuscript tradition (Dahood). This has allowed new and improved translation of many OT passages to be proposed. However, it is not possible to maintain that the biblical Psalter contains Canaanite psalms. The similarities between biblical and Ugaritic literature are based on common thematic, linguistic and stylistic elements (Avishur).

Hebrew is closely related to Phoenician. Both exhibit clear differences from Aramaic. Both have a prefixed definite article (*ha-*), whereas Aramaic uses the determinative suffix *-a*. Also, the first person pronoun *ʾānōḵî* or the noun *ben* («son») contrast with their respective equivalents *ʾānāʾ* and *bar*. There are differences between them both in grammar and lexis such as, e.g. the verbs «to be» and «to have», the form of the relative pronoun, the pronunciation of common Semitic *a*, pronounced *o* in Phoenician but *a* in Aramaic, etc.

The concept of «biblical Hebrew» remains a fiction just like the concept of the «biblical text» or even of the «Masoretic text» (cf. p. 277). The biblical texts reflect a whole millennium of linguistic development and must also reflect different types of Hebrew and must have absorbed different dialects. The differences in dialect between the Hebrew of Judah in the South and of Israel in the North go back to Canaanite dialects of the second millennium BCE. The changes caused in *vocabulary* or in other aspects of the language could give rise to several misunderstandings. Thus, e.g., after murdering his brother Abel, Cain complains to God and says «My punishment is unbearable» (Gn 4:13). The word «punishment» (*ʿāwōn*) later came to mean «crime» or «sin». This change of meaning allowed Jews to change the figure of Cain the assassin into the repentant sinner by translating the sentence from Genesis as follows: «My sin is too great to be forgiven» (Onqelos). This interpretation could have been motivated by a theological scruple, however it is supported by the ambiguity of the biblical text (Kugel).

The formation of the collections of biblical books as well as the transmission, translation and interpretation of the text of these books was completed over the centuries when *Late Biblical Hebrew* and *Qumran Hebrew* were in use. Classical Hebrew and post-exilic Hebrew co-existed for some time. The work of the Chronicler and the books of Qoheleth and Esther exhibit the development of the language in the Persian and Greek periods. The form of the pronoun *ʾānōḵî*, «I», is frequently replaced by *ʾanî*, and the relative *ʾašer* by *še-*. It was precisely this wish to translate the two forms of the pronoun *ʾānōḵî - ʾanî* differently which was to give rise to one of the most conspicuous features of the proto-Theodotion Greek recension: the rendering *ʾānōḵî= ego eimi* in contrast with the simpler and more correct Greek equivalent *ʾānōḵî/ʾanî = egō*. In post-exilic Hebrew the system of the *waw* consecutive also began to break down. The lexical innovations of post-exilic Hebrew are, generally although not always, loans from Aramaic: *qibbēl* («to receive»), *zᵉman* («time»), *kāšēr* («proper, fitting»), *ʿinyān* («matter»), etc. An example of a Persian loan is the term *dāt* («decree»). There is almost no Greek influence on the Hebrew of the canonical books.

During the Hellenistic and Roman periods, biblical or classical Hebrew survived, not only as a spoken language but also as a written language even beyond the confines of the synagogue. This is shown by 4QMMT. Most of the non-biblical manuscripts found in the caves of Qumran are written in the post-biblical Hebrew of that period. The Copper Scroll and the Bar Kochba letters comprise the first witness to the type of Hebrew typical of the later Mishnaic period.

It is no longer possible to repeat as in the last century, in the time of A. Geiger, that *Mishnaic Hebrew* was an «artificial» language, made up of elements from biblical Hebrew and Aramaic, deprived of any support in a living language and intended especially for rabbinic discussions. The grammar, lexicon and *literary* style of Mishnaic Hebrew have as foundation a form of *colloquial* Hebrew, the use of which persisted during this period although it was not used generally (M. H. Segal). Mishnaic Hebrew is not an artificial mixture but fits perfectly in the linguistic development of biblical Hebrew, with its own characteristics, and is a literary language. The Hebrew found in the Copper Scroll and in the Bar Kochba letters is an important link in this development.

Mishnaic Hebrew contains some genuine Semitic elements not found in biblical Hebrew but on the other hand it lacks some elements common to biblical Hebrew and Aramaic. Among such typical differences can be listed the complete replacement of ʾašer by še-, the form šel of the genitive, the restricted use of the «construct state», the disappearance of the *waw* consecutive, more frequent use of the participle which virtually becomes the present tense, etc.

The lexicon has progressed beyond biblical Hebrew. The biblical term ʿôlam («long ago, eternity») comes to mean «world» with a more spatial meaning. Greek now becomes the main source of loanwords: *sanhedrin* (*synēdrion*), *zûg* (*zygón*) = «pair», *qᵉtidrâ* (*kathédra*) = «cathedra», *pinqēs* (*pínax*) = «list». The influence of Aramaic is even greater than Segal supposed; for his study he only used printed editions of the Mishnah.

It is significant that the text of the Mishnah, transmitted by manuscripts of greater authority, provides greater differences in respect of biblical Hebrew and also more frequent Aramaic features. It means that the text of the Mishnah underwent a process of standardisation and adaptation to the form of biblical Hebrew at the expense of the true and original Mishnaic Hebrew of the Mishnaic text.

Throughout the Middle Ages, besides compositions written in an artificial Hebrew far removed from the living language can be found verse or prose texts in an elegant style, comparable to that of the biblical texts, although with clear influences from Arabic models, especially as regards metrical forms and scientific and philosophical terminology.

The 19th and 20th centuries have witnessed a renaissance of the Hebrew language which in actual fact was never abandoned completely.

Dictionaries

AISTLEITNER, J., *Wörterbuch der ugaritischen Sprache*, Berlin 1967³.

ALONSO SCHÖKEL, L., *Diccionario Bíblico Hebreo-Español*, Valencia 1990-1992.

BEN-YEHUDA, E., *Thesaurus totius hebraitatis et veteris et recentioris*, 16 vols., Berlin-Schoönberg 1908, reprinted in 8 vols., in Jerusalem 1948.

BROWN, F.-DRIVER, S.R. -BRIGSS, CH.A., *A Hebrew and English Lexicon of the Old Testament*, Oxford 1974 reprint of 1953 edition.

CLINES, D.J.A., ed., *The Dictionary of Classical Hebrew*, Sheffield I 1993, II 1995, III 1996 -.

COHEN, D., *Dictionnaire des racines sémitiques ou attestées dans les langues sémitiques*, Paris-The Hague 1970.

KOEHLER, L. - BAUMGARTNER, W., *The Hebrew and Aramaic Lexicon of the Old Testament*, trans. and edit. by M.E.J. Richardson, Leiden I 1994, II 1995 -.

KUHN, K.G., *Rückläufiges hebräisches Wörterbuch*, Göttingen 1958.

OLMO, G. DEL - SANMARTÍN, J., *Diccionario de la lengua ugarítica*, vol. I, Sabadell 1996.

OPPENHEIM, A.L., *et al.* (eds.), *The Assyrian Dictionary*, 21 vols. published, Chicago IL 1956-.

SODEN, W. VON, *Akkadisches Handwörterbuch*, 3 vols., Wiesbaden 1965, 1972, 1981.

TOMBACK, R.S., *A Comparative Semitic Lexicon of the Phoenician and Punic Languages*, Missoula MT 1978.

Grammars

BAUER, H.-LEANDER, P., *Historische Grammatik der hebräischen Sprache des Alten Testaments*, Halle 1922.

BROCKELMANN, C., *Grundriß der vergleichenden Grammatik der semitischen Sprachen*, 2 vols., Berlin 1908 and 1913, reprinted in Hildesheim-New York in 1982.

FRIEDRICH, J.-RÖLLIG, W., *Phönizisch-Punische Grammatik*, Rome 1970.

GENESIUS, W., *Hebräische Grammatik*, 29th ed. Leipzig vol. I 1918, vol. II 1929, reprinted in Hildesheim-New York in 1962.

GENESIUS, W.-KAUTZSCH, E., *Gesenius' Hebrew Grammar*, trans. by A. E. Cowley, Oxford 1910.

GORDON, C.H., *Ugaritic Textbook*, Rome 1965.

JOÜON, P., *Grammaire de l'hébreu biblique*, Rome 1947², reprinted in 1982; re-edited by T. Muraoka, *A Grammar of Biblical Hebrew, I: Orthography and Phonetics, II: Morphology*, Rome 1991.

KUTSCHER, E.Y., *A History of the Hebrew Language*, Leiden 1982.

MEYER, R., *Hebräische Grammatik*, 4 vols., Berlin 1966, 1969, 1972, 1972.

MOSCATI, S., (ed.), *An Introduction to the Comparative Grammar of the Semitic Languages: Phonology and Morphology*, Wiesbaden 1964.

OLMO LETE, G. DEL-SANMARTÍN, J., *Diccionario de la Lengua ugarítica* Vol. I (Aula Orientalis Supplementa 7; Sabadell 1996).

PEREZ-FERNANDEZ, M., *La lengua de los sabios, I. Morfosintaxis*, Estella 1992.

QIMRON, E., *The Hebrew of the Dead Sea Scrolls*, Atlanta, GA 1986.

SAENZ-BADILLOS, A., *A History of the Hebrew Language*, Cambridge 1993 (translation by J. Elwolde of *Historia de la lengua hebrea*, Sabadell 1988).

SEGAL, M.H., *A Grammar of Mishnaic Hebrew*, Oxford 1927.

SEGERT, S., *A Grammar of Phoenician and Punic*, Munich 1976.

SEGERT, S., *A Basic Grammar of the Ugaritic Language,* Berkeley CA 1984.

SODEN, W. VON, *Grundriß der akkadischen Grammatik*, Rome 1952.

UNGNAD, A., *Grammatik des Akkadischen*, Munich 1969⁵.

WALDMAN, N.M., *The Recent Study of Hebrew. A Survey of the Literature with Selected Bibliography*, Winona Lake IN 1989.

WALTKE, B.K. - O'CONNOR, M., *An Introduction to Biblical Hebrew Syntax*, Winona Lake IN 1990.

Concordances

EVEN-SHOSHAN, A., *A New Concordance of the Bible*, Jerusalem 1981.

KATZ, E., *A New Classified Concordance of the Bible*, Jerusalem 1992.

LISOWSKY, G., *Konkordanz zum hebräischen Alten Testament*, Stuttgart 1964.

MANDELKERN, S., *Veteris Testamenti concordantiae hebraicae atque chaldaicae*, Berlin 1925², reprinted in Graz in 1955.

Special Studies

AVISHUR, Y., *Studies in Hebrew and Ugaritic Psalms*, Jerusalem 1994.

BAR-ASHER, M., «The Different Traditions of Mishnaic Hebrew», *Working With No Data. Semitic and Egyptian Studies Presented to Th.O. Lambdin*, Winona Lake, IN 1987, 1-38.

BARC, B., «Le texte de la Torah a-t-il été reécrit?», *Les règles de l'interpretation*, ed. M. Tardieu, Paris 1967, 69-88.

BARR, J., *The Semantics of Biblical Language*, Oxford 1961.

DAHOOD, M., «Parallel Pairs and Text Criticism», *Ras Shamra Parallels* I, ed. L.R. Fisher, Rome 1972, 78-79.

FITZMYER, J.A., «The Languages of Palestine in the First Century A.D.», *CBQ* 32 (1970) 501-531.

GOSHEN-GOTTSTEIN, M., «Linguistic Structure and Tradition in the Qumran Documents», *Scripta Hierosolymitana* 4 (1958) 101-137.

KUTSCHER, E.Y., *The Language and Linguistic Background of the Isaiah Scroll (1QIsaᵃ)*, Leiden 1974.

LOEWENSTAMM, S.E., «Ugarit and the Bible», *Biblica* 56 (1975) 103-119; 59 (1978) 100-122.

WALDMAN, N.M., *The Recent Study of Hebrew. A Survey of the Literature with Selected Bibliography*, Winona Lake IN 1989.

WATSON, W.G.E., *Classical Hebrew Poetry: A Guide to its Techniques*, Sheffield 1995².

WATSON, W.G.E., *Traditional Techniques in Classical Hebrew Verse*, Sheffield 1995.

II. ARAMAIC

From the period of exile in Babylon (6th cent. BCE) Aramaic, by then already the international language of diplomacy, began to replace Hebrew as the everyday language of Jews.

The oldest Aramaic inscriptions known come from the 9th cent. BCE. Later, Aramaic became the official language of the Assyrian, Neo-Babylonian and Persian empires. After the conquest by Alexander the Great, when Greek in turn began to replace Aramaic, that language still continued to be the most widespread in the East.

The history of Aramaic can be divided into three periods: ancient, middle and recent.

To the *ancient period* belong the inscriptions of Zinjirli (Sam'al), an archaic dialect written in Western characters, like those of Sefireh (c. 740) which also include expressions known in the Hebrew Bible. Official or Imperial Aramaic was used by the inhabitants of Western regions which became part of the Assyrian empire. It became very important and spread over most of the ancient Near East. A large part of the documents recovered, which comes from the period of the Persian empire, is written in this official Aramaic. The language is fairly uniform, but some works, such as the Sayings of Aḥiquar, are written in an Assyrian dialect.

The short sections of biblical text written in Aramaic are in Imperial Aramaic. However, the spelling seems to have been modernised. Ezra 7:12-26, which copies a decree of the Persian king, and Ezra 4:8-6:18, which also includes official correspondence, is in the Imperial Aramaic typical of such texts. It is not easy to explain, though, why other passages in the OT (Jr 10:11 and Dn 2:4b-7:28) also appear written in Aramaic. On the other hand, the possibility has to be considered that some biblical texts which have come down to us in Greek and even in Hebrew might in fact be translations of originals written in Aramaic.

Middle Aramaic dates to the period between 300 BCE and 200 CE. After the fall of the Persian empire, Greek gradually replaced Aramaic as the lingua franca. Official Aramaic then underwent a process of fragmentation into local dialects. It survived, however, as a literary language and was used in official documents and inscriptions.

The chapters in Aramaic of the book of Daniel (c. 168 BCE) are composed in this literary language, as are some texts found in Qumran: *Tobias, The Dream of Nabonidus,* fragments of *Enoch* and *Melchizedek, Pseudo-Daniel, The Genesis Apocryphon, The Testament of Levi,* the *Leviticus Targum* and the *Targum of Job.* In this literary language also the Onqelos Targum of the Pentateuch and Targum Jonathan (ben ʿUzziʾel) of the Prophets were written in Palestine. Later use of these Aramaic versions in Babylon ensured that their text was influenced by dialectal features peculiar to Eastern Aramaic. Later works such as *Megillat Taʿanit* (c. 100 CE) and *Megillat Antiochus* were also written in this form of literary Aramaic. Given the conservative nature of legal language, it is not surprising that the legal formulas quoted in the

Mishnah and in the Jerusalem and Babylonian Talmuds also reflect the language of the preceding period.

Inscriptions and papyri from Palmyra, Petra and elsewhere provide knowledge of the Nabataean and Palmyrene dialects. Nabataean shows Arabic influence on its vocabulary and syntax; Palmyrene experienced yet other Oriental influences.

The characteristics of *Western Aramaic* are better known today, thanks to a growing number of inscriptions found in Jerusalem in tombs, sarcophagi, ossuaries and other objects. The NT preserves Aramaic expressions such as *talitha koum* (Mk 5:41), *Marana tha* (1 Cor 16:22), *Effatha* (Mk 7:34) and *Elōi elōi lema sabakhthani* (Mk 15:34) as well as proper names and toponyms such as Akeldama, Golgotha, Gethsemani and Bethesda. Jesus and his disciples spoke the Galilean dialect which differed from the one spoken in Judah (Mt 26:73). The letters of Bar Kochba' (132 CE) together with the literature in Aramaic and the inscriptions on ossuaries and tombs mentioned earlier, make up an important source for knowledge of the Judaean dialect (Kutscher).

Written remains in *Eastern Aramaic* are very meagre, among them the text from Uruk from the 2nd cent. BCE and a series of inscriptions and graffiti from Assur and Hatra belonging to the Parthian period (2nd cent. CE).

Consequently, starting with Imperial Aramaic, this language follows a single line of development which goes successively through the Aramaic of the books of Ezra and Dan, of the Targum of Job (second half of the 2nd cent. CE), of the Genesis Apocryphon and finally of the Bar Kochba' letters (Kutscher, Fitzmyer). This development is evident in certain features such as the forms of the relative-demonstrative: zy in Imperial Aramaic, *di* in the Genesis Apocryphon and Bar-Kochba's letters and lastly d^e in Targum Onqelos.

The targums, especially Targum Neophyti allow a different estimation of the history of Aramaic in this period (cf. p. 325). According to research by such scholars as Kahle and Díez Macho (cf. p. 327), Targum *Neophyti* represents the Aramaic spoken in the 1st cent. CE, that is, the period of Christ. According to this view, the Targum of Job and the *Genesis Apocryphon* would represent a contemporary literary Aramaic of the spoken form. However, this synchronic estimate relies on criteria of content and exegetical method (the *halakhah* reflected in the text). Control of these criteria is not so rigorous as for criteria based on texts which have been dated with great certainty thanks to the Dead Sea Scrolls.

The *recent period* extends up to beyond the Arab conquest (from 200 to 900 CE). Knowledge of Aramaic in this period is important for study of the history of transmission, translation and interpretation of the Bible in the Palestinian and Babylonian oriental world in which the traditions of vocalisation and masora of the biblical text were collected and arranged.

In this period Aramaic appears clearly split up into several dialects. The Western group includes Jewish Aramaic (Galilean), Christian-Palestinian Aramaic and Samaritan. In the Jewish Aramaic dialect are written the

Jerusalem Talmud, the Palestinian midrashim (*Genesis Rabbah* and *Leviticus Rabbah*), the Palestinian targums (*Neophyti*, pace Kahle and Díez Macho, the Fragmentary Targum, fragments from the Cairo Genizah and the Targum of the *Ketubim* or Writings), funerary inscriptions from Joppa, Beth-Shearim and Zoar and several synagogal inscriptions dating between the 3rd cent. and the 6th cent. CE. Christian-Palestinian Aramaic was spoken by Jews converted to Christianity and is written in a form of Syriac script.

BIBLIOGRAPHY

cf. the bibliography cited in «Aramaic Versions of the Old Testament», pp. 331-332.

BAUER, H.-LEANDER, P., *Grammatik des Biblisch-Aramäischen*, Halle 1927, reprinted in 1962.

BEYER, K., *Die aramäischen Texten vom Toten Meer samt den Inschriften aus Palästina, dem Testament Levis aus der Kairoer Genisa, der Fastenrolle und den alten talmudischen Zitaten*, Göttingen 1984, *Ergänzungsband*, Göttingen 1994.

DALMAN, G., *Grammatik des jüdisch-palästinischen Aramäisch nach den Idiomen des palästinischen Talmud, des Onkelostargum und Prophetentargum und der jerusalemischen Targume*, Leipzig 1905².

DALMAN, G.H., *Aramäisch-neuhebräisches Handwörterbuch zu Targum, Talmud und Midrasch*, Göttingen 1938³, reprinted in Hildesheim-New York in 1967.

FITZMYER, J.A., *The Genesis Apocryphon of Qumran Cave I*, Rome 1971².

FITZMYER, J.A. -HARRINGTON, D.J., *A Manual of Palestinian Aramaic Texts (Second Century B.C.-Second Century A.D.)*, Rome 1978.

FITZMYER, J.A. -KAUFMAN, S.A., *An Aramaic Bibliography. Part I Old, Official, and Biblical Aramaic*, Baltimore and London 1992.

JASTROW, M., *A Dictionary of the Targumim, the Talmud babli and Yerushalmi, and the Midrashic Literature*, London-New York 1886-1990, reprinted in New York in 1950.

KUTSCHER, E.Y., *Studies in Galilean Aramaic*, Ramat-Gan 1976.

LEVY, J., *Chaldäisches Wörterbuch über die Targumim und eien grosen Theildes rabbinischen Schrifthums*, Leipzig 1881, reprinted in Cologne in 1959.

ROSENTHAL, F., *A Grammar of Biblical Aramaic*, Wiesbaden 1961, reprinted in 1974.

SEGAL, M.H., *A Grammar of Palestinian Jewish Aramaic*, Oxford 1924.

SEGERT, S., *Altaramäische Grammatik mit Bibliographie, Chrestomathie und Glossar*, Leipzig 1975.

SOKOLOFF, M., *A Dictionary of Jewish Palestinian Aramaic of the Byzantine Period*, Ramat-Gan 1990.

VOGT, E., *Lexicon linguae aramaicae Veteris Testamenti documentis antiquis illustratum*, Rome 1971.

III. GREEK

The deutero-canonical books of the OT were written in Greek, although the original text of some, such as Ben Sira, was in Hebrew or Aramaic. The original language of the NT was Greek, although the *logia* or sayings of Jesus and other parts of the NT were transmitted for some time earlier in Aramaic (or Hebrew).

In ancient times, writers did not fail to have an aversion for the language used in the LXX version and the NT, which to them could only seem like a far cry from the canons of classical Greek. The Christian apologists, who had also been educated in Attic Greek and the rhetoric of the classics (Chrysostom, Augustine, Jerome, etc.), tried to justify the style of the biblical writings which was careless and rude yet simple and popular.

The humanists of the Renaissance were also aware of the distance separating biblical Greek from classical Greek. The 17th and 18th cents. experienced a sharp polemic between hebraists, who attributed any deviation of biblical Greek from classical Greek to the influence of Hebrew, and the purists of Hellenism, who could not admit the presence of hebraisms and other barbarisms in the inspired Scriptures. In the 19th cent. there were even some who tried to explain the peculiarities of NT Greek in terms of the special or «inspired» character of that language which was intended to act as a channel to express divine revelation.

The study of papyri found in Egypt (Deissman, cf. p. 340) proved that the language of the LXX and the NT reflects *koiné* or common language, spoken in the Hellenistic period from the time of Alexander the Great until the end of the ancient period in the time of Justinian (6th cent.). The papyri provide parallels to, for example, a typical LXX form such as *ĕltha*, «I came» (*ĕlthon* in Attic Greek).

It should be noted that *koiné* was both the vulgar language of the people and the refined language of the writers of the period (Polybius, Strabo, Philo, Josephus and Plutarch). The Jewish writers of Joseph and Asenath and the Testaments of the Twelve Patriarchs provide examples of a colloquial Jewish Greek *koiné*. This language retained the basic structure of the Attic dialect mixed with Ionic, Doric and Aeolic elements and with syntactic, lexical and stylistic borrowings from other languages. Among these borrowings appear the many Semitisms and Latinisms that are included. Among the Semitisms can be noted the expression *prosétheto* + *toû* + infinitive = «he added to do something...», i.e., «he did again»; *ánthrōpos ánthrōpos* = «man man», i.e., «each one»; *kaì egéneto* + verb clause = «and it happened that...», etc. In the 1st - 2nd cents. CE there was an «Attic» movement which attempted to return the common language to the correctness and style of the Attic Greeks. This movement affected 4 Maccabees, works by Josephus and also the textual transmission of the LXX version. The copyists of this period tried to correct the style of the ancient version, making it conform to Attic canons. So, e.g., the *koiné* form *eîpan*, «they said» was corrected to the classical form *eîpon*.

The estimation of biblical Greek as a *koiné* of the Hellenistic period should not prevent awareness, however, of the peculiar features of biblical Greek, particularly NT Greek, which cannot be equated without further nuances with the «secular» Greek of the papyri. Semitic influence is noticeable not only in the presence of Hebraisms and Aramaisms but also in lexis, semantics and stylistics. These semitisms can be transcriptions of Semitic words or can affect vocabulary, syntax or style (Grelot, Wilcox). As regards lexicography, for example, the term *hypostasis* of the NT (Heb 11:1) can be better explained in terms of LXX Greek and the Hebrew equivalent (*tōḥelet*, «confident and patient hope») than from the Greek of the papyri («document of ownership»). The NT term *parousía* is closer to the meaning given it by Josephus (*Antiq.* 3,203) - as referring to the halo around the tabernacle (i.e. the *Shekinah* or theophanic presence of God) - than to the meaning of coming or royal presence, as in the papyri. The Western text of the gospels, as represented by Codex Bezae, preserves Semitic parallelism in a way not found in other text types (Segert).

Beyond the criticisms made against the tendency of biblical theology to confer a theological meaning on certain words independently of the context in which they occur (J. Barr, cf. pp. 557 and 560), biblical semantics can do no less than recognise characteristics of Semitic thought which correspond to the language and lexis of the LXX version and of the NT. Terms such as *dóxa, diathḗkē, psychḗ, sóma, diánóia, kósmos*, etc. add new and different meanings from the meaning which the equivalent Hebrew terms had. It cannot be forgotten, on the other hand, that the experience lived by the first Christians also had a creative force of language which resulted in the coining of neologisms such as *antíchristos, diábolos, euaggelismós*, etc.

There has also been an attempt to explain the peculiarity of biblical Greek by means of the hypothesis of the existence of a «Jewish-Greek» dialect, written and spoken by Jews in various places and periods (cf. p. 320). In fact, the peculiar features of LXX Greek tend to be explained as a phenomenon due to the actual translation, which justifies and requires close study of translation techniques used. The fact that it is a translation accounts for the strange meaning given to some terms, the indiscriminate use of terms proper to poetry or prose, the coining of neologisms, etc. (Martin, Daniel).

To define NT Greek requires perhaps an eclectic explanation which takes into account very different factors: the synoptic gospels, literary rather than literal; the influence of the LXX, so evident throughout the NT is most obvious in the gospel of Luke like the use in the Pauline epistles of Hebrew concepts such as «justification» or «atonement»; the Apocalypse reflects chiefly the Jewish-Greek speech of the synagogues.

Dictionaries

BAUER. W., *Griechisch-deutsches Wörterbuch zu den Schriften des Neuen Testaments und der frühchristlichen Literature*, eds., Karl and Barbara Aland, Berlin-New York 1988.

BAUER. W.,-GINGRICH, F.W.-DANKER, F.W., *A Greek-English Lexicon of the New Testament and Other Early Christian Literature*, Chicago-London 1979².

LIDDELL, H.G.-SCOTT, R., *A Greek-English Lexicon*, Oxford 1925-1940⁹, reprinted in 1966.

LAMPE, G.W.H., (ed.), *A Patristic Greek Lexicon*, Oxford 1961.

MOULTON, J.H.-MILLIGAN, G., *The Vocabulary of the Greek Testament*, London 1957².

MURAOKA, T., *A Greek-English Lexicon of the Septuagint. Twelve Prophets*, Louvain 1993.

Grammars

BLASS, F.-DEBRUNNER, A., *A Greek Grammar of the New Testament and Other Early Christian Literature*, Chicago IL 1961.

GIGNAC, F.T., *A Grammar of the Greek Papyri of the Roman and Byzantine Periods*, 4 vols., Milan 1976, 1981-.

MOULTON, J.H.-HOWARD, F.W., *A Grammar of New Testament Greek*, 4 vols., Edinburgh I 1949³, II 1929, III 1963, IV 1976; vols. II and IV edited by N. Turner.

SCHWYZER, E., *Griechische Grammatik auf der Grundlage von Karl Brugmanns griechischer Grammatik*, 3 vols., Munich 1953-1959.

THACKERY, H.ST., *A Grammar of the Old Testament in Greek according to the Septuagint*, vol. 1, Cambridge 1909, reprinted in 1978.

Concordances

ALAND, K., *Vollständige Konkordanz zum griechischen Neuen Testament: Unter Zugrundelegung aller kritischen Textausgaben und des Textus Receptus*, 2 vols., Berlin-New York 1975, 1978.

HATCH, E.,-REDPATH, H.A., *A Concordance to the Septuagint and the Other Greek Versions of the Old Testament*, 2 vols., Oxford 1897; vol. 3ʳᵈ Supplement 1906, reprinted in Graz in 1954.

MOULTON, W.F.-GEDEN, A.S., *A Concordance to the Greek Testament*, Edinburgh 1897, ed. by H. Moulton 1978⁵.

Studies

BROCK, S.P., «The Phenomenon of the Septuagint», *The Witness of Tradition*, ed. A.S. Van der Woude, Leiden 1972, 11-36.

DANIEL, S., *Recherches sur le vocabulaire du culte dans la Septante*, Paris 1966.

GEHMAN, H.S., «Adventures in Septuagint Lexicography», *Textus* 5 (1966) 125-132.

GERLOT, P., «Semitisms (dans le Nouveau Testament)», *SDB* 12, fasc. 67, eds. J. Briend É. Cothenet, Paris 1992, 334-423.

HOFFMANN, O. -DEBRUNNER, A. -SHERER., A., *Geschichte der Griechischen Sprache*, Berlin 1969.

MARTIN, R.A., «Some Syntactical Criteria of Translation Greek», *VT* 10 (1960) 295-310.

SEGERT, S., «Semitic Poetic Structures in the New Testament», *ANRW* II 25.1.52, 1433-1462.

SILVA, M., «Bilingualism and the Character of Palestinian Greek», *Biblica* 61 (1980) 198-219.

TURNER, N., *Christian Words*, Edinburgh 1980.

VOELZ, J., «The Language of the New Testament», *ANRW* II 25.1, 893-977.

WILCOX, M., «Semitisms in the New Testament», *ANRW* II 25.1, 976-1029.

IV. THE TRILINGUAL BIBLE AND BIBLICAL TRILINGUALISM

The Bible arose in a multilingual world. Mesopotamian civilization was formed from the symbiosis of two languages and cultures as different as Sumerian and Akkadian (Bottéro).

Almost from its very beginnings the Bible was a polyglot work. The Hebrew Bible includes sections in Aramaic; the Bible transmitted by Christian tradition includes books written in Greek or translated into Greek. The fact that right from the first moment the Bible would be read and interpreted in connection with another language is no less important. From the period of the Exile, the Jews lived in a bilingual or trilingual setting; as a consequence, they read and studied the Hebrew Bible in contact with a second language, Aramaic, starting from the Persian period and Greek during the Hellenistic and Byzantine periods.

The linguistic map of Palestine around the turn of the era and at the moment when Christianity was born is marked by great differences in language. In Jerusalem and Judaea, Hebrew was spoken for preference, with Aramaic as a second language. Hebrew underwent a period of renaissance starting fom the nationalistic revolt by the Maccabees (mid-2nd cent. BCE). At the same time there was also a true renaissance of Hebrew literature (Ben Sira, Tobit, *Jubilees, Testament of Naphtali*, writing of the Qumran comunity, etc.). The coining of money with Hebrew inscriptions is further proof of the revival of Hebrew and of its official importance. Jesus of Nazareth definitely spoke Aramaic, but it cannot be excluded that he also used Hebrew and even Greek. In the Mediterranean coastal area and in the Galilee region they preferred to speak Aramaic somewhat more than Greek. In this area Hebrew was only a literary language.

After the destruction of Jerusalem and the resulting ban on Jews living in Jerusalem and its vicinity, the rabbinic schools fled to Galilee. The literary language in these schools was Hebrew whereas the languages in common use in Palestine at that time were Aramaic and Greek and to a lesser extent,

Latin. If the writings of the Essene comunity of Qumran were still written in a type of Hebrew very close to the Hebrew of the biblical books, the Mishnah, which is a collection of legal texts completed at the start of the 3rd cent. CE, is written instead in Mishnaic Hebrew. The Bar Kochba Letters which date to the second Jewish revolt against Rome (132 CE) prove that Hebrew continued to be a living language at this time.

In the tannaitic and amoraic periods, the reference languages for study of the Bible were Mishnaic Hebrew and Aramaic. Greek influence was evident especially in the use of technical terms and in connection with social and religious institutions.

In the Arab period, especially in the times of Sa'adiah Ga'on, the reference languages were Aramaic and Arabic. The Yemenite Jews have retained the custom of learning the Torah by heart, verse by verse, in trilingual form: the Hebrew text, the Aramaic of the Onqelos Targum and the Tafsîr («commentary») in Arabic of Sa'adiah's translation. Spanish Jews held fierce arguments about the convenience and need of applying to Hebrew the findings and classification systems of the Arabic philologists (Menahem ben Saruq in favour, and Dunas ben Labra against). The end of Muslim Spain put a stop to the growth of Semitic trilingualism.

From the 15th cent. trilingualism revived as Hebrew-Greek-Latin. The return *to the sources* movement of the humanists was not confined to the task of recovering the text of the Vulgate and of the Greek text of the NT, but it attempted to reach the original Hebrew of the OT. In this way *homo trilinguis* arose, the prototype and ideal of the humanist. At the close of the 16th cent., virtually all Hebrew literature (biblical, rabbinic and mediaeval) was already available to Christian Hebraists. However, from the middle of the same century and for different reasons, Catholics and Protestants began to lose direct contact with Jewish sources.

The discovery of Akkadian in the 19th cent. and of Ugaritic and Eblaite in this century has enabled pre-biblical Semitics to be known which contributes to clarifying the early stages of Hebrew and the literary forms of the Hebrew Bible. Modern Hebrew philology is divided into a large number of specialisations, depending on the language used for comparison with the biblical texts: Hebrew-Aramaic-Arabic trilingualism, Hebrew/Aramaic-Greek-Latin trilingualism and Hebrew/Aramaic-Ugaritic-Akkadian trilingualism. The biblical scholar must be trained in at least one of these forms of trilingualism. On the other hand, the intersection of influences between these forms of trilingualism and the relationship with other Oriental languages (Syriac, Ethiopic, Coptic, Armenian, etc.) has to be acknowledged. Study of the many apocryphal writings of the OT and even of the NT requires the analysis of sources which have been preserved only in these languages.

Lexicography is a privileged field of biblical trilingualism, especially as it concerns terms which carry a heavy theological load or refer to social and religious institutions. It is interesting to follow, for example, the history of the use of the Hebrew terms *qahal* («congregation») and *'edâ* («community») and the different translations in the various books by means of the Greek terms *ekklesia* and *synagoge* (*ekklesia* = *qahal*, about 100 times; *syna-goge*=*qahal*, about 35 times; *synagoge*=*ʿēdâ*, about 130 times, mostly in the Pentateuch). The choice of these terms made by different books of the NT and their translation in the Old Latin version and in the Vulgate results in the complete opposition of the terms «church» and «synagogue» exactly as in the title of the pseudo-Augustinian book *Altercatio Ecclesiae et Sinagogae* (5th cent. CE; Peri).

We are used to drawing certain contrasts between Athens and Jerusalem, between Greek thought and Hebrew thought. Greek mentality is said to be abstract, contemplative, static and impersonal and to function by contrasts: matter and form, the one and the many, the individual and the group, time and eternity, appearance and reality. Above all, Greek thought is ahistorical, unconnected with time, based on logic and system. Hebrew mentality, instead, is active, concrete, dynamic, intensely personal, based on the the whole and not on the analysis of opposites. Hebrew thought is historical, focused on time and movement (Boman, Tresmontant, cf. p. 30).

Oppositions of this kind are undoubtedly an artificial construct, the simplicity of which is the key to its success, more the fruit of transferring modern thinking to the Greek and Hebrew worlds that of any direct and critical analysis. The contrast between Greek and Hebrew thought has been exploited by theological movements which tend to shun contact with modern culture. Its appreciation of what is Hebrew is very artificial and does not correspond to what Hebrew was, «historical Hebrew». On the other hand, the ostensible philo-Semitism for that kind of contrast has always been somewhat ambiguous in its relation towards the Judaism of the present day. Many theological movements after the Second World War were thoroughly anti-Greek, in contrast with the previous period. The differences between Greek and biblical thought must be neither reduced to a minimum nor exaggerated (Barr).

Above all, an infinity of nuances have to be brought in, taking into account the differences of the period both in Greece and in Rome, between the beginning of the period and its close; the differences of social groups between philosophers and the illiterate, and the differences among the various schools of philosophy. Contrasts between Greek and Semitic are generally established by taking into account only Platonic Greek thought, very little Aristotelian and absolutely no Stoic and Epicuraean thought, although they were very important in the NT period. The authors of the NT never draw attention to the supposed danger that Greek thought could pose. The basic sources of nourishment for the thought of the early Christians were the OT and Jewish tradition, but these did not make the authors of the NT into purists of Hebraism opposed to Greek thought. As for OT thought, it must be compared more with the ancient near Eastern world than with the Greek world.

It must be stressed that the approach to the study of meaning should be strictly linguistic rather than logical or psychological. On the other hand, the study of meaning has to be specific to each language. A Hebrew word has its meaning only in Hebrew, an Arabic word only in Arabic. One should not fall into a kind of comparative study which defines the meaning of a Hebrew word by asking what it means in another language. In 2 Kgs 4:42, the *hapax* Hebrew term *bᵉṣiqlōnô* can undoubtedly be equated with Ugaritic *bṣql*, but this equation says nothing about the precise meaning of the term in Hebrew. It allows false trails, followed previously, to be excluded; for example, taking the initial consonant *b-* as a preposition and so translating «in his sack» (or «'on the stalk'; perhaps connected with Ugaritic *bṣql*)» (JPS, footnote). It proves, on the other hand, that the term refers to a type of plant, which could already easily be deduced from the context. It cannot be stated unequivocally, though, that the Hebrew term *bṣql* had exactly the same meaning as its Ugaritic equivalent.

A balance has to be found between the polyglot and the pure Hebraist or the pure Hellenist. The purist is jealous of the inner-language example: Hebrew is explained by itself alone and from within. The comparative linguist resorts to the external example: languages and literatures are not understood without reference to an outside context. Sometimes it is convenient not to consider the polyglot so much and pay more attention to the Hebraist or the Hellenist. To know the meaning of Greek literature it is not necessary to refer to the Indo-European languages. In the same way, the meaning of the prophetic oracles is not found in Mari even though it is necessary first to tour Mari and almost the whole ancient East.

The Hebraist usually mistrusts solutions to problems of the Hebrew text which are based on the Greek text. The Hellenist distrusts no less solutions to problems of the Greek text founded on facts from the Hebrew text. Attention must be drawn, though, to the existing connection between Hebrew rabbinic tradition and Greek tradition, without therefore ceasing to be aware of the conflict concerning the antiquity of one or other tradition, as represented by the Masoretic text or as reflected by the Greek version

A good example of this is provided by the titles of the biblical books, especially the books of the Torah. In the LXX version the titles of the books indicate their contents: *Genesis*, the genesis or origin of the world, mankind and the patriarchs; *Exodus*, the exodus or departure of the Israelites from Egypt; *Lauitikon*, Leviticus, or the book about the cult entrusted to the tribe of Levi; *Arithmoi*, Numbers, or the book about the census of the people in the desert; *Deuteronomion*, the Law promulgated a second time or a second Law (cf. Dt 17:18). The Hebrew titles are formed from the first words of each book: *bᵉrēʾšît* («In the beginning»), *šᵉmôt* («Names»), *wayyiqrāʾ* («And he called»), *bᵉmidbar* («In the desert»), *dᵉbārîm* («Words»). The titles of the prophetic books and of the *Kᵉtubîm* are almost the same in Hebrew and Greek.

In the MT, therefore, two different systems co-exist, one to denote the books of the Pentateuch and the other for the Prophets and the Writings. LXX uses a single system which could be older than the MT one. The title *Exagōgē* to denote the book of Exodus appears in the works of Aristobulus, of the tragic author Ezekiel and of Philo. The books of the Pentateuch (except Num) are cited with these titles in Philo's works. Proof of how old the system attested by the LXX is could also be the fact that rabbinism knows a second system to denote the books of the Pentateuch, with titles very similar to the ones in LXX: Genesis = *Sēṗer yᵉṣîrat haʿōlām* ('Book of the creation of the world»), Exodus = *Seṗer yeṣîʾat Miṣrāyîm* («Book of the departure from Egypt»), Leviticus = *Seṗer tôraṯ kohanîm* («Book of the law of the priests»), Numbers = *Ḥōmeš ha-piqqūdîm* («Fifth part of the census»), Deuteronomy= *Seṗer mišnê tôrâ* («Book of the second law»).

It is necessary to make a clear distinction - the way Hebrew dictionaries have to - between the meaning of Hebrew terms in their own biblical context and the meaning derived by means of etymological analyses and from other comparative data. Sometimes, factors of the immediate context, such as poetic parallelism, are more important than external factors.

Study of the Hebrew Bible should not end with analysis of the «canonical» books of the Bible to construct a canonical Hebrew which never existed. Dictionaries of classical Hebrew do not usually go beyond the writings of Ben Sira and Qumran. In certain cases the analysis of biblical Hebrew terms should include the treatment these receive in the other ancient versions. Sometimes this analysis should refer to the interpretation by the rabbis and by Jewish lexicographers and commentators of the mediaeval period. Ancient translations can preserve different meanings or connotations implied by the Hebrew terms. These data cannot provide the exact meaning of the biblical terms in their own context, but they offer another context and other references which can contribute to knowing whether the biblical meaning has been preserved or has been distorted or enriched by a load it did not have.

Dictionaries of Hebrew should certainly take more account of the data from the Greek version of the LXX; on the other hand, they can offer deceptive conclusions about grammatical Hebrew usage. For example, Hebrew grammars and dictionaries (Brown-Driver-Briggs) speak of an absolute use of the negative ʾal in some cases where this particle does not seem to be followed by a verb as is normal («Do not...»). The cases in question are chiefly in the books of Samuel and Kings. The full list is as follows: Gen 19:18; 2 Sm 13:16; 2 Kgs 3:13; 4:16; 6:27; Ruth 1:13 (cf. Jgs 19:23). The textual tradition preserved in Sm-Kgs by the Old Greek and supported by the *old latin*, supposes the presence of a verb after the negative, which invalidates the existence of an absolute use of the particle ʾal. It can always be maintained that the Greek version, which knew the normal use (negative followed by verb) added the verb in those cases where it was missing. However, study of the translation techniques of the books Sm-Kgs proves that such liberties were not permitted and that instead it only reflects the underlying Hebrew text. Therefore, it is preferable to consider the MT as exhibiting a usage, apparently irregular, which the grammars should not make into a rule and that it was usually due to the insertion of a gloss between the negative particle and the verb which comes much later in the context. To base Hebrew grammar only on the masoretic text could mean leaving out of account many phenomena, regular and irregular, which can now be better known thanks especially to the Dead Sea Scrolls.

BIBLIOGRAPHY

BARR, J., *Comparative Philology and the Text of the Old Testament*, Oxford 1968.

BARR, J., *Old and New in Interpretation. A Study of the Two Testaments*, London 1966.

BOMAN, T., *Hebrew Thought Compared with Greek*, New York 1970.

BOTTÉRO, J., «Bilingualism and Its Consequences», in *Mesopotamia. Writing, Reasoning, and the Gods*, Chicago IL 1992, 91-94.

HAMMOND, N.G.-SCULLART, H.H. (eds.), *The Oxford Classical Dictionary*, Oxford 1970².

MCNALLY, R.E., «The 'Tres Linguae Sacrae' in Early Irish Bible Exegesis», *Theological Studies* 19 (1958) 395-403.

PERI, I., «*Ecclesia* und *synagoga* in der lateinischen Übersetzung des Alten Testaments», *BZ* 33 (1989) 245-251.

TRESMONTANT, C., *Essai sur la pensée hébraïque*, Paris 1953.

2

Writing in the Ancient World and in the Bible

To engage in study of the biblical texts requires knowledge not only of the biblical languages but also of the systems, procedures and technical means used for writing in the ancient Near East and in Greek and Roman classical times. It is not easy to envisage the number of obstacles of every kind which the ancients had to overcome in order to transmit their sacred texts faithfully together with the extensive oral and written literature which had accumulated over the centuries.

Writing systems, from hieroglyphics and cuneiform to the Phoenician, Greek or Latin alphabets, had to be created, perfected and spread very slowly and laboriously. Some writing materials, such as clay, stone or metal used for inscriptions, were far too rigid. Others, such as papyrus and parchment, used for writing with ink, were short-lived and decayed easily, and almost inevitably resulted in corruption of the text.

The student of biblical texts needs to know a little about epigraphy and palaeography. In recent decades these «ancillary» sciences of biblical philology have advanced in a surprising way thanks to the discovery of numerous inscriptions (never so many or so monumental, certainly, as those found in Egypt or Mesopotamia) and thanks especially to the discovery of the Dead Sea Scrolls. Today we know in great detail the development of the script in the various alphabets of Syria and Palestine and, more to the point, the development of the script in the Hebrew alphabet. It is also possible to follow in detail the development of the Jewish script (formal, semi-cursive or cursive) during the earliest periods of textual transmission of the Bible, the early, Hasmonaean and Herodian periods.

The study of epigraphic material in Hebrew, Aramaic and other related languages, has considerably extended current knowledge about the spelling and pronunciation of the Hebrew of the biblical period (before and after the Exile). It has also increased our knowledge about many other fields related to the biblical text, such as those concerning the lexicon and Hebrew poetry, not to mention Hebrew toponymy and onomastics, with the results derived from them for the study of the geography and history of ancient Israel. Various factors affect the correct written transmission of the biblical text: the type of writing used (cuneiform, palaeo-Hebrew, Greek uncial, etc.), the material written on (stone, papyrus, parchment, etc.) and the kind of binding (scroll or codex) in which the biblical books were transmitted. The history of the Bible (*ta biblía*, «the books», in Greek) is also the history of writing and the history of the book in ancient times.

I. WRITING IN THE ANCIENT NEAR EAST AND IN GREECE

Historians of the alphabet tend to defend the *theory of a «monogenetic» origin of writing* in general. According to this theory, all the writing systems of the (ancient) Eastern and Western world seem to derive from a single system. The Latin and Cyrillic alphabets are adapted from the Greek script, which in turn is adapted from the Canaanite script. It has to be assumed that the cuneiform writing systems and other equally ancient systems also derive from a single pre-cuneiform system of Mesopotamian origin. Those who study the history of writing from a wider point of view, which includes the Mycenaean, Chinese and Mayan scripts as well as the cuneiform script, tend to cast doubt on the theory, in spite of the many elements which all these types of writing have in common.

The alphabetic script developed in Syria-Palestine, probably in the 13th cent. Before that, other writing systems existed: cuneiform in Mesopotamia and hieroglyphics in Egypt.

1. *Mesopotamia: Cuneiform Writing*

The oldest system of writing, probably invented in Mesopotamia after 3400 BCE., was a *pictographic system*. So, for example, a picture of the solar disc meant «sun» and also expressed the idea of «day» and «light». This *logographic* system was perfected until it became a *phonetic system*. Sumerian, an agglutinative language, is made up of elements which almost always consist of a single syllable. Accordingly, the phonetic value of the signs tended to be syllabic. To differentiate the different possible readings of the same logogram, signs were used which indicated the final syllable of a word or the class of word in question (proper name, name of an object in wood or stone, etc.).

The *signs* were incised with a stylus on a tablet of smooth clay. At first they wrote in vertical columns, as in Chinese, starting from the upper right corner. Later, a simple change in the way the tablet was held produced writing in horizontal lines from right to left. The use of a stylus on clay is better for drawing a straight line than a curve; this prompted stylised marks in the form of wedges.

During the first half of the third millennium BCE, the *Akkadians* adopted this system of «cuneiform» writing. In order to represent the sounds of a Semitic language they had to include new signs and sounds. The excavations of *Ebla* (Tell Mardikh) have shown that Mesopotamian influence in North Syria in the old Bronze Age was greater than could be suspected in the period before the date of these excavations, even though it remains uncertain whether Egyptian writing was also known at Ebla. The cuneiform system, unlike Egyptian hieroglyphics, was very versatile and was adapted as a method of writing for different languages. It also affected the development of two other cuneiform systems: the alphabetic cuneiform of *Ugarit* and the syllabic system of ancient Persian, which comprised 41 signs.

In *Persia*, between 3100 and 2700 BCE, the proto-Elamite script was used which has not yet been deciphered. Towards the end of the third millennium BCE, the linear Elamite script became dominant, but for this period the scribes of Susa had already adopted Mesopotamian cuneiform characters. Cuneiform writing extended through *Anatolia* in the period of the introduction of Assyrian trade colonies in this region (2000-1800 BCE). The Hittites adapted this system to write in their own language and in related languages.

The Hurrians and the peoples of *Urartu* also adopted cuneiform writing in the second millennium.

2. Egypt: Hieroglyphics

Hieroglyphic *writing* arose in Egypt towards the end of the third millennium BCE. It was born, one could say, fully developed and with no traces of prior evolution, unlike the cuneiform script in Mesopotamia. It can be assumed, however, that the Egyptians took some basic elements from Sumer which they imprinted with a new character. Such is the case, e.g., for the use of logograms and of phonetic complements and determinatives. This is a further example of the well-known tendency and ability of the ancient Egyptians to take over inventions made in other areas of the ancient Near East and perfect them.

Hieroglyphic *signs* have features which instead, allow the conclusion to be drawn that they were specifically invented. They appeared suddenly and developed rapidly, with hardly any changes, the opposite of what happened with cuneiform signs. They only represented consonants, not syllables. The uni-consonantal or «alphabetic» signs comprise a striking and unique characteristic of the Egyptian writing system. Its adaptation to this language from the Afro-Asiatic group is perfect.

The complete absence of signs for vowels precludes knowing the *pronunciation* of ancient Egyptian. It can be reconstructed by means of transcriptions of Hebrew terms in syllabic cuneiform and by using Coptic, the final stage in the development of Egyptian, written in Greek characters with the inclusion of vowels.

Egyptian logograms, converted into phonetic signs, contained from one to three consonants. In hieroglyphic writing there were enough signs for single consonants to represent the 24 consonantal phonemes of Egyptian. However, the Egyptians never made the transition from hieroglyphic writing to the alphabet.

Hieroglyphic writing was usually used for inscriptions on stone. Writing on papyrus with quill and ink led, very early on, to the development of a more cursive script called *hieratic*. Towards the end of the 8th cent. BCE *demotic* writing began to be used in letters and official documents. It was even more simplified, using more characters joined by a ligature. The three forms of writing co-existed for several centuries. In the 4th-5th cents. CE, hieroglyphic writing went into decline and towards the 3rd cent. CE, the Greek alphabet was adopted for writing Egyptian and in this manner gave way to Coptic.

3. *Syria and Palestine: the Alphabet*

The alphabet comprises one of the great inventions in the history of mankind. It originated *within the culture of Syria-Palestine*, the crossroads of Mesopotamian and Egyptian civilisations. In 1929, hundreds of tablets were found at Ugarit, dating to the beginning of the 14th cent. BCE and written in a type of cuneiform script which used only 30 signs, so that it was an alphabetic script.

The oldest alphabetic script, however, was found in 24 inscriptions from the Sinai peninsula, and according to many scholars, can be dated around 1400 BCE, but which could well go back to 1800 more or less (during the XII dynasty). These *Proto-Sinaitic inscriptions* were written in a consonantal alphabet derived from Egyptian hieroglyphic writing by the acrophonic system. Each sign represents not the complete word drawn but only its initial sound. By means of this hypothesis, the Egyptologist Sir Alan Gardiner was able to decipher a group of four signs which is repeated five times: *b'lt* = *ba'alat*, «lady». Three somewhat older inscriptions. which come from Gezer, Lachish and Shechem, use the same alphabet. This means that the Semitic slaves of Sinai were not the inventors of the alphabet as had been thought in previous decades. The Proto-Sinaitic inscriptions are only part of a complete corpus of Proto-Canaanite alphabetic inscriptions.

F. M. Cross classifies the oldest alphabetic texts into two groups. The first comprises *proto-Canaanite texts*: ancient Palestinian (17th-12th cents. BCE) and Proto-Sinaitic (14th cent.). The second comprises *Canaanite cuneiform texts*: Ugaritic (14th-13th cents.) and Palestinian (13th- 12th cents.).

The *Proto-Canaanite script* was invented around 1700 BCE by Canaanite Semites who had some knowledge of Egyptian writing. The signs are intended to be written with pen and ink, not impressed like cuneiform. This fact places the origin of the alphabet in the area of Egyptian influence since only Egyptian writing used these writing materials. The Phoenician alphabet cannot be connected with the 30 cuneiform signs used by the scribes of Ugarit. Initially, the consonantal system had 27 letters, but towards the 13th cent. it had been reduced to 22. The signs were pictographic and for the most part had acrophonic values, gradually developing until they became linear characters. So, for example, the sign for «water» became the letter *mem*, from which the letter «M» derives. Similarly, the sign for «eye» became the letter *'ayin*, the form of which was rounded and turned into the letter «O».

Writing could run in any direction. However, vertical writing had already disappeared towards 1100 BCE. Writing from left to right, which is commoner, is another indication for assuming the influence of Egyptian hieroglyphic writing, used in ordinary documents.

From the moment that the number of letters had stabilised as 22 and the writing system had been established as going from right to left, one can no longer speak of the Proto-Canaanite script; it is the *Phoenician script*. The transition from one to the other was completed towards the middle of the 12th cent. BCE. In 1923, the sarcophagus of King Hiram was discovered at Byblos with an inscription in an early form of the Phoenician alphabet dating to around 1000 BCE (Gibson).

Prior to the 11th cent., the Proto-Canaanite script had further derivatives: towards 1300 the *Proto-Arabic script* originated, from which the Ethiopic was derived, and towards 1100 the *archaic Greek script* arose. At present, the adoption of the alphabet by the Greeks is usually dated back to this period.

The alphabet contributed to the spread of writing among the population over a wide range of classes (however, cf. p. 111). The simplicity and adaptability of the new system ensured that it spread quickly at the expense of other systems, from the beginning of the Iron Age. In addition to the Phoenicians, the Aramaeans, Ammonites, Edomites, Moabites and Israelites also adopted the Canaanite alphabet. Phoenician writing gave rise later to the Punic script in the Western Phoenician colonies, especially in Carthage. The spread of Aramaic resulted in the alphabet being widely used at the expense of cuneiform writing. Some Babylonian scribes continued to cling to the cuneiform system up to the 1st cent. BCE. This is a typical example of preserving at all costs a form of writing in order to save a culture which had been inextricably linked with that writing system but was now in its death throes.

The *Aramaic script* of the Syrian city-states eventually became the script used for diplomacy and trade in the Neo-Assyrian, Babylonian and Persian empires. After the fall of the Persian empire, national scripts derived from cursive Aramaic of the late Persian period began to develop. In North Arabia and Transjordan, the *Nabataean script* developed. A cursive form of this script is the immediate ancestor of Arabic writing. In the East, *Palmyrene* and *Syriac writing* were formed and the script of the kingdom of Asoka in North-West India in the 3rd cent. BCE and the late Iranian scripts of the Parthians and Sassanians.

The Bible has no fewer than 429 references to writing and to written documents. This is significant if it is remembered that the *Iliad* provides only one reference to writing and there is none in the *Odyssey*. From the 10th cent. BCE up to the 2nd cent. CE, Hebrew was written in the *Phoenician* or *Palaeo-Hebrew script*, which is still used in some MSS from the Dead Sea (11QPaleoLev^a) and on Jewish coins of the Hasmonaean period. In the 3rd cent. BCE, however, the Jews had already adopted the characters of the *Aramaic* or «*square*» *script*, which had developed independently of the Phoenician script. Jesus' saying, «not one *iota* of the Law will disappear» (Mt 4:18), which refers to *yodh*, the smallest Hebrew letter, only makes sense as refer-ring to this type of square script used in his time. This form of square or Ara-maic script has remained in use until the present day and is used in modern editions of the Hebrew Bible.

The innovations of the square script include the introduction of a special form for some letters at the end of a word and the separation of words by spaces, as can be seen in the Dead Sea Scrolls. There are three phases in the development of the Jewish-Aramaic script: ancient Jewish (240-140 BCE), Hasmonaean (140-30 BCE) and Herodian (30 BCE-70 CE; F. M. Cross, cf. p. 103).

Until the period between the 4th and 7th cents. BCE no system of vocali-sation was developed. The Palestinian and Babylonian vowel systems were supralinear and the Tiberian system was infralinear. The latter, introduced towards the end of the 8th cent., displaced the other two and is used in mod-ern Hebrew Bibles (cf. pp. 272-273). The Ashkenazi script is more angular, the Sephardi more rounded and the Italian script evolved to become what is called the Rashi script (11th cent.)

The *Samaritan script* is a more ornate form of the ancient Phoenician or palaeo-Hebrew script.

4.   *Greece: The Adoption of the Canaanite Alphabet*

On the island of Crete, around 2000 BCE, the Minoan civilisation developed a system of *hieroglyphic writing* which has not yet been deciphered. It is read from left to right or bustrophedically, that is, from left to right on one line and from right to left on the next. In the 17th-16th cents. this system was re-placed by a type of cursive writing known as *Linear A*, also barely deci-phered. These systems are composed of just fewer than 100 signs; the lan-guages of these scripts have not been identified. Most of the documentation preserved consists of economic texts. The most recent texts come from around 1440 BCE. The Mycenaeans, who occupied Crete from 1440 until at least 1374 BCE, introduced the *Linear B* script, which is derived from Linear A and was used until the destruction of that civilisation in continental Greece about 1200 BCE. It is a syllabic script; a syllable comprises a conso-nant plus a vowel or only a vowel. It was written from left to right.

The *adoption of the consonantal Phoenician script* for writing Greek oc-curred towards 1100 (Cross, Bernal), a date which some scholars put for-ward and others put back. Herodotus (4th cent. BCE) refers to a tradition ac-cording to which a legendary person called Kadmos was the one who intro-duced the Phoenician script into Greece. The Semitic origin of the Greek script is proved by the similarity of form, phonetic value and sequence of the letters of both alphabets. In the oldest Greek inscriptions, the letter *sigma* has the shape of an upright *šin* of the 13th-12th centuries. The letter *nu* looks like a *mem* and *omicron* like an *ayin* of the 11th century proto-Canaanite in-scriptions. To this can be added the fact that the Greek names of the letters have no meaning at all in Greek. In Semitic languages these names correspond to well-known words which are related to the signs of the corresponding letters. Some consonantal Phoenician signs which had no equivalent in Greek were used for vowel sounds, which had to be represented in Greek. Thus, the *ʾaleph* sign (ʾ) denoted the letter *a*, *hēʾ* denoted *e*, *ḥêṭ*, long *ē*, *yodh*, *i* and *ʿayin* (ʿ) short *o*. Later, other signs were introduced to represent phonemes missing from Phoenician, particularly those corresponding to the last letters of the Greek alphabet.

At first, writing was from right to left, as was also the case in Syria and Palestine. After a period of writing with the boustrophedic system as in the proto-Canaanite script, it changed definitively to writing from left to right. There was no separation between words. In the mid-4th cent. BCE, the Ionian alphabet displaced all the other local alphabets and became the classic alphabet of 24 graphemes.

Very soon a type of *cursive script* developed, used mostly in accounting. The *uncial script*, in capital letters and generally without accents, survived until the 12th cent. CE. Towards 800 CE, a *script in miniscule letters* was introduced. The Greek alphabet was the origin of all the European alphabets, via Etruscan and Latin in the West and via Cyrillic in the East. To be noted is the frequent use of abbreviations for writing sacred names; examples are ΘC = *Theós* («God»), KC + *Kyrios* («Lord»), XC = *Khristós* («Christ»), etc.

II. WRITING MATERIALS. EPIGRAPHY AND PALAEOGRAPHY

1. *Writing on Stone, Metal and Clay: Epigraphy*

There are very many inscriptions *on stone* in the walls of temples and tombs or on stelae or rock faces in Egypt. In contrast, stone is relatively rare in Mesopotamia. Therefore, cuneiform inscriptions in stone are restricted almost completely to official texts or public stelae, like the famous Code of Hammurabi. In the region of Syria-Palestine a few public inscriptions on stone have been found. Outstanding among them are the stela of Mesha, the Siloam Tunnel inscription and the tombstone of king Uzziah. The inscriptions in Greek prohibiting gentiles from entering the Temple were written on marble. The OT contains several references to writing on stone; the most important is the reference to the tablets of the Law (Ex 24:12; 34:1; Dt 4:13).

Metal is less common than stone. Sumerian, Akkadian and Persian cuneiform inscriptions on objects of gold, silver, copper or bronze have been found. In 1 Mac 8:22 and 14:18.27.48 there is an allusion to writing on plates of bronze. The *Copper Scroll* was found in Qumran and describes the place where the supposed treasure of the Essene community was hidden. A *silver amulet* from the 6th cent. BCE, found in a tomb to the South-east of Jerusalem (Barkay) seems to contain the text of the priestly blessing (Nm 6:22-27).

The valley of the rivers Tigris and Euphrates is formed of alluvial soil which made the *use of clay for writing* very common and cheap. The use of this material influenced the development of the pictographic script, resulting in cuneiform signs. Damp clay was shaped to produce tablets, usually flat on one side and convex on the other. Signs were written with a stylus on the flat side. If necessary, writing was continued onto the convex side. The clay was usually dried in the sun, but baking in an oven made the tablet longer lasting. For greater security, tablets of an official nature could be enclosed in an envelope or case on which was written a summary of the written contents of the text kept inside it. Tablets containing lengthy literary works could have several columns of text. They were kept duly catalogued. When the use of tablets had spread over the whole near East it became a medium for international mail as shown by the Tell el-Amarna letters.

Fragments from pieces of broken pottery comprise a plentiful and cheap writing material, already used in Egypt since the time of the ancient empire, particularly for school exercises, letters, receipts, accounts, etc. These fragments of pottery with writing, called «ostraca» (plur. of ostracon), were written on with pen and ink which only allowed writing in Aramaic characters. This explains the meagre number of ostraca found in Mesopotamia. In Athens, condemnation to exile was expressed by the act of writing on ostraca the names of those condemned to so-called «ostracism». In Palestine, particularly important ostraca have been found in Hazor, Samaria, Lachish and Arad. The collection of ostraca from Tell Arad provides interesting parallels to biblical texts (Gn 43:27; 1 Sm 10:4). The ostraca from Hazor (9th-10th cents.) and Samaria (8th cent. BCE) reflect the Northern dialect. An ostracon from Yavneh-Yam belongs to the period of Josiah. The Lachish ostraca (497-487) belong to a crucial period in the history of the end of the kingdom of Judah. They contain data which have to be connected with data from the book of Jeremiah. Some ostraca are preserved which contain passages from the OT and NT.

In addition to the texts discovered in Ugarit and in the caves of the Dead Sea are the many inscriptions found in places of every kind and from every period. The inscriptions comprise a very important source of data for knowing the linguistic and cultural world in which the Bible originated. So, for example, in the 6th cent., the dialects and spelling of pre-exilic Hebrew gave way to new dialectal forms and different usages of spelling. The discovery of inscriptions from the centuries before the Exile makes available much more certain and accurate knowledge of the archaic forms of the language.

Epigraphy takes us back to forms of the consonantal text which are much earlier than those attested in the biblical manuscripts and allows us to know the types of pronunciation corresponding to those periods. The system of pronunciation we know through the mediaeval masoretes could be the result of a natural evolution from those ancient forms of pronunciation or instead, it could be an artificial reconstruction.

Study of the epigraphic sources provides the linguistic and stylistic parallels between a particular text from the Bible and an inscription of known date. No less important is its contribution to the study of the history, religion and culture of ancient Israel.

Among the *Hebrew inscriptions*, the so-called «Gezer Calendar» (10th cent. BCE) is written in an archaic Southern dialect. It is not a true calendar but rather a list of eight months of the year and the corresponding farming activities. Its interpretation is still discussed. The Southern dialect of Jerusalem seems to be reflected in the Siloam Tunnel inscription (c. 700 BCE). Other inscriptions show that after the Exile, Hebrew continued to be in current use.

The most famous of the *Moabite inscriptions* is the stela of Mesha, king of Moab (9th cent. BCE). It provides correlations with the history of Israel in this period (2 Kgs 3). An *Ammonite* stela from the same century, found in Amman, seems to have been erected in honour of the god Milkom. The rich repertoire of *Aramaic* inscriptions includes the Tell Fekheriyeh inscription (a 9th cent. BCE Akkadian-Aramaic bilingual) and the inscriptions of Sefire, Hamath, etc.

Conspicuous among the *most recent epigraphic finds* are those of: Tell Deir 'Alla, from the mid-8th cent. BCE, in a cursive Aramaic script, mentioning «Balaam, son of Beor», the famous person to which the narrative of Nm 22-24 alludes (Cross, Van der Kooij); Kuntillet Ajrud, with drawings of three figures, two of which could correspond to Yahweh and his consort, if this is in fact the correct interpretation of the inscription accompanying the figures: «Yahweh of Samaria and his Asherah» (*lyhwh šmrn wlʾšrth*; Meshel); Khirbet el-Kom, from the mid-8th cent. with the text of a blessing: «Blessed of Yahweh and his Asherah» (Dever, Lemaire). These texts cannot fail to be tremendously disturbing for the history of Yahwistic monotheism.

The number of seals and stamp-seals has greatly increased in recent decades. The name of Jerusalem is mentioned in the *graffiti* found in Khirbet Beit-Lei. A collection of *bullae* from the period of the prophet Jeremiah provides several personal names including those of persons alluded to in the Bible: «Baruch, son of Neriah, the scribe» (*lbrkyhw bn nryhw hspr*) and «Yerahmeel, the king's son» (*lyrḥmʾl bn hmlk*; Jr 36:4.26; Avigad). The most surprising inscription of all for its connection with the biblical text was found in Jerusalem (Ketef Hinnom) on some silver talismans with the text of a blessing, later known as the «Priestly Blessing», transmitted in Nm 6:24-24. This biblical passage is attributed to the most recent source of the Pentateuch, called the Priestly Document (P). The new find proves that a blessing with similar wording was already widely known in the period before the destruction of Jerusalem by the Babylonians (Barkay).

Epigraphy makes a distinction between formal or chancellory script and cursive script. There are intermediate scripts: semiformal, semi-cursive and vulgar. «Scribal errors» in epigraphic texts are rare, though there are some examples, such as the omission of one word (*yn*, «wine») in an ostracon from Samaria (1:2-3; Naveh).

Papyrus is prepared from the stems of the plant from which it takes its name. It was very common in ancient Egypt. It was cut into fine strips which were placed upon each other in layers crosswise until they formed long strips which were rolled up to form what in Latin was called a *volumen* («rolled up»). It was generally written only on one side, in columns separated by spaces which formed the margins. Only the horizontal fibres («obverse») were written on; when the volumen was rolled up these remained on the inside of the scroll; if necessary the «reverse» was also written on. Until the invention of paper in China and its spread through Syria and Egypt during the 6th-8th cents. CE, papyrus was the commonest writing material in the ancient world.

The oldest written papyrus which has been preserved goes back to the v Dynasty of Egypt (c. 2470 BCE). Papyrus was used for all kinds of texts. It was written on with pen and ink, in hieratic and demotic characters as well as in Coptic, Aramaic and Greek characters. Egyptian papyrus gave rise to the development of a veritable export industry, but the damp conditions of the other countries made preservation of written papyri impossible for long periods except in the region of the Dead Sea, also a very dry region, where important biblical papyri have been found. In Wadi Murabbaʿat, a papyrus palimpsest was found from the period before the Exile. The account of Wen-Amon testifies to the extensive use of papyrus in Syria at the beginning of the 12th cent. BCE. The deed of sale signed by the prophet Jeremiah (Jr 32:10-14) must undoubtedly have been written on folded and sealed papyrus, like those found at Elephantine in Upper Egypt. Paul's letters and other NT texts were also written on papyrus.

The use of leather for writing on goes back to the beginning of the third millennium BCE. The oldest preserved example corresponds to the period of the XII dynasty (c. 2000). During the 2nd cent. BCE, the technique of preparing *parchment* was perfected in the city of Pergamon, from which it took its name. The oldest preserved fragment of a Christian work written on parchment belongs to the Diatessaron of Doura-Europos, from the first half the 2nd cent. CE. No parchment manuscripts of the NT from before the 4th cent. have been preserved.

Writing follows a very erratic evolutionary process, with some letters changing faster than others. From the beginning until a relatively late period, Phoenician, Aramaic or Hebrew letters were written hanging from the top line, not resting on the lower line. For this reason letters should not be studied using tables which arrange the different characters in vertical columns but on horizontal lines (i.e. lineally) so that it is possible to compare the position and length of a letter in relation to the upper line, the size of each letter and with the lower line when it is a question of forms of writing from more recent periods. The form, width, length, shape, etc. of each letter have to be compared in the greatest possible numbers.

Palaeography establishes two types of script, *formal* and *cursive*, with transitional forms in between. When formal script begins to relax and veer towards the cursive, it can be called a *proto-cursive* script. The *semi-cursive* script belongs to the transitional gap between formal and cursive. In the *semi-formal* script, features of formal script are still predominant. The *vulgar* script is the handwriting of non-professionals.

Palaeography permits a chronological sequence to be established, with due allowance for the presence of archaising factors (Cross, Avigad, Birnbaum, Naveh).

1. The *Formal Jewish script* comes from the formal or chancellory Aramaic script of the 4th cent. in the Persian period. The Cursive Jewish script also stems from Aramaic cursive forms and does not derive, therefore, from the formal Jewish script. There are three periods in the development of the formal Jewish script:

a. The *Archaic* or proto-Jewish period (240-140 BCE.) with its variants
– formal, cf. 4QSam[b] and 4QJer[a]
– semi-formal (influenced by 3rd cent. cursive), cf. 4QQoh[a]
– proto-cursive, influenced by the formal script, but more closely related to the vulgar Aramaic script of the 3rd cent., cf. 4QEx[f].

b. The *Hasmonaean* period (140-30 BCE):
– formal (strongly influenced by the semi-formal), cf. 4QDeut[a], 1QIs[a], 4QDeut[c], 4QSam[a]
– semi-cursive, cf. Nash Papyrus, 4QXII[a], 4QDan[e].

c. The *Herodian* period (30 BCE. - 70 CE)
– formal, cf. 4QSam[a] as prototype, 1QM, 4QDan[b], 4QDeut[j]
– semi-formal, cf. 1QNum[b] and 4QNum[b].

2. Knowledge of the gradual development of the *cursive Jewish script* still requires deeper study especially with regard to the post-Herodian period.

3. The *palaeo-Hebrew script*: from the oldest example known, the Gezer Calendar (9th or 10th cent. BCE) until the fall of the kingdom of Judah, two different styles developed: one *lapidary* or *formal,* used especially on seals and stone monuments, the other *cursive,* used principally on ostraca. Against general opinion, Naveh considers that the palaeo-Hebrew script did not fall into disuse during the Persian period. It is certain that it developed very slowly while it was being replaced by the square script (Cross). It belongs to a series of traditional and conservative characteristics which resurfaced in the Maccabaean period. The Hasmonaean kings promoted the use of this type of script, used for the legends on the coins of John Hyrcanus I, Judas Aristobulus, Alexander Jannaeus and John Hyrcanus II. Manuscripts 4QpaleoEx[m] and 11QPaleoLev should be dated to around 100 BCE, like the Hasmonaean coins, also from this period, somewhat later than was customarily thought (Hanson). The last examples of palaeo-Hebrew script are found on coins dating to the years of the two Jewish revolts against the Romans. In the 1st and 2nd cents. CE another form of script developed which gave rise to the Samaritan script.

The contribution of palaeography is decisive not only for the reading, dating and classification of manuscripts but also to resolve many other questions, especially those connected with text criticism. Palaeography allows the possibilities of mistakes in copying the manuscript to be recognised, as in the case of letters with similar shape. For a very extensive period in the development of the script, the letters *dālet* and *rêš* were easily confused both in the palaeo-Hebrew script and in the square script. There was frequently confusion between *waw* and *yodh* in the formal script of the 1st cent. BCE, as can easily be seen in the manuscripts from the beginning of the Herodian period (4QSmᵃ, 1QM, 4QDanᵇ, 4QDeutʲ, 1QNumᵇ and 4QNumᵇ). This explains the frequent cases of confusion of the pronouns *hwʾ* and *hyʾ* or of the pronominal suffixes *-w* and *-y*. Also frequent was the confusion between *waw* and *rêš* in the formal script of the 3rd cent. This confusion gave rise to the MT reading *hʿwyty* in 2 Sm 24:17 against *hrʿh hrʿty* preserved in LXX and 4QSamᵃ (cf. also 1 Chr 21:17; Ulrich, McCarter, Barthélemy).

The bad state of preservation of one manuscript could cause incorrect readings due to letters of which the strokes were only partially preserved. Knowledge of palaeography sometimes allows the process of the corruption of the text to be reconstructed. It also shows, for example, that the Greek version of the book of Job was made from an original written in palaeo-Hebrew characters (Orlinsky). Palaeography has enabled a better knowledge of the rules governing Hebrew spelling (Cross-Freedman) and *scriptio continua* (Millard). The Dead Sea Scrolls have provided much data concerning strophic and stichometric division of the poetic texts, the use of palaeo-Hebrew letters to write the *tetragrammaton* in manuscripts in the square script, the absence of abbreviations and the presence, instead, of several notes introduced by copyists (M. Martin), the procedures for rolling up scrolls and the possibility of reconstructing scrolls using scattered fragments (Stegemann, cf. p. 286), the number of columns and their size in each manuscript, etc.

AHITUV, S., *Handbook of Ancient Hebrew Inscriptions from the Period of the First Commonwealth and the Beginning of the Second Commonwealth*, Jerusalem 1992.

ALBRIGHT W.F., «A Biblical Fragment from the Maccabaean Age: The Nash Papyrus», *JBL* 46 (1937) 144-176.

ANDERSEN, F.I.-FORBES, A.D., *Spelling in the Hebrew Bible*, Rome 1986.

AVIGAD, N., «The Palaeography of the Dead Sea Scrolls and Related Documents», *Scripta Hierosolymitana* 4 (1948) 46-87.

AVIGAD, N., *Hebrew Bullae from the Time of Jeremiah*, Jerusalem 1986.

BARKAY, G., *Ketef Hinnom: A Treasure Facing Jerusalem's Walls*, Jerusalem 1986.

BARTHÉLEMY, D., *Critique Textuelle de l'Ancien Testament*, vol. I, Fribourg-Göttingen 1982.

BIRNBAUM, S., *The Hebrew Scripts*, London 1944-47 and 1972.

BOFFO, L., *Iscrizioni greche e latine per lo studio de la Bibbia*, Brescia 1994.

BORDREUIL, P., «Sceaux inscrits des pays du Levant», *SDB* 12, fasc. 66, Paris 1992, 86-211.

COOKE, G.A., *A Textbook of Northwest Semitic Inscriptions*, Oxford 1903.

CROSS, F.M., *Early Hebrew Orthography: A Study of the Epigraphic Evidence*, New Haven NJ 1942; Winona Lake IN 1990.

CROSS, F.M., «The Development of the Jewish Scripts», *The Bible and the Ancient Near East. Essays in Honor of W.F. Albright*, ed. G.E. Wright, New York 1961, 133-202.

CROSS, F.M., «Early alphabetic scripts», *Symposia celebrating the Seventy-fifth Anniversary of the American Schools of Oriental Research*, ed. F.M. Cross, Cambridge MA 1979, 97-123.

DEVER, W.G., «Iron Age Epigraphic Material from the Area of Khirbet el-Kom», *HUCA* 40/41 (1969/70) 139-204.

DONNER, H.-RÖLLIG, W., *Kanaanäische und aramäische Inscrhiften*, 3 vols., Wiesbaden 1966-70.

FITZMYER, J.A., *The Aramaic Inscriptions of Sefire*, Rome 1967.

FREY, J.B., *Corpus inscriptionum iudaicarum*, 2 vols., Rome 1936 and 1942.

GIBSON, J.C.L., *Textbook of Syrian Semitic Inscriptions*, 3 vols., Oxford 1971, 1974, 1982.

HANSON, R.S., «Palaeography», in *The Paleo-Hebrew Leviticus Scroll (11QpaleoLev)*, by/ed. D. N. Freedman-K.A. Mathews, Winona Lake IN 1984, pp. 14-23.

HOFTIJZER, J. - JONGELING, K., *Dictionary of the North-West Semitic Inscriptions*, 2 vols., Leiden 1994.

JEFFERY, L.H., «Greek alphabetic writing», *The Cambridge Ancient History*, III/1, ed. J. Boardman et al., Cambridge 1982, 819-833.

JENSEN, H., *Sign, Symbol and Script. An Account of Man's Efforts to Write*, London 1970.

LEMAIRE, A., *Inscriptions Hebraïques*, Paris 1977.

LEMAIRE, A., «Les inscriptions palestiniennes d'époque perse: un bilan provisoire», *Transeuphratene* 1 (1989) 87-104.

MCCARTER, P.K., *II Samuel*, Garden City NY 1984.

MARTIN, M., *The Scribal Character of the Dead Sea Scrolls*, Louvain 1948.

MESHEL, Z., *Kuntillet 'Ajrud: A Religious Centre from the Time of the Judaean Monarchy on the Border of Sinai*, Jerusalem 1974.

MILLARD, A.R., «'Scriptio Continua' in Early Hebrew: Ancient Practice or Modern Surmise?», *JSS* 14 (1970) 2-14.

MILLARD, A.R., *Naissance de l'écriture. Cunéiformes et hiéroglyphes*, Galeries nationales du Grand Palais 7 mai- 9 août 1982.

NASSEN, U. (ed.), *Texthermeneutik, Aktualität, Geschichte, Kritik*, Paderborn 1979.

NAVEH, J., *The Development of the Aramaic Scripts*, Jerusalem 1970.

NAVEH, J., *Early History of the Alphabet. An Introduction to West Semitic Epigraphy and Palaeography*, Jerusalem 1982.

ORLINSKY, H.M., «Studies in the Septuagint of Job», *HUCA* 36 (1964) 37-47.

PARDEE, D.-SPERLING, S.D.-WHITEHEAD, J.D.-DION,P.-E., *Handbook of Ancient Hebrew Letters*, Chico CA 1982.

PUECH, E., «ABECEDAIRE et liste alphabétique de noms hébreux du début du IIe s. A.D.», *RB* 87 (1990) 118-126.

RENZ, J.-RÖLLIG, W., *Handbuch der Althebräischen Epigraphik*, I, II/1-2, Darmstadt 1994.

SENNER, W.M., *The Origins of Writing*, The University of Nebraska 1989.

ULRICH, E., *The Qumran Text of Samuel and Josephus*, Chico CA 1978.

VAN DER KOOIJ, G., *Aramaic Texts from Deir 'Alla*, Leiden 1976.

YARDENI, A., «The Palaeography of 4QJerᵃ - A Comparative Study», *Textus* 14 (1990) 233-268.

3

Written and Oral Transmission

I.   PROBLEMS IN THE TRANSMISSION OF TEXTS IN THE ANCIENT WORLD

It is important to realise the enormous difficulties involved in copying a manuscript in ancient times. These difficulties only increased the proliferation of copyist errors. In ancient times writing was much faster than can be imagined today (cf. Ezr 7:6 «swift scribe», if this is the translation of the adjective *mahir*, «rapid», rather than «skilful scribe» as comparison with use of the term in Ethiopic suggests). This factor did not encourage accuracy in the copying of manuscripts either. The use of abbreviations was another cause of frequent mistakes. The Jewish scribes used to make abbreviations with a sign easily confused with the letter *yodh*.

Reading an ancient text, especially if written on papyrus, was much more difficult than a reader used to modern books can imagine. Hebrew writing lacked vowel signs and accents. The punctuation of Greek texts was very rudimentary; spacing between words was not in general use until the Middle Ages. Use of accents began in the Hellenistic period but did not come into use completely until the beginning of Mediaeval times. Before the Hellenistic period, verse was written as if it were prose (an example is in the papyrus of Timothy from the 4th cent. BCE, *P. Berol. 9875*). Aristophanes of Byzantium (c. 257-180 BCE) introduced the practice of indicating metrical units. It is easy to imagine the difficulties which a scenic text entailed devoid of indications of changes of character and even of the names of characters who come on scene. In the Bible, especially in the prophetic books, it is at times not easy to make a clear distinction between passages in prose and passages in verse.

The work of *copying manuscripts* also presented greater difficulties than can undoubtedly be imagined. The originals of the classical period did not supply much help to the copyist. The Alexandrian philologists, dedicated to establishing the texts of the classics, had to transliterate into Ionic spelling books imported from Attica, written in the ancient alphabet. In this alphabet the letter *e* (*epsilon*) could represent short *e* (*e*), closed long *e* (*ei*) and open long *e* (*ē*, *ēta*), etc. Likewise, they had to improve the punctuation system and invent a system of accents. Copying out Hebrew texts presented even greater difficulties of this order (cf. p. 264).

The difficulties of textual transmission in ancient times gained particular importance in a very common and significant case: the *re-editing* or *revision* of works in circulation. Given the conditions of distributing books in those times it was not easy for the second edition to make copies of the first disappear completely. The author could not ensure that the changes and corrections he himself had put into his work were transferred to all the existing copies. Often there was horizontal contamination of the manuscripts of one edition from those of another. In such cases, it is difficult to establish a clear and definite vertical *stemma* of the different manuscripts preserved. Cf. the duplicate editions of several scenes in the works of Plautus (Bickel) and the duplicate editions of certain books of the Bible (cf. pp. 393-404).

II. CRUCIAL MOMENTS IN THE HISTORY OF TEXTUAL TRANSMISSION

In ancient times the history of writing experienced crucial moments for the correct and faithful textual transmission of the books known then. These critical moments coincide with *transitions* due to change of writing materials (transition from tablet to papyrus or from papyrus to parchment), change in the way of binding (transition from volumen or scroll to codex or book), change of the type of letter (transition from palaeo-Hebrew characters to «square» script or of Greek uncial characters to cursive). These critical moments correspond to periods of renewal and cultural rebirth. However, the technical changes effected entailed the complete loss of many literary works and the disappearance of editions or of different versions of the text of the same written composition. Such losses also happened at the time of the invention and spread of printing and will also undoubtedly happen in the transition from printed book to the book stored in computer memory.

1. *The Transition from Tablet to Papyrus and from Papyrus to Parchment*

Tablets were used for Mesopotamian cuneiform writing. Copying very lengthy literary works required a large number of tablets, twelve in the case of the poem of Gilgamesh. A colophon specified the title of the work and the tablet number. A word repeated at the end of each tablet and at the start of the next (*custos*) enabled the order in which the tablets had to be read to be known.

Nothing is known about what happened at the moment when there was a change from the use of tablets to the use of papyrus in Israel. It is impossible to know to what degree it affected the process of formation and transmission of the biblical texts in the initial period. By analogy with what happened in other crucial moments later, it must be thought that this change caused the loss of such texts as were not transcribed onto the new writing material.

The transition from papyrus to parchment took place at the beginning of the Persian period, coinciding with the beginnings of the process of the canonisation of biblical literature, which had to be preserved on a more durable material than papyrus. Adoption of the use of parchment is a further indication of the Aramaising of the ancient Near East and of the Jewish world in this period when Aramaic language and writing were also adopted as were the Babylonian-Aramaic names of the months and many other loans from the same source (Haran).

2.   *The Scroll or Volumen*

The scroll was known in Hebrew as *megillâ* or by the expression *megillat sēper*, translated into Greek as *kephalís biblíou* (Heb 10:7, citing Ps 40:7[8]).

Writing on a volume or scroll of papyrus was much easier than writing on a clay tablet. However, papyrus decayed with the passage of time, especially in damp regions. In fact, almost all the papyri preserved come only from Egypt and the Dead Sea. For better preservation, scrolls of papyrus were usually kept in large pottery jars (Jr 32:14). Some of the manuscripts from the Qumran caves were found inside such jars. This usage was also known in Mesopotamia for keeping tablets and in Egypt for preserving papyri.

A.   THE DEVELOPMENT OF TRANSMISSION BY SCROLLS

In the *pre-exilic* period, scrolls were generally of papyrus in accordance with Egyptian usage.

In the *Persian period* the Jews adopted the Aramaic language and script. At that time writing on parchment became general and was even made obligatory for copying biblical books.

In this pre-Alexandrian period, the length of scrolls was reduced. A scroll could contain a Homeric book (about 700 verses), a tragedy (between 1000 and 1600 verses) or a discourse like those given by Thucydides or uttered by Demosthenes (no more than 600 lines).

The author frequently fitted the size of his work to the size of the scroll he was using. The size of the text was in turn determined by the time required for public recitation of the work. Writings of a philosophical nature, such as the dialogues of Plato or the treatises of Aristotle do not follow this rule or these restrictions for they were not intended for recitation in public but for reading in the Academy or the *Peripatos*.

In the *Alexandrian period* the scroll became much larger. Authors could compose longer works. It is enough to compare the length of the books by Polybius or Diodorus Siculus with the much shorter books by Thucydides.

B.   EDITIONS ON SCROLLS

Plato (*Phaedrus* 278) describes the way an author composed his written work. Everything seemed to consist in «cutting and pasting» [lit., «glueing» (*kollấn* and «sewing» (*aphaireîn*)] the sheets of papyrus to each other (*pròs állēla kollôn te kaì aphairôn*). The author added, removed or inserted separate sheets in the course of composing his text. The autograph did not yet have the form of a scroll. It was only a pile of leaves or layers of papyrus (Prentice). A manuscript by a modern author as delivered to a printer is also usually a pile of numbered sheets of paper from or into which it is easy to remove or insert new pages. Once the author had established the final sequence of pages, the text was copied out again on a continuous scroll. If for any reason the loose sheets became misplaced, various passages of the work appeared in the wrong places. This happened mostly in posthumous editions or in editions which the author had not revised.

This editorial process allowed material to be added chiefly at the beginning or the end of books. The chapters added to the end of the book of Jgs (chs. 17-18 and 19-21) and 2 Sm (chs. 22-24) could have been inserted by means of a similar editorial process applied to writing on a scroll.

C.   THE LENGTH OF BIBLICAL SCROLLS

In ancient times a scroll generally contained the complete text of a single work. If this exceeded the length of the scroll, a second scroll was used, or several more until the work was completely written out. At the time when a scroll was prepared or acquired, the length of the book which had to be copied was taken into account. The writing out of biblical books followed the same procedures. The Qumran manuscripts generally provide the text of each book written on a different scroll.

A scroll could be long enough for a book as lengthy as Isaiah to be copied. Some biblical books were short enough for them to be edited together in a single volume. Such is the case of the five books which compose the *M^egillôt* collection. The Pentateuch, instead, was too long to be copied on a single scroll; usually five scrolls were used, one per book. The books of Sm, Kgs and Chr each filled a complete scroll. The Greek text of the same books took twice the space since the Greek script includes vowels. The doubled length of the Greek text caused the present division of those books into 1-2 Sm, 1-2 Kgs and 1-2 Chr.

Copying the complete work of the Chronicler (1-2 Chr, Ezr, Neh) required two scrolls. To show that after 2 Chr the book of Ezra began, the procedure was used which consisted in writing at the end of a scroll the initial sentences of the next. This is why the text of 2 Chr 36:22-23 anticipates the beginning of Ezr 1:1-3. The first three verses of Ezr belong to this book. Only for technical reasons of editing do they also appear at the end of 2 Chr. The end of this book is actually to be found in 36:21 and not in the text which follows (vv. 22-23). This technique, which the Latins denoted with the term *custos* («catch-line(s)») was used a great deal in copying cuneiform texts and Greek and Latin works (Strabo, Pliny, Eusebius, Porphyry, Theophrastus, etc.). The same procedure was followed in the copying of mediaeval codices, particularly Hebrew manuscripts.

Modern editions of the Bible contain the complete set of books of the biblical canon printed in a single volume, suitably bound. This presentation makes evident and tangible the idea of the unity of the OT canon and of the Bible itself. In ancient times *it was not possible to copy all the canonical books onto a single scroll*, not even a single one of the three major sections into which the canon is divided (Torah, Prophets and Writings). In general, each scroll contained no more than a single biblical book. In such conditions it was difficult therefore to gain an idea of the canon as a single whole, especially in respect of the more fluid collection of writings. The «book-case» of a synagogue could house a larger or smaller number of books of various kinds, including non-canonical books. This did not exactly help in making visible the idea of a closed canon.

3. The Codex

Scrolls had one huge drawback: it was only possible to write on one of the two sides. In addition, to stretch out and read a scroll required both hands. Checking references, therefore, proved very inconvenient. It is not surprising that the scroll was gradually to fall into disuse, becoming replaced by the *codex* made of papyrus leaves at first and later of parchment.

Quaternions of four double leaves formed a codex, of varying thickness and looking something like a modern book with wooden or leather covers. At first the written columns were narrow. Among the most famous codices of the Greek Bible, the Alexandrian has two columns per page, the Vatican three and the Sinaiticus four. As time went on the page generally had one or two columns.

From the 1st cent. CE, the codex increasingly replaced the scroll. It was not used until the 2nd cent. for the edition of literary texts, although already in 84-86 Martial mentions the existence of some works published in codex format, and even indicates the Roman bookshop where such novelties could be bought. In the 4th cent., use of the parchment codex instead of papyrus was already commonplace.

A. CHRISTIAN PREFERENCE FOR THE CODEX FORMAT
Christians very soon used the codex format for the dissemination of their writings even before use of the codex for copying Greek and Latin literary texts became common. The codex offered several advantages over the scroll: lower cost, ease of reference and carrying, greater text capacity and the possibility of numbering pages and including indices, which made it more difficult for other hands to insert interpolations into the text. These features made the codex the most approved medium for publishing religious and legal texts. The ease of transport and the low cost were advantages very much appreciated by Christian missionaries. The codex was also very suitable for compiling imperial constitutions by a process of «codifying» the imperial rescripts into «codices».

It should be noted that the transition from volume to codex, which was more manageable and portable, occurred at the same time as the transition from the loose and voluminous clothing of the classical period to the belted clothing of late antiquity. Belted clothing allowed greater ease of movement especially for journeys. This change even had an effect on the development of ethical outlook. In the classical period, the worker and the traveller used to remove clothing that was too modest, going so far as to strip nearly naked. The Greeks had no objection at all to nudity, an attitude considered as belonging to barbarians. The use of a more practical garment, with a belt, in late antiquity, led to the development of a sense of modesty which brought with it a satisfaction and sublimation of the erotic, forerunners of the courtly love of the Middle Ages.

The codex became the best travelling companion for the missionary. He abandoned the cumbersome volumes which were more suited for being deposited in the *bookcases* of synagogues or in the circular *capsae* of a library.

The oldest preserved texts of the NT (P^{52} from the beginning of the 2nd cent., for example) are all in the form of codices. It has been calculated that of a total of 172 fragments of biblical texts, 158 come from codices and only 14 from scrolls (Roberts-Skeat). In contrast, in the whole range of pagan literature from the 2nd cent., the proportion of use is equivalent to only 2.31%, rising to 16.8% in the 3rd cent., to reach widespread use in the 4th cent. (73.95%).

The swift adoption of the codex on the part of Christians symbolised a break with Jewish tradition which did not authorise the copying of sacred texts in any other format except a scroll or a volume. The gulf between Christians and Jews is also reflected in the techniques used for the edition of their respective sacred books. For example, the Jewish *nomina sacra* («sacred names») were replaced by others of a Christian character. The fact that the Jews did not authorise the copying of sacred books in the new codex format meant that the transmission of the Hebrew texts was not affected by the technical revolutions with an influence on the transmission of classical and Christian texts.

The speed with which the Christians adopted the use of the codex is due, as has been said, to the practical qualities of this format. However, it was certainly also influenced even more by the fact that the Christian books had not yet assumed the character of Sacred Scripture. The general outline of the New Testament canon did not take shape until the close of the 2nd cent. CE. The collections of sayings (*logia*) of Jesus, which were later to become part of the gospels, were at first transmitted possibly on loose sheets of papyrus, as propaganda material and for the apostolate. In the initial period, and urged by the apocalyptic urgency which demanded swift conversion of the gentiles before the imminent parousia, the Christian communities considered it imperative to spread the words of Jesus by means of a quick and practical method like the codex. This was more important than preserving the sacred nature and decorum of the letter and the material on which the texts were written. Only after several centuries and once the definitive canon of the NT had been formed did the process begin of making sacred the actual materials of the new Scriptures. In the mid-2nd cent. the codex format was already used in a general way for all the Christian sacred Scriptures, including books inherited from Judaism. The possibility of copying different writings on a single codex helped bring about the idea of the canon. At first, only collections such as the four gospels or the Pauline epistles could be copied. It is significant that the definitive formation of the NT canon coincided with the period in which codices had enough space to contain the books of the NT in their entirety (Turner).

During the first half of the 4th cent., when the Church had just emerged from the catacombs, parchment was replaced by *vellum* for the preparation of the most cherished books. From this period come the most famous biblical codices such as Vaticanus (B) and Alexandrian (A), mentioned already. John Chrysostom never stopped criticising the lavish way in which some codices were prepared. The best example is the one called *Codex Purpureus Petropolitanus* from the 6th cent.

B.   USE OF THE CODEX IN GREEK AND LATIN LITERATURE

For Greek and Latin literature, the transitional process from the papyrus scroll to the parchment codex ended in the 4th cent., which coincided with a period of renaissance, ephemeral perhaps, but not lacking importance. The renaissance of classical philology and the strengthening of the codex in the 4th cent. contributed to the preservation of classical literature. The 4th cent. «renaissance» is comparable to those occurring later: the Byzantine renaissance in the East and the Carolingian renaissance in the West, both in the 9th cent., and the «Renaissance» par excellence, the humanist renaissance of the 15th and 16th cents.

Our knowledge of the Latin classics derives from the mediaeval manuscript tradition and reaches back to manuscripts which come mostly from the 4th cent. and from the 5th and 6th cents. From this period come the *codices archetypi* («archetypal codices»), the *rescripti* or palimpsests and fragments and loose leaves from ancient manuscripts in capitals and uncials. The archetypal codices basically transmit the works of Virgil, Livy, Terence, Cicero and the national republican legal literature of the *Digests*. The palimpsests and fragments confirm the interest of late antiquity in the works and literary forms of the authors mentioned and complete the range of ancient Latin literature with works by Plautus, Sallust, Pliny the Elder, etc. The discovery of papyri has opened up a wider panorama of classical literature than is provided by the legacy of parchment codices of the 5th-6th cents.

Therefore, late antiquity has bequeathed to us a less extensive *corpus* of Latin literature than existed in the previous period when the scroll format and papyrus were in predominant use.

4.   *The Transition from Scroll to Codex*

The shift from the scroll to the codex meant sifting works which, for one reason or another and chiefly due to the prevailing tastes of the period, ceased to be copied in the new format. Authors and works which failed to form part of this legacy remained forgotten and had no influence at all on later «renaissances». It is only thanks to the modern discovery of the papyri that it has been possible to recover any record of them. The works of Menander are known solely thanks to the papyri. This Athenian writer of comedy was a friend of Demetrius of Phaleron, the prime mover of the Alexandrian cultural renaissance.

The papyri show that mediaeval tradition preserved the texts of classical antiquity very faithfully. The text of a mediaeval manuscript can even be more correct than the text of a papyrus, as in the case of Plato's *Phaedo* compared with a papyrus from the 3rd cent. BCE (1083 P.).

A parallelism can be drawn between the architecture of the great basilicas built in the 4th cent., in the holy places of Christian tradition in Palestine and the great codices of the Greek Bible prepared with painstaking care in that century. The great basilicas of the Byzantine period were built on places revered since the origins of Christianity (the basilicas of the Holy Sepulchre in Jerusalem, of the Nativity in Bethlehem, of the *Pater Noster* on the Mount of Olives, etc.), but at the same time they also buried and destroyed a large part of the remains of earlier periods. It has been necessary to excavate the ground beneath these basilicas to find some of those older remains. Similarly, it can be said that the great biblical codices of the 4th cent., while transmitting the legacy of the earlier period, condemned to oblivion texts written on papyrus or copied on scrolls, which can now only be known thanks to the discovery of the papyri.

The prevailing interest at the end of Antiquity in preserving the literary treasure of the preceding centuries is evident in the use of *subscriptiones* or colophons, which lasted from the close of the 4th cent. up to the 6th cent. These editorial notes can simply provide the name of the reviser of the work copied, or sometimes also add the date, the place and other circumstances of the revision. The most famous are the colophons of some books by Livy, such as the one which runs: *Nicomachus Flavianus v. c. III praef. urbi emendavi apud Hennam* («Nicomachus Flavian, prefect of the city for the third time, made this revision before Henna»).

The use of colophons and *inscriptiones* was well known in the ancient Near East (Hunger). Examples of *inscriptiones* or colophons in collections of laws, in the hymns and in wisdom literature, etc. can be found in the Bible.

Examples of *inscriptiones* in collections of laws are Lv 6:2 («This will be the law of the holocaust»), 6:7 («This will be the law of the cereal offering»), 7:1 («This will be the law for the guilt offering»), 7:11 («This will be the law of the peace offering»). Examples of colophons are Lv 7:37 («This is the law of the holocaust, the cereal offering, the sin offering, the guilt offering ...»), 11:46-47 («This is the law concerning animals, birds, all living creatures ...»), 14:54-57; 15:32-33; Nm 5:29-31 and Nm 6:21 (Fishbane).

The expression «The prayers of David, son of Jesse, are complete» (*kāllû*)», used in Ps 72:20, is the colophon to the collection of Psalms 42-72. The Hebrew term corresponds to *qāti* of cuneiform colophons (Hunger).

A synonymous term is *tammû*, used in Job 31:40: «The words of Job are complete». Examples of colophons in the prophetic literature occur in Jr 48:47b: «Thus far (*'ad hennâ*) the judgment on Moab», and Jr 51:64: «Thus far the words of Jeremiah». The use of blessings and prayers as a colophon is very common (Ps 72:18-19).

The *inscriptio* introducing the second collection of proverbs in Pr 25:1 is particularly instructive: «These too are proverbs of Solomon, which the men of Hezekiah, king of Judah *copied*». The «titles» at the head of many psalms are also examples of *inscriptiones*.

Another aspect of the transition from scroll to codex concerns the change involved in the way the text was divided. The division into books, suitable for texts published in volumes, gave way to the division into chapters (*capita*), more suited to texts intended to be written on codices.

When a text changed from the ancient volume format to the new codex format it was customary to copy the text of the work with all the editorial features of the volume even though these proved unsuited to the new codex format. Each volume usually had a *subscriptio* at the end of the text. However, this was the first thing the reader read, for when starting to unroll the volume around the *omphalos*, the first column to appear was precisely the last column of text. This was, in practice, the oldest system of *subscriptio*, as shown by the history by Thucydides of the Peloponnesian war. Each scroll contained an account of a year's wars and ended with an editorial phrase which provided information on the author, title and ordinal number of each book: «concluding the first (second, third,...) year of the war of which Thucydides wrote the history».[1] These editorial comments could also be found at the beginning of the book (*inscriptio*), i.e. on the inner side of the volume. When a work divided into chapters (one per scroll) was copied onto a single codex, the books continued to keep their own editorial annotations. It is not surprising, therefore, for a codex to repeat the name of an author several times. For example, the Greek codex 485 of Munich (10th cent.) repeats the name of the author in the heading of each one of Demosthenes' long speeches , whereas the five short speeches called *Symbouleutikoi* have only one heading. The reason for this is that they belonged to a single scroll and so were transmitted together.

This means that the divisions of mediaeval codices sometimes allow us to reconstruct the divisions of ancient scrolls and of the works they contained. The transmission of biblical texts in volumes provides similar examples. The five small books which make up the collection of *Mĕgillôṯ* were transmitted originally on separate scrolls until they formed a collection copied in a single volume. The divisions of the biblical text into «open» and «closed» sections given in the mediaeval manuscripts go back to the period of transmission on scrolls, as the manuscripts from the Dead Sea demonstrate.

The edition by Felix Pratensis (1516-17) introduced the division into chapters which Christian Bibles have followed ever since, as well as the di-

---

1. *Thucydides*, trans. by Ch.. F. Smith, 4 vols., Cambridge MA 1980, cf. vol. I, p. 461.

vision into two of the books of Samuel, Kings and Chronicles, which extended to the Bibles and writings of Jewish authors. This system was more practical than the ancient Hebrew system. The renaissance of Hebrew studies among Christians in the 16th cent. contributed, perhaps, to the Jews feeling more involved in a common enterprise and they accepted the form of division widespread among Christians.

The most critical period for the preservation and faithful transmission of the texts of classical antiquity was during the 7th and 8th cents. The material and cultural poverty of this period and the scarcity of parchment contributed to the practice of scraping the text from parchment so as to be able to write a new text on it. This is how *rescripti* codices or palimpsests originated. Today, chemical and photographic techniques enable an erased text to be read. Such texts, usually from a biblical book, were often replaced by penitential or canonical texts.

5. The Change in the Shape of the Letters

A. FROM PALAEO-HEBREW CHARACTERS TO THE SQUARE OR ARAMAIC SCRIPT

The Jewish sages of the Tannaitic period believed that the change from the Palaeo-Hebrew script to the «Aramaic» or square script took place in the time of Ezra. In practice, this belief expresses disapproval of the groups or scribes who continued to use the ancient (Palaeo-Hebrew) script, such as the Samaritans or the men of Qumran.

The shift from Palaeo-Hebrew characters to square characters explains a range of textual mistakes. For example, about forty cases of possible confusion between the letters 'alep and taw can only be explained in the palaeo-Hebrew script (Talmon). Works written in these characters could be lost. In a later period, when the rabbis forbade the use of these characters for copying the Hebrew Bible, biblical manuscripts were undoubtedly lost. Such manuscripts might have contained at least minor textual variants, the study of which could prove interesting today. In Qumran, several manuscripts have appeared in palaeo-Hebrew script (cf. p. 219).

B. FROM CAPITAL LETTERS OR UNCIALS TO MINUSCULE

The Carolingian renaissance from the 9th cent. had as its greatest exponent the Anglo-Saxon Alcuin, to whom are due the Carolingian minuscule letters in which most of classical Latin literature has reached us. In general, the archetypes of mediaeval manuscripts go back to this period. At this time, once the civil iconoclast wars were over, in the age of the patriarch Phoctius a renaissance of Greek literature took place in the East, which also entailed a change of script. The minuscule characters then replaced the uncials of the previous period.

The smaller size of the new characters economised on parchment. A codex in minuscule letters could contain the text of two codices in uncials or capitals. The manuscript *Chigian* R VIII 60 of the *Ancient history of Rome,* by Dionysius of Halicarnassus (10th cent.), contains books I-X, which filled two manuscripts in uncial script. This is the conclusion to be drawn from the close of the manuscript which refers to the «end of the second codex» and also from the distribution of the ten books making up the work into two groups of five, copied on two manuscripts. This grouping of five books per codex is very common in Greek and Latin historical works. Books I-V by Polybius have been preserved, as have books I-V. XI-XV and XVI-XX by Diodorus. Tacitus' *Histories* and the *History of Alexander the Great* by Curtius Rufinus also have this grouping. As this distribution in groups of five books can be dated back to the previous stage of writing on scrolls, the parallel with the transmission of the biblical books can be significant. The Psalter is divided into five books, as is the Pentateuch, and the five books which comprise the collection of the *M^egillôt* were copied into a single volume.

Latin writings were transmitted in four different scripts. One type with square capital letters was reserved for the de luxe editions of Virgil, the national bard. The capital letters used the most and misnamed «rustic» (in contrast to the preceding) were in vogue until the 6th cent. The other two types of letter developed independently of each other, from cursive characters. The first is the majuscule or «uncial», used in the 4th cent. and still in use until the beginning of the 9th cent. The second is the minuscule semi-uncial.

In the Late Empire, shorthand technique developed to an extent not attested in Greece until the 2nd cent. Although the sermons of some Church Fathers were noted down in a form of shorthand, this technique did not play an important role in the transmission of ancient literary texts. The use of abbreviations, on the other hand, was very common and often the cause of copyist's mistakes. Jewish scribes marked an abbreviation with a stroke similar to a small *yôd*.

III. ORAL TRANSMISSION

To gain an idea of the importance of oral tradition three important facts need to be remembered: 1) the formation and interpretation of the Bible depend, to a large extent, on oral tradition; 2) Rabbinic Judaism can be defined as the religion of the double Torah: the written Torah and the oral Torah, just as Christianity is the religion of the two Testaments; and 3) the great arguments between Catholic and Protestant Christians have always focused on the binomination Scripture and Tradition.

Oral transmission played a decisive role in the way the Bible was formed and interpreted. In the initial stages, the living word of narrators and prophets became a written «text». In the closing stages, the written word began to be interpreted, first orally and then using material from oral tradition. In fact, these initial and final stages were not always and not necessarily widely separated in time. The two processes, oral and written transmission, always had to go together. The «sons of the prophets» put into writing the oracles uttered by their masters, but at the same time they interpreted them and brought them up to date, in this manner generating new written texts and by the same token new oral interpretations.

The interaction between orality and writing reaches its highest expression in the phenomenon of textual variants called *Ketib*, «written», and *Qere*, «said».

In the modern Western world the reader of books has become a mute subject. The spread of the Bible in cheap pocket editions has made the Bible into just another book lost among many others on the shelves of any library. Private reading of the Bible has caused the sense of the oral and aural character of biblical texts to be lost. They were not meant to be read in private and in a low voice, but to be declaimed in a loud voice and even accompanied by psalmody in a liturgical assembly. Rabbinic Judaism, Islam, Buddhism and to an even greater degree Hinduism, keep alive to a large extent the oral character peculiar to sacred texts. In the history of religions and in the formation of the Bible, the transition from oral tradition to written transmission marks a definite change. Yet, memorising the Scriptures or simply quoting them presupposed entry of some kind into the sphere of the divine.

Anthropological study of oral tradition has often focused on pre-literary cultures and uncivilised peoples. In the religions of these cultures, but also in the great religions, the word possessed a special force, able to evoke and make present the primordial event of creation and the different landmarks of salvation history. The relationship between saying and doing («he said - and it was done», Gn 1) shapes the literary and theological structure of the Bible (imperative-indicative and promise-fulfilment). In the Koran, Allah «is He who gives you life and death. When He creates a thing, He has only to say 'Be', and it is» (*kun fa-yakun*, Sūrah 40:68)[2].

Rabbinic Judaism and mediaeval Islam knew the divine word revealed in the Torah or in the Koran as something pre-existing and prior to creation. In every order, cosmic, anthropological and historical, the word precedes writing. The seers and the prophets uttered oracles which the disciples later were to put into writing to ensure their remembrance.

In accordance with Jewish tradition, the Torah is learned directly from oral tradition, with the disciples seated at the feet of the rabbi and not just by means of reading books and commentaries. The traditional forms of religious piety turn on the spoken word. It is not surprising that the faithful of a religion can recite from memory extensive passages from their sacred texts. A large number of Jews can recite the whole Torah from memory. Before presenting themselves to their masters some rabbis had repeated the text of the Mishnah 24 or even 40 times (*Ta'anit* 8a). It was not allowed to use books in teaching. A *Tanna'* («repeater») had to know by heart the texts of the Halakah, Sifra, Sifre and Tosefta. The *Tanna'* was a real walking library. At first and for quite some time, the transmission of the Mishnah and later of the Talmud had to be oral only, later changing to written transmission. For pri-

---

2. Ali A(hmed), *Al-Qur'ān. A Contemporary Translation*, Princeton NJ 1988.

vate study the use of texts and the taking of notes was permitted which the pupil could consult outside the room in which the master was teaching. Only after having completed learning by rote could questions be asked about the meaning of the text.

Recitation or reading aloud was common practice in Hellenistic cults such as the cult of Isis. In synagogues, mosques and churches, public reading is an integral part of worship. In monasteries, the recitation of the hours was always chanted. Not even private recitation of the monastic breviary could be in complete silence; it had to be accompanied at least by movement of the lips as in a low whisper.

The text of the sacred books is usually divided into sections for recitation or reading aloud in liturgical assemblies. In all religious traditions there are anthologies of texts for worship and piety, such as the Christian breviaries, psalters, lectionaries and gospels. In Buddhist tradition, the Pomokha selection of the Vinaya is recited as a fundamental element of the Theravad monastic discipline.

Oral transmission can be preferred to written tradition, even though the authority of the text is accepted. To listen to the Koran is more important than reading it. To listen to the Koran recited by a professional cantor allows for better appreciation of the literary and rhythmic qualities of the Arabic text and of its nuances of meaning, which cannot be fully perceived from a simple reading of the written text. After the invention of printing, Islam allowed the printing of profane books, but at first forbade the Koran to be printed. The most sacred texts of Zoroastrianism, written in ancient Persian, are only transmitted through oral recitation until the arrival of Islam motivated the Avesta to be put into writing. It is significant that, long before the writing down of the Avesta, commentaries on the Avesta itself were being transmitted by writing as were other religious books less sacred in character and written in Pahlevi. In Hindu tradition, to speak of «sacred writings» is still a contradiction, for their written transmission was almost never authorised.

Plato attributed to Socrates a suspicious attitude towards writing, which prevents the development of memory and is never a substitute for living dialogue between master and disciple (*Phaedrus* 274C-275A)[3]. In the ancient world, the publication of a text did not consist in publishing it in a volume but in reciting it publicly.

Judaism prior to 70 CE knew the gradual formation of a body of oral tradition and even of a whole doctrine about oral tradition. At the beginning of the Tannaitic period, the oral character of tradition was emphasised, sometimes in controversy with the pagans, and the origin of some oral *halakôt* attributed to Moses himself. The doctrine that the whole of oral tradition goes back to Sinai was not established until the beginning of the Amoraite period, even though it was being fashioned already from the period before Yabneh (P. Schäfer, cf. pp. 165 and 167). The definition of oral tradition became

3. Fowler's translation, Loeb Classical Library, 561-563

a basic element for establishing the difference between the Judaism of the double Torah, written and oral, and the Christianity of the two Testaments, old and new.

At the beginning of Christianity, oral tradition played an important role on many fronts: the character of the Jesus movement, the formation of the canon, the fixing of the text, its interpretation, etc.

In the 1st cent. CE, the reading of documents written on papyrus or parchment was more widespread than is generally thought. However, the spread of literacy in the ancient world must not be exaggerated. Jesus did not write, although it seems that he knew how to. Paul sent epistles to the Christian communities which to some extent were a way of making himself present among them (Gal 4:20; 2 Cor 13:10; 1 Cor 11:34). The collection of official writings of Christianity did not come into being until later. In the second generation of Christians, Papias, bishop of Hierapolis (c. 60-130) still showed his preference for oral tradition (Eusebius, *Eccles. hist.* III, 39:1-7.14-17).

There has been repeated emphasis on the rural setting and therefore on the oral quality of the movement born around Jesus, a figure who is also presented as an oral preacher (Kelber). Surely, not too much stress must be placed on the rural setting of Jesus' ministry (cf. p. 34).

E. E. Ellis has gone so far as to suggest that even in Jesus' lifetime some gospel traditions were transmitted not just orally but also in writing. According to Ellis, the determining factor in writing down such traditions was not so much the passage of time as geographical distance. Certainly, the change of generations required what was transmitted orally to be written down to avoid its loss or corruption, but it was even more important to be able to communicate in writing from the first moment of the Master's teachings with other members of the community who were located in remote places.

The transition from oral to written tradition was a decisive moment in the formation of the NT, especially of the gospels, in particular Mark's gospel. Together with the hermeneutics of the written text it is necessary, therefore, to pay attention also to a hermeneutic of orality, analysing through it the forms and functions distinctive to oral language (Kelber).

BIBLIOGRAPHY

BEIT ARIÉ, M., *Hebrew Codicology*, Jerusalem 1991.

BEIT ARIÉ, M., *The Making of the Mediaeval Hebrew Book. Studies in Palaeography and Codicology*, Jerusalem 1993.

BICKEL, E., *Lehrbuch der Geshichte der römische Literatur*, Heidelberg 1961.

BIRT, T., *Das antike Buchwesen in seinem Verhältnis zur Literatur*, Berlin 1882 (=1959).

FISHBANE, M., «On Colophons, Textual Criticism and Legal Analogies», *CBQ* 42 (1980) 438- 439.

GEVARYAHU, H.M., «Colophons in the Books of Proverbs, Job and Ecclesiastes»,

Studies in the Bible and the Ancient Near East presented to S. E.Loewen-
 stamm, Vol. I, Jerusalem 1978, 107-131 [Hebrew].

GRAHAN, W.A., *Beyond the Written Word. Oral Aspects of Scripture in the History of
 Religion*, Cambridge 1987.

HARAN, M., «Book Scrolls in Pre-Exilic Times», *JJSt* 33 (1982) 163.

HARAN, M., «More Concerning Book Scrolls in Pre-Exilic Times», *JJSt* 35 (1984) 84-
 85.

HARAN, M., «Book-Size and the Device of Catch-Lines in the Biblical Canon», *JJSt*
 36 (1985) 1-11.

HUNGER, H.-STEGMÜLLER, H.-ERSE, H., IMHOF, M.-BÜCHNER, K.-BECK,
 H.G.RÜDIGER, H., *Geschichte der Textüberlieferung der antiken und mittelalter-
 lichen Literatur* I, Zurich 1961.

HUNGER, H., *Babylonische und assyrische Kolophone*, Neukirchen-Vluyn 1968.

KLEBER, W.H., *The Oral and Written Gospel*, Philadelphia PA 1983.

MASON, R., *Preaching the Tradition. Homily and Hermeneutic after the Exile.* Cambridge 1990.

PASQUALI, G., *Storia della tradizione e critica del testo*, Florence 1952².

REYNOLDS, L.D.-WILSON, N.G., *Scribes and Scholars. A Guide to the Transmission of
 Greek and Latin Literature*, Oxford 1991³.

ROBERTS, C.H.-SKEAT, T.C., *Manuscript, Society and Belief in Early Christian Egypt*,
 London 1979.

ROBERTS, C.H.-SKEAT, T.C., *The Birth of Codex*, Oxford 1983.

SARNA, N.M., «The Order of the Books», *Studies in Honor of I. E. Kiev*, ed. Ch.
 Berlin, New York 1971, 407-413.

SCHÄFER, P., «Das 'Dogma' von der mündlichen Torah im rabbinischen Judentum», *Studien zur Geschichte und Theologie des rabbinischen Judentums*,
 Leiden 1978, 153-196.

SKEAT, T.C., «Early Christian Book Production: Papyri and Manuscripts», *The
 Cambridge History of the Bible*, vol. 2, *The West from the Fathers to the Reformation*, ed. G.W.H. Lampe, vol. 2, 66-74.

STEGEMANN, H., «Methods for the Reconstruction of Scrolls from Scattered Fragments», *Archaeology and History in the Dead Sea Scrolls*, ed. L.H. Schiffman,
 Sheffield 1990, 189-220.

TALMON, S., «The Ancient Hebrew Alphabet and Biblical Criticism», *Mélanges D.
 Barthélemy*, Fribourg-Göttingen 1981, 497-530.

TURNER, E.G., *The Typology of the Early Codex*, Philadelphia PA 1977.

WIDENGREN, G., *Religionsphänomenologie*, Berlin 1969.

WILSON, G.H., *The Editing of the Hebrew Psalter*, Chico CA 1985.

ZEVIT, Z., *Matres Lectionis in Ancient Hebrew Epigraphy*, Cambridge MA 1980.

4

Schools and Scribes

In order to know the history of the formation of the biblical collections, the transmission of its texts and their forms of interpretation, it is first necessary to make a study of the schools in which this literary activity was carried out and learn about the role of the heroes of that history, the scribes and copyists.

I. SCHOOLS IN THE ANCIENT WORLD AND IN ISRAEL

«Classical» texts were copied time and again over a very wide area and over very long periods. Textual transmission of this kind is only possible if it runs through established academic channels. The classics quickly became texts and manuals for study in the schools and academies of the Greek and Roman world. They have also been the basis of the humanities in all later periods: Carolingian, Byzantine, mediaeval, renaissance and modern.

In much the same way, in Israel the «classics» of the Bible acquired the didactic function which in other cultures of the ancient Near East were met by «selected» texts of very different kinds: myths, proverbs, hymns, lamentations, rituals, law-codes, lists, historical texts, chronicles, annals, magic or astronomical texts, etc. Cuneiform tablets and ostraca have been found with writing exercises using such texts. They are undoubtedly works of apprenticeship by students with as yet very inadequate and sometimes shaky writing skills.

Abecedaries in many languages are known: Ugaritic, Aramaic, Greek, Etruscan, Latin, etc. Among the Hebrew abecedaries can be noted those from Izbet Ṣartah, dated to the 11th cent. BCE (Canaanite perhaps), Lachish in the 8th or 7th cent., Qadesh Barnea around 600 and perhaps Arad in the 8th cent. The theory has been proposed recently that Hebrew abecedaries contain students' exercises at an elementary level, showing there was a school system in Israel in the monarchic period.

However, apart from a few abecedaries written in ink on ostraca, they do not all have to be considered as school exercises. Equally, the discovery of an abecedary in a particular place does not allow the conclusion that a school of scribes used to exist there. Most of the inscriptions and graffiti with abecedaries are not the work of scribes but of craftsmen or potters who had a limited knowledge of writing signs. Therefore, these epigraphic witnesses are not to be used when studying the level of literacy in the population of Israel.

The relationship of the biblical texts to the epigraphic texts and the teaching institutions of ancient Israel have only been the subject of research in more recent years so that many aspects and problems still await clarification (cf. Lemaire, Puech, Haran, Drake).

The literary formation of the biblical books and the process of making them into a canon also belongs to a *wisdom context* although it is not restricted to such a context. This certainly applies not only to books in the wisdom and teaching genre but also to books with liturgical, juridical or historical content. The Hebrew term *torah* meant «law» but had more the meaning of «instruction». Not only the priests and the kings, holders of the *sacerdotium* and the *imperium* but also wise men and prophets, dedicated to *studium*, imparted «doctrines» which at the same time were true «regulations».

All this took place within the *priestly schools* in the Temple and in the *palace schools*, like the school created by Solomon for the formation of officials for his administration modelled on Egyptian wisdom (Heaton).

In these schools historical works were written and re-edited such as what is called the «history of succession to David's throne» (2 Sm 9 - 1 Kgs 2:1) and the so-called «Yahwistic» history, or ritual codes such as the «Holiness Code» (Lv 17-25) and the writings of the so-called «priestly school» (*Priestercodex*, the P Document). After the exile in Babylonia and during the period of Ezra the cultural, religious and educational heritage of Israel increased with the writings of the exilic prophets, the Chronicler's history (Chronicles, Ezra-Nehemiah), the works of wisdom writers (Job, Qoheleth), etc.

As for the matter of the level of *literacy* in the Israelite population, one may state that in the ancient Near East the number of those able to read and write was very small. They were the few professional scribes who, after hard training in the hundreds of logographic signs, performed their duties in the principal cities of Mesopotamia and Egypt.

The invention of the alphabet made work in schools of professional scribes easier, but it cannot be stated that it therefore made extensive levels of society literate. Illiteracy is a phenomenon which depends on many social, economic and political factors, even more than on the complexity or number of signs which had to be learned by heart (Warner). The scribal class jealously guarded the mystery and mastery of writing. Today one cannot go so far as to say, as did Diringer, that the alphabetic system was revolutionary and democratic and that the systems of Egypt, Mesopotamia and China were, instead, theocratic and elitist.

In the classical world literacy, which was still restricted, fostered critical thinking, made knowledge easier to acquire and was a real instrument of power. In religious circles writing was venerated increasingly, although in practice it was not used very much (Harris).

Learning to write began with exercises such as writing the letters of the alphabet, one's own name, encyclopaedic lists of various objects (gods, geographical terms, titles, liquids, utensils, etc., cf. 1 Kgs 5:13), etc. The training continued with exercises in writing contracts and letters. The higher grade required mastery of the literary conventions used in diplomatic correspondence as well as knowledge of the sciences and wisdom of the period. It can be said that the spread of culture in the region of Syria and Palestine and, in particular, in Israel did not differ significantly from that attained in Egypt and Mesopotamia.

The Scandinavian school, which stressed the importance of oral tradition in the formation of the biblical texts, tended to deny that writing was widespread among the lower classes of the Israelite population (Nielsen, Engnell, Widengren). However, the epigraphic evidence seems to prove that, at least during the last two centuries of the monarchic period (750-689 BCE), written culture was found quite widely in this society.

When synagogues first came into being they were places of worship and libraries of the Jewish community at the same time. The ark in which the scrolls of the Torah were kept could contain up to a dozen books or more. Together with the books Jews accepted for public reading, there could be others of esoteric character (*M^egillōt S^etārîm*, «Scrolls of the secrets»), such as some of the books of the Essenes. Some groups of Christians also kept some books in secret under the «discipline of the arcane». This phenomenon has no equivalent in the literature of the Jewish sages, who expressly forbade reading secret books. This did not prevent them from existing and they reappeared later in cabalistic literature.

II.   THE SCRIBES

The scribe enjoyed great prestige. Enoch, Moses and Elijah were considered the great scribes of Israel (BT *Soṭa* 136). The Hebrew term *sôpēr* (*spr*) and Greek *grammateús* (*grámma*) denote the role and function of a «secretary».

In *Egypt* and *Mesopotamia*, scribes or secretaries carried out their duties in palaces and temples, and were responsible for administration, the collection of taxes, military levies, civil building work, international treaties, etc.

The *Bible* often refers to the character of the scribe, in the monarchic period and also the period after the Exile, when the duties of priests, levites and scribes often overlapped. The best known and most important reference mentions Ezra (Ezr 7:6). Although there are no exact data, very probably the scribes filled an important role in the history of biblical tradition from its beginnings until it was set down in writing, as also in the transmission of the text and exegesis (Fishbane, cf. p. 431). The scribes could follow careers or movements of quite different kinds: priestly, wisdom, apocalyptic, etc. Most of the scribes of the second Temple period were also priests and came from priestly families.

The *Hellenistic world* favoured the formation of an independent class of scribes who were not priests (Bickerman, Tcherikover, cf. p. 000). The activity of the scribes in the Hellenistic period is evident in the immense literature produced in that period. Hellenisation unleashed a degree of secularisation of a scribe's duties which entailed a corresponding loss of prestige.

The book of *Ben Sira* (38:24-39:11) provides a full description of the scribe's role compared with the wise man. It surely tries to enhance Jewish wisdom in the eyes of the Hellenistic intellectual world. The Epistle of Enoch presents Enoch as a scribe in the traditional manner of the wise man (*1 Enoch* 92:1). The first section of the book of Enoch presents him with more prophetic and apocalyptic features, like the scribe sent to announce sentence on the Watcher angels. Enochian traditions seem to come from scribes who were not so enthusiastic about Hellenism and more concerned about the loss of Jewish traditions (Collins).

The author of *2 Baruch*, a book in which the figure of Baruch the scribe appears more prominent than the prophet Jeremiah (2:1; 9:1-104), seems to consider that authority over the community belongs to the scribes and prophets who interpret Scripture by means of apocalyptic visions.

Josephus mentions the scribes, not as a defined group like those formed by Pharisees, Sadducees and Essenes, but as a well known social class able to perform a range of duties and move on very different social levels. The specialised function of a scribe was literary, but he acquired his *status* through his relation to the governing power.

Scribes have generally been described as a group parallel to priests, continually rising in Jewish society in the Hellenistic period. However, the scribes do not seem to have formed a compact group, but were more «individuals» who had various social functions in the different strata of society. The NT and rabbinic literature present the scribes as masters and leaders of the Jewish communities. This image may be correct in respect of some scribes with more prestige. However, this forms part of a more complex and more complete vision of Jewish society.

III. THE RABBIS

The role of the rabbis or «sages», must not be idealised as if they were great leaders whose directives were followed with respect and complete approval in all the Jewish communities. The opposite image is just as false: presenting the sages as a closed group on the margins of Jewish society, concerned only with legal questions, opposed to non-Jews and foreign influence and allergic to any change. There were elitists of this kind in other societies as well, such as the magicians of Persia, the religious philosophy groups in Rome, the Christian episcopate or monastic orders in the Byzantine period.

The development and prestige of rabbinism were in part determined by the political and military crises of 70 and 135. The authority of the rabbis was religious and was bereft of all political or military power. The increase in the urban population and the growing importance of the social institutions of the 3rd and 4th cents. contributed to the creation and development of permanent academies in city centres. In these conditions, the rabbis became an elite devoted to the study of the Torah and the observance of the *miṣwôt*. However, they did not form a homogeneous group, for among them there could be differences of every kind: of origin, social class, attitude towards the Jews themselves, to gentile neighbours, to Hellenism, to Roman authority, etc. They were not always treated with respect by the members of the Jewish communities. Sometimes they turned into a cause of conflict between communities or within the same community, although, generally their authority was acknowledged and respected.

From the 2nd cent. BCE, and in contrast to the previous period, the rabbis acquired for themselves great influence in wide sectors of Judaism on a par with the other elite of the period in their respective societies.

In spite of being eminent religious figures, the rabbis took on responsibilities in the life of the community, especially in the *Bêt-hammidraš* and sometimes also in the synagogue, in the organisations of social welfare in the judicial system and in other institutions. Only on rare occasions did they take on political duties in society. This enabled them to preserve their capacity for influence in the midst of the comings and goings of political change.

The most important academic centre from 200 CE was the Sanhedrin, which had its seat first in Sepphoris, then from the second half of the 3rd cent., in Tiberias and later in Caesarea.

The rabbinic academies of Babylonia go back to the 3rd cent. Information from the Gaonic period tends to exaggerate the antiquity of the Babylonian schools. However, in the Talmudic period there were as yet no great academies in Babylonia. The rabbis taught in their own homes or sometimes in school buildings to a select circle of disciples which was dissolved on the master's death. Information from the Gaonic period is anachronistic and projects to the Talmudic period the situation of a later period. From the beginning of the Islamic period the academies evolved following models taken from Islam.

IV. CHRISTIAN SCHOOLS

A large part of Jewish, Jewish-Christian and even Christian apocryphal writings of non-Jewish origin seem to be ascribed to Enoch, Ezra, Baruch, Solomon or Moses (1Q22, 1Q29, 4Q375 and 4Q376). The works attributed to each of these biblical characters are typical in content and style and seem to belong to a particular social environment. One may suppose that each of these small bodies of literature comes, perhaps, from a different school which transmitted the doctrines set under the authority of one of those biblical characters. Future research will certainly provide new data which will enable the hypothesis of the existence of such schools to be supported. The «school of Ezra» seems to have clearer outlines: the book of *4 Ezra* shows characteristics which recur in *5 Ezra*, in the Jewish-Christian foreword to *4 Ezra* and in the Christian (not Jewish-Christian) works, the *Apocalypse of Ezra*, the *Apocalypse of Sedrach* and the *Vision of Ezra* (Strugnell, cf. p. 195). The «school of Enoch» could even include a Gnostic work such as *Pistis Sophia* (99,134).

The formation of the writings of Paul and John is closely connected with the existence of comparable «Pauline» and «Johannine» schools (cf. p. 238).

From the sociological point of view, the society of the first Christians was comparable to a *«philosophical school»*, like the many which existed in the Hellenistic period. This is how Christianity appeared in the eyes of those viewing it from outside (Wilken). Like the Stoics and the Epicuraeans, the Christians comprised a sect which extended along the whole Mediterranean coast, formed by disciples gathered round a master or rabbi or travelling preacher. The Christians themselves preferred to be compared with a philosophical school, at least guided by a rational principle, to being compared with esoteric cults and mystery religions.

It was possible for Paul to be taken for a Sophist (Judge). Paul's insistence on ethics made him seem almost more philosophical than religious. Although the ultimate goal was communion with God, the means proposed by Paul to gain this end are definitely of an intellectual kind: correct interpretation of the Scriptures and understanding the gospel message.

Ancient Christianity can be considered as the continuation of ancient Greek education, *paideia* (Jaeger). The teaching of philosophy developed in the course of time and was transformed just when Christianity began. Between the 4th and 1st cents. BCE, the teaching of classical schools focused on the art of speaking and on ethics or the art of living; teaching was oral, through dialogue between master and student. Between the 1st cent BCE and the 3rd cent. CE, the teaching of philosophy changed and ultimately consisted of a commentary on written texts. Christianity developed at precisely this moment when Greek philosophy became exegetical in character. Accordingly, Christian theology became basically exegetical and took the form of a philosophy which in practice was the interpretation of texts. On the other hand, from the 1st cent. CE, only six philosophies remained possible: Platonism, Aristotelianism, Stoicism, Epicureanism, Cynicism (Diogenes) and Scepticism (Pyrrhon). From the 3rd cent., Platonism and Aristotelianism combined to form a single system which also included Stoic elements and apart from Cynicism, the other schools vanished almost completely. From this period, up to the end of antiquity, philosophical teaching incorporated many religious and ritual elements. The relationship between Christian theology and the *koiné* philosophy of this period could only become closer still (on the Christian schools of Alexandria, Antioch, Caesarea, etc., cf. pp. 537-544).

V. TECHNIQUES IN THE COPYING OF BIBLICAL MANUSCRIPTS

The pagan who converted to Christianity and the Jewish proselyte could do no less than admire the care which Jews and Christians lavished on their respective sacred books.

1. *Copying Manuscripts within Judaism*

The work of copying a scroll of the Torah was regulated down to the most minute detail with the aim of avoiding absolutely every possible mistake. However, it is not possible to establish precisely in which period - mishnaic, talmudic or earlier - the relevant regulations were set down and to what extent they were put into practice. The copy could not be made under dictation; it had to be made *directly from another* manuscript, so as to avoid typical mistakes from mishearing (cf. p. 371). It seems, however, that in fact copies were made by dictation or from memory; in the case of phylacteries and $m^e z\hat{u}z\hat{o}\underline{t}$, copying from memory was allowed (BT *Megilla* 18b). Authorised copies were derived from a prototype text which was kept in the Temple in Jerusalem. The biblical books could only be written on scrolls or volumes and not in codices.

The *tetragrammaton* had to be spelled out so as to avoid a mistake. Sometimes it is replaced by four points placed below the line as happens in 1QS 8:14 in the quotation of Is 40:3 («the path of ****»).

If a letter was *omitted* through carelessness, it had to be written in the correct place in the upper space between the lines (*Sopherim* 8:2). In view of the sacred nature of the book, letters added inadvertently were not erased but were marked with points generally placed above the letters in question but also below them, with the correct reading written in the margin.

Once the work of copying out a scroll was complete, it underwent one or more *revisions*. The copy of the Torah which the king had to write out, according to the directive of Dt 17:18, was revised by three tribunals, one made up of priests, the second of levites and the third of distinguished Israelites. It was forbidden to keep a text which had not been revised (BT *Ketubot* 19b).

Although not permitted, this did not mean that there were no traditional texts which differed from the authorised text, even of the Torah. It was known, for example, that the Torah of R. Meir and the Severus Scroll provided more than thirty cases of a different text (*Genesis Rabbah*). The more liberal rabbis tolerated one mistake or at most three mistakes per column (JT *Megilla* 1,11,17c). Lists were available which noted cases of differences between the Greek and Hebrew texts so that bilingual Jews could correct their own scrolls personally (Bickerman).

Copyists had to mark clearly the *difference in strokes*, distinguishing similarly written letters so that they could not be easily confused. In the case of letters with two forms, final and medial forms were not to be mixed up. In

Is 9:6 and Neh 2:13, however, two examples of confusion already known to ancient tradition have been retained.

There are even procedures for circumventing holes in the parchment. These techniques and the mistakes which the presence of such holes could cause have been the subject of recent studies (Emanuel).

The officials responsible for revising the biblical manuscripts kept in the Temple of Jerusalem received a wage from the Temple funds (*Ketubot* 16a). It was forbidden to let more than 30 days elapse between the discovery of a mistake in a manuscript and its correction (*Ketubot* 19b).

The written text was not to be touched, ever. If a traditional reading differed from the established reading according to the principle of the majority, the traditional reading was also admitted, but only through the oral transmission. To resolve difficult readings or contradictions about which there was no existing traditional variant, there was no other course except to turn to the midrashic interpretation (cf. pp. 468-478).

2.   *Manuscript Copying in Christianity*

Right from the start Christians made use of the new system of binding codices, so showing their independence from Jewish tradition.

As in Judaism, Christians had at their disposal institutions and professionals (the *lector* and the *didaskalos*) entrusted with watching over the faithful transmission of the sacred text. A list of the authorities who ruled the Christian community of Alexandria refers to the «masters» with authority inferior only to the apostles and prophets. The relative lack of «wild» texts among the manuscripts of the NT, unlike what happened to the text of other works of early Christianity (the *Acta Pauli* or *Shepherd of Hermas*, for example), can only be explained by the existence of persons appointed to watch over the faithful transmission of the text, using suitable mechanisms. However, the scrupulous care of Jewish copyists and scribes in the transmission of the letter of the Bible has no equivalent in Christianity, although much of it was also transmitted to the Church.

As far as we know, at the beginning of the 2nd cent., many hands had a part in the copying of Christian manuscripts, which is an argument against the existence of central *scriptoria*. At the close of that century, the situation has already changed radically, as also happened in many other aspects of the development of Christianity in the 2nd cent. (cf. p. 237). Christian books are already accessible enough to the Christian public. With the founding of the school of Alexandria, the techniques of philological study of classical authors begin to be applied to Christian texts, together with the methods inherited from Jewish tradition

In Alexandria there was a *scriptorium* used as a model for one established later by Origen in Caesarea, and for the library of Jerusalem founded by bishop Alexander after 212. In these centres calligraphy was promoted and methods of shorthand were also developed, generally by women.

VI. BIBLE READING IN THE SYNAGOGUE

There is good information available about the conditions in which the reading of the Torah was carried out in the synagogue liturgy in Palestine in the period after 70 CE, although there is considerable doubt concerning the moment when legislation about it was incorporated into the Mishnah and the Talmud. However, there is no information to prove the existence of public reading of the Torah in the period between Nehemiah and the 1st cent. CE. Attempts at such proof lack solid foundation. Lk 4:16-30 reflects a usage which belongs to the period when the gospel of Luke was edited, after the destruction of the Temple.

To assume that the Bible was central to the Jewish community and that it gave rise to intense midrashic activity is tantamount to refusing to acknowledge the importance which other institutions had in that period, such as the priesthood and the traditions transmitted by the priests. It also does not value sufficiently the variety of ideas and the range of authorities which a Jew could consult in the Hellenistic period. There is not enough information to state that reading the Torah in the synagogues favoured the development of midrashic interpretation. Nor can it be supposed that the creation of midrash was an act of prime importance in Palestinian Judaism before the 1st cent. CE (Wacholder).

The custom of reading the Torah on a sabbath morning was already widespread both in Israel (Acts 15:21) and in the diaspora in the 1st cent. (Philo *De Somniis* 2, 127). The information which has reached us about synagogal reading refers to the 6th-8th cents. CE. At that time there were two main reading cycles: a triennial cycle in Palestine and an annual one in Babylonia. Ultimately, the second cycle prevailed. In this cycle, the readings were distributed throughout the year in 54 weekly sections (*pārāšiyyôt*). The cycle began on the sabbath after the Feast of Tabernacles and ended on the feast of *Simat Tôrâ* on the 23rd of *Tišrî*. The reading of the Torah was followed by another reading with texts taken from the prophetic books (*haptārâ*) which was not specified exactly.

The three-year cycle, of Palestinian origin, distributed the readings over three years in 154 *sedārîm*. In actual fact, one should speak rather of the existence of triennial cycles, given the differences among their various forms. Yet again there is a movement from the many to the one.

The two cycles, annual and triennial, depend on prototypes in the Mishnaic period. As for the situation in the period before 70 CE, we know that from the 3rd cent. BCE in the Egyptian diaspora there were houses intended for prayer (*proseuchae*). Everything seems to indicate that under the influence of the Pharisee movement, synagogues in Palestine were considerably widespread from the mid-2nd cent. BCE. In them the Torah was read on sabbath mornings. This custom was already well established in the 1st cent. CE both in Israel and in the diaspora. However, it is not easy to know the details of this synagogal reading. Reading and teaching undoubtedly went together, and presumably the synagogues responded to the need for promoting instruction. The ancient synagogues of Gamla, Masada and Herodium were not orientated towards Jerusalem. Their architecture seems to have been intended as a reading room in which disciples surrounded a master.

The reading of the Torah and of the *haptārâ* was followed by a homily which later existed separately and was moved to the evening of sabbath or Friday.

Compared with the rich constructions of the synagogues in Antioch and Alexandria, those in Israel were rather poor and cramped, but there were many of them especially in Jerusalem. They could also be found in such remote places as Nazareth. A single reader was responsible for the reading, preferably a *cohen*, a descendant of a priestly family, if one was present in the room. Since it was not possible to have several readers available, though, it was certainly not a requirement for more than one to take on a single reading, as was made obligatory later in the Mishnaic period. The synagogues of Palestine certainly did not have the means required to own all the available scrolls of the *Tanak*, but undoubtedly they had a complete Torah and some other books such as Isaiah, the minor prophets and in some cases, the Psalms.

The officiant handed the book to the reader and after the requisite blessing he «opened» or unrolled the volume and read the passage, standing on a wooden platform. In the diaspora, especially in Egypt, the text read was probably the Greek version of the LXX (but cf. p. 302). The reading was from a manuscript scroll; reciting from memory was not allowed as it could be faulty. It has to be remembered that in Roman religion Cicero rebuked an inexperienced *pontifex* for having recited «without books» (*sine libellis*) when his duty was to read from authorised books (*libellis acceptis*).

In a later period it was the custom for the *meturgeman* to translate from memory the reading from the Torah into Aramaic, without having a written text in front of him, verse by verse and in a lower voice than used by the reader of the Hebrew text. There is no information to substantiate the existence of this custom before 70 CE.

The Targum can be considered as a form of homily or commentary rather than a translation in the strict sense of the term.

The reader first read a previously determined passage chosen from the Torah, although as yet the practice of a continuous reading from the Torah did not exist. It did not succeed in being imposed until the 2nd cent. CE. Some of the titles by which the readings were identifed are known: «about the bramble-bush» (Mk 12:26), «about Elijah» (Rom 11:2). A dozen such titles occur in the works of Philo. The existing divisions in the Masoretic Hebrew text, indicating the various open (*petūḥôt*) and closed (*setūmôt*) sections, is related to the division of the text into sections in the sequence of synagogal readings.

These facts do not allow the supposition that a fixed cycle of synagogal readings already existed before 70 CE. However, some prophetic texts were already connected with other texts from the Torah and were read after them.

Before the Talmudic period, very little is known about the practice of giving a homily. The homiletic *midrašim* are to some extent a reflection of real sermons, although shortened and incorporating a range of previously selected material. The period when these *midrašim* were edited is very late so that it is not easy to draw conclusions about the situation in earlier periods. The sermon of the «*Yᵉlammᵉdēnû*» type is outstanding but it is hardly earlier than the 5th cent. CE. The «Preface» form, so widespread after the 3rd cent., began with some verses (*pᵉtihta*) often taken from the *Ketubîm* or Writings. Genesis Rabbah provides numerous examples of homilies: on the test of Abraham (55:1), on the «Aqedah» or «binding» of Isaac (56:9), on the choice of the Temple mount (99:1), etc. In Hellenistic neighbourhoods synagogal preaching could come under the influence of forms of the Stoic diatribe.

It has been suggested that the *targumim* and the *pᵉtîhôt* could provide information about the practice of synagogal reading (Shinan). The *targumim* translated most verses almost word for word with a limited number of short additions. Some verses contain longer paraphrases, sometimes longer than the actual verse, and placed immediately before them. The topics discussed are usually generic, sometimes going beyond the corresponding verse. For example, in Gn 50:1-12, v.1 includes a long paraphrase while the rest of the section is translated verse by verse, following the biblical text. Longer paraphrases occur in the first or last verse of a *sēder*, known through other sources (cf. Gn 18:1; 28:10; 30:22; 35:9). These, combined with other data, suggest that such paraphrases are related to the division of the biblical text for synagogal reading. In any case it is necessary to be aware of the differences of translation and paraphrase between the various targumim (Targum Onqelos and the Palestinian targum; cf. pp. 326-329).

BIBLIOGRAPHY

BICKERMAN, E.J., *The Jews in the Greek Age*, Cambridge MA-London 1988.

COLLINS, J.J., *The Apocalyptic Imagination*, New York 1984.

CRENSHAW, J.L., «Education in Ancient Israel», *JBL* 104 (1985) 601-615.

DIRINGER, D., *The Alphabet*, London 1949.

EMANUEL, S., «Scribal Errors», *Tarbiz* 58 (1988) 135-145 [Hebrew].

HARAN, M., «On the Diffusion of Literacy and Schools in Ancient Israel», *Congress Volume-Jerusalem 1986*, ed. J. A. Emerton, Leiden 1988, 81-95.

HARRIS, W.V., *Ancient Literacy*, Cambridge MA 1989.

HEATON, E.W., *The School Tradition of the Old Testament*, Oxford 1994.

JAEGER, W., *Early Christianity and Greek Paideia*, Cambridge MA 1961.

JAMIESON-DRAKE, D.W., *Scribes and Schools in Monarchic Judah. A Socio-Archeological Approach*, Sheffield 1991.

JUDGE, E.A., «Die frühen Christen als scholastische Gemeinschaft», *Zur Soziologie des Urchristentums. Ausgewählte Beiträge zum frühgeschichtlichen Gemeinschaftsleben in seiner gesellschaftlichen Umwelt*, ed. W.A. Meeks, Munich 1979, 131-164.

LEMAIRE, A., *Les écoles et la formation de la Bible dans l'Ancien Israël*, Fribourg 1981.

LEVINE, L.I., *The Rabbinic Class of Roman Palestine in Late Antiquity*, Jerusalem-New York 1989.

MANN, J., *The Bible as Read and Preached in the Old Synagogue*, New York 1971, reprint of 1st ed. of 1940, «Prolegomenon» by B.Z. Wacholder, XI-XXV.

MARROU, H.-I, *Histoire de l'éducation dans l'antiquité*, Paris 1948.

PERROT, C., «The Reading of the Bible in the Ancient Synagogue», *Mikra*, 137-160.

PERROT, C., «La lecture de la Bible dans la diaspora hellénistique», *Etudes sur le judaïsme hellénistique*, eds. R. Kuntamann-J. Schlosser, Paris 1984, 109-132.

PERROT, C., *Le lecture de la Bible dans la synagogue. Les anciennes lectures palestiniennes du shabbat et des fêtes*, Hildesheim 1973.

PESCE, M., «Discepolato gesuano e discepolato rabbinico. Problemi e prospettive della comparazione», *ANRW* II 25.1, Berlin-New York 1982, 351-389.

PUECH, E., «Les écoles dans l'Israël préexilique: données épigraphiques», *Congress Volume-Jerusalem 1986*, Leiden 1988, 189-203.

SHINAN, A., «Sermons, Targums, and the Reading from Scriptures in the Ancient Synagogue», *The Synagogue in Late Antiquity*, ed. L. I. Levine, Philadelphia PA 1987, 97-110.

URMAN, D. - FLESHER, P.V.M. (eds.), *Ancient Synagogues. Historical Analysis and Archaeological Discovery*, 2 vols., Leiden 1995.

WACHOLDER, B.Z., «Prolegomenon» to J. MANN, *The Bible as Read and Preached in the Old Synagogue*, New York 1971, XI-XXV.

WARNER, S., «The Alphabet: an Innovation and its Diffusion», *VT* 30 (1980) 81-90.

WILKEN, R.L., «Kollegien, Philosophenschulen und Theologie», *Zur Soziologie des Urchristentums. Ausgewählte Beiträge zum frühgeschichtlichen Gemeinschaftsleben in seiner gesellschaftlichen Umwelt*, ed. W.A. Meeks, Munich 1979, 165-193.

5

Translation in the Ancient World and the Translation of the Bible

To realise the relevance of translation in the study of the Bible it is sufficient to remember a series of facts. Early on, the OT was translated into Aramaic and Greek and later into all the languages of the ancient Christian world. Undeniably, books written in Greek, such as the gospels, have a Semitic background. Many apocryphal books have reached us only in translations since the Semitic or Greek original was lost. Textual criticism makes use of textual variants preserved in ancient versions. Every interpretation of the Bible always implies a previous translation, etc.

The ancients were aware of the difficulties entailed in translating a text from one language to another. The prologue to the book of Ben Sira includes several critical reflections on the accuracy of translations: «You are asked to read with sympathetic attention, and make allowances if, in spite of all the devoted work I have put into the translation, some of the expressions appear inadequate. For it is impossible for a translator to find precise equivalents for the original Hebrew in another language» This agrees with the famous saying from the Gemara of the Babylonian Talmud: «If one translates a verse literally, he is a liar; if he adds thereto, he is a blasphemer and a libeller» (BT *Kiddushin* 49a).[1]

I.   TRANSLATION IN THE ANCIENT WORLD

In ancient times, the practice of translation was known very early on. Lexical texts in Sumerian and Eblaite have turned up at Ebla. The most ancient translations we know about in the Eastern Mediterranean world are official translations made under the auspices of political authorities. An example of this is the bilingual (Sumerian/Akkadian) hymn of Ashurbanipal devoted to the moon goddess, Sin (Brock). Towards 250 BCE, the emperor Ašoka ordered the translation of his edicts from Indian into the two languages (Aramaic and Greek) used in public administration in the region of Qandahār,

---

1. *The Babylonian Talmud, Nashim IV,* trans. by I. Epstein, London 1936.

conquered by Alexander the Great. The translation of the Hebrew Penta-teuch into Greek was probably also promoted by royal initiative just as the letter of Aristeas indicates.

The first known versions of Greek and Latin classical works, made by Lucius Livius Andronicus (*Odyssia*)[2] already show the difficulties presented by translation and the various solutions which a translator could use:
– literal translation, including imitation of the metre: ἤ γούνων λίσσοιτο λαβὼν εὐώπιδα κούρην (*Odyssey* VI 142, «[he pondered] whether he should clasp the knees of the fair-faced maiden»), *utrum genua amplectens / virginem oraret* («Whether to clasp the maiden's knees and beg her»)
– Latinising Greek mythology: ἄνδρα μοι ἔννεπε Μοῦσα πολύτροπον (*Odyssey* I 1; «Tell me, Muse, about the hero of a thousand forms»), *Virum mihi, Camena, insece vesutum* («Tell me, O Goddess of song, of the clever man»). The Roman Camenas, nymphs of the springs, replace the Greek Muses in the translation;
– cultural adaptation: τέκνον ἐμόν, ποῖόν σε ἔπος φύγεν ἕρκος ὀδόντων (*Odyssey* I 64, «my child, what a word has escaped the barrier of your teeth?»),[3] *mea puera, quid verbi ex tuo ore supra fugit* («What word was that, my daughter, that escaped up out of your mouth?»). The term «mouth» replaces the Greek expression «the barrier of your teeth» (S. Mariotti).

Until the 2nd cent. BCE, no private, unofficial translations seem to have been made. One example known is the translation from Demotic to Greek of the *Song of Nectanebo* in about 150 BCE. Translations of the prophetic books and of other biblical books can be numbered, perhaps, among the first known unofficial translations.

The Bible itself includes examples of translation. Laban and Jacob become reconciled in a place which «Laban named Yegar-sahadutha, but Jacob named Gal-ed» (Gn 31:47), corresponding to the Aramaic and Hebrew place-names respectively. The Aramaic name is a late form. This episode has been connected with the Abrahamites' change of language when they moved from Mesopotamian Aramaic to a Canaanite language of the same type as Hebrew. Other examples which allude to translation occur in 1 Kgs 6:38; Est 3:7 and 9:24 (Rabin).

It has also been noted that the speeches of Job, of his friends and of God in the book of Job could be translations from an Aramaic original (Tur-Sinai=Torczyner). Many difficulties of this book seem to be resolved through reconstruction of the original Aramaic.

2. *Remains of Old Latin*, vol. II *Livius Andronicus, Naevius, Pacuvius and Accius*, ed. and trans. by E. H. Warmington, Cambridge MA - London 1967, 24f., 32f.
3. *Homer, The Odyssey Books 1-12*, trans. by A. T. Murray, Cambridge MA - London 1975, pp. 13.16 and 230.

After the Babylonian Exile, when the basic nucleus of the canon of OT books was formed (Torah-Prophets/Psalms and some of the Writings) the Jews already used Aramaic as their normal language, the international language of the Persian period. Therefore, they were not slow in feeling *the need for a translation* into Aramaic of the biblical books written in Hebrew. The official proclamation of the Torah by Ezra could be accompanied by the corresponding translation into Aramaic (Neh 8:8). When a couple of centuries later Greek was widespread throughout the East it very soon became necessary to translate the Torah and the other biblical books into Greek, the new common (*koiné*) and international language of the period.

The translation of the Torah and the other biblical writings into Greek comprised a unique and unparalleled event in ancient times. Like every translation, it involved all the work of interpreting the original Hebrew and at the same time the enormous effort of *translating terms and concepts from the Semitic world to the Greek world*. The spread of the LXX version was a decisive factor in the Hellenisation of Judaism.

In many cases the semantic fields of Hebrew and Greek *terms* do not coincide exactly. For example, the rendering of the term *'emet* («trust») by Greek *alḗtheia* («non-concealment») expresses only one aspect of the Hebrew term. Accordingly, sometimes the LXX translation uses other Greek terms such as *pístis*, *diakaoisýne* and others (Quell).

Translation cannot avoid reflecting typical forms of Semitic thought. In turn, *concepts* peculiar to Greek thought also emerge in translation, altering the sense or meaning of the Hebrew text. Thus, in the translation of Gn 1:31, the adjective *kalós* («beautiful») chosen to qualify what had been created corresponds to the Greek concept of «beauty», but only represents one aspect of the meaning of the Hebrew term *ṭôḇ* which means both «good» and «beautiful» (Grundmann). Hellenistic influence is particularly obvious in the translation of the book of Proverbs, attributed to a Stoic philosopher (G. Gerleman).

On the other hand, some ideas and peculiar Greek terms underwent systematic *rejection* by the translators. The term *hierós*, «sacred», which was loaded with pagan connotations, seems to have been studiously avoided and replaced by the more acceptable term *hágios*, «holy» (O. Sasse). The LXX version comprises an attempt at *bringing together* Hebrew religious concepts and cultural traditions and the spirit and philosophical thought of the Greeks. Philo of Alexandria took on the challenge of reaching a *synthesis* between these two worlds, but his results were not acceptable to later rabbinism.

Reference has already been made to the series of contrasts which are commonly made between *Hebrew thought* and Greek thought. This opposition seems to be particularly valid in the study of the LXX version. It applies especially to the anthropological dichotomy between body and soul peculiar to Greek mentality, and Hebrew anthropology which is unable to imagine a soul separated from the body (T. Boman; C. Tresmontant). However, such appositions are based more on a certain «ethno-psychology» (*Völkerpsychologie*) than on serious linguistic analysis (J. Barr).

The LXX translation received a great *welcome from the Jews of Alexandria*, who celebrated this historic and religious event with an annual festival. Philo thought of the authors of the version «not as translators but as prophets and priests of the mysteries» (*Life of Moses* II, 40).[4] The translation was inspired by God just like the original Hebrew. We have no information for affirming that the LXX version was used in synagogal worship. However, we know that the version of Aquila was used in synagogues, probably replacing the LXX version in official readings.

In Palestine, the LXX version first received a *favourable reception from Greek-speaking Jews*. The fact that copies of the Greek version of some biblical books have been found among the Dead Sea Scrolls is significant. Study of the manuscript 4QLXXNum (4Q121, Num 3:30- 4:14) from Qumran has even yielded the conclusion that the Jews of Palestine felt themselves both qualified and authorised to improve the style of the Greek version (Wevers, cf. p. 000). Some references in rabbinic writings show a favourable attitude towards the Greek version, echoing the situation prior to 70 CE, when the Greek Bible was allowed to be used on an equal footing with the Hebrew text (*Megilla* 1,8; BT *Megilla* 9a).

The first indication of reservations by the Jews towards the LXX version is the revision of the Greek text of several books completed in Palestine towards the end of the 1st cent. BCE or at the beginning of the following century, with the intention of adapting it to the form of the Hebrew text at that time beginning to acquire normative character among the rabbis. The polemic between Jews and Christians provided additional reasons for finally abandoning the ancient version of the LXX and replacing it with new versions, more in tune with the text and hermeneutic of the rabbis. One of these versions was Aquila, who sacrifices Greek grammar and style on the altars of excessive fidelity to the «sacred» Hebrew text. At the end of this process, the feast which the Jews celebrated on the anniversary of the translation of the Torah into Greek was converted into a day of grief and mourning for the damage that version had caused to Judaism (*Sefer Torah I*, 8; *Megillat Ta῾anit* 13).

Throughout its extensive history, *the Bible has almost always been read in translation*. Even in Jewish synagogues, the reading of the Hebrew text was followed by the corresponding Aramaic translation, given in a quieter voice than the original Hebrew. In rabbinic schools, the interpretation of the Bible was made primarily in the context of the Aramaic versions, the targumim, which comprised real anthologies of the exegesis of that period (see pp. 439-443).

4. Philo VI, trans. by F. H. Colson, LCL, Cambridge MA 1966

III. CHRISTIANITY: «A TRANSLATION PHENOMENON»

Christianity spread among the peoples who were on the borders or *limes* of the Roman Byzantine Empire. This was possible thanks to the enormous effort invested in translating the Bible (OT and NT) into the languages of these peoples. *Accordingly, Christianity has been called «a translation phenomenon»*: many of Jesus' *logia* and the gospel accounts as well as many passages from the NT written in Greek allow the original Aramaic (or Hebrew) text to shine through the translation. The same applies to the whole world of ideas and Semitic imagery which they reflect. Christianity formed and spread through the continual effort of creating and translating new terms and concepts. Many peoples located in the frontier zones of the Roman Empire had access to culture on the occasion of their conversion to Christianity. The translation of the OT and NT into the appropriate languages comprised the first literary monument in the history of the national literature of these peoples. This happened with the translation of the Bible into Armenian, Ethiopic and Old Slavonic. In the case of the Armenian version, they even had to invent the script, for until then Armenian culture had remained at the oral stage. Much the same happened in the development of the Arabic script at the time Islam appeared so that it is almost possible to speak of the creation of Arabic script at that time.

If the transition from Semitic to Greek achieved by the LXX version was important, no less important was the transition from Greek to Semitic achieved in the new translations being made by Christians, who needed versions of the LXX Bible available in various Semitic languages, such as Syriac, Ethiopic and Arabic.

The last centuries of Antiquity witnessed the immense labour of translating a whole range of Greek works into Syriac. Most of the population of the Eastern Mediterranean did not speak Greek or had only a smattering of it. Egeria notes that religious services were celebrated in Greek, but one of the officiants immediately made the appropriate translation (*Peregrinatio Aetheriae* 47,3).

In the schools of Nisibis and Edessa, Syriac versions of the works of Aristotle and of other authors were being prepared. These versions have hardly any value for the reconstruction of Greek texts and, in general, the Syriac text must be corrected from the Greek text. There are more versions of Greek works into Arabic than into Syriac and they are better known, although this is no doubt due to the circumstances which influenced the transmission of the manuscripts. The works translated most were philosophical and scientific: Plato and Aristotle, Appollonius of Perga, Philo of Byzantium, Archimedes, Hero of Alexandria, Hippocrates, Galen, etc.

Generally, Arabic translations were based on an existing Syriac version which in this way acted as a bridge between Greek and Arabic. Syriac culture and Christianity fulfilled this intermediary function in many other areas. Syriac architecture, for example, offered construction models for the Umayyad mosque of the Rock in Jerusalem. Translations from Greek to

Arabic, made through Syriac, were naturally subject to twice the danger of distortion, in both text and meaning. However, the Arabic text of a book as short as the *Poetics* of Aristotle does provide some readings which correspond to the original Greek text and a few others worth taking into account.

For the ancient versions of the OT and, in particular, their relation with the original Greek used for them, see the appropriate chapter on biblical versions (pp. 348-365).

IV. «LITERAL» TRANSLATION OR «FREE» TRANSLATION

Whether a translation is literal or free depends on the sacred nature of the book translated and the reading public for which the translation is intended. If respect for the sacredness of the text is paramount in the translation, the version has a more literal character, like a faithful calque of the form of the original text. If the translation is intended more for use in courts of justice, teaching in academies or missionary propaganda, the translation will tend to be freer in nature, closer to the language and to the literary and religious perceptions of the reader.

The Greek version of the Pentateuch is more «Hellenising» than those made later that were tinged with greater literalism. This change of trend reflects the development of Jewish society which, after a period of receptivity to the values of Hellenism in the 3rd cent. BCE Alexandria, returned to traditional and nationalistic values in the Palestine of the Hasmonaeans during the 2nd to 1st cents. BCE, though still remaining deeply under the influence of a Greek life-style.

It seems that Roman writers had a dynamic conception of translation, carried out image for image rather than word for word (Brock). Literal translation was dominant in the mediaeval period. In recent years, there has been a great development in theoretical studies on translation in general and its application to the Bible in particular. The principle of «dynamic equivalence» (Nida) has gained ground. It proposes a three-stage translation process: analysis of the expression in the source language to determine its meaning, transfer of this meaning to the target language and re-structuring of the meaning in the world of expression of the target language (Greenstein).

The biblical text is loaded with such richness of meaning in its smallest details that any translation can offer no more that a few of the many aspects which philological, historical and theological study find in the text. In effect, it is really always necessary to provide several alternative translations. This is one of the reasons why the student of the Bible cannot forego study of the original languages. It is sometimes assumed that modern versions, which are more and more perfect, can save one the trouble of direct contact with the text.

ALONSO SCHÖKEL, L. ZURRO, E., *La traducción bíblica: lingüística y estilística*, Madrid 1977.

BARR, J., *The Semantics of Biblical Language*, London 1961.

BODINE, W.R., *Linguistics and Biblical Hebrew*, Winona Lake IN 1992.

BOMAN, T., *Hebrew Thought compared with Greek*, London 1960.

BROCK, S., «Aspects of Translation Technique in Antiquity», *GRBS* 20 (1979) 69-89.

BUZZETTI, C., *La parola tradotta. Aspetti linguistici, ermeneutici e teologici della traduzione della Sacra Scrittura*, Brescia 1973.

GERLEMAN, G., «The Septuagint Proverbs as a Hellenistic Document», *OTS* 8 (1950) 15-27.

GREENSTEIN, E.L., «Theories of Modern Bible Translation», *Prooftexts* 3 (1983) 9-39.

GRUNDMANN, G., «*kalos*», TWNT III, eds. G. Kittel - G. Friedrich, Stuttgart 1933, 539-553.

MARIOTTI, S., *Livio Andronico e la traduzione artistica. Saggio critico ed edizione dei frammenti dell'«Odyssea»*, Urbino 1986².

MOUNIN, G., *Les problèmes de la traduction*, Paris 1963.

NIDA, E.A. - TABER, C.R., *The theory and practice of translation*, Leiden 1982.

NIDA, E.A., et al., *Style and Discourse: With Special Reference to the Text of the Greek New Testament*, New York 1983.

NIDA, E.A., *Signs, Sense and Translation*, New York 1984.

ORLINSKY, H.M.-BRATSCHER, R.G., *A History of Bible Translation and the North American Contribution*, Atlanta GA 1992.

PRICKETT, S., *Words and the Word. Language, Poetics and Biblical Interpretation*, Cambridge 1986.

QUELL, G., «*aletheia*», TWNT I, eds. G. Kittel - G. Friedrich, Stuttgart 1933, 233-237.

RABIN, C., «The Translation Process and the Character of the Septuagint», *Textus* 6 (1968) 1-26.

RABIN, C., «Cultural Aspects of Bible Translation», *Armenian and Biblical Studies*, edited by M. Stone, Jerusalem 1976, 35-49.

SASSE, O., «*kosmos*», TWNT III, eds. G. Kittel - G. Friedrich, Stuttgart 1933, 867-896.

TRESMONTANT, C., *Études de métaphysique biblique*, Paris 1955.

TUR SINAL, N.H., (H. TORCZYNER), *The Book of Job: A New Commentary*, Jerusalem 1957.

6

The Sacred Book

The idea of «Sacred Scripture» entails the view that all its elements, even the most material, are invested with a sacred character. If a *book* is sacred, so are the *language*, the type of *script*, even the *style* in which it is written. The choice of the canonical books and their transmission and interpretation are very much determined and conditioned by the sacred character of the biblical texts.

The *choice* of books forming a canon of sacred books follows very different criteria from those governing the choice of secular works. The sacred or profane character of the Song of Songs and Esther caused endless discussions about their inclusion in the canon.

The *textual transmission* of a book in which God may have inspired the consonants and even the vowel points, is carried out with care and the use of techniques and principles very different from those governing the transmission of profane texts.

The mere thought that a text could be inspired by God and so possess sacred character, determines the kind of *interpretation* to apply, which is very different when a work is profane.

I.   THE BIBLE AS A SACRED BOOK

The Greek term *biblos* or the diminutive form *biblíon* (plural, *tà biblía*), used more in the LXX version than in the NT, meant at first any kind of written document, whether it was a scroll, a codex, a letter, etc. In the LXX version and in Jewish and Christian sources, the term «sacred book», or *hieraì bíbloi* in the plural, denoted the Pentateuch or the whole OT.

Right from the first, Christians used the Greek term in the plural, *tà biblía*, and the Latin derivative *biblia* to denote the Hebrew scriptures transformed into the Christian Bible by the addition of the books which make up the NT. In the Middle Ages, the Latin term *biblia* began to be used as a feminine singular noun and not as a neuter plural, a usage which has persisted in European languages.

In the NT, the plural term «Scriptures» is used to refer to «Sacred Scripture» or the Bible, and the singular «Scripture» to refer to a particular passage (cf. Lk 4:21 with reference to Is 61:1f.: «this scripture», *hē graphē autē*, Vulgate: *haec scriptura*).

The religions to which the Bible gave birth (Judaism, Christianity and Islam) have been called *«religions of the Book»*. The Koran calls both Jews and Christians the «people of the book» (*ahl al-kitab*). It acknowledges, therefore, that these peoples possess books (*kutub*) of divine origin which, however, have been completely superseded by *the* Book (*al-kitab*) sent by God to Muhammad, i.e., the Koran. The status of *ahl al-kitab* was also granted later to the followers of the religion of Zoroaster and to the Mandaeans, and at a later period, to the Hindus.

The religions of the Book possess «*Sacred Scriptures*»: *tà biblía, miqrā'*, or *qur'an*. This «scriptural» character makes them different from Indo-European religions. In Iran and India as well as in the religious worlds of Latin, Greek and Celt, putting the sacred word into writing was viewed with mistrust. Lycurgus, Pythagoras and Numa renounced the use of writing, even forbidding their words to be put into writing. The druids had the same attitude. However, the very development of these religions meant that there as well writing was to end up by triumphing over the spoken word (cf. pp. 105-106).

In the Hindu book *Bhagavadghita* («Song of the Lord» in Sanskrit) the sacred writings are represented by a cosmic tree: the eternal branches penetrate the sky while the roots and leaves grow in the earth in the form of texts and sacred songs. The ancient cultures of the near East and of the Mediterranean knew the concept of a Book or of some *Heavenly Tablets*. In Mesopotamia, at his coronation the king received the Tablets and the rod as a sign that he was the recipient of divine revelation and possessed hidden knowledge. On his chest the king wore the tablets of the gods as a sign of his rule, and at the New Year Festival lots were cast on them to know the destinies of the coming year.

This concept was passed on to Judaism, Christianity and Islam. The apocryphal books include several references to these tablets under such titles as «Book of those who will be destroyed» (*Jubilees* 30,22; *1 Enoch* 47,3), «Book of life» (*1 Enoch* 108,3) and «The heavenly tablets» containing the astronomical and eschatological doctrine which it is Enoch's mission to reveal (*1 Enoch* 81,1-10).

The heavenly book could have three different forms. It could be considered as a *wisdom book* in which were collected all the resources of divine Wisdom, disclosed to a messenger such as Moses. It could be *prophetic book* in which was written the destiny of the universe and of every living being in accordance with what providence or divine predestination has arranged: «Your eyes saw my deeds and all of them are written in your book» (Ps 139:16; cf. Ap 5:1.3; 6:1-17; 8:1-10:11). In Sūrah 57:22 of the Koran it says: «There is no calamity that befalls the earth or your own selves but in accordance with the law (of causation) before We make it evident». The third conception possible was that of a *judgment book* which kept a record of the deeds, good and bad, of men and women for their reward or punishment in the final judgment. In this book were written the names of God's elect (Ex 32:33; Phil 4:3). This tradition approaches the «Dies irae» of the Middle Ages: *Liber scriptus proferetur in quo totum continetur unde mundus iudicetur*.

Moses received the teachings and laws from the divinity on tablets. It is important to note that in biblical religion, the Tablets of the Law come to be a symbol of divine presence as a substitute for iconographic imagery which the same Law forbade.

According to the Apocalypse (5:5.9.12), God is seated on his throne with a book in his right hand and «the lion of the tribe of Judah» receives this scroll as a sign of his victory over the world.

Ancient iconographic images of the apostle Paul show him seated on a ceremonial chair holding a rolled up book in his left hand. Representations of Christ with a book and a sceptre are common. The sceptre corresponds to the ruling rod already known from ancient Mesopotamian images.

To believe in the truth of his message Muhammad's enemies require the Prophet to offer proofs of having ascended to the heavens and of having brought back the heavenly book. This demand for prophetic legitimacy was the reason for creating the account of Muhammad's ascension. In the Koran it is accepted that Muhammad did not receive revelation from Allah in a single moment and already in the form of a book. A later Arab composition, known only through a Latin version (*Liber Scalae*) shows Muhammad as having gone up to the highest heaven and receiving the Koran from God's hand as a written book.

Hermes, Pythagoras and Zarathustra, all founders of important religious traditions, also received a book from heaven, endorsing their status as messengers of heaven.

The idea of a sacred book concealed for a long time in a hidden place until it is discovered and recognised as bearing an ancient but forgotten revelation is commonplace. Berossus relays the tradition that the Scriptures, which had remained hidden in the city of the Sun-god, were found after the Flood. According to Hermetic tradition, Hermes hid wisdom texts written before the Flood near the sea. The Shiʿite imams believe that they possess esoteric knowledge, the wisdom of Muhammad transmitted through a secret family tradition and contained in the book *al-gafr* attributed to the sixth imam (Gaʿfar al-Ṣādiq).

II. SACRED LANGUAGE

Religion and language are very closely related. We can no better than repeat here the relevant paragraph by E. Coseriu:

«There are also relations which cannot be denied between organised religion as an institution and the formation of common and literary languages and also between religion and the preservation of certain languages, thanks to their use in the liturgy. Most of the oldest liturgical documents available in connection with so-called «primitive» peoples are due to missionaries who studied the particular languages for the purposes of their religious propaganda, and quite often used them in writings which also were concerned with religion. Thus, the continuity of Quechua as a cultural language is due, at least in part, to the Catholic missionaries having used this language as a «lingua franca» in their evangelising efforts and even having raised it to the level of a liturgical language. Also, many of the old languages which we know are «liturgical» languages, i.e., languages used by religious communities or in sacred rituals. Sanskrit, which is such an important language in Indo-European linguistics and has shown us many of the genetic relationships among the Indo-European languages, was originally the literary language of the priestly class of India. That is, it was a «cultural» rather than a vernacular language, and its culture was above all religious. Similarly, what we know of Gothic we owe to the translation of the Bible made by the Gothic bishop Ulfilas into that language. What is called *palaeo-Slavonic* or *Old Church Slavonic* (*Altkirchenslavisch*) is, in origin, a dialect of Old Bulgarian used by Cyril and Methodius in the evangelisation of one part of the Slavs. Later it became a sort of religious *koiné* of the Slavs belonging to the Eastern Church. Avestian is the language of the *Avesta*, i.e. the sacred text of the Zoroastrian religion. We know Umbrian, the language of an ancient village in Italy, chiefly through the Tablets of Gubbio (*Tabulae Iguvinae*) which contain the text of a sacred ritual. The preservation of certain languages is due exclusively to their being the languages of religious communities. This is the case with Coptic, which derives from ancient Egyptian and remained as the liturgical language of that section of the Egyptian people which had adopted the Christian religion. Other languages owe their prestige principally to causes connected with religion. Arabic, for example, was spread over a large part of Africa and Asia by the Islamic religion. And even a Western European language such as German owes much to causes of the same kind: in effect, the literary German common today - the modern «German language» - has its origins in the language used by Luther for his translation of the Bible» (pp. 78-79).

Throughout many centuries the Western Latin Church retained Latin as the only and exclusive medium for liturgical and canonical expression. Something similar happened with the Koran and Arabic, and with the Jewish *Tanak* and Hebrew.

According to a very widespread belief in rabbinic Judaism, Hebrew was the original language of mankind until the confusion of languages created in the tower of Babel (*Genesis Rabbah* 18). It was forbidden to write the Torah in any language except sacred Hebrew. If for a time the use of Greek was allowed (BT *Megilla* 9a) this was due to the fact that the prestige gained by the LXX version led to the belief that Greek could also be a vehicle of inspiration for the sacred texts.

The view that the Greek of the LXX and the NT was a sacred language has been an important factor when it comes to explaining the peculiar characteristics of biblical Greek (cf. pp. 71-72).

III. SACRED WRITING

The relationship between a religion and the type of script used for its sacred texts can be closer even than between a religion and its sacred language. The Jewish rabbis of the Mishnaic period believed that writing had been invented in the six days of creation (Mishnah *Abot* 5,6). This idea reflects a mythical conception of the origin and function of writing to be found in all ancient peoples. Writing, like all the arts, was invented by the gods. In ancient times, therefore, the authorship of the books of wisdom and divination was attributed to one of the gods.

Only the written form of the Torah represents its authorised version. Copying the biblical text was a sacred act regulated down to the minutest detail (cf. p. 115f). Until the 1st cent. CE, copies of some books of the Hebrew Bible were being written in palaeo-Hebrew characters although it had fallen into disuse for centuries. In the celebration of the mysteries of Isis, hieroglyphic characters were used even outside Egypt, although they were utterly unintelligible.

In countries where different races live together and are also challenged for their language and their religion, it is possible to notice utterly astonishing examples of the use of writing. In Albania, Catholic Albanians use Latin characters whereas the Muslims write the same language in Arabic characters. Catholic Croats use the Latin alphabet, Serbs the Cyrillic. Sometimes the differences are completely artificial: in Poland, the Bible Society distributed bibles written in Latin characters for the use of Catholics and bibles intended for Lutherans (of German origin) written in Gothic characters.[1]

The bond between religion and writing can be such that, even when the sacred language is dead, the type of script used in the old sacred texts survives. After the arrival of Muslims in Syria and Iraq, Christians abandoned Syriac for Arabic, but continued to use the letters of the Syriac alphabet to write Arabic (*karšuni*). A similar occurrence is illustrated by Jewish *aljamía* [Hebrew written in Arabic characters] in mediaeval Spain; similarly, after the fall of Granada, the «moriscos» (Spanish Moslems converted to Christianity) wrote Romance languages in Arabic characters.

In every religion there is an inseparable link between Word and Writing. The Word became Writing and Writing is proclaimed and sung or at least recited but never merely read. By the mere fact of being written and being

---

1. When these notes were made an announcement appeared in the press concerning the first indications of political change in Mongolia: « The government has blessed the revival of Buddhism, the traditional Mongolian script is making a comeback... » (*Newsweek*, 30th July 1990).
   When revising this book for publication the following comment could be read in the press: «Across Central Asia and the Caucasus, the newly freed republics plan to toss out the Cyrillic alphabet imposed by Russia in the 1930s. But what to use instead? Tajikistan has announced it will switch to the Arabic alphabet and the Saudis are spreading their Arabic-language Korans far and wide. Turkey, meanwhile, plans to send Latin-lettered typewriters...» (*Newsweek*, 3rd February 1992).

«Scriptures», sacred texts, possess a special aura of authority and respect as well as an immutable fixed character which oral tradition on its own cannot hope to attain.

The sacred texts of Egypt of the pharaohs were as fixed as the pyramids. Sacred Scriptures, the Bible, the Koran, the Buddhist Sutra, etc., even possess a certain magical quality. They are used for auguries and divinations, for formalising oaths and promises, as talismans against evil influences, etc.

The illiterate masses, in the majority up to recent times, felt a special veneration for writing, which was endowed with an aura of mystery they were unable to understand. It is significant in this context that, even though the letters of the Bible were to some extent sacred, the biblical text was never written in unintelligible hieratic characters such as were used, instead, to write magical texts and incantations. The Bible tries to keep a balance between reason and mystery.

For Jews the sacred Scriptures or *Tanak* have a special aura. The scrolls which contain the biblical texts «defile the hands», meaning that they possess sacred character so that before and after touching them in liturgical use it is necessary to make a purifying ablution. The Jew walks towards the synagogue on a Friday evening with the book of the Torah in his hands wrapped in cloth so as not to touch it. The Muslims have a similar veneration for copies of the Koran and Japanese Buddhists for copies of the Lotus Sutra, etc. The early Christians used binding in codices, a novel form of publication, for their sacred texts. They wished to confirm and even consecrate a new way of publishing, one different from what was usual among Jews and pagans, in which to write their sacred books. The development of the art of copying and «illuminating» biblical codices is a result of the increasing awareness of the sacred character of the actual material of biblical texts. The art of calligraphy in copying the Koran, in illustrating the books of Mani or the elegance of the script in collections of the Tibetan Buddhist canon all originate in the same idea of sacred texts.

IV. SACRED STYLE: BIBLICAL CLASSICISM

Sacred style is anointed in some way, the fruit of the religious inspiration which animates the author of a sacred book. E. Auerbach has compared the paratactic style of the Bible with the subordinating style of Homer. Religious language is usually marked by its own tone, intensity, timbre, melody and rhythm. In Church liturgy, the doxology to the Lord's Prayer has rhythm: «For thine is the kingdom, the power and the glory, for ever and ever. Amen». The rhythmic caesura matches the caesura marking the meaning, just before the word *glory*. The break in the rhythm helps isolate this word. Breath is held up to the word *Amen*. Similar remarks can be made about Hebrew texts (cf. p. 116).

The Bible, both in the original Hebrew and in versions in other languages, has a very special style, which drew the particular attention of those comparing the classical style of Greek and Latin with the sacred style of the Bible. The style of the biblical writings is different from the classics in two respects: the public for which they are intended and the writers' point of view.

Petronius wrote for the most educated class of Rome. Sometimes his language is vulgar and common, yet that does not mean Petronius wished to reach the masses and even less the ordinary people of Trastevere. His vulgar style has no other explanation than the pleasure of inserting into the conversations of the pleasure-loving élite of Rome risqué terms and expressions from the language of the street for his own enjoyment and that of his chic readers. Classical epic, tragedy and lyric are always the literature of the ruling classes, intended for the ruling classes. Their main characters are gods, demi-gods or divine heroes. Humans appear only in the role of servants.

The main characters of the Genesis stories are, instead, nomadic patriarchs among whom class distinctions go unnoticed. The authors of the NT are from people who address all peoples and all «gentiles» indiscriminately. This is the more admirable since the opposition between social classes and groups in the OT is not between nobles and serfs but between Jews and gentiles, between pure and impure.

Classical works are faithful to the aesthetic principle of «separation of style»: epic, lyric and tragedy speak of the sublime in elevated and poetic language. Comedy speaks of the vulgar in common prose. The classics always looked at and spoke to the public from a lofty position, up on Olympus with the Homeric gods or on a par with tragic heroes. Biblical characters, at once base and sublime (Noah and his sons, Abraham-Sarah-Hagar, David, Jesus' disciples, etc.) have no place in the Homeric epics or in the histories of Thucydides. All at once they crawl on the ground, punished for their serious offences and just as suddenly their moral stature lifts them up to touch the heavens. They share the punishments of a servant and at the same time have a conversation with God Almighty. Petronius describes the ups and downs of fortune, the uncertainty of fate, what his characters were and what they have become in a decadent Rome, but fortune and poverty, the fortunate and the wretched never come into contact. In the Bible, the same character can fall into the deepest poverty and immediately be elevated to the heights. Scarcely one biblical character escapes the deepest humiliation, from David, the first king of Israel up to Peter, the first «head» of the Church, but they are all equally worthy of God's favour and at critical moments they all have superhuman strength.

The «elevated style» of classical tradition looks from above on a public which is always in an inferior and lower position. It is the typical style of Stoicism and historians like Sallust and Tacitus. The elimination of the principle of separate styles - elevated and common - marks the end of Antiquity. Augustine of Hippo is still close to the classics and writes in a Ciceronian style, but has ceased to be a classical writer. His tone has an element of spontaneity and drama which he gained from biblical tradition where the jump from the sublime to the ridiculous can be sudden. The very kernel of the

Christian message, the *kerygma* of Christ's death and resurrection, is the most extreme example of the fusion of opposites, the human and the divine. Christianity shattered the classical principle, which was pagan as well, of separation of styles. Jesus, neither a hero nor a powerful king, is a human being from lowly social conditions. His followers are fishermen and work-men, publicans, women and children, yet endowed with great dignity. The biblical style does not fit educated rhetoric. It is the *sermo piscatorius*, the language of fishermen, more moving and impressive than classical tragedy: the King of Kings is treated like a criminal, slapped and crucified. Such a story immediately destroys the model of separation of styles. The Bible cre-ates a new elevated style which does not despise ordinary people in life and even sees worth in the ugly, the deformed, the physically hideous. It gives rise to a *sermo humilis*, a low style, though far removed from the vulgarity of comedies and sophists. This mixture of styles, a reflection of the biblical and Christian message, which would mould Christian society, the *civitas Dei* (Augustine), with no distinction between Jew and gentile, man and woman, slave and freeman, rich and poor, black and white (the Wife in Song of Songs), is expressed in Bernard of Clairvaux's commentary on the verse from the Song of Songs where the Wife sings: «My skin is black but beautiful, girls of Jerusalem, like the tents of Kedar» (Song 1:5). Bernard comments: «O hu-mility, O sublimity! [Thou art] the tents of Kedar, and the sanctuary of God; an earthly habitation, and a heavenly palace; a house of clay, and a kingly court; a body of death, and a temple of light; lastly, a scorn to the proud, and the bridge of Christ! *She is black but comely, O daughters of Jerusalem...* If you shudder at her blackness, admire her beauty; if you despise her humble-ness, behold her sublimity».[2] Here, the sublime and the humble are religious and ethical categories and at the same time also stylistic and aesthetic cate-gories in an unmistakable Christian and mediaeval synthesis of the ethical and aesthetic orders. Bernard of Clairvaux exclaims: «O humilitatis sublim-itas!» and after reading the account of the Ascension, urges his readers:«Therefore, dearly beloved, persevere in the discipline which you have taken upon you, so that by humility you may ascend to sublimity, for this is the way and there is no other... for it is humility alone which exalts.».[3]

The question of style had become acute when with the spread of Christian-ity the Scriptures came under the criticism of educated pagans. They could only be horrified at the pretensions of some books which were said to con-tain the highest truths ever revealed, yet were written in an uncouth language which totally ignored the rules of good style. The Fathers of the Church had to react to these criticisms, which opened their eyes and made them realise that Scripture had the capacity to express the most sublime truths in a very vulgar and simple style. Thus a new classicism was born - biblical, Christian

---

2. *Sermones in* Canticum, Pat. Lat., 183, 799; English Translation in Auerbach, E., *Mimesis. The Representation of Reality in Western Literature*, Princeton NJ 1973,152f.
3. In *epiph. Domini sermo*, 1,7; Pat. Lat. 183, 146, and *In ascens. Dom.*, 2,6; Pat. Lat. 183, 304.

and mediaeval - represented by characters such as Augustine and Francis of Assisi and by literary masterpieces such as Dante's *Divine Comedy*. Even the title, «Comedy» yet «divine», inverts the terms used by Virgil to define his Aeneid: «high tragedy». Dante also justified the title of his work through opposition to classical tragedies («elevated»). These tragedies always concluded with an unhappy ending; Dante's comedy has an unhappy beginning and a happy outcome. Even the style he chose, the *modus loquendi*, justifies the title comedy: *remissus est modus et humilis, quia locutio vulgaris in qua et muliercule communicant*. Dante expresses the distinctive character of his poem with the phrase: «il poema sacro, al quale ha posto mano e cielo e terra» (*Paradise* 25,2-3; 'the sacred poem, in which both heaven and earth have had a hand'). The heavens and the earth appear united in the poem and in Christian classicism, the continuation of biblical classicism. Clerical mediaeval poetry is the «art of compromise», popular yet educated (López Estrada). Cultivated knowledge distinguishes the clerk from the cavalryman whose acts are narrated in epic poems (letters and arms). Clerks considered it their duty to write in Latin, the language of the educated, more fitting for their intended goal, namely, spiritual approval by the faithful. At the same time, however, they were the first to be converted to the Romance languages so as to be able to reach a wider public which did not know Latin.

BIBLIOGRAPHY

AUERBACH, E., *Mimesis. The Representation of Reality in Western Literature*, Princeton NJ 1953.
COSERIU, E., *Einführung in die allgemeine Sprachwissenschaft*, Tübingen 1988.
HERNERSON, J.B., *Scripture, Canon, and Commentary. A Comparison of Confucian and Western Exegesis*, Princeton NJ 1991.
GOLDINGAY, J., *Models for Scripture*, Grand Rapids MI 1995.
SMITH, W.C., *What is Scripture?*, London 1993.
WIDENGREN, G., *Religionsphänomenologie*, Berlin 1969.

7

The School of Alexandria and its Philology

The School of Alexandria and its philology exerted *great influence on the whole of Antiquity*. This influence is evident even in the rules and techniques of rabbinic exegesis. The direct heirs of the School of Alexandria were Philo among the Jews and Origen and Clement from among the Christians. The Alexandrians had to carry out the same tasks for ancient Greek literature as the Jewish scribes and rabbis and the Fathers of the Church had to complete for biblical literature. Basically, these tasks were the following: to establish a canon of classical or canonical books, to fix the text of these books and to interpret their contents according to suitable principles and methods.

The creative period of Greek epic poetry ended in the first half of the 6th cent. BCE. At that time, the rhapsodes (*rapsōdoi*) recited the epic poems in public contests, following a traditional text which they had to keep to. These rhapsodes were simultaneously professional reciters, critics concerned with preserving the Homeric text and poets who interpreted the ancient epic poems, making the first steps in allegorical interpretation.

It is not very likely that there were any *public libraries* in the 6th cent. BCE. Nor is it possible to confirm the well-known tradition that Pisistrates collected the songs of Homer which up until then had been scattered, but at least we know that Pisistrates and Policrates owned a large number of volumes in this period. Towards the end of the 5th cent., there were already some private collections or libraries. 5th-4th cent. Athens was familiar with a kind of learned intellectual, the sophist, who boasted of having encyclopaedic knowledge which could be applied to the Homeric texts. According to Strabo, Aristotle succeeded in forming a large collection of volumes in the Lyceum in the 4th cent.

The most famous library in ancient times was the *Museum of Alexandria*, which for a time was a temple dedicated to the Muses, under the supervision of a priest, and also an academic, literary and scientific centre, financed by the royal purse. Until 295, Ptolemy I entrusted Demetrius of Phaleron, a disciple of Theophrastus, with the project of creating the Library of Alexandria, which by the 3rd cent. BCE housed no fewer than 200,000 volumes (Eusebius *Praep. Evang.* 350b). At that time, a scroll contained on average a short work the length of a dialogue of Plato, say, or a play of Attic theatre (cf. p. 96). The cataloguing system of the library is not known, but there is information about the immense work carried out by Callimachus who wrote a sort of bibliographical guide to the literature of antiquity, in 120 volumes (*pínakes*). The splendour of the Alexandrian School began to decline from the moment that Ptolemy Evergetes II persecuted Greek intellectuals, between 145 and 144 BCE.

I. CATALOGUING «CLASSICAL» AUTHORS. THE LITERARY TASK

The first great task of the Alexandrian philologists was to collect and catalogue the texts of «classical» authors. The Alexandrians were the creators of «classicism», and «literature» made its appearance for the first time in Alexandria. By literature is meant the culture of the book, enclosed within the walls of a library for the exclusive benefit of an intellectual elite, far from the oral culture of the public square and immune to the vagaries of time.

In his critical inventory of Greek literature (*pínakes*), Callimachus established the *list of «classical» authors*. Homer and Hesiod headed the list of epic authors. Then came the list of iambic poets, the trio of tragic poets made up of Aeschylus, Sophocles and Euripides, and the writers of ancient comedy (Aristophanes), of intermediate comedy and new comedy, with Menander as the outstanding author. The next categories were formed by the elegiac and lyric poets, prose writers, including the historians (Herodotus, Thucydides and Xenophon) and finally the orators (Demosthenes).

Quintillian used the term «canon» to denote the list of classical authors established by the Alexandrians: until very recently this list comprised the programme for studies in the Humanities. The same term, «canon», has been used to refer to the list of classical authors and also to the list of biblical books. In Alexandria, the Hippocratic *corpus* was also set up, the foundation of medical tradition in the West. Initially, it also served to resolve a problem of cataloguing bibliography, which was solved later by placing numerous anonymous works under the eponymous name Hippocrates. Pseudonymity also developed extensively in biblical tradition and in the formation of the biblical canon (cf. p. 169).

The Museum of Alexandria assured the preservation of the literary legacy of the Greeks and also played a decisive role in the transmission of biblical texts through the translation of the Bible into Greek. In Alexandria, the Greek *logos* and Hebrew wisdom (*ḥōkmâ*) came into contact and fertilised each other. This synthesis breathed life into the works of Philo of Alexandria and later, of the Alexandrian Fathers. From that time, the philological interpretation of classical texts has invariably been the basis for all humanist and Christian thought. Exegesis of biblical texts is carried out at the same time as the interpretation of the secular texts of Greek classics. On contact with classical philology, the Bible was translated into Greek and the methods of interpreting Sacred Scripture were developed. Classical philology and biblical exegesis have common origins, face very similar problems and develop along parallel lines.

In its final moments, Alexandria became open to new influences. Philo shows traces of Stoic influence. Neoplatonism later became the intellectual humous of Christian patristics. In this later period, the god Hermes, whose mission was to guarantee communication between gods and men, became the patron of Hermetism and the occult. Obscurity replaced transparent meaning. The text was searched for hidden meanings, the so-called «alphabets of mystery». A century later, the Jewish mystics of the Cabala even searched the spaces left blank in biblical manuscripts for as yet unexplored revelations of Yahweh.

II.   FIXING THE TEXT OF THE «CLASSICS».
THE TASK OF PHILOLOGY

The second great task of the School of Alexandria was more authentically philological, and consisted in *establishing the text of the classics*. The Alexandrians carried out this task in notes in the margins of the manuscripts and also in longer separate commentaries.

Fragments of Homeric texts earlier than the 3rd cent. BCE are rare. The text of these copies on papyrus is considerably different from the text of our printed editions: some verses are omitted, others added. The Alexandrian scholars established the text they considered to be authentic and in addition succeeded in imposing it on the manuscript tradition to the extent of making other forms of the text which had existed until then disappear from circulation. Similarly, the fixing of the consonantal text of the books of the Hebrew Bible at the beginning of the 2nd cent. CE and the resulting exclusion of alternative forms of the Hebrew text represented an editorial practice comparable in some respects to what the Alexandrian philologists achieved for works of classical antiquity.

The Alexandrians created conventional *signs* (*sēmeía*) to indicate an interesting point or a difficulty in the text. For example, to indicate the fact that the text of a verse was corrupt or that the verse itself was an apocryphal gloss. The most important of these signs was the *obelisk*, used by Zenon to indicate a verse as not genuine. Aristarchus used this sign and others in a systematic way to produce his complete edition of the *Iliad* and the *Odyssey*.

This learned annotation system was very complicated for the public reader, so that over time copyists omitted to reproduce these signs. They soon disappeared from most of the manuscript tradition. No more than about fifteen of the 600 or more papyri preserved and only one mediaeval manuscript, the *Venetus A* of the *Iliad* (*Marc. gr.* 454), preserves these «Aristarchian» signs. Origen used the system of critical annotations of the Alexandrian School to prepare his famous edition of the Hexaplar (cf. p. 311). In this case, too, the complexity of the work and of the annotation system used, caused later manuscript tradition to leave out the editorial signs.

Like many modern exegetes, the Alexandrian scholars were accused of letting themselves be ruled by a certain *tendency to consider particular verses as apocryphal.* For instance, Zenodotus considered vv. 423-426 of canto III of the *Iliad,* where Aphrodite appears to demean herself by offering a seat to Helen, to be a secondary addition like several other passages which portray the gods in unseemly fashion.

Luckily, this type of reasoning, hardly convincing for modern criticism, did not succeed in imposing itself in Antiquity, so that it did not have a great influence on manuscript tradition. Otherwise, many verses by Homer, which the copyists would have removed from the manuscripts thinking them to be spurious, might have been lost. Biblical criticism has to show the same respect for the manuscript tradition, although, like the Alexandrians, they still have to accept the existence of sources and glosses in biblical text tradition.

III. INTERPRETATION OF THE CLASSICS. THE TASK OF HERMENEUTICS

The third great task of the Alexandrians was hermeneutics proper and consisted in the *critique and interpretation of classical writers.* Having established the text, it was necessary to explain the many passages of difficult or enigmatic interpretation.

The *literary criticism of the Alexandrians* achieved acceptable results, such as noticing that the history of Dolon in book I of the *Iliad* does not fit well in its context, nor does its style match the rest of the epic. Aristarchus noted that in the *Odyssey* (book XI 568-626) the episode of the descent to the underworld does not match the plot. Similarly, Aristarchus and Aristophanes considered the ending of the *Odyssey* to be in book XXIII 296. According to modern criticism, the passages which follow were composed in a later period, although perhaps this does not make them apocryphal. The «Homeric question» and the «Thucidydean question» were models for study of the sources of the Pentateuch.

The hermeneutic principle which guided the Alexandrians, especially Aristarchus, was *«to interpret Homer using Homer».* A bad application of this principle could have resulted in deleting from the text terms and expressions which do not seem to match Homeric style. Aristarchus was wise enough to follow the sane criterion that, in principle, many of the *hapax legomena* to be found in the text of Homer must be accepted as authentic readings. Treatment of biblical *hapax legomena* must be ruled by the same standards, as studies in comparative Semitics have shown.

The Greeks of the Hellenistic period, who knew the criticisms directed by Plato and the Sophists against Homeric mythology, perceived that the most pressing problem of interpreting the epic texts was to justify the lack of morality of the Homeric gods. Accordingly, they had to use *allegorical interpretation*. The same epic poetry contained very old «allegorical» elements, for example in the passage about the *Litai* in the *Iliad* (1 502ff.). The rhapsodes of the 6th cent. discovered recondite meanings in many Homeric passages. The Sophists and the great Attic philosophers pursued this work of interpretation, although Plato and Aristotle rejected allegory and in their wake, the Academy and the Lyceum or *peripatos* also rejected allegory. The orthodox Stoics, on the contrary, favoured the allegorical method. For Stoics, the *logos* or reasoning comprises the principle of all things, which necessarily have to be rational, including mythical and legendary poetry, although there, reason can only appear through hidden meanings. Zenon and Cleanthes initiated the allegorical method, Cresippus of Solus developed it and Crates, from the school of Pergamon, perfected it. Cresippus interpreted the Homeric description of the shield forged by Hephaestus for Achilles to mean that ten parts of the shield represent the ten circles of heaven. Under the influence of the Neo-Platonic school, Aristarchus himself seemed, in the last years of his life, to be more inclined towards the allegorical method. It gained importance later as a corrective to the excessively scientific approach dominant in the early period of the Museum of Alexandria.

BIBLIOGRAPHY

GRANT, R.M., *Heresy and Criticism. The Search for Authenticity in Early Christian Literature*, Louisville KT 1993.
REYNOLDA, L.D.-WILSON, N.G., *Scribes and scholars. A Guide to the Transmission of Greek and Latin Literature*, Oxford 1974.
PFEIFFER, R., *History of Classical Scholarship. I. From the Beginnings to the End of the Hellenistic Age, II. From 1300 to 1800*, Oxford 1968 and 1976. II

Chapter II

Collections of Biblical Books.
Canonical and Non-Canonical Books

«I contemplated everthing in the heavenly tablets, I read what was written, I understood everything and read the book about all the deeds of men and of the sons of flesh who were to exist on the earth until the final generation» (Ethiopian Enoch 81, 2).

Chapter II

Collections of Biblical Books.
Canonical and Non-Canonical Books 147

The Literary History of the Canon of Biblical Books

As we have seen, the school and philology of Alexandria had to establish the canon of «classical» books and to fix and interpret its text in accordance with rational methods. Similarly, Judaism and Christianity had as their first and principal task to establish the list of «canonical» books and to fix and interpret their text using procedures similar to those of Alexandria, but from the perspective of the religious principles of Judaism of the twofold Torah, written and oral and of the Christianity of the two Testaments, old and new.

Study of the OT and NT canon has usually been the preserve of theology, especially Christian theology. Here, only problems connected with the literary and social history of the biblical canon will be discussed. Many of these problems, however, still have implications of a theological nature.

Use of the Greek term «canon» comes from New Testament studies. It is typical of a Christian view of the Bible and in addition belongs to a very late period in the history of the formation of the NT canon, the 4th cent. CE.

To apply the term «canon» to the Hebrew Bible, therefore, is quite unsuitable. Hebrew has no term which corresponds to Greek «canon». Rabbinic discussions concerning the canonical or apocryphal character of certain biblical books such as Song of Songs and Qoheleth, turn on the expression «defiles the hands». The supposition is that books of which it is said that «they defile the hands» were considered as canonical, whereas books to which this expression was not applied were excluded from the biblical canon. However, the expression «defile the hands» may have no more significance than to refer to the ritual purification to be performed after having used such books and before starting any other secular activity.

I. CANONS OF SACRED BOOKS

Before going into the details of the literary and social history of the biblical canon, it is helpful to mention three questions connected with the biblical canon. Synchronic comparison of the canon with other canons of sacred books and with the Alexandrian canon of classical books; the diachronic understanding of the biblical canon more as a continuous process than as a single instant and lastly, the systematic concept and the criteria of canonicity which are involved in establishing the biblical canon.

1. *Parallels*

First, a series of parallels between the canon of the Bible and other canons of sacred or classical books have to be established.

«Sacred» text and «canonical» text do not always coincide. A sacred text is not necessarily a canonical text. The sacred books of Jews and Christians are canonical texts; the sacred texts of the Egyptians, however, cannot be said to be classical. The sacred texts of Hinduism and Islam provide closer parallels to the Jewish and Christian Scriptures. The classical texts of the Greek world are very different in character, but comparing them with the canonical texts of the Bible can still provide points in common and parallel developments (Tardieu).

a. Sacred Egyptian texts were for the most part funerary ritual texts; their sacred character was not rooted in their revealed or inspired content but simply in the type of hieroglyphic script in which they were written. The hieroglyphs were a kind of magical substitute for the reality they represent. Sacred Egyptian texts, therefore, do not comprise a suitable comparison for studying the biblical canon.

b. The *Vedas* were transmitted orally among candidates to the priesthood in various oral recensions which could not be written down. The Sanskrit texts, like the biblical texts, underwent a long slow process of canonisation, classification and selection. They can be interpreted with complete freedom but without touching the letter of the text. To alter the sacred text meant expulsion from the Hindu community, though this did not prevent each Hindu «sect» from presuming to possess its own sacred texts (Hernerson).

c. In Islam, the parallelism with the biblical canon is even greater. The *Koran*, like the Bible, is also God's word and revelation. The Koran is a portion of the eternal and uncreated universe of which man perceives no more than a minute part. Koranic language attains the absolute perfection of which human language is capable. The authority of the Koran is absolute. Islam developed a whole body of traditions of interpretation of the Koran (*Sunna*) similar to that created by rabbinic Judaism to interpret the Torah.

d. The idea of the inspiration of poets together with the antiquity of the classics and the religious, ethical, historical and pedagogical significance of these works, indicate some parallelism between the canon of the *Greek classics* and the canon of the Jewish sacred books.

The Greeks had the idea that poets were endowed with a strange force, an «*inspiration*» or possession which could be transformed into madness (*manía*). Plato distinguished four types of *manía*, each inspired by a different god: prophetic by Apollo, ritual by Dionysius, poetic by the Muses and erotic by Aphrodite and Eros (*Phaedrus* 244-245). The Greeks could believe that their poets were inspired by the gods, but they never went so far as to consider them to be gods and still less to listen to them as mouthpieces of the one God, Creator of the Universe, who spoke to Moses and delivered the Law to him. The criticisms against Homer, expelled by Plato from the ideal republic on account of the immorality of the Homeric gods, were unthinkable in the mouth of a Jew in respect of Moses and the God of Israel.

In the Greek world, Homer and the epic poets seem to have enjoyed an *authority* and a standing in some sense comparable to those which the Torah held in Judaism. Therefore it has been possible to say that Homer was the Bible of the Greeks. Homer was considered to be Helade's teacher, but it is uncertain whether he was a Stoic, an Epicurean, a peripatetic or a member of the Academy (Seneca *Epist.* 88, 5).

A certain parallelism can be established between the canon of biblical books and the *lists* («*pínakes*») *of first class authors* («*classics*») drawn up by the Alexandrians. However, the Greek word «canon» was not used to refer to such lists and only in a much later period did it acquire this meaning. These lists of classical authors show the unmistakable respect which the Greeks had for the masterpieces of the ancients, but the criteria for choosing the «classics» were chiefly literary and aesthetic. The Alexandrian critics were not guided by religious concerns; the focus of their interest was basically textual, lexicographic and literary.

On the other hand, the process of setting up the biblical canon was prompted by the exile in Babylon and the return to Zion. In the political and literary history of Greece there was no incident with the religious and literary features and consequences which those events had in the history of Israel and in the birth of Judaism.

Some parallelism can even be seen between the reaction of the pagan Greeks and of the Jews to the challenge posed by the appearance of the new canon of Christian books. Pagans and Jews reacted alike with a movement of return «to their roots», to the traditions and works of the ancients, the Greek classics and the Jewish Scriptures. In the 2nd cent., the writings of the various Greek schools and the Jewish treatise *Pirqê 'Abôt* both attempted to praise the antiquity of their respective traditions to their own people and to foreigners.

The editors of Homer were given the name of «correctors» (*diorthotai*). The Jewish scribes could not accept this name for themselves, since their work consisted in preserving a sacred text which allowed no correction of any kind.

Any parallelism between the biblical canon and the canon of classical poets is nowhere near the essential elements of the first canon. The differences are more important than the similarities (Hengel). The fundamental attitude of Jews and Christians towards the Scriptures is very different from that of the Greeks towards the works of the ancient poets. In Judaism, concern for preserving and faithfully transmitting the sacred text took on the characteristics of a real «religious anxiety» far removed from the textual and literary concerns affecting the editors of Homer. The critical labours of Zenodotus, Aristophanes and Aristarchus lack the unmistakable stamp of zeal and religious commitment characteristic of rabbinic commentaries on the Scriptures.

Accordingly, in spite of common elements which can be observed between the literary history and interpretation of the Jewish Scriptures and of the Greek classics, their ideas and fundamental attitudes cannot be compared.

2.   «*Canonisation» Processes*

The final validation of a canon of sacred books is always the province of a religious authority which, by means of a «conciliar definition» or another form of authoritative decision, fixes the list of canonical books and at the same time excludes books not accepted into the canon. This is an historical event of a social nature, always determined and conditioned by circumstances of a very different kind. The Sassanid Persians set up the Avestan canon at the time of the invasion of Persia by Muslims. By doing so they intended to show the Muslims that the Persian religion was also a «religion of the Book». In this way, they could become eligible for treatment on a par with Jews and Christians in the other countries conquered by the Muslims. Other factors affected the formation of the Avestan canon, such as the dispute with Manichaeism and Christianity and the need to consolidate their own orthodoxy.

a. However important the *final decision* of a religious authority concerning the officially recognised list of books might be, the *historical process* by which particular books come to acquire sacred character and canonical recognition is more important. In general, this process takes several centuries and is affected by many factors of a literary, social and theological kind. Before a canon is established definitively, the idea of a canon does not actually exist. It takes shape as the canon gradually forms. The accumulation of biblical books which make up the collection of *K^etubîm* or *Writings,* probably ran alongside their entry into the canon and the final process by which the canon was formed.

b. The *Old Testament canon* was established as a result of a lengthy process, affected by factors within Judaism and outside it. At a certain moment it became necessary to set out the broad outlines of Judaism in opposition to over-restrictive currents, such as those represented by Samaritans and Sadducees, and in opposition to extremely disruptive trends, such as those championed by some apocalyptic groups in Palestine and by others in the Jewish-Hellenistic diaspora. Later, it also became necessary to mark a clear boundary between Jews and Christians. This forced Jews prepared to accept the new books of the Christians to realise that they could no longer consider themselves as belonging to the people of Israel, or be considered as such.

c. The process which led to the setting up of the *New Testament canon* is connected with anti-heretical disputes. Marcion rejected the OT completely, considerably reducing the canon of Christian books. Montanus, instead, attempted to include his own books and revelations. The Great Church felt forced to react, determining the exact number of books which were to make up the NT canon.

The problems and circumstances which affected the setting up of the NT canon are very different from those which affected the formation process of the Hebrew Bible. Christianity had to establish a canon simply because, besides the four gospels, many others existed which attempted to rival them. It was forced to mark a clear distinction between canonical gospels and apocryphal gospels, and more generally, between orthodox and heretical books. Instead, the «canonisation» of the Torah in the period of Ezra (or even in an earlier period) was not prompted by any of these reasons. Judaism does not seem to have known the problems of orthodoxy and heterodoxy which affected Christianity, in contact with the syncretistic culture of Hellenism. Study of the Temple Scroll and of other writings found in Qumran, however, suggests the existence of alternative or complementary *Tôrôt*. This may indicate that in the struggles between orthodoxy and heterodoxy, Judaism made an attempt at what would emerge later fully developed in Christianity. It is undoubtedly true that just as Christianity rejected the books of Mari or Priscillian, Pharisee Judaism also had to draw up a list of books which would act as an indicator of Jewish identity, against the trend in some Jewish groups to grant canonical authority to new books, purportedly discovered, especially apocryphal writings. The rabbis tried to establish a definitive canon in order to forestall the danger entailed by the large number of heresies within Judaism and especially the growing threat implied by Christianity (Tosefta, *Yadayim* 2:13; BT *Šabbat* 116a-116b). It has been possible to establish a relationship between the books which the rabbis considered «external» or apocryphal and the new Christian writings. However, to equate the term *gylywny* with *tà euaggelía* («the gospels») is incorrect and the heretics to which *Birkat hamminîm* («the blessing of the Minim») refers are not Christians.

3. The Concept of «Canonicity» and its Criteria

a. In respect of the Hebrew Bible, Leiman distinguishes two concepts: *«canonical» book*, authorised for use in religious teaching and practice, and *«inspired» book*, assumed to be written by divine inspiration. By definition, a canonical book did not need to be inspired; an inspired book must be held as canonical, and a book could be both canonical and inspired. In the Tannaitic period, all the books held to be inspired were also canonical, but not all the canonical books were considered to be inspired. *Megillat Ta'anit* was a canonical work, but was not inspired; similarly, Qoheleth was a canonical book even for those who denied its inspired character. The Tannaites considered as Scripture only such canonical books they were convinced to be of inspired character. «Sacred Scripture», then, is a collection of books which combine equally the conditions of canonicity and inspiration.

The concept of a canonical book which was not inspired arose in the 2nd cent. BCE. The idea of a canonical book was unknown to the biblical writers, but instead they did know the concept of inspired literature. When prophecy ceased in the 5th cent. BCE, the production of inspired books also ceased. Probably, only the «sectarian» groups continued to think that the production of inspired books had not ended in the 5th cent.

b. The process of establishing the *Old Testament canon* was guided by the basic criteria of *authority* and *antiquity*. Sacred character was accorded to books which could prove a Mosaic or prophetic origin, going back to a period before the time when the continuous succession of prophets was finally broken. This had happened, it was believed, in the time of king Artaxerxes (465-423 BCE). As a result, books considered to be canonical had to be written before this period. The book of Daniel, edited later, succeeded in getting into the list of canonical books thanks to being written under the name of a prophet, Daniel, assumed to have lived in the Persian period.

Some Jewish groups, such as the *Essenes from Qumran*, probably had a *wider criterion for canonicity*. They thought that prophetic *inspiration* had not ended with the death of Malachi, the last prophet, in the Persian period. New books could present new credentials of prophetic legitimacy. Their authors had access in various ways to new revelations obtained by means of journeys to the heavens, during which they had been authorised to consult tablets and hidden books. The book of *Enoch*, a pseudepigraphical work like the book of Daniel, contains new revelations «according to what he showed me in a heavenly vision and what I know through the word of the holy angel and have learned from the heavenly tablets» (81:2 and 103:3-2).

The term «canon» implicitly includes the distinction between inspired books and those that are not, between authorised and unauthorised books. This distinction is very difficult to apply in the case of books such as Tobit, Wisdom, Ben Sira, *Enoch*, *Jubilees* and some Qumran writings. Perhaps it is preferable to speak of a vast religious literature without exact limits (Sundberg). This could turn out to be far too vague, but perhaps gives a better idea of reality than is suggested by the term «canon» applied to a collection already established in the Maccabaean period (Beckwith).

Into rabbinic discussions on the inspired nature of a book there went such considerations as the *possible secular* nature of the book in question, a suspicion which weighed on the Song of Songs, and the *possible contradictions* of a particular book in respect of the laws or recommendations contained in the Torah, an accusation made against the books of Ez (40-48), Qoh and Pr. The various ways of harmonising conflicting biblical passages, especially in legal matters, led to the formation of different schools of interpretation. They were one more element in the gradual differentiation among the great schools of the Sadducees, Pharisees and Essenes. In many cases, Josephus made an attempt to harmonise conflicting narrative material. Later rabbinic literature tried to resolve every possible contradiction among the texts forming the canon. The most difficult contradictions to reconcile were those occurring within the same book, such as Qoh and Pr, and the contradiction between Ez and the Pentateuch. The many attempts carried out to resolve such contradictions show that the canonical nature of these books was never in doubt since otherwise so many attempts would be meaningless.

Over the book of Qoheleth hung the accusation that it contained *passages bordering on heresy*. Similarly, the book of Esther was accused of relating the story of a marriage between a Jewish heroine and a foreign pagan without adding any criticism at all against such a reprehensible act. One of the «additions» present in the Greek version of this book forestalled just such an accusation, placing in Esther's mouth the avowal that she loathed the matrimonial bed which she had not chosen freely (addition C, 14,15-16).

c. The criteria of canonicity invoked to establish the *New Testament canon* were basically three: the *apostolic origin* of the writing in question, its *traditional use* in the liturgy from time immemorial and the *orthodox nature* of the doctrine expounded.

In both the OT and the NT, ideological criteria of canonicity do not seem to have been so important as the weight of tradition on the sacred and canonical character of a particular book. If the religious group considered it necessary to leave room for a book which did not comply rigorously with the conditions laid down, it did not hesitate to force the ideological criteria which justified those conditions. If received tradition testified to the sacred character of a book which did not fulfil other required conditions, received tradition was respected above all else.

II. TRADITIONAL THEORY ON THE HISTORY OF THE CANON

The OT canon has a three part structure: Torah, Prophets and K^etuḇîm or Writings (*TaNaK*). According to the traditional view of the history of the canon, the diachronic formation of the biblical canon occurred in three successive stages which correspond to the three parts of that synchronic structure. The books of the Torah acquired canonical character possibly in the 5th cent. BCE; the collection of prophetic books entered the canon towards 200 BCE, after the Samaritan schism; accordingly, they never acknowledge the sacred character of the prophetic books. Lastly, the Writings entered the canon in the Maccabaean period towards the mid-2nd cent. according to some, or in the so-called synod of Yabneh towards the end of the 1st cent. CE according to others. At Yabneh the canon was decisively closed with the exclusion of the apocryphal books, called *hîṣōnîm* or «external» in Hebrew.

Against this view of the history of the canon serious objections are raised nowadays:

1. The traditional opinion concerning the history of the canon presumes that the canonisation of the prophetic books occurred *later than the Samaritan schism*, since the Samaritan group did not grant canonicity to the prophetic books. However, even if it were true that the Samaritans restricted the canon to the books of the Torah only, this does not mean that they rejected the prophetic books completely. What the Samaritans did was to place greater emphasis on the primacy of the Torah. In fact, the *Samaritan Chronicles* include much material from the prophetic books, especially allusions to characters from the Northern Kingdom, such as Joshua or Elijah.

On the other hand, it is now considered that the Samaritan schism occurred later than had been supposed, not back in the Persian period but well into the Hellenistic period. The Samaritan question, therefore, cannot be connected with the formation of the canon of prophetic books (cf. p. 213).

2. For a long time it has been reiterated that the closure of the biblical canon took place in the so-called *Synod of Yabneh* in which they resolved the arguments up until then about the canonicity of five of the biblical books: Ez, Pr, Qoh, Song and Est. The closure of the canon at Yabneh was part of the reconstruction programme of Judaism after the fall of Jerusalem, a result of the polemic against Christians or part of the task of fixing the consonantal Hebrew text.

Today, however, it is believed that the «council» of Yabneh was not a council in the Christian sense and that the decisions taken there had no binding force. A parallel cannot be drawn between the academy of rabbis at Yabneh and the Christian councils. The discussions among the rabbis did not refer to the whole of the canon but were limited to the question of the sacred nature of the book of Qoh and possibly also of Song (Lewis, Leiman).

On the other hand, the formation of the canon of sacred books was not so much a question posed and decided in synods or councils. These did no more than sanction what had already been established by long tradition. In Christianity, discussion of the canon did not actually arise in councils until a much later period, towards the end of the 4th cent., when the fundamental contents of the canon was already guaranteed by a long tradition.

3. For a long time it was thought that besides the Palestinian rabbinic canon there was *a second canon circulating in the Jewish diaspora*, especially in Alexandria. This canon was represented by the collection of books form-

ing the Greek Bible of the LXX. Christianity accepted this longer canon before the shorter rabbinic canon was established around 90 (cf. p. 232).

III. HISTORY OF THE FORMATION OF THE BIBLICAL CANON

The history of the formation of the Bible and of the biblical canon runs in parallel with the history of the Temple and of the priestly institutions of Jerusalem.

2 Mc (1:18-2:18) and *4 Ezra* (ch. 14) establish a parallel between the fate of the Temple and of the Book, both at the time of the destruction (587 BCE) and at the restoration of the Temple and of the Scriptures. The loss of sacred objects from the Temple also meant loss of the sacred books. The sacred fire, which disappeared at the time of the destruction, reappeared miraculously in the period of Nehemiah, once the Temple had been rebuilt. Similarly, God inspired Ezra just when he was handing over the Torah to the people, as he had inspired Moses at the moment of the setting up of the Torah on Sinai, so that the sacred books introduced by Ezra after the Exile are identical with those that existed in the «First Temple» period.

The three most outstanding moments of this parallel history between the Temple and the Book are the following: in the times of Josiah, some years before the Exile and the destruction of the Temple of Solomon, in the same Temple is discovered the book of (proto-)Deuteronomy; on the return from the Exile and once the Temple was rebuilt, Nehemiah collects «the books about the kings, the writings about the prophets and David and the royal letters about the offerings»; lastly, after the desecration of the Temple and before celebrating its reconsecration, Judas Maccabaeus collects «all the books scattered because of the war» (2 Mc 2:13-14).

The accepted terminology among Jewish scholars divides biblical history into two long periods: the period of the «first Temple», referring to the period between the building of the Temple by Solomon (c. 950) and its destruction by the Babylonians in 587, and the period of the «second Temple», which begins with the rebuilding of the Temple in 521-515, in the period of Zerubbabel, and its destruction by the Romans in 70 CE.

Recent archaeological discoveries made in the immediate vicinity of the esplanade of the Temple of Jerusalem (Bahat) enable a more precise division of the history of the Temple. Four periods can be distinguished:

– «first Temple», period of Solomon throughout the monarchic period,
– «second Temple», the Restoration in the Persian period until the Hellenistic crisis,
– «third Temple», the Maccabaean period,
– «fourth Temple», the Herodian period in the Roman era.

This division enables a more exact focus on the history of relations between the Temple and the Book in these closing periods, which were decisive for the formation of the biblical canon. The parallelism between the Book and the Temple is especially interesting in the Maccabaean and Herodian periods.

The information from the Mishnah on the limits of *sacred area of the Temple* of Jerusalem matches the dimensions of the Temple of the Maccabaean restoration period. Information from Flavius Josephus refers, instead, to the widening of the perimeter of the Temple carried out later by Herod the Great, who included new areas intended for the outer courtyards and porticos. However, the real sacred space, to which neither unclean Jews nor pagans had access, continued to be the same as in the Maccabaean period.

Similarly, it can be said that *literary space of the sacred Book* stayed fixed in the Maccabaean period, with an almost definitive plan of what later would be the biblical canon. Even so, in the Herodian period, at least some movements of Judaism showed clear tendencies: either for extending this sacred literary space by including new books in the collections of biblical books, or for giving new meaning to the Temple and the Scriptures according to what was said in books which contained new revelations about the true Temple and about the true Israel.

On the other hand, the distinction can be recalled between two types of script - Hasmonaean and Herodian - which correspond to the two periods distinguished here in the history of the Temple and of the Scriptures (cf. p. 90).

1.   The «First Temple» Canon up to the Babylonian Period

In the ancient Near East, the concept of «canonicity» already existed. It was applicable to texts supposed to have been been sent from the heavens, which were transmitted with meticulous accuracy, kept in sacred places and contained blessings for whoever made good use of them and curses for those who destroyed or did not respect them. To some extent it can be said that the concept of canonicity accompanies the formation process of the OT from the beginning. It should not be imagined that the idea of the canon only arose in the final moments of this process (Vasholz).

The history of the biblical canon started, perhaps, from the moment when at the end of the period of the «first Temple», the priests find the book of Deuteronomy in the Temple of Jerusalem in its original version (*Ur-deuteronomium*), the book which Josiah proclaimed as the fundamental Law of the people of Israel (622/21 BCE).

Besides the writings preserved from the monarchic period, which came to form part of the biblical canon, there undoubtedly existed many others which could also have entered the collection of biblical books, but remained marginalised for some unknown reason and their text was lost for ever. Some of these writings are referred to as sources of biblical books: *Book of the Wars of the Lord, Book of the Kings of Israel and Judah, Chronicles of Samuel the Seer*, etc.

A.   THE TORAH

Before the collection of books of the Torah was formed, the final process of the literary formation of the *Pentateuch* underwent three important stages: the composition of Deuteronomy, the composition of the «Priestly work» (the P document or *Priester Codex*) and lastly, the inclusion of the book of Deuteronomy (already separated from the deuteronomistic history) within a longer version of the «priestly» history (Blenkinsopp).

To the extent that during the Persian period there were laws not included in the Pentateuch but considered as the Torah from Sinai in some circles, it is necessary to make a *distinction between Torah and Pentateuch*, for this does not represent the only and complete Torah rooted in the revelation of Sinai (Maier). Study of the Temple Scroll raises new questions on the existence of books of the Torah which are alternative and complementary to the existing Torah. In the Persian period, variants of the Torah could still be quite considerable. It must be assumed that the present text of the Pentateuch is the result of a compromise among the various trends that existed in the Persian period. This does not mean that in some opposition circles traditions not incorporated in the form of the Torah presented by the Pentateuch were not retained for some time. This is one of the more important new items due to study of the so-called «borderline texts» between biblical and non-biblical found in Qumran (cf. p. 295).

The definitive formation of a «Pentateuch», comprising the five books of the Torah, meant abandoning two other possible forms of collecting the books of the Pentateuch and the Historical Books. The first was a *Hexateuch*, comprising the five books of the Pentateuch to which was added the book of Joshua (Wellhausen, Eissfeldt). The second was the *Tetrateuch*, formed of the first four books of the Pentateuch; Deuteronomy would have headed this collection which also included the historical books Joshua to Kings (Noth).

The hypothesis that a *Hexateuch* existed before the present Pentateuch is based on the fact that, from a purely literary point of view, the book of Joshua seems to be the logical and necessary conclusion to the history narrated in the previous books. These proclaim a promise whose fulfilment only becomes reality after the entry of the Israelites into Canaan, exactly as narrated in the book of Joshua, not to mention a series of correspondences with the books that precede it. The fact that the book of Joshua was not included in the collection of books that make up the Pentateuch suggests that the Promise was still open and that its fulfilment narrated in the book of Joshua only seemed to be a partial fulfilment of the patriarchal promises. This means that the Pentateuch composed on the return from Exile has an open structure, which contains a message to the exiles: the Promise continues, it has not yet been fulfilled, it is necessary to wait its final fulfilment.

The hypothesis that a *Tetrateuch* existed before the present Pentateuch refers to the fact that Deuteronomy, by its style and content, is an autonomous and foreign body within the Pentateuch. In many ways, Deuteronomy makes better sense as a prologue to the «deuteronomic history», comprising the books of Jos, Jgs, Sm and Kgs. The fact that Deuteronomy seems to form part of the Pentateuch means that the legislative material contained in Deuteronomy, although not of Mosaic origin, is in any case earlier than the entry of the Israelites into Canaan and so earlier that the facts related in the book of Joshua. In this way it hints that the basic legislation of Israel was already promulgated before the inauguration of the monarchy and that the monarchic institutions lack the necessary authority for establishing the fundamental laws in Israel.

B.   THE PROPHETIC BOOKS

The separation of Torah and Prophets was certainly intentional. This separation could have happened at the time when Deuteronomy was introduced between the books of Nm and Jos. From that time on, two large collections existed: a Pentateuch and a work of history which begins with the book of Joshua (J. Sanders). However, it was certainly not a literary act but a legal decision which decreed that the books of the Pentateuch were accepted as the law of Moses. This probably happened in the time of Ezra.

Before the collection of prophetic books was formed, each one had been through a long process of composition. The development of the prophetic tradition is particularly obvious in the book of Isaiah. The composition of this book was completed by the successive addition of sections of quite different character and length. The literary material in the compilation goes from short glosses placed at the beginning of a collection of oracles (1:2; 2:1), explanatory phrases (23:13), and short oracles (4:2-6) up to very long compositions (13:1-14:24). Some complete units were taken from other sources (36-39 = 2 Kgs 18-20). Chaps. 40-55 are the work of another author called «second» Isaiah. Chaps. 55-66 form a long collection of oracles attributed to various authors («third Isaiah»). The books of Jr and Ez also provide clear evidence of a complex and lengthy literary development.

The formation of a prophetic canon meant making a clear distinction between the prophetic period in which God had spoken to his people through his messengers the prophets, and the later period when the spirit of prophecy ended and history lost all paradigmatic character. There was no other course left but the hope that the eschatological times would bring with them renewal of the spirit of prophecy or that authorised interpretation would allow new meanings to be discovered in the revelations from the mosaic and prophetic past.

C.   THE COLLECTION OF «WRITINGS»

It is usually thought that the collection of Writings acquired shape and canonical character later than the collection of Prophetic books. Certainly, there was no closed list of prophetic books to which another closed list of Writings was added later on. For some time, only two parallel collections must have been in circulation, one of the books of the Torah and one of the prophetic books. To this second collection belonged some books which now feature among the Writings. Such was certainly the case for the Psalter in the early stages, attributed to king David who was considered a prophet like Solomon, the presumed author of the books bearing his name.

Accordingly, it is significant that the *pešārîm* found in the Qumran only comment on texts from the prophetic books and the book of Psalms, which amounts to granting the Psalter prophetic character. The reference in 2 Mc 15:9 and the many allusions in the NT to a division into «Torah and Prophets» can be an indication of such a division into two parts. The headings of the Psalms, with their references to the life of David and the period of the monarchy and exile certainly have no historical value but are rather an indication that the first collections of Psalms were originally related to the collections of the Former Prophets, given that David is considered to be a prophet. In turn the historical books also include an occasional Psalm. In any case, the dividing line between the prophetic books and the Writings was not very clear, as the different distribution of books in the Greek Bible shows. The book of Psalms is positioned at the borderline between the prophetic books and the writings, decidedly leaning towards the latter.

The editing of the *Psalter* was a lengthy process at the end of which the collection of psalms acquired its present structure as five books, marked off by a closing formula, corresponding to the five books of the Pentateuch (I, 1-41; II, 42-72; III, 73-89; IV, 90-106; V, 107-150). Ps 1, the first psalm of the collection, is a wisdom introduction to the whole Psalter on the theme of the «two paths» and allegiance to the Torah. The last Psalm, Ps 150, is a song of praise which closes the fifth book and the whole Psalter. Some psalms of praise were added as a conclusion to small collections. Thus, Ps 100 is added to the collection Pss 93-99, Pss 117-118 to the collection of Pss 111-116, Ps 134 to the collection of Pss 120-133, and lastly, Ps 145 to Pss 140-143. The work of compiling scattered collections had been completed in previous stages. Psalms 3-41 comprise the oldest level of the Psalter, going back to the pre-monarchic period. Next, the unit comprising psalms 42-83, definitely from the Northern Kingdom. The last third of the Psalter is later than the Exile, as shown by linguistic analysis. It is also the section with the greatest textual fluidity. Some of the Psalters found at Qumran add psalms taken from other books of the OT, such as 2 Sm 23, other compositions not included in the Hebrew psalter, such as Psalms 2 and 3 in Syriac, and even pieces composed by the Qumran community itself. These psalters also omit some psalms, especially the whole final part of the Psalter, or give them in a different sequence. 11QPs^a omits Pss 106-108, 110-114 and 116-117, and adds another five poems instead (G. H. Wilson; cf. p. 289).

In the present collection of the Writings, in line with Babylonian tradition, the *narrative books* have been set out in chronological order. The Book of Chronicles comes at the end, certainly with the intention of connecting the beginning and the end of sacred history, which starts from Adam and ends with the return from the Exile. The NT (Mt 23:35 and Lk 11:51) established a relationship between the blood spilt by Abel (Gn 4:3-15) and the blood of Zechariah (2 Chr 24:19-22); in this way it accepts that Chr forms an «inclusio» with the book of Genesis, denoting the Bible as a whole. It also attests indirectly the threefold division of the canon. At present, more attention is paid than in the past to the period of formation of the work of the Chronicler and the remaining late literature of the Bible.

The *poetic books* in the collections of Prophets and Writings appear, instead, in descending order of size, from greater to smaller, with the exception of Song, placed before Lam in order to keep the three books attributed to Solomon together (Pr, Qoh, Cant).

The development of *the apocalyptic tradition* is reflected especially in the two most important books of this genre, Daniel and Enoch. Only the first of these succeeded in entering the Hebrew canon. The court tales of Dn 1-6 appear interpreted in the «apocalypse» of chaps. 7-12. These chapters rework the chronology and update the historic pattern of the four kingdoms (ch. 2), applying it to Antiochus IV. Similarly, the book of Enoch is actually a compilation of several works are so many elaborations of earlier motifs and writings (cf. p. 196).

In summary, the history of the formation of the major collections of the canon (Torah-Prophets-Writings) involved literary and editorial factors, factors of a social nature and certain decisions carried out through authority. This complex history can be reduced to a few more important moments: in the period of the Exile and immediately after the Return (6th cent. BCE) the literary crystallisation process of the Tetrateuch reached its climax, to which can immediately be added the book of Deuteronomy so as to form the canonical Pentateuch. At the same time, the literary corpus of the deuteronomistic history was formed and perhaps a little later the collection of prophetic books, including even the «second» and «third» Isaiah, the books of Jl and Jon and the three last prophets, Hg, first Zach (chaps. 1-8) and Ml; lastly, a collection of Writings took shape, basically wisdom in character.

3.   *The «Third Temple» Canon in the Maccabaean Period*

The first book of Maccabees (4:59-61) describes the first construction work which Judas, Jonathan and Simeon completed in the Temple of Jerusalem. The treatise *Middot* of the Mishnah also refers to this work. Until recent excavations around the Temple esplanade, it was not possible to know to what those construction works corresponded. Basically, they marked out a huge platform of about 230 m. per side. This was the sacred space to which no person in a state of ritual impurity had access. Very close by were basins specifically for purification; foreigners could not approach at all. The Mishnah provides the name of the gates through which one entered the esplanade. Of these gates there remains no trace today, at least in the space actually visible, for Herod's works altered the size of the esplanade. The works carried out in the Maccabaean period assumed the sacred space of the Temple to be marked out exactly. In the later Herodian period, the size of the Temple was altered considerably, but the true sacred space continued to be same as in the Maccabaean period.

Likewise, it can be said that the canonical literary space remained established in the Maccabaean period and continued to be virtually the same in later periods, although already in the Maccabaean period and especially in the later Herodian period until 70, some Jewish groups extended or tended to extend the literary space or canon of sacred books.

The new writing from Qumran, the *Halakhic Letter* (4QMMT) seems to represent the oldest witness of the canon, since it refers to the books of Moses, the Prophets and David.

In the period in which the book of Ben Sira was translated into Greek (132 BCE) the biblical canon already had a three-part structure: Torah-Prophets-Writings. The translator also assumes that already in his grandfather's time (around 190 BCE) there was a tripartite canon. The reference in Lk 24:44 to «the Law of Moses and the Prophets and the Psalms» also seems to presuppose a three-part structure. Other sources indicate that towards the end of the 1st cent. CE the division of the canon into three parts was already widespread throughout all Judaism.

In the 2nd cent. BCE, there was already a collection of prophetic books. The book of Daniel (2nd cent.) says that the hero «read attentively in the book of the prophecies of Jeremiah» (9:2). In the Foreword to the Greek translation of the book written by his grandfather, Ben Sira (2nd cent.) refers three times to «the Law and the Prophets and the other books». The collection of prophetic books was composed of those by Isaiah, Jeremiah, Ezekiel and the twelve Minor Prophets, in that order, exactly as they are cited in Sir 48-49. In about 125 BCE, the second book of Maccabees (2:13) relates that Nehemiah (5th cent. BCE) «collected the annals of the Kings, the writings of the Prophets and David [NEB the works of David]...» with the intention of organising a library. The prophetic books were those used for the *haptārâ* or second reading in synagogal worship. The book of Job is the only book, together with those of the Torah, of which copies have been found in Qumran in the palaeo-Hebrew script and as two copies of an Aramaic Targum. The Babylonian Talmud (*Baba Batra* 14b) attributes it to Moses so that it was considered as a kind of supplement to the Torah. This could mean that in some circles, possibly connected with the Sadducees, the book of Job came to form part of the canon as a supplement to the Torah before the collection of Prophets was granted canonical character.

Thus, in the 2nd cent. BCE, the Jews acknowledged in general a canon formed of the Torah and the Prophets together with «other books», the Writings.

4.   *The «Fourth Temple» Canon in the Herodian Period*

According to Josephus, in the 18th year of his reign (19 BCE), Herod decided to extend the esplanade upon which the Temple stood. Herod followed the model of temples built throughout the length and breadth of the Empire according to the «Caesarean» style. These comprise an immense esplanade surround by columns, some ornamented propylaea and the Temple itself, standing in the centre of the esplanade. In the Southern area, Herod completely reconstructed the supporting wall, cutting two gates into it which can still be seen today, the «double gate» and the «triple gate». To the East, it was not possible to extend the esplanade further since the Kedron valley prevented it. So Herod extended the esplanade towards the West, thus filling in the Tyropoeon Valley. In the North, Herod levelled the hill upon which the *Bîrâ* or fortress stood, putting it at the same level as the Temple Mount, and filled in the depression in the intervening space. In this way all the land to the South of the hill of Baris (Greek, *Bîrâ* in Aramaic, corresponding to the Antonia Tower) was annexed to the Temple Mount.

The newly constructed areas were not affected by the laws of purity. This made it necessary to indicate exactly the boundaries between the ancient sacred space and the new areas added by Herod. For this, a separating wall was built, on which were affixed large inscriptions forbidding entry to the unclean and foreigners. Two of these inscriptions have been found in modern times. In this way the inner courtyard mentioned by Josephus corresponds to the ancient precinct of the Temple Mount and the outer courtyard to the recent extensions. The Eastern part of this outer courtyard was also old and thus was known by the name «portico of Solomon» (*War* v 5:1-2).

If we move from the sacred area of the Temple to the *literary area* of the Scriptures, it is clear that sources of very different origin enable the position of the major movements of Judaism of this period to be known in relation to the biblical canon: the Dead Sea Scrolls attest the extension of the canon among the Essenes; the works of Philo can reflect the extent of the canon in the world of the Greek diaspora or perhaps merely Philo's own position; the other Jewish sources basically represent the viewpoint of the Pharisees regarding the biblical canon; the NT writings allow us to know what the OT canon of the first Christians of Jewish origin was like. Josephus also provides information about the canon of inspired books of the Jews, the number of which he says is restricted to «only 22» (*Contra Apion* 1:37-43). The canon known by Josephus differs from the canon of the Hebrew Bible at most by one book, by omitting the book of Qoh or Song.

One of the most important new facts provided by the Dead Sea Scrolls was to reveal that, at the beginning of the 1st cent. CE, rabbinic circles of Palestine completed a revision of the Greek text of some biblical books. The stimulus for this revision was the fact that the Greek text exhibited differences from the Hebrew text used in those rabbinic circles. Some were minute but others were quite considerable. The revisers set themselves to correct the Greek text from the Hebrew text which they knew and were using. These revisers have been correctly called the «forerunners of Aquila» (Barthélemy) since the literalism typical of this revision was fully developed in the translation made by Aquila at the beginning of the 2nd cent. CE (cf. p. 313). What interests us here is to note which books were revised. It will enable us to gain an idea of the extent of the Pharisee canon towards the beginning of the 1st cent. CE.

Some of the books revised correspond to the Former Prophets (Jos-Kgs) and the Latter Prophets (Is-Ez) which had already formed part of the canon from antiquity. The revision actually reached the book of Judges (a text preserved especially in the subgroup of MSS irua₂), the books of Sm and Kgs (in the *kaige* sections of the Greek text of *I-IV Kings*) and the additions in Greek to the book of Jeremiah, Psalms (Fifth column of the Hexaplar) and the book of the Twelve Minor Prophets, the revised Greek text of which was found in the cave of Naḥal Ḥever in the vicinity of the Dead Sea.

The books whose Greek version had no significant differences from the proto-rabbinic Hebrew did not need to be revised and in fact show no trace at all of having undergone such a revision. These books are Chr, Ezr and Neh.

In the cases of Song, Ruth and Lam, instead, the whole manuscript tradition of these books does show traces of that revision. The fact that no remains have been preserved which allow the existence of an original unrevised version to be supposed may indicate that these books were never revised, but were translated at one go and for the first time by those who revised the other books. The reason for the translation of those books could have been the wish to provide the synagogues of the Hellenistic diaspora with the Greek text for the readings that had to be given in the feasts of Passover and Weeks as well as on the day of mourning on the 9th of Ab.

The book of Qoheleth does not seem to have been translated into Greek until the end of the 1st cent. CE. The characteristics of the version match those of the Aquila recension of the 2nd cent. CE. Until this period, rabbinic circles continued to discuss the canonicity of this book; the school of Hillel admitted it into the canon; the school of Shammai rejected it. Until that time the Jewish diaspora had used the book of Baruch for the liturgical reading on the feast of Tabernacles. The version of the book of Qoheleth ended by displacing the Greek book of Baruch which the authorities of the Palestinian metropolis did not accept into their canon, possibly because they did no longer had a Hebrew original of that book (Barthélemy).

Lastly, the book of Esther, included in the Hebrew canon, and the books of Tobit and Ecclesiasticus (Ben Sira), included only in the Greek Bible, do not seem to have been of any interest in the circles which carried out the revision mentioned above of the Greek text of some biblical books. This lack of interest is particularly surprising in the case of the book of Esther, for the Greek version of this book has very different textual forms: as transmitted by the uncial manuscripts, reflected by the *Old Latin*, witnessed by Josephus and finally as transmitted by the pre-Hexaplar tradition, wrongly called «Lucianic» and preserved in four minuscule manuscripts. All these forms differ from the Hebrew text, especially by the significant additions they provide.

From the former data the conclusion can be drawn that the circles responsible for this revision of the Greek Bible, completed at the start of the

1st cent. CE, already had a canon of sacred books which agreed with the later rabbinic canon. It seems that only two books, Esther and Qoheleth, did not belong to this canon. The book of Esther was already known at that time within the diaspora. The book of Qoheleth was only translated later after opinion favourable to the canonicity of this book had prevailed.

The canon of 22 books, which does not include Qoheleth and Esther, undoubtedly comprises the oldest and most original form of the biblical canon.

5. The Closure of the Canon in the Mishnaic Period

Towards the close of the 1st cent. CE, the canonical character of all (or nearly all) the books of the Hebrew Bible does not seem to allow any discussion. This is what the Jewish and Christian sources from the 1st cent. BCE and the 1st cent. CE attest. The only books without any witness concerning their canonical character are those of Ruth, Song and Esther.

To the period of Yabneh in the broad sense refer the data contained in the tractate of the Mishnah *Sanhedrin* 10:1. According to R. Akiba, the use of the «external books» prevented a share in the world to come. However, this reference certainly has nothing to do with the problem of the canon but rather with something like the Index of Forbidden Books.

The only book referring to the period of Yabneh, Mishnah *Yadayim* 3:5, has the statement that the books of Song and Qoheleth «soil the hands». By this is meant that these books possess a special sacred character but perhaps not necessarily canonical character. In any case it does not seem to have been a definitive decision since the discussion still continued for some time.

If the expression «to soil the hands» has to be granted the strict meaning of a reference to a «canonical book» and if the rabbis decided at Yabneh that the book of *Qoheleth* «soils the hands» and is therefore a canonical book, the rabbis were doing no more than maintain the position of the Hillel school in favour of the canonical nature of Qoheleth.

The sacred and perhaps canonical character of Song had never really been placed in doubt, but the fact that this book was used in secular feasts or could be used in that way, had given rise to a degree of reluctance against its secular use and not so much against its canonicity.

As for the book of *Esther*, R. Akiba had to justify its admission into the canon based on the fact that the author enjoyed prophetic knowledge even though he was never a prophet.

With reference to *Ben Sira*, described as a «book on the border of the canon», the Pharisees were ruled by the principle of not admitting into the canon any book whose origin was considered later than the period of Simon the Just. In spite of that, it continued enjoying at least some canonical status in some rabbinic schools, as shown by the fact that copies of the Hebrew text of this book have been found in Qumran and Masada and that the Babylonian Talmud quotes it, granting it the character of a sacred book.

It is commonly supposed that the apocrypha were excluded from the canon in the period of Yabneh. It has also been stated that the biblical canon was fixed by popular agreement at Yabneh or shortly after and not by a formal and official decision of the Jewish authorities (M.H. Segal, cf. p. 155). However, there is no proof of that.

At Yabneh some books were discussed, but the debate continued and the consensus on the extent of the canon did not crystallise until well into the Tannaitic period. What happened there was a first attempt at declaring Song and Qoheleth as canonical (Schäfer). The canon was not something that would be established by rabbinic authority but took shape little by little, certainly in relation to the practical needs of synagogue worship. A canonical book was one «fit for use in the synagogue» just as previously it had been «fit for use in the Temple».

So then, while it cannot be said that the canon was completely closed without any discussion, mainstream rabbinic tradition considered instead the biblical canon as virtually established. One of the intentions motivating the rabbis was to prevent groups of Jews risking the temptation of granting sacred status to the first NT writings which were already circulating then. The rabbis also took other decisions «on account of the Christians»: they forbade fasting on Sunday, abolished daily reading of the Decalogue which preceded the Šᵉmaʾ, and into the daily synagogal prayer inserted a curse against the minîm: «May there be no hope at all for the apostates...». This addition made it impossible in practice for a crypto-Christian to continue to take part in synagogal worship.

However, this eighteenth petition was not directed exclusively against Christians, as was thought in the past. Its origin stems also from divisions within Judaism. This prayer was directed against the Roman authorities and various heretical Jewish groups, which also included Jewish Christians. However, it is not possible to determine whether at the moment of composition of the hamminîm blessing, the target was in fact the Jewish-Christians.

One current approach of research tends to place the setting up of the canon around 164 BCE, at a moment when one of the great crises in the history of Judaism was overcome, when Judas Maccabaeus collects the scattered Scriptures (2 Mc 2:14-15) which Antiochus Epiphanes had tried to destroy (1 Mc 1:56-57; Beckwith). The OT apocrypha, Philo, Josephus and Christian sources witness that the greater part of the Jewish communities before and after the beginning of the Christian period had a shorter canon available (Leiman, against Sundberg's opinion). Although the question cannot be settled completely, in the 2nd and 3rd cents. BCE the extent of Scripture was not substantially different from that reflected in Josephus, 4 Ezra and the Talmud: only the inspired and canonical books were called Scripture. It is only certain, however, that in the 2nd cent. BCE inspired canonical books and canonical books which were not inspired existed side by side and that the scriptural status of the latter was open to discussion.

The Pharisees represented an intermediate position between those who tended to reduce the borders of the canon to the Pentateuch (and Prophets) and those who tended to consider other books as sacred, especially if apocalyptic, which did not succeed in entering the rabbinic canon. The disputes concerning the canonicity of Ez, Pr, Qoh, Song and Est were not very lengthy, in fact, for they remained within the Pharisee group. Even within this group, discussion was restricted mostly only to the book of Qoh which according to the Hillelites «soiled the hands» but according to the followers of Shammai did not have this effect. Only a very small circle of Pharisees expressed some doubts regarding Song and Est. In any case, whoever placed the canonicity of these books in doubt, as well as that of Ez, Prov and Qoh, seems to have represented a minority. The majority accepted these books, following an old tradition.

The biblical canon was considered closed when it was decided that no more books could be added to the group of those held as canonical and inspired. There are no data for determining the date of this decision or for identifying the authority which took that decision. Everything points to the mid-2nd cent. BCE, the date of the closure of the «Writings» and thus of the biblical canon: the literary activity carried out by Judas Maccabaeus, the canonisation of the present form of Daniel in the Maccabaean period, the existence of the proto-Lucianic recension of the Greek Bible in the 2nd cent. BCE, which indicates that the establishment of the Hebrew text was already under way and that the canon was already fixed.

The closure of the biblical canon did not take place in Yabneh towards the end of the 1st cent. CE. Jewish sources (apocrypha, Philo and Josephus) as well as Christian sources which reflect Jewish practice (the NT and the Fathers) guarantee the idea of a biblical canon which was already closed in most of the Jewish groups throughout the first centuries before and after the Christian era. The only possible indications of a wider biblical canon come from the Jewish sectarian community of Qumran and from Christian sources of the 4th cent. and later. Critical analysis of the book of Daniel, data from the Apocrypha and the biblical manuscripts from Qumran in Hebrew and Greek suggest the possibility and the probability that the canon was closed in the Maccabaean period. Talmudic and midrashic data also support this conclusion (Leimann).

However, it has to be taken into account that this solution does not resolve the problems presented by the existence of a Christian canon of the OT, longer than the Jewish canon, and its possible forerunners in the world of Judaism, and actually in the Essene groups such as those who expressed themselves in the manuscripts from Qumran or in Jewish groups of the diaspora.

IV. THE BIBLICAL CANON IN LITERARY PERSPECTIVE

It is first necessary to separate the problem of the biblical canon from the domain of theology in which it is usually discussed and move it to specifically literary territory. From this literary perspective, study of the canon is related to analysis of literary form of each biblical book and, at a deeper level, to the analysis of archetypes or fundamental symbols which run through the Bible from beginning to end. These archetypes give the Bible an inner tension and dynamic (Law versus Prophecy) and at the same time a tension and movement towards a final outcome (Apocalyptic). These tensions, which run through the biblical canon in every direction, determine its unified structure and the same process of formation of the various collections: Torah, Prophets, Psalms and other Writings.

1. The Formation of the Canon from «Natural Fixed Forms»

The biblical writings and the three collections it comprises (Torah, Prophets and Writings) stem from «natural fixed forms» of Hebrew literature. These nuclear literary forms take shape in certain pieces or literary units. Goethe established the distinction between «natural forms» (*Naturformen*) and «literary genres» (*Dichtarten*; Aguiar 179). Consequently, it can be said that the Torah is born from the «torah» form or instruction, wisdom literature is born from the proverb, prophetic literature from the oracle, history from the story, the psalter from the psalm and in the NT each of the four gospels is born from a gospel pericope. In this sense, each gospel read in the Christian liturgy is a condensed form of the whole Gospel and this, in turn, is the development of the gospel form.

The Bible, before being the book we know, was a group of collections of «booklets» (*tà biblía* in Greek) which are actually read in isolated segments and never in a complete and continuous text. Even when made into a biblical book and written on a complete scroll, only excerpts continued to be used. Separate psalms were recited and commented on but never the complete Psalter. The same happened with the *tôrôt* or laws, the oracles, the proverbs and the stories about the patriarchs, judges, prophets, heroes and heroines of Israel.

2. The Unity of the Canon: Biblical Archetypes

In its canonical form the Bible is a single unit. A whole series of recurring archetypes fom beginning to end contribute to unify the whole and at the same time set up a tension between a Genesis and an Apocalypse, between past and future, as well as a tension between Torah and prophecy, between the principal of reality and the principal of an ideal or utopia.

The biblical archetypes are symbols which run through the whole Bible from beginning to end, conferring unity and a sense of totality to the whole Bible. A familiar example is the symbolism surrounding the figure of the «shepherd» from Yahweh himself (Ps 23), Abel, Abraham, the shepherds of Israel (Ez 34) and in the NT to Jesus of Nazareth. Since it is a universal archetype, the same symbolism is also found in all literature pastoral and Arcadian, from Theocritus and Virgil's fourth Eclogue to Petrarch and Boccaccio, Tasso and J. de Monte mayor.

Archetypes typical of the creation myths reappear in apocalyptic visions which describe the new creation in the last times (the old and new Adam, new heavens, a new paradise, e.g. Is 51:9-11, etc.). Motifs from primeval creation appear the song of Ex 15 on the crossing of the Red Sea: the battle against the chaotic Sea and its leviathans, the crossing of the desert, the rebuilding of the temple on the cosmic mountain, etc. (Cross). Equally, the imagery of Exodus reappears in the prophecies about the Exile and the Return.

It is not surprising that the literary critic N. Frye was able to define the task of the OT critic as *a single archetypal structure extending from creation to apocalypse» (Anatomy of Criticism, 315).* The first function of literature, especially of poetry, is to preserve the human and allegedly child-like ability for creation and expression in a metaphorical language, and to prevent the reduction of language to signs which are too rationalised and conventional, and supposedly more adult, to keep re-creating the first metaphorical phase of language during the domination of later phases (Frye).

3. *The Tension between Law and Prophecy and Tension towards an Eschatological Denouement*

The history of the canon is the history of the myths of creation and of Exodus-salvation which after its reduction to a moral code in the Torah and its testing in the harsh historical experience of Israel as reflected in biblical historical writing, come to give expression to prophetic hope and, ultimately, apocalyptic expectations. The Bible is imbued with historical dynamic, a wish for the fulfilment of the original promise and the realisation of prophetic hope. This yearning for fulfilment, the driving force in every play and every novel, confers on the Bible a projection towards the future, towards an apocalyptic.

The biblical canon is a reflection of the tension buried between myth and history of an irreconcilable conflict between wish and reality, of a polarity between Prophecy and Torah. It is not surprising therefore that at the end of the biblical period the literary forms peculiar to Genesis are copied and that it is difficult to classify some apocalyptic books (or passages from them) as works re-writing Genesis or as true apocalypse, for in fact they exhibit features of both genres. Such, for example, is the case of the book of *Jubilees*.

The archetypes and symbols of Creation and the Exodus-Exile appear fully developed in the Torah and in Prophecy (historical and prophetic books) and reappear, re-interpreted, in wisdom and apocalyptic literature. Frye has distinguished six phases of revelation, each of which broadens the perspective of the preceding and is a type for the following: creation, exodus, law, prophecy, wisdom and apocalypse; if the NT is also considered, gospel must be added.

4. *The Biblical Canon as Generating Parabiblical Literature*

This tension between Law and Prophecy, which determines a utopian projection towards Apocalyptic, tempered only by the counteracting realism of Wisdom, confers on the biblical canon a sense of completeness and perfection which makes it into a «model» generating new parabiblical literature. In the art world the word *kanṓn* means «model» to be imitated. The canon of proportions of the human body established by Praxiteles was the model copied by artists in the Hellenistic period. A «classical» author (*scriptor classicus*) was one whose correctness of language, perfection of style, harmony of work and greatness of ideas could be taken as a model for the creation of new works. Modern literature has to a large extent broken with the principle that literary creation had to be based on «models» and «classical» authors. In the Hellenistic period, artistic and literary creation consisted instead in a *mimesis* or imitation of the classics. Jewish apocalyptic literature in the Hellenistic period created no new genres but imitated and repeated the ancient genres developed in the Bible.

Before being the collection of books in which the «rule» of faith and orthodoxy was expressed, the *kanṓn* was a «list» (*pínakes*) of «selected» (*egkrithéntes*) books or «first class» (*classici*) books, like the lists of the new lyrical poets or of the ten orators of classicism (Pfeiffer, cf. p. 138).

The classical works of the Greek and Latin world and the canonical books of the Hebrew Bible were basically models to be imitated rather than texts for comment and interpretation. The *Aeneid* is a recreation of the *Iliad*; it is therefore an interpretation which is more appropriate and faithful to the original, to the Homeric spirit and verse, than any erudite commentary in prose on the Homeric text. To recreate a story is the best and most faithful way to interpret it. The classical authors and the biblical prophets could not avoid generating new literature which often was even presented under the pseudepigraphic name of a classical author or a prophet.

Accordingly, it is necessary to study the biblical canon not only as the repository of inspired works but also as the source of inspiration for new writings. The inspired works in their turn inspire other new works which pretend to emulate the old ones. The *theologoúmenon* according to which biblical inspiration ended with the last prophet (Malachi) and Christian inspiration with the last apostle (John) has theological value but does not correspond to the true history of the two canons. The canon, even before being a canon, has as a principal characteristic the capacity for generating new literature. The Word is creative; the time has already come for laying channels to the sea.

BIBLIOGRAPHY

ACKROYD, P., «The Open Canon», *Studies in the Religious Tradition of the Old Testament*, London 1967, 209-224.

BAHAT, D., «Le temple de Zorobabel à Hérode», *Le monde de la Bible* 60 (1989) 14.

BAHAT, D., «Les murs secrets de l'esplanade du Temple», *Le monde de la Bible* 60 (1989) 15-20.

BALDERMANN, I. *et al.* (eds.), *Zum Problem des biblischen Kanons, Jahrbuch für Biblische Theologie* 3, Neukirchen-Vluyn 1988.

BARTHÉLEMY, D., «L'état de la Bible juive depuis le début de notre ère jusqu'à la deuxième révolte contre Rome (131-135)», *Le Canon de l'Ancien Testament.*

Sa formation et son histoire, eds., J. D. Kaestly-O. Wermelinger, Geneva 1984, 9-45.

BECKWIRH, R.T., *The Old Testament Canon of the New Testament Church and its Background in Early Judaism*, London 1985.

BLENKINSOPP, J., *Prophecy and Canon. A Contribution to the Study of Jewish Origins*, Notre Dame-London 1977.

CROSS, F.M., *Canaanite Myth and Hebrew Epic. Essays in the History of the Religion of Israel*, Cambridge MA 1973.

DODDS, E.R., *The Greeks and the Irrational*, Berkeley CA 1964.

FRYE, N., *The Anatomy of Criticism*, Princeton, NJ 1971.

FRYE, N., *The Great Code. The Bible and Literature*, Toronto 1982.

GOODMAN, M., «Sacred Scripture and 'Defiling the Hands'», *JThS* NS 41 (1990) 99-107.

HÜBNER, H., «Vetus Testamentum und Vetus Testamentum in Novo receptum. Die Frage nach dem Kanon des Alten Testaments aus neutestamentlicher Sicht», *Zum Problem des biblischen Kanons*, Jahrbuch für Biblische Theologie 3, Neukirchen-Vluyn 1988, 147-162.

KAUFMAN, S.A., «The Temple Scroll and Higher Criticism», *HUCA* 53 (1982) 29-43.

KRAEMER, D., «The Formation of the Rabbinic Canon: Authority and Boundaries», *JBL* 110 (1991) 613-630.

LEIMAN, S.Z., *The Canonization of Hebrew Scripture: The Talmudic and Midrashic Evidence*, Hamden, CT 1976.

LIGHTSTONE, J.N., *Society, the Sacred and Scripture in Ancient Judaism: A Sociology of Knowledge*, Waterloo, Ontario 1988.

MAIER, J., «Zur Frage des biblischen Kanons im Frühjudentum im Licht der Qumranfunde», *Zum Problem des biblischen Kanons*, Jahrbuch für Biblische Theologie 3, Neukirchen-Vluyn 1988, 115-134.

SAEBO, M., «Vom 'Zusammendenken' zum Kanon. Aspekte der traditionsgeschichtlichen Endstadien des Alten Testaments», *Zum Problem des biblischen Kanons*, Jahrbuch für Biblische Theologie 3, Neukirchen-Vluyn 1988, 115-134.

SCHÄFER, P., «Die sogenannte Synode von Jabne. Trennung von Juden und Christen im ersten zweiten Jh. n. Chr.», *Studien zur Geschichte und Theologies des rabbinischen Judentums*, Leiden 1978, 45-64.

STEMBERGER, G., «Jabne und der Kanon», *Zum Problem des biblischen Kanons*, Jahrbuch für Biblische Theologie 3, Neukirchen-Vluyn 1988, 163-174.

TARDIEU, M., *La formation des canons scripturaires*, Paris 1993.

THEOBALD, C. (ed.), *Le Canon des Ecritures. Études historiques, exégétiques et systématqiues*, Paris 1990.

TUCKER, G.M.-PETERSEN, D.L.-WILSON, R.R. (eds.), *Canon, Theology, and Old Testament Interpretation*, Philadelphia PA 1988.

VASHOLZ, R.I., *The Old Testament Canon in the Old Testament Church. The Internal Rationale for Old Testament Canonicity*, New York-Ontario 1990.

WILSON, G.H., *The Editing of the Hebrew Psalter*, Chico CA 1985.

WANKE, G., «Bibel I. Die Entstehung des Alten Testaments als Kanon», *TRE* 6, 1-8.

V. INTERNAL AND EXTERNAL DEVELOPMENTS OF THE CANON

1. Developments of the Biblical Canon

The Bible developed from a few basic collections: the Torah of Moses, the collection of Psalms by David, the historical books (the Former Prophets), the books of the writing Prophets (the latter Prophets) and lastly the collection of wisdom writings attributed to Solomon.

Moses, David, Solomon and the Prophets were the «authors», considered to be inspired. The books placed under their names eventually formed the basic *corpus* of canonical literature.

Until the last stages of its development, biblical literature did not include a collection of edifying stories or any work of the apocalyptic genre. The works belonging to these two categories, Ruth, Jonah and Esther on the one hand and Daniel of the other, came into the well-developed canon of the Persian period.

The inclusion of these new books in the canon made it easy for other new books to enter at the same time the large extant collections of the Prophets and Writings.

a. The Torah. Once the collections of books forming the Torah had been made, no increase at all was allowed which would entail including a new book into the collection of the «Pentateuch». No pseudepigraphical book from those attributed to Moses himself or to a biblical patriarch such as Enoch or Abraham had the slightest possibility of becoming part of the fundamental traditions of Israel collected as the Pentateuch. However, the existence of the «Enochian Pentateuch» and especially the character of complementary or alternative Pentateuch held by the Temple Scroll reveal greater complexity in the history of the Pentateuch than could have been imagined only a few years ago.

b. The Psalter. The collection of psalms also remained virtually intact, apart from additions and changes of a different kind (cf. p. 159).

c. The historical books or Former Prophets. The collection of historical books (Jos, Jds, Sm and Kgs) was augmented by the inclusion of the complete work of the Chronicler: *Chr and Ezra-Neh*, and the other two books of the same genre, *1 and 2 Mc*.

d. The prophetic books or Later Prophets. Once the collection of prophetical books had been formed (cf. p. 159), the book of Jeremiah was the only one to have other books attributed to the tradition of the prophet Jeremiah to be added to it: the book of *Lamentations* entered the Hebrew canon; the book of *Baruch* and the *Letter of Jeremiah* came in later into the list of deuterocanonical books of the Greek Bible.

e. Wisdom books. In the Bible Solomon is said to be a wise king, promoting justice and social order (1 Kgs 3-11; Ps 72). Perhaps Solomon was the initiator of a wisdom tradition which gradually developed to become the

Biblical Books

(Books and texts not belonging to the Hebrew Bible are in italics. These are called deutero-canonical by Catholics and apocryphal by Protestants).

TORAH OR PENTATEUCH: Genesis, Exodus, Leviticus, Numbers, Deuteronomy
HISTORICAL BOOKS: Joshua, Judges, Ruth (LXX sequence), 1-2 Samuel, 1-2 Kings,
    1-2 Chronicles, Ezra and Nehemiah, *1-2 Maccabees*
PROPHETS: Isaiah (I-II-III), Jeremiah, Lamentations (LXX sequence), Ezekiel
    Baruch, Letter of Jeremiah
MINOR PROPHETS: Hosea, Joel, Amos, Obadiah, Jonah, Micah, Nahum, Habakkuk,
    Zephaniah, Haggai, Zechariah, Malachi
PSALMS: Psalter
    Prayer of Azariah (Dan 3,26-45), Canticle of three youths (Dan 3,52-90a)
WISDOM LITERATURE: Job, Proverbs, Song of Songs, Qoheleth
    Wisdom, Ben Sira, 4 Maccabees
NARRATIVES: Daniel 1-6, Esther
    Additions to Esther, Tobit, Judith, Susanna, Bel and the Dragon, 3 Maccabees
APOCALYPTIC: Daniel 7-12

    Apocryphal Literature (Catholic usage)
    or pseudepigrapha (Protestant usage)

Rewritten Pentateuch: *Jubilees, Assumption of Moses, Life of Adam and Eve, Testament of Abraham, Joseph and Aseneth*
History: *1 Esdras* (GK)= *3 Esdras, Biblical Antiquities, Martyrdom of Isaiah, Jewish Antiquities*
Interpretation of prophetic texts: *Paralipomena of Jeremiah*
Hymns: *Psalms of Solomon, Odes of Solomon*
Apocalyptic: *1 Enoch, 2 Enoch, 4 Esdras, 2 Baruch, 3 Baruch*

    Principal Qumran texts related to the Bible

Temple Scroll, Genesis Apocryphon, Pešarim, Hodayot, 5 Psalms, Book of the War between the Sons of Light and the Sons of Darkness, Eschatological Midrash (4QFlor), Aramaic Messianic Text (4QMess ar), Testimonia (4QTest), New Jerusalem (4QNJ ar), etc.

collection of the book of Proverbs. The *Song of Songs* also has its roots in this wisdom tradition of Solomon, developing the distinctive theme of interpreting human love. *Qoheleth* uses the figure of the wise king to confront the problem of evil and an incorrect mechanistic solution to it.

The canonical collection of wisdom books was increased by two wisdom books attributed to king Solomon. They could not enter the Hebrew canon, but did form part of the list of deuterocanonical books. The pseudepigraphical work of the Wisdom of Solomon was added late on to the canonical books Song and Qoheleth, in this way taking on the wisdom tradition of Solomon. Another wisdom book, Ecclesiasticus, by a well-known author (*Ben Sira*) and not a pseudepigraphical work, gained the classification of a deuterocanonical book possibly more through not being excluded than by direct admission.

The book of *Wisdom* turns Solomon into a protector of the ethical and philosophical principles of Hellenistic wisdom. Lastly, the *Psalms of Solomon* express a message of hope, referring to the wisest and most powerful king of Israel. All these books witness the existence of a wisdom tradition transmitted in a sort of «school of Solomon».

f. Biblical narrative. The collection of Writings had included three story-tales, *Ruth*, *Jonah* and *Esther*. To these another two were added, Tobit and Judith, which reflect pious trends of the Jewish diaspora and Palestinian hasidism (cf. p. 176).

g. Apocalyptic. The entry of the book of *Daniel* into the canon gave the stamp of legitimacy to apocalyptic ideas. It happened in spite of mainstream Pharisaism refusing to acknowledge new revelations («apocalypse») placed in the mouths of biblical patriarchs and prophets. No apocalyptic book was put in the deuterocanonical category, although the Qumran group certainly granted the book of *Enoch* a status similar to a canonical book. Some Christian groups, such as the Church of Ethiopia, also showed a clear tendency to grant this book canonical character.

A chart can summarise the literary development of the biblical collections. The Hebrew canon accepted within itself some developments in each collection, except that of the Torah. The Greek Bible accepted some other books in each of the collections, again except the Torah. A whole series of apocryphal books remained outside the biblical canon - Jewish and Christian - but this did not mean that real developments of the previous biblical tradition ended, whether oral or written.

The boundary between deuterocanonical and apocrypha is a fluid and movable line. In the following sections we will examine in greater detail the development of the various biblical collections, with particular reference to the apocryphal works belonging to the sphere of each of these collections without succeeding in forming part of them.

The following presentation also refers to the history of the composition of these works, whether canonical or apocryphal. It is interesting to note how both the canonical books and the apocrypha display a course and problems with many points in common.

Attention is focused especially on the relationship of the deuterocanonical and apocryphal writings with canonical literature, inasmuch as they are «re-writes», exegetical commentaries or re-workings of the biblical material. Many facts and problems are anticipated here which will be discussed in the section on the interpretation of the OT in apocryphal literature (cf. pp. 444-451).

2.   *Canonical Developments Incorporated in the Hebrew Bible*
       (Canonical Books)

The initial nucleus of the OT is composed of the oldest books, which from the beginning formed part of the collections of Torah, Prophets and Writings. The books which came into the canon later comprise a first «re-reading» or interpretation of that initial canon.

Although the Torah did not allow any addition at all, however, several indications show that the book of Job had a special relationship to the Torah, especially in Sadducee circles: the book of Job is the only one, together with Leviticus, on which a targum has been found in Qumran. It is also the only one, together with the Torah, transmitted in the palaeo-Hebrew script.

Biblical history («The Former Prophets») soon admitted other books which rewrote the history of classical Israel in the monarchic period.

A.   DEVELOPMENTS IN HISTORICAL ACCOUNTS: 1-2 CHRONICLES,
       EZRA AND NEHEMIAH

The first great development of the initial nucleus of the canon consists in the Chronicler's work, comprising 1-2 Chr, Ezr and Neh.

For reasons of language and content the most recent opinions of criticism tend to separate into two independent works both 1-2 Chr and Ezr-Neh (Japhet, Williamson), against the theory which supposes a single author for both sets (Rudolph, Myers). The complete work also acquired a series of additions. F. M. Cross has reconstructed its editorial process in three stages.

As sources for his work the author of 1-2 Chr used the Pentateuch and the deuteronomistic history (cf. the references to «The book of the Kings of Israel», 1 Chr 9:1; 2 Chr 20:34, and to «The Chronicles of the Kings of Israel», 2 Chr 33:18). However, it is difficult to determine whether the author of Chronicles knew a form of the books of Sm-Kgs different from and older than the one which has reached us (Rehm, McKenzie).

The books of 1-2 Chr are frequently considered as the work of a «midrashist» rather than as a true historian (Torrey). However, typical of these books is that they comprise a new and original form of «re-writing» the traditions of Israel from the beginnings until the period of Ezra and Nehemiah.

The book of Lamentations comes after Jeremiah in the LXX whereas in the Hebrew Bible it is found among the Writings, forming part of the M^{e}gillôt collection. The book is four fifths a lamentation for the destruction of Jerusalem. The connection of the book with the prophet Jeremiah is secondary, although it could derive from a very ancient period of tradition.

C.   NARRATIVE DEVELOPMENTS: RUTH, JONAH AND ESTHER

The book of *Ruth* likewise is found in the LXX immediately after the book of Judges and refers to its historical period. The Hebrew Bible places it in the collection of M^{e}gillôt. It contains several Aramaisms so that it cannot be earlier than the 4th or 5th cent. BCE, although it does preserve a record of ancient customs. The allusion in 4:7 to a custom laid down in Dt 25:9 insinuates that in the author's time this custom belonged to the past. The fact that David is presented as a descendant of a converted Moabite woman is an indication of a favourable attitude towards the neighbouring peoples. In this, the book of Ruth is very close to Jonah which is also a post-Exilic book.

The book of *Jonah* is not a book of prophetic oracles but a historical novel, a parable or an allegory. These are the terms used in an attempt to define the literary form of this work. Undoubtedly, the fact that it is a narrative work and not a collection of divine oracles transmitted by a prophet determined its place within the collection of the twelve Minor Prophets.

In the Hebrew Bible the book of Jonah comes in the fifth section. It forms part of the first six books (Hos, Jl, Am, Obad, Jon, Mic) which refer to prophets who were active in the period of Assyrian hegemony. The book of Jonah, however, is from a much later period.

In the Greek Bible, Jonah comes sixth within the group of Minor Prophets. The books of this collection seem to be arranged according to size, from the longest to the shortest (Hos, Am, Mic, Jl, Obad, Jon). The book of Jonah is longer than that of Obadiah, but the fact that it is written in narrative prose undoubtedly ensured that it came at the end of the list.

In any case, the book of Jonah is a foreign body in the collection of Twelve Prophets and undoubtedly represents an addition introduced in the collection before it had reached the number 12. The books of Isaiah, Jeremiah and Ezekiel were also formed starting from shorter earlier collections.

The book of *Esther* has a complex position both in the history of the literary formation of the OT and in the history of the OT canon. We will therefore pay considerable attention to this book.

The genre of the book is a historical novel which turns on a historical nucleus mixed with motifs from fiction (Moore). It is difficult to be more precise. As in the case of the book of Judith, the work has been related to erotic novels of Hellenism, assigned a late date, around the period of the Maccabaean uprising (c. 167-140, Stiehl). The term «novel», however, does not seem to be applicable to a work as short as Esther (Cazelles). It has to be set, instead, at the beginning of the Persian period and be defined as «a historical wisdom tale», with emphasis on the aspects of wisdom and the court, in relation to the tales about Joseph, Dn 1-6, Judith and Ahiqar (Talmon). Meinhold thinks that it originated in the exile as a *Diasporanovelle*. Würthwein dates it to before the Maccabaean revolt and accepts the definition «novel» but gives it the meaning «unexpected event», coined by Goethe. Most authors tend to date the work to the Persian period.

Another important factor to define the literary form of this work is its possible connection with the feast of Purim (a word of Babylonian origin which means «destiny», «lot»-«lottery»). It would then be a *Festlegende* (Gaster, Ringgren, Bickerman). The very structure of the work and possibly its inclusion in the canon are connected with a feast of non-Jewish origin which, after being connected with legends and traditions belonging to Judaism, ended up being included within the calendar of Jewish feasts. Consequently, it has been possible to define the book of Esther as a haggadic midrash (Marucq), although this requires giving the term a meaning which is too broad and too vague.

The definitions of historical novel or midrash set out are inexact and lead to inappropriate comparisons with forms of literature (either extra-biblical or post-biblical). Similarly, the description «cultic legend» assumes that the narrative plot and etiological ending form a unit which is far from the unanimous view among scholars. The book ended with the death of Haman on the gallows and the elevation of Mordecai, followed by the annulment of the order to exterminate the Jews and a feast of rejoicing by them; at this point the addition about the carnevalesque feast of Purim is inserted (Torrey).

The best «analytical model» for defining the genre of the book of Esther has surely to be sought within the Bible itself, in the figures of «heroines of liberation» such as Miriam, Deborah and Jael (see below, on the book of Judith) and in the motif of «promoting an exile to the court» (Mordecai) which is also developed in the stories about Joseph and Daniel (Dn 2).

D.   WISDOM DEVELOPMENTS: SONG OF SONGS AND QOHELETH

The *Song of Songs* has a literary structure which is difficult to determine, though it gives unity to the whole work, but on the other hand, it comprises a collection of independent poems and love songs. The composition seems to be from the period of the Exile, although some of the individual poems could go back to a much earlier period. The book forms part of the collection of *M^{e}gillôt*. Song has undergone a long history of literal and allegorical interpretation which comprises one of the most typical developments of biblical hermeneutics (Pope).

Qoheleth or *Ecclesiastes* is the work of an unknown author in the period after the Exile. Later an editor added the epilogue (12:9-14). The language of this book is close to the Hebrew of the Mishnaic period. The repetition of a refrain («futility and utter futility») indicates the structure of the book. The presence of this book in the biblical canon takes on special significance as it confers canonical value on the critique of a certain conventional theology and wisdom and highlights the need for keeping religion within «the bounds of reality».

E.   APOCALYPTIC DEVELOPMENTS: THE BOOK OF DANIEL

The book of *Daniel* took shape shortly before the death of king Antiochus IV Epiphanes in 164 BCE. Chaps. 1-6 contain accounts of Haggadic character, possibly by several authors (Ginsberg, Hartman-Di Lella). The accounts of visions in chaps. 7-12 belong, instead, to the apocalyptic genre. The prayer in 9:4-20, written in better quality Hebrew than the rest of the book, could be a piece of great antiquity included here.

The apocalyptic section, with the exception of chap. 7, is written in Hebrew, while the first part, except for 1:1-2:4a, is in Aramaic. The original language of the work was certainly Aramaic; the beginning and end were translated into Hebrew to ensure the work a place in the canon or perhaps in response to nationalist tendencies. Another possible explanation is that the author of the visions (8-12) collects an already existing collection written in Aramaic, composed of four accounts (2-6) and a vision (chap. 7); the same author completed the work composing and translating into Hebrew the introductory narrative (chap. 1) and the opening verses of the second narrative (2:1-4a). On the various textual forms of the book cf. p. 400.

BIBLIOGRAPHY

BICKERMAN, E., *Four Strange Books of the Bible*, New York 1967.

BARUCQ, A., *Judith, Esther*, Paris 1959.

CAZELLES, H., «Notes sur la composition du rouleau d'Esther», *Lex tua veritas. Festschrift H. Junker*, eds., H. Gross-F. Mussner, Trier 1961, 17-29.

CROSS, F.M. «A Reconstruction of the Judaean Restoration», *JBL* 94 (1975) 4-18.

GASTER, T.H., *Purim and Hanukhah in Custom and Tradition*, New York 1950.

GINSBERG, H.L., *Studies in Daniel*, New York 1948.

HARTMAN, L.-DI LELLA, A.A., *The Book of Daniel*, Garden City NY 1978.

JAPHET, S., *I & II Chronicles. A Commentary*, London 1993.

MCKENZIE, S.L., *The Chronicler's Use of the Deuteronomistic History*, Atlanta GA 1985.

MYERS, J.M., *I Chronicles*, Garden City NY 1974.

MYERS, J.M., *II Chronicles*, Garden City NY 1974.

MOORE, G.A., *Esther*, Garden City NY 1971.

MEINHOLD, A., «Die Gattung des Josephgeschichte und des Estherbuches: Diasporanovelle», I *ZAW* 87 (1975) 306-324; II *ZAW* 88 (1976) 72-93.

POPE, M.H., *Song of Songs*, Garden City NY 1977.

REHM, M., *Die Bücher der Chronik*, Würzburg 1956.

RINGGREN, H., *Das Hohe Lied. Klagelieder, Das Buch Esther*, Göttingen 1958.

RUDOLPH, W., *Esra und Nehemias samt 3. Esra*, Tübingen 1949.

TALMON, S., «'Wisdom' in the Book of Esther», *VT* 13 (1963) 419-455.

TORREY, C.C., «The Older Book of Esther», *HThR* 37 (1944) 1-40.

TORREY, C.C., *Ezra Studies*, Chicago IL 1910.

ULRICH, E.-WRIGHT, J.W.-CARROLL, R.P.-DAVIES, PH.R., *Priests, Prophets and Scribes. Essays on the Formation and Heritage of Second Temple Judaism in Honour of J. Blenkinsopp*, Sheffield 1992.

WILLIAMSON, H.G.M., *Israel in the Books of Chronicles*, Cambridge 1977.

WÜRTHWEIN, E., *Die fünf Megilloth. Ruth, Das Hohelied, Esther*, Tübingen 1969.

3. *Developments of the Canon Included in the Greek Bible (Deutero-canonical Books)*

The *deuterocanonical* books in Catholic terminology, or the apocryphal books, in Protestant terms, comprise the crux of all the confessional discussions concerning the Christian canon of the OT (Meurer). The literary history of these book lies at the origin of many of the problems posed later by theology.

A.   HISTORIOGRAPHICAL DEVELOPMENTS: 1 AND 2 MACCABEES

The two books which include the stories of the Maccabees contain no explicit references to the OT. However, they present the Maccabees as champions of biblical tradition and restorers of the fundamental institutions of Judaism, the Temple and the Torah.

The *first book of Maccabees* was originally composed in Hebrew towards the end of the reign of John Hyrcanus (135-104) or a few years later, at any rate before 90 BCE (Goldstein). Whether the work is a single unit is no longer a subject for discussion although several sources can still be recognised in it: the historical annals mentioned in 14:19, a Seleucid chronicle, an account by Matathias, a life of Judas (the author of which could either be Eupolemos or someone able to use his work) and lastly, other Jewish accounts concerning the reigns of Jonathan and Simon (Schunck). The poetic sections contained in the work could be the creation of the same author. The book of 1 Mc could be based on a Seleucid chronicle, on Hasmonean oral and documentary traditions and on the memoirs of Onias IV (Goldstein).

Undoubtedly, the aim of the book is to justify the legitimacy of the Hasmonean dynasty. The Hasmoneans are presented, in line with Biblical models, as the representatives of God or as priests and judges of Israel. The Hasmonaean dynasty fulfils, then, the traditional expectations of Israel and ushers in the eschatological period (Arenhoevel).

The *Second book of Maccabees* covers a shorter period than 1 Mc. It starts from the events which preceded the revolt and ends with the death of Judas. It is a more complex literary work and has greater pretensions to being a theological work.

The book is a summary of a previous work written in five volumes by Jason of Cyrene, with the addition of two letters and a fragment from a third letter. The book was formed in two stages (Bunger) or more probably in three successive stages (Goldstein). This matter depends on whether the letters quoted were inserted by the author of the summary or whether one or two of them were added by a later editor. The solution to these literary questions is also crucial for determining the date of the book. The summary of the work by Jason, preceded by the first letter, could have been composed in 124 BCE or shortly after (Bunge). The final edited version, which includes the addition of the two letters that precede the summary (Goldstein) could be a litle later than 78-77 BCE.

The work is an amalgam of beliefs of the pietistic groups of the 2nd cent. and of the groups derived fom them, Essenes and Pharisees. Among these, belief in the resurrection of the dead stands out (chap. 7). On the other hand, the work has features which connect it with Greek historical works.

B.   PROPHETIC DEVELOPMENTS: BARUCH AND THE LETTER OF
       JEREMIAH

In the Greek Bible, the book attributed to *Baruch* follows the book of Jeremiah (cf. p. 395) with which it is obviously connected. The introductory narrative, 1:1-14, alludes to the circumstances of the book in the fifth year after the destruction of the Temple. The prayers and confessions of 1:15-3:8 are influenced by the language of Exodus, Deuteronomy, Jeremiah and Second Isaiah and present verbal parallels with the prayer of Dn 9:4-19. The wisdom poem of 3:9-4:4 equates Wisdom and Torah in the tradition of Ben Sira 24 and also paraphrases Job 28. In the poem to Zion, 4:5-5:9 the language of Deuteronomy reappears, but the dominant metaphor - Zion as a mother with her children - comes from Second Isaiah. After remembering the punishments of the Exile, 4:6-20, and two strophes inviting to prayer, 4:21-26 and 4:27-29, the book ends with four strophes addressed to Jerusalem which express hope in salvation, 4:30-5:9.

It is difficult to decide what connection there is between 1:1-3:8, undoubtedly written in Hebrew, and the two final sections, 3:9-4:4 and 4:5-5:9, possibly written in Greek (Burke, Moore). The text of at least 1:1-3:8 was translated into Greek by the translator of the book of Jeremiah. This means that it certainly formed part of the same scroll which contained that book.

The *Letter of Jeremiah* is not really by Jeremiah nor is it a letter but rather a treatise against idol worship based on Jr 10:2-15 and the letter of Jr 29. The text, preserved only in Greek and daughter versions, was composed in Hebrew, as a fragment of it found in Qumran Cave 7 shows (DJD III 143). The writing is earlier than c. 100 BCE as it is cited in 2 Mc 2:2, a little later than this period, to which the manuscript from Qumran just mentioned also belongs. The reference in v.3 to the length of the Exile as seven generations could indicate a composition date of around 317-307 BCE.

C.   HYMNAL DEVELOPMENTS: AZARAIAH'S PRAYER AND THE CANTI-
       CLE OF THE THREE YOUTHS

Among the additions to the book of Daniel are the *Prayer of Azariah* (3:26-45) and the *Canticle of the Three Youths* (3:24-25) and an interlude (3:46-51). The original, Hebrew or Aramaic, which adapted pre-existing liturgical prayers, was inserted into this part of the book of Daniel. The Prayer of Azariah is an entreaty for the community, comparable to the older prayer in Dn 9:4-19 and to those contained in Ezra 9:6-15 and Bar 1:15-3:8. The Canticle of praise by the three youths comprises two litanies like the one in Ps 136. The first is a doxology (1:52-56); the second (1:58-87) is an invitation to all creatures to divine praise, similar to the one in Ps 148 and the litany found in Ms B of Ben Sira, between 52:12 and 52:13 (cf. Skehan-Di Lella).

D.   WISDOM DEVELOPMENTS: WISDOM, BEN SIRA AND 4 MACCABEES

The book of *Wisdom*, written in Greek, is in the form of an edifying exhortation (*Lógos protreptikós* or «encomium») by Solomon addressed to the pagans, to seek wisdom which involves justice and comes from God alone. In the opinion of most scholars, the structure and unity of style indicate single authorship of the work in circles of the Alexandrian diaspora in the first half of the 1st cent. BCE. It popularises Platonic and Stoic concepts adopted in expressions taken from the canonical books of the OT. It combines elements from biblical wisdom tradition, from the salvation history of Israel (Exodus), from apocalyptic and the study of sacred texts, with elements from Hellenistic culture. Some parts of the book comprise a midrash on Exodus (11-19) or on Solomon (7-9). The actual introduction could be a midrash on Is 52:13-15 (Nickelsburg).

The book of *Ben Sira* or *Ecclesiaticus* is the only biblical book by a known author, published towards 180 BCE and translated into Greek 50 years later (cf. p. 401). It comprises a collection of sayings in the style of the book of Proverbs and an attempt at a synthesis between the wisdom tradition and the Torah, to prevent that tradition developing at the margins of Jewish orthodoxy while still in the process of its formation. It belongs to existential wisdom tradition which also finds expression in the books of Job and Qoheleth. In relation to canonical and apocryphal literature, the book of Ben Sira lies «at the borderline of the canon» (cf. p. 165) and is also a book on the border between biblical literature and later rabbinic literature. To a large extent Ben Sira includes a development, a summary or an adaptation of the text of Proverbs. It is enough to compare passages such as 1:4.14.16-177; 2:5.6-9; 3:18; 4:1-6, etc., with corresponding passages from Prov 8:22; 1:7; 8:18-19; 17:3; 3:5-6; 3:34; 17:5; 3:27-28,etc. (Di Lella).

In the guise of a story about the martyrdom of Eleazar together with his mother and his seven brothers, the *Fourth book of Maccabees* is, in fact, a philosophical treatise on the theme of the superiority of reason over emotion. Depending on which aspect of the work is considered, the principal literary form is either the diatribe or the panegyric. Rather than Stoic or Platonic influences, the work reflects commonplaces of Hellenistic philosophy pressed into the service of a panegyric on martyrs and an exhortation in favour of keeping the Torah. The story about the martyrdom is based on 2 Mc or possibly a common source. The work was composed possibly around 40 CE (Hadas).

E.   NARRATIVE DEVELOPMENTS: ADDITIONS TO THE BOOK OF
        ESTHER, TOBIT, JUDITH, SUSANNAH, BEL AND THE DRAGON, AND
        3 MACCABEES.

The Greek version of the book of *Esther* contains a whole series of «*additions*»: the dream of Mordecai and its interpretation (A and F), two letters of the king (B and E), prayers by Mordecai and Esther (C) and the presentation of Esther to the king (D). Apart from the letters of Haman and Mordecai (B and E), these additions already form an integral part of the Hebrew text in the period when it was translated into Greek (cf. p. 399).

The book of *Tobit* was certainly composed in the world of the Eastern Jewish diaspora. It reflects a popular tradition which includes different motifs such as the «fable of the grateful dead man» or «the devil's wife» and other motifs from apocalyptic literature. However, recent research is correct in showing the connections with biblical books. The author is inspired by the book of Joseph (Ruppert) and takes as its model the account in Gn 24 of Isaac's courtship (Deselaers). The aim of the book is to give the Jews of the diaspora confidence. It assures them that God is with them and that one day they will go back to their land, at the same time teaching them what path to take in order to lead a pious life in present circumstances (Nickelsburg).

The book of *Judith* is a story composed in the Persian period and reworked in the Hasmonaean period (Nickelsburg). The didactic and novelistic character of the book has been noted (Zenger) but on the other hand it has also been considered a midrash (Delcor) or a «Passover haggadah» based on the story of the Exodus (Skehan). The story places Judith in the line of biblical heroines: Miriam, Deborah and Jael. It also has features of the genre of interpretation *pēšer* (Nickelsburg).

The place and date of compositon of the story of *Susannah* are the subject of debate. It can be assumed that the original of the work was written in a Semitic language (Moore). The narrative is set in the Jewish diaspora. Susannah is presented as a God-fearing woman, in contrast to some corrupt elders. Susannah proclaims her innocence and begs for her freedom. Elements in common with Gn 39 suggest that the story was influenced by the story of Joseph and Potiphar's wife, although the male and female roles are inverted.

The theme of the persecution and liberation of the just man is also present in Gn 34, Esther, Aḥiqar and Wis 2-5. This theme has also been an influence on the gospel accounts of the sufferings of Jesus.

The two stories about *Bel and the Dragon* have separate origins but share common themes. The same plot which is resolved by the conversion of Cyrus, lends them a degree of unity. They resemble Dn 1-6, with greater emphasis on the polemic against idols. Daniel's opponents are no longer the wise men of the court but pagan priests and «Babylonians». The two stories seem to be later than the accounts in Dn 1-6 and even the formation of the collection Dn 1-6. Their aim is to supply a story which refers to the last of the series of kings which Daniel had to serve (Dn 6:28).

The parallels with Is 45-46 suggest that the two stories began as an exegesis of these chapters from Isaiah. The polemic against idols in Is 46:1-7 ends with exactly the same statement: «Bel has fallen».

The two stories use traditional themes, such as the destruction of idols, which biblical characters such as Abraham and Job also undertook.

The general theme of *3 Maccabees* is the unjust persecution of the Jews and their miraculous deliverance. The stories are set in Palestine and Egypt in the Ptolemaic period after Raphia's victory over the Syrians (217 BCE), well before the Maccabean period. It shows clear parallels with the book of Esther and is also the literary support for a feast similar to Purim.

BIBLIOGRAPHY

ARENHOEVEL, D., *Die Theokratie nach dem 1. und 2. Makkabäerbuch*, Mainz 1967.
BARDTKE, H., *Zusätze zu Esther*, JSHRZ I/I, Gütersloh 1973
BUNGE, J.-G., *Untersuchungen zum zweiten Makkabäerbuch*, Bonn 1971.
BURKE, D.G., *The Poetry of Baruc. A Reconstruction and Analysis of the Original Hebrew Text of Baruch 3:9-5:9*, Chico CA 1982.
DELCOR, M., «Le Livre de Judith et l'époque grecque», *Klio* 49 (1967) 151-179.
DESELAERS, P., *Das Buch Tobit: Studien zu seiner Entstehung, Komposition und Theologie*, Göttingen 1982.
GOLGSTEIN, J.A., *I Maccabees - II Maccabees*, New York 1976 and 1983.
HADAS, M., *The Third and Fourth Books of Maccabees*, New York 1953.
MEURER, S. (ed.), *The Apocrypha in Ecumenical Perspective. The Place of the late writings of the Old Testament among the biblical writings and their significance in the eastern and western church traditions*, New York 1991.
MOORE, C.A., *Daniel, Esther and Jeremiah: The Additions*, Garden City NY 1977.
NICKELSBRUG, G.W.E., *Resurrection, Immortality and Eternal Life in Intertestamental Judaism*, Cambridge MA 1972.
NICKELSBRUG, G.W.E., *Jewish Literature Between the Bible and the Mishnah*, Garden City, NY, 1981.
NICKELSBRUG, G.W.E., «Stories of Biblical and Early Post-Biblical Times», *Jewish Writings of the Second Temple Period*, CRINT 2/2, ed. M. Stone, Philadelphia PA 1984, 33-88.
RUPPERT, L., «Das Buch Tobias - Ein Modellfall nachgestalteter Erzählung», *Wort, Lied und Gottesspruch: Beiträge zur Septuaginta*, ed. S. Schreiner, Würzburg 1972, 109-119.
SCHUNCK, K.-D., *1. Makkabäerbuch*, JSHRZ I/4, Gütersloh 1980.
SKEHAN, P.W.-DI LELLA, A.A., *The Wisdom of Ben Sira*, New York 1987.
SKEHAN, P., «The Hand of Judith», *CBQ* 25 (1963) 94-109.
TOV, E., *The Septuagint Translation of Jeremiah and Baruch: A Discussion of an Early Revision of the LXX of Jeremiah 29-52 and Baruch 1:1-3:8*, Missoula MT 1976.
ZENGER, E., *Das Buch Judit*, JSHRZ I/6, Gütersloh 1981.

4. *Developments of the Canon Outside the Canon: Parabiblical Literature.*

No claim is being made here to give a presentation, even in summary form,
of the apocryphal literature of the OT. It is rather about knowing the relationship of this literature to the canonical books of the OT and the real OT
canon. In this frame of reference, more attention will be paid to some writings than to others and, in discussing each book, more emphasis will be
placed on some aspects than on others.

The term «parabiblical» is applied to writings which, while not biblical,
are re-workings of biblical books or passages and, sometimes, could have aspired to the *status* of scriptural texts. Parabiblica literature comprises real
«rewritings» of biblical books, the 'rewritten Bible' (G. Vermes) or 'expansions of the Old Testament' (Charlesworth).

It is not easy, however, to determine the line of demarcation between this
parabiblical literature and other literature from Qumran, which constantly
refers to Scripture in one way or another: exegetical or midrashic literature
(targumim, pešarim, etc.), eschatological literature (*War Scroll, Rule of the
Congregation, New Jerusalem*, etc.), halakhic texts (4QMMT, *ṭohorot* and
other works), poetic texts (*Hodayot*, wisdom poems, etc.), liturgical texts
(*Songs for the Sabbath Sacrifice*, texts of various prayers, blessings and curses, etc.).

Some of the more important apocryphal books belong to the section
«Rewritten Bible» (Vermes 1962). This type of work has a special relationship with the books of the Torah and with the whole of biblical historical
writing.

Works classified under the heading *«Explained Bible»* refer to the preferred mode of the prophetic books which at one stage included the Psalter.

Apocalyptic literature comprises a very characteristic *corpus* which combines aspects from the previous two: apocalypses continue the cosmological
and historical tradition of the Pentateuch and of the historical books, at the
same time developing the eschatology of the prophets; revelations of hidden
mysteries made to patriarchs or biblical prophets contribute to its contents.

A. PARABIBLICAL LITERATURE: THE «REWRITTEN BIBLE»

The writings listed under the heading «rewritten Bible» are works which
exist because they are the re-working of biblical narratives. Their authors intend to modernise the biblical traditions and make them more intelligible,
more appealing or more edifying for their readers.

Frequently, these works have been studied from the perspective of rabbinic Judaism, making use of the typical categories of this later literature.
Therefore, those writings can be considered as «targumic» works since they
deal with paraphrases of biblical accounts or as «midrashic» works since
they are interpretations of texts from the OT.

Next comes a survey of this «parabiblical literature», classified into five
groups according to the biblical books to which they correspond, rather

grouping them than according to language, genre, content or by other classifications. The six groups are: 1) Narrative writings based on the books of the Torah, 2) Halakhic Writings based on the books of the Torah, 3) Narratives based on biblical historical works, 4) Para-biblical writings based on hymnal literature, 5) Parabiblical writings based on wisdom literature and 6) Apocalyptic type para-biblical writings.

1. Narrative writings based on the books of the Torah: *Genesis Apocryphon, Assumption* (or *Testament*) *of Moses, Life of Adam and Eve* (= *Apocalypse of Moses*), *Testament of Abraham, Joseph and Aseneth, Exhortation based on the Flood, Book of Noah, Apocryphon of Joseph, Second Exodus*

The *Genesis Apocryphon* fully belongs to this group, less so books such as *Assumption* (or *Testament*) *of Moses, Life of Adam and Eve* (= *Apocalypse of Moses*) and the *Testament of Abraham.* Although rather remotely, here also belong the novel *Joseph and Aseneth* and some works from Qumran: *Exhortation based on the Flood, Book of Noah, Apocryphon of Joseph, Second Exodus.*

Some elements from this genre of rewritten Bible are also found in other works such as *Jacob's Ladder*, based on Gn 28, *Jannes and Jambres*, based on Ex 7-8 and *Eldad and Modad* which develops the saying in Nm 11:26-29. Chaps. 71-72 of *2 Enoch* describe the miraculous birth of Melchizedek; similarly, *11QMelchizedek* are literary expansions based on Gn 14:17-24 and show similarities with the most ancient midrashim. These works adapt models from traditional narratives and at the same time reflect the religious and social world of post-biblical Judaism.

1.1. The *Genesis Apocryphon* (1QapGen and 1Q20) is the best example of this type of composition. It is a (haggadic) narrative expansion of a considerable part of the book of Genesis (6-15). In the form of an autobiography, Lamech recounts the wonderful birth of his son, Noah. Faced with the doubt that the real father of Noah could be one of the fallen angels, he goes to his father Methusaleh and asks him to consult his grandfather, Enoch. In the end, Enoch reassures Lamech about Noah's paternity. The main character is then Noah and afterwards, Abraham. In all this, the work could depend on *Jubilees* and *1 Enoch* 106-107 (Fitzmyer), although the dependence could be the other way round (Avigad-Yadin).

In the last section, the text ceases to be autobiography and refers to the kings of Mesopotamia, Abraham's rescue of Lot, Abraham's meeting with Melchizedek and the King of Sodom, and lastly, the promise of an heir. The autobiographical section inserts several extra-biblical elements and follows the biblical text very closely in the manner of a targumic translation.

Written in Aramaic, probably in the first half of the 2nd cent. BCE, this work is a pre-Qumran composition and comes from the same circles as did *Jubilees* and, later, the Qumran community.

1.2. The outline of the book of the *Assumption* (or *Testament*) *of Moses* in effect writes Moses' farewell speech (Dt 31-34) afresh, in apocalyptic terms. It is probable that the author knew the book of Daniel but it is not possible to prove that he depended on it. In its original version, it was most certainly a hasidic or proto-Essene work, written in a situation similar to the book of Daniel, at the time of persecution by Antiochus IV. It provides a global vision of the future history of Israel and ends with an apocalypse (Tromp, cf. p. 400).

1.3. The book of the *Life of Adam and Eve* (in Latin) or the *Apocalypse of Moses* (in Greek) depicts Adam as a sinner and an extremist. Some themes are only tangential to the biblical text: Adam and Eve's repentance and the fall of Satan (*Life* 1-17), Adam's ascent to paradise (*Life* 25-29), the death and burial of Adam and Eve (*ApMoses* 31-43), etc. Other themes are typical of the haggadic midrash on Gn 1-5.

1.4. The *Testament of Abraham* includes no material at all from the OT, apart from obvious references to the hero contained in Genesis. In fact, the work does not include a testament of the patriarch; the Bible makes no mention of Abraham having made a testament. The action takes place on Abraham's death-bed, but a description of the death scene is missing so that this work can correctly be attributed to the testament genre. It is not its literary form, but its content and relationship to the Testaments of Isaac and Jacob which give this work the appearance of a testament. On the other hand it has touches of humour and parody; it presents Abraham as a patriarch who refuses to die and whose excessive zeal in punishing sinners becomes a sin committed by the patriarch himself. The message to emerge from the work is that God prefers mercy to harshness, making no distinction between Jew and gentile.

1.5. The structure, characters and many details of the novel *Joseph and Aseneth* have been taken from Genesis, especially from the story of Joseph. However, the literary form of this work is closer to Greek and Latin novels. It has also been described as a Jewish wisdom novel in a tradition which includes works such as *Ahiqar*, Tobit and Dn 1-6. It should be noted that the vocabulary and expressions of this work have a parallel in the LXX version from which it evidently borrows. Literal quotations are rare and it would be interesting to know to what extent the divergences from the LXX text come from different text forms.

1.6 Among the texts from Qumran, the *Exhortation based on the Flood* (4Q370) uses the biblical account of the flood to elaborate a moralising instruction in sapiential style. It is not exactly a re-writing of the biblical text or even a true paraphrase of it. Instead it re-uses its contents for instructional purposes (C. Newsom).

1.7 The *Book of Noah* (1Q19 and 4Q534-536), was previously known only from references in the *Genesis Apocryphon*, *Jubilees* and *1 Enoch*, and so was probably written in the 3rd cent. BCE, apparently in Aramaic and probably in the same apocalyptic circles from which those works came. The reconstruction of this work is still quite hypothetical. It must have included traditions such as those which refer to the fall of the Watchers and the miraculous birth of Noah. Here, Lamech's doubts are resolved by Enoch, who foretells the boy's future; the parallel has often been noted between this tradition and the gospel account of Joseph's doubts about his paternity and of Jesus' future.

The story of Noah is clearly retold in the form of a sermon and refers in particular to his wisdom and knowledge of mysteries; it included an autobiographical account of his life before the flood, alluding to the Covenant after the flood and its stipulations such as the ban on blood. It ended with instructions given by Noah to his sons about the use of certain plants and the division of the earth among his descendants (on 1Q19, Milik *DJD* I; on 4Q534-536, García Martínez).

1.8. The *Apocryphon of Joseph* (2Q22 and 4Q371-373) contains narrative sections and hymns in the form of thanksgiving psalms. The protagonist seems to be Joseph, although David also features and possibly Pinhas. It alters biblical quotations or allusions to 1st person forms and to fit new historical circumstances. The longest copy preserved, 4Q372, from the second half of the 1st cent. BCE, refers to Jerusalem in ruins, to the building of a «holy place» on a high mountain and to the tribes of Levi, Judah and Benjamin, referring to the exile of the Northern tribes, and to the anti-Samaritan disputes of the Maccabaean period (on 2Q22, Baillet *DJD* III; on 4Q371-373, Schuller).

1.9 The work with the title *Second Exodus* (4Q462) seems to refer to a second exile still experienced by the Jewish people, in spite of «a time of light which has already arrived». It predicts, perhaps, the return of the diaspora and the restoration of Jerusalem (M.S. Smith).

The *Biblical Antiquities* (by Pseudo-Philo) could also belong to this group. It re-writes the Pentateuch but is modelled on the history of Chronicles and continues to the period of Saul's death. For these two reasons it will be discussed later as one of the writings based on biblical historical works (paragraph 3., p.190).

Reference can also be made here to *6QGenesis* (6Q19; Baillet *DJD* III), and *4QReworked Pentateuch* (4Q158; Allegro *DJD* V). Part of the second work is halakhic in content so that it really belongs to the following group.

2.   Halakhic Writings Based on the Books of the Torah: *Temple Scroll*, *Pseudo-Moses* and *Ordinances*

2.1. The *Temple Scroll* (11QTemple^ab = 11Q19 and 11Q20) was probably composed during the reign of John Hyrcanus (135-104). The core document of the book begins with a description of the Temple, followed by a collection of laws relating to its construction (2:1-13:8 + 30:3-47:18) and assorted legal material which adapts the corresponding text of Dt 12-22(51:11-56:21 + 60:1-66:17). A redactor added the calendar of feasts to 13:9-30:2 and the legislation on ritual purity to 48:1-51:10. All these sections, as well as the «Torah of the king» (57-59) were originally separate documents (Willson-

Wills). Wise has made an important study of the sources and redaction of this work, the aim of which was to provide a new Deuteronomy for eschatological times.

The *Temple Scroll* was possibly written by the founder of the Essene sect, who had taken refuge in Qumran. They considered this book to form an integral part of the Torah. Among the members of the group, this Essene Torah seems to have been regarded as comparable to the traditional Torah of the rabbis. The author took complete sections from the Pentateuch, changed other sections to harmonise them with related passages and added new ones known through traditions not included in the rabbinic Torah. The *Temple Scroll* is an additional Torah as valid as the one contained in the Pentateuch (Yadin)

After comparing the *Temple Scroll* with other books such as *Jubilees*, *Enoch*, the *Damascus Document* and rabbinic *halakhah*, Wacholder goes further in his conclusions. He considers that the author of the *Temple Scroll* was not a mere compiler or editor but intended nothing less than «replacing» the Mosaic Torah with this Qumran Torah.

Some facts suggest that the Essene community of Qumran accorded this book «quasi-canonical» status.

The *Temple Scroll* replaces the *Tetragrammaton* and references to Yahweh in the third person with direct speech in the first person, «I». Even laws which have no equivalent at all in the Pentateuch and are only transmitted by the *Temple Scroll* are placed in Yahweh's own mouth, in the first person. In this way, the book is hinting that this Torah comes directly from Yahweh and does not need the mediation of Moses as was the case in the traditional Torah.

In the non-biblical manuscripts from the Dead Sea, the *Tetragrammaton* is generally written in palaeo-Hebrew characters while the biblical text is in the square script. In the biblical manuscripts from Qumran, however, the *Tetragrammaton* is written in the same square script as the rest of the text. This is the system followed in the *Temple Scroll*, which seems to indicate that this text was considered by the Essenes as a biblical or canonical manuscript.

The number of copies found in Qumran (11QTemple[ab], 4QTemple[ab]) and above all the great size of the Scroll (11QTemple[a]) may point in the same direction.

The author of this book, and in particular, of the part concerning the building of the Temple, knew of the existence of a *Temple Scroll*, as named in the *Samuel Midrash* and to which 1 Chr 28:11-19 refers. Whether it was because he considered himself inspired by God or because he knew an earlier tradition, the author of the *Temple Scroll* believed that his book preserved that part of the Torah missing from the traditional Pentateuch and to which reference is made in the passage from 1 Chronicles cited.

The «*Torah of the King*» contained in the Temple Scroll could also correspond to another book alluded to in the Bible and which has not reached us (Dt 17:18; 1 Sm 10:25).

Accepting that *Temple Scroll* is a book of the Torah (*Sefer Torah*), H. Stegemann wonders whether it is the particular and specific Torah of the Essene community of Qumran.

This supposed «Essene» Torah is not mentioned in other Essene writings of the Qumran community, but they frequently quote the Pentateuch as the only Torah. There are clear differences between the *Temple Scroll* and the Essene writings in matters relating to the legislation and construction of the Temple, as well as in the style and language used. In fact, there are only two real copies of the *Temple Scroll*, both of which come from Cave 11.

In Stegemann's opinion, the *Temple Scroll* comprises a very ancient expanded form of the Torah, a sort of sixth book added to the Pentateuch. This expanded form of the Torah was made before the text of the Pentateuch was fixed. It was composed as a reaction to the canonisation of the Pentateuch by Ezra. In 458 BCE, Ezra established a «shortened» Pentateuch imported from Mesopotamia as the Torah from Sinai, excluding traditions and developments of Palestinian «priestly» extraction, precisely those collected in the *Temple Scroll* (the language and style of the *Temple Scroll* are close to those of the Chronicler's work, which is of priestly origin). The edition of this sixth book of the Torah represents the final phase in the formation of Scripture as far as the Torah is concerned. Its editor did not intend to replace the existing Torah but to complete it with a sixth book, with an authority comparable to that of the remaining books of the Torah. Throughout the second Temple period, from the end of the 5th cent. BCE up to the end of the 4th or even the 3rd BCE, at least some priestly families from Jerusalem granted this book the standing of «Torah from Sinai», communicated directly by Yahweh, and used its text to complete and interpret the Torah of the Pentateuch.

J. Maier occupies a position midway between those of Yadin and Stegemann: the final redaction of the work is Qumranic, the traditions give the impression of being ancient.

2.2. The work known as *4QApocryphon of Moses* (1Q 29, 4Q375-376) which is definitely earlier than the formation of Essenism, collects and expands on legal texts from the Torah. Among other questions it deals with the criteria for distinguishing between true and false prophets. Doubts in this respect have to be resolved by means of an expiation ritual carried out by the High Priest. When «the stone of the left side which is at its left side will shine in the eyes of all the assembly» (4Q376, II,1; *DSST*, 279), it means that the prophecy is true. The brilliance of the twelve precious stones of the left pectoral also denotes the happy outcome of the defensive war. The priestly vestment is described in Exodus 28, the text on which the work is based. Josephus refers to the oracular function of the precious stones (*Antiquities* 3,8,9); he is certainly referring to the profanation of the temple in 167 BCE, and states that the precious stones had stopped shining for the last 200 years and that at the same time oracles had ceased (Strugnell).

2.3. To this group also belongs *4QOrdinances*ᵃ (4Q159), a halakhic text which elaborates on the biblical laws of Deuteronomy 23:25-26; Exodus 30:12; Leviticus 25:42; Deuteronomy 22:5 and 22:13-14. A second manuscript, *4QOrdinances*ᵇ (4Q153) is another copy of the same work, related to *4QHalakha*ᵃ and *4QHalakhic Letter* (4QMMT). The preserved fragments refer to the increase in taxes for the Temple in the time of Ezra (Neh 10:33-34). It lays down that the payment of half a *shekel*, as prescribed in Exodus 30:11-16 and 38:26, has to be effective only once in a lifetime. It is difficult to determine the circumstances to which the other regulations of this work refer. Its content, style and details suggest that the circumstances must have been before the formation of the Essene movement (Allegro *DJD* v; Baillet *DJD* vii).

3.   Narratives Based on Biblical Historical Works: *1 Ezra, Biblical Antiquities, Martyrdom of Isaiah, Paralipomena of Jeremiah, Pseudo-Joshua, Visions of Samuel, Apocryphon of Samuel-Kings, Pseudo-Jeremiah*

This group incorporates works which imitate the deuteronomist's and chronicler's historical works, such as *1 Ezra* (Greek), the *Biblical Antiquities*, the *Martyrdom of Isaiah* and the *Paralipomena of Jeremiah*. The last two refer to prophets. *Jewish Antiquities* by Josephus should also be associated with this type of writing.

3.1. Modern editions of the LXX include the work known as *1 Ezra* (Ezra A), the Old Latin version of which appears in the Sixtus-Clementine Vulgate as *3 Esdras*. Its text corresponds to 2 Chr 35-36, followed by the canonical book of Ezra (in a different order) and chaps. 7-8 of Nehemiah. Josephus followed this text and the early Fathers undoubtedly accepted it as canonical. *1 Ezra* is not a free version of the MT as used to be thought. Today it is rather thought to be the original Greek version of a Hebrew edition of the books Ezra-Nehemiah, different from the text transmitted by MT (for similar editorial phenomena, cf. pp. 321-322). Apart from the account in 3:1-5:6 on the three Jewish pages in the Persian court of Darius, it contains hardly anything not also found in the books of Ezra-Nehemiah according to the MT. The story about the triumph of a Jewish wise man at court has a parallel in Dn 1-6.

3.2. The book of *Biblical Antiquities* by Pseudo-Philo, written towards 70 CE or shortly before this date, is a kind of haggadic midrash on events from the Pentateuch and the historical books, up to the episode of Saul's death. It also provides isolated references to the books of Isaiah, Jeremiah and the Psalms. It contains typical interpretative expansions, adding details not known in the biblical text, for example, the name of Jephte's daughter, Seila (Jgs 11:30-40) and the text of the lament she utters (cf. 40:5).

Pseudo-Philo could have used the book of Chronicles as a model, the influence of which is evident in the mix of genealogies, short accounts, speeches, prayers and supplements to biblical narratives, as well as an interest in anything connected with figures and numbers. It shows affinities with *4 Esdras* and *2 Baruch*, both in language and in common apocalyptic motifs. However, in *Biblical Antiquities*, a whole series of ideas present in these two books is missing, together with the historical pattern of the four empires and the idea of a messianic kingdom which was to last for a specified time.

3.3. The *Marytrdom of Isaiah* is the first part of the book of the *Ascension of Isaiah* (1:1-3:12 and 5:1-15). It is also the most ancient material from that book. It is based on 2 Kgs 20:16-21:18 and 2 Chr 32:32-33:20. In the form of a legend, it tells of the martyrdom of Isaiah at the hands of Manasseh and shows similarities with the story of the Teacher of Righteousness. Its origin is Qumranic (Flusser) or it is connected with a world of ideas similar to those expressed in the literature from Qumran (Nickelsburg).

3.4. The *Paralipomena of Jeremiah* has the same source as *2 Baruch*. This source rewrote the history of the final days of Jerusalem before the destruction of that city in 587.

3.5. The writing known as *Pseudo-Joshua (Psalms of Joshua*; 4Q378-379), probably composed in the first half of the 2nd cent. BCE, re-models Joshua using features taken from Moses. The narrative material preserved is sparse, but instead there are plenty of speeches, prayers, exhortations, curses, etc. 4Q387 definitely belongs to the start of the composition, with allusions to the death of Moses and the mourning for him, to the transfer of powers to Joshua and to the speech on entry to the promised land. 4Q388 reproduces the final section of the work, which re-tells the crossing of the Jordan, setting it in one of the jubilee years in agreement with the calendar known from *Jubilees*. This fact and the authority enjoyed by this composition, which is cited in 4Q175 alongside the biblical books of Numbers and Deuteronomy, makes it likely that the work came from the circles in which the Qumran Community originated (C. Newsom).

3.6. The *Visions of Samuel* (4Q160), from the end of the 2nd cent. BCE, inserts a dialogue between Samuel and Eli and a prayer by Samuel (Allegro, *DJD* v; Strugnell).

3.7. The *Apocryphon on Samuel-Kings* (6Q9) is a composition in Hebrew inspired by the accounts in Samuel-Kings and Chronicles (M. Baillet *DJD* III).

3.8. Here, reference must be made also to the work entitled *Pseudo-Jeremiah* (4Q385b, 4Q387b, 4Q389a), an apocryphal composition which contained stories, speeches and dialogues etc., based on the character of Jeremiah. The longest and best preserved copy, 4Q385b, describes Jeremiah addressing the exiles in Babylona (a tradition included in the *Paralipomena of Jeremiah* and in *2 Baruch*) and the exiles in Egypt, an exile he shares (Dimant).

4.   Para-biblical Writings Based on Hymnal Literature: *Apocryphal Psalms* and *Non-canonical Psalms, Hōdāyôt*, Liturgical Texts from Qumran, *Psalms of Solomon, Prayer of Manasseh*

Qumran has provided manuscripts of *Apocryphal Psalms* and *Non-canonical Psalms*, the Qumranic work *Hōdāyôt* and a whole series of liturgical texts.

4.1. *Apocryphal Psalms* are included in three manuscripts of biblical Psalms (4QPsalms^f = 4Q88, 11QPsalm^{a-b} = 11Q5-6). Some were known from the Greek Psalter (Ps 151) or the Syriac Psalter (Psalms 151, 154 and 155). Among them are a hymn to Zion, very like the poems of Is 54; 60; 62 and 66:10-11, a poem which is both an individual lamentation and a thanksgiving, known as Psalm 155 in the Syriac tradition, a short hymn to the Creator with an ending derived from Jr 10:12-13, part of an eschatological hymn and the ending to a composition praising Judah.

These manuscripts had been considered as real biblical manuscripts, which suggests that the sequence, number and identification of the canonical psalms had not yet been definitively established in the Qumran period. They have also been considered to be texts for liturgical use or as library editions (cf. p. 289; J.A. Sanders).

4.2. The remains of one or two collections of *Non-canonical Psalms* have been preserved in two manuscripts (4QNoncanonical Psalms, 4Q380-381), which consistently use biblical motifs and expressions, with wisdom influences, in a form very like the apocryphal psalms included in biblical psalters (Schuller).

4.3. The *Hōdāyôt* or 'Thanksgiving Hymns' (1QH[ab], 1Q35; 4QH[a-f], 4Q427-432) comprise a work of Qumranic character and origin, clearly inspired by biblical language. It has been suggested that the author of these hymns was the Teacher of Righteousness (Sukenik). The «I» speaking in these hymns is someone very aware of his mission («the bearer of the revelation»). In the other hymns, the «I» is less defined and could refer to any member of the community. These hymns are set in the cult of the community, either the daily liturgy or during initiation rites and the annual renewal of the covenant, although it could well be intended for teaching. No precise date can be assigned to these Qumran hymns.

4.4. The liturgical texts from Qumran were intended for use in rituals celebrated daily or weekly or on designated feasts, with no connection with the sacrificial liturgy of the Temple in Jerusalem. Some of these texts, which predate the Qumran community, give information about liturgical practice before the institution of synagogues or at the start of that institution (*Daily Prayers, Festival Prayers, Words of the Luminaries*). Others come from the Qumran Community and throw light on its liturgy and theology (*Songs of the Sabbath Sacrifice*, Blessings and curses; Nitzan).

Daily Prayers (4Q503), recited in the morning and evening and on certain days, follow a lunar calendar, against the solar calendar advocated by *Jubilees* (Baillet *DJD* vii).

Festival Prayers (1Q34, 4Q507-509) were recited on festivals celebrated throughout the year. The Day of Atonement (the tenth of the seventh month) and the First Fruits (the fifteenth of the third month) are mentioned as well as others impossible to identify (Milik *DJD* i; Baillet *DJD* vii).

«*Words of the Luminaries*» (4QDibHam[a-c], 4Q504-506), a title contained in the work. They all have the same structure: a title specifying the day of the week on which each prayer is to be recited, an introductory formula («Remember, Lord», «Praise...»), a prologue which alludes to sacred history, the petition and the reason why it should be heard, a thanksgiving blessing and the exclamation «Amen. Amen». It is possible to see some sort of sequence in the references to sacred history from one weekday to the next: the creation and Adam's sin (Sunday), the trek through the desert (Tuesday), the Sinai covenant (Wednesday), the election of Israel and the glory of Jerusalem during the period of David (Thursday), the exile and restoration (Friday).

These prayers are like the 'entreaties'(*taanûn*) of the later synagogue liturgy (Baillet *DJD* VII).

Songs of the Sabbath Sacrifice, (*Širim ʿOlot ha-šabbat* = 4QShirShabb^{a-h}, 4Q400-407; 11QShirShabb = 11Q17; Masada ShirShabb.). This work, also known as *Angelic Liturgy*, is composed of 13 songs recited on 13 consecutive sabbaths. They refer to the establishment and functions of the angelic priesthood (1st song), its relationships to the earthly priesthood (2nd), Melchizedek among the heavenly priests (badly preserved text, 3rd and 4th), the eschatological war (5th), the psalms of the seven angelic princes and their blessings, comprising seven wonderful words (6th). The song of the sabbath, the 7th and the centre of the circle, includes the praise offered by the components of the heavenly temple (foundations, walls, doors, decorations, etc., including the interior of the sanctuary and the footstool of the divine throne), culminating in the praise of the divine chariot. The songs of the following sabbaths contain the psalms of the seven angelic assistant chiefs or second priests serving in the seven heavenly sanctuaries (8th), praise of all the elements of the heavenly temple considered as angelic creatures (9th), reaching the veil of the sanctuary (10th), the Holy of Holies (11th) and describing the apparition of the divine chariot as a sort of heavenly liturgy, ending with the sacrifices offered by the angelic priests (Newson). Possibly this cycle of 13 songs was repeated four times a year, in each of the four *těqûfah*.

Rule of the Blessings (1Q28b), preserved as an appendix to the *Community Rule* and the *Rule of the Congregation*. The blessings, modelled on the priestly blessing of Nm 6:22-26 (cf. p. 452), were intended for the messianic and eschatological era (Milik *DJD* I).

Blessings (4QBerakhot = 4Q280, 4Q286-287), used in the ceremony of covenant renewal during the feast of Pentecost in the third month of the year, similar in many respects to the *Songs for the Sabbath Sacrifice* (Nitzan).

Here can be mentioned texts from Qumran with prayers and exorcisms, all of a marked religious nature, except for the last: *Songs of the Sage* (4Q510-511), *Apocryphal Psalms* (11QPsAp^a, 11Q11), *Pseudepigraphic Work* (4Q460).

Lastly, the *Apocryphal Lamentations* (4Q179 and 4Q501) represent texts of great beauty, inspired by the biblical Lamentations, on the destruction of Jerusalem and the fate of the people.

Among the hymnal elaborations there are two other works of pseudepigraphic literature:

4.5. The *Psalms of Solomon* appeared in a late period in some Christian lists of the OT canon. It comprises a didactic or polemic work, written in Jerusalem in the mid-1st cent. BCE. The original language was Hebrew although only the Greek translation has been preserved. It includes eighteen psalms.

4.6. The *Prayer of Manasseh* affects to give the text of the prayer mentioned in 2 Chr 33:11-13. It is significant that some Latin Bibles place this text in precisely that position. It is a pentitential psalm.

Reference can also be made in this group to the *Hellenistic synagogal prayers* and *the Odes of Solomon*.

5.   Parabiblical Writings from Qumran Based on Wisdom Literature

Several badly preserved poetic texts from Qumran of a wisdom type continue the tradition of the wise men of the OT: *Wiles of the Wicked Woman* (4Q184), an allegorical poem about Need personified as a woman, inspired by the poem on the 'Foolish Woman' of Pr 7; *Sapiential Work* (4Q185), a recommendation to look for Wisdom or the Torah, surely referring more to the former; *Words of the Sage to the Sons of Dawn* (4Q298); *Sapiential Work* (4Q413); *Sapiential Work* A, B and C (4Q416-418, 4Q419 and 4Q424); *Mysteries* (1Q27, 4Q299-301).

An important text is called *Messianic Apocalypse* (4Q521), inspired by Ps 146 and Is 61:1. It establishes a connection between the resurrection of the just and the announcement of the good news which goes further than the biblical texts in the reply by Jesus to John the Baptist about the signs of the Messiah's arrival, with a parallel only in the NT (Mt 11:4-5 and Lk 7:22-23). This writing presents in an eschatological context the image of the bridge over the abyss, which is Iranian in origin, elaborated in later Muslim tradition (Puech).

Another very important text is the one called *Beatitudes* (4Q525), with strong biblical reminiscences of Proverbs, Qoheleth and Ben Sira (14,20-15,1). It is a clear forerunner to the gospel 'Beatitudes', although the emphasis is sapiential rather than eschatological (Puech).

6.   Apocalyptic Type Parabiblical Writings: *Jubilees, Book of the Watchers (1 Enoch 1-36), Astronomical Book, Book of Giants, Pseudo-Ezekiel, Pseudo-Daniel, New Jerusalem, 4 Esdras, 2 Baruch* and *3 Baruch*, 'Book of the Patriarchs'

The manuscripts found in the Qumran caves have helped to establish a series of facts relating to the origins of apocalyptic in a definitive way. Today it is possible to state that by the 3rd cent. BCE, a tradition of apocalyptic ideas already existed. The apocalyptic social movement is shown to be flourishing, from the creation of several apocalypses. The most outstanding indication of this is the fact that the most authorised and representative work of this movement, the book of Daniel, succeeded in entering the biblical canon at a time when it was virtually already complete.

Four periods can be distinguished in the history of Jewish apocalyptic (Sacchi):

– up to 200 BCE (*Book of the Watchers = 1 Enoch* 1-37, and *Astronomical book = 1 Enoch* 72-82),

– from 200 to 100 BCE (*Book of Dreams = 1 Enoch* 83-90, contemporary with *Daniel*),

– from 100 BCE to 50 CE (*Epistle of Enoch = 1 Enoch* 91-105, *Book of Parables = 1 Enoch* 38-71 and *Ascension of Moses*), and
– from 50 CE to 120 (*Apocalypse of Zephaniah, Syriac Apocalypse of Baruch* and *4 Esdras*).

There are two types of apocalypse, one cosmic and the other historical. The first is older than the second. As yet, apocalypses of the cosmic type do not show eschatalogical hope and the conception of history characteristic of historical apocalypses.

Known *cosmic apocalypses* are the Book of Watchers, the Astronomical Book and the book of Parables contained in *1 Enoch* as well as the books *2 Enoch, 3 Baruch, Testament of Abraham, Testament of Levi, Apocalypse of Zephaniah* and some works unknown until the discovery of the Dead Sea Scrolls, such as *4QVisions of Amram* and *4QNew Jerusalem*.

The *historical apocalypses* which have reached us are the canonical book of Daniel, the *Apocalypse of the Animals* (*1 Enoch* 85-90), the *Apocalypse of Weeks* (*1 Enoch* 93; 91:11-19), *4 Ezra, 2 Baruch, Jubilees* and other works, also previously unknown: *4QPseudo-Daniel, 4Q246, 4QPseudo-Ezekiel* (Stone).

In the 1st cent. BCE, both types of apocalypse are already combined in longer compositions which include both genres. For example, 4QEn^c is a collection of various Enochian traditions (*Book of the Watchers, Book of Giants, Book of Dreams*, and the *Epistle of Enoch*) which later were formed into the Book of Enoch as it has reached us in the Ethiopic version.

The oldest apocalypses are earlier than the Hellenistic crisis and the Maccabaean wars. Accordingly, it cannot be said that the type of the oldest apocalyptic is the result of a reaction against Hellenism. The apocalyptic literary genre, the Apocalypse, is possibly the only new genre created in this final biblical period.

The books of *1 Enoch, 4 Ezra, 2 Baruch* and *3 Baruch* comprise true interpretations of biblical narratives, related anew and incorporating new elements frequently based on already existing traditions or on others imagined by the author.

Apocalyptic literature revolves round the problem of evil around which many others are developed: hope in a sudden change, the end depicted as a cosmic catastrophe (pessimism), the relationship between the last times and the previous history of the cosmos and of mankind (determinism), the dependence of earthly history on the afterlife by means of an intermediate world, good and evil angelic beings, the restoration of a remnant of the people after the catastrophe (as yet not a universalist vision), the divide between this evil world and the good future (dualism), an intermediary with royal functions as bringing about future salvation (messianism), and «glory» as the final stage of the merging of the earthly and heavenly spheres. This whole gamut of elements gave rise to apocalypic and helped it flourish (Koch).

6.1. The most typical work among the apocalyptic type parabiblical texts is the book of *Jubilees*. The *Book of Watchers*, the *Astronomical Book* and the *Book of Giants* also belong to this group, as do other works from Qumran:

Pseudo-Ezekiel, Pseudo-Daniel, New Jerusalem. Important works are *4 Esdras, 2 Baruch* and *3 Baruch*. Lastly, reference should be made to the 'Book of the Patriarchs'.

The book of *Jubilees* is probably the oldest work of the genre. The only complete text to reach us is the Ethiopic version. It was made from a Greek translation and reproduces the original Hebrew very closely (VanderKam).

The work adapts and applies to the present the narratives of Genesis and Exodus (up to chap. 12). It also uses expressions and information taken from the books of Kings, Isaiah, Jeremiah, Ezekiel and some Minor Prophets, Psalms, Chronicles and Ezra-Nehemiah. The episode of Abraham's temptations (chaps. 17f.) elaborates on a motif also found in the book of Job. *Jubilees* also refers to older Enochian writings such as the books *of the Luminaries, of the Watchers, of Dreams,* and possibly also to the *Epistle of Enoch.*

The title '(The Book of) Jubilees', emphasises the peculiar division of history into periods of 49 years (7 weeks of 7 years) to which are assigned the events that took place in each jubilee. It advocates a 364-day calendar and is concerned with the correct observance of feasts which always fall on the same days of the week, though never on the feast of the sabbath. The book claims to be a 'new Torah' revealed to Moses on Sinai, which supplements what was revealed 'in the book of the first Torah which I wrote for you' (6:22). The *halakhah* characteristic of *Jubilees* differs on many points from traditional pharisee *halakhah* and instead corresponds substantially to the *halakhah* of other Qumran writings. The worlds of angels and demons appear to be very hierarchical, in accordance with a strong dualistic view which also affects the world of human beings. The hostility between Israel and the nations is also what separates angels from demons. All this is in agreement with the typical characteristics of the Essene writings from Qumran and the formation period of the Community before it broke completely with the Temple of Jerusalem.

The surprising number of copies of this book found in the Qumran library shows the importance this community attributed to that work. There are 12 copies, of which the oldest comes from a date around 100 BCE (according to new identifications proposed by M. Kister). The Ethiopic version comprises the only complete text preserved. It was made from a Greek translation and reproduces the Hebrew original very faithfully (VanderKam).

6.2. The *Books of Enoch* have acquired new importance thanks to the discovery of several copies of the Aramaic original in Cave 4. *1 Enoch*, already known before the Qumran finds, actually comprises five separate books: the *Book of the Watchers* (*1 Enoch* 1-36), the *Book of the Parables* (37-71), the *Astronomical Book* (72-82), the *Book of Dreams* (83-90) and the *Epistle of Enoch* (91-105). The last book includes the 'Apocalypse of Weeks' (chaps. 91-93). Two appendices follow, one from the *Book of Noah* (*1 Enoch* 106-107) and the other an extract from 'another book written by Enoch' which is a conclusion of the complete work (*1 Enoch* 108).

The *Book of Watchers* (*1 Enoch* 1-36) is an expansion of Gn 6:1-4. The oldest part of this section is found in chaps. 6-11 in which Enoch is not yet mentioned. The fact that the *Book of Watchers* was known by the author of

Jubilees proves that its origin is earlier than the second half of 2nd cent. BCE. The spelling of the manuscripts compels composition to be dated to the end of the 3rd cent. BCE (Milik). This fact proves that cosmic type apocalypses are earlier than those of historic type and that in general, apocalyptic is earlier than and therefore independent of the Hellenistic crisis.

6.3. The *Astronomical Book* or *Book of the Courses of the Heavenly Luminaries* (*1 Enoch* 72-82) is the oldest part of *1 Enoch*. It mixes astronomical and geographical elements with apocalyptic elements of a moral nature. This part, which was already in circulation at least towards the end of the 3rd cent. BCE, is included in chaps. 72-78; 82:9-20 and 82:1-8. The astronomical and geographical elements go back to traditions of Mesopotamian origin and are now found inserted in the narrative context of a revelation; Enoch transmits to his son Methuselah the revelations received from Uriel concerning the sun, the moon, the stars, the winds, the cardinal points and the heavenly sphere. The oldest part includes a calendar of 364 days (VanderKam). Even if this oldest section cannot yet be classed as a true apocalypse, it contains enough elements of apocalyptic character for it to become an authentic apocalypse, by the later addition of chaps. 80-81.

The *Book of Dreams* (*1 Enoch* 83-90) was composed in the period between the beginning of the Maccabeean wars and the death of Judas Maccabeus. It had its origin in Hasidic or pietistic circles, partisans of the Maccabaean revolt, or perhaps comes from the Qumran group, to the formation of which 90:6-7 alludes (Dimant). It relates two dreams or visions of Enoch: the first, not preserved, refers to the flood; the second tells the history of mankind from the first man up to the last times, using representations and symbols of animals.

The seventy periods into which the *Book of Dreams* divides history are changed into a cycle of ten «weeks of years» in the *Epistle of Enoch* (*1 Enoch* 91-105). The first seven weeks refer to the history of mankind and the last three to the eschatological period. This scheme combines two others, one of 70 multiplied by 7 and the other of 10 multiplied by 49, both known from unpublished fragments from Qumran. All this makes up the *Apocalypse of Weeks* (chaps. 91-93), a work from a period before the Hellenistic crisis, like those indicated earlier.

So then, we have a corpus of Enochian writings, possibly composed half a century before the Maccabaean revolt and before the canonical apocalypse of Daniel. These are apocalypses which can be considered the oldest, the *Astronomical book* and the *Book of Watchers* and the *Apocalypse of Weeks*, which makes no allusion to the desecration of the Temple by Antiochus Epiphanes. This apocalypse was inserted into the *Epistle of Enoch* and could have formed part of it from the beginning. Given its polemical character against idolatry, the same Epistle most probably comes from a period earlier than the Maccabaean crisis.

6.4. The existence of a *Book of the Giants* had been known from indirect sources. The text found in Turfan (Iran) contains translations of a «Book of the Giants» written by Mani, inspired by a lost apocryphal book. These Manichaean texts allow us to assign four or five manuscripts found in Qumran Cave 4 (4Q203 and 4Q530-533) to this apocryphal work, as well as another four previously published as copies of unidentified works (1Q23, 1Q24, 2Q26, 6Q8; Milik).

The work is about the «giants» who, according to Gn 6:1-4, were born from the union of the angels with the daughters of men and survived the Flood. They were as tall as the cedars of Lebanon, had wings to fly with, were invisible like the angels and tempted humans to do evil. The book gives names to the most famous of them. The members of the Essene community had to keep these names secret, for merely to know them meant having control over them. The gift of healing, highly appreciated among the Essenes, consisted in the power to conjure the demons which caused illnesses. The *Book of the Giants* is important for understanding the accounts of the expulsion of demons by Jesus as well as the reticence shown by some NT texts towards the world of angels (cf. 1 Corinthians 6:3; 11:10).

The complete work must have included a summary of the *Book of Watchers* and established in detail the ancestry of the giants. It differentiated between the punishment inflicted on Azazel from the one reserved for Semihaza. It recounted some of the giants' actions before their imprisonment and the discussions between Semihaza and the imprisoned giants. Also included were the two dreams of the giants 'Ohyah and Hayhah, to interpret which required a double embassy of Mahaway to Enoch in order to demand its interpretation. The Manichaean work contained information not referred to in the Aramaic fragment from Qumran, such as references to the battles between the giant 'Ohyah and the monster Leviathan and Mahaway, and to other combats between giants, the separation of men from giants, the chaining up of men in cities reserved for them and the final destruction of the giants by the angels (Milik, Reeves, García Martínez).

6.5. The work known as *Pseudo-Ezekiel* (4Q385-388), written in Hebrew, could have come from the Essene period, but possibly it has to be dated towards the middle of 2nd cent. BCE. Within the framework of an autobiography it collects Ezekiel's visions of a whole panorama of sacred history, as in other apocalypses. The most noticeable of these visions are those of the divine chariot (Ez 10) and of the bones brought to life again (Ez 37). The visions are explained within the framework of dialogues between God and the prophet, like those of later apocalypses (*4 Esdras* and *2 Baruch*). The work poses the question of how and when the resurrection of the just will occur (Strugnell, Dimant).

6.6. *Pseudo-Daniel* (4Q243-245) preserved in Aramaic. Daniel reads out to the King and his courtiers an ancient document or revealed book which records history from the earliest times to the period of Daniel, and how long the Greek kingdoms will last. The last part, which is eschatological, proclaims the reunion of the elect and the destruction of enemies (Eisenman - Wise).

6.7. The work, written in Aramaic and known as *New Jerusalem* (1Q32, 2Q24, 4Q554, 4Q554a, 4Q555, 5Q15, 11Q18) is based on chaps. 40-48 of Ezekiel. The author receives a revelation; he is shown a book with the plans of the future Jerusalem. This work has similarities with the *Temple Scroll*, allowing its origin to be placed within the founding circles of the Qumran community. This apocalypse lies midway between the description of a future Jerusalem as in the book of Ezekiel and the heavenly Jerusalem as described in the NT Apocalypse. The description of the new Jerusalem as a city prepared by God in heaven is comparable to the one in in NT Apocalypse (chap. 21), though the author neither used nor knew the document found in Qumran, for it says it did not see a temple in the new city (21,22), whereas the description of the Temple forms a substantial part of the Qumran text, as also does the text of Ezekiel (Baillet *DJD* III; Milik *DJD* III; García Martínez).

6.8. *4 Ezra*, known in the Vulgate as 4 Esdras, has only been preserved in a Latin version. The Hebrew or Aramaic original has been lost, as has the Greek version. The work comprises three separate sections. The first (1-2) and the third (15-16) are Christian works. The second (3-14) is the *Apocalypse of Ezra*, generally known as 4 Esdras. It is a Jewish work from 90-120 CE. It contains six scenes with dialogues and visions. The sixth vision (chap. 13) has similarities with the description of the Son of Man in 1 Enoch. In the seventh vision (chap. 14), Ezra is told to write down the 24 books of Writing and the 70 hidden books, after which Ezra is taken up to heaven.

6.9. The pseudepigraphical tradition under Baruch's name includes two very important works.

The work known as *2 Baruch* or *Syriac Apocalypse of Baruch*, was known by means of a single manuscript of the Syriac version made from a lost Greek translation. Bogaert considers the original language to have been Greek. It comprises a Jewish apocalyptic composed between 95 and 120 CE. The letter to the exiles incorporated in chaps. 78-87 acquired canonical status among Syrian Christians; this explains why 36 copies have been preserved.

4 Ezra and *2 Baruch* provide us with the Jewish reaction to the capture of Jerusalem by the Romans, just as the Apocalypse represents Christian reaction to the same events. *4 Esdras* (3:1-2) uses the framework of the destruction of Jerusalem by the Babylonians to refer to the destruction of the city at the hands of the Romans. The same happens in *2 Baruch* 6:1-2.

The work called *3 Baruch* or *Greek Apocalypse of Baruch*, was composed in Greek, perhaps in Egypt, between 70 and 150 CE. Later, several Christian interpolations were inserted in the text. It shows similarities with *2 Enoch* and *Paralipomena of Jeremiah*.

6.10. The «Books of the Patriarchs» form a special genre within para-biblical literature.

These writings have been preserved only in fragments, mostly in Aramaic, even in the case of the works called *Visions of Jacob* and *Visions of 'Amram*. Their origin is earlier than the setting up of the Qumran community, although it is not possible to determine precisely the date of composition or the original setting. Apart, from the case of the *Visions of 'Amram* perhaps, their authorship cannot be ascribed to the Qumran community (Milik 1978).

Visions of Jacob (4Q537) describes a vision in which an angel shows Jacob (or Levi) the heavenly tablets foretelling his future and containing the ban on building an altar at Bethel. Jacob (or Levi) speaks to his sons in the form of a 'testament', telling them the future and warning them to keep on the right path.

The *Aramaic Testament of Judah* ((?); 3Q7, 4Q538), from the middle of the 1st cent. BCE, narrates Joseph's meeting with his brothers, using the first person (perhaps in the mouth of Judah or Benjamin) It is not a 'testament', but a narrative based on the biblical account (Baillet *DJD* III; Milik).

In the *Aramaic Testament of Joseph* (4Q539), Joseph speaks in the first person to his descendants and tells them about an event also known in the *Testament of Joseph* (15-16; Milik).

The *Aramaic Testament of Levi* (1Q21, 4Q213-214, 4Q540-541) also comes from the priestly circles from which the Qumran group was to emerge later. Levi counsels his descendants, telling them about his visions and prayers (Stone-Greenfield, Puech).

The *Aramaic Testament of Qahat* (4Q542) also comes from the same pre-Qumran circles mentioned earlier. It includes the farewell address by Levi, son of Qahat, to his son 'Amram and his descendants. It stresses the importance of the levitical line to which the care of the ancient writings has been entrusted. It exhibits dualistic features ('light-darkness') similar to those which also mark the *Visions of 'Amram* and the *Aramaic Testament of Levi* (Puech).

The *Visions of 'Amram* (4Q'Amram, 4Q543, 4Q544. 4Q545, 4Q548) describes 'Amram, Qahat's son and Aaron's father, on his death-bed just as he is remembering the past in the presence of his sons and is about to reveal a vision to them in which two angels fight over the patriarch's soul. The work goes back to at least the mid-second century BCE and comes from the same circles in which the Qumran community had its origin (Puech).

As far as the age of these works is concerned, then, most of the manuscripts found in the Qumran caves provide the text of biblical writings or of other works dating back to a period before Essenism or the first Essene period. In contrast, there are very few works of an Essene origin which are later than 160 BCE.

The parabiblical literature described above is completed by writings from a period earlier than the formation of the Essene community of Qumran. The importance and number of these works is noteworthy: 1. *Genesis Apocryphon* and *Pseudo-Joshua*; 2. *Temple Scroll*, *Pseudo-Moses* and *Ordinances*; 3. *Pseudo-Ezekiel* (?) and *New Jerusalem*; 4. *Jubilees*, *Astronomical Book* or *Book of the courses of the heavenly luminaries* (*1 Enoch* 72-82), *Book of the Watchers* (*1 Enoch* 1-36), *Book of the Giants*, *Visions of Jacob*, *Aramaic Testament of Judah*, *Aramaic Testament of Joseph*, *Aramaic Testament of Levi*, *Aramaic Testament of Qahat*, *Aramaic Testament of 'Amram*.

Literature earlier than Essenism and the Hellenistic crisis also includes other works of different genres which cannot be discussed here, such as *War Scroll* (1QM and copies from Cave 4), the *Songs of the Sabbath Sacrifice* (7 copies), the *Calendrical Document* (4QMishmarot, 4Q320-330), *Words of the Luminaries* (4Q504-506), various wisdom texts and other texts. Nor is it suitable to discuss here the exegetical literature of Qumran which features a special relationship with the biblical text and a strong apocalyptic bent.

The division established here between 'parabiblical literature' and 'exegetical literature' remains artificial and provisional. The second type is also an extended and elaborate form of biblical literature, with the specific purpose of commenting on and interpreting the biblical texts, not only to re-write and embellish them. Some of the works classified as «re-writings of the Bible» could belong to this group of «biblical commentaries», and vice versa.

1.   The *Pešārîm* of the Prophets and the Psalms

In the *pešārîm*, a form of interpretation called *pēšer* ('interpretation') and typical of Qumran, is developed. They provide a continuous commentary, section by section, of certain prophetic books and of the book of Psalms, which is usually eschatological and messianic in tone, and refers to the history of the Qumran community and of the last days. The interpretation and occasionally the explicit quotations of biblical texts are introduced by formulas which usually contain the word *pēšer*, such as «its interpretation concerns X, who/which ...».

The system of interpretation used consists in establishing some type of connection between the biblical quotation and the present day history of the Jewish community from which such works originated. So, for example, the Pešer on Habakkuk assumes that the oracles of that prophet speak about mysteries (1QpHab 7:1-2.4) which refer to the history of the community (2:9-10; 7:11) the interpretation of which had been revealed to the Teacher of Righteousness and his disciples (7:4-5; 2:7-10).

The Teacher of Righteousness is presented as the authorised interpreter of the Torah. Its meaning is what refers to the community founded by the Teacher of Righteousness. The *Pešārîm*, therefore, are related to the apocryphal writings *1 Enoch*, *4 Ezra* and *2 Baruch* which can be called «prophecy by interpretation» (Collins). The *Pešārîm* are closer to the apocalyptic genre of the book of Daniel than to the midrashic genre of later rabbinism. However, in comparison with interpretation by means of dreams as developed in the book of Daniel, the interpretation *pēšer* is very close to a continuous commentary on the biblical text.

Since the books of Isaiah and the Psalms are those most cited in the Qumran writings it is not surprising that a large number of copies of commentaries or *pĕšārîm* on those biblical books were written. Nor is it suprising that the book of Psalms was commented on as if it were a prophetic book once it is remembered that David was considered as its author and held to be a prophet (11QPs[a] 17,11).

Pešārîm of Isaiah: 3QpIs = 3Q4 (Baillet *DJD* III); 4QpIs[a] = 4Q161, applies Is 10:27 to the Prince of the Congregation in the context of the eschatological battle; 4QpIs[b] = 4Q162, Is 5:11-14 is applied to the enemies of the sect, the «insolent men who are in Jerusalem»; 4QpIs[c] = 4Q163, 4QpIs[d] = 4Q164, interprets Is 54:11-12 in connection with the Community, the New Jerusalem (Allegro *DJD* v).

Pešārîm of Hosea: 4QpHos[a] = 4Q166, an eschatological interpretation of Hos 2:5-11 4QpHos[b] = 4Q167 (Allegro *DJD* v).

Pᵉšārîm of Micah: 1QpMiq, 1Q14 (Milik *DJD* 1) and 4QpMiq = 4Q168 (Allegro *DJD* v)

Nahum Pēšer: 4QpNah = 4Q169, the only *pēšer* which provides proper names and helps to identify people and events: Kittim = Romans; Demetrius = Demetrius III Eukerus; Antiochus = Antiochus IV Epiphanes; «Angry Lion» = Alexander Jannaeus; «Those looking for easy interpretations» or «Ephraim» = the pharisees; «Manasseh» = the Sadducees; «Judah» or «Israel» = the Qumran Community (Allegro *DJD* v).

Habakkuk Pēšer: 1QpHab is the longest and best preserved, copied towards the end of the 1st cent. BCE by two different scribes. The second scribe copied out the final section (12,13 - 13,4) and inserted the corrections to be found throughout the text. The work does not comment on Hab 3. The interpretation, which is strongly eschatological in character, mentions the Teacher of Righteousness (1,13; 2,2; 5,9-12; 7,4-5; 8,3; 9,9-12; 11,4-8) the «Man of Lies» (2,1-2; 5,11) or «Spreader of Deceit» (10,9-13), as well as the «Wicked Priest» (8,8-13; 8,16-9,2; 11,4-8; 11,12-15; 12,2-6; 12,7-10; Burrows).

Pᵉšārîm of Zephaniah: 1QpZeph = 1Q15, with the text of Zeph 1:18-2:2 and the beginning of a *pēšer* (Milik *DJD* 1); 4QpZeph = 4Q170, with a quotation from Zeph 1:12-13 and what appears to be a *pēšer* (Allegro *DJD* v).

Malachi pēšer: 5QpMal?, 5Q10 (Milik *DJD* III).

Pᵉšārîm of Psalms: 1QpPs = 1Q16 on Ps 68. (Milik *DJD* 1): 4QpPsᵃ = 4Q171, on a selection of psalms (37, 45 and 60). The Qumran community is called «the converted to the Law» (2,2-3), «the congregation of his elect» (2,5; 3,5), «the congregation of the poor» (2,10; 3,10), «those who have returned from the wilderness » (3,1), or «the congregation of the Community» (4:19). The Teacher of Righteousness is described as the «Interpreter of Knowledge» (1,27) and the «Founder of the Community» (3,16), with priestly characteristics (3,15). The punishment of the wicked was to happen after a period of 40 years (2,7-9), the same period that follows the death of the Teacher (CD 2,13-15) and the length of time the final battle would last (1QM 2,6-14); 4QpPsᵇ, 4Q173: on Ps 129 and possibly also on Ps 127 (Allegro *DJD* v).

2.   Thematic Midrashim

The thematic midrashim are collections of texts referring to the same theme, taken from different biblical books, following a similar interpretation and using equivalent introductory formulae.

In spite of the different literary form, the different origin and the difference in content, the compositions analysed here are all distinguished by preserving for us various aspects of exegesis - a feature of inter-testamental literature - and thus shows us the very great importance which the biblical text had within this literature.

4QTanḥumim = 4Q176: Under the title of 'words of consolation', it refers mostly to texts from Second Isaiah (Is 40,1-5; 41,8-9; 43,1-2.4-6; 49,7.13-17; 51,22-23; 52,1-3; 54,4-10). Besides the biblical text, it is possible that the author also used other works such as the *Book of Jubilees* (Allegro *DJD* v).

4QFlorilegium = 4Q174, and *4QCatenaᵃ* = 4Q177 (Allegro *DJD* v). These two works comprise the *Eschatological Midrash*.

The first manuscript, known as *Florilegium*, reproduces sections from the beginning of the work, and the second, with the title *Catena*, preserves elements from the end of the work. This was a thematic *pēšer* on the last days.

The *Florilegium* (= 4QEschatological Midrash[a]) interprets Nathan's oracle (2 Sam 7,10-11) with reference to the eschatological Temple built by God himself at the end of time (according to Ex 15:17f.), which, unlike the Temple of Israel, would not be destroyed. Another Temple, distinct from these other two, the 'Temple of man', is in fact the Community considered to be a temple in which the sacrifices were 'works of praise'. The text of 2 Sam 7:11-14 is interpreted as an announcement of the coming of the Messiah, «shoot of David» or royal Messiah (described in terms of Amos 9:11) together with another messanic person, «the Interpreter of the Law», priestly Messiah or eschatological Prophet. Ps 1:1 is applied to the Council of the Community , with the support of Is 8:11 and Ez 37:23. The combined commentary on Ps 2:1-2, Dn 12:10 and 11:32 seems to allude to the eschatological war between the nations and «the chosen ones of Israel» (Brooke).

The *Catena* (=4QEschatological Midrash[b]) continues eschatological interpretation in the form of a commentary on Psalms 6-17, with quotations from and references to other biblical passages. The interpretation of Ps 17:1 (3:6-9) opposes Michael and Belial, the respective leaders of the forces of light and darkness. The commentary on Ps 6:4-5 (4:9-16) concludes this confrontation with the destruction of Belial, the reunion of the sons of light and their return to Jerusalem. The interpretation of the various psalms uses texts mostly from Isaiah, as well as from other prophetic books: Mic 2:10-11 in the commentary on Hos 11:1-2; Zac 3:9 for Ps 12:7; Ez 25:8 for Ps 13:5 and Hos 5:8 for Ps 17:1 (Steudel). 4QCatena[b] = 4Q182 (=4QEschatological Midrash[c]) is similar to the foregoing work.

4Q(Pesher) Ages of Creation (4Q180 and 4Q181) is a thematic *pēšer* on the history of mankind, predetermined by God and written on the Heavenly Tablets. 4Q180 refers to the first of these ages, which covers ten generations, the first of which is marked by the sin of the angels and the last by the sin of Sodom and Gomorrah. With 4Q181, the system of 70 weeks is introduced (Allegro *DJD* v).

4QHistorical Work (4Q183) is an historical and exegetical work which uses stereotyped formulae to refer to the fidelity of members of the Community and the evil of their enemies (Allegro *DJD* v).

Genesis Pesher (4Q252-254): This work could be termed a targum rather than a pesher, but part of it does have the characteristics peculiar to a pesher.

4QGenesis Pesher[a] (4Q252), previously published as *4QPatriarchal Blessings*. It interprets the 120 years (Gn 6:3) as the time which has to elapse until the flood. The commentary on Gn 7:11-8:15 with respect to the flood centres on the chronology of the biblical text. It solves problems using the 364-day calendar adopted by the Qumran community. Citing Gn 9:24-27, it comments on the fact that the biblical curse affects Canaan and not the real guilty party, his father Ham. With the help of 2 Chr 20:7, it identifies 'the tents of Shem' as the land of Israel granted to Abraham. It then comments on the death of Terah at the age of 205 (Gn 11:32) and to Abraham's plea on behalf of Sodom and Gomorrah, to the sacrifice of Isaac, the counsel given to Reuben (Gn 49:3-4, explained in connection with Gn 35:22 by the act of intercourse with Bilhah) and the reference to Amaleq in Gn 36:12, explained by that person's importance in the future history of Israel (with reference to Dt 25:19 and 2 Sm 15:7). It interprets the blessing of Judah, of Gn 49:10, in messianic and eschatological terms in respect of the Community. There follows the commentary on the text of the blessings of Jacob (Allegro, Lim).

4QGenesis Pesher[bc] (4Q253 and 4Q254). The second of these manuscripts cites Gn

9:24f. and comments on the blessings of Jacob in connection with Zac 4:14. It is a decisive text on the two messiahs of Qumran. A third manuscript, 4Q254ᵃ, refers to Gn 9:7 and 6:5 in connection matters concerning chronology and the calendar.

BIBLIOGRAPHY

BECKER, J., *Die Testamente der zwölf Patriarchen*, III/1, Gütersloh 1974.

BERGER, K., *Das Buch der Jubiläen*, JSHRZ II/3, Gütersloh 1981.

BLACK, M., *Apocalypsis Henochi graece*, and DENIS, A.-M., *Fragmenta pseudepigraphorum quae supersunt graeca*, Leiden 1970.

BLACK, M., *The Book of Enoch or I Enoch. A new English Edition with Commentary and Textual Notes*, Leiden 1985.

BOGAERT, P.-M., *Apocalypse de Baruch*, Paris 1969.

BROCK, S.P., *Testamentum Iobi*, and PICARD, J.-C., *Apocalypsis Baruchi graece*, Leiden 1967.

BURCHARD, CH., *Joseph und Aseneth*, JSHRZ II/4, Gütersloh 1983.

CAZEAUX, J.-PERROT, C.-BOGAERT, P.-M., *Pseudo-Philon, Les Antiquités Bibliques*, Paris 1976.

COLLINS, J.J., «Jewish Apocalyptic against its Hellenistic Near Eastern Environment», *BASOR* 220 (1975) 27-36.

DE JONGE, M., *The Testaments of the Twelve Patriachs. A Critical Edition of the Greek Text*, Leiden 1978.

DELCOR, M., *Le Testament d'Abraham. Introduction, traduction du texte grec et commentaire de la recension grecque longue*, Leiden 1973.

DELLING, G., *Jüdische Lehre und Frömmigkeit in den Paralipomena Jeremiae*, Berlin 1967.

DIETZFELBINGER, CH., *Pseudo-Philo: Antiquitates Biblicae (Liber Antiquitatum Biblicarum)*, JSHRZ II/2, Gütersloh 1975.

FLUSSER, D., «The Apocryphal Book of Ascensio Isaiae and the Dead Sea Sect», *IEJ* (1953) 30-47.

FRANXMAN, TH.W., *Genesis and the «Jewish Antiquities» of Flavius Josephus*, Rome 1979.

HAMMERSHAIMB, E., *Das Martyrium Jesajas*, and MEIDNER, N., *Aristeasbrief*, JSHRZ II/1, Gütersloh 1973.

HARRINGTON, D.J., *et al.*, *Pseudo-Philon. Les Antiquités bibliques*, 2 vols., Paris 1976.

HARRINGTON, D.J., *The Hebrew Fragments of Pseudo-Philo's Liber Liber antiquitatum biblicarum Preserved in the Chronicles of Jerahmeel*, Missoula, MT 1974.

HERZER, J., *Die Paralipomena Jeremiae. Studien zu Traditionen und Redaktion einer Haggada des frühen Judentums*, Tübingen 1994.

HOLLANDER, H.W.-DE JONGE, M., *The Testaments of the Twelve Patriarchs. A Commentary*, Leiden 1985.

KLAUCK, H.J., 4. *Makkabäerbuch*, JSHRZ III/6, Gütersloh 1989.

KOCH, K., *Ratlos vor der Apokalyptik. Eine Streitschrift über ein vernachlässigtes Gebiet der Bibelwissenschaft und die schädlichen Auswirkungen zur Theologie und Philosophie*, Gütersloh 1970.

KOCH, K.-SCHMIDT, J.M. (eds.), *Apokalyptik*, Darmstadt 1982.

KRAFT, R.A.-PURINTUN, A.-E., *Paraleipomena Jeremiou*, Missoula, MT 1972.

POHLMANN, K.-F., 3. *Esra-Buch*, JSHRZ I/5, Gütersloh 1980.

SACCHI, P., «Il 'Libro dei Vigilanti' e l'apocalittica», *Henoch* 1 (1979) 42-92.

SCHECHTER, A. (ed.), *Fragments of a Zadokite Work*, 2 vols., Cambridge 1910, reprinted 1970.

SCHREINER, J., *Das 4. Buch Esra*, JSHRZ V/4, Gütersloh 1981.

STONE, M., *The Testament of Abraham: The Greek Recensions*, Missoula MT 1972.

STONE, M., *Scriptures, Sects and Visions. A Profile of Judaism from Ezra to the Jewish Revolts*, Oxford 1980.

STONE, M., «Apocalyptic Literature», *Jewish Writings of the Second Temple Period*, ed. M. Stone, COINT II/2 (Assen 1984) 383-441.

STONE, M., *Fourth Ezra*, Minneapolis 1991.

TROMP, J., *The Assumption of Moses. A Critical Edition with Commentary*, Leiden 1993.

UHLIG, S., *Das äthiopische Henochbuch*, JSHRZ V/6, Gütersloh 1984.

WAHL, O. (ed.), *Apocalypsis Esdrae. Apocalypsis Sedrach. Visio Beati Esdrae*, Leiden 1977.

WALTER, N., *Fragmente jüdisch-hellenistischer Historiker*, I/2, Gütersloh 1976.

VAN DER HORST, P.W., *The Sentences of Pseudo-Phocylides with Introduction and Commentary*, Leiden 1978.

VANDERKAM, J.C., *Textual and Historical Studies in the Book of Jubilees*, Missoula MT, 1977.

VANDERKAM, J, *Enoch and the Growth of an Apocalyptic Tradition*, Washington DC 1984.

VERMES, G., *Scripture and Tradition in Judaism: Haggadic Studies*, Leiden 1961.

Texts from Qumran

AVIGAD, N.-YADIN, Y., *A Genesis Apocryphon*, Jerusalem 1956.

BETZ, O., *Offenbarung und Schriftforschung in der Qumransekte*, Tübingen 1960.

BROOKE, G.J., *Exegesis at Qumran. 4QFlorilegium in its Jewish Context*, Sheffield 1985.

BROWNLEE, W.H., *The Midrash Pesher of Habakkuk*, Missoula MT 1979.

BURROWS, M.-TREVER, J.C.-BROWNLEE, W.H., *The Isaiah Manuscript and the Habakkuk Commentary*, New Haven NJ 1950.

DIMANT, D., «An Apocryphon of Jeremiah from Cave 4 (4Q385^b = 4Q385 16)», *New Qumran Texts and Studies. Proceedings of the First Meeting of the International Organization for Qumran Studies, Paris 1992*, Brooke, G.J. (ed.) with García Martínez, F., Leiden 1994, 11-30, Pl. 2.

DIMANT, D., «The Merkaba Vision in Second Ezekiel (4Q385 4)», *RQ* 14 (1990) 331-348.

DIMANT, D., «A Quotation From Nahum 3:8-10 in 3Q385 6», *The Bible in the Light of Its Ancient Interpreters. Sarah Kamin Memorial Volume*, Sara Japhet (ed.), Jerusalem 1994, 31-37 [Hebrew].

EISENMAN, R.-WISE, M., *The Dead Sea Scrolls Uncovered. The First Complete Translation and Interpretation of 50 Key Documents Withheld for over 35 Years*, Shatesbury 1992.

ELLIGER, K., *Studien zum Habakkuk-Kommentar vom Toten Meer*, Tübingen 1953.

FLINT, P.W., *The Dead Sea Psalms Scrolls and the Book of Psalms*, Leiden 1995.

FITZMYER, J.A., *The Genesis Apocryphon of Qumran Cave I: A Commentary*, Rome 1971^2.

GARCÍA MARTÍNEZ, F., *The Dead Sea Scrolls Translated. The Qumran Texts in English*, Leiden 1994.

GARCÍA MARTÍNEZ, F., *Qumran and Apocalyptic. Studies on the Aramaic Texts from Qumran*, Leiden 1992.

GARCÍA MARTÍNEZ, F., «The 'New Jerusalem' and the future temple of the manuscripts from Qumran», *Qumran and Apocalyptic. Studies on the Aramaic Texts from Qumran*, Leiden 1992, 180-213.

GARCÍA MARTÍNEZ, F., «4QMess Ar and the Book of Noah», *Qumran and Apocalyptic. Studies on the Aramaic Texts from Qumran*, Leiden 1992, 1-44.

GARCÍA MARTÍNEZ, F., «The *Book of Giants*», *Qumran and Apocalyptic. Studies on the Aramaic Texts from Qumran*, ed. F. García Martínez, Leiden 1992, 97-115.

GARCÍA MARTÍNEZ, F., «Contribution of the Aramaic Enoch Fragments to our understanding of the Books of Enoch», *Qumran and Apocalyptic. Studies on the Aramaic Texts from Qumran*, Leiden 1992, 45-96.

HORGAN, M.P., *Pesharim. Qumran Intrerpretations of Biblical Books*, Washington DC 1979.

KISTER, M., «Newly-identified Fragments of the Book of Jubilees: Jub 23:21-23; 30,31», *RB* 12 (1987) 527-536.

LIM, T.H., «The Chronology of the Flood Story in a Qumran Text (4Q252), *JJS* 43 (1992) 288-298.

MILIK, J.T., *The Books of Enoch. Aramaic Fragments of Qumrân Cave 4*, Oxford 1976.

MILIK, J.T., «Ecrits préesséniens de Qumrân: d'Hénoc à 'Amram», ed. M. Delcor,

NEWSON, C., «4Q370: An Admonition based on the Flood», *RQ* 13 (1988) 23-43, pl.1.

NEWSON, C., «The 'Psalms of Joshua' from Qumran Cave 4», *JJS* 39 (1988) 56-73, pl.1.

NEWSON, C., *Songs of the Sabbath Sacrifice: A Critical Edition*, Atlanta GA 1985.

NITZAN, B., *Qumran Prayer and Religious Poetry*, Leiden 1992.

NITZAN, B., «4QBerakhot (4Q286-290): A Preliminary Report», *New Qumran Texts and Studies*, eds. G.J. Brooke - F. García Martínez, Leiden 1994, pp. 53-71.

PUECH, E., «Fragments d'un apocryphe de Lévi et le personnage eschatologique, 4QTestLévi^{c-d} (?) et 4QAJa», *The Madrid Qumran Congress*, vol. II, eds. J. Trebolle Barrera - L. Vegas Montaner, Leiden - Madrid 1992, pp. 449-502, pls. 16-21

PUECH, E., «Le Testament de Qahat en araméen de la grotte 4 (4QTQah)», *RQ* 15 (1991) 23-54.

PUECH, E., «Une apocalypse messianique (4Q521)», *RQ* 15 (1992) 475-522.

PUECH, E., «4Q525 et les péricopes des béatitudes en Ben Sira et Matthieu», *RB* 98 (1991) 80-106.

REEVES, J.C., *Jewish Lore in Manichaean Cosmogony. Studies in the Book of Giants Traditions*, Cincinnati KT 1992.

SANDERS, J.A., *The Psalms Scroll of Qumran Cave 11 (11QPsª) DJD* IV, Oxford 1965.

SCHULLER, E.M., *Non-Canonical Psalms from Qumran. A Pseudepigraphical Collection*, Atlanta GA 1986.

SCHULLER, E.M., «A Preliminary Study of 4Q372 1», *The Texts of Qumran and the History of the Community*, ed. F. García Martínez, Vol. II, Paris 1990, 349-376.

SCHULLER, E.M., «A Preliminary Study of 4Q373 and Some Related (?) Fragments», *The Madrid Qumran Congress*, vol. II, J. Trebolle Barrera – L. Vegas Montaner (eds.), Leiden-Madrid 1992, 515-530.

SMITH, M., «4Q462 (Narrative) Fragment 1: A Preliminary Edition», *RQ* 15 (1991) 55-77.

STEGEMANN, H., «The Origins of the Temple Scroll», *Congress Volume Jerusalem 1986*, Ed. J.A. Emerton, Leiden 1988, 235-256.

STEUDEL, A., *Der Midrasch zur Eschatologie aus der Qumrangemeinde (4QMidr-Eschat[a.b]). Materielle Rekonstruktion, Textbestand, Gattung und traditions-geschichtliche Einordnung des durch 4Q174 ('Florilegium') und 4Q177 ('Catena A') repräsentierten Werkes aus den Qumranfunden*, Leiden, 1994.

STONE, M.E. - GREENFIELD, J.C., «The First Manuscript of *Aramaic Levi Document* from Qumran (4QLevi[a] aram)», *Le Muséon* 107 (1994) 257-281.

STRUGNELL, J., «Moses-Pseudepigrapha at Qumran. 4Q375, 4Q376, and Similar Works», *Archeology and History in the Dead Sea Scrolls*, ed. L.H. Schiffman, Sheffield 1990, 221-247.

STRUGNELL, J., «Notes en marge du volume v des 'Discoveries in the Judaean Desert of Jordan'», *RQ* 7 (1970) 163-276 (79-183).

STRUGNELL, J. - DIMANT, D., «4QSecond Ezekiel», *RQ* 13 (1988) 54-58, pl. II.

SUKENIK, E.L., *The Dead Sea Scrolls of the Hebrew University*, Jerusalem 1955.

SWANSON, D.D., *The Temple Scroll and the Bible. The Methodology of II QT*, Leiden 1995.

WACHOLDER, B.Z., *The Dawn of Qumran. The Sectarian Torah and the Teacher of Righteousness*, Cincinnati KT 1983.

WILLSON, M.A. - WILLS, L., «Literary Sources in the Temple Scroll», *HTR* 75 (1982) 275-288.

WISE, M.O., *A Critical Study of the Temple Scroll from Qumran Cave 11*, Chicago IL 1990.

YADIN, Y., *The Temple Scroll*, 3 vols., Jerusalem 1984.

General bibliography on apocalyptic literature

CAQUOT, A. (ed.), *La littérature intertestamentaire. Colloque de Strasbourg (17-19 octobre 1983)*, Paris 1985.

CARLESWORTH, J.H. *The Old Testament Pseudepigrapha*, 2 vols., Garden City, NY 1985.

DE JONGE, M., *Outside the Old Testament*, Cambridge 1985.

DENIS, A.-M., *Introduction aux Pseudépigraphes grecs d'Ancien Testament*, Leiden 1970.

DUPONT-SOMMER, A., et al., *La Bible. Écrits intertestamentaires*, Paris 1987.

KAUTSCH, E., *Die Apokryphen und Pseudepigraphen des Alten Testaments*, Tübingen 1900.

NICKELSBURG, G.W.E., *Jewish Literature Between the Bible and the Mishnah*, Philadelphia PA 1981.

NICKELSBURG, G.W.E., «Stories of Biblical and Early Post-Biblical Times», *Jewish Writings of the Second Temple Period*, ed. M.E. Stone, CRINT II/2, Philadelphia PA 1984, 33-87.

RIESSLER, P., *Altjüdisches Schrifttum ausserhalb der Bibel*, Heidelberg 1928, 2. ed. 1966.

ROST, L., *Einleitung in die alttestamentlichen Apokryphen und Pseudepigraphen ein-schliesslich die grossen Qumran-Handschriften*, Heidelberg 1971.

TURDENANU, É., *Apocryphes slaves et roumains de l'Ancien Testament*, Leiden 1981.

UBIGLI, L.R., «Gli apocrifi (o pseudepigrafi) dell'Antico Testamento. Bibliografia 1979-1989», *Henoch* 12 (1990) 259-322.

2

The Social History of the Biblical Canon

I. INTRODUCTION

The history of any literature, particularly of biblical literature, is closely linked with the social history of the people or of the social groups in which that literature has its origin and is transmitted throughout the centuries.

The social history of the Bible opens a vast field of study, ranging from study of the social setting (*Sitz im Leben*) in which the various literary elements that make up the Bible originated and were transmitted, up to study of the relationship each canonical or apocryphal book could have with the various socio-religious groups of Hellenistic Judaism. It is this second aspect which interests us here.

In the Judaism of the Hellenistic period there was a wide spectrum of socio-religious groups: Samaritans, Sadducees, Pharisees, Essenes, Hellenists and various others, more or less connected with them, to which the various Jewish-Christian groups were added later. As was to happen later in Christianity, the Bible was an issue of both harmony and discord among all of them. The disagreements could be about the extent of the accepted canon, the text used in each book and the approach to interpreting the Bible as a whole. These differences crystallised later into different ways of visualising Judaism and putting it into practice.

This description starts with the group which has a narrower concept of the biblical canon and the conditions for belonging to the «true Israel», i.e., the Samaritans. It ends with reference to the groups displaying a broader and more open concept: the apocalyptic movements and the Hellenising movements and, connected with these, the Jewish-Christian group.

First, we have consider two preliminary questions. The first concerns the criteria which permit apocryphal writings to be assigned to one or other of the various Jewish groups of this period. The second concerns the relationship between Jewish literature, canonical and apocryphal, and the ideological movements from which post-exilic Judaism arose.

It is difficult to determine the authorship of «pseudepigraphical» works, which by definition conceal the identity of their author or authors. At the beginning of this century, attempts were made to assign each apocryphal writing to a Pharisee, Sadducee or Essene author. The Zealots and Hellenists did not count, for they had not actually been independent groups but were connected more with the others.

To assign a work to a Sadducee, Pharisee or Essene author, a *thematic criterion* was used: the presence in a work of doctrines typical of Sadducees, Pharisees or Essenes was a decisive factor in determining the author of that work. The doctrinal differences separating these three «schools», as used for such a classification, were as follows. The Sadducees denied the existence of angels, the resurrection of the dead and a possible judgment of the individual; they rejected the oral tradition produced by the Pharisees and held their own opinions concerning certain regulations about ablutions and sacrifices. The three groups differed from each other over a matter as important as the calendar, which had to govern all aspects of life, especially the cult and the festivals. In theodicy and ethics, the Essenes placed more stress on divine sovereignty, whereas the Sadducees stressed human responsibility more, while the Pharisees looked for a middle road (Le Moyne).

Using these differences as a criterion, it is still possible to attempt to assign each book Sadducee, Pharisee or Essene authorship, although this is more than hypothetical and difficult to verify.

The *oldest writings, earlier than the appearance of the three groups*, exhibit anti-Sadducee tendencies. These writings include the books of Tobit, Ecclesiasticus, the first and third books of *1 Enoch* and also the LXX version; the LXX inserts references to angels into passages where the Hebrew and Samaritan text do not mention them (Gn 6:2; Ex 4:24; Dt 32:8.43; 33:2). Ecclesiasticus is a proto-Pharisaic book, as is the Greek text of the Pentateuch, the text of which lends support to the date given by the Pharisees to the presentation of the first sheaf and the feast of Pentecost (Lv 23:11.16). The first and third books of *1 Enoch* are proto-Essene.

Among the *writings of the later period in which the three groups co-existed*, the books *1 Ezra* and *2 Ezra* (*4 Ezra*) show non-Sadducee trends; the book of Judith is probably Pharisee as also seem to be the books of Wisdom, (which follows a lunar calendar in 7,2), 1 Maccabees and 3 Maccabees.

The book *2 Ezra*, like the *Parables of Enoch* (*1 Enoch* 37-71) and the *Assumption of Moses* exhibit both Essene and Pharisee features.

The remaining pseudepigraphical books are non-Sadducee. *Jubilees* is Essene (the calendar in 2:9; 6:30-32.36-38 is Essene), as are also the fourth and fifth books of *1 Enoch*.

2 Baruch could be a purely Pharisee work. The *Psalms of Solomon* and also the *Letter of Aristeas* probably have a Pharisee origin. The *Sibylline Oracles* may have the same origin. The *Biblical Antiquities* exhibit Pharisee features.

The *writings of the Qumran community* are Essene. With regard to Hellenistic writers it can be noted that the tragedian Ezekiel and Eupolemos were not Sadducee authors.

2.   *Jewish Literature and Social Movements in the Persian and Hellenistic Periods*

Canonical and non-canonical Jewish writings after the exile can be divided into two large groups, depending on whether they reflect one or other of the ideological trends and social movements of the Judaism born after the Exile. For this purpose, the distinction between canonical and apocryphal books is totally unsuitable. The classification proposed cannot avoid a certain amount of subjectivity, but it is at least indicative and can serve as an introduction to later developments.

A series of writings come from *hierocratic circles*, concerned for the continuity of the institutions and the safekeeping of traditional doctrine. Its notion of the breadth of the canon tends to be reductive and closed. Other writings are the work of *visionaries*, for whom the experience of the Exile was the irrefutable proof that Yahweh utterly rejected the structures and institutions of ancient Israel, of the period before the monarchy. For these visionaries it was only possible to wait for the arrival of the new order of things. Its notion of the size of the canon tends to be open-ended and broad.

The first tendency, which maintains tradition, seems to be reflected in deuteronomistic theology, the book of Ezekiel, the priestly edition of the Pentateuch and the work of the Chronicler.

The second trend has antecedents in the eschatology of 8th and 7th century prophets, in Jeremiah and in Second Isaiah. Towards the end of the 6th cent. and throughout the 5th, the Zadokite party, allied to the Persian Empire, dominated the visionary prophets. The thrust of the missions of Ezra and Nehemiah, whose intention was to reinforce the Torah and the hierocratic structures, ignored that movement, though its critical viewpoint remains obvious in works such as Malachi, Joel, Is 24 and 27, Zac 9-14 and Ez 38-39.

In later periods, the first movement is represented, with the requisite differences in each case, by the books of Ben Sira, 1 Maccabees, Wisdom, the *Sibylline Oracles*, the Greek additions to the Book of Esther, Tobit, the novel *Joseph and Aseneth* and 3 Maccabees. The works which can be assigned to this second critical movement, also with evident differences among them, come mostly from the 2nd and 1st cents BCE. They are *Jubilees, 1 Enoch, Testament of Levi* and the *Temple Scroll*. From Second Isaiah the Essenes took the metaphors of the new creation, the new exodus and the cosmic conflict and applied them to their idea of a universal renewal and of a final restoration of Israel.

To a large extent, apocalyptic is the fruit of this tension between the two trends of post-Exilic Judaism, hierocratic and visionary (Hanson).

II. THE CANON ACCORDING TO THE SAMARITANS

The answer to the question about who the Samaritans were and how they came to be comes after the answer to the question about the nature of the Samaritan Bible and how the Samaritan Pentateuch was formed.

This question about the Samaritan Pentateuch was exactly what scholars were concerned with from the moment they came to know about the existence of the Samaritan Pentateuch, rather than questions about the history of the Samaritans. In 1616, Pietro della Valle got hold of a copy of this Pentateuch which was made known in the West through the polyglot bibles of Paris and London (cf. p. 271). At that time, many thought that the text of the new Pentateuch was more faithful to the original of the Bible than the text known through Medieval Hebrew copies. The Samaritan text provides about 6,000 cases where it differs from the text reproduced in modern editions of the Hebrew Bible, based on those mediaeval manuscripts. In general, they are worthless variants, but the 1900 variants which it shares with the LXX version against the Masoretic Hebrew are very important (cf. p. 297).

These two questions, about the origin and character of Samaritanism and of the Samaritan Pentateuch, are so intertwined that it is neither easy nor advisable to discuss them separately. This shows that Samaritanism is one more variation of Judaism of which the characteristic feature seems to be a sort of «Torah alone» principle.

1.   *The Origin of the Samaritan Pentateuch and the Schism of the Samaritans*

Since ancient times and until only a few years ago, the question of the origin of the Samaritans has been answered in three different ways: by the Samaritans themselves, by their opposites, rabbinic Jews, and by the historian Flavius Josephus.

a. The Samaritans' point of view. The Samaritans date their origins back to the tribes of the house of Joseph, Ephraim and Manasseh. They also consider themselves to be descendants of the Levite priests. From the moment of the Israelites' entry into Canaan, this priestly dynasty never ceased living permanently in Shechem, the capital of the kingdom of Israel, located at the foot of Mount Garizim, upon which the temple of the Samaritans was built. They considered themselves to be the «true Israel», the only descendants of the people of Israel who had faithfully kept the Torah of Moses, that is, the law established by Joshua in Shechem (Jos 24).

The Samaritans accused the Jews of being heretics and schismatics. By dating their origins back to the period of the Judges, they also dated the Jewish schism back to the 11th cent. BCE, when the priest Eli set up a sanctuary in Shiloh rivalling the temple of Shechem. This schismatic action was followed by others, no less important: the foundation of a temple in Jerusalem and the introduction of a false version of the Torah, which made no mention at all of Shechem and Garizim. The people most insulted by the Samaritans were, consequently, the priest Eli, the instigator of the schism of

Shiloh, king Solomon, the builder of the temple of Jerusalem and Ezra the scribe, the falsifier of the text of the Torah.

This view of Samaritan history, written by and for Samaritans, is offered by the book *Sēper Hayyāmîm* or Samaritan Chronicles (McDonald). The historical value of these Chronicles is very problematic. The book is probably a forgery made in the 19th century, although it is still based on ancient documents.

b. The rabbis' point of view. Jewish rabbinic tradition gave a very different version of the history of the Samaritans. They descended from a mixed population which the Assyrians had deported from Syria to the territory of the kingdom of Israel in 722, after the destruction of Samaria. The rabbis gave the Samaritans the name *kûtîm*, considering them to originate from a city in Mesopotamia called Cutha.

The rabbis based this explanation on 2 Kgs 17:24-41, which alludes to the events mentioned and to the pagan origin of the half 'Yahweh-ised' population, from which the Samaritans come. However, the passage from the book of Kings does permit the conclusion to be drawn that the Samaritans are descended from an ethnically half-caste population with a syncretistic religion, the result of a deportation over many years by the Assyrians. This is a statement which the rabbis add off their own bat, without providing any proof at all.

c. Josephus' point of view. Josephus attributed the Samaritan schism to a dispute between Jews. Some priests from Jerusalem became Samaritans and established a temple on Mount Garizim, rivalling the Jerusalem temple. This desertion by Jewish priests, who switched to the Samaritan ranks, took place when the leading Jews of Jerusalem opposed marriage between Manasseh, Yaddua's brother, high priest of Jerusalem, and Nicaso, daughter of Sanballat, governor of Samaria. According to Josephus, these events happened in the time of Alexander the Great, who granted Sanballat the privilege of building a temple on Mount Garizim.

Josephus' testimony presents serious difficulties. The first is to make Sanballat a contemporary of Alexander, when (until recently) the only Samaritan known by the name of Sanballat was a contemporary of Nehemiah (5th cent. BCE). On the other hand, the account by Josephus of the prohibition by the leading Jews of the projected marriage between members of the ruling dynasties of Jerusalem and Samaria, shows too many similarities with another account in the book of Nehemiah (13:18). However, that account does not say that the opposition to the marriage between members of the Jewish and Samaritan dynasties had given rise to the Samaritan schism.

Many historians considered that Josephus was referring to a schism which happened in the Persian period and not the Greek period. Others relied on the testimony of Josephus, who sets these events in the Greek period (Rowley). Josephus' testimony has given rise to two different theories about the period when the Samaritan schism took place: in the Persian period or in the years following the appearance of Alexander in Palestine. There is even a third hypothesis: the schism took place in the Persian period, but the building of the Samaritan temple, the true expression of the schism, was completed in the Greek period.

d. The viewpoint of current research. Recent discoveries allow a much more complex panorama of the history of the Samaritans to be drawn than was known until very recently.

The first and most important discovery for reconstructing this history concerns precisely the *text of the Samaritan Pentateuch*.

One of the great surprises caused by the discovery of the Dead Sea Scrolls has been to prove that the text of some Qumran manuscripts is very similar to the Samaritan

Pentateuch. They all go back to the same «Palestinian» textual tradition (cf. p. 298) which is distinguished by frequent harmonisation and expansion of the text. On the other hand, the Samaritan Pentateuch still shows obvious agreements with the Masoretic Hebrew text. It requires the supposition that the editor of the Samaritan text used a text belonging to the proto-masoretic («Babylonian», according to Cross) tradition. Such an agreement between the Samaritan text and the Jewish proto-masoretic text could not have happened after the schism between Samaritans and Jews, when contacts between them had ceased. On the other hand, the spelling of the Samaritan Pentateuch is characterised by the frequent use of *matres lectionis* («vowel letters»), a type of spelling peculiar to the Hasmonaean period. In this same period, the type of Samaritan script began to be different from the palaeo-Hebrew script, to which it is related.

As a result, the textual, palaeographic and orthographic data available show that the edition and promulgation of the Samaritan Pentateuch could not be earlier than the Hasmonaean period, i.e., the second half of the 2nd cent. BCE (Cross, Purvis).

This conclusion concerning the origin of the Samaritan Pentateuch entails another concerning the origin of the *Samaritan schism*. The possibility arises that the Samaritan schism would have taken place well into the Greek period and not already in the early part of the Hellenistic period.

The archaeological finds confirm this late dating of the Samaritan schism. In the first place, the excavations of Tell Balatah (ancient Shechem) show that, after a period of being almost completely abandoned during the Persian period, the city of Shechem regained its ancient importance at the beginning of the Greek period. On the other hand, the excavations at Tell-er-Ras (Garizim) prove that the construction of the temple on the rock of Garizim was carried out in the Hellenistic period. Lastly, the papyri discovered in Wadi-Deliyeh have shown that, besides the Sanballat we already know as a contemporary of Nehemiah (Sanballat I) there existed another Sanballat (II) who could well be the grandfather of Sanballat (III), Alexander's contemporary (Cross). These papyri have shown that the Samaritan dynasty practised the system of papponymy (imposing the grandfather's name on the grandson) which has enabled a sequence of Samaritan governors to be established. This is favourable to accepting Josephus' testimony that the temple of Garizim was built by a Sanballat (III) in the time of Alexander.

The information given above allows a *history of the Samaritans* in several stages to be sketched out.

At the beginning of the Greek period, the Macedonians deprived the nobility of Samaria of all political power. They rebuilt and repopulated the city of Shechem. Relations between Samaria and Jerusalem continued to be unfriendly, as they had been in previous centuries. At that time, the Samaritans built a temple to Yahweh, but at they same time they worshipped Nergal (possibly a god of Cutha). This building follows a sort of historical law according to which the creation of a Greek colony generally resulted in the indigenous population reviving worship in an ancient ancestral sanctuary as a symbol of the unity and identity of the people (Bickerman).

There is no information favouring the assertion made by Josephus, that the priests of Samaria were descendants of Jewish priests who had broken with the temple of Jerusalem. The Samaritan priesthood had its own genealogy, independent of Jerusalem. On the other hand, the building of the temple on Garizim did not necessarily mean a religious split with Jerusalem. There were similar Jewish temples elsewhere: the Tobiads had a temple in Transjordan and the high priest Onias IV, banished from Jerusalem, had set up a temple in Leontopolis (Egypt).

The relations between Samaritans and Jews were worsening to such an extent that *in 128 BCE, John Hyrcanus destroyed the temple of Garizim* and in 107, the city of Shechem. These events were due to several causes: the tensions created by the alliances of both parties with Ptolemies or Seleucids; the resentment of the Jews towards the Samaritans for accepting the Hellenism of Antioch instead of opposing it as the Maccabees had done; the hostilities between Samaritans and Jews in their respective communities in the diaspora of Egypt under Ptolemy VI Philopator (180-145) and, lastly, the expansionist policy of the Maccabees, especially of John Hyrcanus.

In this historical context, *the edition of the Samaritan Pentateuch* was the Samaritan reaction to the attacks by the Jews which culminated in the destruction of the temple of Garizim. The twin columns of Judaism, Torah and Temple, were also the fundamental institutions of Samaritanism as a version of Judaism. The Samaritans were not prepared to submit to the Hasmonaeans. They had always been independent of Jerusalem and were prepared to continue that way, convinced of being the only transmitters of the letter and spirit of the Mosaic law. Accordingly, when the Samaritans saw the Temple destroyed by the Jews, they hoisted the banner of the Torah and completed an edition or recension of the Torah in opposition to the Jewish version. They accused the Jews of having distorted the text of the Torah, misrepresenting the true and ancient traditions. These connected the history of the Israelites with Shechem and Garizim and not with Jerusalem and Zion, as recorded in the Jewish version of the Torah, From that moment on, the continuing disagreements between Samaritans and Jews no longer focused so much and solely on the matter of the Temple but shifted to revolve round the legitimacy of each other's Torah. This is the reconstruction of the history of the Samaritan «schism» as given nowadays (Cross, Purvis, Coggins, etc.).

Thus, summarising the historical events outlined above, the Samaritan edition of the Pentateuch was not completed in the period of the *construction* of the Samaritan temple, as an act of schism against Judaism, but took place after the *destruction* of the temple at the hands of John Hyrcanus, in reaction to what the Samaritans considered an attack by the Jews. Similarly, the so-called Samaritan «schism» did not happen in the Persian period, or even at the beginning of the Greek period, as had been stated previously, but already well into the Hellenistic period.

2.   *Samaritanism: the «Torah alone»*

Now that we know the origin of Samaritanism and of the Samaritan Pentateuch, it is necessary to determine the text type of the Samaritan Torah and the nature of Samaritanism as a variety within Judaism. The peculiarities of the Samaritan Torah reveal to us the kind of Judaism represented by the Samaritans.

The discovery at Qumran of manuscripts which show certain similarities with the Samaritan Pentateuch and represent a type of *«Proto-Samaritan Palestinian text»* is, in a certain sense, a more important find that the appearance of other manuscripts agreeing with the text of rabbinic Judaism (MT) and/or with the Greek text of Hellenistic Judaism (LXX). The rabbinic Hebrew text was already well documented previously. The text of the Greek Bible allows the reconstruction, with varying degrees of probability, of the Hebrew textual tradition underlying the Greek version. On the other hand, and with reference to the Samaritan Pentateuch, if the «proto-Samaritan» manuscripts of Qumran had not been discovered, it would never have been suspected that in fact the text of the Samaritan Pentateuch is made up of two different layers.

The first layer corresponds to a kind of «Palestinian» text as attested by the «Proto-Samaritan» manuscripts just mentioned. The second is more recent and corresponds to the actual *Samaritan recension*. This recension was superficial. The changes which were inserted are easily identifiable and thus it is easy to separate them from the more ancient layer of text into which they were inserted. This is the case particularly for readings which reflect Samaritan theology, such as those which make the text say that the place chosen by Yahweh is not the Mount Zion of the Jews but Garizim of the Samaritans.

Samaritanism should not be considered as something opposed to Judaism and thus independent of and free from any influence from Judaism (McDonald). Instead, it comprises *a variant of Judaism*. Although undoubtedly more extreme than other variants of Judaism, it is comparable to those variants which, after the imposition of the strict criteria of Pharisaism, ended up being rejected by rabbinic Judaism.

It is obvious that the Samaritans belong to the Jewish world from the claim made by the Samaritans of being the true heirs of the traditions of ancient Israel. This claim placed them in a state of constant conflict with the Jews. The fact that the *War Scroll* (1QM) still relies on the possibility of a reconciliation between the Judahite (Jewish) and Josephite (Samaritan) branches of Israel shows clearly that both were aware of originating from a common stem and continued to nourish hope in a possible reunion.

The opposition of the Samaritans to the *Temple* of Jerusalem and, as a result, to the priesthood and festival calendar of Jerusalem, could be no more than the more extreme element of similar attitudes, also shared, although with less virulence, by other Jewish groups, such as the Essenes. The Hellenist branch of the church of Jerusalem (Acts 7) and the Christian community behind the gospel of John, also present a view of Jerusalem and of the Temple which it has been possible to interpret as an expression of hostility towards the Jews, but may be only a reflection of more widespread opposition to the cult of Jerusalem.

It has been possible to establish a relationship between Samaritan traditions and Hellenistic-Christian traditions, such as those referring to the prophet at the end of time (Dt 18:15.18; cf. Jn 4) and the *Taheb*, the Samaritan Messiah who was to restore the universe, although there is not enough information allowing the existence of any form of messianic belief among the Samaritans in the 1st cent. CE. to be affirmed with any probability. It still remains significant that there were Samaritans among the very first Christians, converted at the time of the mission narrated in Acts 8:1ff. Very few groups of the early Christians shared the prejudices of the Pharisees towards the Samaritans (Mt 19:5). Jesus seems to have taken no notice of such prejudices (Lk 19:33).

The *Torah*, together with the Temple, comprises the second of the fundamental pillars of Judaism. The Samaritans knew the rabbinic distinction between written and oral Torah, but they did not give them equal status. Tradition is not a different manifestation of the actual Torah nor can it ever surpass it. At most, tradition is an aid to understanding it. As a result, Samaritanism was ruled by a sort of principle of *Scripture alone*.

The Samaritans disputed whether the authority for interpreting the Torah belonged to priests or to experts. The priests had the last word concerning the transmission of secret doctrines and the calendar as well as the reading of the Torah in the synagogue. As for what touched on matters of *hălākâ*, one stream of tradition defended the authority for decision as belonging to the priests. Another stream ascribed this authority to the experts, whether they were priests or not.

A matter of prime importance in Samaritanism was the correct pronunciation of the words in the text of the Torah. The experts, whether priests or not, had the authority to express an opinion about matters of *hălākâ* or about a doctrine or interpretation of Scripture and to teach the text, its pronunciation and the correct understanding of the Torah. The people retained the right to accept or reject a halakhic opinion and to declare the other opinions as not binding, although later, the experts or the priests generally used to impose their own authorised opinions.

The sect of Dositeans, which originated before the 1st cent. CE from a movement made up of lay-people, had a tremendous impact on the Samaritan community. They held their views about matters of *hălākâ*, the calendar, eschatology, etc., which were similar to those of Pharisee Jews (Isser). Dositheus, the founder of the movement, considered himself to be a second Moses, so that he felt authorised to insert into the text changes based on tradition, of the kind found in the *Temple Scroll* of Qumran. The author of this text re-wrote the Torah to make it say what in fact it does say if interpreted according to what tradition and exegesis require (cf. p. 184).

The Dositean movement (or perhaps other later movements equated with it) developed clear antinomian tendencies. This opposition to the Law explains why rabbinic references to the Samaritans are hostile. It also explains, on the other hand, the favourable reception which the Christian message received among some Samaritans, given the obvious antinomian connotation of the first message of Jesus. The authority which Jesus assumed over the

Torah has no equivalent in contemporary Judaism or even in the more official Samaritanism, although Jesus seems to have presented himself as one who fulfils the law. It may have some similarities with the antinomic trend of the Dositean movement, which was developed even further in Christianity.

The Samaritans considered decisions in matters of *hălākâ* as unobtainable from the text of Scripture. In this they differed from the men of Qumran and the Karaites who considered it possible and necessary to gain knowledge of *hălākâ* by means of midrash. Similarly, the Samaritans did not accept the pharisee and rabbinic principle of the two Torahs, oral and written, in agreement here with the Sadducees (Boíd 632).

III. THE CANON ACCORDING TO THE SADDUCEES

The Sadducees seem to have represented a position similar to the extremely conservative position of the Samaritans, who accepted virtually no evolution at all in the canon, restricting it to the five books of the Torah.

It is not surprising that with the passing of centuries and from a perspective very distant from those events, the Fathers of the Christian Church even confused Sadducees and Samaritans. This confusion was all the more feasible if it is remembered that the Samaritans were usually confused with the Dositean group.

Study of everything relating to the Sadducees is strongly determined by the fact that the writings of the Sadducees themselves have not been preserved. All that is available are isolated references in Pharisee or Christian sources which were not exactly favourable to those who were their enemies.

The question of what the Bible of the Sadducees was or what use they made of it is closely connected with the question of who the Sadducees were.

1.   *The Origin and Character of Sadduceeism*

The origin of the Sadducees has to be dated around 200 BCE (Mansoor) or not long before the reorganisation of Judaism under the Maccabees (Sundberg). All that can be stated with certainty is that in the 1st cent. BCE, the Sadducees already comprised a recognised social group (Le Moyne).

The *disappearance* of Sadduceeism is commonly associated with the destruction of the Temple in 70 CE. This assumes a reduction of the Sadducees to the circle of the priesthood, which virtually ceased to exist once the Temple was destroyed. However, the disappearance of the Sadducees could be due simply to the fact that they lived mostly in Jerusalem and as a result were the ones to suffer most the consequences of the destruction of the city (Sundberg).

From the name by which they are known, the «Sadducees» seem to be related to the *běnê Şadōq* («Zadokites»), the *descendants of Zadok the priest*, who had been priests in the Temple of Jerusalem from the time it was built by Solomon. The Sadducee priests were, in practice, those who best represented Sadducee tendencies. Some high priests were Sadducees (Josephus, *Antiq.* 20,9 no. 199; BT *Yoma* 18b). The Sadducees feature alongside the high priest (Acts 4:1-4; 15:17-18). However, no known source equates the Sadducees with the priestly party. The most that can be said is that some priests were Sadducees.

The Sadducees are also usually presented as the aristocracy of Palestine at that period (Mansoor, J. Jeremias, Schürer-Vermes-Miller). Again, this statement relies on the testimony of Josephus who says that the Sadducees gave their support to the rich upper class: «but this doctrine is received but by a few, yet by those still of the greatest dignity» (Josephus, :, *Antiq.* 18,1,4 no. 17). It must not be forgotten, however, that there were also priestly families whose power and money were quite meagre.

Being the upper class, the Sadducees were also portrayed as *the most Hellenised class*. It is not true, though, that some groups of Jews were more Hellenised than others. The Pharisees were certainly as Hellenised as the Sadducees, although the reaction of both groups towards Hellenism was very different (Sundberg).

The Sadducees are also usually considered as *the most nationalistic group*. Because of their relationship to the priesthood, the Sadducees were the group which had most to lose if, confronted by the onslaught of Hellenism, the cultural, national and religious roots of Judaism were dissolved. However, the Sadducees must be considered as the most Hellenised and the most nationalistic, without any evident contradiction at all between these two adjectives (Baron).

The conservatism of the Sadducees in respect of the biblical canon and the principle of *Scripture alone* changes, on the other hand, to a liberalism open to the lifestyle and ideas of the State and *polis* peculiar to Hellenism. This *mix of conservatism and liberalism*, both sceptical and ironic, is evident in the attitude of the Sadducees towards the only two questions about which we have information concerning Sadducee doctrine. According to the NT, Josephus and rabbinic sources, the Sadducees rejected the idea of resurrection (Mk 12:18ff.; Josephus, *Antiq.* 18,16) as well as the existence of angels and spirits (Acts 23:8). As a result, the punishment and reward due to human deeds are carried out only in this earthly life, with no conception of providence or destiny. The resurrection and the existence of angels could not be proved only from the texts of the Torah. The Sadducees were attached to the oldest traditional doctrine, which only knew the idea of the dead existing as shadows in *She'ôl*. They rejected both the Greek idea of a separate soul and the Persian-apocalyptic idea of a resurrection, as reflected in the book of Daniel, the last to be included in the Bible. This shows the doctrinal conservatism as well as the secular and sceptical mentality which governed the day-to-day life of the Sadducees. On the other hand, they also stressed the freedom and trust of man in himself, and not only the religious idea of God's intervention in man's life.

Some very Hellenised priests, such as the Zadokite family of the Oniads, placed traditional Jewish life in jeopardy, as well as the very independence of the Jewish State, to the extent of provoking the Maccabaean revolt. This was more an internal reaction against Hellenised Jews than against Greek Seleucids. However, after the revolt, the Sadducee priests supported the Maccabees. Kings John Hyrcanus, Aristobulus I and Alexander Jannaeus depended to a large extent on the Sadducees, who did not have the slightest intention of Hellenising the cult in Jerusalem, although they themselves led a fairly Hellenised life. The survival of the Jewish state of the second

Temple, from the Maccabaean period up to the destruction in 70 CE, was very largely due to the political vision of the Sadducees, conservative yet compliant.

Other «sons of Zadok», hostile to the Hasmonaean priestly dynasty, founded the Essene community of Qumran, combining Sadducee, Pharisee and apocalyptic ideas in a precipitate which mixed the claim to supremacy of the priesthood and of the Aaronite messiah, the preparedness to accept halakhic interpretation and openness to new apocalyptic revelations concerning the end of time.

From a Christian and NT viewpoint, it is common to make Jesus an apocalyptic figure, opposed on the one hand to the pharisees over the Torah and legalism in observing it, and on the other, opposed to the Sadducees, over the Temple which Jesus declared to be obsolete (Schürmann). However, Torah and Temple were two inseparable pillars of Judaism: the Sadducees tended to reduce the canon to the Torah because in it are found the laws concerning Temple worship; in turn, the Pharisees, laymen but not secularising, interpreted the laws of the Torah concerning the support of cult and clergy with great generosity, thus showing great reverence to the oldest institutions of the people of Israel.

The confrontation of Jesus with Sadduceeism took place particularly after the scene of the purification of the Temple (E.P. Sanders) and on account of the sayings of Jesus about its destruction, which brought about the accusation and condemnation before the Jewish tribunal. However, it is no less certain than in the early period of Christianity, important sectors of Sadduceeism had to convert. Of some significance in this connection could be the fact that a NT book, which soon circulated under the title of «Letter to the Hebrews», has as its theme the priesthood of Christ, absent from the rest of the NT. On the other hand, the influence of the OT cult on Christian worship is surprising, especially when Judaism went in the opposite direction after the destruction of the Temple in 70, which led to the abandon or replacement of the priestly and cultic aspects of earlier Judaism.

2. The Sadducee Bible

It is reasonable to imagine that the first settlers to arrive in Qumran brought with them biblical manuscripts copied previously. Palaeographic study of the Qumran manuscripts shows that the oldest are, in fact, copies of biblical texts: 4QEx^f (250 BCE), 4QSam^b (second half of the 3rd cent. BCE), 4QJer^a (c. 200 BCE), 4QXII^a and 4QQoh^a (3rd cent. BCE; Cross). On the other hand, the manuscripts copied in palaeo-Hebrew characters can be connected with conservative elements for whom the use of this archaic script was important. The fact that the manuscripts in palaeo-Hebrew script are precisely and only the books of the Torah is significant: 2 MSS of Gn, 2 of Ex, 4 of Lv, 1 of Nm and two of Dt (as well as one of Job). This fact is not to be interpreted as the result of a revival or an archaising use of the ancient script, for that would mean that these copies were from originals in the square script, which is inconceivable. Certainly, the use of this type of script corresponds to a tradition kept alive among conservative groups, different from and earlier than the Qumranites. In principle, the books written in palaeo-Hebrew script can be connected both with the Samaritans and the Sadducee movement.

The fact that, apart from the Torah, Job is the only book of which a copy has been found at Qumran in the palaeo-Hebrew script (together with copies of a targum of the same book) could suggest that some Sadducees considered the book of Job as canonical, added to the Torah. In this respect it may also be significant that one passage from the *Midrash Tanḥuma* (*Bereʾšit* 5), even though late and suspect, presents the Sadducees having a discussion on a passage from Job (7:9): «The Sadducees deny the resurrection and state: 'As a cloud fades away, so whoever goes down to *Šeʾôl* will never return'» (Barthélemy). It does not seem that from this passage the conclusion can be deduced that the Sadducees never rejected the canonical character of the Prophets and Writings (Le Moyne). However, it is certain that Josephus and rabbinic literature list the friction between Pharisees and Sadducees, though they never suggest that the rejection of the books of the Prophets and the Writings by the Sadducees features among these points of confrontation.

Another connection between the Zadokite world and the history of the biblical text is the possible relationship between the «Palestinian» textual family (which differs from the «Tiberian» and «Babylonian» families) and the Greek text of the LXX, the common origin of which could go back to priestly circles of the Temple of Jerusalem (Sacchi, Chiesa, cf. pp. 272 – 274). This poses the question of the relationships among Sadducees, Qumranites and Karaites (cf. p. 483).

Evidence from many Christians (especially Hippolytus and Origen) seems to indicate that the Sadducees, like the Samaritans, had as their Bible only the Torah of Moses, thus excluding the books of the prophets and the remaining biblical books. However, Jewish sources, rabbinic literature and Josephus do not seem to confirm this statement. Certainly, in controversial issues the Sadducees apparently used no other proofs except those derived from the text of the Torah. In debate with the Sadducees about the matter of resurrection, Jesus argued exclusively from texts from the Torah (Mk 12:26), which seems to suggest that Jesus agreed not to use other texts not accepted by the Sadducees. Jesus would have been able to argue more easily and with more weight using texts from the prophetical books and the Writings, which contained statements closer to belief in the resurrection. In the Torah, instead, exactly as the Sadducees asserted, it is difficult to find references to the resurrection or to future life.

However it is difficult to imagine that the Sadducees completely rejected the books of the Prophets and the other biblical writings. It is possible that one of the more extreme movements within Sadduceeism came close to the Samaritan position, but undeniably mainstream Sadduceeism did no more than set up a sort of «canon within the canon», regarding only the books of the Torah as canonical in the strict sense of the term. This is not surprising given that the Pharisees also accorded greater authority to the Torah than to the books of the Prophets and the Writings.

The Samaritans had their own reasons for rejecting the prophetical books. Most of the prophets had originated in the kingdom of Judah and in addition had preached against the kingdom of Israel. Some prophetic movements had been very much in favour of the hegemonist presumptions of Jerusalem and the Temple of Zion. This applies to the Isaianic tradition, which runs from the historical Isaiah (8th cent. BCE) to the anonymous prophets known as Second and Third Isaiah (from the period of the Babylonian exile, 5th cent. BCE).

The Sadducees could also have their own reasons for not granting binding force to other books which were not the five of the Torah. Since they were a group with special relationships to the priesthood of Jerusalem, the Sadducees considered everything connected with the legislation about the Temple and the cultic institutions as essential. This is precisely the legislation included in the Torah.

However, the argument according to which the Sadducees, by their links with the Temple and the cult as regulated by the Torah, restricted themselves to the exclusive use of the Pentateuch certainly cannot be pushed to such an extreme. The high priests who succeeded John Hyrcanus and those who had this office in the final years of Herod's reign, as well as most of the priests forming the entourage of the high priest, were all Sadducees. It remains significant that the gospel of Matthew (2:4-6) describes the «princes of the priests», together with the scribes, citing a passage from a prophetic book (Mic 5:2) referring to the Messiah's place of birth and the hope in «Christ» (Anointed) and «Son of David». These are prophetic or messianic themes to which allusion is made in the books of the Prophets and in the Psalms, but not in the Pentateuch.

On the other hand, the fact that the Sadducees controlled the cult and the Temple in which were kept the authorised copies of all the Scriptures and not only of the Torah, makes one think that these copies were already found in the Temple towards the end of the second cent. BCE, when the Sadducees took control of the Temple. The Scriptures, including the books of the Prophets and the Writings, certainly comprised the common inheritance of the Jews at that time, which the Sadducees accepted and kept with conservative scruple.

The Sadducees would accept no development at all which went beyond the written Torah, rejecting an oral Torah as a construct of the halakhic tradition of the Pharisees: «and say that we are to esteem those observances to be obligatory which are in the written word, but are not to observe what are derived from the tradition of our forefathers» (Josephus, *Antiq.* 13,10,6).

The possibility of legislation which would break with the established Torah and its Sadducean interpretation presented the danger of seeing a reduction in the power the Sadducees had in their own domains, the temple and the cult. The tension between priests of this Sadducee tendency and laypeople of Pharisee tendency is reminiscent of the tension in Samaritanism between priests and experts who disputed the authority for making legal decisions based on interpretation of the Torah.

BARTHÉLEMY, D., «L'état de la Bible depuis le début du notre ère jusqu'à la deuxième révolte contre Rome (131-135)», *Le Canon de l'AT*, Geneva 1984, 9-45.

BÓID, I.R.M., *Principles of Samaritan Halachah*, Leiden 1988.

COGGINS, R.J., *Samaritans and Jews: The origins of Samaritanism Reconsidered*, Oxford 1975.

CROSS, F.M., «Papyri of the Fourth Century B.C. from Daliyeh», *New Directions in Biblical Archaeology*, Garden City NY 1971, 45-69.

CROWN, A.D. (ed.), *The Samaritans*, Tübingen 1989.

HALL, B.W., *Samaritan Religion from John Hyrcanus to Baba Rabba. A Critical Examination of the Relevant Material in Contemporary Christian Literature, the Writings of Josephus, and the Mishnah*, Sydney 1987.

HANSON, P.D., «The Matrix of Apocalyptic», *The Cambridge History of Judaism*, II: *The Hellenistic Age*, eds., W.D. Davies-L. Finkelstein, Cambridge 1989, 524-533.

ISSER, S.J., *The Dositeans: A Samaritan Sect in Late Antiquity*, Leiden 1976.

JEREMIAS, J., *Jerusalem in the Time of Jesus*, Philadelphia PA 1967.

LE MOYNE, J., *Les Sadducéens*, Paris 1972.

MANSOOR, M., «Sadducees», *Encyclopaedia Judaica*, vol. 14, Jerusalem 1972, 620-622.

MCDONALD, J., *The Theology of the Samaritans*, Philadelphia PA 1964.

MCDONALD, J., *The Samaritan Chronicle No. II (or Sepher Ha-Yammim)*, Berlin 1969.

PORTON, G.G., «Sadducees», *ABD* V, New York 1992, 892-895.

PURVIS, J.D., *The Samaritan Pentateuch and the Origin of the Samaritan Sect*, Cambridge MA 1968.

SANDERS, E.P., *Jesus and Judaism*, Philadelphia PA 1985.

SCHÜRMANN, H., «Wie hat Jesus seinen Tod bestanden und verstanden», *Orientierung an Jesus. Zur Theologie der Synoptiker. Festschrift J. Schmid*, eds., P. Hoffmann et al., Freiburg 1973, 325-363.

SCHUR, N., *A History of the Samaritans*, Frankfurt 1989.

SUNDBERG, A.C., «Sadducees», *The Interpreter's Dictionary of the Bible*, vol. 4, Abingdon Nashville 1981, 160-163.

IV. THE CANON ACCORDING TO THE PHARISEES: WRITTEN TORAH AND ORAL TORAH

Opposed to the tendencies of Samaritans and Sadducees on the one hand and to those of the Essenes and Hellenisers on the other, the Pharisees represented a middle road of gradual acceptance of a three-part canon (Torah-Prophets-Writings), with a list of books already defined in the mid-second cent. BCE. In this, the history of the canon set out above (cf. pp. 161-167) is to a large extent a history of the Pharisee canon or of a Pharisee understanding of the canon, which develops the doctrine of the two Torahs, one written and the other oral. There is no need to repeat here what has been said and what will be said in the chapter on rabbinic hermeneutics (cf. p. 481).

The Pharisees represent mainstream Judaism, which leads to the rabbinism of the period of the Mishnah and the Talmud. Information about the Pharisees comes mainly from sources of this later period, so that it is easy to make the mistake of extrapolating facts or situations from that time to the earlier period.

Phariseeism has usually been considered as an «orthodox» and official variant of Judaism and Pharisees have been considered as real leaders, political even, of the Jewish people (Moore, Finkelstein, Baron, Simon). This view of Phariseeism, however, depends on the witness of rabbinic literature and on Josephus, who provide a distorted version of Judaism before 70 CE.

The Judaism of the Hellenistic period, however, took on very many forms. The Pharisees comprised one of the many groups that did exist, the largest and later the most influential, but not the only representative of «normative» Judaism. The Pharisees had no control at all over political power. If Josephus in the *Jewish Antiquities* portrays the Pharisees as a very influential group, this is only to persuade the Romans to grant power over the Jewish population to the Pharisees. In *War*, written much earlier, Josephus says nothing about this influence of the Pharisees and even devotes more space to the Essenes (Smith).

It is not easy to ascertain the moment when the Pharisee group was formed: in the time of Ezra (Zeitlin), of Jonathan (Guttmann) or of Hyrcanus and Alexander Jannaeus (Simon). Possibly they began to be organised into a group only from the beginning of the 1st cent. CE, although their origins could go back to the 2nd cent. BCE (Meyer).

The characteristic which most differentiates the Pharisees from their opponents, the Sadducees, was their idea of the Torah. The Pharisees acknowledged one written Torah and one oral Torah, whereas the Sadducees only acknowledged written tradition (Black). However, judging by the number of rabbinic traditions which concern matters of ritual purity (67% of the total) it must be supposed that the main characteristic of this group was concern for ritual purity. The Pharisee was someone «separate», always remote from unclean things and persons, particularly the «people of the land» (Neusner). This concern for purity, however, does not cease to be connected with the typical Pharisee idea of the oral and written Torah.

It is usually thought that Judaism in the Persian and Hellenistic period was a religion focused on the Torah. The Samaritans restricted themselves to the Torah alone and the Sadducees also seemed to have done the same, at least in practice. 1 Mc 1:56 only refers to the books of the Torah: «the books of the Law which they found... which they found in house a book of the Covenant». Later rabbinic Judaism undoubtedly revolves around the Torah.

However, the references to the central character of the Torah in apocryphal literature are ambiguous, for the word «Torah» means both Jewish tradition and secular law. Ben Sira accepts the importance of the Torah, but considers that common sense and experience are equally valid sources of knowledge and the creation of an authorised tradition. Ben Sira makes hardly any reference to laws which are more important than the Pentateuch. Books such as *Enoch* and *Wisdom* are evidence of the kind of literature in circulation in the inter-testamental period together with the Torah and the other biblical books. Wisdom and apocalyptic literature have biblical prototypes, but they do not confirm the Torah as central.

BIBLIOGRAPHY

BLACK, M., «Pharisees», *The Interpreter's Dictionary of the Bible*, vol. 3, Abingdon Nashville 1981, 774-781.
DAVIES, D., *Introduction to Pharisaism*, Philadelphia PA 1967.
GUTTMANN, A., *Rabbinic Judaism in the Making: A Chapter in the History of the Halakhah from Ezra to Judah*, I, Detroit MI 1970.
MEADE, D.G., *Pseudonymity and Canon. An Investigation into the Relationship and Authority in Jewish and Earliest Christian Tradition*, Grand Rapids MI 1985.
MEYER, R., *Tradition und Neueschöpfung im antiken Judentum: Dargestellt an der Geschichte des Pharisäismus*, Berlin 1965.
NEUSNER, J., *The Rabbinic Traditions About the Pharisees Before 70*, 3 vols., Leiden 1971.
SALDARINI, A.J., «Pharisees», *ABD* v, New York 1992, 289-303.
SIMON, M., *Les sectes juives au temps de Jésus*, Paris 1960.
SMITH, M., «Palestinian Judaism in the First Century», *Israel: Its Role in Civilization*, ed., M. Davis, New York 1956, 67-81.
SMITH, M.S., *Parties and Politics that Shaped the Old Testament*, New York 1971.
ZEITLIN, S., «The Origin of the Pharisees Reconsidered», *JQR* 52 (1969) 97-128.

V.   THE CANON ACCORDING TO THE ESSENES

1.   *The Origins and Character of the Qumran Community*

In the early years of study of the Dead Sea Scrolls, in the fifties and sixties, there were several different *theories about the origin and history of the Qumran group*. It was identified in turn as the mediaeval sect of the Karaites (a false hypothesis proposed by Zeitlin), a Jewish-Christian group (Teicher), a Zealot group connected with the events of the Jewish war in 70 CE (Roth, G.R. Driver) or a group from the period of Alexander Jannaeus, Aristobulus or Hyrcanus II (De Vaux, at first). The Qumran group has also been connected with the Pharisees (Rabin), the Sadducees (R. North) or the Zealots (Roth, Driver).

The theory which has gained greatest acceptance puts the origin of the Qumran community *in the time of the Maccabees* (Dupont-Sommer, Milik, Cross, De Vaux, Vermes, Hengel, etc.), possibly in connection with the circumstances arising from the assassination of Onias III or from the change of calendar imposed in 167 (VanderKam). The members of the Qumran community are usually identified *as a group of Essenes* formed from the ḥasîdîm movement (Stegemann, Beall).

Recently, some scholars tend to set the remote origins of the Qumran community in a period before the period of the Maccabees, either in Palestine or in Babylon.

The theory of a *Babylonian origin* assumes that the Essene group was formed in Babylon, from where it returned to Palestine at the time of the Maccabaean revolt. There, it soon came into conflict with the other existing groups and movements and as a result of this conflict formed itself into a small group. This group, led by the Teacher of Righteousness, broke away from mainstream Essenism and took refuge in the desert, so beginning the Qumran community (Murphy-O'Connor).

The «Groningen hypothesis» (Van der Woude, F. García Martínez) supposes that the Essene movement *originated in Palestine* within the Palestinian apocalyptic tradition, before the Antiochene crisis, that is, towards the end of the 3rd cent. BCE or at the beginning of the 2nd cent. BCE. The Qumran group began as a result of a split within the Essene movement itself and in consequence the group faithful to the Teacher of Righteousness left Jersualem and settled permanently in Qumran. This hypothesis starts from two prior suppositions. The epithet «wicked priest» has to be applied to more than one Hasmonaean leader and not only to Jonathan or another Maccabee. Also, a clear distinction must be drawn between the origins of the Qumran group and the origins of the Essene movement, while apocalyptic tradition must be dated back to the 3rd cent. BCE.

In any case, Essenism has its roots deep in apocalyptic tradition. In studying this tradition, it is necessary to distinguish clearly and study separately three different aspects: the literary form of the «apocalypses» and the works belonging to this genre (to which reference has been made in the section on apocalyptic re-written works, p. 194); «apocalyptic» as a social movement from which the Essene movement and the Qumran community derive (to which reference will be made below), and «apocalyptic» eschatology, i.e. the world of ideas and symbolic images which find expression in the apocalypses and determine the viewpoint from which these writings interpret the canonical books of the OT. Apocalyptic was in the air at that time. It is not surprising that ideas and motifs of apocalyptic form frequently occur in works belonging to other literary genres and writings by authors from religious circles which were not specifically apocalyptic.

The fact that over a period of more than 150 years, numerous works of apocalyptic style and genre were written, can only mean that *an «apocalyptic» movement and social group* existed which produced these literary works. The apocalypses, in fact, include references to groups with these characteristics (*1 Enoch* 1:1; 90:6; 93:5.9-10). *Apocalyptic movements, ideas and literary forms* crystallised into the *Essene movement* and later became institutionalised as the *Qumran community*, separated from mainstream Essenism.

Nowadays, the origins of the *apocalyptic movement* are generally sought in the Mesopotamian world (VanderKam), although it cannot be forgotten that Greek, Latin and Persian literature also has writings of an apocalyptic nature. Apocalyptic, born in Mesopotamia not later than the 3rd cent. BCE, crystallised into the *Essene movement*, the most characteristic features of which are precisely apocalyptic in nature: determinism, an interest in anything related to the world of angels (*Angelic liturgy, Book of War* 7:6), the idea of the eschatological Temple (with the resulting rejection of the Temple of Jerusalem) and the method of biblical interpretation. At Qumran, interpretation is changed to the category of revelation: this is obtained by means of the interpretation of dreams and of secret books or heavenly tablets. Prophetic interpretation now passes through the sieve of apocalyptic tradition (cf. p. 446).

The Qumran community originated from the Essene movement, from which it detached itself. It is not easy to determine the moment when this separation occurred. What is certain is that in the period of John Hyrcanus' high priesthood, the group of Essenes which had followed the Teacher of Righteousness was already settled in Qumran. There they lived in a state of very high tension between two apparently contradictory tendencies: eschatological hope in an end foretold by the Scriptures which was to become a reality in the community itself, and the strict observance of the regulations of the community's own *hălākâ*. In the *Damascus Document* (1:5-12) it says that «(God...) raised up for them a Teacher of Righteousness, in order to direct them in the path of his heart and to make known to the last generations what he had done for the final generation». These two clauses express the twofold mission of the Teacher of Righteousness: eschatological revelation and halakhic interpretation. Similarly, they express the polarity between the two characteristics and tendencies evident in the Qumran community and lead to the interpretations found concerning the meaning of the writings of this community.

The problem of the calendar highlights the twofold source, at once eschatological and halakhic, of the writings and lifestyle of the Qumran community. The calendar of feasts has legal import, as the fundamental premiss of the regulation of the cult. In addition, it has the function of dividing history into periods as well as the function of calculating the end of times, both themes which belong to earlier apocalyptic tradition. If the Teacher of Righteousness or the Qumran community allow themselves to change legal directives by invoking a new interpretation of the appropriate biblical passages, this is due to them all believing in having access through revelation to the correct interpretation of Scripture. This is shown by the text of *1QH* 2:13-14: «You have set me like... a wise interpreter of marvellous mysteries...».

Thus, within the Qumran group are combined the two poles around which the Judaism of the period revolves: halakhic interpretation and apocalyptic revelation.

The Qumran community was an «apocalyptic community», which originated in the setting of apocalyptic movements, so widespread at the time. The Teacher of Righteousness and the «Man of Lies» were prophetic figures from the mid-second cent. BCE, whose concerns revolved around matters of both a halakhic and an apocalyptic nature (Collins). It is not possible to draw more exact conclusions with certainty. The thesis of the Babylonian origin of the Qumran community seems to contradict the very specific facts of the

Damascus Document. On the other hand, the hypothesis according to which the withdrawal from the sect was caused by a dispute about succession in the high priesthood, lacks support in the texts. Similarly, the hypothesis that the Teacher of Righteousness functioned as a high priest during the *intersacerdotium* does not seem likely. Nor are there proofs that the «Man of Lies» was an Essene leader.

2. The Biblical Canon of the Qumran Community

To gain an idea of the biblical canon used in the Qumran community, it is necessary to look at the contents of the library found in the Qumran caves. Three sets of data guide us in respect of the books which the Qumran community particularly valued or perhaps even considered as canonical.

The first set of data is made up of the number of duplicates preserved: 31 copies of the book of Psalms, 25 of Dt, 18 of Is, 14 of Gn and Ex, 8 of Dn and the Minor Prophets, 7 of Lv, 6 of Ez, 4 each of Nm, Sm, Jr, Job, Ruth, Song and Lam, 3 of Jgs and Kgs, 2 of Jos, Pr and Qoh and lastly, 1 copy of Ezr and Chr.

The second is the number of commentaries on each biblical book: 5 copies have been found of commentaries on the book of Is, 3 on Pss, 2 on Hos and Mic and 1 copy of a commentary on the books of Hab and Zeph.

The third consists of the introductory formulae («it is written», etc.) by which books considered to be authorised or canonical are quoted: books cited in this way are Is, Jr, Ez, Dn, Minor Prophets and Pss.

The data set out indicate that for the Qumran community the Torah and the Prophets comprised a sort of «canon within the canon». The Torah formed part of the oldest deposit for it is represented by 4 palaeo-Hebrew MSS of Lv, 2 of Gn, Ex and Dt, 1 of Nm and Job. The *pĕšārîm* or Qumran commentaries to Isaiah, the Minor Prophets and the book of Psalms (which was possibly joined to the collection of Prophets) attest to recognition of canonical value of this collection

As for the «other books», Qoheleth is represented by 2 copies. Its inclusion in the canon was recommended by its supposedly Salomonic authorship. The Song of Songs, also attributed to Solomon and certainly already interpreted allegorically, is represented by 4 copies. The book of Lamentations, for certain already attributed to Jeremiah, has appeared in 4 copies. It is questionable whether the book of Ruth was listed in the Qumran library among the prophetic books, as happened later, or among the Writings, as in the masoretic tradition.

The book of Esther is the only one of which no copy at all has appeared. Unless due to chance, this fact seems to suggest that the Qumran community did not accept the book, nor did they celebrate the Feast of Purim. The Essenes of Qumran could have objected to this book since it portrays Esther as a Jewish woman married to a pagan foreigner, without adding any condemnation of an act reprehensible in every way. The same accusation could also be made of the book of Ruth, although it does appear among the books of the Qumran library. The gravest objection which the Essenes, and only the Essenes, could raise against the book of Esther is the reference to its contradictions with the Essene calendar of 364 days (cf. the «Astronomical book» in *1 Enoch* 72-82). Certainly, the book of Esther was the last to be included in the biblical canon. The book of Daniel is already to be found in the Qumran library.

At Qumran, several types of Psalter seem to have co-existed, some of which included apocryphal poems.

The Qumran community seems to have granted at least a degree of canonical value to other books of which multiple copies have been found. The Enochian Pentateuch was very much in use at Qumran. 4 Copies of the *Astronomical book* have appeared, 5 of the *Book of Watchers*, 15 of the *Book of Giants*, 4 of the *Book of Dreams* and 2 of the *Letter of Enoch*. Also significant is the number of copies of the *Book of Jubilees*, 12 in all.

In such a situation it is logical to ask the question whether the Essenes used a more extensive canon than did the Pharisees, and included those books found in multiple copies in the Qumran library, such as *1 Enoch*, the *Testament of Levi, Jubilees* and the *Temple Scroll*. One school of modern research tends to think that the Essenes did not intend to add new books to those of the Torah and the Prophets but merely to give them a new interpretation based on a new revelation. The Essenes ranked the pseudepigraphical books below the canonical books. This is shown by the fact that the writings of the Qumran community very often cite canonical literature with suitable formulae, whereas quotations from Essene pseudepigraphical writings are very rare and in any case are not accompanied with the formula peculiar to a biblical quotation (Beckwith, cf. p. 432). However, the decisive element, when speaking of the canon of the Qumran Essenes, is not so much to determine which collection of books they considered canonical, as to be aware of the viewpoint, possibly not all that «canonical», from which they read canonical books and produced a re-reading very different from the biblical texts. This viewpoint is determined by «apocalyptic» ideas (cf. p. 194).

BIBLIOGRAPHY (cf. p. 458-459)

BEALL, T.S., *Josephus' Description of the Essenes Illustrated by the Dead Sea Scrolls*, Cambridge 1988.
COLLINS, J.J., «The Origin of the Qumran Community: A Review of the Evidence», *To Touch the Text*, eds., P. Kobelsky-M. Horgan, New York 1990, 159-178.
COLLINS, J.J., «Was the Dead Sea Sect an Apocalyptic Movement?», *Archaeology and History in the Dead Sea Scrolls*, ed. L.H. Schiffman, Sheffield 1990, 25-52.
COLLINS, J.J., *The Apocalyptic Imagination. An Introduction to the Jewish Matrix of Christianity*, New York 1984.
DAVIES, P.R., «The Birthplace of the Essenes: Where is 'Damaskus'?», *The Texts of Qumran and the History of the Community*, RQ 14 (1990) 503-519.
DRIVER, G.R., *The Judaean Scrolls: The Problem and a Solution*, Oxford 1965.
DUPONT-SOMMER, A., *Les écrits esséniens découverts près de la Mer Morte*, Paris 1957.

GARCÍA MARTÍNEZ, F., «A 'Groningen' Hypothesis of Qumran Origins and Early History», *RQ* 14 (1990) 521-541

KNIBB, M.A., *The Qumran Community*, Cambridge 1987.

MURPHY-O'CONNOR, J., «The Essenes and their History», *RB* 81 (1974) 215-244.

MURPHY-O'CONNOR, J., «The Damascus Document Revisited», *RB* 92 (1985) 223-246.

NICKELSBURG, G.W.E., «Social Aspects of Palestinian Jewish Apocalypticism», *Apocalypticism in the Mediterranean World and the Near East*, ed. D. Hellholm, Tübingen 1983, 641-646.

NORTH, R., «The Qumran 'Sadducees'», *CBQ* 17 (1955) 44-68.

QIMRON, E.-STRUNGNELL, J., «An Unpublished Halakhic Letter from Qumran», *Biblical Archeology To-day: Proceedings of the International Congress on Biblical Archeology*, Jerusalem 1985, 400-407.

RABIN, CH., *Qumran Studies*, Oxford 1957.

RABIN, CH., *The Zadokite Documents, I. The Admonition, II. The Laws*, Oxford 1958².

ROTH, C., *The Historical Background of the Dead Sea Scrolls*, Oxford 1958.

ROWLAND, CH., *The Open Heaven. A Study of Apocalyptic in Judaism and Early Christianity*, New York 1982.

RUSSELL, D.S., *Apocalyptic: Ancient and Modern*, Philadelphia PA 1978.

SACCHI, P., *L'Apocalittica guidaica e la sua storia*, Brescia 1990.

STEGEMANN, H., *Die Entstehung der Qumrangemeinde*, Bonn 1971.

TEICHER, J.L., «The Dead Sea Scrolls-Documents of the Jewish-Christian Sect of Ebionites», *JJS* 2 (1951) 67-99.

VANDERKAM, J.C., *Enoch and the Growth of an Apocalyptic Tradition*, Washington DC 1984.

VAN DER WOUDE, A.S., «Wicked Priest or Wicked Priests? Reflections on the Identification of the Wicked Priest in the Habakkuk Commentary», *JJSt* 33 (1982) 349-359.

VAUX, R. DE, «Esséniens ou Zélotes: à propos d'un livre récent», *RB* 73 (1966) 212-235.

ZEITLIN, S., *The Dead Sea Scrolls and Modern Scholarship*, Philadelphia PA 1956.

VI. THE CANON IN THE HELLENISTIC JEWISH DIASPORA

1. *Hellenistic Judaism*

The expression «Hellenistic Judaism» refers to the Judaism of the communities scattered the length and breadth of the Greek and Roman world during the period beginning with Alexander the Great (336-323 BCE). In Palestine, it extends to the period of Hadrian. The Jews of these communities adopted and absorbed Hellenistic language, customs and culture in an attempt to combine Greek culture and the Jewish faith.

The movements of the population caused by ceaseless wars, the development of trade in these centuries and the attraction of life in Hellenistic cities were the main causes producing the Jewish diaspora in this period. In the 1st cent. CE, the Jewish population of the diaspora was greater than in their own metropolis in Palestine.

The Jewish diaspora, however, maintained close links with the metropolis and with Jerusalem. Jews more than 20 years old had to contribute to the upkeep of the cult in Jerusalem with an annual tribute of half a shekel (Ex 30:11-16 cf. Mt 17:24-27 Mishnah *Sheqalim*) or two Greek drachmas (Philo, *Legatio ad Gaium* 23; Josephus, *Antiq.* 14,7,2; 18,9,1). On the occasion of the three annual feasts of pilgrimage, large crowds of Jews came to Jerusalem from the diaspora (*War* 6,9,3).

There were great contrasts between Hellenistic Judaism and the Judaism of the Palestinian metropolis, although the differences must not be over-exaggerated, for it has to be remembered that Palestinian Judaism was also very Hellenised. However, it remains clear that Palestinian Judaism was rooted in the post-exilic theocracy and culminated in Pharisaic rabbinism. The Judaism of the diaspora seeks greater integration in the world of Hellenistic syncretism, while trying not to lose its Jewish roots.

The Jewish communities provided themselves with the requisite organisation for safeguarding their rights and preserving their signs of Jewish identity. The systems of organisation varied from place to place. In general, the Jews were organised into independent groups, even within well-defined territory. The basic organisation system comprised the *políteuma*. Other ethnic groups had a similar organisation, which generally went back to the period of military service carried out during the Ptolemaic period.

In Alexandria, the Jews had succeeded in forming a single semi-autonomous political corporation, endowed with administrative, financial and legal functions (Aristeas 310). The Jews were not real citizens of the Greek *polis*. The *polis* tended to establish a single *politeia* based on kinship connected with municipal worship (*syggéneia*). As a result, the *polis* tended to abolish the Jewish *politeia*. Jews, therefore, were usually called «foreigners» or «permanent residents» (*metoíkoi*).

The Jewish *politeia* tried to guarantee the preservation of Jewish ancestral customs and at the same time the participation by Jews in the life of the city. The Jews of Alexandria fought to retain their *politeia* not merely to acquire full incorporation in the *polis*. They tended to place their trust in the central government, in the Ptolemaic kings and Roman emperors.

As a result, the population of Alexandria, in confrontation with the Ptolemies and the Romans, unleashed their hatred against them on the Jews.

There is not enough information to suppose that the Jews, as an organised group, wished to infiltrate the Alexandrian gymnasium and, by that means, attain full citizenship and full integration in the *polis*. In fact there are indications of a rejection of the gymnasium and of all that it signified.

In Rome, the Jews formed small private societies of unassuming character, given the name *synagōgē*. The powers that be allowed the Jews free practise of their religion and the enjoyment of other privileges. They also punished attempts to suppress these rights (Josephus, *Antiq.* 14,8,5; 10,12,3-6;

16,6,2-7). In the Roman Empire, Judaism enjoyed the legal status of *religio licita* (Tertullian, *Apologeticum* 21).

The Jews were exempt from being obliged to take part in the cult of the emperor, a privilege Caligula did not respect (Josephus, *Antiq.* 19,5,2-3). They were allowed to administer the resources of their own communities, including the collection and payment of contributions for the temple of Jerusalem (Philo, *Legatio ad Gaium* 23 Josephus, *Antiq.* 16,6,2-7) and held jurisdiction to settle civil lawsuits between Jews.

Recognition of the privilege of observing the Sabbath also entailed a long series of privileges, including exemption from military service (*Antiq.* 18,8,4 14,10,11-14.16.18-19) and from attending tribunals on the Sabbath (16,6,2.4). However, there is no clear information enabling a satisfactory answer to the question of whether the Jews had civil rights in Greek cities, with a full share in public life.

In the religious sector and from the Greek point of view, Judaism was one more cult among many in the Hellenistic world. Greek-speaking Jewish writers put particular emphasis on what they considered to be specific to Judaism: obedience to the law of Moses (4 Mc 5:19-26 9:2; Josephus, *Ag.Apion* II 39; Philo, *Life of Moses* 2,3.5 3; Mc 2:31-33; *Sibylline Oracles* III 573-85 762-71), faithful compliance with the ancestral customs of the people, strict monotheism and an aniconic cult, moral ideals and the precepts related to Sabbath observance, circumcision and the ban on eating pork. The Jews' belief in a single, all powerful and just Creator was in contrast with the crude polytheism of their pagan neighbours. The Jews frequently expressed their pride in it, mocking polytheism and the worship given to images (Wisd 13:10-19 15:7-17).

However, the Jews could not remain immune to the influence of Hellenism, particularly the Greek language. Towards 250 BCE, there were sufficient numbers of Greek-speaking Jews to feel the need for translating the Pentateuch into Greek which had become the language of synagogal worship owing to increasing ignorance of Hebrew.

Proselytism continued to give life to Judaism in the diaspora. Even at the margins of missionary activity, the Jews by their mere presence and through contacts of all kinds and their synagogues open to all made themselves noticed among the gentile population. Particularly attractive to the pagans were Jewish monotheism, insistence on the original unity of the human race, on ethical behaviour, judgment by God, promise in eternal salvation, etc. In the eyes of many, Judaism appeared to be a philosophy, and synagogal worship an assembly of teachers and disciples of a foreign school of philosophy. To others it was like the Oriental mystery cults which claimed to offer a path to eternal life. The most salient feature of Judaism was undoubtedly fidelity in keeping the Sabbath, fasts and dietary rules.

Circumcision, however, was a real obstacle to conversions. This explains the fact that most of the proselytes were women. Many gentiles followed Judaism in an uncompromising way as «fearers of God» (*sebómenoi, phoboúmenoi tòn theón*). The swift Hellenisation of Christianity to a large extent followed the path already traced out by Jewish proselytism. Many gentiles, who saw circumcision as an insurmountable obstacle, were now prepared to accept gentile Christianity.

However, a degree of anti-Jewish feeling did not fail to grow. Although Hellenism was open to innumerable cults and gods, the monotheism of the Jews which did not acknowledge the pantheon of Greek and Roman gods, was very often portrayed as true atheism and their social exclusiveness as hatred of humanity. The privileges and exemption granted by the Romans provoked envy as also did the continuous flow of contributions by the Jews to Jerusalem. The proselytes to Judaism broke their ties with family and friends which heightened resentment by the gentiles.

2.   *The Canon of the Hellenistic Jewish Diaspora*

The Greek Bible, transmitted with Christianity, differs from the rabbinic Bible in the number and sequence of books and their text. The Greek Bible adds several books (Tobias, Judith, Maccabees, etc.) and inserts new chapters into some books (the «additions» to Daniel, Jeremiah, Job, etc.).

Contrary to what was thought for a long time, a real «Alexandrian canon» in Greek which could be considered as parallel to the «Palestinian canon» in Hebrew never existed (Sundberg; cf. p. 155-156).

The traditional theory on the existence of an «Alexandrian canon», which was supposed to include more books than the Palestinian canon, was based, among other data (see below) on the fact that the codices of the LXX contained several apocryphal books. However, it should be remembered that the great codices of the 5th cent. were very much longer than codices in previous centuries. In any case, they are all of Christian origin, for from the 2nd cent. CE on, the Jews ceased to use the LXX version which they replaced with other Jewish versions. In fact, Greek codices reflect the situation of the 4th and 5th cents., which cannot be compared in any way with that of previous centuries.

It is commonly supposed that Philo and the Hellenist Jews did not share the view of the rabbis of Palestine that the spirit of prophecy had ended centuries ago. The Hellenist Jews preferred to consider that a wider literature than outlined by the Pharisees also enjoyed the privilege of prophetic inspiration. However, even if that were the case, the conclusion cannot be drawn that Hellenistic Judaism used a wider canon than rabbinic Judaism. In fact, the works of Philo do not cite the apocryphal books even once, which invalidates any hypothesis about the existence of a Hellenistic canon. On the other hand, it would be very strange if a book like 1 Mac, which insists that for some time prophecy had ended (4:46 9:27 14:41) could form part of a supposed Hellenistic canon, the existence of which depends precisely on the statement that prophecy had not yet ended, even in a previous period.

The theory of the Alexandrian canon had two other mainstays which have also collapsed. The first was that Hellenistic Judaism and Palestinian Judaism were both different and remote. The second was that the apocryphal books were mostly composed in Greek on Egyptian soil.

Certainly Ben Sira and 1 Mc come from Palestine and many of the apocrypha are translations from Hebrew or Aramaic originals from Palestine, with the exception of the other three books of Maccabees and, also in part, the book of Wisdom. On the other hand, the preface to the book of Ben Sira, written in Egypt, mentions three times the threefold division of the canon and there is no evidence at all to support the statement that any of the apocrypha had a place in the three established divisions.

In conclusion, the Judaism of the Hellenistic diaspora was no different from Palestinian Judaism in respect of the extent of the canon, although it could have very great esteem for books written in Greek, in the way that the Essenes of Palestine also had great esteem for other books written in Hebrew or Aramaic. The rivalry among Pharisees, Sadducees and Essenes, which exploded in the years of Jonathan Maccabeus' high priesthood (152-142 BCE) must have had repercussions in the breadth of the canon accepted by any one group. However, the fact is that they all agree in accepting a canon which in general lines had already been established shortly before the explosion of rivalry among them (Beckwith, cf. p. 165).

It should not be forgotten, however, that Judaism prior to 70 was marked by a huge variety of forms. Some Pharisee circles did not rigidly apply the principle that the chain of prophetic succession had been broken in the Persian period, which in principle left the book of Ben Sira outside the canon. If in the Judaism of the Greek diaspora a man such as Philo could witness a conservative Judaism centred on the Torah, other devout circles of that diaspora were prepared to consider as canonical several writings such as, for example, the «additions» to the books of Daniel and Esther. At the beginning of the 1st cent. CE, the book of Wisdom came to increase the number of pseudepigrapha attributed to Solomon, later becoming part of the Greek Bible. These groups, like the Qumran community, were not at all concerned about closing the canon of biblical books completely. The Christian Greek Bible does no more than reflect this situation which dominated before 70, in which it is not possible to speak of the existence of a closed canon (Sundberg).

This present discussion concerning the OT canon moves between acknowledging the Pharisee canon as already well fixed in the mid-second cent. BCE (Beckwith, who suggests that the Christians changed a well established Jewish practice, cf. p. 234) and supposing that, at the start of the Christian period, in both Palestine and Alexandria, the canon as yet had no exact limits (Sundberg, cf. p. 234).

VII. THE CHRISTIAN CANON OF THE OLD TESTAMENT

The Christian canon adds the books of the NT to the end of the Jewish canon. This addition radically alters the meaning of the whole.

At the beginning of Christianity, the first Christian writings, which later came to form part of the NT, could still be viewed as simply yet more writings in the vast Jewish literature of the period. These writings referred to the whole, comprising the Torah, the Prophets and the Writings as the only accepted Scriptures to exist. However, they soon became an entity in their own right, eventually proclaimed as a «New» Testament, parallel to the Scriptures of the Jews, now changed to an «Old» Testament.

The frequent *quotations* of the OT in the NT present a picture very like that shown by the Qumran library. The books cited most in the NT are, first of all the Psalms, followed by Isaiah, Deuteronomy and the other books of the Torah. The Apocalypse owes a great deal to the books of Ezekiel and Daniel. The book of Daniel is quoted as the work of a «prophet» (Mt 9:27) or within the category of «the prophets» (1 Pt 1:10-12).

The OT of the first Christians was basically the same as that of the Jewish community. The disputes between Christians and Jews do not show important differences with regard to the list of authorised books. If at a later period the Christian Church granted canonical status to some books which did not form part of the Hebrew Bible, that is due more to a tradition of using such books than to a conscious decision to extend the biblical canon (Ellis).

There are two different *explanations of the Christian canon of the* OT. The first supposes Christianity to have inherited a Jewish canon of 22 books (24 in the MT). Christianity differed from Judaism in the way it interpreted the OT, but not in the number and content of the books of the Bible. The LXX version, as transmitted in Christian codices from the mid-2nd cent. CE, formed a *mixed corpus* of books, which to some extent was equivalent to a Jewish canon differing from the canon of rabbinic tradition (Beckwith, Ellis). Instead, according to another school of thought, the Christian Church did not inherit from Judaism a canon which was already closed. The Church had already followed an independent road, different from Judaism, when the rabbinic canon was permanently closed (Sundberg). Christianity had the idea of an open OT canon. This is the reason why the Christian canon is not exactly the same as the Jewish one.

The final establishment of the Christian canon of the OT occurred at quite a late period, in the 4th cent. CE, when the definitive lists of books considered as canonical were fixed. Up to that time, one has to speak of «authorised» writings but not of canonical books. In Judaism, the «formative process» of the OT canon is found already almost complete in the mid-2nd cent. BCE, but the definitive list was not drawn up until the close of the 2nd cent. CE, or at least, the final discussions about some of the books were not settled until that period. In Christianity, the closing decades of the 2nd cent. comprise the decisive period in the «formative process» of the canon, but the definitive list was not established until the 4th cent. (cf. p. 237).

COLLINS, J.J., «Was the Dead Sea Sect an Apocalyptic Movement?», *Archaeology and History in the Dead Sea Scrolls*, ed. L.H. Schiffman, Sheffield 1990, 25-52.

COLLINS, J.J., *The Apocalyptic Imagination. An Introduction to the Jewish Matrix of Christianity*, New York 1984.

DAVIES, W.D., *Paul and Rabbinic Judaism*, London 1948.

SALDARINI, A.J., *Pharisees, Scribes and Sadducees in Palestinian Society*, Edinburgh 1988.

STRECKER, G., «On the Problem of Jewish Christianity», *Appendix to Orthodoxy and Heresy in Earliest Christianity*, eds., R. Kraft-G. Frodel, Philadelphia PA 1979, 241-285.

WACHOLDER, B.Z., «The Ancient Judaeo-Aramaic Literature (500-165 BCE). A Classification of Pre-Qumranic Texts», *Archaeology and History in the Dead Sea Scrolls*, ed. L.H. Schiffman, Sheffield 1990, 257-281.

3

Early Christian Literature: Collections of Canonical and Apocryphal Books

I. INTRODUCTION

Discussion about matters connected with the NT canon has usually been in the hands of those studying patristics, the history of theology and the history of the Church. The biblical scholar or NT theologian has generally considered his task complete when, historically speaking, he has reached the last work to be included in the NT corpus (2nd epistle of Peter). The same applies, theologically speaking, when he has reached the critical moment of the «death of the last apostle», the instant when Scripture gave place to the Tradition of the Church as a new source of revelation. This hiatus of time between the NT writings and the writings of the apostolic Fathers, between the apostolic and «sub-apostolic» periods, is completely artificial, as is the literary distinction between canonical and apocryphal literature.

The discovery of the Gnostic library of Nag Hammadi has revived interest in study of the NT canon, just as the discovery of the Qumran library revived interest in the OT canon. The discovery of the apocryphal literature of the OT has also had its counterpart in renewed interest in the apocryphal literature of the NT.

The historical perspective from which the NT canon is studied has also changed. It focuses less on the final moment of council decisions on the «list» of canonical books and more on the earliest moment of the gradual process by which, through very many controversies and vicissitudes, the NT canon was finally established. Study of the history of the canon cannot be restricted to an analysis of «lists» of canonical books from the patristic period. It is necessary to relate these lists to each other, in respect of time and place, and to set them within the context of the formative process of Christian theology and the history of the Church in the first centuries.

Accordingly, as happens in respect of the OT canon, today more emphasis is placed on the plurality and diversity of writings which make up the NT, in its structure, in its diachronic formation and in its theological meaning

Lastly, the problem of the canon has become a crucial question in modern theology, decisive no less for a definition of Christian being in general and the way of being Christian specific to each of the great confessional faiths and Christian Churches (Käsemann). In this way, historical problems seem very closely connected with theological problems.

As was said with regard to the OT, the history of the NT canon cannot be separated (as happened in the past) from the history and criticism of the text and from the history of NT exegesis (Hanson).

II. THE HISTORY OF THE COLLECTIONS OF CANONICAL BOOKS OF THE NEW TESTAMENT

It is necessary to make a distinction between what the word «canon» can refer to: the historical *process* by means of which the collection of canonical books was formed and the *closed list* of canonical books established by the Church.

If the canonical nature of the NT books lies more in their apostolic *origins* than in mere inclusion in the conciliar lists, it has to be said that the NT was already established from the moment when the various books it comprises were written. However, the compilation of the *lists* of the councils required a long period and underwent a complex historical process until it had been defined which books were to belong to the canon and which were to remain outside it.

According to the classic theory of the history of the NT canon, the second half of the 2nd cent. CE is the period of the decisive events leading to the formation of the canonical corpus of the NT.

Towards the end of the 2nd cent., the basic «nucleus» of the future NT canon had already been formed. This nucleus comprised the four gospels, the thirteen epistles of Paul, Acts, 1 Pt and 1 Jn. The Fathers of the end of the 2nd cent. and of the beginning of the 3rd cent., as well as the Muratonian Fragment, already know this corpus of Christian literature and cite it as canonical scripture on the same footing as the OT, the only Scriptures of the Christians until shortly before.

In the following two centuries, a consensus was gradually reached on the canonical status of the other books, so that towards the end of the 4th cent. the NT canon had already acquired its final form. The Easter Letter of Athanasius in 367 gives a list which already agrees fundamentally with those transmitted from then on.

Five periods can be distinguished in the formation of the canon.

1.   *The Apostolic Period: until 70 CE*

At that time, the primitive Church had no other Scriptures except «the Law and the Prophets», i.e., the OT, read however, in the light of Christology and Christian eschatology.

The apostolic period knew the beginning of the transition process from oral message to written document. This process corresponds to an absolutely unbroken line of transmission from the preaching of the first apostles of Christianity to the written legacy which emerges in the closing decades of the 1st cent. At the beginning of the following century, Papias had such an awareness of continuity linking him with apostolic tradition that he seized on its oral transmission in preference to the written form.

2.   *The Sub-apostolic Period: from 70 to 135* CE

In this period the collection of the gospels and the collection of Pauline letters were formed. The other traditions which go back to Paul were put together in the deutero-Pauline letters. The definitive collection of Johannine writings was also formed. Just as the Jewish Bible was known as «the Law and the Prophets», the Christian Bible of this period could be called «the Prophets and the Apostles».

The formative process of the NT consisted in making a large collection from smaller collections. The gospels and the Pauline letters comprise the two nuclei of the canon, and the book of Acts, which showed the apostolic character of Paul, served to unite both. Acts, the catholic letters and the Apocalypse circulated at first as separate writings, not forming part of any collection.

A statistical study on the frequency with which ecclesiastical writers used the NT books allows the probable conclusion that the gospels acquired some authority shortly before the collection of Pauline letters.

a. The collection of gospels. In the period of the apostolic Fathers, the gospel traditions were known by means of oral rather than written tradition (Köster 1957). In the mid-2nd cent., at the time of Justin, the various gospels or *memoria* of the apostles are known already. The *Diatessaron* of Tatian, which merges the synoptic gospels into one, shows that in the 2nd cent. there was a tendency to prefer a single gospel to several, two, three or four gospels.

The *Gospel of Thomas* represents an independent redaction of an ancient gospel tradition. The same can also be said, perhaps, of the other works of the library of Nag Hammadi (*Gospel of Peter, Dialogue of the Saviour, Apocryphon of John*). Today, the apocryphal gospels cannot be rejected as if they were late products dependent on the canonical gospels (Köster 1971, 1980).

For a long time the gospels circulated separately, independently of each other. Later, two or more gospels began to be used simultaneously. It used to be said that the collection of four canonical gospels was established at the time of Irenaeus (Von Campenhausen 1972). However, it is generally thought that by the mid-2nd cent. matters were still somewhat fluid. In some churches, acceptance of one or another of the four gospels was still being discussed, or some other gospel which failed to enter the canon was added. The collection of four gospels was not finally imposed until the end of the 2nd cent.

b. The Collection of Paul's letters. Towards the end of the 2nd cent., all the

Christian churches also knew the collection of Pauline letters and used it in the liturgy and in teaching. However, the question as to the number of letters which formed part of the first and oldest collection of Paul's letters can be answered in several ways, although all more or less concur:

1. A Christian writer, who was interested in Paul's personality and knew Acts, published in Ephesus a corpus of ten letters, all except the pastoral letters (Goodspeed) and also composed a letter as an introduction to the collection: the letter to the Ephesians.

2. The redaction of some Pauline letters, the composition of some pseudepigraphic writings attributed to Paul and the compilation of all Paul's literary legacy were possibly the work of the «Pauline school», a group of persons who knew and admired the character and work of the apostle. This school compiled the authentic letters and composed further «new» ones: Col, Eph, 2 Thess, 1 and 2 Tim and Tit, eventually publishing the complete corpus (Schenke).

3. The Pauline corpus underwent two editions: the first contained the letters to the seven churches; the second added the pastoral letters, finally reaching the number thirteen (Dahl).

4. Until 90 CE, there were several ancient collections of Pauline letters (*Ur-Corpora*) of varying length, in various places, which included some or all of the following letters: 1 and 2 Cor, Heb, Rom, Gal, Eph and Phm (Aland).

5. The first *Pauline corpus* contained the following seven letters: 1 and 2 Cor, Heb, Rom, Php, 1 and 2 Thess and Rom (W. Schmithals).

c. The Book of the Acts of the Apostles acted as a connecting link between the two large collections, the gospels and the Pauline letters. It bonded the characters of Peter and Paul, the two apostles who had a decisive influence on the formation not only of Christianity but also of the Christian Bible. (Farmer).

The essential elements of the NT canon, represented in the gospels, Acts and the Pauline letters, stem from the agreement which Peter and Paul reached in Jerusalem, possibly also an agreement with James, three years after Paul's conversion.

d. Among the *remaining writings* which later came to form part of the NT canon, the *catholic letters* had, at first, limited circulation only in certain areas. Only the letters 1 Pt and 1 Jn seem to have enjoyed wide circulation in the 2nd cent. The *Apocalypse* was well known in the West but hardly at all in the East. The opposite happened to the *Letter to the Hebrews*.

So, towards the end of the 2nd cent., the four gospels, the letters of Paul, Acts and the First Letters of Peter and John were generally accepted as authoritative. However, the situation was not the same everywhere. These are the writings cited most by Irenaeus, Tertullian and Clement, but there was still no agreement yet about the authority of the other books in that period. Differences of opinion lasted throughout the 3rd cent. and until well into the 4th.

The fact that there were four different gospels continued to cause problems. Several times and in different ways attempts were made to unify the gospel tradition: Tatian reduced the four gospels to one (the *Diatessaron*), Marcion reduced the canon to the gospel of Luke alone.

In the initial stages some churches knew only a single gospel: in Palestine, Matthew's was the most widespread; in some areas of Asia Minor only John's was used; the same thing happened to the gospels of Mark and Luke in these areas respectively.

3. *The Period of Early Gnosticism: from 135 to the Death of Justin in 165 CE*

In this period Christianity detached itself from its Jewish roots and acquired forms characteristic of Gentile Christianity. The Church which had risen from paganism did not succeed in rejecting the OT but sometimes felt it as a weighty legacy.

In these years Gnosticism developed strongly and Christianity saw itself destined to take various measures against it at the same time, none easily reconcilable: acknowledging the legitimacy of Christian Gnosticism, retaining the OT as an integral part of Christian revelation, preserving the historical character of the message of Christian salvation and, lastly, developing Christian exegesis of the OT according to principles and models established in the apostolic traditions.

The Gnostic idea that there were «secret apostolic traditions» opened the door to all types of doctrine and writings. The development of Gnosticism already made it impossible to be limited to oral tradition and required an acceptable way of interpreting the OT.

The concept of a closed canon was already latent in the sub-apostolic period, but it was the development of Gnosticism which forced this idea to become a reality. Marcion made the problem of the canon a matter of urgency, but it was the Gnostics who to some extent determined the direction that was actually taken: a reaction to them.

In the period of *Justin*, the NT known *in Rome* included two thirds of the total of what later was to be the definitive NT. Several tasks remained: to separate the books of Lk and Acts, placing Lk together with the other evangelists (Mt, Mk and Jn) so as to form a canon of four gospels; to extend the *Marcionite* Pauline corpus of ten letters to include other letters of Paul and letters of other apostles and, lastly, to make Acts a connecting bridge between the collection of four gospels and the collection of apostolic letters.

4. *The Anti-Gnostic Period: Irenaeus, Clement of Alexandria, Origen and Hippolytus of Rome*

The canon known by *Irenaeus* and the church of *Gaul* which he represented contained the essence of the definitive canon: the four gospels, Acts, the letters of the apostles and the Apocalypse. The *Gospel of Peter* was excluded, owing to its docetist character; the Gnostics detracted from the meaning of martyrdom and the value of suffering.

Against the Gnostics and especially against the Marcionites, the most important work undertaken by Irenaeus was to establish the principles and arguments for Christian understanding of the Scriptures, OT and NT, as a coherent and harmonious whole.

The canon of *Clement of Alexandria* (150-c. 215) had fairly wide and not very exact limits. Clement used a collection of books like the one used later in the other churches, with the possible or probable exceptions of James, 3 Jn and 2 Pt. It included Heb, which other churches of that time did not accept; it made limited use of the letters of Barnabas and the first *Letter of Clement* as if they were apostolic in origin and it acknowledged as inspired the work *Shepherd of Hermas*. In the Egyptian church, however, Ap and Acts do not seem to have enjoyed more than relative importance.

While he was living in Alexandria, *Origen* (185-254) seems to have granted canonical status to the *Didache*, the *Shepherd of Hermas* and the *Letter of Barnabas*. Later, he rejected some of the books accepted by Clement: *Preaching of Peter, Apocalypse of Peter, Gospel of the Egyptians, Gospel of Matathias* and possibly the *Gospel of the Hebrews*.

Clement and Origen agree on a list of 22 books: the four gospels, Acts, the fourteen Pauline letters (including Heb), 1 Pt, 1 Jn and Ap. Origen accepted five of the books considered canonical by Clement - *Jud, Letter of Clement, Letter of Barnabas, Shepherd of Hermas* and 2 Jn - but warned that they were «disputed». On his part, Origen included three other books, also «disputed», which do seem to have been used before Clement: 3 Jn, James and 2 Pt.

Hippolytus of Rome (†235) knew a list of 22 books: 4 gospels, Acts, 13 Pauline letters (without Heb), 1 Pt, 1-2 Jn and Ap. This list is virtually identical with the list of 22 «undisputed» books mentioned by Origen, which includes 2 Jn, in spite of his awareness that this books was the subject of discussion. The «undisputed» books of Origen are closely related to the canon of Hippolytus and Irenaeus, both in number and in titles.

Accordingly, Eusebius could say later that the undisputed books were accepted by almost all the churches. However, at the beginning of the 3rd cent. it is not certain that the wider and rather amorphous canon of Clement reflected better the practice of some churches and certainly of the Egyptian church than the more restricted canon of Irenaeus and Hippolytus.

5.   *Definitive Composition of the Canon in the 4th Century*

Eusebius of Caesarea (†340) provides a list of canonical books which seems to be identical with the one presented by Athanasius some years later. However, it does not mention Heb and refers to some books with are subject to discussion: James, Jud, 2 Pt, 1-3 Jn and Ap. He also gives a list of books which he does not consider as «authentic», although they were read publicly in apostolic and orthodox churches: *Acts of Paul, Shepherd of Hermas, Apo-*

calypse of Peter, Letter of Barnabas and the *Didache* (cf. *Hist.Ec.* 3.31.6).

The NT canon which was to be imposed later in the Council of Chalcedon (451) is the same as found already in *Athanasius* (296-373): 4 gospels, Acts, 7 catholic Letters (James, 1-2 Pt, 1-2-3 Jn, Jud), 14 Letters of Paul (including Heb) and Ap. Many manuscripts of Egyptian origin which go back to the 4th cent. follow this sequence of books.

The same list is found in Amphilochius, bishop of Iconium (†394), in the sequence of books which prevailed later: Heb after Phm and the catholic letters after the Pauline letters.

Even the churches which failed to accept the decisions of the council of Chalcedon accepted this list of 27 canonical books, the same one included in the list established very much later at the council of Trent.

III. UNSUCCESSFUL CANONS

The history of the canon did not run in a single straight line from start to finish. As happened with the history of the text and interpretation, the canon proceeded to open up the road and left behind dead ends and abandoned paths. Some of these unsuccessful efforts contributed to the success of the final form, others led to solutions which failed, sooner or later.

From the beginning of Christianity until the 6th cent., when the official version of the canon was imposed, quite different collections of books existed which, if added to the OT, could have ended up as so many different canons. Some of these embryonic collections or canons were not only set in motion but actually formed real canons, though they did not succeed in gaining the consensus of all the Christian churches (Harnack).

These pre-canonical forms, in various stages of completion, were as follows, all preceded by the OT: a collection of *logia* or sayings of the Lord; a written gospel or a collection of several gospels; one or more gospels combined with a shorter or longer collection of teachings of the Lord and the twelve apostles (the *Didache* is the beginning of such a collection); a collection or summary of messianic prophecies such as found in the *Letter of Barnabas*, etc. (Farmer).

It is important to remember that the form acquired by the NT towards the end of the 2nd cent. was by no means the only one imaginable which the Christian canon could have assumed.

The history of the NT canon is, yet again, the history of a process which starts from diversity and ends in unity. The formation of the Christian Bible towards the end of the 2nd cent. CE runs in tandem with the formation of the Great Church. In both, the line of evolution leads from diversity to unity. The theological perspective tends to consider that the principle of unity of faith (*regula fidei*) had already been established at the beginning and that diversity arose through a break (*haíresis*, «heresy») with that original unity. In fact, this view is only gained *a posteriori*. W. Bauer has questioned the supposition that at the start of Christianity some sort of orthodoxy did exist (critique of the thesis of Bauer in Metzger and Harrington). In accordance with traditional and patristic doctrine concerning the origin of heresies, from the beginning the Church preserved the purity of Christian doctrine and of apostolic tradition. Orthodoxy, therefore, is earlier than all the heresies, which are nothing but deviations from orthodoxy and attributable to Satan, to unhealthy curiosity, to the sectarian spirit of some, to Greek philosophy considered to be the «mother of all heresies», etc. The Church preserves the unique truth, the sects unceasingly fragment the truth and each other.

This static conception of orthodoxy does not correspond to historical fact. History cannot be approached with rigid concepts. What was understood as orthodoxy in the 2nd cent. was not the same orthodoxy known in the 4th and 5th centuries. According to Harnack, heresies were a stimulus to the formation of orthodox dogma and the Gnostics were the first Christian theologians. According to M. Werner, dogma gradually replaced eschatology, following a process of increasing «de-eschatologisation» of Christianity. Heretics, particularly Gnostics, were the first to perceive and draw attention to this change. Accordingly, one could speak of a «legitimate belonging of heresy to Christianity» (Werner).

According to Bauer's thesis, in the beginning of Christianity, heresy and orthodoxy were not yet consolidated powers. In some respects, heresy, or what later was considered such, anticipated orthodoxy. As examples, Bauer studies the churches of Syria and Egypt. In the early stages there was no clear difference between orthodoxy and heresy; the two could co-exist side by side. Only with the passage of time did the difference between orthodoxy and heresy gain importance. In this development Rome played a decisive part (cf. p. 252).

On the other hand, it should not be forgotten that primitive Christianity seemed like a *haíresis*, a Jewish group with special characteristics, known as the «sect of the Nazarenes» (Acts 24:5.14; 28:22). The NT itself contains information about the existence of conflicts among Christian groups, between Hebrews and Hellenists (Acts 6:1-7), between Paul and his Judaising opponents, among different groups of Corinth (1 Cor 1:10-17) as well as allusions in the letter to the faithful of Colossians.

It is important to note here that according to Bauer's thesis, the «question of the OT» (cf. p. 513) was the cause of disagreement among the Christian groups and later decided the interplay of forces within Christianity.

IV. CHRISTIAN LITERATURE IN THE SUB-APOSTOLIC PERIOD: THE DEVELOPMENT OF NT GENRES

Over the past there has been a great lack of interest in the apocryphal books of the NT. Several reasons seemed to account for this: the material contained in these writings depends, in general, on the canonical books, compared with them it adds hardly any reliable information, it does not belong to mainstream Christian theology, etc. Before the first World War, the number of apocrypha known was very small. The edition by Kautzsch included thirteen apocryphal works, and the one by Charles' seventeen. The editions of Hennecke, Riessler and M. R. James gradually extended the number of published apocrypha. The English edition by H.F.D. Sparks (1981) and the American edition by J. H. Charlesworth (1983 and 1985) broke the methodological reductionism of the beginning of the century. The discoveries at Qumran and Nag Hammadi awoke interest in the apocrypha. However, Schneemelcher (who prepared the 3rd edition) still tends to choose a smaller number of what are considered «true» apocrypha of the NT.

«Apocryphon» means concealed, secret, either referring to writings not accepted in the canon, to Gnostic writings or, in a pejorative sense, to books considered as heretical. The Gnostics, instead, gave the term «apocryphon» a positive sense, considered these secret and hidden works to be too sacred to expose to general distribution among the public.

From the point of view of formal analysis, the apocryphal books can be defined as those writings which imitate the style of the NT and, while not actually being in the canon, both for the title given and the statements made about them, had pretensions of being considered canonical (Schneemelcher). This definition, however, pays no attention to other writings of the sub-apostolic period or to various forms of Gnostic literature which are undoubtedly connected with the writings called apocryphal.

The apocryphal books of the NT belong to several different literary forms, similar in any case to those of the canonical books which they try to imitate. In spite of that, the first four gospels and the fictional or Gnostic gospels have more differences from each other than similarities.

Within a single genre further large differences are possible: some apocrypha are in a more refined or more popular style than others; they are more orthodox or more heterodox, they maintain a more original style or are made up from material from different periods, they are very old (2nd cent.) or very recent (5th and 6th cents.). In every case it is always necessary to distinguish between ancient material and interpolations and later re-workings.

Possibly there were cycles of apocryphal writings, each one of which set under the authority of a biblical or New Testament character such as Daniel, Ezra, Mary, Pilate, the apostles and other characters of primitive Christianity. These cycles were perhaps connected to schools which followed a master and represented a certain line of tradition.

Study of the apocrypha includes the *agrapha*: every isolated word attributed to Jesus by tradition and not included in the canonical gospels. The *agrapha* can be found in interpolations or variants of the manuscripts of the gospels or other canonical books, in writings of the Fathers of the Church or ecclesiastical authors, in liturgical texts or texts on church discipline and in apocryphal gospels and acts. They are mostly short sayings or dialogues. After the discovery of the Oxyrynchus papyrus (3rd cent.) and of the finds at Nag Hammadi, J. Jeremias accepts 21 genuine *agrapha*. For quite some time the authority of the fourfold gospel did not prevent the transmission of certain oral traditions.

The contribution of the apocryphal writings to the *history of the NT text* is meagre. However, as far as the *literary history of the NT* is concerned, the apocrypha allow us to glimpse the existence of very ancient collections of the *logia* of Jesus, of *testimonia* from Scripture and perhaps also of collections of stories about Jesus or the apostles. These collections developed absolutely independently and by very different routes from the moment they ceased being under the control and influence of the canonical collections. The letters and the apocalypse are not so important.

The apocryphal writings are of undeniable interest for the study of *the history of ancient Christianity*. They are not merely useful for highlighting the superiority of the canonical writings. They also help one to realise that primitive Christianity was not absolutely monolithic and thus it is not possible to reduce Christian literature to two large blocks: mainstream orthodoxy and a heretical fringe.

The apocrypha reflect specific trends of popular piety and show how the Church tried to adapt to these different trends, unsuccessfully at times.

The Apocrypha of Jewish-Christian origin and background prove the survival of apocalyptic forms to express Christian doctrine. The Jewish-Christian gospels display an archaism which very soon moved towards Ebionism or Gnosis. They reveal features of popular piety: concern for the infancy of Jesus, his mother and the mysteries of the afterlife and of the last times. They retain a degree of theological significance which sometimes does not go beyond mere curiosity or even borders on bad taste, as occurs in descriptions of marked anti-docetic realism. The contribution of the apocrypha to the history of art and literature is far above their intrinsic merit.

The imitation of NT genres entailed a degree of risk owing to the use the Christian sects could make of them, especially Gnosticism.

The choice and use of the apocrypha varied a greatly according to time and place. The deutero-canonical writings of the OT, or the OT apocrypha according to the terminology in use among Protestants, were accepted into the canon of the Church, but not the NT apocrypha. For a limited time and in some places, however, several did enjoy a degree of canonicity, for example, the *Acts of Paul* and the *Apocalypse of Peter*. The *Didache*, the *Letter of Barnabas* the first *Letter of Clement* and the *Pastor of Hermas* nearly entered the NT canon.

Though less concerned with the deutero-canonical writings, the Christian Church did not leave the preservation of the apocryphal writings of the OT to chance, for a variety of reasons. Books 2-3-4 Maccabees were a source of inspiration to Christian martyrology. The books of Judith, Tobias, *Prayer of Esther*, *Psalms of Solomon* and the novel *Joseph and Aseneth* provided models of piety and asceticism. *Bel and the Dragon* and the *Letter of Jeremiah* dealt with the fight against paganism. The book of Wisdom and the works of Philo interpreted the Law by means of symbols and allegories. The preservation of the Enoch cycle shows how important apocalyptic was for Christians. The works of Josephus were worth being preserved even, but only to keep the *Testimonium Flavianum*.

1.   GOSPELS

Mark (65-70)
Matthew (70/80)
Luke (70/80)
John (90)

       Gospel of the Hebrews or Nazarenes (100-150)
       Gospel of the Egyptians (100-150)
       Gospel of the Ebionites (100-150)
       Apocryphon of John (Nag Hammadi)(100-150)
       Gospel according to Peter (130-150)
       Egerton Papyrus w (140-160)
       Proto-gospel of James (150-200)
       Gospel of the Truth (Nag Hammadi)(150-200)
       First compilation of the *Gospel according to Thomas* (Nag Hammadi)(150-200)
       Gospel of Philip (Nag Hammadi)(200)
       Gospel of Thomas (Nag Hammadi)(200-250)
       Arabic History of Joseph the Carpenter (4th cent.)
       Gospel according to Thomas (Manichaean work, extant form later than 6th cent.)
       Translation of Mary
       Gospel of Pseudo-Matthew (6th cent.)

2.   ACTS OF THE APOSTLES

Acts of the Apostles (70/80)

       Acts of John (140-160)
       Acts of Paul (150-200)
       Acts of Peter (150-200)
       Acts of Thomas (200-250)
       Acts of Andrew (200-250)
       Acts of Pilate (250-300)

3.   LETTERS OF THE APOSTLES

Pauline letters

       1 Thessalonians (51)
       2 Thessalonians (51 or 90)

       Galatians (54-57)
       Philippians (56-57)
       1 Corinthians (57)
       2 Corinthians (57)
       Romans (58)

       Philemon (56-57 or 61-63)
       Colossians (61-63 or 70/80)
       Ephesians (61-63 or 90/100)
       Titus (65 or 95-100)
       1 Timothy (65 or 95-100)
       2 Timothy (66 or 95-100)

       Hebrews (60 or 70/80)

Catholic letters
>	1 Peter (64 or 70/80)
>	James (62 or 70/80)
>	1 John (90)
>	2 John (90)
>	3 John (90)
>	2 Peter (100-150)

Apocryphal letters of Paul
>	*3 Corinthians*
>	*Letter to the Laodiceans*
>	*Correspondence of Paul and Seneca*

Apocryphal letters of Peter
>	*Preaching of Peter*
>	*Kerygmata Petrou*

4.	APOCALYPSES
Apocalypse of John (90)
>	*Apocalypse of Peter*
>	*Apocalypse of Paul*
>	*Apocalypse of the Virgin*
>	*Apocalypse of Thomas*
>	*Apocalypse of John*
>	*Apocalypse of Stephen*

5.	CHRISTIAN INSERTS in the apocryphal books of the OT
>	*Greek Apocalypse of Baruch (3 Baruch)*
>	*Apocalypse of Ezra (3 Ezra and 4 Ezra)*
>	*Apocalypse of Sidrach*
>	*Apocalypse of Elijah*
>	*Apocalypse of Zephaniah*
>	*Ascension of Isaiah*
>	*Sibylline Oracles*
>	*Book of the parables (1 Enoch)*, etc.

6.	WRITINGS OF THE APOSTOLIC FATHERS
>	*First Letter of Clement to the Corinthians* (90-100)
>	*Second Letter of Clement to the Corinthians* (c.90 or 100)
>	*Letters of Ignatius of Antioch* († c. 110)
>	*Letter of Polycarp to the Philippians* (somewhat later than the letters of Ignatius)
>	*Letter of Barnabas* (c. 130)

7.	DOCTRINAL OR MORAL TREATISES
>	*Didache or Doctrine of the Twelve Apostles* (end of 1st or beginning of 2nd cent.)
>	*Pastor of Hermas* (beginning of 2nd cent.)

The Jewish-Christian gospels include the *Gospel of the Hebrews and/or Nazarenes* and the *Gospel of the Ebionites*, probably the same as the *Gospel of the Twelve Apostles*. When mentioning the gospels of the Hebrews, of the Nazarenes or of the Ebionites, it is difficult to know whether the reference is to three different gospels or to a single work. The *Gospel of Peter*, written in Syria around 130, belongs to a setting close to the Jewish-Christian churches. The *Gospel of the Egyptians* was composed for Christians who used to be pagans.

Like the canonical gospels, all these gospels attempt to collect and transmit the teachings of Jesus. The fictional gospels, however, intend to give information which popular curiosity found missing in the canonical gospels: facts about Mary and Joseph, the childhood of Jesus and to a lesser extent, details of the Passion. They were written between the 3rd and 4th centuries. Of these, the *Proto-Gospel of James*, and to a lesser degree, the *Translation of Mary* are transitional forms. The *Gospel of Thomas*, combined with the *Proto-Gospel*, led to two derivatives in Syriac, which in turn resulted in the *Armenian Book of the Infancy* and the *Arabic Book of the Infancy*. The *Gospel of Nicodemus*, to which were added the *Acts of Pilate*, is a compilation of ancient material made at the beginning of the 5th cent.

The Gnostic gospels merit a separate chapter. Gnosis emerged in Syria at the beginning of the Christian era. It found the right terrain in Jewish and Christian apocalyptic thought. At the beginning of the 2nd cent., it moved from Syria to Egypt, and afterwards underwent considerable development in the whole Christian world, eventually giving rise to Manichaeism.

The *Gnostic Gospel according to Thomas*, or the *Secret Sayings of Jesus to Thomas,* is a collection of 114 words or *logia* of Jesus which sometimes are very old variants or even represent a more ancient stage of tradition, either already fixed in writing or still in the process of oral transmission, than that reached in the actual synoptic gospels. Their origin may go back to oral tradition (8, 14, 15, 24, 29, 78, 82, 101, 106, 113). Those listed as numbers 8 and 82 display the oldest style (J. Jeremias).

Initial studies on the *Gospel of Thomas* from Nag Hammadi tended to assume that it represented a gospel tradition independent of the canonical gospels (Quispel 1957). Today, instead, predominant opinion is that the *Gospel of Thomas* is dependent on the canonical gospels. The facts are that the author of the Gnostic gospel must have known the three synoptics, the changes inserted by this gospel are not always Gnostic in character and, sometimes, it seems to be more primitive than the synoptic tradition. It can be said that the *Gospel of Thomas* contains: 1) elements of authentic tradition, 2) elements in parallel with (although perhaps independent of) the synoptic gospels, but from a later stage in the development of that tradition, and 3) elements derived from the synoptic gospels.

It is generally considered to be a Gnostic work, but it could simply be a work of Encratic character. In any case, it seems to be the outcome of an evolutionary process now difficult to reconstruct (Köster).

It should be noted that many texts from Nag Hammadi are also in gospel form or under the name of an apostle: *Apocryphon of John*, *Gospel of the Egyptians*, *Apocalypse of Paul*, *Apocalypse of James* (3 works), *Epistle of Peter to Philip*, *Acts of Peter*, *Apocalypse of Peter*, *Gospel of Philip*, *Book of Thomas*, *Gospel of Truth*, *Prayer of the Apostle Peter*, etc.

2.　　*Apocryphal Acts of the Apostles*

The Apocryphal Acts of the Apostles are writings composed between 160 and 230. They are narratives in a popular style, and highly inventive. Towards the end of the 4th cent., they eventually formed a kind of corpus which the Manichees set in opposition to the canonical book of Acts. They come from Asia or Syria and have Encratic or Gnostic aspects, in some cases original and in others the product of later embellishment.

They are the following writings: *Acts of John, of Paul, of Peter, of Peter and Paul, of Thomas, of Andrew and Thaddeus*. The *Acts of Paul* has three parts: *Acts of Paul*, *Martyrdom of Paul* and *Correspondence of Paul with the Corinthians*. Possibly, there was a single edition incorporating all three, the title of which could have been *Acts of Paul and Thecla*.

The apocryphal Acts are essentially different from the work of Luke in respect of genre, literary form, and content (Schneemelcher).

3.　　*Apocryphal Letters of the Apostles*

The most important work among the apocryphal Letters of the apostles is the *Letter of the Apostles* or *Testament of Our Lord in Galilee*, probably written between 140 and 160.

The apocryphal letters attributed to Paul are the *Third Letter to the Corinthians*, the *Letter to the Laodicaeans* and the *Correspondence of Paul and Seneca*. The Petrine apocrypha include the *Preaching of Peter* and the *Kerygmata Petrou*.

4.　　*Apocryphal Apocalypses*

Not all apocryphal works with the title apocalypse strictly belong to this genre, especially the two works from Nag Hammadi bearing the name of James. The apocryphal apocalypses known are *of Peter, of Paul, of the Virgin, of Thomas, of John and Stephen*.

5.　　*Christian Interpolations in the OT Apocrypha*

Among the apocryphal literature of the NT must be listed also the first Christian interpolations inserted in some apocryphal books of the OT, especially in the *Apocalypse of Baruch in Greek (3 Baruch)*, of Ezra (*3 Ezra and 4*

Ezra), *of Sidrach*, *of Elijah and Zephaniah*, as well as the *Ascension of Isaiah*. The *Book of the Parables* from *1 Enoch* and from the *Slavonic Book of Enoch* have been attributed to Christian authorship (Milik). The *Sibylline Oracles* also contain Christian interpolations; books 6-8 of this work could be completely Christian in origin.

It has to be remembered that the traditional division between OT apocrypha and NT apocrypha is in question nowadays. On the other hand, just as the problem of defining the limits of what is canonical has to be posed, so too must the definition of the canon of what is «genuinely apocryphal» (Schneemelcher 1964).

6. Writings of the Apostolic Fathers

The writings of the apostolic Fathers date to 90-150 CE. The mere fact that the text of some of these writings features in certain biblical codices does not prove that they were considered as Scripture, although other facts certainly point in that direction.

In the Protestant world, especially in the theological movement represented by K. Barth, it has been quite common to establish a radical separation between the NT and the apostolic Fathers or the early Church, in which Catholic tendencies appear. Catholic and Protestant positions have moved closer together, forcing both to acknowledge the historical complexity of the development of the Church which arose from a blend of the Jewish priestly system and another system based on the orders of bishops and deacons. A great deal of emphasis has been placed on the importance of Jewish elements, but just as much also on elements from Hellenism and Gnosis (cf. p. 30). With the exception of Polycarp, the steady influence of oral tradition on the apostolic Fathers should not be forgotten (Köster).

Study of the apostolic Fathers has been very much influenced by W. Bauer's thesis concerning orthodoxy and heresy, taken even further by Köster. Others, however, deny that forms of Christianity later considered as heretical were dominant everywhere from the beginning and that the idea of a normative Christianity played such an important role.

The writings of the apostolic Fathers include letters, sermons and treatises. The *Letter to the Corinthians* by *Clement of Rome* comes from the 90's. It contains Greek and Roman elements, especially Stoic elements, but also some which are biblical. The relationship it established between the OT and the NT is particularly interesting (Hagner).

The *Second Letter to the Corinthians* is not by Clement nor it is really a letter. Instead it is a sermon, the oldest one known, from the end of the 1st cent., or the beginning of the 2nd cent., or perhaps even later.

Ignatius of Antioch, martyred around 100 CE, wrote seven letters: five addressed to the Christian communities of Ephesus, Magnesia, Tralles, Philadelphia and Smyrna, one to the bishop Polycarp, and the most important addressed to the community in Rome (cf. p. 515).

Of *Polycarp*'s letters, only the one addressed to the Philippians has reached us.

The *Letter to Barnabas* is a theological treatise in the form of a letter, from the beginning of the 2nd cent., which probably makes use of existing *Testimonia*. In the first part, which is doctrinal (chaps. 1-7) the allegorical method of interpretation is used. The second part (18-21), moral in content, develops the doctrine of the two ways, of life and of death.

Christian martyrologies undoubtedly have Jewish roots, but the cult of martyrs almost certainly reflects the Hellenistic cult of the dead.

7. Doctrinal and Moral Treatises

The *Didakhé* or *Doctrine of the Twelve Apostles*, from the end of the 1st cent. or the beginning of the 2nd, is the oldest ecclesiastical code known. It develops the doctrine of «the two ways», the path of life and the path of death, which goes back to Jewish sources and has similarities with the *Manual of Discipline* from the Qumran community.

The work known as the *Pastor of Hermas*, from the beginning of the 2nd cent., does not really belong to the writings of the apostolic Fathers. It belongs to the group of apocryphal apocalypses. It owes a great deal to Judaism, although it also contains undeniable Hellenistic elements.

V. HISTORICAL AND SOCIAL FACTORS IN THE FORMATION OF THE NT CANON

It is generally thought that the formative process of the NT canon was greatly affected by *the polemic against the great heresies of the period*. On the one hand, against Marcionism, which unduly reduced the number of authorised books (a slimmed down version of Luke's gospel and ten Pauline letters). On the other, against Montanism, which included the written canon of its own sect with purported and new revelations (Von Campenhausen). The Gnostics, on the other hand, were not concerned with increasing or decreasing the number of authorised books. Their interest, instead, was centred on giving a Gnostic interpretation to the texts accepted by everyone.

In Von Campenhausen's opinion, Marcion was the decisive factor in the formative process of the canon which took place in the period between Marcion and the Muratonian Fragment. The disputes of the 3rd cent. or the decisions of the councils in the 4th and 5th cents. then move into the background compared with the important events of the 3rd cent.

Certainly, the polemic against the heterodox movements of the period and the reaction to them was an important factor, but it cannot be considered as the principal cause which triggered the formative process of the NT canon. It is certainly incorrect to assign too much importance to Marcion's role in the formation of the Christian canon (Balas).

The unification process which led to the formation of the Great Church and of the Christian Bible had to fight its way between two extremes: to cast off the «old» Testament, as Marcion and the Gnostics proposed, or remain in the OT as the Jewish-Christians did. The «ecumenical» character of the Great Church and of the Christian Bible was certainly the factor which made the consolidation of both possible. The provincialism and elitist separatism of the «heretical» communities resulted in their being marginalised and disappearing.

Many other factors of very different kinds influenced the formation of the NT canon: the shift from the first generation of Christians to the second, once the generation of the apostle had disappeared; the exhaustion of oral tradition fed directly from apostolic sources; the use of Christian writings in the liturgy; the needs of catechesis and apologetics, and finally, the impossibility of establishing Christian theology only on the basis of the OT. The NT canon arose, according to Kümmel, at the moment when oral tradition ceased and the Church felt itself forced to look in the apostolic writings for the «irreplaceable norm of the Lord and of the Apostles». The problem of the canon is the problem of the second generation of Christians and of the «transmission of authority» (*Übertragbarkeit der Autorität*; Marxen).

On the other hand, with the passing of time, the influence of the councils and synods gained increasing importance. There was also a more general trend, especially in the 4th cent., to codify bodies of legislation and set up lists of classical writers (cf. p. 536).

From the start, but especially in the anti-Gnostic period, the contacts which the various churches were initiating with a view to setting up a canon, all passed through the church of Rome. This *«Roman connection»* had great importance for the development of the NT canon (Gregory).

The formation of the canon, besides excluding certain books which could not be considered as the «norm» of faith of the churches, performed an equally important task: to bind and unite the traditions of the churches of the Christian East and West. Irenaeus, Hippolytus and Origen reached Rome in this period, more or less. In Rome, then, they took the decisions and basic compromises which later led to the final establishment of the Christian canon.

The churches and the great Christian figures which helped to set up of the Christian canon also made connections with Rome or through Rome: contacts were established by Ignatius between Syria and Asia Minor and Rome, by Polycarp between Asia Minor and Rome, by Irenaeus between Asia Minor and Gaul, by Irenaeus and Hippolytus between Gaul with Rome, by Hippolytus and Origen between Rome and Alexandria, by Origen between Alexandria and both Caesarea and Cappadocia, by Eusebius and Athanasius between both Caesarea and Alexandria and Constantinople, etc. Evidently, Rome was the centre and axis of all these movements.

VI. LITERARY CRITERIA FOR CANONICITY

A look at the literary genres of the NT books seems to suggest that apostolic writings accepted as authentic could belong to only *two literary forms*: *narrative* as in the gospels and *epistolary* as in the apostolic letters. This literary criterion certainly allowed immediate disqualification of works in neither genre. The letter to the Hebrews seems to confirm the existence of such a criterion as does the fact that the apostolic Church produced no other kind of literature. The true genre of this «letter» is really a theological treatise, to which was added an ending, as in a Pauline letter, giving the whole thing the look of an apostolic work. The fact that the canonicity of this letter to the Hebrews was disputed for a long time, as was the Apocalypse, neither narrative nor epistle in genre either, strengthens the hypothesis of only two apostolic genres, gospel and apostolic letter.

However, it is certain that the early Church never seems to have used this literary criterion to determine the apostolic or non-apostolic nature of a Christian text. In the OT, the Torah or Pentateuch originated in a literary unit comprising a torah or commandment and prophetic literature originated in an oracle and wisdom literature originated from the proverb. Similarly, the gospels also originate from a piece of gospel narrative and the extensive epistolary literature of early Christianity stems from the missive sent by an apostle to keep in contact with the Christian communities.

VII. THEOLOGICAL CRITERIA FOR CANONICITY

In Christianity, the criteria for canonicity are primarily *of a theological nature*, to a greater extent than in Judaism, if that is possible.

The NT canon and its formative process are built on three foundation pillars: 1) the message and person of Jesus, as known through the oldest form of the synoptic tradition, 2) the oldest kerygma of the early Church concerning Christ's death and resurrection, and 3) the first theological reflections on this kerygma, developed in Pauline theology (Kümmel).

As a result, the criteria now being applied to determine the canonical nature of a text were basically as follows: the apostolic origin of the text in question, widespread use or degree of universality and, lastly, conformity with the *regula fidei* or faith of the Church (*ho kanṓn tḗs písteōs*). This combination of historical and theological criteria is not applied equally in every case. They are rather rationalisations, justifying established traditional practice in the churches (Ohlig).

The Fathers of the Church thought that the books of the Scriptures were inspired by God, but apparently they did not consider inspiration as a criterion to distinguish between orthodox canonical writings and other writings which, though not necessarily heterodox, were not canonical. The Scriptures are inspired, but this is not the reason why the Scriptures are canonical as well as inspired. The inspiration of the Scriptures was written into the framework of the inspirational activity of the Spirit in many other fields and aspects of the life of the Church.

Like the two possible meanings of the word *kanón*, the NT canon has a twofold theological value, one active and the other passive. In the first meaning, the canon is the collection of books which contain the Christian norm of faith and life (*norma normans*); in the passive sense, the canon is the list of books established by the Church as normative or deposits of the rule of faith (*norma normata*).

In the first sense, the books of the canon are assumed to have *intrinsic value*, rooted in its own origin and nature, before it formed a collection. In the second sense, to belong to a collection authorised by the Church confers an *extrinsic authority* on them which they did not have before. In one case the Church acknowledges the authority inherent in the Scriptures. In the other, it confers its own authority on the books, combining them into a collection with its seal of canonicity.

VIII. A CANON WITHIN A CANON?

Tensions within the canon affect fundamental theological views. Far from securing the unity of Christianity, the canon allowed confessions to multiply. The contradictions among various books or within the same book make it necessary to establish a critical canon within the actual canon. The canon cannot be the basis for the unity of the Church but is, instead, the basis for multiple confessions in the Church (Käsemann).

The eschatology of Luke and Acts cannot be harmonised with Paul's; the view of the Law presented in Rom is incompatible with Mt 18. The Epistle of James attacks the Pauline doctrine on justification by faith alone. Not only is there no unity within the canon, it is even useless to hope that the Christian Church can lay the foundations of its unity on the base of the NT canon. Therefore, from a Protestant and particularly a Lutheran viewpoint, the problem of the existence of a «canon within the canon» has often been posed.

Ultimately, the question consists of establishing the hermeneutical criterion to determine which elements of the canon are faithful to the «gospel» and which are not in agreement with it.

On the other hand, there is also the problem of the relationship between Scripture and Tradition. The canon of Scripture is deeply rooted in tradition. To acknowledge the authority of the canon is to acknowledge the authority of tradition. This is a Catholic idea to which Protestants today pay more attention. Modern exegesis has emphasised up to what point the books of the canon are the product of an earlier tradition, demolishing any clear distinction between scripture and tradition. It is more correct, perhaps, to speak of written and non-written tradition (oral and written Torah in the terms specific to Judaism). This does not mean that the Catholic principle of Tradition is taken for granted or that the Protestant principle of *Scripture alone* is bereft of authority.

In fact, it is a hermeneutical problem: to know whether Scripture can be interpreted on its own (*Scriptura sola*) or whether the interpretation of Scripture needs the complement of an external principle (*Scriptura et traditio*). The traditional Catholic and Protestant positions have come closer to each other, but they are still far from complete agreement. Historical studies show that Scripture and Tradition were not separate categories but intertwined realities which Christian theology has to restore to true unity.

The attempts made to establish a principle of some kind («justification by faith» or any other), as a rule for deciding the authority of a particular book of the canon has merely led to unilateral positions which can only diminish some important aspects of Christian faith or life. Early Christian thought as reflected in the whole spectrum of the 27 books of the NT canon is very rich and varied. The differences among the books reflect the theological diversity that existed in the early Christian communities, to the extent that a «primitive catholicism», a «primitive protestantism» and a «primitive (Eastern) orthodoxy» can be found. in the writings of the apostolic period.

Each book of a movement counteracts the danger brought by an interpretation which takes to extremes the tendency evident in the writings of the opposing movement. The canon acknowledges as valid the diversity of theological expression and marks out the limits of the diversity acceptable within the Church (Metzger).

BIBLIOGRAPHY

ALAND, K., «Die Entstehung des Corpus Paulinum», *Neutestamentliches Entwürfe*, Munich 1979, 302-350.

BALAS, D., «Marcion Revisited: A 'Post-Harnack' Perspective», *Texts and Testaments*, ed. W. E. March, San Antonio CA 1980, 102-105.

BAUER, W., *Rechtgläubigkeit und Ketzerei im ältesten Christentum*, Tübingen 1964[2].

CAMPENHAUSEN, H. VON., *The Formation of the Christian Bible*, Philadelphia PA 1972.

CHARLESWORTH, J.M., *The New Testament Apocrypha and Pseudepigrapha: A Guide to Publications, with Excursuses on Apocalypses*, Metuchen NJ-London 1987.

DAHL, N.A., «The Origin of the Earliest Prologues to the Pauline Letters», *The Poetics of Faith*, ed. W.A. Beardslee, Missoula MT 1978, 233-277.

ELLIS, E.E., «The Old Testament in the Early Church», *Mikra*, CRINT 2,1, ed. J.M. Mulder, Assen/Maastricht-Philadelphia PA 1988, 653-690.

EVANS, C.C., *Noncanonical Writings and New Testament Interpretation*, Peabody MA 1992.

FARMER, W.R., «Peter and Paul: A Constitutive Relationship for Catholic Christianity», *Texts and Testaments. Critical Essays on the Bible and Early Church Fathers*, San Antonio CA 1980, 219-236.

FARMER, W.R.-FARKASFALVY, D.M., *The Formation of the New Testament Canon. An Ecumenical Approach*, New York-Ramsey-Toronto 1983.

FONBERG, T., «Textual Criticism and Canon. Some Problems», *Studia Theologica* 40 (1986) 45-53.

GAMBLE, H.Y., *The New Testament Canon Its Making and Meaning*, Philadelphia PA 1985.

GOODPSEED, E.J., *New Solution of the New Testament Problems*, Chicago IL 1927.

GREGORY, C.P., *Canon and Text of the New Testament*, New York 1924.

HAGNER, D.A., *The Use of the Old and New Testaments in Clement of Rome*, Leiden 1973.

HANSON, R.P.C., *Tradition in the Early Church*, Philadelphia PA 1962.

HARNACK, A., *Das neue Testament um das Jahr 200*, Freiburg 1889.

HARNACK, A., *Marcion. Das Evangelium vom fremden Gott*, Leipzig 1924^2.

HARRINGTON, D.J., «The Reception of Walter Bauer's *Orthodoxy and Heresy in Earliest Christianity* during the Last Decade», *HThR* 73 (1980) 289-298.

HAYS, R.B., *Echoes of Scripture in the Letters of Paul*, New Haven-London 1989.

KÄSEMANN, E. (ed.), *Das Neue Testament als Kanon. Dokumentation und kritische Analyse zur gegenwärtigen Diskussion*, Göttingen 1970.

KÄSEMANN, E., «Paulus und der Frühkatholizmus», *ZThK* 40(1962) 75-89.

KÖSTER, H., «Apocryphal and Canonical Gospels», *HThR* 73 (1980) 105-130.

KÖSTER, H., «One Jesus and Four Primitive Gospels», *Trajectories Through Early Christianity*, eds., J.M. Robinson-H.Köster, Philadelphia PA 1971, 158-204.

KÖSTER, H., *Ancient Christian Gospels. Their History and Development*, Cambridge MA 1990.

KÜMMEL, W.G., «Notwendigkeit und Grenze der neutestamentlichen Kanons», *ZThK* 47 (1950) 227-313.

MARCH, E. (ed.), *Texts and Testaments. Critical Essays on the Bible and Early Church Fathers*, San Antonio CA 1980.

MARXEN, W., «Das Problem des neutestamentlichen Kanons aus der Sicht des Exegeten», *Das Neue Testament als Kanon, Dokumentation und kritische Analyse zur gegenwärtige Diskussion*, ed. E. Käsemann, Göttingen 1970, 233-246.

METZGER, B.M., *The Canon of the New Testament. Its Origin, Development, and Significance*, Oxford 1987.

MILIK, J.T., *The Books of Enoch: Aramaic Fragments of Qumran Cave IV*, Oxford 1976.

OHLIG, K.-H., *Die theologische Begründung des neutestamentlichen Kanons in der alten Kirche*, Düsseldorf 1972.

OUTLER, A.C., «The 'Logic' of Canon-making and the Tasks of Canon-criticism», *Texts and Testaments. Critical Essays on the Bible and Early Church Fathers*, San Antonio CA 1980, 263-278.

RINALDI, G., *Biblia Gentium. A First Contribution towards an Index of Biblical Quotations, References and Allusions made by Greek and Latin Heathen Writers of the Roman Imperial Times*, Rome 1989.

SCHMITHALS, W., «On the Composition and Earliest Collection of the Major Epistles of Paul», *Paul and the Gnostics*, New York 1972, 239-274.

SCHNEEMELCHER, W., *Neutestamentliche Apokryphen*, 2 vols., Tübingen 1987 and 1989.

SUNDBERG, A.C., *The Old Testament of the Early Church*, Cambridge MA 1964.

SUNDBERG, A.C., «The Making of the New Testament Canon», *The Interpreter's One-Volume Commentary on the Bible*, Nashville TN 1971, 1216-1224.

WERNER, M., *Die Entstehung des christlichen Dogmas*, Tübingen 1953^2.

WILSON, R.MCL., *New Testament Apocrypha, the New Testament and Its Modern Interpreters*, eds., E.J. Epp-G.W. MacRae, Atlanta GA 1989, 429-455.

ZAHN. T., *Geschichte des neutestamentlichen Kanons*, Erlangen 1888-1892.

Chapter III

The History of the Text and Versions of the Old and New Testaments

«Any commentary which does not refer to punctuation and accents is not necessary for you; take no notice of it»
(Abraham Ibn 'Ezra').

Chapter III

The History of the Text and Versions of the Old and New Testaments 259

I

Introduction

After knowing which books became part of the biblical canon it is necessary
to know whether the text of these books has reached us in a good state of
preservation or whether it has undergone important alterations, either by
unintentional mistake or through deliberate tampering by copyists. Discoveries of papyri of the NT and especially of the Dead Sea Scrolls have completely revitalised study of the history of the transmission and criticism of
the biblical text. Before these discoveries, quite a number of variants of the
Hebrew text of the OT were known, but almost always by indirect means,
such as the ancient versions. Now, not only are variants in Hebrew itself
available, but there is also manuscript evidence of different textual forms,
connected in some biblical books, with a whole complex editorial process of
those books.

I.   FACTS JUSTIFYING TEXTUAL CRITICISM OF THE OLD TESTAMENT

Two facts account for study of the history and textual criticism of the OT.
The first is the *loss of the autographs or «originals» by the biblical authors*.
The second is the presence in the biblical manuscripts of all kinds of *variants,
gaps, glosses and mistakes made in copying* them over the centuries. In addition, it should also be remembered that the great Hebrew codices come from
the mediaeval period and are more than a millennium later than the original
texts. The great codices of the NT come from the 4th cent. and so are only a
couple of centuries later than their autographs.

The Dead Sea Scrolls, copied between the 3rd cent. BCE and the 1st CE,
bring us considerably closer to the period when the biblical writings were
composed. Similarly, the NT papyri (from the 2nd and 3rd cents. CE) allow
closer approach to the oldest periods of the transmission of the NT text.
However, the state of preservation of the manuscripts from Qumran and the
care with which they were copied leave much to be desired.

Faced with these facts, the biblical scholar cannot help posing a series of questions: Does the text which has reached us match faithfully the text written by the biblical authors? Is it possible to reconstruct the history between the manuscripts preserved and the autographs of each biblical book? Is it possible to reconstruct the «original» text, purified of all the dross of mistakes, additions and gaps which have marred the text over the centuries?

Textual criticism of the Bible has two objectives. The first reflects the great number of variants in the manuscript tradition and consists of the *reconstruction of the history of transmission of the biblical text* from the moment it was put down in writing until the present. The second is determined by the loss of the autographs of the biblical authors and consists of the *restoration of the text to its original form* or the form closest to the autographs.

II. THE IMPORTANCE OF THE HISTORY OF THE BIBLICAL TEXT

To rehearse *the history of the biblical text* from the beginning of manuscript transmission up to the invention of printing (and even up to modern critical editions) is the same as rehearsing *a complete history of Judaism and Christianity*. All the great events and many of the lesser happenings in the history of Jews and Christians, all the great theological questions and many of the lesser scholastic disputes of both parties have left their mark on the biblical texts, even in the original languages, but especially in the numerous versions of the Bible made in the languages of the peoples converted to Christianity.

In the early years, the history of Jews and Christians was almost a common, shared history, but quite soon it began to run on parallel lines and sometimes on opposing lines. Judaism seemed to be more and more concerned with *preserving faithfully the Hebrew text* of the OT down to its last jot and tittle; with it the survival or at least the preservation of Jewish identity and religious, ethnic and cultural unity were at stake. Christianity showed greater missionary concern and even an urgency to *translate the text of the Bible* and make it reach all the peoples of the world. In so doing, it contributed to consolidating the cultural and religious identity of many churches and peoples at the risk of internal unity and of very marked differences among the biblical texts used in the various churches.

To write the history of the text of the Bible, therefore, also amounts to writing the history of *the origins of national literature of many nations* and of their writing systems. The translation of the Bible, particularly of the NT, set in train Gothic, Slavonic, Coptic, Armenian, Georgian and Ethiopic literature. In the case of some translations, such as the Armenian version, even several characters of the script, which did not yet exist, had to be created, since Armenian had remained at the level of oral tradition exclusively (cf. p. 125).

Textual criticism of the Bible was a *pioneering discipline of the humanist Renaissance*. The great humanists such as Erasmus or Nebrija devoted their knowledge to editing the biblical texts in their original languages. Textual criticism of the Bible has always been a link between biblical philology and classical philology. In the Renaissance period and even in the 19th century, these disciplines were not so far apart from each other as today. A person such as Lachmann, a top theoretician of textual criticism and an editor both of classical texts and of the NT, represents a figure linking both types of philology.

Textual criticism of the Bible has also been the field in which some of the most crucial discussions between *Protestants* and *Catholics* have taken place, each group tied to its own text and biblical canon: the Protestants tied to the *received text* and the Hebrew canon, and Catholics, to the Latin text and the canon of the Vulgate.

From the Renaissance, especially in the 17th and 18th cents., textual criticism of the Bible was also a battlefield between *Hebraists* and *Hellenists*.

During the 19th cent. until the period of Lagarde and Wellhausen, there was a sort of *personal union* joining the grammarian, the editor of texts, the textual critic, the literary commentator, the historian and the theologian of the Bible. In the 20th cent., the demands of greater specialisation have determined the development of these disciplines as autonomous, reducing textual criticism to splendid *isolation vis à vis the other fields* of philology, history and theology.

However, the discovery of the Dead Sea Scrolls and the NT papyri have revived text-critical studies of the Bible which had declined in the periods before these discoveries. At the same time, there seems to be a rebirth, more dream than reality, of the global and «holistic» vision which attempted to connect textual criticism with the other philological disciplines: comparative Semitics, biblical exegesis (commentaries, source criticism, literary forms, redactional criticism, etc.) and the history of the interpretation of the biblical text, as reflected in the versions, apocryphal literature, the NT, the Targumim and Midrashim, the Mishnah and Talmud and in the huge field of patristic literature.

III. MODERN RESEARCH ON THE HISTORY OF THE BIBLICAL TEXT

The task of reconstructing the «original» text of the Bible requires, first, knowledge of the history of transmission of the biblical text from the instant it was put into writing up to modern editions of the Bible.

History is usually told from start to finish, from the oldest to the most recent. However, historical research proceeds in the opposite direction. Historians have to *recreate history and go back in time*, starting from the most recent and best documented until finally reaching the oldest and least known. The history of biblical research, from the Renaissance up to the most recent archaeological finds, is the history of a gradual discovery of the oldest sources.

Initially, and for some time after, the modern biblical critic had available only later mediaeval manuscripts and a «received text» (*textus receptus*) as reproduced in printed Bibles.

Gradually, modern criticism discovered and studied older and more authorised manuscripts: the mediaeval Hebrew manuscripts from the purest masoretic tradition and the Greek manuscripts and papyri from the first centuries of Christianity.

At a later period, it became interested in discovering and studying the manuscripts of the ancient versions and the biblical quotations contained in the works of the Fathers and the Church. This provided knowledge of the biblical text exactly as it was transmitted in the first centuries of Christianity.

Finally, and only in recent decades, the discovery and analysis of the Dead Sea Scrolls have provided knowledge of biblical texts in Hebrew and Greek which are earlier than the emergence of Christianity, very close to the period when the Bible was translated into Greek (3rd-2nd cents. BCE) and the final redaction of the latest biblical books.

As a result, it is absolutely indispensable to know the history of transmission of the biblical text throughout more than two thousand years for further work in criticism and restoration of the «original» biblical text. It is necessary to know the wealth of variants which the manuscripts in Hebrew, Greek and other versions have transmitted to us, including rabbinic and patristic quotations. It is also necessary to determine which of these variants are guaranteed to go back to the oldest stages of textual transmission and which are the work of later revisions or the result of some type of textual corruption.

2

The Hebrew Text of the Old Testament

The history of modern research on the Hebrew text of the Bible (with short passages in Aramaic) is a history of gradual recovery. First, recovery of the *vocalised text*, which reached a state of equilibrium towards the end of the 10th cent. CE; next, of the *consonantal text*, which was fixed towards the end of the 1st cent. CE; and lastly, recovery of the *texts known in the 3rd and 2nd cents. BCE*, i.e., before and after the translation of the Bible into Greek.

There are significant differences between *the* Hebrew text, transmitted with great consistency and *the various* Greek texts and texts in other versions, known in various recensions. Right from the start, these differences are the challenge confronting the modern critic, whose first task is to establish which text has to be printed in a modern edition of the Hebrew Bible. There have been different answers to this question and as a result different editions or ways of editing the Hebrew Bible.

Following a reverse order, and going backwards through the course of history, we will study: 1) *establishing the printed text* in modern times, 2) *establishing the vocalised text* of the Masorah in the mediaeval period, 3) *establishing the consonantal text* in the Roman period through a process which culminated towards the beginning of the 2nd cent. CE, and lastly, 4) the *stage of «textual fluidity»*, when the biblical books were transmitted in the Persian and Hellenistic period.

I. ESTABLISHING THE PRINTED TEXT (15TH-20TH CENTS)

The Hebrew Bible is usually read and studied using printed editions. Direct access to manuscripts is not easy, and in the initial stages not necessary either.

1. *Modern Editions*

Towards the end of the last century, printed editions of the Hebrew Bible had established an «authoritative printed text» in respect of the consonants and vowels of the Hebrew text and, to a lesser degree, in respect of the masoretic accents and notes.

Until that time, and since the Renaissance period, there were simultaneously *three «recensions»* of the printed text. The differences among these recensions were due to differing reasons and circumstances. First came the very limited possibilities which the Renaissance editors had for collating manuscripts for their editions. There could be a few or several of these manuscripts which could vary in quality. Another factor which made some editions different from others was the degree of attention paid to the punctuation, accentuation and masoretic notes of the Hebrew text. Lastly, the public for which the edition was intended matched to some extent its character. Jews, naturally, preferred a text based on masoretic tradition.

The first recension is represented by *the Soncino edition of 1494*, used by Martin Luther for his famous translation of the Bible into German. The text of this edition is very inaccurate in respect of the masoretic notes. Once it was revised by comparing it with the text of other manuscripts, it was used for the first rabbinic edition and also for later editions by R. Estienne (1539 and 1544-46) and S. Münster (1535).

The second recension is that of the *Complutensian Polyglot (1514-17)*. The special feature of this edition is that it is based directly on manuscript tradition, without relying on earlier printed editions.

The third recension is represented by *the second rabbinic Bible* by Jacob ben Hayyim (1524- 25). For a long time it was considered as the *textus receptus/received text* or what might be called the Vulgate and authorised edition of the Hebrew Bible.

The editions which followed the publication of these three recensions provide a «mixed» text, dependent in one way or another on the recensions mentioned. Such is the case, for example, for the Biblia Regia or Polyglot of Amberes.

The *Ginsburg edition* (of 1908 and 1926), based on the second rabbinic Bible recension by Jacob ben Hayyim, still used the masorah uncritically and an eclectic selection of manuscripts, with no preliminary classification or discrimination of their readings. This edition was superseded by those that followed.

The edition known as the *Biblia Hebraica*, completed by R. Kittel, is the one used most in this century. The first two editions (1906 and 1912) still followed the text of the second rabbinic Bible. At P. Kahle's suggestion, the third edition of 1937, and successive editions, reproduced the *text of the St Petersburg Codex* (B 19^A), copied in 1008 CE. Kahle considered the text of this codex to represent a pure masoretic text, written by Aaron ben Moses ben Asher (cf. p. 274).

In 1977, a new edition was completed, known as the *Biblia Hebraica Stuttgartensia*, edited by K. Elliger and W. Rudolph. It, too, is based on the St. Petersburg Codex. G. E. Weil was in charge of editing the masorah. This edition tries to forestall the criticisms made of previous editions by R. Kittel. These were censured for excessive use of «readings» from the ancient versions and of conjectures by modern scholars on order to correct presumed corruptions in the Hebrew text. The critical apparatus of the *Stuttgartensia* edition reflects a new trend of contemporary textual criticism (cf. p. 386), although it does not completely abandon the practice of suggesting corrections to the text based on literary criteria.

The Hebrew University of Jerusalem is preparing a *new edition* of the biblical Hebrew text, primarily *based on the Aleppo Codex*, dated to the first half of the 10th cent. This codex represents a «Ben Asher» text of better quality than the St. Petersburg Codex (cf. p. 274). According to Ben-Zvi and Goshen-Gottstein, this codex is none other than the famous manuscript authorised by Maimonides (died 1204) who conferred the prestige of his authority on a codex which contained the text of the whole Hebrew Bible he had used in Egypt. This codex had previously been used in Jerusalem as a model for copying other manuscripts.

A feature of this edition is that in various sets of critical apparatus it collects masoretic variants from rabbinic sources and from the Dead Sea Scrolls, with a great deal of material extracted from the versions and from ancient writers. It refrains completely from proposing any conjectures and from attempting to correct the Hebrew text. Up to now, two volumes corresponding to the book of Isaiah have appeared: Goshen-Gottstein, M. H. (ed.), *The Book of Isaiah*, I *Isaiah 1,1-22,10*, II *Isaiah 22-44*, Jerusalem 1975 and 1981 respectively.

Reference must also be made to the edition which N. H. Snaith planned in 1933. On the basis of MSS Or. 2626-2628, Or. 2375 and the Šem-Ṭôb of 1312, Snaith thought he would be able to recover a masoretic text from the Ben Asher tradition.

2.   *The First Printed Editions*

The invention of printing very quickly ousted the method of copying by hand and thus a very considerable source of mistakes in the transmission of the biblical text, called «copyist's errors». These were replaced by «printing errors», which continued to be reproduced and multiplied in successive printed editions.

The first printed book is the *Latin Bible of Gutenberg*. In 1477, the first edition (*editio princeps*) of the psalms in Hebrew came out in Bologna. The first edition of the Pentateuch also appeared in 1482 and in the same city; the books of the Prophets in 1485-86, in Soncino; the Writings in 1486-87, in Naples; the complete OT with vowels and accents, although without comments, in 1488, in Soncino. This edition did not follow the rules established concerning opened and closed sections and was very careless in respect of the masorah and the question of Qĕrê-Ketîb.

The most important printed editions were the Complutensian Polyglot (1514-17) and the so-called second rabbinic Bible, the work of Jacob ben Ḥayyim (1524-25).

a. The Complutensian Polyglot. This edition was completed by cardinal Francis Ximenez of Cisneros, archbishop of Toledo. The first four volumes of the work contain the text of the OT. The first reproduces the Hebrew, Aramaic (Onqelos Targum), Greek and Latin texts of the Pentateuch. Since it was the work of learned Christians, the Vulgate has a central position between the Hebrew and Greek texts and the order of the biblical books follows that of the Vulgate. Similarly, the masoretic division into sections is replaced by division into chapters, introduced into Latin Bibles by Stephen Langton in the 13th cent. The accents of the Hebrew text were almost completely omitted and the vowel pointing is very erratic. However, the reproduction of the consonantal text is very careful. It is assumed that the base text used for this edition was *Codex no. 1* of the Library of the University of Madrid, dated by Ginsburg to 1280.

b. The Rabbinic Bible. Between 1516-17, Daniel Bomberg published the first edition of the rabbinic Bible in Venice, which was prepared by the convert Jew Felix

Pratensis. More famous, however, is the second edition, already mentioned, supplied with a masorah and undertaken by Jacob ben Ḥayyim in 1524-25 in Venice with the same printer, D. Bomberg. For the first time an edition was available which gave due attention to masoretic pointing and accents. Until well into the 20th cent., it was considered as the *received text* of the Hebrew Bible and was used in successive editions of it. It acquired the name «rabbinic» Bible, since besides the Hebrew text it contained the Onqelos Targum and the commentaries by Rashi and Ibn Ezra in vol. I (the Pentateuch); Targum Jonathan and the commentaries by D. Kimchi, Ralbag (R. Levi ben Geršom) and Raši in vol. II (the Former Prophets); the targum and commentaries of Kimchi (on Jeremiah and Ezekiel) and of Ibn Ezra on the other books in vol. III (the Later Prophets), and lastly, the targum of Daniel, Ezra-Nehemiah and Chronicles and commentaries on all the *Ketubim* by various Jewish exegetes in vol. IV (the Writings). In an appendix to this last volume, on 65 folios and in 4 columns, part of the *masorah magna* is reproduced, which was too long to be included in the upper and lower margins of the text. It is also the first edition which notes in the margin the consonants of the official readings or *Qěrê* as well as the *sěbirim* («unexpected» textual forms).

c. The Polyglot editions of Antwerp, Paris and London. The polyglot editions prepared in Antwerp (1569-72), Paris (1629-45) and London (1657-69) are adaptations of the Polyglot of Alcala and of the second edition of the rabbinic bible.

The *Antwerp Polyglot*, also known as «Regia Biblia» (Royal Bible) since it was published at the expense of king Philip II, was prepared by Benito Arias Montano and printed by Christophe Plantin in 1569-1572 in eight volumes, the first four dedicated to the OT.

The *Paris Polyglot* only reproduces the OT text of Antwerp, adding the Samaritan Pentateuch and its targum.

The *London Polyglot* is the work of Brian Walton; it supersedes its predecessors in its care for the texts. Besides the Hebrew text of the Samaritan Pentateuch and of the Samaritan Targum, this Polyglot adds the Greek text of the LXX, fragments of the *Old Latin*, the targums and parts of the Ethiopic and Persian versions, complete with the corresponding Latin translation in (where necessary) a very appropriate synoptic arrangement.

All these printed editions were based on mediaeval manuscripts of very recent date and scant critical worth. Therefore, it was soon realised that it was necessary to collate all the variants of the mediaeval manuscripts which could have been preserved. The response to this concern, very much in keeping with the encyclopaedic spirit of the 18th cent., was the monumental work by Kennicott, *Vetus Testamentum Hebraicum cum variis lectionibus* (1776-80), followed by that of De Rossi, *Variae lectiones Veteris Testamenti* (1784-88).

After this effort of compiling manuscripts, the 19th cent. saw the first attempts to establish a text which would incorporate due guarantees of authenticity. For that, it was necessary to establish the principles and methods of critical analysis and to put to the test all the textual variants preserved by the manuscript tradition (cf. p. 370). However, the edition by Baer and Delitzsch (1869-92), prepared with this intention, was strongly criticised for the low academic quality of its masorah.

Thus, after 500 years of history of the printed Bible, the question remains:

which is the *«best text»* to reproduce in a printed edition? The reply to this question cannot be obtained without first analysing all the data relative to the history of the biblical text in the Middle Ages and in previous periods. It is necessary to know which text represents the best tradition of the *consonantal text* and which best corresponds to the *oldest* and most original *form* of the text. Nowadays, this question is more pressing, given the new information which the Dead Sea Scrolls have provided about the plurality of texts in existence before the fixation of the consonantal text undertaken at the beginning of the Mishnaic period.

The history of the biblical text in its various phases has always been the *history of successive attempts at unifying diversity* and not the other way round. Up to now, we have seen how the history of the printed Bible has been the history of the progressive establishment of a printed text, starting from the three recensions published in the Renaissance period.

Next, we will retrace the steps by which the vocalised text was established, starting from traditions, systems and schools with different pointing. Later, we will retrace the steps of the progressive establishment of the consonantal text, obtained after filtering the various texts to be found circulating in the pre-Christian period.

II. FIXING THE VOCALIC TEXT AND THE MASORAH. THE MANUSCRIPT TRADITION AFTER THE NINTH CENTURY

1. *Fixing the Vocalic Text*

Until the beginning of the Middle Ages, the biblical text was transmitted only in consonantal characters without any vowel pointing at all. The treatise *Sopherim* of the Babylonian Talmud refers to various aspects of scribal activity, but as yet does not mention the existence of a vocalisation system. On the other hand, at quite a late date, in the 12th cent., the prayer-book of *Maḥazor Vitry* opposed the practice of vocalising the text of the Torah. His reason is that the pointing does not «come from Sinai» and consequently does not form part of the sacred text. The prayer-book contains information about the existence of three different systems of vocalisation: Babylonian, Tiberian and Palestinian or «from the land of Israel».

a. The *Babylonian system*, developed in the 8th cent., is supralinear: the vowel signs are written above the consonants. It is still used in some editions of Targum and in Yemenite texts (Roberts). It has precursors in the system devised by Syrian Christians after the 4th cent. to distinguish words written the same way. The process was perfected by the Nestorian Eastern Syrians in the 7th cent., and by the Western Jacobites in the 8th cent. The Babylonian Jews developed a system of vocalisation and accents which consisted in writing letters and points placed above the consonants. The Karaite sect made a decisive contribution to perfecting the Babylonian and Palestinian systems.

b. The *Palestinian system* was used between 700 and 850 CE and evolved until it gave way to the Tiberian system (Chiesa).

c. The *Tiberian system* is used in current editions of the Hebrew Bible. Modern Hebrew grammars explain the details of the system. It is sublinear and consists of 10 signs, three of which are composite. The period when the Tiberian school flourished spans 780 to 930 CE. During this time there were six successive generations of the most famous family of the masoretes, *the Ben ʾAšer.* The best known and most authoritative member of the family is the last in the series, Aaron ben Moses ben ʾAšer, who edited a complete text of the Hebrew Bible with vowels, accents and the appropriate masora. The Aleppo Codex seems to be a faithful copy of this text. It was common practice of a member of the family or of the Jewish community to write the consonantal text and for a «pointer» (*naqdān*) to be entrusted with writing in the masoretic pointing and accents. In this way Moses ben ʾAšer pointed the El Cairo Codex (895) and Aaron ben Moses pointed the St. Petersburg Codex.

Another family of masoretes, contemporary with the Ben ʾAšer but less well known, is *the Ben Naphtali* family, whose system of vocalisation seems to be more rigid and consistent. This tradition is represented by the three codices known as the *Erfurtenses* Codices and in the *Codex Reuchlinianus*, a codex of the Prophets from 1105.

The two families represent *two different traditions* of textual transmission.

The study which P. Kahle (1941) was to complete on the fragments of manuscripts found in the previous century in the Cairo Genizah has provided better knowledge of the evolutionary process of the systems of vocalisation, although there are still many unanswered questions. According to Revell, the differences between the Palestinian and Tiberian vocalisations reflect different Palestinian dialects, so that they are not to be attributed to different systems of the masoretes.

The masoretes developed very meticulous techniques for copying manuscripts, ensuring perfect preservation and transmission of the consonantal and vocalic text. There are four mediaeval codices which claim to be text of the Ben ʾAšer tradition (cf. p. 270).

The *Aleppo Codex* (c. 980), used as the basis for the new edition by the Hebrew University of Jerusalem, and considered an authentic Ben ʾAšer text (cf. p. ooo). According to Dotan, the vocalisation of the masorah does not match the vocalisation of the text. Sometimes it differs from the Ben ʾAšer tradition and sometimes it contains readings from Ben Napthali. It cannot be ruled out, therefore, that it is a copy and not an authentic Ben ʾAšer text.

The *Saint Petersburg Codex* (B 19[A]), dating to 1008/9, also includes Ben Napthali readings, so that it cannot be considered as a «pure» Ben ʾAšer text.

The *El Cairo Codex* contains only the text of the former and latter prophets. The colophon says that it was written and annotated by Moses ben ʾAšer in 895. However, Kahle questioned the purity of its text. This codex originated and circulated in

Karaite circles (A. Schenker) which raises a question about the relations between the Karaites and the «Rabbanites». The former believed that the characters and pronunciation of the Bible were revealed so that they felt more obliged to fix and perfect a system of vocalisation for which the need had not been felt in previous periods.

The *MS. Or. 4445* of the British Museum preserves only the text of Gn 39:20-Dt 1:33.

These are both the oldest and the most complete manuscripts preserved. From the 11th cent. and later centuries, quite a few manuscripts have been preserved, but they tend to diverge from the Ben ʾAšer text and include mixed readings, especially from the Ben Naphtali tradition. The Yemenite manuscripts have preserved the use of the Babylonian pointing system up to present times, though it is contaminated with Tiberian elements. The largest collection of Hebrew manuscripts is the Firkowitch collection of St. Petersburg.

2. *The Masorah*

The term *masorah* derives from the Hebrew root *ʾsr*, «to tie». According to some authors, it comes instead from the post-biblical verb *msr*, «to transmit». The term *masorah* means «tradition». It denotes the whole set of notes which accompany the text in which the «masoretes» (*bʿly hmsrh*) have collected the accumulation of rabbinic tradition concerning the biblical text. The masorah has two functions: to preserve the text in its entirety and to interpret it. The masoretic text is the consonantal Hebrew text which the masoretes vocalised, accented and provided with a masorah. The masorah is the best reflection of the care with which the masoretes preserved the text they themselves had received through tradition from their predecessors.

The masoretes were active from 500 to 1000 CE. They were the successors to the scribes or *sopherim* of previous periods (cf. p. 281).

A. MASORETIC NOTES AND TRADITIONS

The *masoretic notes* are very varied in character. They usually refer to letters or words which could occasion misunderstandings, as was the case with spellings with or without *vowel letters*.

Among the most important notes occur the following:
– *Litterae suspensae*: in Jg 18:30 a superscript *nun* in the name «Moses» (*mšh*) so that it is read «Maⁿasseh» (*mⁿšh*). In this way, an attempt was made to avoid any possible connection between Moses and one of his descendants who became a priest of a pagan temple. The manuscript tradition of the Greek version reflects this double reading: the Antiochene or Proto-Lucianic text (together with the OL and Vulg.), which represents the old Greek text, preserves the original reading «Moses»; the Vatican Codex (*kaige* text) and the Alexandrian Codex (hexaplaric text) give the reading «Manasseh».
– One type of masoretic notation points out, for ex., that «the *central word* of the Torah» is found in Lv 8:8, «the *central letter* of the Torah» in Lv 11:42 and «the *sum of the verses* of the book (which is) 1534» at the end of Genesis. In Dt 6:4, the two let-

ters which make up the word *ʿēd*, («testimony») appear in *larger characters*; this is to draw attention to the importance of this passage where the *šᵉmaʿ* («Listen, O Israel...») occurs.

– *Qᵉrê/Kᵉtîb*: other notes in the margin warn that a particular word is not to be exactly pronounced as it appears written in the text (*Kᵉtîb*) but according to the pronunciation transmitted by oral tradition (*Qᵉrê*). It was thought to be a system to preserve variants from very old MSS or a way of correcting incorrect, difficult or uncommon words or expressions. Gordis thinks that in the roughly 1350 cases of *Qᵉrê-Kᵉtîb*, the two forms of the text are of equal value. What is written (*Kᵉtîb*) is not always inferior to what is considered to be the official reading (*Qᵉrê*). In only 18% of cases is the *Qᵉrê* better than the *Kᵉtîb* and only in 12% is it the other way round. In the remaining 62% both are of equal value.

– *Qᵉrê wᵉlōʾ kᵉtîb*: another type of note marks cases in which a word has to be read although it does not appear written in the text. In *BHS*, there are 10 cases where the consonants of a word appear written in the margin while in the actual text of the corresponding line only the vowels are written (Jgs 20:13; 2 Sm 8:3; 16:23; 18:20; 2 Kgs 19:31.37; Jr 31:38; 50:29; Ruth 3:5.17).

On eight occasions the reverse phenomenon occurs: what is written is not to be read and therefore the vowels are not written. They are as follows: 2 Sm 13:33; 15:21; 2 Kgs 5:18; Jr 38:167; 39:12; Ez 48:16; Ruth 3:12.

Fifteen times a word written as one unit is to be read as if it were two separate words (Gn 30:11; Ex 4:2; Dt 33:2; Is 3:15; Jr 6:29; 18:3; Ez 8:6; Pss 10:10; 55:16; 123:4; Jb 38:1; 40:6; Neh 2:13; 1 Chr 9:4; 27:12). There are also cases of the reverse (Lam 1:6, etc.). In Ez 42:9 the two words which appear written as *wmtḥth lškwt* (*Kᵉtîb*) are to be read as *wmtḥth hlškwt* (*Qᵉrê*); the letter *h* is the article which precedes the second word, which now becomes correct: «Underneath these rooms...».

There are *two* different *traditions* of the *masorah*, one *in Babylon* and the other *in Palestine*, the two great centres of Jewish life after the second Jewish revolt against the Romans (132-5 CE). Babylonian Judaism and Palestinian Judaism developed two schools of interpretation which have been collected in their respective Talmud.

For some time it was thought that it was R. Akiba who, after establishing the consonantal text, had also fixed the masorah which was to accompany the text. If that were the case, the differences between the Babylonian masorah and the Palestinian masorah would have been the result of the corruption of his text over the centuries. However, P. Kahle has shown that such differences reflect the different traditions known in Babylonia, in the schools of Nahardea, Sura and Pumbedita («Eastern masoretes») and in Palestine chiefly in Tiberias («Western masoretes»).

The *masorah parva* is written in the margins between columns. It comprises very short notes, usually in the form of an abbreviation. Sometimes a small circle (*circellus*) or an asterisk was written above the word to which the note referred. Generally, the notes deal with doubts or possible misunderstandings affecting a letter or word, such as the spelling with or without a *vowel letter*, or for example, problems concerning some vowels, accents, grammatical forms, word combinations open to incorrect interpretation, etc. They also mark other passages for comparison. The terminology is Aramaic which is an indication of the period of composition. The editions of *BHK* and *BHS* provide a list of signs and abbreviations with the corresponding meanings.

The *masorah magna* is written in the upper and lower margins and sometimes also on the sides. It contains, besides other information, all the words or parts of verses which exhibit any kind of unusual form.

The *masorah finalis* collects lists for which there is no room in the masorah magna.

Thus the ultimate objective of the masoretic work was to fix in a definitive manner the vowels and accents of the consonantal text which had already been established in an earlier period.

B.   MASORAH AND EXEGESIS

The neglect and sometimes the distaste with which modern criticism has usually treated mediaeval Christian exegesis is perhaps even greater in respect of the masorah and mediaeval Jewish exegesis (cf. p. 487). A few examples will be enough, however, to show the great importance of many masoretic notes which to the non-expert could seem tedious and useless.

Exegesis by means of biblical references. In Is 43:21 the masorah parva notes by means of a simple letter, *ghimel* (= the number 3) that the expression *'am zô* is found twice more in the Bible: Ex 15:13 and 15:16. This simple note summarises the parallelism established by modern biblical theology between the Exodus from Egypt and the Exile in Babylon (the «second Exodus») and between the Song of the Sea (Ex 15) and the passage Is 43:16-21 which seems to be a sort of midrash on the earlier text (J. A. Sanders).

Exegesis by means of accents. The accents are important elements, bearing the meaning, either by association or by disassociation of the elements making up the text. The accents have a function similar to the legatos and rests in a musical score. Musical interpretation consists largely in the art of «phrasing» which is connected with rhythm. In a similar way, biblical rhythm is largely semantic. Rhythm and meaning run in parallel. If due attention is not paid to the accents there is a danger of losing the meaning of the text (Weil).

The masoretic accents (*ṭeʿāmîm*) were quite hierarchical. They are divided into *melāḵim* or *śārîm* («kings» or «princes»), and *mešārĕṭîm*, «servants». The former are disjunctive, the latter conjunctive. In the books written in prose there are 12 disjunctive accents and 8 conjunctive; in the poetic books there are 8 disjunctive and 10 conjunctive accents. The most important rule governing accentuation is that a «prince» accent cannot descend to the level of «servant», and a «servant» cannot rise to a higher class.

Three important examples are enough; the first two concern disjunctive accents and the third a conjunctive accent, according to the Tiberian system.

In Ex 23:12, the various accents establish the following phrasing: «Six days - shall you do your work - and on the seventh day - you will rest/so that they rest - your ox and your ass - and have relief the son of your handmaid - and the foreigner». The disjunctive accent *'aṭnāḥ* falls on the verb «you will rest», drawing attention to this key word around which the whole verse revolves with reference to the story of creation.

Gn 28:25 refers to «... Rebecca, mother of Jacob, and of Esau». The disjunctive accent *ṭarḥā* accompanying the name Jacob has the purpose of drawing attention to the fact that Rebecca is before everything and above all a mother of Jacob, the heir of the patriarchal blessing; only in a very secondary sense is Rebecca also the mother of Esau.

In Ex 17:7-8 we read: «(We will see) if Yahweh is with us, or not. Amalek rose up and attacked Israel...». The masorah suggests, instead, shifting the accent (or the mark dividing the two clauses), leading to a new meaning: «We will see if Yahweh is with us. Instead, Amalak rose...». The masoretes connect this shift of the accent with an interpretation based on the numerical value of the name «Amalek» which is the same as that of the word *sāpēk* («he doubts»). In this way it is possible to interpret the passage from Exodus in the sense that every time that Israel «doubts» its identity, Amalek rises, the prototype of anti-Semitism which threatens and attacks Israel again.

Exegesis by means of Qᵉrê-Kᵉtîb. A typical example is Nm 7:1: «The day on which Moses finished (*kallôt*) erecting the tabernacle...». The Midrash (*Numbers Rabbah* 12:8) and Rashi follow the defective reading, without *wāw*, *kallat*, «bride»: the day on which the Tabernacle was erected, the people of Israel seemed like a bride (*kallâ*) preparing to enter the bridal chamber.

Exegesis by means of paragraph division. These masoretic divisions serve to indicate cuts in the text and mark off sense-units in the text. This is the case in 1QIsᵃ 51:17-52:6.

It is very important to realise that the different reading traditions, as witnessed by the masoretes, in turn generate a diversity and an enormous wealth of meanings and interpretations of the text.

Thus, the history of the masoretic text emphasises the amazing faithfulness with which the masoretic text was transmitted in the Middle Ages, as well as the rabbis' concern to preserve the different traditions of vocalisation and accentuation of the text. Of the three systems developed at the beginning of the mediaeval period (Babylonian, Palestinian and Tiberian), ultimately the Tiberian dominated. Of the two families of masoretes of the Tiberian school, the Ben ʾAšer and the Ben Naphtali, the former prevailed. Of the members of this family, the last, Aaron ben Moses ben ʾAšer, stood out. Yet again the history of the text of the Bible is the history of uniting and purifying earlier traditions in a difficult attempt to save the best of received tradition and at the same time to include the best knowledge of the time. The knowledge of the masoretes was at once grammatical and exegetical.

It has been possible to state that «There never was, and there never can be, a single masoretic text of the Bible!» (Orlinsky, *Prolegomena*, xviii). The tradition of the Ben ʾAšer is not itself uniform (Ph. Cassuto). For this reason, modern editions of the Hebrew Bible have elected to reproduce the text of a single manuscript, the one considered to be the best representative of masoretic tradition, either the St. Petersburg Codex or the Aleppo Codex (cf. p. 268). The reproduction of the chosen codex tries to be absolutely faithful even to the extent of reproducing the mistakes of the manuscript which are conveniently indicated for the attention of the reader.

This means that modern criticism refrains from establishing an «eclectic» edition of the masoretic Hebrew text, as if a single manuscript had contained *the* masoretic text and as if all existing manuscripts had derived from this manuscript. In this way, the bond which unites the text of a codex and the masorah which accompanies it is also acknowledged. In an eclectic codex it would be impossible to establish even the slightest match between a text reconstructed from various manuscripts and the masorah which forms an integral part of each manuscript.

A single system of vocalisation and accentuation or of masorah never existed. Yet it can be said instead that the transmission of the Hebrew consonantal text was already quite consolidated and unified from the beginning of the mediaeval period, since the variants provided by the manuscripts from this period are not, as a whole, of much importance. It is necessary to sketch out the earlier history of the establishing of the consonantal text carried out in accordance with a process of unification very like those considered up to now.

BIBLIOGRAPHY

CASSUTO, PH., «La lettre comme forme. Les bases d'une édition des divergences de la Bible hébraïque», *Henoch* 11 (1989) 3-16.

CHIESA, B., *The Emergence of Hebrew Biblical Pointing*, Frankfurt 1979.

CHIESA, B., *L'Antico Testamento Ebraico secondo la tradizione palestinese*, Turin 1978.

DÍEZ MACHO, A., *Manuscritos hebreos y arameos de la Biblia*, Rome 1971.

FERNANDEZ TEJERO, E.-ORTEGA MONASTERIO, M.T., *Estudios masoréticos (X Congreso de la IOMS) en memoria de Harry M. Orlinsky*, Madrid 1993.

GINSBURG, CH.D., *Introduction to the Massoretico-Critical Edition of the Hebrew Bible*, London 1897, reprint New York 1966.

GORDIS, R., *The Biblical Text in the Making. A Study of the Ketib-Qere*, Philadelphia PA 1937.

GOSHEN-GOTTSTEIN, M., «The Authority of the Aleppo Codex», *Textus* 1 (1960) 17-18.

GOSHEN-GOTTSTEIN, M., «Hebrew Manuscripts: Their History and Their Place in the HUBP (= 'Hebrew University Bible Project') Edition», *Biblica* 48 (1967) 243-290.

KAHLE, P. DE, *Masoreten des Ostens*, Leipzig 1913.

KAHLE, P. DE, *Masoreten des Westens*, Stuttgart 1930.

KAHLE, P. DE, *The Cairo Geniza*, Oxford 1959².

KÖNIG, J., «L'activité herméneutique des scribes dans la transmission du texte de l'Ancien Testament», *Revue de l'histoire des religions* 161 (1962) 141-174; 162 (1963) 1-43.

MALONE, J.L., *Tiberian Hebrew Phonology*, Winona Lake IN 1993.

MCCARTHY, C., *The Tiqqune Sopherim and Other Theological Corrections in the Masoretic Text of the Old Testament*, Fribourg-Göttingen 1981.

ORLINSKY, H.M., «The Origin of the Khetib-Qere Systems: A New Approach», *VT.S* 7 (1960) 184-192.

ORLINSKY, H.M., «The Massoretic text: A Critical Evaluation», *Prolegomena* to the reprint of Ginsburgh 1966.

PÉREZ CASTRO, F., *et al.*, *El Códice de Profetas de El Cairo*, Madrid 1979-1988.

REVELL, E.J., *Biblical Texts with Palestinian Pointing and Their Accents*, Missoula MT 1977.

SANDERS, J.A., «Text and Canon: Concepts and Method», *JBL* 98 (1979) 5-29.

SCHENKER, A., «Die Lehre vom Ursprung des biblischen Schrift- und Aussprache systems im Kairoer Prophetenkodex und das karäische Bekenntnis Mosche Ben Aschers», *Judaica* 43 (1987) 238-247.

WEIL, G.E., «La Massorah», *REJ* 131 (1972) 5-104.

YEIVIN, I, *Introduction to the Tiberian Masorah*, Chico CA 1980.

III. ESTABLISHING THE CONSONANTAL TEXT (70 CE - 150 CE)

The *consonantal text* transmitted by mediaeval manuscripts goes back to the final years of the 1st cent. CE at least. In this period or at the beginning of the 2nd cent. CE, the consonantal text was established definitively and had to remain unchanged from then on (*ne varietur*). At the same time, the final questions concerning the inclusion of certain books in the *biblical canon* were resolved. Apocryphal Jewish writings and writings distributed by Christians remained completely excluded from the Jewish canon and, as a result, from rabbinic libraries. At the same time, the work of compiling the *juridical and exegetical traditions* was begun which was to result in the legal corpus of the Mishnah and the exegetical body of midrashic literature.

This whole project of restricting the canon of inspired books, fixing their text and compiling a corpus of authorised juridical and exegetical interpretations (canon-text-interpretation) responded to the need for *rebuilding Judaism on the Tanak* after the loss of the Temple in the disaster of 70 CE.

Representative of this period is *R. Akibah*, martyred in 132. His contribution to the restoration of Judaism consisted above all in working to fix the consonantal Hebrew text. His connection with the second Jewish revolt (132-135 CE) is important and the fact that the manuscripts from Wadi Murabbaʿat and Naḥal Ḥever (Dead Sea), also connected with that revolt, show a text already established, very close to the later masoretic text. These manuscripts reflect the culmination of a process of fixing the consonantal text which had begun some time earlier. For fixing the text, the rabbis did not proceed so much using the system of combining various texts, selecting the commonest variants (as used to be thought). Among the different forms in which the text was transmitted before 70 CE, the rabbis selected one type of text, which could be called proto-masoretic, more or less as a unit.

The process of fixing the text, undertaken towards the end of the 1st cent. CE, had antecedents in an earlier period. The tradition of the masoretes perpetuates a textual form or «a masoretic recension» (Roberts) already in existence before 70 CE. A proof of this is the fact that 1QIs^b^ shows surprising agreement with MT in both text and spelling. The differences, greater than at first thought, are no more than those in mediaeval manuscripts.

It has been thought possible to find traces of a school of proto-masoretes, before the period of Aquila. Indications of this would be, for example, the variant readings which occur in the actual masoretic text, added at the end of a passage (cf. 1 Kgs 22:48), in the middle of a passage (cf. 1 Kgs 6:15, an example of an addition in the caesura) or simple placed side by side (cf. 1 Kgs 10:21). In many cases, the doublet was inserted after the LXX version which is unaware of one or other variant of the doublet (Zimmermann).

The existence of a very established form of the text of the Torah in a period before the appearance of Christianity is also borne out by other data. Dt 17-18 and Jos 1:8 assume that well before the OT canon was set up, the text of the Torah had already acquired a sacred character which made it immutable. According to *Numbers Rabbah* (11:3), a Torah scroll was kept in the Temple of Jerusalem as the archetype for copying other scrolls. The Jerusalem Talmud (*Ta'anit* 4:2) says that from the period of return from Exile, three scrolls of the Torah were kept in the Temple. In the case of differences among them, the reading accepted as authoritative was when two manuscripts agreed against a third. The *Letter of Aristeas* (nos. 176-179) and the writings of Philo and Josephus also indicate the existence of a more or less authorised text of the Pentateuch.

However, as we will see in what follows, the range of texts that existed in the second Temple period, before 70 CE, is much more varied and richer than was supposed from the information known up to a few decades ago.

It should be noted that sometimes it can be difficult to classify a text as «masoretic» or «pre- masoretic». Thus, the text of 4QEz^a^ could be classed as masoretic (Lust) or pre-masoretic (Sinclair).

The masoretic text has evident antecedents in a textual form which became dominant from the close of the 1st cent. BCE, but there was also a movement in the opposite direction, although it was less noticeable. It consisted in the *survival of readings from non-masoretic text forms in later masoretic tradition*. The author of the book of Chronicles had already made use of a Palestinian text of the books of Samuel and Kings with a different text from the one known through the masoretes. In this way, the masoretic text of Chronicles becomes a witness to variants of a text form differing from the masoretic text form in those books. However, the phenomenon alluded to refers properly to the variants preserved in mediaeval Hebrew manuscripts which agree with readings from the LXX version and do not need to be attributed to «copyists' idiosyncrasies», which tend to produce similar variants independently of each other (Goshen-Gottstein). It is necessary to accept that they go back to a common ancestor belonging to a non-masoretic textual tradition.

This persistence of non-masoretic readings within the consonantal tradition from which the *received text* arose occurs in a special way in the Palestinian textual family, independent of the Tiberian and Babylonian. The convergence of the Palestinian Hebrew text with the Greek text of the LXX (and with its daughter versions) is not a sporadic happening. It indicates «a connection between the P(alestinian) text and the model text of the LXX» (Chiesa, cf. p. 320). Possible the P text and the LXX text have a common origin in priestly circles of the Temple (Sacchi).

2. The Work of the Sopherim

Parallel to the process of establishing the consonantal text, *the sopherim, forerunners of the masoretes*, began the type of study which throughout the whole millennium ultimately led to the stabilisation of the vocalisation and cantillation and the establishment of an authorised (masoretic) interpretation of the consonantal text. The *sōp̄ĕrîm* initiated the work carried out later by the masoretes, basically «counting» (*spr* in Hebrew) the words of text and marking the central letter, word and verse of the text of the Torah (cf. BT *Qidduŝin* 30a).

It is not possible to specify an exact *period* for the activity of the *sōp̄ᵉrîm*. We have information that the members of the Temple personnel were entrusted with revising and correcting the biblical manuscripts (BT *Ketubot* 106a). All the scrolls of the Pentateuch had to undergo an annual inspection in the Temple (BT *Mo'ed qaṭan* 18b), where they were compared with the official model kept there which had been established using three different manuscripts (BT *Ta'anit* 4.2).

The *sopherim* have their *antecedents* in the guise of the scribes of the royal chancelleries of Israel and Judah (2 Sm 8:16-18; 1 Kgs 4:1-6; 2 Kgs 18:18, etc.) and in other prototypes from Mesopotamia and Egypt (cf. p. 111). Tradition connected the scribes with Ezra and Simeon the Just in the time of the «Great Assembly».

The scribes did not confine themselves to making copies of biblical scrolls. They also used various signs to indicate those passages about which tradition knew some kind of doubt or difficulty. Among the typical types of annotation of the sopherim the following can be noted:
– «Omissions of the scribes» (*'itturê sōp̄erîm*): the Babylonian Talmud (*Nedarim* 37b) lists five cases in which a word has to be read but does not appear in the text. On the other hand, there are another five where the word which does appear written is not to be read (cf. p. 275).
– «Corrections of the scribes» (*tiqqunê sōp̄ᵉrîm*): in the oldest sources the number of these corrections varies between seven and thirteen. Mediaeval masoretic lists list as many as 18 cases. In general they consist of some kind of change the aim of which is to avoid an anthropomorphic reference to the deity. For example, according to 1 Sm 3:13 the sons of Eli uttered a curse against God; to prevent the simple reading of this

text becoming an actual and effective utterance of a curse against God (mere utterance made the curse effective) the scribes inserted a slight change in the text: the curse by Eli's sons is against «them» themselves (*LāHeM*) and not against «God» (*'eLōHîM*). A simple change of consonant (') causes the change in meaning.

The clause in Gn 18:22, «Yahweh remained standing before Abraham», is likewise unacceptable since the expression «to remain standing in front of someone» implies the idea of subservience. In this case, all the *sopherim* did was to reverse the order of words: «Abraham remained standing before Yahweh».

Besides the «corrections of the scribes» transmitted by Jewish tradition, the masoretic text underwent other corrections of which later Judaism has kept no record. These corrections were guided by theological scruple. Dt 32:8-9 is an example for different reasons: the contradictory facts from deuteronomic tradition concerning the 70 sons of Jacob (Dt 10:22) and of the priestly tradition which, instead, numbers 75 sons of Jacob (LXX Gn 46:27 and Ex 1:5) need to be harmonised. As a result, this requires changing the texts referring to the descendants of Noah so that the number of the peoples is also be 70 or 75. The corrector chose the number 70 which, according to Barthélemy, was the number attested in the earliest tradition.

– Euphemisms: in order to avoid any chance juxtaposition of words which could mean disparagement of the divine Name, the *sopherim* did not hesitate to use some kind of euphemism: adding a word («you have blasphemed against the enemies of Yahweh», 2 Sm 12:14), substituting the name of a pagan deity in theophoric names, replacing it with a distorted form (*'eš-bāʿal*, 1 Chr 8:33; 9:39, distorted to *'iš-bōšet*, 2 Sm 2:8.10.12.15, etc.), replacing an expression with a pagan tinge with another more acceptable one (in Dt 32:8, the expression *bᵉnê 'ᵉlōh(îm)*, «the sons of El/of the gods» of the LXX and Qumran is changed in the MT to «the sons of Israel») (cf. p. 319), etc.

– *Extraordinary Points*: the procedure of writing points above the words and sometimes under them has not yet been explained convincingly. *Sifre* Numbers (69) lists 10 cases in the Pentateuch: Gn 16:5; 18:9; 19:33; 33:4; Nm 3:39; 9:10; 21:30; 29:15 and Dt 29:28. In the last case, the *extraordinary points* are placed above each letter of the words *lānû ûlᵉbānênû* («to us and to our sons») within the sentence: «Concealed failings belong to the Lord, our God and overt failings to us and to our sons until the end of times». The prophetic books provide another four cases and the *Kᵉṯûḇîm* one more (Ps 27:13).

– It is not possible to determine whether the practice of *increasing the size of some letters* comes from this pre-masoretic period; examples are the *w* of *gāḥôn* («belly») in Lv 11:42 since it is the letter marking the mid-point of the Pentateuch. The same happens in the various ways known through tradition of writing the *šᵉmaʿ yiśrā'ēl* (Dt 6:4).

The antiquity of the process of *dividing the text into sections* is already attested in manuscripts from Qumran and of the LXX version (Oetsch, Langlamet). In Hebrew Bibles (*BHK, BHS*) the «open» sections (*pārāšâ pᵉtuḥâ*) are marked with a *p* and «closed» sections with an *s* (*setumâ*).

Thus, the consonantal text, transmitted in mediaeval manuscripts and vocalised by masoretes, goes back to the centuries before the destruction of Jerusalem, to the second Temple period. Traces of this text or allusions to it can be found in witnesses from the 1st cent. BCE and the 1st cent. CE (the proto-Theodotion recension). The initial fixation of this text, inherited by the masoretes from the hands of the ancient *sopherim*, can be connected with the final stage of the formation of the Hebrew canon, which culminated at the start of the Mishnaic period. The process of fixing the «rabbinic canon» set off a parallel process of fixing the «proto-rabbinic text» (Cross). The manuscripts from Wadi Murabbaʿat and Naḥal Ḥever confirm that the text of this tradition had stabilised towards the end of the 1st cent. CE. The faithful transmission of this form of text at the hands of later copyists turned the MT into an indispensable reference text, although it is by no means the only one, and it will always be necessary to take account of traces of earlier text traditions.

BIBLIOGRAPHY

ALBREKTSON, B., «Reflections on the emergence of a standard text of the Hebrew Bible», *VT.S* 29, Leiden 1978, 49-65.

BARTHÉLEMY, D., *Les Devanciers d'Aquila*, Leiden 1963.

BARTHÉLEMY, D., «History of the Hebrew Text», *The Interpreter's Dictionary of the Bible, Supplement*, ed. K. Crim, Nashville 1976, 878-884.

BARTHÉLEMY, D., «L'état de la Bible juive depuis le début de notre ère jusqu'à la deuxième révolte contre Rome (131-135)», *Le Canon de l'AT. Sa formation et son histoire*, eds. J. D. Kaestly-O. Wermelinger, Geneva 1984, 9-45.

GREENBERG, M., «The Stabilization of the Text of the Hebrew Bible, Reviewed in the Light of the Biblical material from the Judaean Desert», *JAOS* 76 (1956) 157-167.

LEIMAN, S.Z., *The Canon and Masorah of the Hebrew Bible*, New York 1974.

LUST, J., «Ezekiel Manuscripts in Qumran. Preliminary Edition of 4QEza and b», *Ezekiel and his Book*, ed. J. Lust, Leiden 1986, 9-100.

MCCARTHY, C., *The Tiqqune Sopherim and Other Theological Corrections in the Masoretic Text of the Old Testament*, Fribourg-Göttingen 1981.

MCKANE, W., «Observations on the Tikkune Sopherim», *On Language, Culture, and Religion: In Honor of E.A. Nida*, eds. M. Black-W. Smalley, The Hague 1974, 53-77.

ROBERTS, B.J., «The Textual Transmission of the OT», *Tradition and Interpretation*, ed. G. W. Anderson, Oxford 1976, 1-30.

ROBERTS, B.J., *The Old Testament Text and Versions. The Hebrew Text in Transmission and the History of the Ancient Versions*, Cardiff 1951.

SACCHI, P., «Rassegna di studi di storia del testo del Vecchio Testamento ebraico», *Rivista di Storia e Letteratura Religiosa* 2 (1966) 257-324.

SANDERS, J.A., «Text and Canon: Concepts and Method», *JBL* 98 (1979) 5-29.

SEGAL, M.H., «The Promulgation of the Authoritative Text of the Hebrew Bible», *JBL* 72 (1953) 35-47.

SINCLAIR, L.A., «A Qumran Biblical Fragment: 4QEzekᵃ (Ezek. 10,17 - 11,11)», *RQ* 14 (1989) 99-108.

ZIMMERMANN, F., «The Perpetuation of Variants in the Masoretic Text», *JQR* 34 (1934-44) 459-474.

IV. THE PERIOD OF INSTABILITY AND FLUIDITY OF HEBREW TEXTS BEFORE 70 CE

The finding and study of new Qumran manuscripts in the years following the first discovery in 1947 changed the scene in a way that was unimaginable a few decades earlier. The new material is a millennium older than the great mediaeval manuscripts. Until the discoveries of Qumran, the Samaritan Pentateuch and the Greek version of the LXX were virtually the only two important sources able to provide reliable information on the existence of consonantal variants in the period before 70 CE. Witnesses after this date only reflect isolated variants which escaped the process of making the text uniform. In addition, they are very minor variants to be found here and there in rabbinic quotations, in the versions of Theodotion, Aquila and Symmachus and in the hexaplaric text of Origen (the *Fifth* column and transcriptions of the second column), in the Vulgate, Peshitta and targumim and lastly, in mediaeval manuscripts. The variants transmitted in biblical quotations in the apocryphal books, in Jewish-Hellenistic literature and in the NT are infrequent.

The only pre-masoretic Hebrew text known before 1947 was the Nash Papyrus (2nd cent. BCE) which does not actually match the biblical text. It reproduces the passage of the Ten Commandments with a mixed text taken from Ex 20 or rather from Dt 5, at the end of which it adds the text of the *Šĕmaʿ*. The text of this papyrus has some variants with respect to the MT. Examples of harmonising similar to those presented by this papyrus have been found later.

The biblical manuscripts from the Dead Sea provided two contrasting surprises. The manuscripts from Cave 1 and, in particular, the second Isaiah scroll (1QIs^b) show surprising agreement with the text known through the masoretes of the 9th and 10th cents. CE. On the other hand, manuscripts from Cave 4, particularly the book of Samuel (4QSam^abc) and the second Jeremiah MS (4QJer^b) differ considerably from the MT and agree significantly with the text of the LXX. Other manuscripts agree with the Samaritan Pentateuch. In the case of the book of Jeremiah, the Qumran manuscripts provide copies which reproduce different text forms.

Thus, next to the more or lest straight line of textual transmission reaching us through mediaeval manuscripts, there now appear other lines of textual transmission which were abandoned towards the end of the 1st cent. CE and the start of the following century. Of this, only refections have been preserved in the sources listed above: the LXX, the Samaritan Pentateuch, quotations from apocryphal writings or from the NT, etc.

As a result, the importance of the biblical manuscripts from Qumran is twofold. They confirm the antiquity of the text of masoretic tradition and they testify to the existence of a degree of textual pluralism in the centuries just before the change of era. The biblical text at that time remained fluid to some extent, due to the diversity of textual forms which existed and to the normal process of stabilisation of texts.

The biblical manuscripts from Qumran have additional value since they cause the witness of other sources to be re-appraised. Though already known, their value was very much debated, at least in some quarters. Such is the case particularly for the LXX version.

However, when appraising the witness of the Dead Sea Scrolls, it is always necessary to bear in mind that in most of these manuscripts there are many examples of textual corruption. In addition, they are texts transmitted within a very specific socio-religious group which has very marked or «sectarian» characteristics, compared with mainstream Judaism. For these reasons, it must always be remembered that the range of texts provided by the manuscripts from Qumran may be very incomplete and biased.

1.   The Biblical Dead Sea Scrolls

Analysis of the biblical Dead Sea scrolls has *important repercussions in a wide range of fields*: the history of the Hebrew language, the history of the transmission of the biblical text, the historical process of the translation of the Bible into other languages, the development of biblical and Jewish interpretation of the biblical text, textual criticism which aims to trace «original» variants and lastly, literary criticism which has the aim of reconstructing the history of the formation of the biblical books.

The structure and syntax of *Qumran Hebrew* are the same as in biblical Hebrew, especially if both are compared to Mishnaic Hebrew. For example, the *wāw*-consecutive system continues to be used, the relative (particle) continues to be biblical Hebrew *ʾašer* and the genitive particle *šel* characteristic of Mishnaic Hebrew is not yet in use.

However, the Hebrew of Qumran has features which distinguish it from Hebrew. The Dead Sea Scrolls frequently exhibit fuller spelling. Among the morphological features, the pronoun forms *hwʾh* and *hyʾh* stand out, which could be pronounced *huʾa*, *hiʾa*. Also, the forms of the imperfect with a suffix such as *yšwpṭny* (*yišpᵉṭēni* in the Tiberian vocalisation), which seem to correspond to a primitive form with a vowel after the first radical. The lexicon of the manuscripts from Qumran is peculiar to post-biblical Hebrew, with some typical terms: *pēšer* («interpretation»), *sereḵ* («rule»), *mᵉbaqqēr* («overseer»), *qēṣ* («period»), *yaḥaḏ* («community»), etc. Some terms show Aramaic influence but on the whole this influence is slight.

The Dead Sea Scrolls provide information about the state in which *the biblical text* was transmitted between the 3rd cent. BCE and the 2nd cent. CE, not only in the Qumran community but *in the whole of Palestine*, for many, if not most of the manuscripts were copied in various places in Palestine outside Qumran. The manuscripts found at Masada, Naḥal ever and Wadi Murabbaʿat were written elsewhere and deposited in the caves in which they were found, although some of those found in Masada could have been copied on site. According to Tov, at Qumran only those were copied with certain linguistic features (lengthened pronominal forms such as *hwʾh/hyʾh* and verb forms such as *mlkkmh*, [*w*]*ʾqṭlh*, [*w*]*qṭltmh*, etc.) and spelling (*kwl*, *ki*ʾ, *zwʾt/zʾwt/zwt*, etc.). Among the characteristics of these manuscripts copied in Qumran can be included also, still in Tov's opinion, the use of special marks by the scribe, of initial or medial charcacters at the end of a word, of stronger and more durable writing material and of palaeo-Hebrew characters for writing the divine names *ʾel(ōhîm)* and *YHWH*. Most of the biblical texts written in the «Qumran system» come from the period between 50 BCE and 68 CE and some form an earlier period. These include 1QDeutᵃ, 1QIsᵃ, 2QNumᵇ, 4QSamᶜ and the biblical paraphrases 4Q158, 4Q364, 4Q365 and 11QTemple.

It is not possible to classify these manuscripts on the basis of the contents of the various caves (except for Cave 7, in which only Greek manuscripts were found). More problematic are Caves 1, 4 and 11, owing to the variety of languages, contents, types of script, spelling systems, textual types, etc.

It is even more difficult to determine the *type of collection* of the books found at Qumran. It is not a Genizah (Del Medico) nor can it be said that there is no connection between the manuscripts and the Qumran community, as if all the scrolls came from other places, possibly from the Temple library (Golb). The only plausible explanation is that some members of the Qumran comunity lived in the caves close to the place and that at a time of crisis they deposited the manuscripts there for safekeeping.

It is now necessary to run through all the biblical books - copies of all of which have been found in Qumran, except for the book of Esther - in order to know the new material and their contribution to critical study and exegesis (see below). The detailed description of each of the manuscripts discovered in Qumran can be found in the corresponding edition, usually in the series *Discoveries in the Judaean Desert*. H. Stegemann calculates that 823 manuscripts were found in the Qumran caves, 580 from Cave 4. F. García Martínez's list includes 668 manuscripts, 426 from Cave 4.

Genesis (and Exodus): The manuscripts of Genesis and Exodus from Cave 4 have two types of text; in Exodus there is also a third type which corresponds to a recension (Davila). They are as follows: 1 QGn = 1Q1 (Barthélemy *DJD* I); 2QGn 1QGn = 1Q1 (Barthélemy *DJD* I); 2QGn = 2Q1 (Baillet *DJD* III); 4QGn-Exᵃ = 4Q1contains the text of Gn and Ex, joined; 4QGnᵇ⁻ᵍ = 4Q2-7, identical to the MT in 4Q2 and close to the masoretic and Samaritan texts in 4Q5; 4QGnʰ⁻¹, 4QGnʰ⁻², 4QGnʰ⁻ᵖᵃʳᵃ, 4QGnʰ⁻ᵗⁱᵗˡᵉ = 4Q8 and 8abc; 4QGnⁱ = 4Q9, of a text type close to the Samaritan text; 4QGnᵏ = 4Q10, with portions of Gn 1-3 (Davila *DJD* XII, pp. 31-78). Three manuscripts are in the palaeo-Hebrew script: 4QpaleoGn-Exˡ = 4Q11, portions of Gn 50,26 and of Ex 1-36; 4QpaleoGnᵐ = 4Q12, with portions of Gn 26 (Skehan-Ulrich-Sanderson *DJD* IX); 6QpaleoGn = 6Q1, portions of Gn 6 (Baillet *DJD* III). 8QGn = 8Q1 preserves portions of Gn 17- 18 (Baillet *DJD* III).

Exodus (and Leviticus): 1QEx = 1Q2 (Barthélemy *DJD* I); 2QExᵃ = 2Q2; 2QExᵇ = 2Q3, and 2QExᶜ = 2Q4; 2Q3 gives the text of Ex 19:9 inmediately after Ex 34:10 (Baillet *DJD* III).

4QExᵇ = 4Q13, six fragments with portions of Ex 1-5 (Cross *DJD* XII); 4QExᶜ = 4Q14, 36 fragments with portions of Ex 7-18 (Sanderson, *DJD* XII 97-125); 4QExᵈ = 4Q15, and 4QExᵉ = 4Q16, the first with the text of Ex 13:15-17, followed immediately by Ex 15:1, and the second with portions of Ex 13,3-5 (Sanderson *DJD* XII, 127-131); 4QEx-Lv^f = 4Q17, copied in about 250 BCE, could be the oldest biblical text from Qumran; portions of Ex 38 - Lv 2, with a text virtually identical to MT (Cross *DJD* XII, 133-144); 4QEx^g = 4Q18; 4QEx^h = 4Q19 and 4QEx^j = 4Q20, fragments with portions of Ex 14,21-27, Ex 6,36, Ex 36,9-10 y Ex 36,9-10 respectively (Sanderson *DJD* XII, 145-151).

4QpaleoEx^m = 4Q22, from the first half of the 1st cent. BCE, contains 6:25-37:16. It is a text of the Samaritan Pentateuch type, with typical additions taken from Ex or Dt, except for the additions of the «sectarian» Samaritan text (Sanderson *DJD* IX, 51-130).

Phylacteries and $m^e z\hat{u}z\hat{o}\underline{t}$ from Cave 4 provide fragments of Ex 12:43-13:18. The «pharisee» phylacteries follow a text very like the later masoretic text (4Q130, 4Q133); the older «Essene» phylacteries follow an unspecified text, which at times agrees with the Samaritan Pentateuch or the LXX and at others is completely different (4Q128-129; 4Q134-142). 4Q149 only contains the Decalogue, in the Samaritan form, a mixture of Ex 20:1-7 and Dt 5:11-16. 4Q141 only seems to contain the Song of Moses (Dt 32) in a text related to the Samaritan text and the LXX (Milik *DJD* VI,33-85 pls. V-XXVII).

Leviticus and Numbers: 1QpaleoLv = 1Q3 (Barthélemy *DJD* I); 2QpaleoLv = 2Q5 (Baillet *DJD* III); 4QLev-Num^a = 4Q23, with numerous fragments; 4QLev^b = 4Q24, thirty fragments with portions of Lv 1-3 and 21-25 (Ulrich *DJD* XII, 153-187); 4QLev^c = 4Q25, nine fragments with portions of Lv 1-8, one of them writtennn by two different hands; 4QLev^d = 4Q26, portions of Lv 14-15; 4QLev^e = 4Q26a, nine fragments with portions of Lv 3 and 19- 22, y 4QLev^f = 4Q26a, portions of Lv 7,19-26 with the tetragrammaton in palaeo-Hebrew characters (Tov *DJD* XII, 189-204). 6QpaleoLev = 6Q2, portions of Lev 8 (Baillet *DJD* III); 11QpaleoLev^a = 11Q1, portions of chs. 4 to 27 (Freedman-Mathews); 11Q Lev^b contains 9:23- 10:2 and 13:58-59. Its text cannot be set within known co-ordinates; at times it agrees with the LXX.

Numbers: 2QNum^{a-d} = 2Q6-9 (Baillet *DJD* III); 4QNum^b = 4Q27, from the Herodian period, has a very developed type of text on the lines of the Samaritan Pentateuch, but still closer to the LXX text; it inserts Dt 3:21 after Nm 27:23 and Dt 3:23-24 after Nm 20:13 (Jastram *DJD* XII, 205-267).

Deuteronomy: 16 copies of this book have been recovered from Cave 4. 4QDeut^j contains portions of chs. 4, 6, 8, 11 and 32 and sections of Ex 12-13, which confers a «frontier» type character on the text of the manuscript (cf. p. 000) as between the biblical and the non-biblical (Duncan, *DJD* XIV). 4QDeut^n has chapters in a different order and a harmonising text in the Decalogue (White *DJD* XIV; cf. p. 000). 4QDeut^q contains the Song of Moses, Dt 32.

Phylacteries (*Tĕpillîn*) and $m\check{e}z\hat{u}z\hat{o}\underline{t}$ from Cave 4 (4Q128-131; 4Q134-144; 4Q146; 4Q150-153) preserve sections of the text of Dt, sometimes agreeing with MT, the Samaritan Pentateuch and with a large number of its own readings (Milik *DJD* VI, 35-38 pls. V-XXVII).

Joshua: 4QJosh^a = 4Q47 has the chapters in a different order from the traditional masoretic sequence. In the order as attested by this manuscript, Joshua built the first altar in the land of Canaan at Gilgal, after crossing the Jordan (i.e. after Jos ch. 4), and not later on Mount Ebal as in the masoretic Hebrew text (8:30-35) or in the LXX Greek text (9:3-8). The sequence of passages as in the Qumran manuscript is supported by the text of Flavius Josephus (*Jewish Antiquities* V, 16-19; Ulrich *DJD* XIV). 4QJos^b = 4Q48 has a text which seems similar to 4QSam^a.

Judges: 4QJudges^a contains sections of the text of Jgs 6:2-13, with the important omission of vv. 7-10 and variants agreeing with the proto-Lucianic Greek text and the OL (cf. p. 349). 4QJudgesᵃ preserves text from 9:5-7 and 21:12-25, with a type of masoretic text, although the reconstruction of the lines raises problems about the relationship between both texts (Trebolle *DJD* xiv).

Samuel: Three copies of Samuel have turned up in Cave 4. 4QSamᵃ contains quite a long section of text. Its frequent agreement with the text of the LXX confirms the Hebrew origin of very many variants of the Greek text (cf. p. ooo). 4QSamᵇ is the oldest document from Qumran; Cross dates it towards the close of the 3rd cent. BCE; the text, distinguished by defective spelling, belongs to a primitive period in the evolution of the Palestinian textual tradition (cf. p. 293; Cross, Ulrich; on 4QSamᶜ, cf. Ulrich 1979).

Kings: 7 fragments of a single manuscript are preserved with parts of the text of 1 Kgs 7:20- 8:18. It preserves a reading missing from the MT due to homoioteleuton (1 Kgs 8:16; Trebolle).

Isaiah. 1QIsᵃ was copied by a single scribe around 125-100 BCE, although it has also been suggested that possibly there were two copyists of the manuscript. The same scribe and others later filled in gaps in the first copy. The spelling is quite plene and the text has several harmonising and easier readings. The language and spelling of 1QIsᵃ show traces of the influence of the language spoken in Palestine towards the end of the 2nd cent. BCE. The MT preserves, instead, the oldest textual tradition without being affected by linguistic innovations (Kutscher). Kutcher's position has been criticised for relying too much on the MT. 1QIsᵃ readings which may be preferable to the MT: 3:24; 11:6; 14:4b; 21:8a; 37:27-28 (line six); 40:6; 49:17.24; 51:5; 59:11; 60:19a; 62:11. Giving the surprising agreement of this manuscript with the consonantal text of the masoretic tradition, it was thought that it would make an earlier stage in the transmission of the book more accessible, but in most cases where the two texts differ, the manuscript reading is inferior to the masoretic text.

It is important to study the text of this and of every manuscript, paying attention to the structure formed by their variants, independently of the critical value the text may have. The variants of this manuscript are the work of a scribe whose intention was to update the prophetic text in the manner of the *Pesharim*, reflecting the viewpoint of the Qumran community (Van der Kooij).

1QIsᵇ was edited by Sukenik in 1954 (7 fragments were edited later by Barthélemy-Milik). The 22 fragments preserved correspond mostly to chs. 38-66, with large gaps in the lower parts of the columns. The manuscript comes from 100-75 BCE. Its spelling is more defective than 1QIsᵃ but its text has fewer re-workings. Its resemblance to the MT has also been exaggerated. According to Loewinger, there are about 300 variations from the MT, but the almost all of them concern only the use of the *matres lectionis wāw* and *yôd*. The dependability of the text transmitted is not comparable to that of later manuscripts. On the other Isaiah manuscripts, cf. Skehan (DBS).

Jeremiah: 4QJerᵃ, c. 200 BCE, corresponds to the longer text of the masoretic tradition. 4QJerᵇ, instead, from a later period, corresponds to the shorter text reflected by the Greek version. 4QJerᶜ, from the close of the 1st cent. BCE or the start of the 1st cent. CE, contains text from chs. 8; 19-22; 25-27; 30-33, in a text form close to the MT (Janzen, Bogaert, cf. Tov 1989 on the new division of the manuscripts; cf. p. 393)

Ezekiel: Four fragments of 4QEzᵃ, in late Hasmonaean or early Herodian script, preserve portions of 10:5-15; 10:17-11:11; 24:14-18.44-47 and 41:3-6. Four small fragments of 4QEzᵇ, in the Herodian script, contain portions of Ez 1:10-11-12.13.16-17.20-24. The text of the two manuscripts is very close to the MT (Lust). Sinclair attributes the text of 4QEzᵃ to a pre-masoretic form of the text (cf. p. 281).

Minor Prophets: Cave 4 has supplied 7 manuscripts from this collection of books, although some only preserve parts of the text corresponding to one or two of the books which form the collection. The text is substantially the same as the MT (Fuller).

Psalms: Cave 4 has provided 20 manuscripts. Its contribution to the study of the text of the Psalter seems to be rather meagre (Skehan). 4QPsᵃ, from the mid 2nd cent. BCE, preserves fragments of the text of Psalms 5-69; the psalms are in their normal sequence except for Ps 71 which comes after Ps 38; in 135:21 it provides a better reading. 4QPsᵇ, from the Herodian period, runs from Ps 91 to Ps 118; it has a stichometric layout in columns of 16 to 18 lines and omits Pss 104-111. 4QPsᶜ, slightly earlier than 68 CE, has fragments from Ps 5 to Ps 53. The last manuscript from Cave 4, 4QPsˢ, from the second half of the 1st cent. CE, preserves part of the text of Ps 88:15-17, with a variant possibly already known from the Greek version ('*apûrâ* instead of the hapax '*apûnâ* in MT).

11QPsᵃ, from the beginning of the 1st cent. CE, contains passages from 41 psalms from the fourth and fifth book of the psalter, in a different order from the Hebrew Bible. At the end, seven non-biblical psalms are inserted («Plea for Deliverance», «Apostrophe to Zion», «Hymn to the Creator», etc.; Sanders). According to Talmon and Goshen-Gottstein, they comprise a collection of psalms intended for the liturgy of Qumran, a sort of prayer-book; however, they do not allow the supposition, made by Sanders and Yadin, that it is a variant and open canon. Sanders sees confirmation of this in the statement in column 27 that David wrote 3,600 psalms and 450 poems by the gift of «prophecy», known through God. According to Skehan, it is not possible to speak of a canon in Qumran and the collection of psalms represented by 11QPsᵃ is a secondary derivation from the collection of 150 psalms which had already been established in the Persian period (Skehan, Cross, Ulrich, Flint).

11QPsᵇ, from the same period as the first, adds the same «Plea for Deliverance» as 11QPsᵃ. The other manuscripts from Cave 11, 11QPsᶜᵈᵉ, exhibit features peculiar to the spelling at Qumran. Sometimes they substitute an archaic word for the normal, contemporary word and its text is close to MT. 11QPsᶜ preserves material from Pss 2:1-8; 9:3-7; 12:5-13:6; 14:1-6; 17:9-15; 18:1-12; 36:13-37:4; 77:18-78:1; 86:11-14. The text of 11QPsᵈ corresponds to Pss 39:13-40:1; 43:1-3; 59:5-8; 68:1-5.16-18; 78:5-12; 81:3-9; 105:34-45. 11QPsᵉ has the text corresponding to Pss 36:13-37:4 and 86:11-14 (Van der Ploeg, García Martínez).

Daniel: Eight manuscripts of this book have been found. 4QDanᵃ, from the mid-1st cent. BCE, preserves the change from Aramaic to Hebrew in 8:1 and the short form of the text, although it also has several additions to the MT (2:20.28.30.40; 5:7.12; 8:3.4...), variants which agree with the LXX or papyrus 967 plus other readings of its own. In 2:28, 4QDanᵃ and the original of the LXX seem to go back to a different text tradition from the one represented by MT and Theodotion (Ulrich). 4QDanᵇ witnesses Hebrew-Aramaic bilingualism as does 4QDanᵃ. 4QDanᶜ is very interesting since it comes from the end of the 2nd cent. BCE, no later than 50 years after the definitive composition of that book. 4QDanᵈ, in a bad state of preservation, does not include the text of the prayer as in the Greek text of ch. 3. 4QDanᵉ corresponds to the prayer of ch. 9, and is thus a witness to its existence in Hebrew.

In some cases the Dead Sea Scrolls witness a text which is very close to the masoretic text, but in others they confirm the existence of a Hebrew text as reflected in the Greek version of the LXX, and at times show some affinity with the Samaritan Pentateuch. However, each text also has its own characteristics and has to be evaluated on its own merits and not merely with reference to the three forms of text known since antiquity (Van der Woude, Tov).

As for the text of the Pentateuch, it is true that the greater the number of manuscripts known, the greater the number of textual variants to be studied. However, the text of the Pentateuch attested by the Qumran manuscripts is very consistent and relatively free of significant variants, as is also the Pentateuch in the Greek version.

Two stages in the history of the Palestinian text of the Pentateuch can be distinguished: an older form, close to the original of the LXX, and another, more developed form, close to the Samaritan recension. With regard to the book of Genesis, the texts found show a degree of stability. As for Exodus, 4QEx^b represents a short text; 4QpaleoEx^m, instead, although dating to the beginning of the 2nd cent. BCE, has a longer text. 4QNum^b, from the Herodian period, is based on a text closely related to the LXX, with interpolations of a Samaritan type (cf. p. 295). 4QDeut^q (Dt 32) is a mixed text with readings known from the LXX.

Over several centuries very differing Hebrew texts were in circulation. This situation gave way to a very different situation towards the end of the 1st cent. CE with the establishment of a uniform and unalterable consonantal text in a form of textual tradition which originated far away and is found already attested among the manuscripts from Qumran.

The history of the consonantal text, like the history of the fixing of the vowels, is the history of a transition from a situation of textual fluidity to one of textual uniformity.

BIBLIOGRAPHY

BURROWS, M.-TREVER, J.C.-BROWNLEE, W.H., *The Isaiah Manuscript and the Habakkuk Commentary*, New Haven NJ 1950.

CROSS, F.M., «The Old Testament at Qumrân», *The Ancient Library of Qumrân and Modern Biblical Studies*, Sheffield 1995, 121-142.

FREEDMAN, D.N.-MATHEWS, K.A., *The Paleo-hebrew Leviticus Scroll (11Qpaleo-Lev)*, Winona Lake IN 1985.

FULLER, R., *The Minor Prophets Manuscripts from Qumrân, Cave IV*, Dissertation Harvard University 1988.

GOLB, N., *Who Wrote the Dead Sea Scrolls? The Search for the Secret of Qumran*, New York 1996.

GOSHEN-GOTTSTEIN, M.H., «The Psalms Scroll (11QPs^a): A Problem of Canon and Text», *Textus* 5 (1966) 22-33.

KOOIJ, A. VAN DER, «1QIs^a Col. VIII, 4-11 (Isa 8,11-18): A Contextual Approach of Its Variants», *RQ* 13 (1988) 569-581.

SANDERS, J.A., *The Dead Sea Psalms Scroll*, Ithaca NY 1967.

SANDERS, J.A., «The Qumran Psalms Scroll (11QPs^a) reviewed», *On Language, Culture and Religion. In Honor of E.A. Nida*, The Hague 1974, 79-99.

SANDERSON, J.E., *An Exodus Scroll from Qumran: 4QpaleoExod^m and the Samaritan Tradition*, Atlanta, GA 1986.

SKEHAN, P.W., «Qumran. IV, Littérature de Qumran - A. Textes bibliques», *DBS* 9, Paris 1979, cls 805-822.

SUKENIK, E.L., *The Dead Sea Scrolls of the Hebrew University*, Jerusalem 1955.

TALMON, S., «Extra-Canonical Hebrew Psalms from Qumran - Psalm 151», *The World of Qumran from Within. Collected Studies*, Jerusalem - Leiden 1989, 244-272.

TOV, E., «The Orthography and Language of the Hebrew Scrolls Found at Qumran and the Origin of These Scrolls», *Textus* 13 (1986) 31-58.

TOV, E., «Hebrew Biblical Manuscripts from the Judaean Desert: Their Contribution to Textual Criticism», *JJSt* 39 (1988)5-37.

TOV, E., «The Jeremiah Scrolls from Cave IV», *The Texts of Qumran and the History of the Community, RQ* 14 (1989) 189-206.

TOV, E., «Groups of Biblical Texts found at Qumran», *Time to Prepare the Way into Wilderness. Papers on the Qumran Scrolls by Fellows of the Institute for Advanced Studies of the Hebrew University, Jerusalem, 1989-1900*, eds. D. Dimant & L.-H. Schiffman, Leiden 1995, 85-102.

TOV, E. (ed.), *Companion Volume to the Dead Sea Scrolls on Microfiche Edition*, Leiden 1995².

TREBOLLE BARRERA, «Textual Variants in *4QJudg^a* and the Textual and Editorial History of Judges», *RQ* 14 (1989) 229-245.

ULRICH, E., «Daniel Manuscripts from Qumran. Part 1: A Preliminary Edition of 4QDan^a», *BASOR* 267 (1987) 17-37; «Part 2: Preliminary Editions of 4QDan^b and 4QDan^c», *BASOR* 274 (1989) 3-26.

ULRICH, E., «4QSam^c. A Fragmentary Manuscript of 2 Samuel 14-15 from the Scribe of the Serek Hayyahad (1QS)», *BASOR* 235 (1979) 1-25.

VERMES, G., *The Dead Sea Scrolls in English: Revised & Extended Edition*, Harmondsworth 1995.

WHITE, S., «4QDt ⁿ: Biblical Manuscript or Excerpted Text?», *Of Scribes and Scrolls: Studies on the Hebrew Bible, Intertestamental Judaism, and Christian Origins*, eds. H.W. Attridge-J. Collins-T.H. Tobin, Lanham 1991, 13-20.

WOUDE, A.S. VAN DER, «Pluriformity and Uniformity. Reflections on the Transmission of the Text of the Old Testament», *Sacred History and Sacred Texts in Early Judaism. A Symposium* in Honour of A.S. van der Woude, eds. J.N. Bremmer - García Martínez, F., Kampen, 1993, 151-169.

YADIN, Y, *The Ben Sira Scroll from Masada*, Jerusalem 1965.

2.   *Theories on the Origins of the Biblical Text*

Before the discoveries at the Dead Sea, knowledge about the history of the Hebrew text was limited to the masoretic tradition and, for the pre-masoretic period, to the indirect witness of the versions. The encyclopaedism of the 18th cent. led to two large collections which assembled textual variants contained in the mediaeval manuscripts, one by B. Kennicott (1776-1780) and one by J. B. de Rossi (1784-1788; cf. p. 271).

a. The «Single Recension» Theory: Rosenmüller. Although the number of variants was enormous, E. F. K. Rosenmüller developed the theory of the «single recension» (1797-1798, the theory is earlier than Rosenmüller, Chiesa) according to which all existing codices are very much later than the original texts, full of mistakes, lack significant variants and belong to a single recension or source, so that they are of little use for restoring possible corruptions in the Hebrew text.

b. The «Single Archetype» Theory: P. de Lagarde. A century later, Paul de Lagarde (1863) still voiced a similar and if possible more extreme opinion: «our Hebrew manuscripts of the OT go back to a *single exemplar*» (emphasis ours) and even its mistakes have been copied. Lagarde assumes the existence of a «single archetype» from which the whole of Hebrew tradition comes. It is impossible to go back beyond it except by means of conjectures or through the Greek version which translates a Hebrew manuscript from a different family. According to Lagarde, the single Hebrew exemplar from which all the rest derive represented the «Palestinian recension» and the single Greek exemplar from which all the LXX manuscripts preserved derive, represented the «Egyptian recension». Thus the early history of the Hebrew and Greek texts run in parallel.

Lagarde applied the same model to the textual history of the LXX version. The Greek manuscripts preserved go back to three basic recensions (Origen, Hesychius and Lucian) and from them it is possible to go back to the single exemplar of the original Greek version (cf. p. 381).

c. The «Vulgar Texts» Theory: Paul Kahle. Some years later this scholar elaborated exactly the opposite theory (*The Cairo Geniza*). Kahle noted that the manuscripts found in the Cairo Geniza (built in 882) which come from the 9th cent. or even earlier, as well as the biblical quotations contained in rabbinic literature and the NT and lastly, the ancient versions, sometimes contain considerable textual differences, contrary to the supposition that all the Hebrew texts go back to one single text.

Kahle proposes, therefore, what is called the theory of «vulgar texts»: the Hebrew and Greek archetypes envisaged by Lagarde are only the final precipitate of a very lengthy process by which a large number of vulgar texts was becoming unified under the efforts of Jewish, Samaritan and Christian copyists until it developed into the official texts of these three religious communities: the proto-masoretic text of the Jews, the Samaritan version of the Pentateuch and the Greek text of the LXX transmitted by the Christians. Within each official tradition there survived remnants of older vulgar texts which never actually disappeared completely.

Kahle interprets the history of the Hebrew text in the light of the history of the Aramaic targums which circulated in different text forms and initially without official control. Kahle also applies the same model to the history of the Greek text which originated from differing targumic versions made from the Hebrew «vulgar texts» mentioned earlier. Study of the biblical manuscripts from the Dead Sea, however, has discredited Kahle's theory, particularly in respect of the history of the Greek text (cf. p. 306).

d. The Theory of «local texts»: F. M. Cross. After the discovery of the Dead Sea Scrolls, F. M. Cross formulated the theory of «local texts». The variety of texts reflected in the manuscripts from Qumran is not as chaotic as supposed by the theory of «vulgar» texts. This variety can be reduced to just three types or forms of text, the uniformity and persistence of which over the centuries is explained by factors of geographical isolation.

In the Pentateuch and the historical books three types of text are found; in the prophetic books, only two.

The three types of text of the Pentateuch seem to have taken shape by means of a slow process between the 5th and 1st cents. BCE in the three great centres of Judaism: the Palestinian metropolis and the Eastern and Western diasporas of Babylon and Egypt. In a situation of isolation - in Babylon and Egypt - a text acquires its own form and character. In a situation where there are contacts - Palestine - some texts become contaminated by others. In both cases the text diverges from its original archetype.

– The *Palestinian type* is «expansionist». It is distinguished by its many glosses, double readings, additions of parallel passages or harmonisations and other traces which reflect intense editorial activity.

– The *Egyptian type* is an intermediate text, which does not provide the expansions of the Palestinian type and the omissions of the Babylonian type. The Egyptian and Palestinian types show a close relationship. The former seems to be a branch of the latter.

– The *Babylonian type* is a short text. In the Pentateuch it is an old and conservative text with very few traces of revision, expansion or modernisation. In the books of Samuel, however, the text is worthless, corrupted by frequent omissions.

The oldest manuscripts from Qumran belong to the Palestinian type and only on rare occasions do they come from Egypt. The Babylonian type is seen for the first time in the historical books through the Greek proto-Theodotion recension, with no equivalent of any kind in the Hebrew manuscripts from Qumran.

F. M. Cross reconstructs the history of the Hebrew text, in parallel with the history of the Greek text of the LXX, in the following four stages:

– In the *Persian period*, probably in the 5th cent. BCE, different local texts began to emerge, which evolved separately in Palestine and in Babylonia. The priestly edition of the Tetrateuch as well as the definitive deuteronomistic edition of the historical books are no earlier than the *closing decades of the 6th cent. BCE*. The Pentateuch and the historical books certainly gained their final form in Babylonia in the 6th cent; the «local texts» stemmed from copies of these works. In any case, it is necessary to backdate the *«archetype» of all local texts* to the period of the Restoration.

– At *the start of the 4th cent. BCE*, the *Egyptian text* of the Pentateuch became independent of the Palestinian to go its own way. Up to this period, the author of Chronicles used an early form of the *Palestinian text*. The separation of the Egyptian text of Jeremiah probably occurred at an earlier stage while the separation of the historical books was somewhat later. At the same time, *a third textual type* developed *in Babylonia* which remained in isolation until its return to Palestine, perhaps in the Maccabaean period, when the deportations by the Parthians and the worries about the return to Zion made many Jews go back to Palestine. It may possibly be later, *in the 2nd cent. or at the start of the 1st cent.* BCE. In any case, the proto-Lucianic recension of the 2nd cent. or the beginning of the 1st BCE did not yet use the Babylonian text type which, however, was the basis for the proto-Theodotion recension.

– The *base-text of the later masoretic text* was formed *in the period between Hillel and the first Jewish revolt*, that is, between the close of the 1st cent. BCE and 70 CE. The proto-Theodotion Greek recension probably coincided with the first attempts at a recension of the Hebrew text of the Pentateuch and of the historical books. This Hebrew recension did not use only a single text type but mixed together local texts in various books. Thus, for the Pentateuch it used the Babylonian text, which had been brought to Palestine shortly before, rejecting the Palestinian text and even the palaeo-Hebrew script. For the historical books it also selected the Babylonian text in spite of the existence of a better text preserved by the ancient Palestinian type. In the prophetic books different text types were mixed together, due perhaps to the lack of originals of the Palestinian type.

– At *the start of the 1st cent. CE*, the *proto-masoretic text*, still undeveloped, was used for the proto-Theodotion text. This text is well known though the manuscripts from Qumran, whereas not a single copy of the MT or traces of its influence have been found. This last *rabbinic recension* comprises the official text in all the Jewish communities *from 70 CE*. Soon, the remaining competing text traditions began to disappear, preserved only in ancient translations or in the text of an isolated community such as the Samaritan Pentateuch.

Thus, in accordance with the theory of local texts, the picture of the text before the textual unification of the *sopherim* is not so simple and straightforward as Lagarde assumed nor so chaotic and «vulgar» as Kahle imagined. In general, the discoveries from the Dead Sea have come to confirm Lagarde's theory. However, the Hebrew *Urtext* of Lagarde has had to be some five centuries earlier, until it becomes an archetype (5th cent. BCE) from which various types with their own development derive. To some extent Kahle has also been proved right. He insisted on the plurality of the Greek text tradition and had dared to set research back beyond the *terminus non ante quem* which Lagarde considered could not be crossed once the *Urtext* had been reached.

Several *objections to the theory of local texts* proposed by Cross *have been expressed* (Goshen-Gottstein, Talmon, Barthélemy). Nothing is known about possible literary activity by the Jews in Babylonia during the period between Ezra and Hillel. Little is known either about whether the Jews in Egypt used texts in Hebrew. On the other hand, the LXX version was not fully completed in Egypt nor was it made from Hebrew texts which came exclusively from Egypt. Finally, it is not easy to explain the fact that a community as closed in on itself as the Essenes of Qumran could make use over two centuries of texts with such different origins (the book of Jeremiah, for example) as supposed in the theory of local texts.

In Talmon's opinion, the number of text traditions in existence was much greater than Cross supposed, but they disappeared through not having been accepted by any religious group, as did the Synagogue with the masoretic text, the Church with the LXX text and the Samaritan community with the text form of the Pentateuch, which they accepted granting them special character.

E. Tov, chiefly on the basis of study of the MS 11QpaleoLev[a] published in 1985, insists on the need for paying more attention to the discrepancies than to the agreements of the biblical manuscripts from Qumran with the MT, the text of the LXX or the Samaritan Pentateuch. Tov proposes that the peculiar character of each text has to be recognised even to the extent of calling into question the concept of text «type». This proposal is in agreement with Augustine's complaint, referring to what happened in his time: «there are as many texts as codices». The individual character of each manuscript should not make us blind to characteristics which assign it to a particular movement of text transmission. The criterion of identical mistakes, typical of Lachmann's critical method, is decisive here (Cross 1992 and reply by Tov, Chiesa, Catastini).

e. The New «Parabiblical» Texts. In recent years, a series of new Qumran texts has been published which have considerably altered the range of biblical texts known and require theoretical constructions elaborated earlier to be modified. It is not without significance, within the overall history of discoveries at Qumran, that the manuscripts showing most agreement with the MT were the first to be published. They were followed by those agreeing with the LXX and the Samaritan Pentateuch, and only very recently has any attention been paid to a whole series of manuscripts published earlier, with their own peculiar character with respect to the texts known before. Research seems to have been conditioned very much by the MT and by the desire to see the antiquity of the MT confirmed. In the early editions it even led to partiality for the MT readings in the interpretation of cases with a doubtful reading in the new manuscripts.

Problems have already been raised by 4QpaleoExod[m] in connection with the «Samaritan text» and by 4QpaleoLev[a] in connection with the separate and individual character of each manuscript from Qumran. The manuscripts of the Torah published recently have some additions taken from halakhic traditions but not included in the canonical texts (4QDeut[n], 4QDeut[j]) or rewrite halakhic texts from other canonical books (4QNum[b], Jastram; cf. p. 287). Similar phenomena can be seen in other non-biblical texts such as the Temple Scroll (cf. p. 187), in some texts which from their titles are clearly anthologies (4QFlorilegium, 4QTestimonia and 4QCatena[a], Allegro DJD v) and texts published recently such as *Pseudo-Ezekiel* (4Q385-390, Strugnell-Dimant) and *Apocryphon of Moses* (4Q375-376, Strugnell); in addition there is the *Apocryphon of Elisha* (4Q481a, Trebolle).

The most important text is the 'Reworked Pentateuch' (= 4Q158, 4Q364-367), edited by E. Tov (*DJD* XIII). A large number of fragments from 4Q364 and 4Q365 have been preserved and only a few from 4Q366 and 4Q367. 4Q364 contains parts of Gn 2 and 25-48, Ex 16-26, Nm 14 and 33 and portions of Dt 1-14 in abundance. 4Q365 only provides a fragment of Gn 21 and plentiful material from Ex 8-38, Lv 11:26, Nm 1:38 and two fragments of Dt 2 and 19. 4Q366 has texts from Ex 21-22, Nm 29 and Dt 14 and 16. The passages preserved in 4Q367 correspond to Lv 12, 15, 19, 23 and 27. These manuscripts are interesting because the text gives the passages in an order different from the traditional Pentateuch, omits whole sections of the known biblical text, combines the traditional text with commentaries of an exegetical type, joins together passages which in the biblical text are distributed in different books or in different positions in the same book, and above all adds passages which are not biblical or at least are not to be found in other biblical books. This work had already been partly known through 4Q158, published by J.M. Allegro at the beginning of Qumran research (*DJD* v, 1-6). It is only by a strange coincidence that this manuscript has been separated from the others published.

The type of biblical text represented by the *Paraphrase on the Pentateuch* corresponds to what is called «pre-Samaritan». Its agreement with 4QNum[b] is significant, therefore (Jastram). The extent of the paraphrase suggests that it is not an «aberrant» form of the «biblical» text but a para-biblical composition which goes completely beyond the boundaries of what is biblical.

All this requires criteria to be established which enable the boundary between the biblical and the non-biblical to be defined. In this way, a text can be classified as a biblical manuscript or can be assigned to a sort of no-man's land, to which the new *«frontier»*, «anthological» or «periphrastic» texts belong. It also involves posing a whole series of questions connected with the problem of the biblical canon (Ulrich).

BIBLIOGRAPHY

Qumran Cave 4. VIII: Parabiblical Texts, Part 1, eds. H. Attridge, T. Elgvin, J. Milik, S. Olyan, J. Strugnell, J. VanderKam, S. White & E. Tov, *DJD* XIII, Oxford 1994.

BARTHÉLEMY, D., *Études d'histoire du texte de l'Ancien Testament*, Fribourg-Göttingen 1978.
CHIESA, B., «Textual History and Textual Criticism of the Hebrew Old Testament», *The Madrid Qumran Congress* II, Leiden 1992, 257-272.
CROSS, F.M.-TALMON, S., *Qumran and the History of the Biblical Text*, Cambridge MA- London 1975.
FITZMYER, J.A., *The Dead Sea Scrolls: Major Publications and Tools for Study*, Atlanta GA 1990³.
NEWSOM, C.A., «The 'Psalms of Joshua' from Qumran Cave 4», *JJSt* 39 (1988) 56-73.
RABIN, CH., «The Dead Sea Scrolls and the History of the Old Testament Text», *JThS* 6 (1955) 174-182.
STRUGNELL, J.-DIMANT, D., «4QSecond Ezekiel», *RQ* 13 (1988) 46-58.
STRUGNELL, J., «Moses Pseudepigrapha at Qumran. 4Q375, 4Q376, and Similar Works», *Archeology and History in the Dead Sea Scrolls*, ed. L. H. Schiffman, Sheffield 1990, 221-247.

TALMON, S., «The Old Testament Text», *The Cambridge History of the Bible* I, Cambridge 1970, 159-199.

TALMON, S., «The Three Scrolls of the Law that were found in the Temple Court», *Textus* 2 (1962) 14-27.

TOV, E., «A Modern Textual Outlook Based on the Qumran Scrolls», *HUCA* 53 (1982) 11-27.

TOV, E., «The Nature of the Hebrew Text Underlying the LXX. A Survey of the Problems», *JSOT* 7 (1978) 53-68.

V.   THE SAMARITAN PENTATEUCH

The Samaritan Pentateuch (SP) was unknown until 1616 when Pietro della Valle obtained a copy of it in Damascus. The Paris and London polyglots reproduced this text, which was even considered at that time to be more faithful to the original than the MT. However, in 1815, Gesenius rejected nearly any critical value to SP, explaining its very numerouis variants as corruptions or interpolations to a Jewish text. Geiger considered the SP to comprise one of the text traditions eliminated by the rabbis in the 1st cent. CE.

According to Kahle, the SP represented one of the many «vulgar» traditions. The agreements between the SP and the LXX were due to the fact that the first Greek translations were made from «vulgar» Hebrew texts such as the SP. The discovery at Qumran of texts related to the Proto-Samaritan text tradition has provided new data to explain the relationship between SP, MT and LXX. According to the theory of local texts, the SP represented the Palestinian text tradition from which the Egyptian tradition derives, represented by the LXX. The differences between the SP and MT, where the SP is more developed in respect of text and spelling, are due to their respective text traditions: Palestinian in the Samaritan and Babylonian the masoretic tradition. On the other hand, the agreements between both texts suggest that the Samaritan text was re-worked on the basis of the Babylonian tradition, which must have happened before the schism between Samaritans and Jews.

Study of the manuscripts from Qumran has shown that, judging by the textual, palaeographical and orthographical data, the editing of the SP is not earlier than the Hasmonaean period (2nd cent. BCE). Likewise, study of these manuscripts and of the Samaria papyri from Wadi Daliyeh, as well as excavations at Shechem (Tell Balatah) and on Mount Garizim (Tell er-Ras) have shown that the formation of the Samaritan sect occurred at this time, against previous opinions based on the testimony of Josephus (cf. p. 211).

There are approximately 6,000 variations of the SP from the MT. In about 1,900 cases, it agrees with the LXX against MT, although they are mostly unimportant variants. On the whole, the SP agrees more with the MT than with LXX. It differs from both, for example, in information concerning the age of the antediluvian patriarchs (Gn 5:19-31) and Shem's descendants (Gn 11: 10-26).

The SP text is longer than the MT text. It often includes elements like the one after Gn 30:26, taken from 31:11-13. It inserts speeches by God to Moses in the discussions with pharaoh. It completes passages of Nm with some from Dt and viceversa. It inserts explanations into the text with continual additions and repetitions of words or phrases.

Some readings reflect Samaritan theology. The place chosen by Yahweh is Mount Garizim and not Mount Zion. As part of the tenth commandment it inserts, after Ex 20:17, a gloss taken from Dt 27:28 and 11:29-30, with the aim of restating the divine comandment to build an altar on Garizim.

The changes made to the texts taken from other passages are minimal: «or his field», «of the Canaanites», «the stones», etc. The important changes concern the exclusive legitimacy of the Samaritan place of worship: «Garizim», «near Shechem». Besides the change of «Ebal» to «Garizim» (we will not go into the matter of which is the original reading) the most important fact is precisely the insertion which brings in a reference to building an altar on Garizim precisely in the context of the tenth commandment. By introducing into the decalogue the commandment to build an altar on Garizim, the Samaritan text wishes to confer Mosaic authority, as a law from Sinai, on that commandment.

Other examples show the harmonising procedure of the SP and the interest provided by comparing it with other parallel texts found in Qumran (4QDeut^n and 4QpaleoEx^m).

Like the Samaritan text, the MS 4QDeut^n adds Ex 20:11 after Dt 5:15, juxtaposing in this way two parallel passages concerning the third commandment of the Decalogue:

(Dt 5:12)«You shall observe the sabbath day to keep it holy *(l^{e}qadd^{e}šô)* as Yahweh, your God, has command you. (13) Six days shall you labour and do all your work; (14) but the seventh day is of rest, consecrated to Yahweh, your God. You shall not do any work, neither you nor your son nor your daughter nor your male or female slave, nor your ox, nor your ass, nor any of your cattle, nor the stranger who dwells within your gates, so that your male and female slave may rest as you do. (15) And you shall remember that you were a slave in the land of Egypt, and Yahweh, your God, brought you out from there with a mighty hand and outstreched arm; therefore, Yahweh, your God, has commanded you to oberve the sabbath day to keep it holy (+ Ex 20,11:) for in six days Yahweh made the heavens and the earth, the sea and all that is in them, but on the seventh day he rested. Therefore Yahweh belssed the sabbath day to keep it holy. (Dt 5,16:) Honour your father and your mother...» (S. White).

The agreement between the Samaritan Pentateuch and 4QDeut^n is explained by the common dependence of both texts on another earlier text, called «proto-Samaritan». The editor of this text combined the parallel passages from Dt and Ex, juxtaposing the separate reasons justifying the sabbath precept. One reason, more social in character, refers to the history of slavery in Egypt: the Israelites rested and also made their servants rest to signify that, after their entry into the land of Israel, they would never go back to being slaves and let them be enslaved. This is the reason provided by the Deuteronomist source of the Pentateuch (*D*, 7th-6th cent. BCE). Another, given by the

You shall not covet your
neighbour's house; you
shall not covet his wife **or
his field,** or his slave or his
maid-servant or his ox or
his ass, or anything that is
your neighbour's.

And when Y. your God has brought you into the land that you are about to enter to posses it, you shall pronounce the blessing on Mt Gerizim and the curse on Mt Ebal	And when Y. your God has brought you into the land **of the Canaanites** that you are about to enter to posses it,	When you cross the Jordan to enter the land which Y. your God gives you,

you shall erect large stones   you shall erct large stones
and plaster them with lime.   and plaster them with lime.
You shall write on the stones   *You shall write on them*
all the words of this law   *all the words of this law*

in your path,
so that you enter the land
which Y. your God gives
you, a land which flows
with milk and honey, as Y.
god of your fathers fore-
told you.

When you have crossed   When you have crossed
the Jordan you shall erct   the Jordan you shall erect
these stones which I com-   these stones which I command you today, on Mt   mand you today, on Mt
Garizim.   Ebal.
And you shall build an   And you shall build an
altar an altar to Yahweh....   altar an altar to Yahweh....
And you shall rejoice be-   And you shall rejoice before Y. your God.   fore Y. your God.
                              You shall write on the
                              stones all the words of this
                              law

These mountains are be-   **This mountain** is beyond
yond the Jordan behind   the Jordan behind the path
the path of the west, in the   of the west, in the land of
land of the Canaanite, who   the Canaanite, who lives in
lives in the Arabah, oppo-   the Arabah, opposite Gil-
site Gilgal, near the oak/s   gal, near the oak of Morah,
of Moreh   **near Shechem**

Priestly source (*P*, 6th-5th cent. BCE) is more ritual in character and refers to Yahweh's rest on the seventh day of creation: the *homo faber*, tired from the work of the week, must rest and celebrate the sabbath as a feast day, in imitation of Yahweh the creator.

It is even easy to recognise the technique («resumptive repetition» or *Wiederaufnahme*) used by the redactor to combine the two passages: after inserting the text from Ex into Dt, all he needed to do was repeat the Hebrew term *leqaddešô* («to make it holy») to return to the thread interrupted by the insertion he had made.

The frequent use of this type of combination and harmonisation is characteristic of the proto-Samaritan text. One more example can be added, this time taken from a narrative passage: the MS 4QpaleoEx^m, written in palaeo-Hebrew characters, agrees with the Samaritan Pentateuch in making explicit the execution of the commandment given by God to Moses and Aaron. Before each plague they admonished the pharaoh about his obstinacy (Sanderson).

Other manuscripts from Qumran, which provide a type of proto-Samaritan text, are 4Q364, 4QNum^b, 4QTest(175), the first two published recently (cf. p. 000).

From quotations by St. Jerome it is known that a Greek version of the SP existed, called *Samariticon*, which sometimes follows the LXX text more than the Samaritan Pentateuch itself. The Aramaic version was published in the London Polyglot by Walton. The oldest and most complete codex of the Samaritan Pentateuch dates to 1149-50 (Cambridge). The first printed edition was the Paris Polyglot (1632). The edition by Von Gall (1914-18), which is eclectic, has been the one used most.

BIBLIOGRAPHY

VON GALL, A.F., *Der hebräische Pentateuch der Samaritaner*, Giessen 1914-18 = Berlin-New York 1966.

PÉREZ CASTRO, F., *Sefer Abisaʾ*, Madrid 1959.

SKEHAN, P.W., «Exodus in the Samaritan Recension from Qumran», *JBL* 74 (1955) 182-187.

WALTKE, B.K., «The Samaritan Pentateuch and the Text of the Old Testament», *New Perspectives on the Old Testament*, 1970, 212-239.

LANGLAMET, F., «Les divisions massorétiques du livre de Samuel. À propos de la publication du Codex Caire», *RB* 91 (1989) 481-519.

SANDERSON, J.E., *An Exodus Scroll from Qumran. 4QpaleoExod^m and the Samaritan Tradition*, Atlanta GA 1986.

TOV, E., «Proto-Samaritan Texts and the Samaritan Pentateuch in the Wake of the Discovery of the Qumran Scrolls», *Proceedings of the First International Congress of the Société d'Etudes Samaritaines (Tel-Aviv, April 11-13, 1988)*, eds. A. Tal-M. Florentin, Tel Aviv 1991, 293-303.

WHITE, S., «4Q364 & 365: Pentateuchal Traditions in the II Temple Period», *The Madrid Qumran Congress*, vol. J. Trebolle Barrera-L. Vegas Montarer (eds.), Leiden-Madrid 1992, cf. p. 309 BCBJ.

3

The Greek Septuagint Version

The history of the Hebrew text of the OT is described retrospectively here. When considering the history of the Greek Bible, it is helpful to go into reverse, retracing its course from modern times to the Hellenistic period. Modern research from the Renaissance up to our day was obliged to take this difficult road, which of necessity had to start with the scant material available in the Renaissance period. It led to the gradual discovery of new material and the development of exact methods for knowing ancient texts and, if possible, the original texts of the Greek version. Before taking this path, it is first necessary to have some knowledge of an introductory nature.

I. INTRODUCTION

1. *Historical Importance of the LXX Version*

The importance of the LXX version is not confined to the field of biblical studies but affects the cultural and literary history of Eastern and Western Europe and of the Semitic Near East, with all the ramifications these cultural centres (Byzantine, Latin and Semitic) have had throughout history.

This version is the first example of the translation of the complete corpus of sacred, legal, historical and poetic literature of one people, in a language of the Semitic cultural world, to the language of classical Greek culture.

Until the discovery of the Dead Sea Scrolls, the Greek version was the most important and almost the only source for studying the history of the text of the Hebrew Bible, as well as for studying the theological and exegetical ideas of Alexandrian and Palestinian Judaism.

The LXX version has an added value since in it, the NT authors and the Christian writers found an arsenal of terms and concepts for expressing the content and symbols of the Christian faith. It therefore comprises a bridge joining the two Testaments; this relationship is highlighted in a special way in the quotations made in the NT from the OT through the LXX version.

The first Christians adopted the Greek version as their «Old» Testament.

The various communities of the Jewish diaspora knew the Greek Bible in collections which certainly differed greatly from each other. The number of books included in a collection could be greater or smaller and the text of each book could be the original of a version or a revised form agreeing with the most up-to-date Hebrew text. The Christian communities accepted this pluralism of books and texts in the Greek version. They even contributed to making the Greek text increasingly different, so that it needed Origen to try and introduce some logic into the transmission of the Greek text of the Bible.

2.   *The Importance of LXX Studies Today*

At present, research on the LXX version has entered a new period of growth.

The stimulus for this research came, first of all, from A. Deissman's studies on *papyri and inscriptions* of the Roman period, which enabled the language of the LXX to be situated within Greek *koiné*.

The second stimulus was provided by the discovery of the *Dead Sea Scrolls*, which brought about a re-evaluation of the LXX when it was realised that the text of some books and variants represented a different Hebrew original from the masoretic text and, at times, one to be preferred.

Studies over the past decades on the *targumic versions* (especially after the discovery of Codex *Neophyti* 1) and on «intertestamental» literature supplied a third stimulus to research on the LXX. This literature and those Aramaic versions transmit reading traditions and theological interpretations of the OT which also have a parallel in the LXX version.

A final element in the revival of studies on the LXX version is the *cessation of apologetic stances* which had made Paul and the NT the absolute beginning of Christian theology without reference to their OT presuppositions. Among scholars today there is a greater readiness to see a thread of continuity (rather than of division) between the Jewish reading of the *Tanak* in the periods before and after the birth of Christianity and the reading of the OT by the first Christians (Harl).

Thus, the importance of the LXX comes from two aspects of that version: its *critical value* as a translation of a Hebrew original, differing at times from the text of masoretic tradition, and its *exegetical value* as a translation reflecting the traditions of interpretation and theological ideas of Hellenistic Judaism.

3.   *The Proposed Translation - Place, Date and Authors*

The translation of the Pentateuch into Greek, as a version of the LXX, was made *in Alexandria* probably *towards the middle of the 3rd cent. BCE*, during the reign of Ptolemy II Philadelphus (285-247 BCE). According to the apocryphal Letter of Aristeas, at the request of the king, the high priest Eleazar sent from Jerusalem 72 wise men, 6 for each tribe of Israel, with the task of translating the Hebrew Torah for the library of Alexandria.

This letter is actually a historical fiction, very inexact on some details, but in essence based on truth. It was written by a Jew from Alexandria in the second half of the 2nd cent. BCE or somewhat later. The information of the *Letter of Aristeas* on the Palestinian contribution to the work of translating the LXX matches verifiable data. On the other hand, the attribution of the origin of the version to the initiative of the librarian Demetrius, who had suggested presenting the Alexandrian library with a translation of the Jewish Torah, has aroused the suspicions of modern criticism. The completion of this version has been attributed instead to liturgical (Thackeray), educational (Brock and Perrot), motives, to proselytism etc.

Bickerman and others, however, go back to the explanation given by Pseudo-Aristeas, considering the version as the *product of a royal initiative*, in response to needs of a juridical nature (Rost) or connected with the Jewish *políteuma* of Alexandria (Barthélemy). According to Mélèze-Modrzejewski, the Greek translation comprises an official version, intended for use in the law courts of the Lagides system, just as similar versions of native Egyptian customary law were made so that they could be used in courts of law. It seems beyond doubt that the Jewish *políteuma* was ruled by a special law, but it cannot be said that this law was exactly the Pentateuch of the Greek version. Possibly, the attribution of the translation to the librarian Demetrius includes an element of truth in supposing that, hidden behind the royal initiative of undertaking that version lies an intention of cultural politics.

Other information about the origins of the version, which more or less agrees with that given by Pseudo-Aristeas, can be found in Aristobulus (1st half of the 2nd cent. BCE), Philo of Alexandria, Josephus, in rabbinic sources and in Christian writings.

Study of the *translation techniques* together with *lexicography* helps to establish the *geographical origin of the translation of each book* of the Greek Bible.

The books of the Torah, Jgs, 1-4 Kgs, 1-2 Paralipomena, 3 Mc, Prov, Job, XII Prophets, Is (Van der Kooij), Jr, Bar, Letter of Jeremiah, Ez, etc., were translated in Alexandria.

The books of Ruth, Est, Qoh, Song, Lam, Jdt, 1 Mc, etc. were translated in Palestine. The translator of Wisdom was evidently an Alexandrian Jew of Palestinian origin, as was also the translator of Ben Sira.

Continuing contact between Alexandria and Jerusalem prevented too sharp an opposition being set up - as had happened (cf. p. 232) - between these two Jewish centres, who competed for the honour of being the place of origin of the translation of the various books of the LXX. Recent research no longer allows it to be said that the translation of the Bible into Greek entailed its Hellenisation. A better balance has to be acknowledged, instead, between the part corresponding to the Greek *expression* of the translation and what corresponds to the Jewish *content*, and continues to be the basis of that translation (R. Marcus, D. Barthélemy).

The title «LXX version» at first referred to the translation of the Pentateuch only. The other biblical books were translated later, up to the middle or at most the end of the 2nd cent. BCE. It thus includes translations made by different writers. On the whole the translation is of high quality, more literal in some books, freer in others. In addition to the books of the Hebrew canon, the Greek Bible includes - with variations from one manuscript to another - the following works: 1 Ezra, Wis, Sir, Jdt, Tob, Bar, Letter of Jeremiah and 1-2 Mc In some books of the Hebrew canon the LXX version adds new texts, such as the additions to the book of Esther, the Greek text of which is more than twice as long as the Hebrew text. Some LXX manuscripts add various hymns to the end of the Psalter.

II. MODERN EDITIONS AND FIRST PRINTED EDITIONS

1.   *Modern Editions (19th and 20th cents.)*

Modern editions of the LXX have taken two different approaches:

a. The *Cambridge edition*, discontinued in 1940, follows the tradition of Holme Parsons. The editors were A. E. Brooke, N. McLean and H. St J. Thackeray (the last-named only from the historical books onwards).[1] They represent a *diplomatic edition* which is a completely faithful reproduction of the text of a single manuscript, the Vatican Codex (B). In the critical apparatus it gives the variants from the manuscript tradition and other variants from daughter versions and from quotations in the Fathers, without making any value judgment about these variants. The edition includes the Pentateuch and the historical books, with the exception of the book of Maccabees.

The hand-book edition by H. B. Swete also reproduces the text of the Vatican Codex; it completes some of its gaps with text from other uncials.[2]

b. The *Göttingen edition*, instead, represents a *critical edition.*[3] It follows the principles and methods established by Lagarde, which consist of classifying the manuscripts according to recensional families in order to make a judgment on their variants, so as to obtain and establish a critical text which corresponds to the text of the original Greek version (cf. p. 381). The edition goes up to the books of the Pentateuch and all the Prophets, Est, Jdt, Tob, Ezra A, 1, 2 and 3 Mc, Jb, Wis and Ben Sira. In this edition, which A. Rahlfs began, W. Kappler, J. Ziegler, R. Hanhart, J. W. Wevers, U. Quast and O. Fraenke have collaborated. Ziegler tended to assume too much stability in the textual groups and to acknowledge the Vatican Codex as the highest authority. Hanhart and Wevers, its later editors, pay more attention, instead, to the translation characteristics of each book in particular (Hanhart). Even although more attention is also given to the versions (especially the Coptic and

1. *The Old Testament in Greek according to the Text of Codex Vaticanus* (Cambridge 1906-1940)
2. *The Old Testament in Greek According to the Septuagint*, 3 vols, (Cambridge 1887-1894).
3. *Septuaginta Vetus Testamentum Graecum auctoritate Societatis litterarum Göttingen editum*, Göttingen 1931.

Latin versions), the readings from the versions do not move out of the critical apparatus to be reflected in the Greek text of the edition.

The critical edition by A. Rahlfs in hand-book form is based principally on the Vatican, Sinaitic and Alexandrian codices and also includes recensional variants from Origen, Lucian and the *Catenae.*[4]

2.   *First Printed Editions (16th-17th cents.)*

The *editio princeps* of the LXX was completed in the *Complutensian Polyglot* of cardinal Cisnos (1514-1521). The later polyglots of Antwerp, Heidelberg, Hamburg and Paris are based on it. Some of the manuscripts used in the Complutensian reproduce a Lucian text.

The *Aldine edition* of Venice (1518), contemporary with the Complutensian, gives a text of lesser critical value. The *«Sistine» Bible* was published in Rome in 1586, commissioned by Sixtus V. Its importance lies in its using the Vatican Codex (B) as the basic text of the edition for the first time. Almost all the later editions are based on the Sistine edition and on Codex B, among them the London Polyglot or Walton's polyglot (1657) and the *Holmes-Parsons edition* (1798). In this edition the first large-scale compilation of textual variants was undertaken.[5]

The *Grabe edition* of 1707-20 is based on the Alexandrian Codex (A) and already represents an attempt at a critical edition, marking the hexaplaric texts and those passages with no matching text in the Masoretic Hebrew text.

III.   THE MANUSCRIPT TRADITION

The LXX are classified as uncials and cursives or minuscules (cf. p. 103). The value of a manuscript, however, depends on its script. *Cursive manuscripts*, in spite of being more recent, can represent forms of text which did not succeed in being preserved in the uncial manuscripts. Such is the case for the Lucianic textual tradition in the books of Samuel-Kings, preserved only in the minuscules b (=Rahlfs 19+108) o (=82), c_2 (93), e_2 (127).

About thirty *uncial manuscripts* of the LXX have come down to us. The most important have already been mentioned: Vatican (B), from the 4th cent., Sinaiticus (א) from the beginning of the 4th cent., both written in Egypt or in Caesarea, and the Alexandrian (A) from the 5th cent., which comes from Egypt.

The most important *papyri* are as follows:
– *Rylands* Papyrus gr. 458 (=Rahlfs 957) dated to the first half of the 2nd cent. BCE and for that reason written a century after the Alexandrian version had begun. It contains texts from Dt 23-28.

---

4. *Septuagint, id est Vetus Testamentum graece iuxta LXX interpretes*, 2 vols, Stuttgart 1935.
5. R Holmes-J. Parsons, *Vetus Testamentum Graece cum variis lectionibus*, 5 vols.

– *Fouad* Papyrus 266, dated around 50 BCE. It preserves extracts from Gn 7 and 38 (Rahlfs 942) and of Dt 11 and 31-33 (Rahlfs 847).

– *Chester Beatty* Papyri from the 2nd cent. CE or from the beginning of the 3rd cent. CE (Rahlfs 963). It contains fragments of Nm and Dt.

Among the *manuscripts of the LXX found in the caves of the Dead Sea* the following can be noted:

_ 4QLXXXLev^a, skin scroll from the close of the 2nd cent. BCE (Skehan 1957), containing Lv 26:2-6.

_ 4QLXXXLev^b (4Q120), papyrus scroll from the close of the 1st cent. BCE or the beginning of the following century with remains of Lv 2:3-5.7; 3:4.9-13; 4:4-8.10-11.18-20.26-29; 5:8-10.18-24; 6:2-4 (Skehan 1957; Ulrich).

_ 4QLXXNum (4Q121), leather scroll from the 1st cent. BCE or the start of the 1st cent. CE (Skehan 1977) with the text of Nm 3:40-43; 50-51 ; 4:1.5 and 4:11-16; contrary to what Skehan at first supposed, it does not contain the text of an old revision which attempted to accommodate the text to the form known from later codices, but is in fact a revision made in pre-Christian times the purpose of which was to make the Greek closer to a form of the Hebrew text closely related to MT (Wevers).

– 4QLXXDeut (4Q122) from the 2nd cent. BCE, with the text of Dt 11:4 and unidentified fragments (Ulrich 1984).

– Two papyrus scrolls from cave 7, edited by M. Baillet, contain the text of Ex 28:4-7 (7Q1) and the Letter of Jeremiah (Baruch 6) 43-44 (7Q2) (Baillet, *DJD* III 1962, 142-43, pl. 30).

– Finally, the copper scroll 8HevXIIgr from the 1st cent. CE with the text of the minor prophets. This manuscripts has enabled D. Barthélemy to identify the proto-Theodotion recension, forerunner of the work accomplished later by Aquila (cf. p. 314).

One example is enough to show the *importance of the new material discovered*. A fragment of a papyrus in Greek from the book of Job (papyrus no. 3522 in the series *The Oxyrhynchus Papyri*, vol. 50, ed. P. J. Parsons) from the 1st cent. CE, of Jewish origin, seems to omit vv. 16c-17 from chap. 42. This omission is attested in the Sahidic version and in Latin quotations. It also occurs marked with an asterisk in Greek manuscripts. The Greek text of this passage is taken from Theodotion. Thanks to the papyrus just mentioned we now have a direct witness the oldest form of the Greek text.

To the manuscript tradition of the codices and papyri of the LXX have to be added the quotations from this version found in the NT and in the writings of Philo, Josephus and the Greek Fathers.

IV. THEORIES ABOUT THE ORIGIN AND HISTORY OF THE LXX VERSION

Two main theories have competed for the privilege of giving a satisfactory explanation for the origins of the Greek version of the LXX. The discovery of the Dead Sea Scrolls has certainly tipped the balance in favour of one of them.

1. According to *P. De Lagarde* (†1891), *all preserved codices of the LXX*

derive from three recensions, as known through the ancient tradition of Origen, Hesychius and Lucian. As a result, the first task of criticism is *to identify the text of each of these recensions*. The quotations by the Fathers as well as the daughter versions of the LXX are of great assistance in this task. For example, the Armenian text reflects Origen's hexaplar recension, the Bohairic (Coptic) text of Daniel reflects a Hesychian text and the text of Theodotion of Cyrus enables the text of the Lucianic recension of Kings and Chronicles to be identified.

Once the critical editions of these three recensions have been prepared, Lagarde believed it was possible *to establish from them the archetypal Text or original (Ur-Text)* of the LXX version (Lagarde). Lagarde also began this enterprise with the edition of what he thought was the Lucianic text of Gn and Est. Later studies showed that the Lucianic manuscripts do not represent a strictly Lucianic homogeneous text in all the books of the OT (Fernández Marcos - Sáenz Badillos). A. Rahlfs continued his erstwhile teacher's work and began the project of the Göttingen edition (cf. p. 304). The new discoveries from Qumran have come to confirm Lagarde's critical principles as well-founded and they are followed even today by many scholars (Montgomery, Kappler, Ziegler, Gehman, Wevers, Orlinsky, Katz, etc.).

b. In P. Kahle's opinion, instead, Lagarde's supposed archetype is nothing but the end result of a whole process of unifying the text from an *assortment of Greek versions* which circulated earlier. These versions had been made *from «vulgar» Hebrew texts* and the nature of the translation would be similar to the Aramaic targumim (cf. p. 324).

According to Kahle, the *Letter of Aristeas* has to be interpreted as propaganda in favour of a translation of the Pentateuch made shortly before that letter was written. Thanks to this work of propaganda the version of the Pentateuch made by the LXX succeeded in being more widely spread than others already in existence which were consigned to oblivion. As for the remaining books of the OT (the Prophets and the Writings), there never was an official text of them; multiple translations co-existed, represented by the different recensions of the LXX.

Among scholars this theory was less accepted than the theory developed by Lagarde. The discoveries from the Dead Sea have resulted in it being discarded completely. The history of the Greek version is not comparable, as Kahle supposed, to the history of Targumim, nor can its origin be explained by «vulgar» Hebrew texts. If Kahle were followed, the LXX version would have hardly any value as a witness for the critical study of the Hebrew text. Barthélemy's study of the Greek manuscript of the Twelve Minor Prophets has confirmed that there was once a single original version, as Lagarde supposed.

Other theories on the origins of the LXX version were less accepted. According to M. Gaster, the LXX version originated in Palestine and not in Egypt as is generally recognised. In Thackeray's opinion it had a liturgical origin as a book of the people and for use in the synagogue. According to Wutz, the Greek translators worked with a Hebrew text transliterated into Greek characters and not with a text written in Hebrew characters.

ALAND, K., *Repertorium der griechischen Papyri, I. Biblische Papyri. AT, NT, Varia, Apokryphen*, Berlin-New York 1976,

BARTHÉLEMY, D., «Pourquoi la Torah a-t-elle été traduite en grec?», *Études d'histoire du text de l'Ancien Testament*, OBO 21, Fribourg-Göttingen 1978, 322-340.

BICKERMAN, E., «The Septuagint as a Translation», *Studies in Jewish and Christian History*, vol. I, Leiden 1976, 167-200.

BROCK, S.P.-FRITSCH, C.T.-JELICOE, S., *A Classified Bibliography of the Septuagint*, Leiden 1973.

BROCK, S.P., «The Phenomenon of Biblical Translation in Antiquity», *Studies in the Septuagint: Origins, Recensions, and Interpretations*, ed. H. M. Orlinksy, New York 1974, 541-571.

FERNÁNDEZ MARCOS, N., «La Septuaginta y los hallazgos del Desierto de Judá», *Simposio Bíblico Español. Salamanca 1982*, eds. N. Fernández Marcos-J. Trebolle Barrera-J. Fernández Vallina, Madrid 1984, 229-244.

FERNÁNDEZ MARCOS, N.-SAENZ BADILLOS, A., *Anotaciones críticas al texto griego del Génesis y estudio de sus grupos textuales*, Madrid-Barcelona 1972.

HANHART, R., Zum gegenwärtigen Stand der Septuagintaforschung», *De Septuaginta. Studies in Honour of J. W. Wevers*, Mississauga, Ontario 1984, 3-18.

HARL, M.-DORIVAL, G.-MUNNICH, O., *La Bible grecque des Septante. Du judaïsme hellénistique au christianisme ancien*, Paris 1988.

JELLICOE, S., *The Septuagint and Modern Study*, Oxford 1968.

KAHLE, P., «Untersuchungen zur Geschichte des Pentateuchtextes», *Opera minora*, Toronto 1964, 58-77.

KOOIJ, A. VAN DER, *Die Alten Textzeugen des Jesajabuches*, Fribourg-Göttingen 1981.

LAGARDE, P., *Anmerkungen zur griechischen Übersetzung der Proverbien*, Leipzig 1865.

MARCUS, R., «Jewish and Greek Elements in the Septuagint», *L. Ginzberg Jubilee Volume*, New York 1945, 227-245.

ORLINSKY, H.M., (ed.), *Studies in the Septuagint: Origins, Recensions,and Interpretation. Selected Essays with a Prolegomenon by S. Jellicoe*, New York 1974.

RAHLFS, A., *Verzeichnis der griechischen Handschriften des Alten Testaments*, Berlin 1914.

ROST, L., «Vermutungen über den Anlass zur griechischen Übersetzung der Tora», *Wort-Gebot- Glaube*, ed. H.J. Stoebe, Zurich 1970, 39-44.

SKEHAN, P.W., «The Qumran Manuscripts and Textual Criticism», *VT.S* 4, Leiden 1957, 148-160.

SKEHAN, P.W., «4QLXXnum: A Pre-Christian Reworking of the Septuagint», *HthR* 70 (1977) 39- 50.

SWETE, H.B., *An Introduction to the OT in Greek*, Cambridge 1914, 2nd revised edition by R.R. Otley.

THACKERAY, H.ST.J., *The Septuagint and Jewish Worship. A Study in Origins*, London 1923.

ULRICH, E., «The Greek Manuscripts of the Pentateuch from Qumrân, Including Newly-identified Fragments of Deuteronomy (4QLXX Deut)», *De Septuaginta*, Mississauga, Ontario 1984.

WUTZ, F.X., *Die Transkriptionen von der Septuaginta bis zu Hieronymus*, Stuttgart 1925-1933.

V. CHRISTIAN RECENSIONS OF THE LXX VERSION

The history of the LXX text is very complex. The text was revised several times. There could have been three *reasons for these revisions*. The first was the need to correct the many mistakes which inevitably crept into the text in its successive copies. The second was the desire to improve and up-date the language and style of the Greek translation. The third was the desire to adapt the Greek text of the LXX to the proto-masoretic Hebrew text in cases where by addition, omision or other changes, the Greek text differed from the Hebrew. This last mentioned work of adaptation to a Hebrew original (*Vorlage*) is what is meant by the term «recension».

According to S. P. Brock, besides these reasons of critical nature there was one of an apologetic nature. In the controversies between Jews and Christians, both sides needed to have their own authentic text available as well as needing to know the textual tradition presented by the adversary in cases where it differed from their own. The Jews felt the need for their Greek translations to be faithful to the proto-masoretic Hebrew text, declared the official text at the beginning of the 2nd cent. CE. This was why the revisions ascribed to Aquila, Symmachus and Theodotion were made. The Christians, besides preserving faithfully the Greek text of the LXX, accepted by the Church, also needed to know those Jewish versions which reflected the Hebrew text better.

In his prologue to the book of Chronicles in 396 CE, St Jerome states that at that time the text of the LXX was known in *three different recensions*. The oldest was by Origen, in Caesarea; a second recension, somewhat hypothetical, was by Hesychius in Alexandria, and the third and last by Lucian in Antioch (Syria) (*totusque orbis hac inter se trifaria uarietate conpugnat*).[6]

It is therefore necessary to know the recensions of the LXX made by Christian authors (Hesychius, Lucian and Origen) and afterwards the first revisions of the LXX or the new translations made previously by Jews (Symmachus, Aquila, Theodotion).

1. *Hesychius*

Little or nothing is known about a recension made in Egypt and attributed, not without reservations, to bishop Hesychius (†311). Quotations from Egyptian Fathers, especially Cyril of Alexandria (†444), are possibly the means of recognising the text of that recension. However, in most of the books of the LXX it has not been possible to identify the supposed «Hesychian» text. It is not possible to ascertain whether the revision was made using a Hebrew text; possibly it was only a stylistic revision. In the prophetic books it would be represented by the text of Codex *Marchalianus* (Q). Some scholars have thought that Codex Vaticanus (B) preserves the Hesychian text in some books. Possibly it was not a systematic recension or even

---

6. «Prologus in libro paralipomenon», *Biblia Sacra*, ed. R. Weber, Stuttgart 1969, 546.

an edition, but was a text used chiefly in Egypt. Egyptian Christianity had independence and a sufficiently strong tradition to be able to distribute a biblical text with its own characteristics which made it different from other the texts of Caesarea and Antioch. Proof of this lies in the fact that the emperor Constantius commissioned Athanasius of Alexandria to send off biblical codices, just like his predecessor, Constantine, who had requested copies from Caesarea. Codex Vaticanus (B) could have originated in this commission by Constantius.

2.   *Lucian and the «Proto-Lucianic» Text*

In Syria, the text of the LXX was known in a recension ascribed to Lucian martyr (†311-312), founder of an exegetical school in Antioch, a rival of the Alexandrian school in Egypt. This Lucianic or Antiochene recension is recognisable from the lengthy quotations in the works of Theodoretus of Cyrus and St. John Chrysostom. The Lucianic or Antiochene recension has been identified in the prophetic books; in the book of Judges and in the group K Z g l n w and in the sub-group d p t v, and in the books of Samuel-Kings in the group b o $c_2 e_2$.

As for the Pentateuch as a whole, identification of a Lucianic text is very difficult. In this respect Lagarde's edition is completely incorrect (cf. p 306). There are traces of the work of a non-Hexaplar recension made under the influence of the Hebrew text; these traces are found in the text of families *d* and *t* according to the classification by J.W. Wevers; it is not impossible that they represent the Lucianic recension but then it would be inexplicable why the quotations in Chrysostom and Theodoretus do not follow this text.

It is not easy to determine precisely what was the work Lucian carried out, both in respect of the pre-Hexaplar tradition and in respect of Origen's work. However, the *characteristics of the Lucianic text* are quite obvious: frequent additions, inserted into the text to adapt it to the rabbinic Hebrew text; many duplicate readings in which the old *Septuagint* is juxtaposed to the Hexaplar reading, which in turn is closer to the rabbinic text; grammatical corrections and stylistic improvement of the text; the insertion of explanatory elements, such a proper names, pronouns, articles, etc.; replacement of Hellenistic forms by the Attic equivalents, etc. (Metzger).

Two observations gave rise to the hypothesis of the existence of a *«proto-Lucianic text»*. The *Old Latin*, from the close of the 2nd cent. CE, translates a Greek text very like the one used by Lucian as the basis of his recension (B. Fischer; cf. p. 352). Also, the text of Flavius Josephus (1st cent. CE) contains Lucianic readings which seem to suppose the existence of a «Lucian before Lucian» (Thackeray, Mez, Ulrich). The agreement of Hebrew readings from 4QSam[a] with readings from Lucianic manuscripts in the books of Samuel now give considerable support to this hypothesis (Cross, Ulrich).

However, it is difficult to determine whether the proto-Lucianic text is 1) the same text as the original version «more or less corrupt» (Barthélemy), or 2) the result of a recension intended to adapt the Greek original to the Hebrew text type current in Palestine in the 2nd cent. BCE (F.M. Cross), or whether it is simply 3) the LXX version or another ancient Greek version (E. Tov).

One remaining task of current research is precisely to identify proto-Lucianic readings and differentiate them from those of the later Lucianic text (S.P. Brock). Attempts have been made to date the 4th cent Antiochene text type to Jewish circles in Antioch of the 1st cent CE (N. Fernández Marcos). However, there are no proofs that Antiochene Judaism made recensions of any kind. It seems, instead, that the characteristic of the Antiochene text in its oldest stage was to have remained immune to the influence of the intense recensional activity carried out in Palestine (Bogaert).

3.   *Origen. The Hexaplar Recension and the Pre-Hexaplar Text*

In 245, Origen completed a work of enormous proportions in which he displayed a critical sense far ahead of his times. In the six columns of the *Hexaplar* he compiled the Hebrew text known at the time (col. 1), this same text transcribed into Greek letters (col. 2), the text of the version by Aquila (col. 3), and by Symmachus (col. 4), the text of the old Greek version (col. 5) and of the version by Theodotion (col. 6). The most important is the «fifth», with a text corresponding to the LXX.

It is not easy to determine whether the text of this column was the LXX as known by Origen or a text he had already revised which he supplied with the appropriate hexaplaric signs and additions. It can be assumed that the mere arrangement of the texts in columns enabled the differences between the different texts and columns to be noted without the need for adding the signs (asterisk and obelus) which indicated an addition or an omission respectively in one of the columns (Mercati, Barthélemy, Bogaert).

Origen certainly completed a *later, truly hexaplar edition*, which has therefore to be distinguished from the Hexaplars described above. This later edition contained only the text of the LXX; the lacunae in the LXX in respect of the MT (shorter) are completed by the text of Theodotion. As a result, this edition was supplied with the requisite diacritical signs. The hypothesis of this hexaplar edition replaces the other hypothesis, according to which the *fifth* column of the Hexaplar contained the text revised by Origen, marked by asterisks and obeli, the same text later made into the edition of the LXX alone.

In any case it is necessary to distinguish clearly the work of the Hexaplar and the later hexaplar edition. The confusion is due to the fact that the witnesses of this hexaplar edition tend to include in the margins readings from other Greek revisions, so that they to some extent they look like the edition in columns. The use of the signs which Zenodotus had employed in Alexandria for the edition of the Homeric texts allowed the actual text of the LXX version to be recognised and at the same time drew attention to the differences between the Greek text and the Hebrew text of rabbinic tradition. When the LXX contained a word, sentence of passage not found in the Hebrew text, Origen marked the beginning and end of this addition with an obelus (÷) and a metobelus (ɣ) respectively. If, instead, the LXX text omitted a passage which was in the Hebrew text, he inserted at that point a Greek translation of it, usually taken from Theodotion. To warn the reader, he marked the beginning and end of the omission with an asterisk (※) and a metobelus respectively.

Origen's work gave rise, later, to a *confusion and mix of texts* far greater than he had known. The enormous difficulty involved in copying all the columns of the Hexaplar or even just the four columns in Greek meant that this work was no longer copied and was to be lost forever. In time, the Aristarchian signs accompanying the hexaplar edition of the LXX were no longer copied either or were copied in the wrong place, which led to even more confusion of the text. In this way, a mixed text was formed and transmitted, comprising the old Greek of the LXX and fragments from the other versions. This mixed text gradually became part of preserved manuscript tradition. It should be noted that, at the request of the emperor Constantine, Eusebius sent fifty copies of the text of the LXX on parchment from Caesarea to Constantinople.

The *recovery of the pre-Hexaplar text prior to Origen* is now only feasible though those manuscripts which did not suffer hexaplar influence, as is the case for the Codex Vaticanus (B). The Syro-hexaplar version (cf. p. 360) also contributed to the recovery of the old *Septuagint*, that is to say, of the original text of the LXX version. The Syro-hexaplar version translates the hexaplar text of the LXX in a completely literal way, but in addition it preserves with great accuracy the signs differentiating the hexaplar readings from the pre-hexaplar readings. In this way it is possible to know which was the text of the LXX and which the hexaplar additions. The recovery of the pre-hexaplar text also makes it possible, though a palimpsest found in 1896 in the Ambrosian Library of Milan by cardinal G. Mercati, which preserves verses and various Psalms with the text of all the columns of the Hexaplar, except for the first Hebrew column.

The third, forth and fifth columns, corresponding to the versions by Aquila, Symmachus and Theodotion, have been lost together with the complete work of the Hexaplar. However, many readings of these versions have been preserved in marginal readings of manuscripts and in quotations by the Fathers.

VI. ANCIENT JEWISH VERSIONS OR RECENSIONS

Before the great Christian recensions of the 3rd and 4th cents., Judaism had already felt *the need to revise the old version of the LXX*. The aim was always the same: to adapt the text of the LXX to the type of Hebrew text which had been imposed in rabbinic circles and was definitively established at the beginning of the 2nd cent. CE.

The fact that the Christians made the LXX translation their own and had used it in disputes with the Jews led to increasing rejection of that version by the Jews, who ended by replacing it with new translations, more faithful to the rabbinic Hebrew text. A typical example of the difference between the Hebrew and Greek texts, quoted in all the disputes between Jews and Christians, was Is 7:14, where the LXX translates the Hebrew term *'almâ*, «(married or unmarried) girl», by *parthénos*, «virgin» instead of *neânis* which was more appropriate. The Jews rejected this translation by the LXX in which the Christians saw a prophecy of the virgin birth of Christ (cf. p. 511).

There is information about the existence of various Greek translations before Origen, but nothing is known about their origin or character. Origen himself cites three versions, calling them *Quinta*, *Sexta* and *Septima*; the first was discovered by Origen in Nikopolis (on the West coast of Greece), the second in Jericho.

1. Symmachus

Symmachus was, perhaps, a Samaritan converted to Judaism, or an Ebionite. In about 170 CE he completed a translation which, like those by Aquila and Theodotion, could also have had antecedents in a previous version (Fernández Marcos; cf. below). The starting point of this revision could have been a translation made by Ebionites of Cappadocia. The translation by Symmachus is both faithful and literal, accurate yet elegant. For example, in 1 Kgs 2:46-3:1, Symmachus follows the MT against the LXX which inserts additional material, but it does not follow the paratactic construction of the Hebrew: «The kingdom was secure in Solomon's hands. And Solomon allied himself by marriage with Pharaoh...» but uses the subordinate construction of the Greek text: «With the kingdom secure in Solomon's hands, he married...».

Two other Jewish versions, made before Symmachus, are more literal and therefore more significant for knowledge of the underlying Hebrew text of these translations.

2. Aquila

Aquila was a Jewish proselyte from Pontus and a disciple of R. Akiba (although the Jerusalem Talmud, *Megillah* 71a, connects him instead with R. Eliezer ben Hyrcanus and R. Yehoshua). In about 140 CE he completed an extremely literal translation of the Hebrew according to the methods of rabbinic interpretation. Rather than a completely new translation it is to a large extent a recension or systematic revision of the LXX which was the ultimate consequence of the tendency already begun a century earlier by «the forerunners of Aquila» who had made the recension known as proto-Theodotionic or *kaige* (cf. p. 314). The Hebrew text used by Aquila for his revision of the LXX was the *proto-masoretic Hebrew text*, of which the consonantal text had been established a few years before. However, the presence in Aquila's Greek text of variant readings in respect of the MT suggests that the process of fixing the Hebrew text was not completely finished in Aquila's time, which always demands some restraint in statements about the definitive stabilisation of the consonantal Hebrew text in this period (cf. p. 279).

Owing to its *extreme literalism*, Aquila's version tended to be virtually incomprehensible for anyone now knowing Hebrew. It reproduces the Hebrew text word for word in the same order as in Hebrew. It translates into Greek petty details of the Hebrew, such as the particles (*'et* = *syn*+accusative), the locative (*-āh* = *-de*) or the elements which make up a Hebrew particle, without at all being afraid of breaking the most elementary rules of Greek grammar. In 2 Kgs 19:25, for example, the composite Hebrew particle *lᵉ-mē-rāhôq*, «until from afar» = «since ancient times», is translated by decomposing it into its three lements: *eis apò makróthen*.

Aquila's translation of the first sentence of Genesis: «In the beginning God created the heavens and the earth» (Gn 1:1), would be as follows in English: «In the head (the beginning) God created with (*'ēt*) the heavens and with the earth». The translation of the particle *'êt* (= «with») is justified by giving it an inclusive meaning, in agreement with the rules of rabbinic hermeneutics. The translation of the text of Aquila in a continuous text would be: «God created the heavens, *together with* the sun, the moon and the stars, and the earth, *together with* the trees, the plants and paradise».

On the other hand, Aquila replaced translations using words which had acquired Christian connotations with new ones. Thus, the version of the title *māšîaḥ* = *Khristós*, «Messiah», is replaced by *ēleîmmenos*. This increased its appreciation among the Jews.

Besides the fragments of Psalms published by Mercati (cf. p. 312), the text of Aquila is known from readings preserved in the margins of LXX manuscripts, patristic quotations and the Talmud and from fragments of Psalms and Kings found in the Cairo Genizah (Burkitt).

3. *Theodotion and the Proto-Theodotionic Recension*

Little is known about Theodotion, by tradition dated to the 2nd cent. CE. According to Irenaeus he was a Jewish proselyte from Ephesus. Epiphanius adds that he became a proselyte after following Marcion for a time.

The text of Theodotion had and still has great importance. It was so *widespread* that it replaced the original LXX version in most of the manuscripts which have reached us. Origen used it in his Hexaplar to fill in the lacunae of the LXX text, for example in the book of Job.

The theodotionic text of Daniel became the prevailing text of that book. The question of the theodotionic text of Daniel has been one of those most discussed in previous decades. Ziegler noted already that the text ascribed to Theodotion could not be connected with him. A. Schmitt goes further and states that the text of Theodotion does not fit into the textual tradition represented by «proto-Theodotion» (*kaige*) which has been recognised in other OT books (against the opinion, therefore, of Barthélemy and other scholars). A. Schmidt's opinion has not found much acceptance.

It can be assumed that the «theodotionic» text of Daniel is a translation of the Hebrew- Aramaic form of the book which was made by a Jew who also took into account the existing LXX version. This version could have come Syria or Mesopotamia (Koch). In any case this version cannot be considered a recension in the strict meaning of the term.

Other books of which large theodotionic fragments have been preserved are Is, Jr, Ez and Pr. Numerous quotations of the Greek OT contained in the NT reproduce the text of Theodotion. The Apocalypse quotes the book of Daniel according to the text of Theodotion and not the LXX. Heb (11:33) and 1 Cor (15:54) quote the book of Isaiah according to the text of Theodotion. Clement of Rome (*1 Clement* 3:46) also seems to have used the theodotionic text of Daniel.

All this means that a text with theodotionic characteristics already existed *before the historical Theodotion*. This strange fact, to solve which the hypothesis of an *Ur-Theodotion* or *proto-Theodotion* was proposed in the past, could find no satisfactory explanation until the discovery of the scroll of the Twelve Prophets of Naḥal Ḥever in the Desert of Judah (cf. p. 306).

In an earlier study on the text of this scroll, D. Barthélemy (1953) indicated the points of agreement between the quotations by Justin and the text of this scroll. He noted that it could not by any means be considered a completely fresh translation but a revision of the oldest Greek text, the *«proto-Theodotionic recension»* of a Hebrew text older than Aquila's. This study came to the firm conclusion that P. Kahle's hypothesis should be set aside - he assumed the existence of a number of translations, among which the LXX was only one of many, widespread among Christians (cf. p. 292).

The conclusions from study of this scroll have supposed a change in direction of studies on the origins of the LXX version and the history of its development in parallel with the Hebrew text. Study of this scroll has made it possible to know that, before the great Christian recensions and the Jewish versions or revisions mentioned above, in about 50 CE (Barthélemy) or perhaps towards the end of the 1st cent. BCE, Palestinian Judaism undertook the laborious task of revising the text of the early Greek version. The aim of this revision was to correct the Greek text from the Hebrew text which then had status in rabbinic circles in Palestine.

This «missing link» (Barthélemy), now found, of the history of the Greek version provides knowledge of an intermediate stage in the process of fixing the Hebrew text on the road to its definitive canonisation. It should not be surprising that the NT includes OT quotations which correspond to a Greek text revised slightly in terms of the Hebrew.

The new recension is recognisable from a series of *characteristics* which differentiate it from the old version. The most important include:
_ Translation of the particle *gam/wᵉgam*. «also»/«and also», by *kaige* instead of translation by the simple conjunction *w-* = *kaí*, «and».
– Translation of *ʾîš* by *ʾanēr* = «man» when the context requires *hékastos* = «each one», as in the old version, which was replaced by *ʾanēr* of the recension.
– Translation of the pronoun *ʾānōḵî*, «I» by *egṓ eimí* = «I am». The recensionist tried

to differentiate between the translation of this pronominal form *'ānōkî* and the form *'ānî*. The old version translated the two forms *'ānōkî* and *'ānî* indiscriminately by the pronoun *egō*. The Hebraising recension, however, does not notice the possibility that the construction *egō eimí* can precede a finite verb resulting in a construction completely impossible to Greek ears. For example, the recensionist translates 2 Sm 12:7 *wᵉ'ānōkî hiṣṣilka*, «*and I* have saved you» by *Kaì egó eimí errysámēn se*, «*and I am* have saved you», a construction which is a complete travesty of Greek syntax.
– The Hebrew negative *'ên*, «not, no» is translated by the corresponding Greek negative *ouk* followed by the form *esti*, «it is not» (present tense), but again without paying attention to the possible distortion which could be caused to the agreement of tenses in the immediate context (past or future).

Other characteristics of the *kaige* recension have been identified by M. Smith, J.A. Grindel, J.D. Shenkel, K.G. O'Connell and W.R. Bodine (Bodine).

The authors of this revision could justifiably be considered as the «*forerunners of Aquila*» (Barthélemy). This led to unheard of excesses, even if intolerable to Greek ears, in the tendency to literalism which had already started in the proto-Theodotionic recension (cf. p. 313).

Consequently, this recension began the process of revision of the LXX, which in the Jewish world culminated in the literalist version by Aquila and in the Christian world with the hexaplar recension of Origen. The proto-Theodotionic recension resulted in the Greek translation of Lamentations and, probably, of Song of Songs and Ruth, the text B of I-IV *Reges* (in the sections marked with the sigla *bg*, 1 Sm 10:2-1 Kgs 2:11, and *gd*, 1 Kgs 22:1-2 Kgs), the text of Judges attested by the groups of MSS i r u a₂ and B e f s z, the text of the Theodotionic recension of Daniel, the Theodotionic additions to the LXX of Jb and Jr, and column of Theodotion of the Hexaplar, the *Quinta* version of Psalms and, obviously, the Greek text of the Twelve Minor Prophets of Nahal Ḥever.

All this means that there was a «*Theodotionic text before Theodotion*» (cf. p. 311). Barthélemy has even suggested that the Theodotion known to us in history, who is said to have lived in the 2nd cent. CE is in fact the author of this proto-Theodotionic recension at the start of the 1st cent. CE, and so prior to Aquila. However, it does not look as if *the traditional person of Theodotion* of the 2nd cent. can be completely erased from history. This is because there is external testimony in his favour and because of the complex nature of the Theodotionic material, the author of which is still in dispute (A. Schmidt).

It is significant that *the three Jewish translators*, Symmachus, Aquila and Theodotion have been *compared to tannaitic persons*, considered to be the authors of the targumim or translations of the Bible into Aramaic. The Jerusalem Talmud knows or seems to know the three recensions of Theodotion, Aquila and Symmachus (in chronological order, from the oldest to the most recent) rather than in the traditional sequence, Aquila-Symmachus-Theodotion, derived from the text of each of the hexaplaric columns of Origen (3rd, 4th and 6th respectively).

Theodotion is none other than Jonathan (= «Theodotion» in Greek) ben

'Uzzi'el, Hillel's disciple, to whom the Babylonian Talmud (*Megilla*) mistakenly ascribes authorship of the Targum to the Prophets, when it could equally be the author of the proto-Theodotionic Greek recension. Likewise, the Babylonian Talmud ascribes to Onqelos the traditions of the Palestinian Talmud which at first refer to the Greek translation of Aquila, who then became Onqelos (*'nqls* = Aquila). Similarly, Symmachus could only have been Sunkos ben Joseph, R. Meir's disciple.

All this poses the question of knowing what were the relationships among the revisions of the LXX by Jewish authors and the Aramaic translations or targumim, especially in respect of their common development of translation methods and of the principles of OT interpretation established by the rabbis (cf. pp. 436 and 439).

BIBLIOGRAPHY

BARTHÉLEMY, D., «Origen et le texte de l'Ancien Testament», *Epektasis. Mélanges patristiques offerts au Cardinal Jean Daniélou*, Paris 1972, 247-261.

BARTHÉLEMY, D., «Redécouverte d'un chaînon manquant de l'histoire de la Septante», *RB* 60 (1953) 18-29.

BARTHÉLEMY, D., *Les Devanciers d'Aquila*, Leiden 1963.

BODINE, W.R., *The Greek Text of Judges. Recensional Developments*, Chico, CA 1980.

BOGAERT, M., «La Septante», *SDB* 12, Paris 1993, 538-692.

BROCK, S.P., «Lucian *redivivus*», *Studia evangelica* 5, Berlin 1968, 176-181.

FERNANDEZ MARCOS, N., *El texto antioqueno de la Biblia griega, 1 1-2 Samuel*, Madrid 1989.

FERNANDEZ MARCOS, N., «The Lucianic Text in the Books of Kingdoms: From Lagarde to the Textual Pluralism», *De Septuaginta. Studies in honour of J.W. Wevers*, eds. A. Pietersma-C. Cox, Toronto/Brandon 1984, 161-174.

FIELD, F., *Origenis Hexaplorum quae supersunt*, Oxford 1875 = 1964.

JELLICOE, S., «The Hesychian Recension Reconsidered», *JBL* 82 (1963) 409-418.

METGER, B.M., «The Lucianic Recension of the Greek Bible», *Chapters in the History of NT Textual Criticism*, Leiden 1963, 1-41.

O'CONNELL, K.G., *The Theodotionic Revision of the Book of Exodus*, Cambridge MA 1972.

RAHLFS, A., *Lucians Rezension der Königsbücher*, Göttingen 1911 = 1965.

SCHMIDT, A., *Stammt der sogenannte «O»-Text bei Daniel wirklich von Theodotion?*, Göttingen 1966.

SOISALON-SOININEN, I., *Der Charakter der asterisierten Zusätze in der Septuaginta*, Helsinki 1959.

SCHENKER, A., *Hexaplarische Psalmenbruckstücke*, Freiburg-Göttingen 1975.

SHENKEL, J.D., *Chronology and Recensional Development in the Greek Text of Kings*, Cambridge, MA 1968.

TOV, E., «Lucian and Proto-Lucian», *RB* 79 (1972) 101-113.

ULRICH, E., «Origen's Old Testament Text: The Transmission History of the Septuagint to the Third Century CE», *Origen of Alexandria. His World and his Legacy*, eds. Ch. Kannengiesser-W.L. Petersen, Notre Dame IN 1988, 3-33.

WALTERS, P. (formerly Katz), *The Text of the Septuagint. Its Corruptions and Their Emendation*, Cambridge 1973.

WEVERS, J.W., «Proto-Septuagint Studies», *The Seed of Wisdom*, Homage to T. J. Meek, Leiden 1956, 3-37.

WEVERS, J.W., «An Early Revision of the Septuagint of Numbers», *Eretz-Israel* 16 (1982) 135-139.

VII. THE TEXT OF THE ORIGINAL VERSION OF THE LXX

The LXX version has intrinsic value, as a translation into Greek. It also has extrinsic value, in respect of its contributions to Hebrew textual criticism and to the history of OT exegesis.

1. *The LXX as a Translation: What Kind of Version?*

The Greek Bible is really an anthology of translations and revisions of very differing types and styles. It has been affected by two factors. The first factor is external: the great codices were made by combining copies of scrolls with very different origins and characters. The second factor concerns the actual translation: various authors translated with very different styles and techniques in the various books which make up the Greek Bible.

The LXX is more *literal* in some books and more *free* in others. The literal version assumes a «formal equivalence» between the original language and the target language. The result in a free version is a «functional equivalence». Study of translation features has to proceed book by book. Even sections of the same book can sometimes have different characteristics. For example, some sections of the translation of the books of Sm-Kgs (I-IV *Reges*) preserve the text of the original translation, made from a non-masoretic Hebrew text type (1 Sm-2 Sm 10:1 and 1 Kgs 1:12-21:19); the other sections have the text of a more literal recension, based on a text close to the MT (1 Sm 10:2-1 Kgs 2:11 and 1 Kgs 22:1-2 Kgs). Thackeray had attributed the authorship of different sections to various authors. Barthélemy has shown that they are not translations by different authors but a (proto-Theodotionic) revision using the text of an older version. It is important to note that the history of the transmission of the Greek text (as in the Old Latin version) is the history of becoming more and more literal, first evident in the proto-Theodotionic recension and culminating in the works of Origen and Jerome.

The *criteria of «literalism»* of a translation studied by J. Barr and E. Tov, consist basically in the unchanging translation throughout a book or a section of elements in the original Hebrew (words, particles, roots, reconstructions, etc.) by the same Greek equivalents. For example, most translators systematically give Greek *dikaio-* for the Hebrew root *ṣdq* (*ṣaddîq = dikaios*, «just»). Similarly, it is possible to identify statistically the characteristics of the version by Aquila (Hyvärinen) or by Symmachus (Busto).

A quick run through the various books of the Greek Bible will highlight the character of the version of each book.

The version of the *Pentateuch* is faithful and correct within the characteristics of the *koiné* of the period. In spite of a great number of variants of small importance and a few changes in the order of the texts (as in Ex 30ff., and in Nm), the text of the LXX conforms, basically, to the MT. This agreement in textual tradition does not mean that there were was absolute uniformity in the Hebrew tradition. The Greek version shows agreements with the Dead Sea Scrolls and the Samaritan Pentateuch which indicate some fluctuation in the text. The version of the Pentateuch was a model and a source of technical and theological vocabulary for later versions of the other OT books (Tov). The first translators had to face the problem of looking for equivalents for very important Hebrew terms, such as *kābôd*, translated as Greek *dóxa*, «glory». Comparison with later translation of other books emphasises the boldness and originality of the translators of the Pentateuch.

The version of the Pentateuch is more «Hellenising» than later versions which are tinged with more literalism. This change in tendency reflects the evolution of Jewish society which started with complete openness to Hellenism in Alexandria in the 3rd cent. BCE but reverted to traditional and nationalist values in the Palestine of the Hasmonaeans during the 2nd and 1st cents. BCE.

The translation of *Isaiah* is very free. It is barely of use for textual criticism of the Hebrew of this book. It represents, instead, an invaluable source of data for the study of old Jewish exegesis as it is based on exegetical traditions which resurface later in the Targum and the Peshitta. The many quotations of the text of Is in the NT and in Christian and Jewish apologetics confer additional worth to this translation.

The text of the version of *Jeremiah* is one eighth shorter than the MT. It also has significant variations in the sequence of chapters. It exhibits a metrical regularity missing from the MT. It is based on a form of Hebrew recension which differs from the MT (cf. p. 395).

The version of *Ezekiel* is an attempt at a literal translation of the Hebrew text which is different from and shorter than the MT. The original text of the Greek version of this book has been preserved in only two manuscripts. The Christian Church replaced this text with Theodotion's, already cited in the NT, which is a much more literal translation (cf. p. 397).

The Greek *Psalter* translates the masoretic Hebrew with greater and lesser success. It underwent many revisions no doubt due to its continual use in the liturgy.

The version of *Proverbs* and *Job* is excellent, certainly the work of the same author. Its Hebrew original is very different from the MT. The book of Job in the LXX is one sixth shorter than the Hebrew text; modern editions use the text of Theodotion for the missing sections. The text of Pr has many double readings. They are the result of considerable revision which consisted in adding a more literal version to the first translation.

The book of *Lamentations* and perhaps also those of *Song of Songs* and *Ruth* were translated very much later, in a very literal manner (cf. p. 164).

The translation of *Qoheleth* (= *Ecclesiastes*) is extremely literal and unintelligible to someone not knowing Hebrew. It is a version made by Aquila or very much influenced by his style (cf. p. 165). It is not easy to see the reasons why the Christian Church adopted this type of text.

Current research is directed towards study of the translation techniques of each book of the Greek OT and in particular to characteristics of morphology, syntax and lexis. Study of the lexis of Jr, Ez and the Minor Prophets leads to the conclusion that they were translated by the same person (Tov). The same type of study enabled D. Barthélemy to identify the proto-Theodotionic recension and indicate which books were affected by it. The books of Pr and Job are certainly the work of the same translator (Gerleman). Study of translation procedures combined with lexicography helped establish the geographical origin (Alexandria or Palestine) of the translation of the different books (cf. p. 302).

Although studies of translation techniques are dry, they are very fertile when it comes to producing results. The most significant works are by Ziegler, Seeligmann, Orlinsky, P. Walters (previously Katz), G.B. Caird, E. Tov, J. de Waard, A. Aejemelaeus, etc.

Hebraisms and Aramaisms are to be noted which occur in the LXX version. Sometimes translators assign to an OT term the meaning which it acquired in post-biblical Hebrew or in Aramaic, the language spoken at the time of the Greek translation. With regard to studies of syntax, the Scandinavian school is particularly important. Through analysis of the way parataxis is translated, A. Aejmelaeus shows that each book of the Pentateuch has its own translator. The translations of Genesis and of Ex 1-34 are fairly free and Hellenising; the translation of Numbers is pedestrian; of Deuteronomy it is very accurate. J.W. Wevers has reached similar conclusions.

The LXX version, therefore, has intrinsic value which requires special study. It should be read as an independent text with its own consistency, not only in relation to external values, on which perhaps modern research has laid more emphasis and are studied in what follows.

2. *The Hebrew Original (Vorlage) of the LXX*

The LXX version is the largest and most important storehouse of data for critical study of the Hebrew text. Its witness is in direct since it is a translation. However, the many agreements between the LXX and the Hebrew manuscripts from Qumran has *re-evaluated the witness of the Greek text* in contrast with prevailing opinion before their discovery (1947), according to which the Greek text had no critical worth but was very valuable instead as witness of contemporary Jewsi exegesis in the period of the translation.

The relations between the LXX and some manuscripts from Qumran have already been mentioned (cf. p. 286). They are particularly close in 4QDeut[q] ,4QSam[ab], 4QJer[b], etc. Each manuscript contains, however, countless idiosyncratic readings, so that they have to be considered as witness of independent but interrelated traditions. The most important information provided by the biblical manuscripts from Qumran is, undoubtedly, the fact that in some books the LXX version reflects *a different Hebrew text from the one known in later masoretic tradition.* Such is the case in Jr and Sm. In other books the data are more complex. For example, the problem about the original Hebrew of Chr, Ezr and Neh cannot be solved without also determining their relationship to *3 and 4 Esdras* (as they are called in the Vulgate). In Qumran have been found Hebrew or Aramaic texts of books of which the text had only been preserved in translations in other languages. This applies to Sir and Tob, of which four manuscripts in Aramaic have been found and one in Hebrew.

Without doubt the most conspicuous examples is in Dt 32:8-09 where the Hebrew text of 4QDeut^q also reflected in the Greek, has mythological elements («according to the sons of *God*», an expression commonly replaced in the LXX by «the angels of God») which have been censored in the text of masoretic tradition: «according to the number of the sons of *Israel*» (cf. p. 282). The correction tries to avoid considering Yahweh as one of the 70 sons of God or, rather, if Yahweh is the same as the Most High, as the instigator of polytheism (Barthélemy 1963).

The Greek translators often did not know the meaning of the Hebrew terns they were translating so that some terms and expressions in the Greek version are no more than guesses (Tov). This has to be borne in mind when studying the *Vorlage* of the LXX.

3.   *The LXX as a Work of Interpretation and Exegesis*

From the point of view of textual criticism the LXX sometimes reflects a Hebrew text unlike the MT. From the point of view of targumic interpretation and the history of religion, the LXX *reflects both the theological ideas and hermeneutical tendencies of the Judaism at that time*. To consider the LXX purely as text tends to reduce its value merely to a tool for correcting the MT and in a more recent variation of the same tendency, to a tool for finding lost forms of the Hebrew text.

However, the value of the LXX is much greater. The translation of a whole body of Hebrew literature into Greek is a unique effort of interpretation in every sense: spelling, morphology, syntax, semantics, theology, etc. The unvocalised script, the Semitic verbal system, the conceptual world and Hebrew poetry, the OT theology, forced the translators to make an effort of interpretation in which sometimes the Hebrew component of the original prevails and sometimes the Greek of the translation dominates. Besides the Hebraisms and Aramaisms, there occur intentional or unavoidable Grecisms and Egyptianisms. This applies both to the literary expressions and to the expression of ideas and concepts. In the LXX the list of feminine accessories in Is 3:18-24 is replaced by a list of items more familiar to a Greek.

The «School of Religions» paid great attention to this *transfer of expressions and concepts from the Hebrew Bible to the Greek*, following an approach developed by G. Bertram and applied in the well-known *Theological Dictionary of the New Testament* (*Theologisches Wörterbuch zum Neuen Testament*) edited by G. Kittel and G. Friedrich from 1933 (cf. p. 30). For example, there is an obvious reluctance by the translators to admit Greek expressions which had pagan overtones. The Old Latin translation shows similar disapproval. The Hebrew word *torah* is generally translated by the Greek term *nómos*. However, the Hebrew concept of «law» is much wider than is expressed by the Greek term. A more suitable equivalent would be *didakhé*, «teaching», which is precisely the title of an important early Christian work. The choice of *nómos* could have led to unreasonably legalistic or nomistic interpretations of Hebrew law and even of Judaism as a whole (cf. p. 519).

However, we have to remember J. Barr's criticisms of the *Theological Dictionary of the New Testament*: in principle over hasty leaps to theological conclusions are to be distrusted as without a sufficient linguistic foundation. For example, Bertram developed on the supposed theological implications of the version of the Hebrew divine epithet *šadday* («the Almighty») by Greek *ho hikanós* (Ruth 1:20-21). In fact, the Greek translator has only given an etymological interpretation of the term *šadday* as *še-day* («the one who is enough»). The Greek version represents a Hellenised form of the Hebrew Bible, but one made by Jews for Jews in a Jewish way. The translation of the Scriptures into Greek Judaised the *koiné* more than it Hellenised Judaism. It loaded with typically Israelite echoes terms which until then had had a secular and pagan meaning (Barthélemy).

The LXX is a true work of Jewish exegesis, comparable at times to a targum (cf. the chapter «The interpretation of the OT in the Greek version of the Septuagint», p. 436).

BIBLIOGRAPHY

AEJMELAEUS, A., *Parataxis in the Septuagint*, Helsinki 1982.

AEJMELAEUS, A., «Translation Technique and the Intention of the Translator», *VII Congress of the IOSCS. Louvain 1989*, ed. C. Cox, Atlanta GA 1991, 23-36.

ALLEN, L.C., *The Greek Chronicles: Part I: The Translator's Craft*, Leiden 1974.

BARR, J., *The Typology of Literalism in Ancient Biblical Translations*, Göttingen 1979.

BARR, J., *The Semantics of Biblical Language*, Oxford 1961.

BARTHÉLEMY, D., «L'Ancien Testament a mûri à Alexandrie», *ThZ* 21 (1965) 358-370 = *Études d'histoire du texte* 127-139.

BARTHÉLEMY, D., «Qui est Symmaque?», *CBQ* 36 (1974) 451-465.

BARTHÉLEMY, D., «Les tiqquné sopherim et la critique textuelle de l'Ancien Testament», *Congress Volume. Bonn 1962*, VT.S 9 (1963) 285 - 304 = *Études d'histoire du texte* 91-110.

BERTRAM, G., «'IKANOS' in den griechischen Übersetzungen des Alten Testaments als Wiedergabe von *schaddaj*», ZAW 70 (58) 20-31.

BROOKE, G.J.-LINDARS, B. (eds.), *Septuagint, Scrolls and Cognate Writings. Papers Presented to the International Symposium on the Septuagint and Its Relations to the Dead Sea Scrolls and Other Writings (Manchester, 1990)*, Atlanta GA 1992.

BUSTO SAIZ, J.R., *La traducción de Símaco en el libro de los Salmos*, Madrid 1978.

CAIRD, G.B., «Towards a Lexicon of the Septuagint», *JTS* NS 19 (1968) 453-475; 20 (1969) 21-40.

HYVÄRINEN, K., *Die Übersetzung von Aquila*, Lund 1977.

OLOFSSON, S., *The LXX Version. A Guide to the Translation Technique of the Septuagint*, Stockholm 1990.

ORLINSKY, H.M., «The Septuagint as Holy Writ and the Philosophy of the Translators», *HUCA* 46 (1975) 89-114.

PIETERSMA, A.-COX, C.(eds.), *De Septuaginta. Studies in Honour of J.W. Wevers*, Mississauga, Ontario, 1984.

REIDER, J.-TURNER, N., *An Index to Aquila*, Leiden 1966.

SEELIGMANN, I.L., *The Septuagint of Isaiah*, Leiden 1948.

SOISALON-SOININEN, I., *Die Infinitive in der Septuaginta*, Helsinki 1965.

SOLLAMO, R., *The Renderings of the Hebrew Semiprepositions in the Septuagint*, Helsinki 1979.

TOV, E., «Three Dimensions of LXX Words», *RB* 83 (76) 529-544.

TOV, E., «Did the Septuagint Translators Always Understand their Hebrew Vorlage?», *De Septuaginta*, eds. A. Pietersma-C. Cox, Mississauga, Ontario, 1984, 53-70.

TOV, E., *The Text-Critical Use of the Septuagint in Biblical Research*, Jerusalem 1981.

ULRICH, E., *The Qumran Text of Samuel and Josephus*, Missoula MT 1978.

ULRICH, E., «The Greek Manuscripts of the Pentateuch from Qumrân, Including Newly- Identified Fragments of Deuteronomy (4QLXX Deut)», *De Septuaginta, Studies in Honour of J.W. Wevers*, ed. A. Pietersma - C. Cox, Mississauga, Ontario, 1984, 71-82.

WAARD, J. DE, «Homophony in the Septuagint», *Bib.* 62 (1981) 551-556.

WALTERS, P. (formerly Katz), *The Text of the Septuagint, Its Corruptions and Their Emendation*, Cambridge 1973.

WEVERS, J.W., *Text History of Greek Numbers*, Göttingen 1982.

4

Aramaic Versions of the Old Testament.
The Targumim

I. INTRODUCTION - CHARACTERISTICS, LANGUAGE, PERIOD

During the Persian period, the Jews adopted Aramaic as the language for common use (cf. p. 68). It created the *need* to have available Aramaic translations (*Targumim*) of the Bible. At first they were oral, periphrastic translations, which accompanied the synagogue reading (Neh 8:8). When they were put into writing later and as they became more complex paraphrases, they started to be used outside the synagogue and to acquire a more marked literary character. The existence and use of such versions in synagogal worship in the NT period are amply testified.

In *Qumran*, large fragments of a Targum on Job (11QTgJob = 11Q10) have been found, dating from the end of the 2nd cent. BCE. The Targum is written in an Aramaic somewhere between the Aramaic of the book of Daniel and that of the *Genesis Apocryphon*. It could well correspond to the text which Gamaliel I ordered to be hidden away, though years later his nephew Gamaliel II was using it (Tosefta, *Šabbat* 13:2). It comprises a fairly literal translation from a Hebrew original close to the MT. It follows the same sequence of chapters, but ends with 42:11, leaving the rest of the column blank. It poses the question whether the Hebrew original translated by this targum was unaware of the traditional ending of 42:12-17, which refers to Job recovering his prosperity. After 42:17, the Greek version, instead, adds a list of Job's descendants. In 42:6, the biblical Job, a repentant sinner, seems to have become a man who although suffering is perfect and does not need to loathe himself. It has been assumed that this targum is a copy used by Mesopotamian Judaism and is not actually the product of the Essenes of Qumran (Van der Ploeg-Van der Woude, Sokoloff). Another copy of the Targum of Job (4Q157) has been preserved, dating to the middle of the 1st cent. CE, which is a very literal translation although it varies slightly from the MT (Milik *DJD* VI).

The fragments of the Targum to Leviticus (4QTgLev = 4Q156), which correspond to Lv 16, may come from a complete targum or perhaps from a ritual for the Feast of Atonement. Unlike the Palestinian targumim, these two targumim from Qumran, written in literary Aramaic, provide a literal version.

The discovery of these two targumim as well as the edition of Palestinian targum texts of the Pentateuch completed by Kahle in 1930, and the discovery of *Codex Neophyti I* by A. Díez Macho in the Vatican Library in 1956, have in the last few years revived interest in Aramaic translations and in questions connected with their origin, language and exegetical characteristics.

Targumim to the Pentateuch, the Prophets and the Writings do exist, but not to Ezra-Neh and Dn. The differences among the targumim concern the type of translation (more literal in Onqelos and more a paraphrase in the Palestinian targumim) and the place of origin and development of each targum (either Babylonia or Palestine). The Onqelos Targum was used in Babylonia, the Jonathan Targum in Jerusalem and the Yĕrûšalmî and/or Targum *Neophyti* in Galilee and Tiberias (M. Kasher).

1. These versions have common *characteristics*. Most significant is the tendency to paraphrase. They insert mainly short accounts, midrashic in character, and points of doctrine connected with the translated text. In the references to God they tend to avoid anthropomorphisms and anthropopathisms, not in a completely systematic way, but generally to avoid any direct reference to the divinity. Instead, they use substitutes such as *Memrâ* («the Word»). They carry out «derashic» exegesis (*drš*) with the intention of extracting the abstruse meaning or to explain the difficulties of a text.

The Targumim lie halfway on the path between a literal version and the long midrashic commentaries of the rabbinic period. Accordingly, the presentation and discussion of everything related to the Targumim are in the section dealing with the Jewish interpretation of the OT (cf. pp. 468-489)

2. The *language* of the old Palestinian targumim is standard literary Aramaic. It exhibits influences from the Aramaic dialect of Galilee which were particularly strong after the Bar Kokhba revolt when rabbinic Judaism had to take refuge in Galilee. As a result, and to judge from the linguistic character of the targumim, none of them is earlier than the second half of the 2nd cent. BCE.

3. Since they are works composed of elements from very different periods and in view of the extreme fluidity of the text of the targumim, it is impossible to give them an absolute date. Comparison with the haggadic and halakhic traditions contained in these Aramaic versions with similar traditions preserved in other works of better known date, allows a *relative chronology* to be established for those traditions. In this way it is possible follow the history of a specific exegetical or juridical tradition and locate the targumic reference to that tradition within that history.

So, for example, texts from apocryphal literature, from the Dead Sea Scrolls and from the NT interpret the expression «the sons of the gods» (*bᵉnê ᵉlōhîm*) of Gn 6:3 as a reference to the «angels». However, early on in Jewish as well as Christian circles, this expression was interpreted as a reference to men of flesh and blood, to the «sons of the judges» (*Genesis Rabbah* 36:5). The targumim reflect the exegetical history of this expression. The translations of *Neophyti*, «the sons of the judges» and of Onqelos, «the sons of the nobles», represent the new interpretation. The old interpretation appears in a marginal reading in *Neophyti* and in the text of the following verse (6:4) according to the Targum of Pseudo-Jonathan.

In general, the targumim reflect the type of exegesis which became official in the period around 150 CE, but retained traces of interpretations from earlier periods which escaped the «censure» of the Mishnaic period.

As for halakhic or juridical traditions, Kahle formulated a criterion for dating by which *«what is anti-Mishnaic is pre-Mishnaic»*. This criterion is based on the logical supposition that an interpretation opposed to the authorised interpretation of the Mishnah must be earlier than its promulgation. However, this principle has to be applied with extreme caution and never in an automatic way.

Another criterion for dating the targumim is provided by several *geographical references* which they contain. For example, Targum Neophyti interprets the geography of the map of the nations (Gn 10) in connection with the geography of a particular historical period, i.e., between the 3rd and 4th cents. CE, into which fit references to Phrygia, Germany, Media, Macedonia, Bithynia, Asia, Thrace, etc.

It is important to note that the LXX is one of the literary sources of the Onqelos and Jonathan targumim. More than half the cases of definite Greek borrowing found in the targumim match corresponding passages in the LXX. The inclusion of a Greek term in the targum is the result of a type of interpretation already attested precisely in the LXX (Brown).

II. TARGUMIM OF THE PENTATEUCH

1. *The Palestine Targum*

The Palestine Targum of the Pentateuch comprises Targum Pseudo-Jonathan (= *Y^erûšalmî* I), the Fragmentary Targum (=*Y^erûšalmî* II), Cairo Genizah Fragments and *Codex Neophyti I*. These versions differ among themselves but provide a common paraphrase. They suppose the existence of a tradition of oral interpretation of the OT, the main nucleus of which seems to be earlier than the Mishnaic period. This has to be assumed from the fact that the halakhic or legal paraphrase of these targumim sometimes does not agree with what is established in the Mishnah. Another school of thought, based on study of the Aramaic texts from Qumran, sets a later date for the Palestinian targumim.

A. TARGUM PSEUDO-JONATHAN (= *Y^erûšalmî I*)

This targum, wrongly attributed to Jonathan ben 'Uzzi'el (due to confusing the initials T.Y. which refer in fact to Targum *Y^erûšalmî* and not to Targum

Jonathan) is a composite work in which are mixed old and new elements and it includes very many paraphrases which virtually double the length of the translation in respect of its Hebrew original. Some of these paraphrases have a parallel in the Onqelos Targum or in the Palestinian Targumim, others derive from midrashic works (e.g. Ex 14:2) and some which no doubt are of ancient origin (e.g. Ex 6:2.4) are peculiar to this targum.

The oldest sections go back to a pre-Christian period. The more recent interpolations refer to the wife and daughter of Mohammed (Gn 21:21; cf. similarly *Pirqê Rabbi Eliezer* 30).

According to some scholars Targum Pseudo-Jonathan is in fact the Onqelos Targum completed from the text of the Palestinian Targum (Dalman, Kahle, Grelot). According to others it is a Palestinian Targum reworked from the Onqelos Targum (Bacher, Bloch, Díez Macho). The *editio princeps* of 1590-91 is reproduced in the London Polyglot and in rabbinic bibles.

B.   THE FRAGMENTARY TARGUM (= *Yĕrûšalmî* II)

The targum contains sections from all the books of the Pentateuch. In Genesis it covers one third of the book. Five manuscripts of this targum, from the 13th-18th cents., go back to the same original and agree with the *editio princeps* included in the first edition of the rabbinic bible of Bomberg (Venice 1516-17). Another four manuscripts represent the same number of recensions of the Fragmentary Targum which have to be added to the recension represented by manuscripts which agree with the Bomberg edition.

The Fragmentary Targum, notable for being an anthology of selected passages, could have originated as a supplement to a complete Palestinian Targum or to the Onqelos Targum, in the manner of the *tôsāpôt* or additions of this targum. However, the Fragmentary Targum seems to be more systematic; it appears to correspond to a deliberate intention of making an extract from a complete recension of a Palestinian Targum. It probably comprises, then, an extract from a complete Palestinian Targum in Western Aramaic. Its paraphrase is sometimes very lengthy, sometimes older and more authentic than the other Palestinian Targum texts. At times its translation is literal and faithful to the Hebrew.

C.   THE FRAGMENTARY TARGUM OF THE CAIRO GENZIAH

The fragments of the Palestinian Targum from the Cairo Genizah go back to the 9th-13th cents., which gives it special value, since most other manuscripts known are not earlier than the 16th cent. The fragments from the Genizah prove the existence of different recensions of the Palestinian Targum.

D.   TARGUM NEOPHYTI

Codex Neophyti 1 was discovered by A. Díez Macho in the Vatican Library, where it was catalogued as a copy of the Onqelos Targum. In fact, it was a copy of a Palestinian Targum, virtually complete and divided into liturgical sections (*pārāšîyôt*). A colophon informs us that the copy, by three different hands, was made in Rome in the year (5)264 in the Jewish calendar (1504 CE).

This text is in a vernacular and popular form of Northern Aramaic, earlier than the Galilean Aramaic of the Jerusalem Talmud and of the midrashim. Its paraphrase is more restrained than in the other targumim. According to Díez Macho, the version was made in the pre-Tannaitic period (1st cent. CE). Wernberg-Møller, however, considers that the data provided by Díez Macho do not allow such an early date. In some sections it seems to have been under the later influence of the Onqelos Targum, although the facts could also indicate the opposite.

Other material from the Palestinian Targum is found in the *tôsāp̄ôt* or interpolations inserted into manuscripts of the Onqelos Targum, as well as in collections of texts for reading on certain feasts and of Sabbaths of special festive nature.

2.   The Onqelos Targum

The Onqelos Targum covers the complete text of the Pentateuch. It was the targum with the greatest authority and even had its own masorah, which includes a list of the differences in reading between the schools of Nahardea and Sura. The Babylonian Talmud (*Megilla* 3a) attributes it to Onqelos, evidently confused with Aquila, the author of the Greek translation which bears that name. The textual transmission of this targum is much more stable than it is for the Palestinian. Targumim.

Targum Onqelos is of Palestinian origin. Its language is different from that of the Babylonian Talmud. It is a literary Aramaic as used in academies. Targum Onqelos could have originated either in Palestine or in Babylonia. However, some facts indicate a Palestinian origin (Kutscher). Its Aramaic is very close to the *Genesis Apocryphon* found in Qumran. On the other hand, the translation is very consistent with the Hebrew text. The paraphrase is very restrained and is only implicit in the actual translation. The very many agreements with the Palestinian targum could indicate that Onqelos is a very concise extract from a Palestinian targum. It is a further indication of a Palestinian origin for that targum.

However, the definitive edition of the Onqelos Targum was made in Babylonia where it became the official text and authorised interpretation of the rabbinic schools of Sura and Nahardea. The linguistic character of the targum was not altered. It retained the Western form of established literary Aramaic. It testifies to the respect felt by Babylonian Judaism for Palestinian Judaism.

Likewise, the spread and the authority of Targum Onqelos in the centuries following the talmudic period reflect the dominance of Babylonian Judaism throughout the Middle Ages. Targum Onqelos and Targum Jonathan of the Prophets did not succeed in displacing the other targumim, but their spread determined the formation of the Fragmentary Palestinian Targum, which had to supply the passages lacking in those two targumim that were marked by simpler paraphrase.

Since Onqelos comprises a sort of compendium to a Palestinian Targum, it shows that the shortest text is not always the oldest. In the history of textual transmission, two opposing tendencies can co-exist: the tendency to expand on the text of a tradition and the tendency to abridge and summarise it.

The differences among the manuscripts of Onqelos set the textual critic the task of recovering the Babylonian form of its text. This requires study of several Yemenite manuscripts which to a large extent preserve the text of the Babylonian.

The Samaritans also had available translations of their own Pentateuch in their (own) Aramaic dialect. Compared with the Jewish targumim, which are largely very periphrastic, the Samaritan Targum gives the impression of being an extremely literal translation in the form of each Hebrew word corresponding to one in Aramaic (Tal).

III. THE TARGUM OF THE PROPHETIC BOOKS

Targum Jonathan of the «former» Prophets (Josh-Kgs) and the «latter» Prophets (Is-Jr-Ez) is attributed to Jonathan ben 'Uzzi'el in the Babylonian Talmud (*Megilla*, 3a), once again through confusion with another Greek translator, Theodotion (= Jonathan). It originated in Palestine, but the final redaction was probably made in Babylonia (3rd-4th cents.).

It is not possible to indicate which parts of the text correspond to the original and which to the final redaction. The aim of making the translation correspond to the Hebrew text was certainly the reason why a large part of the paraphrase was removed, although this removal was not as systematic as in Targum Onqelos. The nature of the paraphrase differs from one book to another. In Is it exhibits archaic features close to those of the Palestinian Targum to the Pentateuch.

The targum to the Prophets includes traditions not found in rabbinic literature. It imparts an urgency to the biblical prophecies in contrast to the projection into distant times which rabbinic writings make of them. Similarly, the figure of the priestly Messianic figure occurs also in Qumran and the NT but is missing from rabbinic literature. The targum to Ezekiel develops the mystical doctrine of the *Merkābâ* as a substitute for messianism; this doctrine has no equivalent at all in rabbinism (Ribera).

The transmitted text is as stable as Onqelos, but there are still important variants among the manuscripts. The chief problem, then, consists in determining the relationship between the Yemenite manuscripts with supralinear vocalisation and the Western manuscripts with Tiberian vocalisation. There seem to be two slightly different recensions in this targum, one Western and the other Yemenite. The recension represented by the Yemenite manuscripts is much closer to the Babylonian tradition.

IV. THE TARGUMIM OF THE WRITINGS

Even though not much use is made of the Writings in synagogal worship, there are targumim of all the books which make up this section of the Bible, except for Ezra-Neh and Dn. They are not earlier than the Talmudic period (5th cent.). Some are even later. The language is basically Palestinian Aramaic.

Depending on the translation techniques used, three groups can be distinguished: one composed of the five rolls or *Mĕgillôt*, one comprising the books of Jb, Pss and Pr, and lastly the targum to Chr. The text of these targumim has been transmitted in a state of extreme fluidity; in most of the books different recensions have been transmitted. The language of the targumim to the *Mĕgillôt* is a mixture of Western Aramaic and the Aramaic of the Babylonian Talmud; the paraphrase is quite elaborate. In Lam, the Yemenite manuscripts transmit one recension and the Palestinian manuscripts, another, but while the vocalisation of the Yemenite MSS is better than in the Western MSS, the text of the recension represented by the latter is better than in the former, and older. In the targum to Song and Qoh, it seems that two traditions of textual transmission have to be distinguished, one Yemenite and the other Western. The rabbinic bible of Bomberg distinguishes two targumim of Esther to which the Antwerp Polyglot (1569-72) adds a third, the most periphrastic of all the targumim.

In the targumim to Jb and Pss, old material is mixed with new and there are numerous haggadic additions. The language of Prov is close to Syriac; the paraphrase in this targum is very restrained.

The language, translation techniques and paraphrase of the targum to Chr make it close to the Pseudo-Jonathan Targum to the Pentateuch.

V. TARGUMIC EXEGESIS

The targum texts, especially Onqelos, follow the masoretic text faithfully. The presence in the targumim and in the Pešiṭta of readings which reflect variants to the MT shows the origin of such readings to be earlier than the period when the consonantal Hebrew text was fixed (Isenberg; cf. p. 378). However, the fundamental value of the targumim lies in their contribution to Aramaic (cf. p. 68), on the one hand and to Jewish exegesis, halakhic and haggadic, on the other. To this exegesis and its methods is related the exegesis by NT writings of OT texts. Jesus seems to have made use of targumic traditions, more specifically, of the traditions contained in the targum to Is (Chilton). These seem to have had some influence on the transmission of the sayings of Jesus.

Targumic exegesis will be discussed again in the chapter on «The interpretation of the OT in the targumim» (cf. p. 439).

VI. THE TARGUM AND THE SYNAGOGUE

In the synagogue, the reading of the biblical texts, Torah and *Haptārâ* was followed by the corresponding translation into Aramaic, to avoid as far as possible confusing written tradition with the oral tradition expressed in the targum tradition. The reader and the translator had to be different people; one had to limit himself to reading the sacred text, the other had to recite from memory. The translation was made immediately after the reading. The reading of each verse of the Pentateuch was followed by the corresponding translation but translation of the prophetic texts could be made in blocks of two or three verses.

This concern for safeguarding the separation between Scripture and Targum, however, seems complemented by just as much insistence on the close relationship between sacred text and targumic interpretation. The targumic version was not a simple translation of the sacred text but its authorised interpretation in agreement with rabbinic «orthodoxy» and remote from any theological deviation. Without touching the letter of the text, targumic interpretation imposed a specific interpretation on it. The targum is at once translation and commentary.

The use of the targum, however, goes beyond the setting of synagogue worship. Some targumim may have originated outside the synagogal setting. Only in this way can it be explained that there are targumim to the books of Job and Prov, which are not easily placed in synagogal reading. The targum was study material in the schools (*bêt ha-sēper*) which no doubt had decisive importance in the composition and transmission of the targumim. They do not comprise literature of popular origin and character. This can be deduced from a consideration of the targumim as translations almost exclusively for liturgical use, made for the attention of a people unable to understand Hebrew.

Its liturgical use started to decline when Aramaic began to be replaced by Arabic as the spoken language of the Jews. The targum was also reading material for individuals and nourished personal piety.

BIBLIOGRAPHY (cf. p. 70)

Editions of targum texts

BERLINER, A., *Targum Onkelos* I-II, Berlin 1884.

CLARKE, E.G., et al., *Targum Pseudo-Jonathan of the Pentateuch: Text and Concordance*, Hoboken NY 1984.

DÍEZ MACHO, A.(ed.), *Neophyti I: Targum Palestinense* MS *de la Biblioteca Vaticana*, I-VI, Madrid-Barcelona 1968-79.

DÍEZ MACHO, A. (ed.), *Biblia Polyglotta Matritensia*, Series IV, Madrid 1965-1988 (with a Spanish translation).

KLEIN, M.L., *Genizah Manuscripts of the Palestinian Targum to the Pentateuch*, 2 vols., Cincinnati KT 1986.

KLEIN, M.L., *The Fragment-Targums of the Pentateuch: According to Their Extant Sources*, Rome 1980.

LE DÉAUT, R.-ROBERT, J., *Targum des Chroniques*, Rome 1971.

LEVINE, E., *The Aramaic Version of Ruth*, Rome 1973.

LEVINE, E., *The Aramaic Version of Lamentations*, New York 1976.

RIBERA FLORIT, J., *El Targum de Isaías: la versión aramea del Profeta Isaías. Versión crítica, introducción y notas*, Valencia 1988.

LEVINE, E., *The Aramaic Version of Qohelet*, New York 1979.

SPERBER, A., *The Bible in Aramaic* I-IVB, Leiden 1959-1973=1992.

STEC, D.M., *The Text of the Targum of Job. An Introduction & Critical Edition*, Leiden 1994.

TAL, A., *The Samaritan Targum of the Pentateuch*, 3 vols., Tel Aviv 1983.

VAN DER PLOEG, J.P.M.-WOUDE, A.S. VAN DER, *Le targum de Job de la grotte XI de Qumran*, Leiden 1971.

Studies

BEATTIE, D.R.G.-MCNAMARA, M.J. (eds.), *The Aramaic Bible. Targums in their Historical Context*, Sheffield 1994.

BROWN, J.P., «The Septuagint as a Source of the Greek Loan-Words in the Targums», *Biblica* 70 (1989) 194-216.

CHILTON, B., *A Galilean Rabbi And His Bible. Jesus' Own Interpretation of Isaiah*, London 1984.

GORDON, R.P., *Studies in the Targum to the Twelve Prophets. From Nahum to Malachi*, Leiden 1994.

GROSSFELD, B., *A Bibliography of Targum Literature*, 3 vols., Cincinnati-New York 1972, 1977 y 1990.

ISENBERG, SH.R., «On the Jewish-Palestinian Origins of the Peshitta to the Pentateuch», *JBL* 90 (1971) 69-81.

KAHLE, P., *Masoreten des Westens* I-II, Stuttgart 1930.

KASHER, M.M., *Torah Shelemah. Talmudic-Midrashic Encyclopedia on the Pentateuch*, vols. 1-7, Jerusalem 1927-1938 (Genesis); vols. 8-23 1944-1969 (Exodus); vols. 25-33 1971-1980 (Leviticus).

SOKOLOFF, M., *The Targum to Job from Qumran Cave XI*, Ramat-Gan 1974.

VERMES, G., «The Targumic Versions of Genesis 4:3-16», *Post-Biblical Jewish Studies, Studies in Judaism in Late Antiquity* 8, Leiden 1975, 92-126.

WERNBERG-MØLLER, P., «An Inquiry into the Validity of the Text-Critical Argument for an Early Dating of the Recently Discovered Palestinian Targum», *VT* 12 (1962) 312-330.

5

The Greek Text of the New Testament

I.   THE PROBLEMS IN OUTLINE

The NT has had a far greater influence on Western culture than any other ancient book. As a result its text has reached us in an incomparably greater number of copies than for any other work from the classical world. About 5,000 Greek manuscripts of the NT are known to which should be added about 10,000 manuscripts of the various ancient versions as well as thousands of quotations contained in the writings of the Fathers and the Church. All this material (manuscripts, versions and quotations) contains a number of variants calculated as between 15,000 and 250,000 or perhaps more. There is not one single phrase of the NT for which the manuscripts tradition has not transmitted some variant.

Comparison with the transmission of classical Greek and Latin texts is of great interest. Many classical works have reached us in only two or three copies from the mediaeval period, often separated from the original by more than a millennium. The discovery of papyri has come to remedy this situation in some way. Instead, the time intervening between the period when the gospels were redacted and the period to which most of the witnesses preserved belong to the gospel text is not more than three or four centuries and in some cases is reduced to only two hundred years or even less. A papyrus fragment (P^{52}, about 125 CE) of John's gospel is older than the date specified by some critics for the redaction of that gospel.

The state of preservation of the NT text is far superior to that of many classical texts. To reconstruct the original text of the tragedies of Aeschylus and correct the corruptions in the preserved manuscripts, the editor of these works has no other recourse except frequent textual «conjectures». In the vast majority of cases the original reading of each passage of the NT text is always preserved in one or other of the manuscripts which have reached us.

The greater part of existing variants in NT manuscripts concern spelling or matters of grammar and style. Variants affecting the meaning of the text are very rare. Many comprise deliberate changes inserted in the text by copyists. However, even in cases where the inserted changes affect or alter the meaning of the text, in general they do not touch on matters of substance which would later become Christian dogma. Some cases are more impressive, such as the variant «son» or «God» in Jn 1:18 for its concerns no less a matter than the divinity of Christ (cf. p. 409).

The inspired character of Scripture is no guarantee of a well-preserved text. The Letter to the Hebrews develops an important point of its Christological doctrine on the basis of what is in fact a textual error: a supposed reference in Ps 40:6 to the incarnation of Christ in a body destined for sacrifice. The expression of Heb 10:5 «a *body* (*sōma*) have you prepared» is presented as a quotation of Ps 40:7 (MT 39:7) «you have given me and opened an *ear*». The Letter to the Hebrews refers to the preparation of a body for Christ who comes to the world. The immediate context confirms this (10:10). However, the Hebrew text of Ps 40:7(39:7) does not use the Hebrew term «body» and neither does the LXX, which has the term *ōtia*, «ears», corresponding to the Hebrew original. The argument of the Letter to the Hebrews is based on two mistakes in reading: doubling of the sigma (the last letter of the preceding word) and confusion of the letter M with the two consecutive letters TI; the result of these two mistakes is that the reading -s *ōtia* gave rise to the reading -s *sōma*. This incorrect reading in the Letter to the Hebrews later passed into many manuscripts of the Psalter. Christian copyists granted more authority to the reading in the NT quotation than to the actual Psalter.

On the other hand, a reading error can originate a new text considered as inspired, even though its does not mean that the doctrine expressed is based on the textual error. The most impressive case is the quotation in Mt 1:22 of Is 7:14 «the virgin will conceive a son». In this case it is not a matter of a copyist's error or of an incorrect translation. What has occurred is a shift in meaning. The Greek translators knew perfectly well the meaning of the Hebrew word *'almâ* which they translated *parthénos* with the meaning «girl» and not «virgin». The Christians, who believed in the mysterious birth of Christ, interpreted the text of Is as a prophecy of «virgin» birth of the Messiah, giving the meaning «virgin» to the term *parthénos*.

The original autographs of the books which comprise the NT have been lost for ever. There were many factors which could affect inadequate preservation of the NT text. In the early period the NT writers copied onto papyrus, a material which decayed very quickly, except in such climates as Egypt or the Dead Sea. The greater part of the variants preserved come from a period earlier than the canonisation of the MT books, at a time when not much care was taken in the copying of manuscripts. The canonisation of the NT books caused greater care in copying them, but this did not stop new variants and new changes in the text. Once the canonical character of the books was accepted, copyists were even more inclined to correct the text, concerned with expurgating from it anything that could seem erroneous, incorrect or even inappropriate in a sacred text.

In antiquity, copyists were not interested in the «original» reading so much the concern of modern critics. Their interest centred on the «true» reading, the one which corresponded to church tradition and was in agreement with it. This does not mean to say that copyists and scribes in antiquity had no critical concern. It is enough to think of Origen's work which remaining faithful to the text transmitted by the tradition of the Church is not therefore unworthy of more modern and demanding criticism.

Interest in the «better» and original text and in the history of the versions was not developed until the Renaissance period. It remains important even so that, after the first period of the Renaissance and of the Reformation, there would emerge a new «tradition» of the so-called *textus receptus*, the authority of which was almost undisputed until the last century.

II. THE PRINTED TEXT OF THE NEW TESTAMENT. THE TEXTUS RECEPTUS

After the invention of printing and for quite a few years only Latin texts were printed. The first Greek texts of the NT to be printed were the *Magnificat* and the *Benedictus*, printed together with a Psalter in Greek in 1481, in Milan.

The first printed edition of the Greek text of the NT was in the *Complutensian Polyglot* (cf. p. 270). The fifth of this six volume work contains the text of the NT. The printing work was completed in Alcalá on the 10th January 1514, but the complete edition did not appear until 1522. It is not possible to determine exactly which manuscripts were used to make this edition. We know that some (*antiquissima et emendatissima*) were sent for the purpose from Rome. Sometimes the editors correct the Greek text from the Vulgate Latin text. This applies to the so-called *Johannine comma* (1 Jn 5:7-8).

In 1515, *Erasmus* (1466?-1536) prepared an edition of the NT which appeared the following year. Erasmus prepared this edition at the request of the printer J. Froben, established in Basel, whose intention was to publish the Complutensian. The edition by Erasmus reproduced in parallel columns the Greek text and a revised text of the Vulgate. The work was carried out in less than six months, so that edition was inevitably marred by typographical errors. Erasmus based himself on manuscripts from the library of the University of Basel which were late and of little critical worth. The manuscript used for the edition of the Apocalypse only contained the passage 22:16-21. All Erasmus could do was to fill the gap in manuscript with his own version made from the Latin text.

Erasmus' work, published in 1519, 1522, 1527 and 1535, was criticised at the time, not so much for the mistakes it contained as for the changes made to the Latin text. The text quoted by Erasmus does not match the quality of the Complutensian Polyglot. However, since it had been published a few years earlier, it soon became the most widespread and authorised text. If so many years had not elapsed between the printing and publication of the Alcala Polyglot, the NT text of that edition would certainly have become the *textus receptus* of later tradition.

In 1546 and 1549, the humanist and printer *Robert Estienne (Stephanus)* published in Paris two editions of the NT which in fact were nothing but an adaptation of the editions by Cisneros and Erasmus. The third edition of 1550 (regia) faithfully follows the text of the fifth edition of Erasmus and in the margin places readings from the Complutensian edition and manuscripts largely from the royal Library of Paris. The fourth edition of 1551 introduced the division of the text into verses, copied from then onwards in every edition of the NT.

Estienne's edition was the basis for two other editions: by the Frenchman *Theodore of Beza*, with ten editions between 1565 and 1611, the edition by the brothers *Bonaventure and Abraham Elzevier* in *Leiden* (The Netherlands) in 1624. In 1623, the same Elzevier brothers produced an edition which from then onwards was considered as the *textus receptus* of the Greek NT. Only in Britain was the Estienne edition of 1550 considered the *textus receptus*, used in the *London Polyglot* edited by *Walton* in 657. As well as the Greek text and the Latin Vulgate text, this Polyglot included the texts of the Peshitta, Ethiopic, Arabic and Persian versions (in the gospels). A Syriac version filled the gaps in the Peshitta of the NT text. Each of the versions was accompanied by its Latin translation. In 1675, J. Fell published an edition which also included the texts of the Coptic and Gothic versions.

J. Mill's edition of 1707, also based like previous editions on Estienne's, includes 30,000 variants, with a critical assessment on their value. Mill was the first to realise the importance of the ancient versions and the quotations in the Fathers for critical study of the NT text.

J.A. Bengel's edition, completed in Tübingen in 1734, started the gradual disuse of the *textus receptus*. However, this edition failed to include readings not already known in previous editions. In 1751-52 *J.J. Wettstein* published an edition marked by an enormous amount of material, including quotations from Greek and Latin classics as well as from Talmudic and rabbinic writings in some way connected with the corresponding biblical passages. Wettstein was the first to use capital letters to denote uncial manuscripts and Arabic numbers for the minuscules. Other editions worth mentioning are those by J.J. Griesbach (1775-77), D.F. Matthaei (1982-88) and J.M.A. Scholz (1830-36).

III. MODERN CRITICAL EDITIONS

C. Lachman was the pioneer of textual criticism of the NT and of classical literature. He was the first to break with the tradition of the *textus receptus*. His edition of 1831, based on old manuscripts, attempted to establish the text of the NT as it was known in the 4th cent. The work completed by S.P. Tregeles (1857-1872) was also a model of critical exactness in this respect.

L.F.K. Tischendorf published no fewer than 24 editions of the NT. The most important, *Novum Testamentum Graece. Editio Octava Maior* (Leipzig 1869-1872) was based on the famous Codex Sinaiticus (ℵ) which he himself had discovered in the monastery of Sinai. He attempted to recover the «best» text, although this was not exactly the oldest. The critical apparatus of this edition continues to be *de rigueur* even today.

The edition by *B.F. Westcott and F.J.A. Hort* of 1881, *The New Testament in the Original Greek*, has enjoyed enormous authority among critics. In essence it is based on the text of the Vatican Codex.

H. von Soden published an edition which featured an enormous number of minuscule manuscripts: *Die Schriften des Neuen Testaments in ihrer ältesten erreichbaren Textgestalt hergestellt auf Grund ihrer Textgeschichte* (Göttingen 1913). Von Soden developed a new classification system for the manuscripts and a new theory of the history of the text.

Besides the important editions mentioned there are others in the form of manuals. Those by *J.M. Bover, Novi Testamenti Biblia graeca et latina* (Madrid 1943) and of *A. Merk, Novum Testamentum Graece et Latinae* (Rome 1933), provide the Greek and Latin text, as their titles indicate. The most widespread edition of the NT in Greek has been the one by E. Nestle (1898), revised in successive editions. Since the 25th edition, K. Aland has been responsible for its revision (*Novum Testamentum Graece*, Stuttgart 1963).

K. Aland, M. Black, B. M. Metzger and A. Wikgren published an «eclectic» edition (*The Greek New Testament*, London 1966) intended as a tool for translators into modern languages. The variants chosen are those which in some way affect the translation. They are smaller in number than in the Nestle edition, but the mass of witnesses used is much greater. The editors give a judgment on the value of each variant, expressing the degree of certainty which they assign their decisions on scale of greater to less (A-B-C-D). A companion volume, edited by B.M. Metzger (*A Textual Commentary on the Greek New Testament*, London 1971) explains the reasons for these decisions.

In 1967-68, the Institute for Research on the Text of the NT (*Institut für neutestamentliche Textforschung*, Münster) in collaboration with other centres of study, planned a new, large format edition: *Novi Testamenti Graeci Editio Maior*. This new project is completely justified since the manuscript documentation available today is much greater than was known in the time of Tischendorf. This documentation includes all the papyri (except for P[11], already used by Tischendorf), 80% of uncials, 95% of the minuscules and 99% of the lectionaries, as well as the text of some versions known today. Furthermore, at that time there were still no critical editions of the patristic texts. This edition accepts the existence of three textual forms: the *Koiné*, text D (a more suitable siglum than «Western text») and the Egyptian text. It attempts to go back to the text underlying these three forms, i.e., the form of the text of the NT writings in the earliest moments of its transmission.

IV. MODERN RESEARCH ON THE NT TEXT. THEORIES AND METHODS

The aim of modern criticism on the text of the NT is to locate and reconstruct the «best» text, by which is meant the closest to the original. The history of this search, from the Renaissance until today, has undergone various stages.

1. The first advance of modern criticism consisted in *realising that the original text of the NT was to be sought in Greek manuscripts, not Latin*. Between the 5th and 16th cents., the Latin text, particularly in the form of the

Vulgate, had enjoyed absolute dominance in the West. The fall of Constantinople in 1453 caused many experts in Greek to leave for the West. They took with them a large quantity of Greek manuscripts and opened the eyes of Westerners to the need for tracking down the original of the NT in the Greek MSS.

However, the text copied in the manuscripts taken from Constantinople was in fact a late mediaeval text which was quite widespread in the Byzantine East. The first printed editions reproduced these manuscripts without any differentiation between the texts. If variant readings were quoted, this did not go beyond pure decoration or as a show of learning.

Only variants of one type aroused fierce controversy at that time: when the new Greek texts brought from the East were different from the Latin text, considered as the normative text in the West. The fact that Erasmus and Estienne presumed to correct the Latin text could only provoke criticism and, for Estienne, even condemnation.

2. The next step of modern criticism consisted in *noting that the Greek text* was not only different from the Latin text of the Vulgate but *also from the text of the other ancient versions and from the text of patristic quotations*. In 1716 *Bentley* planned an edition, never actually issued, in which he established the principle of preferring the oldest manuscripts. Also, he was the first to accept the value of the ancient versions as a means of approaching the Greek text. On the other hand, *Bengel* stated the principle, according to which the *«more difficult reading»* had preference over the others. Later, it became a rule of textual criticism. Bengel also tried to classify the manuscripts into families, making a distinction between Asiatic and African. Wettstein set out a series of critical principles which included preference for the *«shortest reading»* (cf. p. 409).

3. Modern textual criticism of the NT really began with *Griesbach*, who *classified the manuscripts into three large groups*: the *Western*, very old but corrupt; the *Alexandrian* which corrected the former, and the *Constantinopolitan*, reproduced in most of the manuscripts preserved. Griesbach did not consider the evidence of individual manuscripts as important, especially in cases of agreement between the Western and Alexandrian families.

4. *C. Lachmann* was the first to break with the tradition which considered the «best» text to be the *textus receptus* of the printed bibles, based on very late manuscripts. As both a classical philologist and a scholar in Germanic studies, Lachmann established the critical principles of the *genealogical method* which has determined the progress of textual criticism right up to the present. According to Lachmann, the best text is the oldest, the one with the best genealogical tree and, in principle, the least exposed to copyists' errors.

5. *Westcott and Hort* gave the coup de grâce to the *textus receptus,* with its authority based on the criterion of majority. According to this criterion the commonest and most frequent reading in manuscript tradition had preference. However, a reading attested in many manuscripts could stem from a single manuscript which could itself be corrupt. In addition, Westcott and

Hort established the distinction between *four* different *types of text*: Syro-Byzantine, *Western, Alexandrian and neutral.* The relations among these text forms can be represented in the following diagram

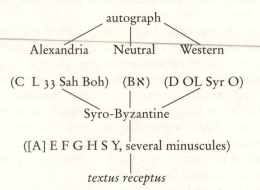

autograph

Alexandria   Neutral   Western

(C L 33 Sah Boh)   (B ℵ)   (D OL Syr O)

Syro-Byzantine

([A] E F G H S Y, several minuscules)

textus receptus

6. *B. H. Streeter* (1874-1934) never succeeded in publishing a critical text but he developed the idea of classifying the manuscripts into groups of «*local texts*» according to the various geographical centres and the different local churches: Alexandria in Egypt, Antioch in Syria, Caesarea in Palestine, Carthage in Africa and Italy and Gaul in Western Europe. The text from Byzantium, which is reproduced in most of the uncial and minuscule manuscripts, probably represents the text of the Lucianic recension and combines earlier texts, until it resulted in the *textus receptus*:

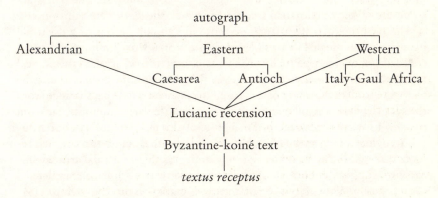

autograph

Alexandrian   Eastern   Western

Caesarea   Antioch   Italy-Gaul Africa

Lucianic recension

Byzantine-koiné text

textus receptus

H. Lietzmann (1875-1942) distinguished *three families in the Pauline letters*: the *koiné*, the most recent; the Western, of great antiquity, and the Egyptian, often the most primitive. In any case it is always indispensable to examine each and every one of the variant readings and to judge the probability of each based on internal evidence.

7. With *Burkitt, internal criticism* of the variants acquired greater importance than the codicological study of the manuscripts and their grouping into families. There were various reasons for this change of direction. Since all the manuscripts were corrupt, a sort of pure sacred text could not exist in

the best manuscripts. On the other hand, most of the variants known originated in the first two centuries of Christianity, before the period of the great codices. Furthermore, the application of the genealogical method to study of the NT text does not permit more precise conclusions since the variants were due more to deliberate change than to accidental error.

At the end of this long process and since the time of *H. von Soden*, at the beginning of the 20th cent., it is accepted that the genealogical method is not adequate to resolve all the problems of textual criticism in the NT. Accordingly, there is a trend towards an *«eclectic» method*, considering the best text is the one which, after a detailed study of all the variants preserved and the application of the rules of internal criticism, provides the highest probability of corresponding to the original form of the text.

Von Soden distinguished three recensions: Jerusalemite (I) by Origen, Egyptian by Hesychius (H) and Byzantine or *koiné* (K) by Lucian. The first corresponds to the Western text of Westcott-Hort, the second to the neutral and Alexandrian text and the third to the Syrian text. Having reconstructed these three recensions, Von Soden tried by means of internal criticism to reconstruct their archetype, the text known as I-K-H. Von Soden's work received much harsh criticism. It is very complicated, especially for those beginning to study text criticism of the NT.

Textual criticism, therefore, has to examine all the variants preserved and to select the one with the highest probability of corresponding to the original form of the text. For this it has first to reconstruct the texts which at any time and in each region were known by the Christian community of that time and place. The textual critic, therefore, has to know and take into account the whole of Christian tradition in which the texts were transmitted.

The most important variants are those due to corrections of a doctrinal nature. Also, those due to a whole range of editorial work, influenced by factors of a political nature such as the triumph of Christianity, and theological factors such as anti-heretical apologetics. The editing and transmission of the text was also influenced by countless circumstances. These could range from the geographical and linguistic isolation of a particular community, far from the new forms of text developed in a great city, to interference by church authority which made its weight felt much more in these cities than in such remote places. All this accumulation of data forces the NT textual critic, while carrying out his specific task of philologist and text-restorer, to complete all the work on the history of Christianity and Christian theology (cf. p. 348).

V.   MANUSCRIPTS OF THE NEW TESTAMENT

1.   *Papyri*

Most of the papyri found in Egypt are not literary texts but receipts, letters, commercial documents, etc., although papyri with classical texts have also been found. A. Deissmann emphasised the importance of studying the papyri in order to know the *koiné* language as well as the ordinary way of life in the Greek and Roman periods.

Up to the last century only 9 papyri of the NT were known. At present, 98 papyri have been catalogued, including some talismans and lectionaries which are of no interest for the history and criticism of the text. The papyri cover about 40% of the NT text. Almost all of them come from Egypt and they were also copied there. They date from the 2nd to the 8th cent., but more than half are from the 3rd and 4th cents., earlier therefore than the formation of the textual types of the NT.

Owing to their antiquity the papyri are of enormous importance for NT textual criticism. However, in many cases the fragments preserved are, tiny or barely usable. The two most famous collections of papyri are named Chester Beatty (P45-47, now in Dublin) and Martin Bodmer (P66, P72, P74 P75, in Geneva). The most important papyri, with the type of text they provide indicated, are as follows:

P45: from the beginning of the second half of the 3rd cent. The 30 leaves preserved contain fragments from the 4 gospels and from Acts. The text of Mark is close to the Caesarean text; in the other gospels it lies between the Alexandrian and the Western.

P46: dated towards 200 CE. It had 140 leaves of which 86 are preserved, and contained the text of the Pauline letters in a different sequence (Rom. Heb, 1-2 Cor, Eph, Gal, Phlp, Col and 1-2 Thess). The pastoral letters were certainly missing. The text is closer to the Alexandrian than the Western. It is therefore a witness of a «neutral» text of the Pauline letters which antedates by a century and a half all the other preserved witnesses of this type of text.

P47: comes from the last third of the 3rd cent. It agrees more with Sinaiticus than with any other manuscript, although it retains marked independence.

P52: dated towards 125 CE. It is the oldest known fragment of the NT, very close in date to the redaction of John's gospel, about 90-95. It testifies to the spread of this gospel in Egypt at the beginning of the 2nd cent. It is now in the John Rylands Library, Manchester.

P66: comes from about 200 CE. It contains the text of John, chaps. 1-14, with few gaps; chaps. 15-21 are in a worse condition. It is a mixed text, with Alexandrian and Western elements.

P72: of the 3rd cent., with the text of Acts and the catholic letters, very eclectic and close to the late text.

P75: dated about 200 CE. It is the oldest copy known of Lk and one of the oldest of Jn. Its text is very similar to the Vatican Codex which makes this form of the text go back to the 2nd cent. and shows that the neutral text did not undergo recension in the 4th cent.

2.   *Manuscripts in Uncial Characters*

The name «uncial» is given to manuscripts written on parchment with a type of letter derived from the majuscules (capital letters) used in inscriptions (cf. p. 103). Up to the 9th cent., only uncial characters were used in manuscripts of the NT. They continued to be used for some time in copying lectionaries.

268 uncial manuscripts of the NT have come down to us. They are known

by Arabic numbers, with a zero prefix. Some are also given the Latin, Greek or Hebrew letters by which they were identified before the numerical reference system was introduced (01=ℵ, 02=A, 03=B, etc.). Owing to their antiquity they were considered as the most important source for study of the NT. After the discovery of the papyri, which are earlier than the uncials, and once the appropriate analysis of internal criticism was complete, there was in fact no course except to accept that the text of the uncial manuscripts contains mistakes requiring correction.

The more important uncial manuscripts, with comments on the type of text they represent, are as follows:

01=ℵ *Codex Sinaiticus (S)*, written in the first half of the 4th cent. It contains the OT and the NT as well as the *Letter of Barnabas* and the *Shepherd of Hermas*. There are four columns per page (43 cm x 37,8 cm) except in the poetic books, where every page has only two columns. Three different consecutive hands copied the manuscript and until the 13th cent. new correctors inserted various changes into the text. Tischendorf discovered it in the library of the Monastery of St. Catherine in Sinai. It was given as a present to the Tsar of Russia and later acquired by the British Museum in 1953. It is one of the important witnesses of the NT. Its text is generally of the Alexandrian type, although there are Western elements. Notable among its characteristics are the placing of the end of Mk in 16:8, the omission of the adulterous woman (Jn 7:52-8:11) and the location of the doxology in Rom after 16:23.

02=A, *Alexandrian Codex* (in the British Museum) from the beginning of the 5th cent. It contained the whole of the Greek Bible, plus the first and second letters of Clement and the *Psalms of Solomon*. Passages from Mt, Jn and 1 Cor are missing. It is written in two columns per page. It is the oldest witness of the Byzantine text of the gospels. For the rest of the NT it represents the Alexandrian text type. It is the best available witness of the text of Ap.

03=B, *Vatican Codex* (in the Vatican Library), from the early 4th century. It contained the complete text of the Greek Bible with the exception of the *Prayer of Manasseh* and the books of Maccabees. As it is now the text has lost passages from Gn, 2 Sm, Pss, Heb, the pastoral letters and Ap. It had 920 leaves, with two columns per leaf in the poetic texts and three in the others.

04=C, *Ephraim rescriptus* or palimpsest codex of St. Ephraim (Paris) from the beginning of the 5th cent. The palimpsest on which it has been preserved dates to the 12th cent. Originally, the codex contained the whole Bible, but the OT preserved the text of Jb, Pr, Qoh, Wis, Sir and Song, and parts of all the NT books except for 2 Thess and 2 Jn. It has 209 leaves, with one column per leaf. Its text, reconstructed by Tischendorf, shows a mixed character, but in general agrees with the Byzantine text.

05=*Codex Bezae* (Cambridge). It is a Greek and Latin codex, the oldest preserved bilingual codex. It dates to the 5th or 6th cent. It contains the gospels and Acts. The gospels are in the so-called Western sequence: Mt-Jn-Lk-Mk. It had 510 leaves or more, with the Greek text on the lefthand page, Latin on the right. The text is very special since it has numerous additional words and complete phrases. In Acts, the text is one tenth longer than in the other manuscript traditions.

06=Dp, *Claromontanus Codex* from the 6th cent. It contains the Pauline letters (as the letter *p* indicates).

022=N, *Codex Purpureus Petropolitanus* (St. Petersburg), its most striking feature being the de luxe form of the codex, hence its name.

040=*XII*, *Codex Zacynthius* (from the Greek island of Zakinthos). It is on an 8th (or 6th?) cent. palimpsest. It contains the text of Lk in an Alexandrian type text. It is the oldest of the manuscripts which contain a *catena* or commentary formed of patristic quotations.

3.   *Manuscripts in Minuscule Letters*

Manuscripts written in cursive or minuscule characters are called minuscules. Their spread covers the period from the 9th cent. up to the invention of printing. As in the case of the uncials, the oldest manuscripts were written more carefully and with less embellishment. Today, 2,792 minuscule manuscripts are known, denoted by Arabic numerals. Since they are not so old as the uncials, for some time it was thought that their text was also remote from the original. In fact most of them have the Byzantine or *koiné* text. However, this is not always the case. The factor which determines the value of the readings of a text is not the *antiquity of the manuscript* but the quality of the *archetype used* for copies. For example, MS 33, which dates to the 9th cent., has an Alexandrian text of great value.

Manuscripts which have associated readings comprise a «family». Several *families of minuscule manuscripts* are known. Family 1, comprising MSS 1, 118, 131,209 (from the 12th-14th cents.) has a text close to codex Θ and reflects a Caesarean type of text. Family 13 or the Ferrara group (from the 11th-14th cents.) with three sub-groups headed by MSS 13, 69 and 983 respectively, also shows Caesarean affinities, which in fact enabled this type of text to be identified. The archetype comes from the East and was brought to southern Italy. That region underwent a period of cultural splendour under the Normans and Greek monks fleeing from the Moslems found refuge there.

Other minuscules worth mentioning are numbers 28, 33, 61, 69, 81, 157, 383, 565, 579, 614, 2344, the family comprising MSS 1678, 1778 and 2080, and the family made up by the MSS 1016, 1841, 2582 and 2626, etc. Notable for their external appearance are MS 16, written in four colours according to content, MS 461, which is tiny and also the oldest to contain a specific date (835), and the large-sized *Codex Gigas* or «giant codex».

4.   *Lectionaries*

Very early on, the Christian liturgy selected several passages from the gospels and from the rest of the NT, with the sole exception of the Apocalypse. These passages were read in the celebrations of each day of the year, and especially on Sunday feast days. There are about 2,193 lectionary manuscripts catalogued, none earlier than the 9th cent. The oldest were written in uncial characters which were still in use up to the 11th cent. for lectionaries. They are denoted by the letter *l* followed by the appropriate number (*l* 1, *l* 2, *l* 3, etc.). Recent research has emphasised the value of the lectionaries for the textual study of the NT. However, ostraca and amulets which contain brief fragments of the NT text, have no critical value since there is no check on their text.

VI. VERSIONS OF THE NEW TESTAMENT

In ancient times the translation of books into other languages was not common. The few translations made were very free and did not allow any precision regarding the text of the original used for the translation. The translation of the LXX was the first to break with this model of translating. The versions made from the LXX followed the example of that version.

Christians in the new countries through which Christianity spread very soon felt the need to have translations into their own languages available. At first the translations were very literal. This gives them high critical value, for they permit recognition of the characteristics of the original text from which the translation was made. The approximate date and the area of spread of the various translations are also so many indicators of the form of Greek text used in each period and in each area. The importance of the versions for textual criticism, then, is rooted in antiquity and in their literal nature. The oldest versions are the Latin and the Syriac (on the origin and nature of each version cf. pp. 352 and 358).

VII. PATRISTIC QUOTATIONS

Besides the biblical manuscripts and the versions, the quotations from the NT in commentaries, sermons and other writings of the Fathers provide such a wealth of material that it virtually spans the whole NT. The importance of patristic quotations lies in the fact that the text quoted in them is often older than most of the biblical manuscripts preserved. On the other hand, the quotations of the Fathers allows identification of the type of text used in a particular period and in a particular area. They also provide knowledge about the origin and range of spread of a particular manuscript. For example, the quotations by Cyprian of Carthage (c. 250) agree with the text of MS *k* of the OL. It can then be deduced that this manuscript, from the 4th or 5th cent, goes back to a copy which was in circulation in North Africa until 250 (cf. p 351).

To be able to make use of the quotations by the Fathers, it is first necessary to determine the original text of the patristic writings, for these underwent a process of corruption and revision comparable to the biblical manuscripts. On the other hand, in each case it is necessary to determine whether the quotations are literal or paraphrases, made from memory or taken straight from a biblical manuscript. More recent study has shown that quoting from memory was not so common as used to be thought. It could be that quotations with texts that do not correspond to the manuscripts known today belong to different and older texts.

Of special interest are cases where the same author, such as Origen, cites different texts or compares different readings. Jerome notes three variants of the text of 1 Cor 15:15, one known only in Latin manuscripts (*Epist.* 119). Boismard draws attention to the importance of patristic quotations through which a shorter form of the gospel texts can be known.

The Fathers or Church writers who have transmitted the greatest number of NT quotations include Marcion (†c. 150-160), Tatian (†c. 170), Justin (†c. 165), Irenaeus (†202), Clement of Alexandria (†212), Tertullian (†220), Cyprian (†258), Hippolytus of Rome (†235), Origen (†253/4), Ephraem Syrus (†373), Lucifer of Cagliari (†370/1), Ambrose of Milan (†397), Chrysostom of Constantinople (†407), Jerome (†419/20), Cyril of Alexandria (†444), Theodore of Mopsuestia (†428), Augustine (†430), etc.

VIII. CHARACTERISTICS AND WITNESSES OF THE VARIOUS TEXT TYPES

It is important to know the characteristics of each type of text, the class of readings each usually provides and the type of mistakes to be found in them.

1. The *Alexandrian* or *«neutral»* type is usually considered as the best and most trustworthy witness. In general it is shorter than the others and has not undergone the grammatical and stylistic revision shown by the Byzantine text and to a lesser extent by the Caesarean. It is no longer possible to repeat the statement (Bousset) according to whom it is text with a recension dating to the 4th cent., a period from which the best witnesses come, the Vatican (B) and the Sinaiticus (ℵ). The discovery of papyri (P^{66}) and (P^{75}) which are copies from the close of the 2nd cent. or the beginning of the 3rd, proves that the Alexandrian type goes back to a 2nd cent. archetype.

Witnesses of the Alexandrian text type (manuscripts, books or writings by authors marked with an asterisk (*) belong only partially to the text-type indicated; the brackets indicate that the manuscript has a mixed text) are:
   a. Proto-Alexandrian Text: P^{45} (in Acts) P^{46} P^{66} P^{75} ℵ B Sahidic*, Clement of Alexandria, Origen* and most of the papyrus fragments of the Pauline epistles.
   b. Later Alexandrian Text:
– Gospels: (C) L T W* (X) Z (in Mark) X Ψ (in Mk, Lk* and Jn) 33 579 892 1241, Bohairic version.
– Acts: P50 A (C) Ψ 33 81 104 326
– Pauline Letters: A (C) 1 33 81 104 326 1739
– Catholic Letters: P^{20} P^{23} P^{72} P^{74} A (C) Ψ 3 81 104 326 1739
– Apocalypse: A (C) 1006 1611 1854 2053 2344. P^{47} and ℵ are of lesser value.

2. The *Western type* is so called because it is a text attested in Western sources such as OL, in quotations of the Latin Fathers up to 400 and in the Greek and Latin Manuscripts Bezae and Claromontanus. However, this form of text was recognised later in quotations by the Greek Fathers, including those

from the 2nd cent. such as Justin and Irenaeus as well as Marcion and Tatian, in P[38] and P[48] and in other sources from the East. It is the oldest known form of the NT text. Some critics therefore considered that the other text forms are due to reworking this Western text. Others think that this text has lost its value because of the many additions, omissions and harmonisations it exhibits.

The Western text of Acts is very interesting and very different in character from the actual Western text of the gospels and Paul. It is roughly a tenth longer than the Alexandrian text and, generally, more lively and colourful than the alternative short text, which is sometimes more enigmatic. Sometimes, it is also the shortest. For example, in 28:6 it omits the words «blood and fire and smoke». In the closing chapters of Lk it also has important omissions such as 24:6 where it leaves out the angel's words «He is not here but has risen».

Westcott-Hort and Kenyon undervalued this text which they considered to have been interpolated in the 1st and 2nd cents. According to Ropes it is a revision of the Alexandrian text. For Clark the relationship is the reverse. Some authors have emphasised the Semitic colouring of the Western text (Black, Torrey). The more eclectic schools favour this text more (Kilpatrick) although the Nestle-Aland edition and *The Greek New Testament* are against it.

According to Boismard, Luke wrote a first redaction which is reflected in the Western text. Years later, Luke himself revised his work for style and content. The Alexandrian text, purer in form than the extant text, is the result of the combination of both those redactions by Luke.

Witnesses of the Western Text:
– Gospels: D W (in Mk 1:1-5:30 and Jn 1:1-5:11) 0171 (Lk 22:44-56.61-63), OL, Syro-Sinaiticus, Syrocuretanian*, the first/early Latin Fathers, Tatian's *Diatessaron*.
– Acts: P[20] P[38] P[48] D E 383 614 1739, the earliest Latin Fathers, Ephrem's Commentary (preserved in Armenian and, in part, in Syriac).
– Pauline Letters: the Greek-Latin bilinguals D F G, the Greek Fathers to the end of the 3rd cent., manuscripts of the OL, the older Latin Fathers, the Syrian Fathers up to 450.
– For the Apocalypse no specifically Western witnesses have been identified.

3. The *Byzantine type* or *koiné* is the one most attested in the minuscule manuscripts. Through the edition by Erasmus it entered into the *textus receptus*. It is related to the Lucianic recension (K. Aland). Characteristic are the tendency towards a longer text and to double readings, correction of style, the addition of explanatory elements, modernisation of the vocabulary, etc. This all fits the intention of producing an elegant text which reads fluently. The discovery of papyri P[45], P[46] and P[66], which have readings known only through the Byzantine text, has proved the value of this text. It does not justify, however, the attempts to make this type an earlier text.

Witnesses of the Byzantine and *koiné* text (also called Syrian or Antiochene):
– Gospels: A E F G H K P S V W (in Mt and in Lk 8:13-24:53) π ψ (partly in Lk and Jn) 3 and most of the minuscules, the Gothic version and the Peshitta.
– Acts: H L P 049 and most of the minuscules.

4. The *Caesarean type* was discovered later than those above, after study of the group of manuscripts from Ferrara or family 1. It presents a smaller number of peculiar readings and has affinities with the Alexandrian and Western texts.

Witnesses of the Caesarean text:
– pre-Caesarean: P⁴⁵ W (Mk 5:31-16:20) 28
– Caesarean: Θ 565 700, the Armenian and Georgian versions, Origen*, Eusebius, Cyril of Jerusalem.
Apart from the gospels, no Caesarean text has been identified.

BIBLIOGRAPHY (cf. pp. 414-415)

6

Ancient Versions of the Bible: Old and New Testaments

Having discussed matters connected with the texts of the OT and NT in their respective original languages, as well as what concerns the versions in Greek and Aramaic of the OT, here, the ancient versions which translate the OT and NT together are described and discussed. The growing number of Christians unable to understand Greek and speaking other languages, especially in the frontier zones of the Empire, made inevitable a process of translating the Bible, OT and NT into these languages. In respect of Latin, Syriac and Coptic, this process had already begun around 180 CE.

The *history* of the ancient versions of the Bible is, in fact, a history of the development of Christianity and of the language, theology, liturgy, etc., of the various churches and peoples making up the *Oikouménē*.

The *origin* of some of these ancient versions presents problems, like those just noted for explaining the origin of the LXX version (cf. p. 306). The question consists in knowing whether the known text of each of these versions comes from a single ancient version or whether it is the final precipitate of various versions already in existence. The dilemma which has to be resolved is as follows: was there a single original version which underwent successive revisions to give rise to the variety of texts transmitted, or did different translations co-exist from the beginning which, by means of a process of unification converged into a more uniform text, although not without variants. Only in the case of the Gothic and Slavonic versions is it known for certain that there was a single version right from the start.

As for the *critical value* of these versions, modern criticism tends to be divided into two movements. One tends to grant great value to these versions for reconstructing the original texts of the OT and NT. The other, instead, tends to deprive them of critical value and to consider them more as testimony of the exegesis and dominant theological ideas of the time when the versions were made.

I.   THE LATIN VERSIONS

Up to the 3rd cent CE, the language of the Roman Church continued to be Greek. Clement of Rome, Hermas, Hippolytus and Irenaeus of Lyons all wrote in Greek. In North Africa, a Tertullian could write just as easily in Greek or Latin. *Christian literature in Latin* originated in the 2nd cent. in North Africa and not in the Roman metropolis.

Study of the epigraphic material preserved enables the population movements of this period to be known. 74% of Jewish inscriptions from Rome are written in Greek (413 in Greek and 137 in Latin). Until the beginning of the 4th cent., the epitaphs of popes were also written in Greek. Many Christian burial inscriptions from the West refer to the origin of the person buried as being somewhere in the East. When the extensive slave-trade of the East ended, Latin gained ground among the lower classes, while the upper classes lost contact with Greek culture.

There is not enough information to assume that biblical texts in Latin originated in Jewish communities. Such communities were very oriental in outlook which did not favour interest in having a Latin version available. On the other hand, there is no reference at all to the use of Latin in synagogue worship. However, in the period of Tertullian, some Jewish communities in North Africa definitely spoke Latin. It has to be assumed that the Latin version of the Pentateuch really did have a Jewish origin.

The Latin Bible is of supreme *importance* for two main reasons: the first is textual, the second exegetical. It contributes to knowledge of the oldest Greek text and even at times of Hebrew variants unknown in the remainder of manuscript tradition. It has also had a fundamental role in the history of the Bible from the beginnings of Western Christianity up to the present century. The Latin Bible has had a decisive influence on the history of Latin and on European languages and literature. This influence has not been confined to literature in Romance languages but has also affected Saxon and Germanic languages. It has also coined the most important terms of Western theology and numerous expressions and formulas of the Latin liturgy.

1.   *The Old Latin*

The term «Old Latin» does not refer to a single and complete translation of the Bible into Latin but denotes all the translations prior to Jerome's *Vulgate* (end of the 4th cent.). It might be the case, however, that some stages of the text of the OL are later than Jerome.

A.   ORIGIN, LANGUAGE, CHARACTER AND HISTORY

Christian literature in Latin had its beginnings in Africa at the close of the 2nd cent., with Tertullian. Tertullian's writings already contain many biblical quotations. However, these quotations cannot be attributed with certainty to a Latin translation in existence at that time. A few years later, *Cyprian of Carthage* (†258) in his books *Ad Quirinum* (248-9, a work also known as

Testimonia) and *Ad Fortunatum*, provides numerous biblical quotations which are lengthy and faithfully transmitted. Cyprian was already using a translation known in his time and its text agrees substantially with later manuscripts.

This version is known as the «*African*» *version* not only because it has certain linguistic idiosyncrasies requiring it to be located in Africa, or because it reflects a supposed African dialect, nor for the possible African origin of the translator, but simply because this was the Latin translation circulating in Carthage from a period before 250. There is no known documentation testifying to the existence of other versions in Latin in the rest of the Christian world.

The manuscript tradition of the OL has reached us in very much as fragments. In addition, the manuscripts which preserve part of this version are not very old, although it has always to be taken into account that manuscripts of recent date can preserve quite ancient texts very faithfully. The text of some books has reached the present day in a form very close to the text used by Cyprian; this is the case in the books of Wis and Ben Sira as well as deuterocanonical books such as Mc and Bar.

The African text underwent continual adaptations to the liturgical vocabulary of the various places where it spread. Towards the end of the 4th cent., different *recensions known as «European»* were already circulating in Italy, Gaul and Spain. The differences among these recensions should not create the impression that different original translations existed, since they all retain traces of the archetypal African text. This is particularly certain in the case of books which underwent a slow process of development, such as Pr and even Gn.

Saint Augustine complained in his time that, given the enormous spread of Greek manuscripts and the knowledge that Latin-speaking Christians had of Greek, many believed themselves authorised to insert corrections into the Latin text so much so that there seemed to be as many versions as codices. This situation led to a state of such textual confusion (= *vitiotisissima varietas*) that it soon became intolerable (however, cf. p. 399)

The ancient version was written in the *vernacular* of the people, a far cry from the literary language of the time. The literary character of the OL is attested by: the frequent carelessness in pronunciation (*famis* for *fames*, Gn 41:57), the use of vulgar or late Latin terms (*manducare* for *comedere*, Hos 9:3), Greek loanwords (*agonia*, Sir 4:33; *zelus*, Wis 5:18), the imitations of Greek (*paranymphus*, Gn 26:26), the Aramaic loanwords (*mammona*, Mt 6:24), the grammatical or syntactical deviations in respect of classical Latin (*magis bonus*, Wis 8:20), the constructions introduced by *quod*, *quia*, instead of the classical construction with accusative and infinitive (*et vidit deus lucem quia bona est*, Gn 1:4), etc.

Sometimes the *Greek loanwords* take on new connotations in Latin. Thus, the Greek term *ággelos*, which translates Hebrew *mal'ak*, «messenger», is translated by the Greek loan-word *angelus*, but restricts the meaning of the term to «heavenly messenger». To refer to an earthly messenger the Latin text uses the term *nuntius*. At times the translator is forced to decide which was the term and its meaning in a particular case. For example, the OL confers on Haggai the title of *angelus* whereas the Vulgate recognises only the mission of *nuntius* (Hg 1:13).

Frequently, a similar fluctuation can be seen between a Greek loanword and a Latin term with different shades of meaning: *diabolus - adversarius*; *synagoga - congregatio*; *eleemosyna - iustitia*. Some Latin terms acquire new meaning owing to biblical influence: *fides*, «trust» also means «religious faith» (Hb 2:4); *gentes*, «nations», is applied to «pagans» (Ps 79:10); *peccatum*, «failing» also means «sin» or «fault» (Gn 18:20); *testamentum*, «will», «testament», means «covenant» (Gn 17:2); *saeculum*, «generation», means «eternity» (Ps 37:27).

The history of the OL is the history of a *constant and continuous revision of its text* to adapt it to Greek texts which differ from those used in the primitive version as well as to the tastes, style and vocabulary changing with the development of Latin. For example, the term *cenapura* was replaced by *parasceue* («Easter/passover»), *sacramentum* by *mysterium*, *itaque* by *ergo* and *igitur*, etc. African vocabulary was replaced by European vocabulary. This allows manuscripts of the OL to be classified into two groups: the *afra* version and the *itala* version.

All the factors mentioned (numerous text forms, textual corruption, careless language and style, etc.) were determinative in making the need felt in the 4th cent. for completely revising the old version and making a new Latin version. From this century on, the *Vulgate* version of Jerome, a mix of old revision and modern translation, gradually replaced the old version. However, the manuscripts of the OL remained in circulation until the close of the 8th cent.

Among the few *preserved manuscripts of the OL* of the OT there is a copy of the Heptateuch of the Visigoth tradition from the second half of the 6th cent. The very conservatism of the liturgical tradition explains the fact that copies of the Psalter are the most numerous, and palimpsests and papyri are included among them. Until very recently, local recensions of the Psalter continued to be used in Rome, Milan and Toledo.

The textual tradition of the OL has often been transmitted together with Jerome's *Vulgate*. This is the case for manuscripts preserved in Spain, with important remains of the OL. A palimpsest bible of the 8th cent. of the Cathedral of León (Cat. 15) contains text from Mc and 4 Ezra as well as from Acts and the catholic epistles. Complutensis 1, which comes from the South of the Peninsula, contains the Visigothic Psalter and Song, plus other books. A family of Spanish bibles reproduces in the margin, in the form of glosses, a considerable number of readings from the OL gathered from very different sources. Among them the *Codex Gothicus Legionensis* deserves special mention; it is a manuscript of the Vulgate from the close of the 10th cent. with marginal readings taken from the OL (Morano).

The *quotations from the Fathers* also comprise an important source for the text of the OL. These quotations are often very free, but sometimes they are instead very faithful to the original. This is the case for the work *Speculum de Divinis Scripturis* of Pseudo-Augustine or the works of Lucifer of Cagliari. Still indispensable is the collection of quotations compiled by P. Sabatier in his work *Bibliorum sacrorum latinae versiones antiquae seu Vetus Itala* (1745-49).

In 1949 in the Benedictine monastery of Beuron, publication of the *critical edition* of this version began. Up to now the volumes corresponding to Gn and Wis have appeared, and for the NT, the letters of Paul (from Eph to Phm) and the catholic epistles. Still in preparation are the volumes of Is (Gryson), Sir (Thiele) and Heb. Because they are so many and the quoted text so long, particularly important are the quotations by Cyprian, Lucifer of Cagliari, Tyconius, Jerome, Augustine and some florilegia such as the *Liber de diuinis scripturis* (or *Speculum*, a pseudo-Augustinian work).

B.   CRITICAL VALUE

The Old Latin was the Bible of the Latin Fathers, who in general did not follow the principle of *veritas hebraica* at all.

The textual tradition represented by the Latin and Coptic versions is much richer and more varied than the Greek tradition. The OL translates a Greek text of the 2nd cent., earlier than the Origen recension. It supposes that its text is very old and so has considerable critical value.

Sometimes the OL preserves its own readings which have great critical value. For example, in Gn 31:46 the clause which in MT, LXX and Tg is «Jacob said...» in the OL has «Laban» as subject, a reading supported by the context.

In the *historical books* the OL text represents a proto-Lucianic Greek text, very close to the original Greek version, which reflects a Hebrew text which differs from the one which has reached us through the masoretic tradition.

In the book of *Ez* the OL text and the text of a single Greek manuscript (967) are the only witnesses preserved which show that the order of chapters 37-39 according to the MT is not original; the oldest text followed the sequence 38-39-37 and omitted 36:23c-28.

Similarly, in the book of *Dn* the OL reproduces the chapter sequence 7 - 8 - 5 - 6 characteristic of the old Greek.

Even more important is the case of *Sir*. Here the OL preserves the original sequence of the text whereas the whole Greek manuscript tradition places the text of 33:13b-36:10 before 30:25-33:15a (cf. p. 401).

In the book of *Job*, the Latin text and the Coptic reflects a better and older Greek textual form of which no trace has remained in the Greek manuscript tradition (Bogaert)(cf. p. 399).

In *Tob* the OL provides a longer textual form, also preserved in the Greek in *Sinaiticus*. The antiquity and originality of this textual form seem confirmed by the Aramaic fragments of this book which have been found in Qumran (Milik).

The OL of *Est* is the only surviving witness of a lost Greek text form (Schildenberger). Several fragments of Aramaic 4QprotoEster published by Milik will give new impetus to study of the book of Esther and its old Latin text. This is a text which combines narratives and sources like those of the various known versions of Esther and agrees surprisingly enough with the OL text (cf. p. 399).

Similarly in the case of *Ezr* (Esdras B in LXX) some OL readings are witness to a lost Greek text (Bogaert).

Thus, the OL goes back to the oldest levels of the Greek textual tradition and at times is a witness of exceptional value to the oldest Hebrew tradition. Textual criticism has to trace «the oldest witnesses» which, starting with the «Old Latin» text lead to the «Old Greek» and ultimately to the «Old Hebrew» (Trebolle, cf. p. 14).

As for the *text of the NT*, 32 incomplete manuscripts of the gospels have been preserved, 12 of Acts, 4 (with some fragments) of the Pauline letters and a single manuscript (with other fragments) of Ap. The dates of these manuscripts run from the 4th to the 13th cents. The OL reflects and is witness to a Western Greek text. The African text of OL has greater differences from the Greek than the European text. The OL of NT is also marked by its literalism and its popular speech and style.

The manuscripts of the OL are given minuscule letters of the Latin alphabet. The most important manuscripts of the African text are *e*, *h* and *k*. The last mentioned was copied in about 400 and so is earlier than the translation of the NT *Vulgate*. Its text is closely related to the quotations by Cyprian. Among manuscripts representing the European text are *a*, *b*, *c*, *d*, *j*, *f*, etc.

2.   *The Vulgate*

From the 16th cent. the name *Vulgate* was given to the translation made by St Jerome towards the end of the 4th cent. From the Carolingian period it became the «divulgated» and official version of the Latin Church. The text of the old version (OL), in common use at the time, even though in a coarse and unpretentious style, had fallen into a state of irritating corruption. Reaction against this situation combined with the growing appreciation for the Alexandrian Greek text and the great Greek uncial manuscripts of the 4th century, which were better suited to the more refined circumstances of the period, prepared the ground for Jerome to take on the work of translating which later was to become the «divulgated» version or *«Vulgate»*.

A.   JEROME'S TRANSLATION

Jerome was born in 347 or a little later. He is the *vir trilinguis* (triple-tongued man) *par excellence*. During 360-367 he had a good literary education in Rome. Later (374-380) he visited the best exegetical schools of the Greek Orient and learnt Hebrew from Jewish rabbis. In 382 he returned to Rome. There he made an arrangement with a Jew who provided him with texts purloined secretly from the synagogue. The opinion is not correct according to which towards 382 pope Damascus officially entrusted Jerome with making a complete translation of the bible. The assignment referred at most to a translation of the gospels (Gribomont).

Jerome spent the last part of his life (385-420) in Bethlehem. He knew the library which Origen and Eusebius had formed in Caesarea and there he could consult Origen's famous Hexaplar.

Jerome had an excellent knowledge of Hebrew, in spite of opinion to the contrary (Burkitt). He frequently consulted Jewish scholars and he himself recommended doing so in cases of doubt (*sicubi dubitas, Hebraeos interroga, Epistulae* 112,20). For Jerome, Hebrew was the *matrix omnium linguarum* (6,730). He even considered the vocabulary of Greek and Latin to be poorer than Hebrew (*propter... ad comparationem linguae Hebraeae, tam Graeci quam Latini sermonis pauperiem, Epistulae* 4,488). Probably Jerome also learned some Aramaic or Syriac (*Epistulae* 17,2; *Prologus in Job*). Even in some of the cases where Jerome makes some kind of mistake, he is only intentionally following current interpretations of his time, as reflected in contemporary Jewish commentaries. A famous example is the translation of *qeren* by «horn» instead of «ray» (Ex 34:29). This interpretation gave rise to representing Moses with a horn on his forehead as in Michelangelo's well-known sculpture. However, it is not a mistake. Jerome could well have translated in accordance with the LXX text («glorified»). However, he chose an etymological interpretation, already to be found in Aquila, which confers «horns» on Moses as a sign of power and majesty (*Epistulae* 6,321; 4,68).

Jerome's work did not follow a systematic plan or a consistent method. He completed a first version of the Psalter from the Greek text, which was lost later. It cannot be identical with the Roman Psalter used in Italy during the Middle Ages and the Basilica of St. Peter in Rome until very recently (De Bruyne). The Gallican Psalter, given this name because it was used by Charlemagne for the French Empire, is the result of a new recension made from the Greek hexaplar text. This is the text used by the *Sixto-Clementine Vulgate* (1592). The text of Job and several fragments of Song and Pr correspond to this version, based on the hexaplar text.

After revising the version of Gn in 392, Jerome changed direction. He switched to working on the Hebrew text, guided by the principle of preference for *veritas hebraica*. It has to be noted that for Jerome «Hebrew truth» refers not so much to the actual Hebrew text but to the versions made by Hebrews, i.e., the versions by Symmachus, Aquila and Theodotion (C. Estin). Jerome began this new work with the Psalter called *iuxta Hebraeos* and continued it with the prophetic books, which included Dn and the obelised supplements. Between 392-394 he translated I-IV *Reges*, Job and Ezr-Neh; in 394-396, the first and second books of Chr; in 398 Pr, Qoh and Song, and towards 400, the Pentateuch. He completed the translation of the Hebrew Bible in 405 with the books of Est and its obelised additions, Jos, Jgs and Ruth.

Jerome did not translate the deuterocanonical books of the OT, which did not form part of the *veritas hebraica*. However, again using the OL text, he did translate Tob and Jdt, for which he did not devote more than a few hours' work. However, the Church was neither willing nor able to do without these books, so that the manuscript translation of the *Vulgate* did not delay in including a translation of these books not made by Jerome. This explains why the tradition of the OL is so constant in those books.

The expression *«Vulgate»* is not equivalent to «translation by Jerome». Not everything included in the Vulgate was translated by Jerome and not all his translations became part of the Vulgate. It includes the translations by Jerome made from the Hebrew text (except for the Psalter), the version of Tob and Jdt, the revision of the gospels and his revision of the Psalter made from Origen's Hexaplar. The text of the remaining deuterocanonical books and the NT comprises old revisions of the OL included in the Vulgate. The hexaplar revisions made by Jerome do not form part of the Vulgate (except for the Psalter).

To equate the *Vulgate* with everything translated by Jerome only adds further to the confusion in the 4th cent. One example is enough to show that the need for distinguishing between the translations made by Jerome from Hebrew and those he merely revised. When Jerome translates the Hebrew text, the term $b^e r\hat{\imath}t$ («covenant») is translated by Latin *foedus* or *pactum*; when Jerome revises a Latin text by means of the Greek LXX, the equivalent of *diathḗkē* is *testamentum*.

As for the NT, Jerome began by translating the gospels which were the texts most used in the liturgy. He also began translating the MT with the Psalter, the OT book most used in the liturgy. This translation is still the work of a beginner, but on the whole it is of good quality. Jerome did not always keep to his twofold aim of not changing the text of the OL beyond what was required by the Greek original, yet retain in his own translation the traditional character of the old Latin version. This explains why, for example, different renderings of the same Greek expression are found: *princeps sacerdotum* in Mt, *summus sacerdos* in Mk and *pontifex* in Jn. Essentially, Jerome followed the Alexandrian text for his translation.

An as yet unresolved question is to know when and how Jerome revised the rest of the NT. Today it is generally accepted that the version of the Epistles, Acts and Ap is not the work of Jerome although he could well have begun and set in train the translation. Probably it is the work of one of his pupils, Rufinus the Syrian, who followed more systematically his teacher's principles and completed the work in Rome in 405 (B. Fischer). The best witnesses of the Vulgate are codices A F G M R Z Σ (Sangallensis) and the palimpsest of Autun in Italy.

B.   THE CRITICAL VALUE OF THE VULGATE

Jerome's work merges the textual and exegetical traditions of three languages: Latin, Greek and Hebrew. In each book, and even in sections of a single book, an element peculiar to one or other language could predominate. Jerome's respect for the OL is most evident in Gn, especially in the oracular and prayer formulae consecrated by the liturgy. In the narrative sections, Jerome works with greater freedom. The frequent Septuagintisms and Semitisms of the version show that Jerome used the best Greek witnesses he could obtain and the form of the Hebrew text known at his time. This was already virtually identical to the mediaeval masoretic text, with very rare variants. Therefore, one of the interesting points of the *Vulgate* lies in the readings of Aquila and Symmachus which the Latin text allows to be traced. All this confers incalculable critical value on the Vulgate, although Jerome's intention was not exactly to establish a critical text.

Very soon the *Vulgate* was contaminated by readings from the OL which Jerome himself continued to quote in his commentaries, as did all those who did not accept the innovations he had introduced. The OL survived not only in manuscripts of the *Vulgate* but also in copies of the OL itself, which continued to be made until the 12th cent.

Augustine showed his reservations towards the *Vulgate*, considering that the Greek text of Church tradition should not be passed over in favour of the Hebrew text. Augustine also feared that the new version would be the cause of a schism between the Greek and Latin Churches. In addition, Jerome and Augustine disagreed on the matter of the inspiration of the LXX. Augustine believed that version to be inspired.

C.   THE TEXTUAL TRANSMISSION OF THE VULGATE

In the centuries following Jerome's translation, the Western world moved more and more away from the Byzantine world and no further attempts were made to correct the Latin text in accordance with the Greek original. Concern for revising the text of the translations shifted to the Syriac East, where throughout the 6th and 7th cents. various revisions were made of the Syriac text, all earlier than the Syro-hexaplar (cf. p. 360).

During the 8th-9th cents. the *Vulgate* replaced the OL, although it refused to disappear. The contamination of both texts and the process of corruption of the *Vulgate* manuscripts led to the revisions by Cassiodorus (†570) and Alcuin (730/735-804). The traces of «ciceronism» in the Vulgate are to be attributed to Alcuin rather than to Jerome. Although Jerome was very often inspired by classical Latin, he retained more «vulgarisms» than the text transmitted to us allows to suspect.

Other revisions of the Middle Ages (such as those by Theodolph of Orleans (†821) and Stephen Harding (†1134) in fact only corrupted the text of the *Vulgate* even further. The more than 8,000 manuscripts preserved suffer from this complaint. Besides the texts of the OL which still continued to circulate and the texts of these recensions of the *Vulgate*, there were different forms of the text of this version in Italy (C. *Amiatinus*, c.700), France (C. *Bigotianus*, 8th-9th cent.), Ireland (C. *Armachanus*, c. 812) and Spain (C. *Cavensis*, 9th cent.).

In the Renaissance period, beginning with Lorenzo Valla (1440) there was a reaction against the corrupt condition of the text of the *Vulgate*, which coincided with the start of a return to the original Greek text (cf. p. 546).

The Council of Trent (1456) declared that the *Vulgate* was the authentic version of the Church. However, this did not mean neglect of an obvious reference to the original texts, Hebrew and Greek. Half a century later, in 592, the publication of the *Sixto-Clementine Vulgate* supposed the culmination of the publishing efforts of an official text.

Since 1907, Benedictine monks of the Monastery of St. Jerome have been working on a critical edition which was completed in 1987 (except for 1-2 Mc, still in preparation). The *«Neo-Vulgate»* attempts to include in the edition of the *Vulgate* text the most certain findings of modern exegesis, respecting as far as possible the language and text of the ancient translators.

BIBLIOGRAPHY

Biblia Sacra iuxta Latinam vulgatam versionem iussu Pii PP.XI, 17 vols. (Città del Vaticano, 1926-1987).
Nova Vulgata Bibliorum Sacrorum editio, Rome 1979.

AYUSO MARAZUELA, T., *La Vetus Latina hispana I. Prolegomenos*, Madrid 1953.
BERGER, S., *Histoire de la Vulgate pendant les premiers siècles du moyen âge*, Nancy 1893 = Hildesheim, Olms, 1976.
BILLEN, A.V., *The Old Latin Texts of the Heptateuch*, Cambridge 1927.
BOGAERT, P.-M., «Bulletin de la Bible Latine», *RB en.S.* (1964-).
BOGAERT, P.-M., «La Bible latine des origines au moyen âge», *Revue théologique de Louvain* 19 (1988) 137-159 and 276-314.
BROCK, S.-ALAND, K.-REICHMANN, V.-ALAND, B.-MINK, G.-HANNICK, CH., «Bibelübersetzungen, I. Die alten Übersetzungen des Alten und Neuen Testaments», *Theologische Realenzyklopädie* VI, Berlin - New York 1980, 160-216.
BURKITT, F.C., *The Old Latin and the Itala*, Cambridge 1896.
CASSUTO, U., «The Jewish Translation of the Bible into Latin and its Importance for the Study of the Greek and the Aramaic Versions», *Biblical and Oriental Studies*, Jerusalem 1973, 285-298.
ELLIOT, J.K., «The Translations of the New Testament into Latin: The Old Latin and the Vulgate», *ANRW* II/26.1, ed. W. Haase, Berlin-New York 1992, 198-245.
FISCHER, B., (ed.), *Die Reste des altlateinischen Bibel nach Petrus Sabatier*, Freiburg 1949-.
FISCHER, B., *Novae concordantiae bibliorum sacrorum iuxta Vulgatam versionem critice editam*, 5 vols., Stuttgart 1977.
FISCHER, B., «Palimpsestus Vindobonensis. II. Manuscript 115 of the Books of Kingdoms», *Beiträge zur Geschichte der lateinischen Bibeltexte*, Freiburg 1986, 315-333.
FISCHER, B., *Novae Concordantiae Bibliorum Sacrorum iuxta Vulgatam Versionem critice editam, I-V,* Tübingen 1977.
FISCHER, B.-FREDE. H.I.-GRIBOMONT, J.-SPARKS, H.F.D.-THIELE, W., *Biblia Sacra iuxta vulgatam versionem*, Stuttgart 1984³.
GLARE, P.G.W. (ed.), *Oxford Latin Dictionary*, Oxford 1968-1982.
GRIBOMONT, D., «Les plus anciennes traductions latines», *Le monde latin antique et la Bible*, Bible de tous les temps II, eds. J. Fontaine - Ch. Pietri, Paris 1985, 43-65.
GRYSON, R. (ed.), *Esaias. Vetus Latina*, Die Reste der altlateinischen Bibel 12, Freiburg 1993.

MORANO, C., *Glosas marginales de Vetus Latina en las Biblias Vulgatas españolas. 1-2 Samuel*, Madrid 1989.

MORANO, C., *Glosas marginales de Vetus Latina en las Biblias Vulgatas españolas. 1-2 Samuel*, Madrid 1989.

STUMMER, F., *Einführung in die lateinische Bibel*, Paderborn 1928.

THIELE, W. (ed.), *Sirach (Ecclesiasticus). Vetus Latina*, Die Reste der altlateinischen Bibel 11/2, Freiburg 1993.

II.   THE SYRIAC VERSIONS

The versions into Syriac are of special importance. Through Syriac language and literature Greek culture passed to the East and later to the Islamic world. These versions are in a Semitic language and so closer than the other versions to the Hebrew and Aramaic of the biblical texts. Therefore, they incorporate the different textual and exegetical traditions, both Jewish and Christian.

1.   *The Old Syriac Version: Vetus Syra*

The *Old Syriac Version of the OT* has had a long history which is better known to us today thanks to the discovery of new manuscript material. Together with the Pentateuch it included the Psalms and the Prophets. The original of this versions shows a relationship with the Palestine targumim (Baumstark, Kahle, Vööbus). The Jewish or Jewish-Christian origin of this ancient Syriac version is disputed. The royal house of Adiabene, East of the Tigris, converted to Judaism in 40 CE. The translation could have its origin in this event, but it could also be the work of Jewish Christians who brought the gospel to Adiabene. In any case, the translation was made from a targum.

A revision of the *Vetus syra* resulted in the Pešiṭta or «simple» version. It was given this name from the 9th cent. to distinguish it from the Syro-hexaplar version, which is more carefully prepared and learned (cf. p. 360). The old version continued in circulation and was used later for the version known as Syro-Palestinian.

The *Old Syriac version of the NT* is especially interesting. It is derived from the *Diatessaron* or harmony of the four gospels, made around 170 by Tatian, a disciple of Justin. This work is a true monument of ancient Christian literature which had a wide circulation in the Syriac Church and enormous influence even on other Churches. The literary qualities of the text are combined with interesting the reader: it provides a continuous life of Jesus which gives meticulously all the details from the four gospels. For the Syriac Christians the *Diatessaron* also provided additional interest by including a series of readings taken from apocryphal sources which could be of particular interest to readers of Syriac.

Determining the origin and character of this version, however, is one of the more difficult problems of the textual history of the NT. Against the view that the *Diatessaron* is a translation from a Greek original (H. von Soden, Vogels), internal criticism seems to support those who maintain that it was originally written in Syriac, from the four gospels in Greek (Baumstark, Vööbus). Its text has reached us only in quotations. However, a manuscript has been found which contains the commentary of Ephraim of Edessa (†373) based on the text of the *Diatessaron*. The neglect and disappearance of this work is the result of the rejection during the 5th cent. provoked by its Encratic tendencies. Theodoretus of Cyrus († c. 450) had more than 200 copies destroyed, which shows how widespread it had been previously. Ancient Syriac literature preserves traces which suppose the existence of an old text of Acts and of the Pauline letters with characteristics similar to the *Diatessaron*.

Tatian's work gained great significance in early Christianity. It enjoyed enormous popularity in both East and West, far beyond the geographical limits of the Syriac language. For his translation Tatian used a form of the Greek text which was in circulation in Rome in the mid-second cent. It means that the reconstruction of the *Diatessaron* would also be an important contribution for the history of the Greek text of the NT.

The Old Syriac version of the NT originated with the *Diatessaron*. It tries to adapt its material to the original form of the gospel in the four gospels. This version follows, in general quite loosely, the Western type of text. It is preserved in two manuscripts, codex Syro-Curetonianus and Syro-Sinaiticus representing two independent textual traditions of this version. It exhibits good knowledge of the topography and customs of Palestine and uses expressions typical of Palestinian Aramaic unknown in classical Syriac. The translation was completed in the 3rd cent., and later underwent extensive revision. Its text was used as the basis of many Eastern versions of the gospels, among them the old Armenian, old Ethiopic and old Arabic versions. Only the text of the gospels, fragments of Acts and Pauline quotations have been preserved.

2.   *The Common Version: the Pešiṭṭa*

The *OT Pešiṭṭa* has a complex history which is reflected in the many variations of its text and style. It exhibits influences from the targumim (Gn 2:8 and 4:7) and the LXX (Gn 49:10). The translation was made in various periods and by different authors, Jewish or more probably Christian.

The version is very literal in Jb, not so literal in Song, freer in Pss, Is and the Minor Prophets, and a paraphrase in Ruth. In the Pentateuch, Ez and Pr it follows a targumic model and in Chr it shows the influence of targumic and midrashic traditions. The text on which the version is based also differs from one book to another. The Pešiṭṭa has affinities with the text of Isaiah known in Qumran. It gives this version critical value. The influence of the LXX is obvious in the oldest manuscript tradition but it is not easy to determine whether this influence was exerted on the first revision which gave the Pešiṭṭa its form, or only in the stages of later revision. There are interesting differences between the text of the Jacobite and Nestorian Pešiṭṭas (e.g., in Ps 68:19).

The text of the Pešiṭṭa most used has been the one prepared by Gabriel the Zionite and published in the Paris Polyglot (1645). This text was included in the Walton Polyglot and in Samuel Lee's edition (1823). At present the critical edition is being prepared in Leyden.

The *NT Pešiṭṭa* is the result of a revision of the old Syriac version with the text adapted to the Greek text known in Antioch. However, many elements of the old Syriac are preserved. The version has a good style without impairing its faithfulness to the Greek. For some time the author of this version was considered to be Rabbula, bishop of Edessa (Burkitt). New data discounts this possibility since the text which Rabbula used for the period before his death has been discovered and it is an old Syriac text (Vööbus). The Pešiṭṭa translation has to be dated in the last decades of the 4th cent. The canon of this version reflects the canon current in Antioch in the 4th cent.; it leaves out 2 Pt, 2-3 Jn, Jgs and Ap. Remains of this version have been found in a manuscript copied in Edessa in 411.

Sometimes this version of the NT occasions surprise by its Western type readings. It shows a large variety of translation techniques and lexical usages. This indicates that it was the work of several translators in agreement with Syriac tradition which attributes the work to an anonymous author. The text tradition is very old and careful, almost without variant readings, to the extent that the first critical edition of the gospels (P.E. Pusey-G.H. Williams 1901) provides a text very like the first printed edition of 1555.

3.   *Other Syriac Versions*

The *Philoxene version* of the OT is based on a more ancient text than the Pešiṭṭa text, revised in accordance with the Antioch Greek text. The version is attributed to Polycarp who had to complete it in 507/8, commissioned by archbishop Philoxenus. A commentary by Philoxenus based on this version has been found. Study of this commentary shows that in fact it was not a new translation but an adaptation of the Pešiṭṭa with the intention of being more literal in respect of the Greek original. This version included the NT writings not forming part of the old Syriac canon (2 Pt, 2-3 Jn, Jgs, Ap).

The *Syro-Palestinian version* is independent of the other Syriac versions. Its language is the Western Aramaic dialect spoken by the Christian of Palestine. In the 4th and 5th cents., the population of Palestine was almost completely Christian, with Greek as the dominant language. Fragments of this version are preserved in lectionaries, especially of the text of Psalms. It exhibits archaic characteristics with targumic influences which assume a base text in Greek. Recent discoveries confirm its Palestinian origin (Vööbus) rather than a possible origin in Antioch or Egypt as scholars previously supposed. The first indications on the origins of the translation are found in references by Jerome to the liturgy celebrated in Bethlehem. In 700 an Arab writer also used this version, in current use by the Melchite community of Palestine.

Among the Syriac versions, the Syro-Palestinian version of the NT is the closest to the Byzantine text type although it shows similarities with the Origen's text and the old Syriac version (cf. p. 346).

The *Syro-hexaplar version of the OT* is better known today thanks to recent finds (Vööbus). The text of most of the books of the OT have been preserved. It was made before 619 by Paul, bishop of Tella (Mesopotamia), in Alexandria where he took refuge after fleeing the invasion of the Persian Sassanids. It translates very literally Origen's hexaplar text. It does not shrink from forcing Syriac syntax to reflect the original Greek better. It also copies the diacritical signs of the hexaplar. In the margin it preserves many readings from «the three» (Aquila, Symmachus and Theodotion), as well as from the Quinta and the Sexta in the Psalter. It therefore is of great value for the reconstruction of the hexaplar text and the old Greek of Dn.

The *Harklean Version* is the NT equivalent of the OT hexaplar version. It is obviously scholarly in character. It continues in the line developed by the Philoxenian version. It aims at absolute faithfulness to the original Greek with no respect at all for Syriac grammar and style. The text is supplied with diacritical signs and marginal variants. In Acts it follows the Western text. It was the work of Thomas of Herakla during his exile in Alexandria. He completed it in 616.

The *version of James of Edessa* is the final example of the intense activity displayed by Syriac-speaking Christians in translating the Bible. Fragments corresponding to Sm-Kgs have been found, translated in 705. This version was an attempt to improve the literary quality of the Syro-hexaplar version in relation to the Pešiṭṭa. The first systematic compilation of a Syriac masorah was made using this version and includes marginal notes on pronunciation and variants.

BIBLIOGRAPHY

Vetus Testamentum Syriace iuxta simplicem Syrorum versionem, Leiden 1972- .
BROCKELMANN, C., *Syrische Grammatik mit Paradigmen, Literatur, Chrestomathie und Glossar*, Leipzig 1951, reprinted in 1976.
DIRKSEN, P.B., «The Old Testament Peshitta», *Mikra*, CRINT 2/2, ed. M.J. Mulder, Assen/Maastricht 1988, 225-297.
GOSHEN-GOTTSTEIN, M.H., *The Bible in the Syropalestinian Version*, I, Jerusalem 1973.
NÖLDEKE, T., *Compendious Syriac Grammar*, London 1904 (based on the 2nd edition Leipzig 1898).
PAYNE SMITH, R., *Thesaurus syriacus*, 2 vols., Oxford 1879, 1901.
UNGNAD, A., *Syrische Grammatik mit Übungsbuch*, Munich 1932.
VÖÖBUS, A., *Studies in the History of the Gospel Text in Syriac*, Louvain 1951-1987.
VÖÖBUS, A., *The Hexaplar and the Syro-Hexapla*, Stockholm 1971.

III. COPTIC VERSIONS

Coptic is the final stage of ancient Egyptian. It was the language spoken by the Egyptian population long before the Christian era. However, it did not become a written language until 200 CE, which happened precisely because of Bible translations. It was written in Greek characters to which had to be added a further seven characters taken from the Demotic script. Coptic developed seven dialects: Sahidic, which extended from Cairo to Heraclopolis; Bohairic, spoken in the Western Delta; Akhmimic, a dialect of Akhmim, ancient Ponopolis in Upper Egypt; sub-Akhmimic, south of Aswan (Lycopolis);

the Middle Egyptian dialect and lastly, Fayyumic, used West of the Nile and South of the Delta.

Of these dialects, Sahidic is the most important for studying the early Coptic versions. In the 4th cent. it became the literary language of the Nile. The oldest version in this Sahidic dialect is earlier than 270 CE. A century later all the books of the Bible were already translated into Sahidic. The manuscript tradition shows that there were several translations in this dialect which later underwent a whole series of successive revisions. In this dialect are written the «Sahidic» codices of the Gnostic library of Nag-Hammadi.

Over time the Bohairic version, made possibly inn the 4th cent., replaced the others. It continues to be used in the Coptic liturgy. The manuscripts of it which have been preserved are also very numerous, although most of them are of relatively recent date (12th-14th cents.).

The versions of the OT were made from the Greek of the LXX. The Sahidic version of Job seems to have used a pre-hexaplar text; the version of Dn was made from a Theodotionic text. The Bohairic version of the prophetic books is textually close to the recension of Hesychius. In the NT the Sahidic and Bohairic versions mostly follow an Alexandrian text type.

Of the versions in the other dialects only fragments have been preserved, relatively small, except for an important manuscript of John's gospel in sub-Akhmimic, from the 4th cent. There is still much research to be done on the date, text types and relations among the Coptic versions.

IV. THE GOTHIC VERSION

It is the first version where we know the translator's name which is bishop Ulfilas, apostle to the Goths in the provinces of the Danube in the mid-4th cent. It is one of the versions for which an alphabet had first to be created. It is the oldest literary work in a Teutonic language. Six manuscripts are preserved, of which the most complete is a very de luxe copy, the *Codex argenteus* («Silver codex») of the 5th or 6th cent. (Uppsala) where the gospels are in the Western sequence (Mt-Jn-Lk-Mk). The version is very literal and follows a Byzantine text. Into the Pauline letters are inserted Western readings taken from the OL. Of the OT only some fragments have been preserved based on a Lucianic Greek text.

V. THE ARMENIAN VERSION

At the beginning of the 5th cent., Patriarch Sahug (Isaac the Great, 390-439) and Mesropius (†439), who is credited with the invention of the Armenian script, began a translation of the Bible and the liturgy into Armenian, the national language, as a reaction to the use of Syriac in Armenian worship. The version of the OT was made, initially at least, from the Syriac version, although ancient Armenian historians inform us that it was made on the basis of the Greek text. In any case, the manuscripts preserved indicate that it was a text strongly influenced by the hexaplar tradition, in some cases was revised on the basis of a Syriac text.

With regard to the NT text, it has been debated whether the version was made from a Greek original or through a Syriac version. The inclusion of Paul's third letter to the Corinthians as well as other data which reflect Semitic syntax, point to Syriac influence.

Most of the manuscripts preserved, however, present a more Hellenised form of text. Probably the original version underwent recension between the 5th and 8th cents. To judge from some indications, the first form of the gospels was a «harmony» similar to Tatian's *Diatessaron*. On the whole, the Armenian version is of great literary merit which has earned it the title «queen of the versions». As a source of critical analysis it also merits more attention than it has been paid.

VI. THE GEORGIAN VERSION

Christianity reached Georgia, between the Black Sea and the Caspian Sea, in the first half of the 4th cent. Georgian is an agglutinative language which has no connection with any other known language. It is not easy to determine exactly the date of the first versions which books were translated and which base text was used for the translation; it could have been Greek, Syriac or Armenian.

The version of the OT was made in several periods from various texts; the version of the Octateuch was made from the LXX, the prophets from an Armenian translation.

The version of the NT, which according to ecclesiastical tradition was made directly from a Greek text, seems however to be based on the Syriac or more probably on the Armenian. Five versions or recensions of the gospels in ancient Georgian have been distinguished all earlier than a revision undertaken by Euthymius towards end of the 10th cent.

VII. THE ETHIOPIC VERSION

The version of the Bible into Ethiopic began possibly towards the middle of the 4th cent. or shortly after, when bishop Aksom Frum was consecrated, the first historical figure in Ethiopian Christianity we know about.

The manuscript tradition of this version is later than the 13th cent. and exhibits a mixed text with traces of strong contamination by Arabic and Coptic mediaeval texts.

The version of the OT seems to have been made from the LXX, although some scholars think they can detect influences from Hebrew. In 1 Kgs text B of the LXX is followed, with strong Lucianic influence.

The text of the NT is very mixed, sometimes very literal, elsewhere very free. In the Pauline letters, the agreement with P[46] is striking. The oldest layer of this version reveals a mixed text, with the Byzantine text type predominating.

VIII. ARABIC VERSIONS

The exact date when the first translation into Arabic was made is not known. It is generally thought that until the time of Muhammad (†632), the language of the Christians in Arabia was Syriac and only in a later period was the need felt for a version in Arabic. Some scholars believe, instead, that the Arabic-speaking Christians, already before the spread of Islam, needed a translation of the Bible into their own language. The oldest texts preserved do not seem to be earlier than the 9th cent.

The different Arabic versions come from very sources. The version by Sa'adiya Gaon (†942), which gained great authority in the rabbinic school of Sura in Mesopotamia, is from Hebrew and includes elements of Talmudic exegesis and of its author's philosophy. The version of the Prophets, incorporated in the Paris and London Polyglots, was from the Greek text. Other versions translate forms of the Syriac text. The version of the gospels by Isaac Ibn Velasquez of Cordoba in 946 is from a Latin text. Other versions are from Coptic.

IX. THE SLAVONIC VERSION

The first Slavonic version of the gospels, psalms and other texts read in the liturgy, was the work of Cyril (†869) and Methodius (†885). The version was completed towards the end of the 9th cent. Subsequently, it underwent several recensions which reflect the dialectal development of Slavonic. A manuscript from 1499 reproduces the version by Gennadius, archbishop of Novgorod. It follows the Byzantine Greek text and has become the text for church use. The St. Petersburg edition of 1751 is the current text of the Slavonic Bible.

BIBLIOGRAPHY

BIRDSALL, J.N., «Georgian Studies and the New Testament», *NTS* 29 (1983) 306-320.
BOTTE, B., «Versions Coptes», *DBS* 6 (1960) 818-25.
COWE S.P., *The Armenian Version of Daniel*, Atlanta GA 1992.
COX, C., «Biblical Studies and the Armenian Bible: 1955-1980», *RB* 89 (1982) 99-113.
CRUM, W.E., *A Coptic Dictionary*, Oxford 1939.
LAMBDIN, T.O., *Introduction to Sahidic Coptic*, Macon GA 1983.

LAMBDIN, T.O., *Introduction to Classical Ethiopic (Ge'ez)*, Ann Arbor MI 1978.

PETERS, M.K.H., *A Critical Edition of the Coptic (Bohairic) Pentateuch*, Septuagint and Cognate Studies SBL.

STEINDORFF, C, *Lehrbuch der Koptischen Grammatik*, Chicago IL 1951.

SMITH, A., *A Concise Coptic-English Lexicon*, Grand Rapids MI 1983.

STONE, M.E. (ed.)., *Armenian and Biblical Studies*, Jerusalem 1976.

STONE, M.E. (ed.)., *Selected Studies in Pseudepigrapha and Apocrypha With Special Reference to the Armenian Tradition*, Leiden 1991.

TILL, W.C., *Koptische Grammatik (Sahidischer Dialekt)*, Leipzig 1955.

Chapter IV

Textual Criticism of the Old and New Testaments

Si qua tamen tibi lecturo pars oblita derit, haec erit e lacrimis facta litura meis: aut si qua incerto fallet te littera tractu, signa meae dextrae iam morientis erunt.

«If, when you read this letter, a part has vanished,
it must have been my tears that smudged it out:
or if you cannot make out the shaky letters,
they are the signs my hand is close to death»
(Propertius, Arethusa's Letter to L, Elegies...)

Chapter IV

Textual Criticism of the Old and New Testaments 367

Textual Criticism of the Old Testament

Textual criticism studies the process of transmission of the text from the moment it is put into writing or its first edition. Its aim is to determine the oldest biblical text witnessed by the manuscript tradition. *Literary criticism* (in the sense of the German term *Literarkritik*) studies instead the process before the formation of the biblical writings in order to determine their author and date. Even though in theory the domains and methods of these two disciplines are quite separate, in practice they often overlap. The meeting point causing friction between them is in the editorial process where the previous process of collecting material and of composition and of editing the text ends and the next process, textual transmission, begins.

During the manuscript transmission of a text, especially if the process is extended through several centuries and covers far flung places, there is no avoiding the introduction of many *changes in the text*, some accidental, others intentional. There are almost a thousand years between the oldest texts of the Bible and the last book to be included in the biblical canon, that is between the Song of Deborah (11th cent. BCE?) and the book of Daniel (2nd cent. BCE). From the fixing of the consonantal Hebrew text, carried out at the beginning of the 2nd cent. CE, up to the copying out of the St. Petersburg codex, finished in 1008 CE, almost another thousand years elapsed. Throughout all this time, accidental mistakes by the copyists and intentional changes made by the same copyists, by glossators and by interpreters have undoubtedly accumulated.

Textual criticism establishes the *principles and methods* which make it possible to identify and correct these changes in order to re-establish the text in the form closest to the original text. Variants in the Hebrew manuscripts, the versions and biblical quotations provide the *data* which allow a judgment to be made on the critical value of one or other form of the text.

The best *example* of the kind of problem which textual criticism tries to deal with is provided by parallel or repeated passages. For example, the texts of 2 Sm 22 and of Ps 18 represent two different versions of the same poem.

2 Sm 22	Ps 18
(v.2) Yahweh is my rock	*Yahweh is my rock,*
my fortress and my deliverer, (v.3)	*my fortress and my deliverer,*
God of my rock,	*my God, my rock,*
I will trust in him,	*I will trust in him/it,*
my shield and horn of	*my shield and horn of*
my salvation,	*my salvation,*
my bulwark	*my bulwark*
and my refuge,	
from violence you save me,	
(v.4) I invoke Yahweh...	*(v.3) I invoke Yahweh...*

Faced with the agreements and differences of these two poems, textual criticism asks: Is one of these two texts a modification of the other? Do both derive from a common source? In that case, which is the text of the original poem? If this assumption is not certain or if it is still not possible to reconstruct the original poem, which of the two versions is older or preserves older elements, even though it could also include later elements?

The answer to these questions is extremely important. From it depends further research which has to be made on the literary history of any text, historical, legal, prophetic or hymnic, etc. and on the interpretation of their contents.

I. CHANGES IN THE TRANSMISSION OF THE TEXT OF THE OT

There are two types of alteration which can be introduced into the text during the process of copying manuscripts: accidental and deliberate. A textual variant can be related simultaneously to different phenomena of corruption or change in the text. The causes of textual corruption can be as varied and accidental as the one mentioned in the text from Propertius quoted above.

1. *Accidental Changes or Copyists' Mistakes*

Confusion of similar letters in the Aramaic or square script. In this type of script the letters *d/r* are often confused. For example, in 2 Kgs 16:6 translators and commentaries usually replace the MT reading ʾĂrām with ʾĔdôm. The reasons in favour of this substitution are the facile confusion of the consonants *d/r* in the square script and agreements with geographical and historical references in this passage, easily seen in the context. This confusion between Aram and Edom happens much too often for the confusion to be thought purely accidental. Possibly, on some occasions at least, historical reasons lie behind it, or else the wish to make either the Edomites or the Aramaeans the «arch-enemies» of Israel, depending on the date and the tendency of the different redactors (Lemaire).

Similar cases of confusion occur in 2 Sm 22:11: «he showed himself» (*wayyērā'*) upon the wings of the wind» - Ps 18:11: «he glided (*wayyēde'*) on the wings of the wind». Cf. similarly 1 Sm 17:8 and 2 Sm 8:12 (in comparison with 1 Chr 18:12).

Also frequent is the confusion between *b* and *k*: Is 28:21 «For Yahweh will arise *as* (*k-*) (upon) Mount Perazim, *as* (*k-*) (in) the Valley of Gibeon he will rouse himself» - 1QIs^a: «...he will arise *in* (*b-*) Mount Perazim, *in* (*b-*) the Valley of Gibeon....». In 2 Sm 13:37 there is an example of confusion between *h* and *ḥ*.

Confusion between similar letters in the palaeo-Hebrew script. In Pr 9:1 the parallelism attested in the Greek version: «Wisdom *built* her house/ erected (*hiṣṣîbâ*) her seven columns» seems preferable to MT «*she built* her house/hewed (*ḥāsebâ*) her seven columns». The MT is the result of a confusion between the signs *h* and *ḥ* in the palaeo-Hebrew script.

In 1 Sm 14:47, critics usually correct the MT reading, «he did evil» (morally), replacing it with LXX «he defeated» which fits the context better (cf. Barthélemy 1982). The letters *w* and *r* are easily confused in the palaeo-Hebrew script (MT: *yrš'y^ʿ* and LXX: [*ywš^ʿ*]).

Other letters easily confused in the palaeo-Hebrew script are '/*t*, *k*/*n*, *d*/', *b*/*r* and *m*/*n*.

Confusion between homophonous words or of similar pronunciation. This confusion can be produced by dictation error. In Ps 49:8, some manuscripts have the reading *'āḥ*, «brother» («a brother can in no way redeem another»), whereas others have the similar sounding reading *'ak*, «surely» («surely no-one can redeem himself»). Similarly, in Ps 100:3 some manuscripts have *lô* («to him») and others have *lō'* («not»).

Transposition of letters or words (metathesis). The immediate context of Ps 49:12 speaks of the death of wise and wicked alike («In truth the wise die...(v.11)»)., The reading of the LXX, Targ., Peshitta and Vulg. - «*their tomb* (*qibrām*) is their eternal homes...» - seems less suitable in this context and is certainly the result a metathesis or transposition of letters. Faced with this reading, mediaeval Jewish commentaries were perplexed. Rashi attempted to make the best of the masoretic reading: «their inner (thought is that) their houses (would last) for ever...». Ibn Ezra, as usual taking a more rational approach, was aware that there was an opinion according to which *qrbm* is a transposition (*hpk*) of *qbrm*. Certainly, since there was no authorised tradition to support a correction of the transmitted text, the mistake was perpetuated without anyone daring to correct the text. However, the Babylonian Talmud (*Mo'ed qatan* 9b) already attests that *qrbm* has to be read, not *qbrm*. Other examples of metathesis can be seen in 1 Sm 14:27; Is 9:18; etc.

Haplography or omission by homoio-arcton or homoio-teleuton. The copyist jumps unintentionally from one word or expression to another which has the same beginning (-*arcton*, e.g. Gn 31:18; 1 Sm 10:1; Is 5:8, etc.) or the same ending (-*teleuton*, e.g., 1 Sm 13:15; Is 4:5-6, etc.).

An example of a jump through *homoioteleuton* occurs in the MS 1QIs^a, in the passage corresponding to 4:5-6: «Yahweh will create over all the region of Mount Zion and upon its assemblies a cloud [*by day* (*yômām*) and smoke and a glow of flaming fire by night, because on top of all the (Glory of Yahweh) it will be like canopy and a cabin and will serve for shade], *by day* (*yômām*), against the heat, and as protection and shelter against downpour and rain» (Cantera-Iglesias), In the Qumran manuscript the text between parentheses has been lost due to skipping from the first *yômām* to the second.

When two letter or two words are consecutive it is easy for one of them to disappear. In Is 5:8, where the MT is «house against house» (*bayît bᵉbayît*), 1QIsᵃ omits the preposition *b-* through *homoioarcton* (identical beginning), which results in the meaningless «house house».

The Hebrew text of 1 Sm has many cases of haplography. The lost text can be reconstructed using the LXX and some Qumran fragments. For example, 1 Sm 11:1 has lost part of the text which, however, has been preserved in Ms. 4QSamᵃ. The text of this manuscript enables the original beginning of the narrative to 4QSamᵃ be recovered (the missing text is in parentheses):

«[And Nah]ash, king of the Ammonites, oppressed the sons of Gad and the sons of Reuben and gouged out a[ll] their right eyes and instilled fe[ar and terror] in Israel. No-one among the sons of Israel remained on [the other side of the Jordan whose] right eye had not been [go]uged out by Naha[sh king] of the Ammonites. Only seven thousand men [fled before] the Ammonites and came to Jabesh-gilead and a month later it happened that...» (Cross).

However it needs to be determined whether the text preserved in 4QSamᵃ is original or whether it is a midrashic type of expansion (Rofé).

The reader can make his own comparison between the different translations given in modern bibles for 1 Sm 3:15; 4:1; 10:1; 13:15; 14:41 and 29:10.

Dittography. It occurs when the first letter, word of sentence is written twice successively. For example, in 1QIsᵃ the expression *wᵉhišmîaʿ* is repeated twice in Is 30:30 as is *laʾăser* in Is 31:6. In 2 Kgs 7:13 there are seven repeated words, «which have remained in it, behold they are like the whole multitude of Israel» (*ʾăser niš'ārû-bah hinnām kᵉkol-hā*[!]*hāmōn yiśra'ēl ʾăser niš'ārû-bah kᵉkol-hāmōn yiśra'ēl*). This repetition could have been intended to preserve a variant (*hhmwn/hmwn yśr'l*) which allows the insertion of «Israel» in the text (the article before the *nomen regens* is incorrect).

In 2 Sm 6:3-4, the MT also repeated seven words: «new; and they took it to the house of Abinadab which is on the hill». 4QSamᵃ and LXX do not have this dittography which, however, may not be a dittography but a repetition by an editor due to the convergence at this point of two different versions of how the ark was transported (Trebolle 1989).

The presence of the term *ʿôd* («again») has been understood as a case of dittography in 1 Sm 20:3: «However, David swore again». The Greek version omits this term, and its insertion in the MT must have been due to accidental repetition of two consonants in a continuous text (*wayyiššābaʿ* [*ʿôd*] *dāwiḏ*): the ʿ of the preceding verb and the *d* of the following noun. The context does not mention a previous oath by David which seems to support the view that it is a case of dittography (however, cf. Barthélemy 1982).

Other examples can be found in 2 Kgs 19:23 (compare Is 37:24) and Ez 28:23.

Incorrect division or join of words. This kind of mistake may seem strange to a modern reader but it was very common in the continuous consonantal script which left no space between words. It was easy to separate two consonants incorrectly, dividing a word in two or making two words into one. This mistake could even happen in texts in English, for instance, 'lighthouse keeping' and 'light housekeeping'.

An example of *incorrect word division* occurs in Ps 42:6. In the MT, the sentence «(He) is the salvation of my face and my God» (*yšwʿt pny wʾlhy*) is cut off so that the last word, «my God» (*ʾlhy*) forms part of the following verse. A mistake has been made in the division of words in a continuous consonantal text (*yšʿtpnywʾlhy*). Repetition of the same refrain at the end of the psalm and also at the end of the following psalm shows that undoubtedly there has been a mistake in the MT. The two psalms (42 and 43) at first comprised a single poem, divided into strophes by repetition of the refrain mentioned.

In Jr 23:33, the reading in MT is unintelligible: «If... they ask you: 'What is the Lord's burden?', you will say to them: '*what burden*?'. It is the result of a mistake in word division: three words, *ʾt mh mśʾ* instead of two: *ʾtm hmśʾ*. The LXX translation, «(you will say to them:) *You are the burden* of the Lord...» corresponds to the LXX reading which reflects a consonantal Hebrew text with those two words. Similar examples can be found in 1 Sm 9:1; Is 30:5; Ez 26:20; Hos 6:5 and Ps 89:45.

The reverse, *incorrectly joining* consonants in a single word, can be seen in Am 6:12. The translation «to plough *with cows*» corresponds to the Hebrew word *bbqrym* (MT), whereas «to plough *with cattle in the sea*» translates two Hebrew words, *bbqr ym* (BHS). The context speaks of impossible or difficult things such as ploughing the sea or galloping on rocks.

2. *Intentional Changes*

Intentional changes belong to interpretation and should be considered under hermeneutics. However, there are many cases where it is possible to distinguish the original reading from a secondary reading. This is precisely the task of textual criticism.

Replacement by «trivialisation» or modernisation. In the course of textual transmission, linguistic changes are inevitably inserted in order to modernise the text, such as replacing the piel by the hiphil as the causative, or replacing some prepositions with others (*ʿl/ʾl*), some terms with others, the perfect with the imperfect, etc.

In Is 39:1 there is an example of an archaic term being replaced by a more modern one. The verb *ḥzq* here has the old meaning of «to heal» («he had been ill and had recovered»); in 1QIs^a it is replaced by the verb *ḥyh* which was the term current in the Qumran period for that meaning. Similarly, in 1 Sm 20:34 the expression «he rose» (*wyqm*) replaces older «he sprang up» (*wypḥz*) attested in 4QSam^b and the LXX which has the added peculiarity of expressing a degree of arrogance in Jonathan's attitude (McCarter, 339).

1QIs^a provides many examples where the imperfect replaces the perfect: 41:6; 43:20; 44:17; 45:24 and 54:15. The reverse, with the perfect replacing the imperfect, occurs in 48:18 and 66:2.

Harmonisation. Gn 2:2 (MT) runs as follows: «and Elohim having finished on the *seventh* day the work he had done, he rested on the seventh day». The Samaritan Pentateuch, the Peshitta and *Jubilees* (2:16) have the variant «the sixth day». This variant tries to harmonise the two sentences. Possibly, this harmonisation is not necessary for the Hebrew text also allows the other meaning according to which Yahweh had already finished his work on the seventh day.

Assimilation to parallel passages. In Lv 5:25-26 the text is as follows: «Then Yahweh he shall present to Yahweh, as his sacrifice of expiation, a ram without blemish from the flock, according to your valuation, in sacrifice for the misdeed, *to the priest.* (v.26) The priest will make expiation for him...». The reference in v.25 *to the priest* (*ʾl hkhn*) is absent from the text of the Samaritan Pentateuch, LXX and Siphre. Nor is there a reference to the priest in v.15. The MT took it from v.18 by assimilation to this passage.

Double readings. Double readings occur through juxtaposition of two or more alternative variants. The Qumran manuscripts have several examples of double readings inserted in the margin or between the lines. Such doublets prove the existence of different textual traditions and reflect the fluid state in which the biblical text was transmitted at the time. Doublets are easily noticed by comparing two or more text forms of the same passage. They are more common in more recent texts with an extended history of transmission, as is the case in the Greek Lucianic text. S. Talmon has established a typology of such doublets consisting in the juxtaposition of synonymous words or expressions, alternative grammatical forms, syntactic variants, etc. Doublets demonstrate the respect copyists had for every variant attested in tradition, as well as the efforts they made to ensure that no variant of the biblical text could be lost (cf. p. 115).

In Ez 1:20 the MT has a doublet which has the function of preserving a variant, *šm/šmh* («there»/«thither»): «To *there,* wherever *the Spirit* made them *go,* they went [*thither the Spirit go*]» (*ʾl ʾšr yhyh šm hrwḥ llkth ylkw* [*šmh hrwḥ llkt*]). Some Hebrew manuscripts, the LXX and the Peshitta as well as Cantera-Iglesias' translation omit the text between square brackets.

Corrections for moral or theological reasons. Theophoric names referring to the god Baal, such as ʾIshbaʾal, can occur in a disparaging form as ʾÎšbōšet (1 Chr 8:33 and 2 Sm 2:8; cf. LXX^L.

For euphemism, the expression «to curse Yahweh» (Jb 1:5.11; 2:5.9) is replaced by «to bless Yahweh» even though the first expression fits the context better. Similarly, the expression «Yahweh incited David to count the Israelites» (2 Sm 24:1) is corrected in the parallel text of 1 Chr 21:2, with the name «Yahweh» simply replaced by «Satan».

The tendency of late Judaism to avoid anthropomorphisms in reference to the divinity is evident in a special way, although not always, in the Targumim (cf. p. 441). Most of the *sebirîm* or «conjectures» of the masoretes are for theological or moral reasons.

Glosses. In Jos 1:15 «then you .will return to your land [and you will take possession of it], which Moses gave you...», the clause «you will take possession of it» is an added gloss (BHS). It is missing from the LXX and also interrupts the syntactic sequence between the foregoing clause and the following relative (however, cf. Barthélemy 1982).

In 1 Sm 2:2: «There is no holy one like the Lord (there is no other beside you), there is no rock like our God», the clause placed in parentheses breaks the poetic parallelism formed by the other two clauses. In the LXX this clause is added at the end of the verse. A glossator had attempted to give more force to the statements on Yahweh's uniqueness.

Addition of epithets. In the book of Jeremiah, the introduction to an oracle, «Thus says Yahweh», is common, to which MT adds an epithet such as «(Yahweh) of hosts, the God of Israel» (39 times), «(Yahweh) of hosts» (14 times). «(Yahweh) the God of Israel» (3 times), etc. In the LXX these additional epithets are found only 19 times.

Addition of the names of the subject and object. In the book of Jeremiah, the MT adds the name «Nebuchadnezzar» on 8 occasions (27:6.8.20; 28:3.11.14 and 29:1.3); the LXX text completely omits this addition and in 27:8; 28:3 and 29:1 it even omits expressions referring to Nebuchadnezzar.

II. DATA FOR CRITICAL ANALYSIS

The variants attested in the biblical manuscripts or contained in the ancient versions and in patristic and rabbinic quotations form the basic material for textual criticism. After presenting the manuscripts and versions of the OT (cf. pp. 273 and 301) it is necessary to give a critical assessment of this material as well as to patristic and rabbinic quotations.

1. *The Biblical Manuscripts*

The *manuscripts from the Dead Sea* (the Dead Sea Scrolls) have confirmed the value of the textual tradition represented by the MT, with the text of mediaeval manuscripts agreeing substantially with the text now found in the Dead Sea Scrolls. This is especially the case in 1QIs^a (cf. p. 288). In other books, such as Sm and Jr, the manuscripts from Qumran support the tradition attested by the LXX version, although it also has its own peculiarities.

However it must also be remembered that the manuscripts found in the caves of the Dead Sea have reached us in a bad state of preservation and in general give us a very fragmentary text, at times no more than portions of lines or words. In addition, the quality of the copyists' work is somewhat careless, so that one has to be very cautious when making a critical analysis of the variants attested in the manuscripts from the Dead Sea.

One example will be enough to give an idea of the contribution of the Dead Sea Scrolls to the textual criticism of the OT and to many other fields such as the literary history of the biblical books or the history of the religion of Israel. It is taken from the Pentateuch, which in spite of its colossal textual stability still allows cases of textual variation as striking as the much-quoted Dt 32:8-9 and 32:43.

The MT of Dt 32:43 is shorter than in the LXX. The MS 4QDeut^q preserves the longer Hebrew text reflected in the Greek version:

MT	LXX / 4QDeut^q
«Acclaim, *nations (gwym)*, his people,	«Acclaim, *heavens (šmym)*, his people, *and lie prostrate before him all gods*
for he will avenge the blood of his *servants*, he will wreak vengeance on his foes, *on those who hate him*	for he will avenge the blood of his *sons*, he will wreak vengeance on his foes, *he will (re)pay them*
and will make expiation for *his land*, his people»	and will make expiation for *the land of* his people»

The MT reading, «pagan nations» looks as if it is secondary to the reading «heavens» attested in the LXX and transmitted by 4QDeut^q. It demythologises a text with obvious mythological connotations for it compares in synonymous parallelism, «heavens» and «gods». The reference to the «sons» of god makes the mythological nature of the oldest text very clear. For if there were any doubt, v. 8 of the MS 4QDeut^q has the reading «according to the number of the sons of El» (*lemispār benê ʾEl* or perhaps *ʾElîm* or *ʾĒōlōhîm*), agreeing with the reading in the Greek version (*katà arithmón aggélōn theoû*). The MT has changed «sons» to «servants» of God. However, there are clear references in vv. 5, 19 and 20 to the «sons» of God with which the oldest reading undoubtedly agrees.

On the other hand, the reading in the genitive «the land of his people» (LXX and 4QDeut^q) makes more sense and belongs to the context better than MT reading «his land, his people».

P. W. Skehan, the editor of 4QDeut^q, suggested a possible reconstruction of the oldest form of the text as follows:

harnînû šāmayim ʿimmô	Shout for joy, heavens, with him,
weʿhābû ʿōz lô kōl benê ʾelîm	and give power to him, all you gods,
kî dam bānā(y)w yiqqōm	for the blood of his children he will avenge,
wekippēr ʾademat ʿammô	and he will make expiation for the land of his people»

The hemistich in the MT «he will wreak vengeance on his foes» belongs to the parallel which follows in LXX/4QDeut^q «those who hate him he will repay». The proof is that these two hemistichs form a complete verse in v.41. It has to be supposed that in v.43 the verse made up of these two hemistichs comprises an addition taken from v.41. The proof is obtained by the simple observation that this addition breaks the parallelism between the two hemistichs of the verse: «for he avenge the blood of his sons, [...] he will make expiation for the land of his people».

Thus, before the discovery of the Dead Sea Scrolls, it was possible to suspect that the Greek text contained in Dt 32:43 some older elements than those present in MT. Now, 4QDeut^q leaves no room for doubt that in this case the Greek text did not change the Hebrew text but faithfully translated a Hebrew original similar to 4QDeut^q.

The *mediaeval Hebrew manuscripts* provided with vocalisation and masora contribute very important data for work on criticism. The masoretic vocalisation can agree or otherwise with the vocalisation supposed by the ancient versions (compare Is 7:11 *š^eʾālâ/ š^eʾōlâ*). Many times, together with the «written» (*k^etîb*) text there is another variant written in the margin indicating how it «has to be read» (*q^erê*). According to Orlinsky, these *q^erê* readings correspond to true textual variants. About 350 marginal notes suggest «conjectures» (*s^ebirîm*) some of which are very certain (cf. p. 274).

The masoretes succeeded in establishing the Hebrew text in the minutest detail. As a result, the mediaeval manuscripts do not transmit variants of much significance, although it is still important to study them. It is significant that in the book of Kings, the readings of mediaeval Hebrew manuscripts frequently agree with variants of the ancient Greek text (LXX^L, OL, Targ., Arm.) attesting to a Hebrew text different from the masoretic text (Wevers; Trebolle 1980). Such agreements cannot simply be ascribed to the tendencies and habits of the copyists (Goshen-Gottstein) but may go back to pre-masoretic forms of the Hebrew text (cf. p. 280). The vocalic variants are not necessarily less important than consonantal variants.

Ultimately, the MT is a text which has been transmitted with the utmost care in every period of its history, even from the period before the consonantal text was fixed in the 2nd cent. CE. The MT is therefore the starting point and obligatory reference for all work on OT text criticism (cf. p. 382). However, the MT is neither the only nor always the best text (cf. p. 385).

2.   *The Ancient Versions*

In general, the ancient versions have great critical value. They sometimes reflect non-masoretic forms of the Hebrew text which can have their origin closer to the original text than the MT itself. However, the witness of the versions is only indirect. Therefore, for the to use its text critically requires as perfect a knowledge as possible, both of the original language and of the target language. This knowledge has to include not only morphology and syntax but also the way each language represents reality. It is also necessary to have suitable knowledge of the «translation characteristics» of each book, especially its exegetical and theological tendencies. Also it is necessary first to carry out a critical study of the text of the versions themselves to avoid the mistake of considering as a reading or peculiarity of the original version what is nothing more than a corruption or later revision of its text (Wevers).

The *LXX version* is the most important of the versions, for its greater antiquity (3rd-2nd cents. BCE) and because it embraces all the books of the OT. In some books (Sm, Jr, Job, etc.) it also represents the text of lost forms of the Hebrew text which have only partially reappeared in fragments of the Qumran manuscripts. In other books such as Is and Pr, the more periphrastic nature of the version considerably reduces its value as a witness for criticism of the Hebrew text.

Among the *Aramaic versions*, targum Onqelos is very literal; *Neophyti* and Yerushalmi are more periphrastic as is the targum Jonathan of the prophets. However, sometimes the targumim and Peshitta also preserve variants which reflect pre-masoretic texts. These «primary variants» are, as far as the Pentateuch is concerned, those in which the Samaritan text and/or the LXX agree against MT (Isenberg). In Sm-Kgs the primary variants are where the Aramaic text coincides with the Greek (proto-)Lucianic text and with the Hebrew text of Chr (Trebolle 1980).

The *Old Latin Version (OL)* - in spite of meagre and fragmentary material preserved, its complex recensional history and the mix of vulgar and literary style (Ulrich) is, however, a witness of great value for knowing the Greek text before the period of the great uncial manuscripts of the 4th cent. *The Vulgate*, instead, in general represents the text of masoretic tradition, known through «the three» (Aquila, Symmachus and Theodotion) and also, although to a lesser extent, directly from the Hebrew text of the end of the 4th cent.

3.   *Quotations from the Old Testament*

The quotations from the OT contained in the Mishnah, the Talmud and rabbinic writings sometimes include variations from the MT. Similarly, the writings of the Syriac, Greek and Latin Fathers transmit in translation variants of great value. The witness of the quotations has, however, to be used with extreme care since these quotations were committed to memory (although not so many as was once thought) and could also reflect recensional forms or corrupt forms of the text (cf. p. 344).

III.   THE PRINCIPLES AND METHODS OF TEXTUAL CRITICISM

The aim of text criticism is to restore the text to its original condition, purified as far as possible of all elements extraneous to the autograph copy, the first edition or the various editions of the text if there were any (Wevers). The critical edition of a classical text transmitted in mediaeval copies proceeds in two stages according to the genealogical method developed by C. Lachmann and followed by modern philology from the last century until today (cf. p. 336).

1. The aim of textual criticism is first to determine the relationships among the various witnesses or manuscripts preserved as well as the affiliation of one or other to their common archetype. For this *the preserved manuscripts and their documentary and historical analysis are stored*. These manuscripts are collated and compared, their variants are determined and if possible their genealogical tree is established (*stemma codicum*).

2. The next procedure is the *examination of the variants* of the manuscripts and the selection of those which best correspond to the archetype. In the case where the whole manuscript tradition has been damaged by corruption it will be necessary to resort to conjecture.

When examining the variants of a particular passage and choosing those considered to be original, textual criticism becomes more an art than a science. A keen critical sense is needed combined with a large capacity for intuition to grasp all the nuances of the text.

Textual criticism has evolved some basic rules but their value is only as a guide. They cannot be applied too rigidly or merely mechanically. These four basic rules are as follows:

a. In the transmission of a text «banalisation» and «trivialisation» occur. When the copyist comes across a lexical, grammatical, historical or theological difficulty he tends to make the text easier to read, replacing the expression which presents a difficulty with an easier one. Thus the reading which is «more difficult» (*lectio difficilior*) has more probability of being original, unless the difficult is due to corruption. See the examples note above (Is 39:1; 1 Sm 20:34; cf. p. 374).

b. In the course of the manuscript transmission there is inevitably a tendency to expand the text which leads to the insertion of glosses, for example, or the repetition of parallel passages. For this reason the «shorter» reading (*lectio brevior*) is also in principle the older, unless there has been a mistake through haplography. See the examples given under the headings of doublets, glosses, additions of epithets or names, etc. (pp. 375-376).

c. The *reading which accounts for the origin of the other* variants is preferable to them in principle (cf. p. 409).

d. Given the tendency of copyists to harmonise texts, the *reading which differs from its parallels* is preferable to one exhibiting signs of similarity to them. See the examples of harmonisation or similarly to parallel passages (pp. 374-375).

IV. TEXTUAL CRITICISM OF THE GREEK VERSION

Since it is a translation the LXX version presents special problems of text criticism. This happens in two stages: the first tried to recover the text of the Greek recensions (Origen, Lucian and Hesychius) and the second the recovery of the text of original version. To these two stages a third is added which does not affect the textual criticism of this version but of the Hebrew text. The aim of this third stage is the reconstruction, to the extent it is possible, of the original Hebrew reflected in the Greek translation. These three stages have very complex problems.

1. *Recovery of the text of the LXX recensions.* The first objective noted by Lagarde for textual criticism of the Greek text of the LXX is the recovery of the archetypes of the great recensions of Origen, Hesychius and Lucian.

The first step to be taken is to establish the genealogical tree of the LXX manuscripts with the object of reaching through them the archetypes from which the manuscripts derive. This requires study of the characteristics and filiation of each manuscript (cf. p. 338). The origin of a particular textual family can be ascertained in many cases through the quotations of the Fathers of the region in which that textual family was known. For example, the quotations of the Antioch Fathers allows the text of manuscripts b o c_2 e_2 of Sm-Kgs to be assigned to the Lucianic recension.

2. *Recovery of the text of the original version.* Once the text of those three great recensions is recovered, an attempt is made to reconstruct the original text of the Greek version. The numberless interconnections among the various text families make the task of reconstructing the original text very complex and difficult. To regain the original text of the LXX it is also necessary to identify the variants inserted by recensions earlier than Origen, as are the proto-Lucianic and proto-Theodotion or *kaige* recensions. Sometimes the original text of the LXX will have to be given up as lost. However, to a very large extent the original text of this version is still recognisable as emphasised by the critical edition of the LXX completed in Göttingen according to the principles established by Lagarde (cf. p. 305).

In this task the principles and general method of text criticism have to be applied (cf. p. 379). For example, when evaluating a variant of the LXX it is not much the number but the quality of supporting witnesses which counts. A reading witnesses by the Greek hexaplar text, the Vulgate and the syro-hexaplar and Armenian versions can have less value than another attested only in the OL but which goes back to an older Greek text. The reasons for this is that a variant which is repeated in several manuscripts can have originated in a single manuscript of inferior quality but very widespread, whereas a reading preserved in a single manuscript can be preferable for reasons of internal criticism.

3. *Reconstruction of the original Hebrew (Vorlage).* The LXX text is of great value for criticism of the Hebrew text in that it provides the possibility of reconstructing the original Hebrew used to make the translation and at times shows considerable differences from the MT which has reached us.

Reconstruction of the original Hebrew is very often hypothetical, especially as regards morphological and syntactic details. However, the existence of parallels in manuscripts from Qumran and the presence of Hebraisms in the LXX provoke attempts at retroversion from the Greek text to Hebrew. This is feasible especially through study of the equivalents in the respective vocabularies. In 2 Kgs 17:20, for example, the MT has «and he afflicted them» (*way^e'annēm*) whereas the Greek text *kaì esáleusen autoús* assumes the Hebrew to read *way^{e}ni'ēm*, «and he moved them»; one of these readings is the result of metathesis (Tov 1981, p. 103).

V. HISTORY AND CRITICISM OF THE HEBREW TEXT

To apply correctly the methods of textual criticism first a correct theory about the history of the biblical text is required. The principles and methods of textual criticism do not change, but their application varies considerably depending on how the history of transmission of the biblical text is envisaged. It is either a single straight line (*geradelinnig*, Noth) which starting from the first edition reaches present editions or it resembles rather a bundle of lines which intersect and coincide (like a «multilinear» edition as Fischer called his edition of the *Old Latin* text).

The history of the biblical text comprises a process of gradual separation into different text forms and of later unification around a single type of text, the proto-rabbinic or proto-masoretic text. To determine the existence of this twofold process of separation and unification has important consequences for the practice of textual criticism and of later exegesis. It requires adopting a methodology of work which consists of progressive approach to the text in four moves.

1. The analysis has to begin with the most recent textual witnesses to reach, later, the oldest. This work, therefore, has to start with the mediaeval *masoretic text* since it is the only text which has been transmitted in its entirety and with great accuracy over the centuries.

2. With knowledge of the masoretic tradition and its forerunners in the period before the 1st cent. CE, criticism has to carry out a parallel movement of *approach to the ancient Septuagint*. This approach consists in retracing the path taken by the recensions of the LXX which departed from the original Greek version influenced by the (proto-)masoretic Hebrew text type (cf. p. 381).

3. The next move consists in an *approach to the original Hebrew (the Vorlage) of the LXX* made possible by the recognised literalism of the Greek version in many of its books and texts. Even when an accurate reconstruction of the original used by the translator it is not possible in many cases, there is still no doubt about the existence of such an original, nor can the bulk of the variants found in most of the books of the LXX be ascribed to the translator. A valid criterion is that the shifting of verses, the additions and omissions are best explained by supposing a different Hebrew text, whereas isolated vari-

ants are more easily due to the intervention of the translator (Bogaert).

4. The next move consists of approaching the forms of Hebrew text which existed in the Persian and Hellenistic periods. Critical analysis is carried out by a synoptic comparison of the different texts transmitted (MT, Hebrew original of the LXX, the Dead Sea Scrolls, etc.).

The aim of criticism can then be directed at all or any particular one of the following levels of textual crystallization: 1) the *text form closest to the original* although no longer attested in any surviving manuscript, 2) the *oldest attested text form* even though it is not the most original or even canonical, or, lastly, it can aim at the 3) *«authorised» form based on careful tradition,* but is not always the most original nor the oldest known by surviving manuscript tradition.

These three objectives correspond to the three stages which can be distinguished in the history of the biblical text:

a. The first stage corresponds to the *original form and composition*; study of this stage corresponds to literary criticism. The moment a book becomes sacred within a particular religious community its literary form stays stable and allows no further major alteration. The *process of literary development* of the Pentateuch culminated in the 5th cent. BCE at the time when the literary corpus comprising the deuteronomic history (Jos-Kgs) was being formed, as was the collection of prophetic books including the texts of so-called Second and Third Is, Jl and Jn and the last three prophets, Hg, proto-Zac (chaps. 1-8) and Ml (Blenkinsopp). At the same time the collection of Writings began to form (cf. pp. 158-159).

b. The second stage corresponds to the *earliest form or text forms attested in texts preserved in the manuscript tradition*. With stage one complete, *the process of textual transmission* begins during which, in spite of the careful techniques for copying manuscripts, very many variants and also corruptions of all kinds are inserted in the text of each book. During this period, *different editions or recensions of the same book co-exist* which can come into contact with and contaminate each other. This happens in the duplicate editions of the books of Sm and Jr.

c. The third stage is that of the *proto-masoretic consonantal text,* declared as official after 70 CE. After the previous stage there could only be *a stabilisation process* marked by a tendency to determine the limits of the canon of sacred books and at the same time to react against the diversity of texts often very corrupt. This process culminated at the beginning of the 2nd cent. CE with the final definition of the unsolved questions about the limits of the Hebrew canon, the exclusion of books considered to be apocryphal and the almost total imposition of a particular type of consonantal text for each book admitted into the canon. On the whole, the uniformity of the text tradition and the faithfulness of its transmission is greater in the books of the Pentateuch, decreases in the prophetic books and is very low-grade in some of the Writings. These were edited much later and for some time it was disputed whether some of these writings were sacred books.

To these three stages a third can be added, which corresponds to the *ma-*

soretic text of the 9th-10th cents. CE. Each of these stages has to be studied separately and not only in terms of an earlier or later stage (Barthélemy 1982).

Synoptic comparison among the different texts preserved takes on special importance in books in where the variety of texts reflects prior redaction and editing. This is the case for the historical books and for some prophetic and wisdom books of which different literary traditions have reached us: the books of Sm and Kgs, of Jr, Pr, Dn, Ezr, Est and other sections of smaller texts (cf. pp. 393-404).

The transmission of these books in two or more forms of text can only be adequately explained by a very broadly based study which should include *study of the history of literary redaction and of the editorial process of the book*. The discrepancy between the masoretic text and the LXX in Jr in both the length and the arrangement of the material goes beyond what is usually typical of these two types of text (Bogaert, Tov). The two text forms, short (LXX) and long (MT) of the book of Jr had already crystallised during the literary redaction of the book, before transmission of the text began, at least of the second edition of the book (cf. p. 395).

The existence of many different texts and recensions of the same book and the attempts to unify and fix the text of each book pose a series of question which are not easy to answer: Which of the three levels of the history of the biblical text distinguished earlier should text criticism try to reconstruct? What is the oldest level which text criticism can and should attain? These questions entail others such as: Which of the text levels noted above corresponds to the canonical or authorised (Jewish, Catholic or Protestant) text? Which text is to be translated into modern languages?

If we retain a theoretical difference betwen the fields of text criticism and literary criticism, the following holds true. Text criticism considers it possible and therefore its aim to reconstruct the second stage of those noted above: the earliest form or forms of text attested by texts which have reached us. Literary criticism aspires to reconstruct the original form and literary composition of the text of a book. Barthélemy (1982) considers that in the case of Pr, Jr and Ez mentioned above and several others, the MT and the text represented by the LXX are the result of independent literary developments, which makes it impossible to attain the point of textual stability assumed to exist around 300 BCE. Textual criticism on its own does not allow one to go back to the text stage before these developments. In such cases the proto-masoretic text has to be imposed as «the reference text within the limits of the Hebrew text» (Barthélemy 1982). As a result, the «Committee for the textual analysis of the Hebrew OT» chooses to follow the tradition of the MT in cases where it differs from the tradition given in the LXX at the literary level and not only at the textual level.

Childs follows the same line from a more theological and «canonical» perspective. For him the masoretic text «is the *vehicle* both for recovering and for understanding the canonical text of the Old Testament». It is justified by the fact that the Hebrew text would have been fixed towards the end of the

1st cent. CE and formed part of an absolutely established canon, whereas for a long time the Greek text of the OT remained in a very fluid and undefined state and did not gain stability except in relation to the Hebrew text thanks to Origen's critical work. In favour of the «canonical» priority of the masoretic text also figures the quality and faithfulness of masoretic oral tradition with respect to the vocalisation of the consonantal text. Throughout history the pharisee movement and rabbinism were «the living vehicle of the whole canon of Hebrew scripture» (Childs). On the other hand, the Greek-speaking Jewish community in Egypt or the Qumran community ended up by disappearing or ceased to exert meaningful influence. The Samaritan community only preserved part of the Hebrew canon, the Torah, so that it denied itself any possibility of influencing the course of the history of the biblical canon and text. The same Greek-speaking Jewish communities accepted the authority of the proto-masoretic Hebrew text as the recensional history of the LXX proves.

However, the position of Childs leads to the contradiction of considering canonical and normative for Christians a Hebrew text which was fixed and declared official by the Jewish Synagogue in a period after the birth of Christianity. Childs justifies opting for the MT from the fact that «the early Christian community of the New Testament never developed a doctrine of scripture apart from the Jewish». Christians never presumed to use their own text which was better than others, unlike the Samaritans who appropriated a text which they considered as authorised or canonical. However, right from the start, the Christians used the Greek text as the text of the Scriptures. On the other hand, the NT shows great freedom in the use of different textual traditions and so reflects current practice in the period before the proto-Masoretic text was stabilised (cf. p. 495). Similarly, it can be said that an inadequately transmitted text may go back to an original which is more authentic and older than another text transmitted with less care. The question of the better text refers less to the better preserved text than to the the text which preserves a better original or reflects better the oldest forms of that text.

Insofar as it is considered impossible to reconstruct critically a level prior to the proto-Masoretic text, there is a tendency to contrast *literary authenticity*, which modern criticism before and after Wellhausen has always aimed for, to *canonical authenticity*, to which the Comité mentioned above seems to pay more attention (Brock). Underlying this is the old opposition between rational criticism and traditional criticism.

Critical-historical exegesis cannot abandon its primary objective: to know the form and meaning of the original texts. Accordingly, it cannot close itself to the possibility of resorting, if necessary, to textual conjectures in spite of its misuse in the past (Albrektson, and Barthélemy's reply 1982).

A reconstruction of the biblical text completed from a selection of variants as a guide to translations into modern languages (as carried out by the Comité) does not explore the possibilities for approaching the older forms of the text than represented in MT. These possibilities are undoubtedly greater than such work would suppose. It may be possible to accuse the crit-

icism of past generations of yielding to «expertise» (Barthélemy) and looking for no other solution to the problems of the MT than using the variants
from the versions and hypothetical conjectures. It is, then, equally possible
to predict that in the future, a whole movement of biblical studies would be
guilty of no less an expertise in considering that only the MT variants merit
attention and that they can be resolved within masoretic tradition. By this
road, the text is explained through the grammar and the lexicon of masoretic tradition and Hebrew grammar and lexis are based on that text. In this
way, if a vicious circle is not produced, the range of movements is reduced in
every case to masoretic tradition alone. This same tradition is understood on
many occasions in a very restricted sense, for no attention is paid to the consonantal variants of mediaeval manuscripts,, which in cases where they agree
with readings from the versions are not mere mistakes which arose independently in the manuscripts and versions (Goshen-Gottstein) but the remains
of genuine pre-Masoretic readings (Wevers, Trebolle; cf. p. 281). Nor is it
usual practice to take any notice of the variants in Palestinian manuscripts
related to the Hebrew textual tradition reflected in the versions (cf. p. 273).
Masoretic tradition completely ignored the existence of different translations
which the discoveries near the Dead Sea have brought to light.

One example is enough to emphasise that the different textual traditions
are all interconnected and cannot be studied separately, at least if one claims
to reach the oldest levels of the text, quite a justified claim as this example
shows. In 2 Kgs 13:23 the Greek text of Codex B and its dependent manuscripts omit the MT expression «up to now» (*'ad 'āttâ*). Most critics give preference to the short reading of LXX^B. Barthélemy (1982) considers this omission is due to a modernising tendency of the Greek translator. The text represented by LXX^B certainly does not correspond to that of the original Greek
translation but to the text of a later recension (*Kaige*). The text of the *Septuaginta* is represented here by the proto- Lucianic text, the position of which
does not correspond to MT 13:23 but to 13:7. At this point (13:7), the ancient
Greek text has the MT reading (13:23) «until now». Accordingly, preference
cannot be given to an assumed short reading of the LXX, nor can one speak
of modernisation by the translator. Both texts agree on the reading but position it differently; the differences in the order of the passages in MT and LXX
are connected with the history of the deuteronomic redaction of that book
(cf. vv. 3-7). Global rather than atomistic comparison between the different
textual traditions allows each variant to be placed in its context. It also allows
one to go back to the oldest levels of textual tradition, represented in the
Greek version by the proto-Lucianic text.

Existing editions of the Hebrew text reproduce a diplomatic text, i.e., the
text of a codex (of St. Petersburg in the *Biblia Hebraica*) and not a critically
established text (cf. p. 277). It can be stated that the OT textual critic is still
governed by external criticism and is indebted to the cult of the great
codices, a stage already superseded in textual criticism of the LXX and the NT.
It should no longer be surprising that in practical exegesis and even in historical and diachronic studies, the text of a single mediaeval codex is used,

the one reproduced in *BHS* as if it were the only biblical text to exist throughout all biblical history and even up to the present. Since this approach is no longer tenable in critical studies, translations, exegetical commentaries and historical studies insert numberless corrections and exceptions to be able to face the problems of every kind presented by the biblical text, from grammatical problems to literary and historical problems.

A critically reconstructed text can be, and many times is, more authentic, i.e. closer to the original, than the documented text. The reconstruction of texts involves problems very like those in artistic restoration: Which «Sistine Chapel» is truer and would be recognised by Michelangelo as his own, the one seen up to a few years ago and blackened by age or the one on show now, with brightened up colours?

Textual criticism of the past erred in undervaluing what was late and traditional (= «masoretic»), canonical and confessional. Much of modern textual criticism errs, instead, in abandoning the diachronic approach, in not seeking to face the challenge of the original and the distance separating the original and the traditional. It is precisely this distance, however, which sets in motion a whole hermeneutic process which has allowed the texts to be freed from the accumulation of centuries and enabled them to tell their own story.

The knowledge of countless readings from one or other text tradition and the comparison of these readings among themselves and with the MT enable the relationships between the two dimensions and fundamental values of the biblical text, *authenticity* and *canonicity*, to be considered in a richer and more varied way. The two aspects and meanings of «traditional», i.e., the fact of coming from the «tradition of the origins» and enjoy the nature of «sacred tradition», do not necessarily go together. In the case of the Bible, however, they are not so far apart as to reach the point of a complete break between the original and the canonical, between the scope of criticism and of canonical tradition.

The history of the biblical text and the make-up of the biblical canon have to be conceived as a plurality and not as a single line of transmission which ends up as the proto-masoretic text. Comparison of the various biblical texts preserved allows one to get closer to the oldest and most original edited form of the biblical books. Study of *the Bible as a pluri-textual and polyglot work*, like the Renaissance Polyglots or the Hexaplar of Origen, allow closer approach to the Bible as a literary and historical work and at the same time, a religious work which enjoys canonical recognition by Judaism and by Christianity.

VI. TEXTUAL CRITICISM AND COMPARATIVE SEMITIC PHILOLOGY

Although textual criticism keeps to the witness of preserved biblical documents which do not go back further than the end of the 4th cent. BCE, it cannot avoid taking into consideration the advances of comparative Semitic philology, although this refers to texts of much older periods. This itself makes it very evident that study of the bible cannot set up barriers between disciplines or absolute divisions between historical periods.

Study of Hebrew epigraphy and Ugaritic literature in particular has improved our knowledge of Hebrew a well as of the orthography and lexicography in the period before the exile, a period to which a very large part of the sources and texts of the OT go back (cf. p. 87). The grammatical or lexical difficulties of the oldest texts of the bible, often already quite unintelligible to the translators of the Greek version, were resolved in previous decades by resorting too frequently to textual variants of that version or to conjectures by modern critics. The advances of comparative Semitic philology can often dispense with this resort to the versions and to conjectures. Knowledge of Ugaritic helps to resolves many difficulties of the Hebrew text (Dahood) although this tendency should not be made so radical as to undervalue the testimony of the versions and declare text criticism virtually obsolete for the study of ancient poetic texts.

Comparative philology is a good antidote to the abusive correction of the Hebrew text as at the beginning of the century. However, it too sometimes exaggerates in correcting the consonantal text. Correction of the vocalic text can be even more arbitrary. Comparative philology tends to rewrite the text according to the semantic meaning it attributes to the text. If the practice of conjecture and correcting the text, so common at the start of the century, assumed the abandon of the written tradition attested in the manuscripts, comparative philology tends to put on one side the semantic tradition in respect of the meaning of the Hebrew words, ascribing to them meanings derived from other Semitic languages and sources. Comparative study of the Semitic languages has improved knowledge of Hebrew and still has much to contribute. Therefore, the history and criticism of the text can at least continue to pay attention to this branch of modern research. The work of text criticism achieved by Barthélemy and the other members of the Committee is based on the supposition that comparative philology is only useful on very few occasions. The use they make of comparative philology is, accordingly, very cautious and restricted. Their work is text criticism and comparative philology, always keeping to readings attested in the manuscript tradition.

Although modern translations, especially those made in the 60's and 70's, profess not to wish to change the text or to accept textual conjectures, it remains true that they still alter the text, which in fact on many occasions was unavoidable.

ALBREKTSON, B., «Difficilior lectio probabilior: A Rule of Textual Criticism and its Use in Old Testament Studies», *Remembering All the Way...*, OTS 21 (1981) 5-18.

BARR, J., *Comparative Philology and the Text of the OT*, Oxford 1968.

BARTHÉLEMY, D., *Critique textuelle de l'Ancien Testament*, vol. 1 Fribourg-Göttingen 1982, vol. 2 1986.

BARTHÉLEMY, D., «L'enchevêtrement de l'histoire textuelle et de l'histoire littéraire dans les relations entre la Septante et le Texte Massorétique», *De Septuaginta*, eds. A. Pietersma-C. Cox, Ontario 1984, 19-40.

BARTHÉLEMY, D., 'Notes critiques sur quelques points d'histoire du texte', *Études d'histoire du texte de l'Ancien Testament*, Fribourg-Göttingen 1978, 289-303.

BARTHÉLEMY, D. -GOODING, D.G. -LUST, J. -TOV, E., *The Story of David and Goliath. Textual and Literary Criticism*, Fribourg-Göttingen 1986.

BLENKINSOPP, J., *Prophecy and Canon. A Contribution to the Study of Jewish Origins*, Notre Dame-London 1977.

BOGAERT, P.-M., «Les trois rédactions conservées et la forme originale de l'envoi du Cantique de Moïse (Dt 32,43)», *Deuteronomium*, ed. N. Lohfink, Louvain 1985, 329-340.

CHILDS, B.S., *Introduction of the Old Testament as Scripture*, London 1979.

DAHOOD, M., «Northwest Semitic Texts and Textual Criticism of the Hebrew Bible», *Questions disputées d'Ancien Testament*, Louvain 1974, 11-37.

DELITSCH, F., *Die Lese- und Schreibfehler im Alten Testament*, Berlin-Leipzig 1920.

EHRLICH, A.B., *Randglossen zur hebräischen Bibel*, 7 vols., Leipzig 1908/1914.

GOODWIN, D.W., *Text-Restoration Methods in Contemporary U.S.A. Biblical Scholarship*, Naples 1969.

GOSHEN-GOTTSTEIN, M.H., «The Textual Criticism of the Old Testament: Rise, Decline, Rebirth», *JBL* 102 (1983) 365-399.

GRABBE, L.L., *Comparative Philology and the Text of Job: A Study in Methodology*, Missoula MT 1977.

KLEIN, R.W., *Textual Criticism of the Old Testament*, Philadelphia PA 1974.

LEMAIRE, A., «Hadad l'Édomite ou Hadad l'Araméen?», *BN* 43 (1988) 14-18.

MCCARTER, P.K., *Textual Criticism. Recovering the Text of the Hebrew Bible*, Philadelphia PA 1986.

ROBERTS, B.J., *The Old Testament Text and Versions*, Cardiff 1951.

SANDERS, J.A., 'Text and Canon: Concepts and Method', *JBL* 98 (1979) 5-29.

SKEHAN, P.W., «A Fragment of the «Song of Moses» (Deut. 32) From Qumran», *BASOR* 136 (1954) 12-15.

TOV, E., *The Text-Critical Use of the Septuagint in Biblical Research*, Jerusalem 1981.

TOV, E., «Criteria for Evaluating Textual Readings. The Limitations of Textual Rules», *HThR* 75 (1982) 429-448.

TOV, E., *The Textual Criticism of the Bible. An Introduction*, Minneapolis-Assen/Maastricht 1992.

TOV, E., *The Text-critical Use of the Septuagint in Biblical Research*, Jerusalem 1981.

TREBOLLE BARRERA, J., «The Text-Critical Use of the Septuagint in the Books of Kings», *VII Congress of the IOCS. Louvain 1989*, ed. C. Cox, Atlanta GA 1992, 285-299.

TREBOLLE BARRERA, J., *Centena in libros Samuelis et Regum. Variantes textuales y composición literaria en los libros de Samuel y Reyes*, Madrid 1989.

TREBOLLE BARRERA, J., *Jehú y Joás. Texto y composición literaria de 2 Reyes 9-11*, Valencia 1984.

TREBOLLE BARRERA, J., *Salomón y Jeroboán. Historia de la recensión y redacción de 1 Reyes 2-12; 14*, Salamanca-Jerusalem 1980.

ULRICH, E., «Characteristics and Limitations of the Old Latin Translation of the Septuagint», *La Septuaginta en la investigación contemporánea (V Congreso de la IOCS)*, ed. N. Fernández Marcos, Madrid 1985, 67-81.

ULRICH, E., «Horizons of OT Textual Research at the Thirtieth Anniversary of Qumran Cave 4», *CBQ* 46 (1984) 613-636.

WEVERS, J.W., «The Use of Versions for Text Criticism: The Septuagint», *La Septuaginta en la investigación contemporánea (V Congreso de la IOCS)*, Madrid 1985, 115-24.

WÜRTHWEIN, R., *Der Text des Alten Testaments*, Stuttgart 1974.

WEINGREEN, J., *Introduction to the Critical Study of the Text of the Hebrew Bible*, Oxford 1982.

WONNERBERGER, R., *Understanding BHS. A Manual for the Users of Biblia Hebraica Stuttgartensia*, Rome 1984.

VII. TEXTUAL CRITICISM AND LITERARY CRITICISM. GLOSSES AND DOUBLETS

Textual criticism and literary criticism have very different fixed fields and limits of activity. *Textual criticism* aims at recovering the text exactly as it left the hands of the author or last the redactor. It analyses the process of *textual* transmission and tries to eliminate from the text any corruption which could have occurred during that long process. *Literary criticism* (*Literarkritik*) attempts to recreate the process of literary *formation* of the work up to the moment of its definitive redaction; it de-composes the text into its literary units to reassemble it following the various stages through which, starting from the first written and oral sources, the redaction and composition of the work was completed. Textual criticism tries to reconstruct the history of the text with the aim of recovering the *Urtext* or original text. Literary criticism tries to reconstruct the history of the composition and redaction of the work with the objective of reaching the initial form (*Urform*) and the original stage of composition. In theory the distinction between these disciplines is clear, but in practice the boundary separating them is very movable making necessary the use of both methods in combination.

The *variants produced in the course of textual transmission* whether by copyists' mistakes or by intentional changes at the hand of glossarists and exegetes (cf. p. 371) are not usually very large or very important. In general they are easy to detect and usually it is possible also to find a suitable solution.

The lengthier variants, instead, and those which are more important and more complex are usually *variants which arose in the editorial process of the book*. In the text of the NT also the more important variants are those which originated in the earliest phase, that is, in the period before the first half of the 2nd cent. CE. These variants determine the difference between existing text forms. In the study of such variants the fields of text criticism and literary criticism combine which makes a dialogue between these two specialties of biblical criticism necessary.

The historical books provide special interest for an all-round study of text criticism and literary criticism.

The sequence reflected in the LXX at the end of the book of *Jos* (death of Joshua and the elders, start of transgressions by the people, Eglon's oppression) clearly matches the original order of the text exactly as it would have appeared on a scroll of the second Temple period which the Greek translator translated (Rofé). In this respect, the text of the LXX is preferable to the MT.

As for the book of *Jgs*, the MS 4QJudg[a], edited by the author of that book, is of extraordinary interest since it omits a literary unit which modern criticism had long since considered as inserted into the Gideon narrative. It omits Jgs 6:7-10 where an unnamed prophet addresses the Israelites in a moralising tone using stereotyped language which criticism at first ascribed to an Elohist source but today is usually attributed to Deuteronomist editor (perhaps a nomist, DTR-N). I drew attention for the first time to the connection between the omission in 4QJudg[a] and the deuteronomistic redaction in an article the title of which «History of the text of the historical books and history of the deuteronomistic redaction (Judges 2:10-3:6)» attempted to emphasize the importance of this manuscript for the textual and literary history of the book of Judges and the whole deuteronomistic history (Trebolle 1986 and 1992).

Here we will focus attention exclusively on two aspects which require the interdisciplinary approach of text criticism and literary criticism: the gloss, usually not very large, and re-editing, which can affect a whole book.

1. *Explanatory Glosses*

Glosses, when considered as explanatory, belong to hermeneutics, to be dealt with in the chapter 'The OT Interprets Itself' (cf. pp. 430-435). Here they are considered as interpolations in the text, either as part of literary criticism or of textual criticism, depending on whether they had been added during the redaction or the transmission of the text.

Glosses can be inserted into a work during the literary editing of the text or in the later period of text transmission. To identify the presence of a gloss there are in general no other criteria than those intrinsic to the actual text so that a certain element of doubt can never be avoided in the conclusions reached. Among these criteria stand out linking repetition (*Wiederaufnahme*), comparison with parallel passages in the MT or the versions, repetitions or inconsistencies, the presence of particular indicators, etc. (Driver).

a. A *resumptive repetition* can mark the presence of a gloss. An example is to be found in Ps 68:9 «When you arose, Elohim, before your people... the earth trembled, the skies rained also *before Elohim, the one of Sinai* (zh syny), *before Elohim*, the God of Israel». W. F. Albright suggested that *zeh*

Sînay is a divine epithet, «the (God) of Israel», but it must surely be a gloss which attempts to refer to the revelation on Sinai. The repetition of the terms «before Elohim» (*mippenê ʾĕlohîm*), a repetition which is not in the LXX text, is probably further confirmation of the late nature of the intrusive «the one of Sinai».

b. The presence of a gloss can be determined by *comparison of parallel passages*. The gloss in question can consists of a lexical substitution in order to explain ambiguous or inexact terms or bring them up to date. For example, the expression «to oppress them» (*leʾannôtô*, 2 Sm 7:10) is replaced in the parallel passage in Chr by another which is not so harsh: «to destroy them» (*leballotô*, 1 Chr 17:9[suffix: people]). Similarly, the expression «according to your desires» (*ḥepṣekâ* 1 Kgs 5:22) is replaced by «according to your needs» (*ṣorkekā*, 2 Chr 2:15).

c. The presence of certain *indicators* allows the presence of a gloss to be identified. These are the pronouns *hwʾ* or *hyʾ* («he/she is»), the particles *hinnēh* («behold»), *ʾēt* (object marker) and *ʾ(w)ô* («or»), the generic expression *kol-* («all»), the formula *kēn-taʿśeh* («you shall do the same»), etc.

a. The pronouns *hwʾ* and *hyʾ* («he/she is..») can introduce, for example, a gloss which explains a toponym or patronymic. In Josh 18:13 «Luz, that is (*hwʾ*) Bethel», the gloss shows that the ancient place-name «Luz» was later known under the name of Bethel. Similar cases are «in the Valley of Shaveh, that is (*hwʾ*), the Valley of the King» (Gn 14:17) and «Jerusalem, that is (*hwʾ*), Jebus» (1 Chr 11:4), etc. (Fishbane).

In Gn 36:1 there is a gloss typical of many others: «Esau, that is (*hwʾ*), Edom». The gloss in Ez 31:18 wishes to make it absolutely clear to whom the prophet's oracle refers: «that is, to pharaoh and all his hordes» (cf. v. 2).

b. In Hg 2:5a, the particle *ʾet* introduces the gloss «this is (*ʾet*) the word which I promised you on leaving Egypt». This interpolation is missing from the LXX.

The case of Is 29:10 is quite important: «(Yahweh) has closed your eyes, [which are (*ʾet*) prophets], and has covered your heads, [which are (*ʾet*) the seers]». The double interpolation introduced by the particle (*ʾet*) transforms what was an oracle against the people into censure of the false prophets.

c. The particle *ʾ(w)ô* («or») is used to introduce glosses in texts of a legal nature. In Num 6:2, «If a man [*or* a woman] has made a solemn nazirite vow...», the Hebrew verb is in the masculine singular which indicates that the phrase «or a woman» is a gloss, extending the scope of the law in question to the woman (cf. Nm 30:3-4).

d. Expansions of a legal nature can be introduced by the generic expression *kol-* («all»). In Ex 22 there is whole series of casuistic laws on property rights; v.8. is an interpolation introduced by *ʿal-kol debar-* («concerning everything...»), an expression which extends the scope of the application of the law to many more than were envisaged in the context and in the original text.

e. The formula *kēn-taʿśeh*(«You shall do the same...») can be used to introduce glosses in legal texts. In Ex 22:29a, the expression extends to the first-born of animals the law affecting first-born sons: «You shall give me the first born among your sons. [You shall do the same (*kēn-taʿśeh*) with your cattle and your flocks]. Seven days shall he stay with his mother and on the eighth you shall give it to me». There is a similar gloss in Dt 22:3 in respect of the two preceding verses.

f. Narrative texts provide many quotations from other biblical texts, usually of a legal nature; these quotations are often inserted by means of technical terms or expressions such as *kakātûb* («as it is written:», 1 Kgs 2:3), *lē'môr* («as it says:») (2 Kgs 14:6; 2 Chr 25:4; Ezr 9:11), *'ašer* («that:»), *ka'ašer ṣiwwâ* or *'ašer ṣiwwâ* («as he commanded:»).

This section also includes the *inscriptions* and colophons (cf. pp. 101-102).

2. Duplicate or Double Editions

The overlap of text criticism and literary criticism becomes very obvious in books where the process of literary formation went beyond the first edition, ceding place to what could be called a second edition, «corrected and enlarged» in common parlance. Cases of duplicate editions occur in the canonical, deuterocanonical and apocryphal books of both the OT and the NT and also in the writings of the apostolic *Fathers* or in a rabbinic writing as important as *'Aboth*.

It is common to have «duplicate editions» in all literatures of any period. The second edition can affect a story, a poem or a complete work. The author or editors of later periods can be directly responsible for the new editions. New copies of the first edition continued to circulate, especially in isolated places which the second edition could not reach and never succeeded in replacing the first edition. The various editions were transmitted in parallel and their texts contaminated each other giving rise to an endless number of variants.

Until a few years ago, the variants attested in the LXX used to be explained as the result of intervention by the Greek translators (Nyberg). Instead of restricting themselves to translating the Hebrew text in their hands, the translators recast the text to the extent of changing it into a new edition of the book in Greek. After the finds at Qumran this explanation can no longer be upheld. Duplicate editions generally originated in the original language, either Hebrew, as in the case of the extended («Palestinian») text of the book of Ex, or Aramaic, as in the case of Dn 4-6 which in MT are in a different sequence from the LXX.

Double editions of the biblical books have great transcendence. They pose questions as controversial as which of the two editions is the authentic original, which is canonical and which of them ought to be translated in modern versions, especially if it was a matter of establishing the official, authorised version of a particular Christian confession.

A. 1 SM (1 SM 17-18)
The masoretic Hebrew text, followed by the Greek of the hexaplaric and Lucianic recensions, represents the text of a «second edition» of the story of David and Goliath (1 Sm 17-18). The Greek version, instead, reflects the text of a shorter «first edition», comprising the following literary units: 17:1-11.32-54*; 18:6*-9 and 18:12a.13-16.20-28*.29a (the * means that there are other variants in the text).

The second edition added a series of literary units related to each other (cf. 17:25

and 18:17-19) and to episodes included in the first edition:

– 18:10-11 refers to 16:14-23.

– 18:1 and 4 allude to episodes about Jonathan and David (1 Sm 14:20.23; 2 Sm 9).

– The account in 17:12-30 (31), described as «romantic», contrasts with the more «heroic» narrative in 17:1-11.32-54*.

– The scene about Saul's jealousy in 18:10-11 repeats 19:6-9.

– Similarly, the episode about Merab in 19:17-19 is parallel to the one about Mikal in 18:20-28.

– According to 18:5, Saul, pleased by David's success against the Philistines, puts him at the head of his army. In 18:13-15, however, Saul seems to be seized by jealousy and tries to get rid of David, sending him to the riskiest position in the battle. The text of the second edition makes these successive episodes. In this way the two episodes, originally independent of each other, now seem to correspond to two consecutive stages in David's life: separate accounts have been made into a continuous story.

1st Edition: MT = LXX	*2nd Edition: MT +*	
STORIES	STORIES	JOINS
David & Goliath I 17:1-9(10)11		
	David & Goliath II 17:12-30(31)	
17:32-33(34-36)		v.41
17:37-40(42-47)		
17:48a		v.48b
17:49		v.50
17:51-54		
	David before Saul 17:55-58	
	18:1.4	
	18:2(3a)5	v.3b
Saul's jealousy I 18:6ab-8a.9.		v.6aα
	Saul's jealousy II 18:10-11	
18:12a		v.12b
18:13-14.15.16		
	David & Merab 18:17-19	
David & Mikal 18:20-21a		v.21b
18:22-27		
18:28a.b(LXX)/b(MT)		
18:(29a)		vv.29b-30

It can no longer be said that the Greek translator shortened a longer Hebrew text. The Greek version reflects a Hebrew original with a shorter text which corresponds to a first edition of the David and Goliath story. MT transmits the text of a second «corrected and enlarged» edition (however, cf. the arguments of Barthélemy and Gooding).

AULD, A.G., «The Cities in Joshua 21: The Contribution of Textual Criticism», *Textus* 15 (1990) 141-152.

BARTHÉLEMY, D.-GOODING, D.W.-LUST, J.-TOV, E., *The Story of David and Goliath. Textual and Literary Criticism*, Fribourg - Göttingen 1986.

LUST, J., «The Story of David and Goliath in Hebrew and in Greek», *EpThLov* 59 (1983) 5-25.

ROFÉ, A., «The Battle of David and Goliath: Folklore, Theology, Eschatology», *Judaic Perspectives on Ancient Israel*, eds. J. Neusner - B.A. Levin- E.S. Frerichs, Philadelphia PA 1987, 117-151.

ROFÉ, A., «The End of the Book of Joshua According to the Septuagint», *Henoch* 4 (1982) 17-36.

TOV, E., cf. D. BARTHÉLEMY.

TREBOLLE BARRERA, J., «Historia del texto de los libros históricos e historia de la redacción deuteronomística (Jueces 2,10-3,6)», *Salvación en la Palabra. Targum-Derash-Berith*, Homenaje al Prof. A. Díez Macho, Madrid 1986, 245-258.

TREBOLLE, J., «Textual Variants in 4QJudg^a and the Textual and Editorial History of the Book of Judges», *The Texts of Qumran and the History of the Community. Proceedings of the Groningen Congress on Dead Sea Scrolls*, ed. F. García Martínez, *RQ* 14 (1989) 229-245.

TREBOLLE, J., «The Story of David and Goliath (1Sam 17-18): Textual Variants and Literary Composition», *BIOSCS* 23 (1990) 16-30.

TREBOLLE, J., «Histoire du texte des livres historiques et histoire de la composition et de la rédaction deutéronomistes avec une publication préliminaire de 4Q481a (Apocryphe d'Élisée)», *Congress Volume. Paris 1992*, ed. J.A. Emerton, Leiden 1995, 327-342.

B.   JEREMIAH

The Hebrew and Greek texts of the book of Jeremiah are considerably different in respect of the text (variants, additions and omissions) and of the order of the material which makes up the book. They represent two different editions, both attested in the manuscripts from Qumran: the text of the Greek version corresponds to the first edition and the MT text to the second.

The *text* of the LXX is one eighth shorter that the MT (there are 2,700 words missing). This fact is particularly significant if it is remembered that the Greek version of the other biblical books usually has a longer text than MT. The material added in the MT and unknown by the Greek version, consists of epithets of Yahweh, redactional additions to various literary units, the formula «oracle of Yahweh» (added some fifty times to the MT), etc. The second edition gives more importance to the prophet Jeremiah. It often adds the title «Jeremiah the prophet», which only occurs four times in the first edition (42:2; 43:6; 45:1; 51:59) and is found an additional 26 times in the second (MT 20:2; 25:2; 28:5.6.10.11.12.15; 29:1.29, etc.). This fact is significant for the history of prophecy (Auld, Vawter). Baruch plays an important part in the first edition (cf. *2 Baruch*) whereas in the second, Jeremiah is more prominent (Bogaert).

The *sequence* of the chapters is also different in the MT and the LXX. The collection of «Oracles against the nations» occurs in different contexts in each. The literary material given by the LXX in 25:14-20; 26-32 corresponds to 46-51; 25:15-38 in MT. In the Greek text the collection of «Oracles against the nations» comes after 25:1-13, a summary of the first part of the book. In the MT, instead, the «Oracles against the nations» come after the fourth section MT: 46-51) and the order of the oracles is also different. In this way the MT breaks the connection between the first part of the book (oracles of disapproval against Judah) and the second (oracles of disapproval against the nations). In spite of this it is still possible to identify in the MT the existence of an earlier link between both parts. After the summary of the first part the MT adds a reference to a magical action against the nations plus a list of those nations (MT 25:15-38). The reference to «everything written in this book» in 25:13, suggests that the «Oracles against the nations» formed a separate collection and its original position is attested in the LXX.

After the poems and the appendix to the first part, the order reflected by the LXX is in three parts: judgment against Judah - judgment against the nations - conditional salvation of Judah. One edition is not to be corrected by the other; the two forms of the text should be respected and interpreted independently of each other (Janzen, Tov, Bogaert). A. Rofé's opinion should be noted: he thinks that the general arrangement of the LXX, like other data such as the use of the divine title $s^e\underline{b}\bar{a}$'$\hat{o}\underline{t}$ and the addition of 39:4-13 in the MT, indicate that the features characteristic of the LXX are secondary in respect of the MT.

The two editions belong to a deuteronomistic school of thought. The deuteronomistic revision of the book of Jeremiah is much more complex than is generally supposed (Tov). The deuteronomistic redactional level of this book (denoted by the letter C by Mowinckel) is the product of a comparable development which gave rise to the editorial stages represented by Dt and the deuteronomistic redaction of Jos and Kgs.

Three fragments of Jeremiah found in Cave 4 (4QJer[abc], cf. p. 288) and one from Cave 2 (2QJer) throw new light on the textual and literary history of the book of Jeremiah. The fact that texts of the shorter type (as reflected by the Greek version) and of the longer (transmitted by the MT) have turned up in Qumran, shows that these two textual traditions of the book of Jeremiah developed in parallel from the 5th cent. to the 2nd cent. BCE. Both forms of the text could co-exist in the same setting and in the same place. 4QJer[b] reproduces the shorter («Egyptian») text. The other manuscripts correspond to proto-masoretic Palestinian textual families with a tendency to lengthen the text, as characteristic of the MT.

Cases in which the Greek version has a longer text than the masoretic text are few and far between. The greater originality of the text reflected by the LXX is evident from the absence of double readings which, instead, are common in the MT (1:15; 7:24; 10:25; 14:3b.4b; 25:6-7; 29:23; 41:10, etc.). Duplicate readings in the MT are usually cases of harmonisation. There are also many cases of Q[e]rê and K[e]tîb. All this emphasises the long history of textual transmission which underlies the MT of this book. Although there are more than a few cases of textual corruption, the MT of Jeremiah is not as unsatisfactory as the books of Sm, Hos or Ez can be.

The rare duplicate readings in the Greek text cannot be easily explained. Some may be due to recensions made on the basis of the MT. The Hebrew original (*Vorlage*) of the Greek version, instead, seems to have undergone hardly any recensional activity (Janzen).

The Wirceburgensis codex of the OL omits Jr 39:1-2 of the MT and Origen's Greek text marks them with an asterisk. This agreement shows that originally, these verses did not appear in the text of the LXX and neither did vv. 4-13. This is another example showing the importance of the OL (Bogaert 1990).

AULD, A.G., «Prophets and Prophecy in Jeremiah and Kings», *ZAW* 96 (1984) 66-82.

BOGAERT, P.-M., «De Baruch à Jérémie: Les deux rédactions conservées du livre de Jérémie», *Le livre de Jérémie: Le Prophète et son milieu, les oracles et leur transmission*, ed. P.-M. Bogaert, Louvain 1981, 168-173.

BOGAERT, P.-M., «La libération de Jérémie et le meurtre de Godolias: le texte court (LAA) et la rédaction longue», *Studien zur Septuaginta - R. Hanhart zu Ehren*, eds. D. Fraenkel - U. Quast - J.W. Wevers, Göttingen 1990, 324-322.

CROSS, F.M., *The Ancient Library of Qumran and Modern Biblical Studies*, Sheffield 1995³ (Grand Rapids MI 1980).

JANZEN, J.G., *Studies in the Text of Jeremiah*, Cambridge MA 1973.

MOWINCKEL, S., *Zur Komposition des Buches Jeremia*, Kristiania 1914.

ROFÉ, A., «The Arrangement of the Book of Jeremiah», *ZAW* 101 (1989) 390-398.

SODERLUND, S., *The Greek Text of Jeremiah: A Revised Hypothesis*, Sheffield 1985, 193- 248.

STIPP, H.-J., *Das masoretische und alexandrinische Sondergut des Jeremiabuches. Textgeschichtlicher Rang, Eigenarten, Triebkräfte*, Fribourg-Göttingen 1994.

TOV, E., *The Septuagint Translation of Jeremiah and Baruch: A Discussion of an Early Revision of the LXX of Jeremiah 29 - 52 and Baruch 1:1 - 3:8*, Missoula, MT, 1976.

TOV, E., «Some Aspects of the Textual and Literary History of the Book of Jeremiah», *Le livre de Jérémie: Le Prophète et son milieu, les oracles et leur transmission*, ed. P.-M. Bogaert, Louvain 1981, 145-167.

TOV, E., «The Literary History of the Book of Jeremiah in the Light of its Textual History», *Empirical Models for Biblical Criticism*, ed. J.H. Tigay, Philadelphia PA 1985, 213-137.

ULRICH, E., «Double Literary Editions of Biblical Narratives and Reflections on Determining the Form to Be Translated», *Perspectives on the Hebrew Bible: Essays in Honor of W. J. Harrelson*, ed. J.L. Crenshaw, Macon, GA, 1988, 101-116.

VAWTER, B., «Were the Prophets *nābī's*?», *Biblica* 66 (1985) 206-220.

C.   EZEKIEL

The book of Ezekiel has also undergone a process of editorial revision, the result of which is the form of the text represented by the MT (distinguished by the present order of chapters 36-39). The MT has additions of various kinds throughout the book. Particularly important are 36:23c-38 in connection with a change in the original order of the text as attested by the LXX.

In the past, the differences between the Hebrew and Greek texts of the book of Ez were attributed to changes caused during the process of textual transmission. The masoretic text of this book is one of the most corrupt of the biblical books (Cornill, Smend, Cooke). In his commentary on this book, Cornill kept a degree of balance between text-critical analysis and literary criticism. Smend, instead, did not think it was possible to recover the original text by means of textual criticism; accordingly he tried instead to reconstruct the various stages of the literary formation of the text. More recent commentaries and studies attempt a new balance between textual and literary study (Zimmerli, Greenberg, who in principle is more favourable to the MT).

As happens in the books of Josh, Sm, Jr and others, the more important differences between the Hebrew and Greek texts of the book of Ez go back to the period of literary formation of the book and have little to do with later activity by Hebrew copyists or the Greek translator.

The Greek version of Ez is one of the more literal as a study of his translation techniques shows: he tends to use the same order of words in Greek as in the original Hebrew and regularly uses the same lexical equivalents. As a result, the «omissions» in the LXX against the MT (about 4 or 5% of the text) cannot be blamed on the translator. The Hebrew original of the Greek version did not have these passages. The MT has given rise to additions of words or parallel phrases, exegetical notes, explanations of context, harmonisation with other passages, stereotype formulas, etc.

The MT exhibits a more developed form the text than is reflected in the LXX. One example, 2:3, is enough: «I sent you to the Israelites, *to the nations* of rebels who have rebelled against me». The expression «the nations», unknown to the Greek versions and its Hebrew original, has been added in the MT to soften the impact of the adjective «rebels» which originally referred only to Israel and now is also applied to the other nations. The syntactic construction shows the late and secondary character of the insert: the article is added to the second term (*goyîm ham-mordîm*) as is common in Mishnaic Hebrew but is not used in biblical Hebrew.

Another and more significant example is the absence of deuteronomistic formulas in the Greek text: this applies to expressions such as «and they have provoked me again» (8:17) and «and they shall cry loudly for me to hear but I will not listen to them» (8:18) which are missing from the Greek text.

The Geek text has one important omission, the existence of which is known to us only from the pre-hexaplaric text of papyrus Chester Beatty 967 and the Old Latin version (Codex Wirceburgensis). These witnesses do not have the text corresponding to 36:23c-38. The vocabulary and style of the Greek text of this passage are considerably different from the immediate context, as Thackeray had already noticed. The transliteration of the divine name is typical of late Jewish recensions and translations. These facts prove that this passage did not belong to the original text of the Greek version.

On the other hand, the theme of this passage is the restoration of Israel, expressed in stereotyped phrases and, in particular, using the metaphor of the new heart. This passage was added to the MT. It is inspired by the neighbouring chapters and by 11:19; it is also reminiscent of the language of Jr. The insert is due to the well-known technique of link-repetition (*Wiederaufnahme*): «... and the nations will know that I am Yahweh [.... and they will know that I am Yahweh]» (vv. 23 and 38).

Ez 7:3-4 duplicates 7:8-9. The Geek version repeats both texts consecutively (vv.8-9.3-4). It might be thought that this is due to the Greek translator. In fact, as in many other cases, since the repetition occurs in both the Hebrew and Greek texts, and since the repeated material occupies a different position in each, it is better explained if the repeated passage is considered to be an insertion in both cases (Zimmerli). The Greek version only reflects a different Hebrew text from the masoretic text (cf. also the parallel passages in Ez 1:1-3a = 1:2-3b; 1:13 = 1:14; 4:10.11.16.17 = 4:9.12-15; 9:5 = 9:7).

BOGAERT, P.-M., «Le témoignage de la Vetus Latina dans l'étude de la tradition des Septante: Ezéchiel et Daniel dans le papyrus 967», *Bibl* 59 (1978) 384-395.

BOGAERT, P.-M., «Montagne sainte, jardin d'Éden et sanctuaire (hiérosolymitain) dans un oracle d'Ézéchiel contre le prince de Tyr (Éz 28,11-19)», *Le Mythe. Son langage et son message*, Louvain la-Neuve 1983, 131-153.

LUST, J., «Ezekiel 36-40 in the Oldest Greek Manuscript», *CBQ* 43 (1981) 517-533.

LUST, J., «The Use of Textual Witnesses for the Establishment of the Text. The Shorter and Longer Texts of Ezekiel. An Example: Ez 7», *Ezekiel and his Book. Textual and Literary Criticism and their Interrelation*, ed. J. Lust, Louvain 1986, 7-20.

TOV, E., «Recensional Differences Between the MT and LXX of Ezekiel», *EpThLov* 62 (1986) 89-101.

ZIMMERLI, W., *Ezechiel*, 2 vols., Neukirchen-Vluyn 1969.

D.   JOB

The text of the books of Job and Hosea poses one of the most difficult problems of text criticism. The Greek text is considerably shorter that the MT. This situation is comparable to the book of Jr where the Greek version also represents a shorter text. From the version by Theodotion Origen took the approximately four hundred verses missing from the text of the LXX. Many consider the longer form in MT to be more original than the shorter LXX text. The Greek translator eliminated the difficulties of the text by removing difficult passages. Certainly, the omissions from the Greek text increase rather than resolve these difficulties. In many passages the Greek version seems more like a paraphrase than a translation and only on rare occasions does it help to correct the Hebrew text.

However, against the opinion that the translator allowed himself to be influenced by theological tendencies which altered the meaning of the Hebrew text, Orlinsky defends the Geek text from such an accusation and in addition, notes that the Hebrew texts is also not free of such tendencies. For example, in 13:15, against the text critical reading (*Kĕtîb*) «Though he slay me, *I shall not tremble* (in hope or fear)», the rabbis proposed the reading «Although they slay me, *I will trust in him*». The simple change of the negative *l^c* («not») to the preposition + pronoun *lw* («in him») makes a protest by a mistrusting Job into a statement of trusting submission.

E.   ESTHER

No copy of the book of Esther has been found among the Qumran manuscripts and it is one of those which cause the greatest critical difficulties. The canonical status of the book of Esther was debated for a long time. This could have had an influence on the book being transmitted in three different forms of text: as represented by MT, as reflected in the LXX (text B) and as another Greek text known as text A. To judge from the colophon to the Greek version (F 11), the translation was made around 114 BCE.

The Greek version of the LXX or *text B* is a «literary» version. In spite of the presence of a few Hebraisms, it is a free and occasionally periphrastic version. The best proof for that is there is hardly a verse of the text which has not been affected by the hexaplar version.

Text A is considerably shorter, in spite of a few «additions». The most striking «omissions», apart from personal names, dates and repeated elements, include 1:19; 2:12-14; 5:3.11.12; 6:2 and 9:16.

Almost all scholars have followed P.A. de Lagarde's opinion (*Librorum Veteris Testamenti Canonicorum pars prior*, Göttingen 1883) according to which text A of Esther is a Lucianic revision of the LXX. C.A. Moore, instead, thinks that it is an independent translation of the Hebrew text: there are passages which seem to have the same Hebrew original but are translated differently in texts A and B; there are very few exact agreements between both texts and in text A various Hebraisms are evident. According to Moore, text A reflects a Hebrew text which differs both from the MT and from the text used by the LXX. According to Tov, the «Lucianic» text is a translation based on the text of the LXX which it corrects from a Hebrew (or Aramaic) text different from the MT. It is a sort of midrashic re-write of the biblical account.

Study of the book of Esther has been enriched by the recent publication, by Milik, of five manuscripts from three separate works containing «models», «archetypes» or «sources» of the versions preserved in Hebrew, Greek and Latin(4Q550 = 4QProto-Ester^{a-e}).

F.   DANIEL

The original language of the twelve chapters which make up the book of Daniel according to the MT could have been Aramaic. In that case, the sections of the book now in Hebrew were translated from Aramaic. The difficulties which the existing Hebrew text presents seem to be solved by supposing there to be an Aramaic original (Hartmann-Di Lella). The Greek of Daniel represents a form of tradition which is earlier than the Aramaic of Dn 2-7. It goes back to Hebrew and Aramaic originals of the 4th/3rd cent. BCE (Albertz).

The Greek text of Dn has reached us in two forms: as transmitted by the Old Greek and as represented by the text of Theodotion (cf. p. 314).

Papyrus 967 of the LXX (according to the Göttingen catalogue), dated to the 3rd cent. BCE, preserves almost the whole text of Dn. The text represents an older and more original form of the Greek text. A fundamental difference from the masoretic text and other witnesses known up to 1968 (the date when the Cologne fragments, chs. 5-12, were published by Geissen) concerns the sequence of chapters and of the additions to the book Dn. MS 967 has the following order: chs. 1-4; 7-8; 5-6 and 9-12, followed by the stories of Bel and the Dragon and of Susannah. Origen's hexaplar text (88, *Chisianus*) is a revision of the old Greek version made in terms of the standard Hebrew-Aramaic text; it keeps quite close to the old Greek to the extent of enabling the lacunae of 967 to be filled and even to correct its mistakes.

The sequence of chapters of the old *Septuagint*, witnessed by 967, is dependent on the MT, which divides the book into 2 parts. The first part is narrative in character and refers to prophecies already fulfilled (1-6 and 7); the second part is prophetic and contains visions which are to be fulfilled in the future (7 and 8-12). In the first part, Daniel passes various tests in the court of kings Nabuchadnezzar, Balthazar and Darius (1-6). In the second part he shows himself to be a real prophet who can predict the succession of four great empires and the downfall of the last of them (7-12). The order in the text translated by the LXX tries to correct the chronology of the traditional Hebrew text. Accordingly, it puts chs. 7-8, where king Balthazar is still assumed to be alive, before ch. 5, which ends with the death of that king (Geissen). Thus, the text reflected by the LXX is concerned about historicity. In 9:25-27, the old Greek (or its Hebrew original) has several changes from the MT which can easily be shown using a synoptic chart (Bogaert).

When comparing the masoretic text and the Greek texts of the LXX and Theodotion, important cases are where the LXX differs from Theodotion and those where MT agrees with the LXX or Theodotion against later versions (Montgomery). Cases of agreement between any of the MSS of Dn from Cave 4 of Qumran (4QDan^{abc}) and the text of the LXX against the MT and Theodotion are also important (Ulrich).

G. SUSANNAH

Among the additions to the book of Dn, the story of Susannah has been preserved in two very different text forms: the text of the old version and the text of Theodotion. The second could be a re-edited form of the first (Schüpphaus) or an independent translation (A. Schmitt) or depend on the first and oldest translation (Moore).

BIBLIOGRAPHY

ALBERTZ, A., *Der Gott des Daniel. Untersuchung zu Daniel 4-6 in der Septuagintafassung sowie zu Komposition und Theologie des aramäischen Danielbuches*, Stuttgart 1988.

GEISSEN, A., *Der Septuaginta-Text des Buches Daniel. Kap. 5 - 12 zusammen mit Susanna, Bet et Draco sowie Esther 1,1a - 2,15 nach dem Kölner Teil des Papyrus 967*, Bonn 1968.

HARTMANN, L.F. -DI LELLA, A.A., *The Book of Daniel*, Garden City NY 1978.

JEANSONNE, S.P., *The Old Greek Tradition of Daniel 7-12*, Washington DC 1988.

MILIK, J.T., «Les modèles araméens du livre d'Esther dans la Grotte 4 de Qumrân», *Mémorial J. Starcky*, eds. E. Puech-F. García Martínez, Paris 1992, 321-406.

MONTGOMERY, J.A., *The Book of Daniel*, Edinburgh 1927.

MOORE, C.A., «A Greek Witness to a Different Hebrew Text of Esther», *ZAW* 79 (1967) 351-358.

MOORE, C.A., *Daniel, Esther and Jeremiah: The Additions*, Garden City NY 1977.

ORLINSKY, H., «Studies in the Septuagint of the Book of Job», *HUCA* 28 (1957) 53-74;   29 (1958) 229-271; 30 (1959) 153-167.

POPE, M.H., *Job*, Garden City NY 1986³.

SCHMITT, A., *Stammt der sogenannte «The»-Text bei Daniel wirklich von Theodotion?*, Göttingen 1966.

SCHÜPPHAUS, J., «Das Verhältnis von LXX- und Theodotion-Text in den apokryphen Zusätzen zum Danielbuch», *ZAW* 83 (1971) 49-72.

TOV, E., «The 'Lucianic' Text of the Canonical and the Apocryphal Sections of Esther: A Rewritten Biblical Book«, *Textus* 10 (1982) 1-25.

ULRICH, E., «Daniel Manuscripts from Qumran. Part I: A Preliminary Edition of 4QDan^{a}», *BASOR* 268 (1987) 17-37.

ZIEGLER, J., *Susanna, Daniel, Bel et Draco*, Septuaginta. Vetus Testamentum Graecum 16/2, Göttingen 1954.

H. BEN SIRA

The fact that this book did not form part of the rabbinic OT canon certainly caused the loss of its Hebrew original. Up until a century ago, the Greek and Syriac versions, from which the other versions are derived, were the only texts in which this book was transmitted. The Hebrew text was known only from a few quotations in rabbinic literature. These quotations represent text forms which are different from those preserved in the Hebrew MSS of Ben Sira known today. Starting from 1896, the gradual identification of the manuscripts found in the Synagogue of Old Cairo provided almost 70% of the Hebrew text. Among this material were found fragments corresponding to four different manuscripts of the book of Ben Sira (A, B, C, D).

Manuscript A (11th cent.) preserves the text of 3:6b-16.26.

Manuscript B (12th cent.) contains 30:11-33:3; 35:11-38:27b; 39:15c-51:30 (two sheets published later have the text of 10:19c-11:10; 15:1-16:7).

Manuscript C (older than the other two) is a florilegium which contains 4:23.30.31; 5:4-7.9-13; 6:18b.19.28.35; 7:1.2.4.6.17.20.21.23-25; 18:31b; 20:5-7; 37:19.22.24.26; 20:13; 25:8.13.17-24; 26:1-2a (in that order). Two sheets published later preserve the text of 3:14- 18.21-22; 41:16; 4:21; 20:22-23; 4:22-23b; 26:2b.3.13.15-17; 36:27-31. Another fragment contains 25:8 and 25:20-21.

The portion of text preserved by manuscript D (11th cent.) corresponds to 36:29-38:1a.

In 1931, a sheet from a fifth manuscript (E) was discovered with the text of 32:16-34:1. A sheet assigned by Scheiber to manuscript D, seems instead to belong to a sixth manuscript (F), probably from the 11th cent., preserving 31:24-32:7 and 32:12-33:8 (Di Lella).

The finds at the Dead Sea have also revealed manuscript material of the Hebrew text of Ben Sira: 2Q218, from the second half of the 1st cent. BCE, contains very meagre material from 6:20-31 and 6:14-15 (or possibly 1:19-20; Baillet, *DJD* III), and 11QPs², from the first half of the 1st cent. CE, has the text of 51:13-20.30b (J.A.Sanders; cf. p. 000). In 1965, 26 fragments of the scroll found in Masada were published, dating to the first half of the 1st cent. BCE, with seven columns of text corresponding to 39:27-44:17. The discovery of the Masada scroll has solved the question of the authenticity of the El Cairo manuscripts, which today is beyond doubt (Yadin).

We can now speak of an original Hebrew from of the book of Ben Sira (HTI) and of a second enlarged edition, the product of one or more recensionists (HTII). The original Greek version, made Ben Sira's own nephew, translates the original Hebrew edition (GI); most of its text is to be found in the uncials A, B, C, S and in the cursives dependent on them. A Greek version of the longest text corresponds to the second enlarged Hebrew edition (GII); it is to be found in the «O» group of hexaplaric MSS (Origen) and in the «L» group of Lucianic MSS (with the subgroup «l»); the translator of GII did no more than add to GI the correct passages from the enlarged Hebrew edition (Ziegler). The Greek text of Ecclesiaticus is one of the most corrupt in the Greek bible so that it presents great problems of textual criticism (C. Kearns).

The enlarged edition adds words which can alter the meaning of a sentence or a verse (e.g., 1:30e; 2:11a) and complete verses or hemistichs (e.g. 1:5.7.10cd.12cd.18cd.21; 2:5c.9c). The edition of the Greek text, completed by J. Ziegler, gives the additional verses (about 300) in the actual text, but printed in smaller type.

The OL is witness to the longer text. It has the merit of preserving the correct sequence of chapters after 30:24, whereas the whole of Greek tradition inverts the sequence of 30:25-33:13a and 33:13b-36:16a. The reason for this inversion was simply a change in page order of the first archetype.

The OL of Sir became part of the collection of versions of the Vulgate since Jerome did not complete any translation of this deuterocanonical book. The lengthy history of textual transmission of the OL ensured that its text is more studded with doublets, variants and glosses than any other book of the Latin bible.

The Syriac version was made directly from the Hebrew somewhat before the beginning of the 4th cent. Towards the end of the same century, a revision was made of the first version. The Hebrew text from which the translation was made has characteristics of both Hebrew recensions, but the Syriac version was also influenced by the Greek version, which had a lot in common with GII (Nelson). The Syriac version has 70 of the approximately 300 additions in GII, besides other variants it also has in common with GII.

Analysis of the translation techniques used by the Greek translator of this book (copying the Hebrew word order in Greek, dividing Hebrew words or splitting them up into their component parts in sequence to reflect each one in the Greek version, matching the length of the Hebrew text or reflection in the version each one of the terms making up a unit, and lastly, regular use of a Greek term for the corresponding Hebrew word) emphasises that Ben Sira's nephew and his translator did not intend to make a literal, word for word, translation nor did he generally consult existing translations as an aid to his own translation work (B.G. Wright).

As for the possibility of reconstructing the Hebrew text used for the version, the conclusion of the study on the translation techniques is rather pessimistic. Although in certain passages it is possible to reconstruct some aspects of the underlying Hebrew text, there is little likelihood of recovering a continuous and complete text.

The book of Ben Sira is a book in transition between the OT and intertestamental literature. It has, therefore, been described as a book «on the frontier of the Canon». The book of Ben Sira opened the road towards rabbinism which developed later (cf. p. 165).

I.   TOBIT

Two recensions of the book of Tob are known: one long, represented by Codex Sinaiticus and the OL, and one short, witnessed by the Vatican and Alexandrian Codices. The long version seems to be closer to the manuscripts found at Qumran (4 in Aramaic and 1 in Hebrew), which seem to indicate that the short recension is a compendium of the longer. Deselaers, however, defends the priority of the short version, by basing himself on a study of its sources which, after they were written in Greek, were enlarged twice in succession.

J.   TESTAMENT OF ABRAHAM

The Testament of Abraham is a Jewish work, composed in Egypt in Greek around 100 CE. Its text has reached us in two different text forms: one long (A), the other short (B). These two recensions are probably not dependent on each other but both derive from a common original. Text A preserves the original narrative structure better (Nickelsburg). The conclusion is that the structure of form A corresponds better to the original but form B generally has the older text (E.P. Sanders).

K.   JOSEPH AND ASENETH

The text of the work Joseph and Aseneth is known though four textual families (a, b, c, d). Text d corresponds to a shorter and older version of the work (Philonenko), although in fact it is a shortened edition of the text. The long version is represented by the other three families: family b is the oldest of this textual form and family a is the most recent of the three. Any attempt at reconstructing the original text has to be given up and we must be content with the two versions that exist, one shorter and the other more expanded.

BARTHÉLEMY, D., «L'enchevêtrement de l'histoire textuelle et de l'histoire littéraire dans les relations entre la Septante et le Texte Massorétique. Modifications dans la manière de concevoir les relations existant entre la LXX et le TM, depuis J. Morin jusqu'à E. Tov», *De Septuaginta*, Mississauga, Ontario, 1984, 21-40.

BARTHÉLEMY, D., «Problématique et tâches de la critique textuelle de l'Ancien Testament hébraïque», *Études d'histoire du texte de l'Ancient Testament*, Fribourg-Göttingen 1978, 365-381.

BARTHÉLEMY, D., «Notes critiques sur quelques points d'histoire du texte», *Études d'histoire du texte de l'Ancien Testament*, Fribourg-Göttingen 1978, 289-303.

BARTHÉLEMY, D., «La qualité du Texte Massorétique de Samuel», *The Hebrew and Greek Texts of Samuel, 1980 Proceedings IOSCS*, Jerusalem 1980, 1-44.

BURNEY, C.F., *Notes on the Hebrew Text of the Books of Kings*, Oxford 1903.

DESELAERS, P., *Das Buch Tobit: Studien zu seiner Entstehung, Komposition und Theologie*, Göttigen 1982.

DI LELLA, A.A., *The Wisdom of Ben Sira*, New York 1987.

KEARNS, C., «Ecclesiasticus, or the Wisdom of Jesus the Son of Sirach», *A New Catholic Commentary on Holy Scripture*, ed. R.C. Fuller *et al.*, London 1969.

NELSON, M.D., *The Syriac Version of the Wisdom of Ben Sira Compared to the Greek and hebrew Materials*, Atlanta GA 1988.

NICKELSBURG, G.W.E., *Studies on the Testament of Abraham*, Missoula, MT 1976.

ORLINSKY, H.M., 'The Kings-Isaiah Recensions of the Hezekiah Story', *JQR* 30 (1939-40) 33-49.

PHILONENKO, M., *Joseph et Aséneth: Introduction, texte critique, traduction et notes*, Leiden 1968.

REHM, M., *Textkritische Untersuchungen zu den Parallelstellen der Samuel-Königsbücher und der Chronik*, Münster 1937.

SCHECHTER, S. -TAYLOR, C., *The Wisdom of Ben Sira: Portions of the Book Ecclesiasticus from Hebrew Manuscripts in the Cairo Genizah Collection*, Cambridge 1899.

STIPP, H.J., «Textkritik - Literarkritik - Textentwicklung. Überlegungen zur exegetischen Aspektsystematik», *EphThLov* 46 (1990) 143-159.

TOV, E., «Some Sequence Differences Between the MT and LXX and Their Ramifications for the Literary Criticism of the Bible», *JNSL* 13 (1987) 151-160.

WRIGHT, B.G., *No Small Difference. Sirach's Relationship to its Hebrew Parent Text*, Atlanta GA 1989.

ZIEGLER, J., *Sapientia Iesu Filii Sirach*, Septuaginta 12/2, Göttingen 1965.

YADIN, Y., *The Ben Sira Scroll from Masada*, Jerusalem 1965.

Textual Criticism of the New Testament

Once the manuscripts have been classified and each assigned to a specific group or a specific text type, it is necessary to proceed to internal examination of each readings and its variants with the aim of establishing, ultimately, an «eclectic» text.

I CHANGES IN THE TRANSMISSION OF THE TEXT OF THE NEW TESTAMENT

The story told by Jerome about the six copyists sent him by Lucinius, a wealthy Spaniard of the period, commissioned to copy some of the works of the famous biblical scholar, gives some idea of the lack of expertise and the carelessness with which some copyists worked. Jerome complained to Lucinius as follows: «If a mistake or omission is found which contradicts the meaning it should not be blamed on me but on your servants. They are the product of ignorance or carelessness by the copyists who do not write down what they find but what they think the meaning to be and only display their own mistakes when they try to correct those of others» (*Epist.* 71,5). However, it has to be said at once that on the whole the text of the NT shows faithful transmission and care. The variants, which could be called substantial, in Hort's appraisal, hardly affect a thousandth part of the NT.

1. *Unintentional Changes*

A copyist can easily make mistakes either writing under dictation or copying from an original.

a. Dictation Error. For example, a copyist can confuse the sound of a short vowel with a long vowel. This type of confusion explains the variants in Rom 5:1: «we have peace» (*eirēnēn ékhomen*) and «may we have peace» (*eirēnēn ékhōmen*).

After the period of composition of the NT the diphthong *ai* and the vowel *e* had the same pronunciation which could lead to mistakes. In Mt 11:6, part of the manuscript tradition confuses *hetérois* = «others» with *hetaîrois* = «companions». In *koiné* Greek the vowels *ē, ī, y*, the diphthongs *ei, oi, yi* and the improper diphthong *ē* (with *iota* subscript) eventually had the same pronunciation (*iota*). Thus, in 1 Cor 15:54 the expression «death was absorbed in victory» (*nîkos*) could become «death was absorbed in conflict» (*neîkos*) according to the text of P⁴⁶ and B. The clause in 1 Cor 13:3 «I deliver my body to glorify myself»(P⁴⁶ ℵ A B 6 33...) in several manuscripts appears as I deliver my body to burn myself» due to confusion between the consonant sounds *kaukhēsōmai* and *kauthēsōmai*.

b. Confusion of Letters. In the uncial script it is easy to confuse the letters C, E, Θ and Ω. In 1 Tim 3:16 the best and oldest manuscripts read OC, «he who»; other more recent ones read ΘC, an abbreviation for *theós*, «god».

The letters Γ, π and T are also easily confused: 2 Pet 2:13 ΑΓΑπΑIC= «agapes» / ΑπΑΤΑIC = «deceptions».

c. Incorrect word division in continuous script. In Mk 10:40, the saying of Jesus «to sit at my right or my left is not for me to grant, *but it is for those to whom* it is reserved», is translated in the old versions (OL Syr Eth): «..., *but it is reserved for others*». Instead of the two words ΑΛΛ OIC, «... but for those who...» the word ΑΛΛOIC, «for others» has been read.

The use of abbreviations is fairly common which is an additional source of mistakes. In 2 Pet 1:21 the more original reading seems to be «some men spoke on God's behalf» (P⁷² B P 614...). The reading «some holy men of God spoke» originates from it through confusion of the letters ΑπΟΘY read as ΑΓΙΟΙΘY.

d. Homoioteleuton. In Jn 17:15 «I do not ask you to remove them [from the world, but to keep them] from the Evil One», Codex Vaticanus omits the text in parentheses, due to jumping between identical words (...*autoús ek toû* [...].*autoús ek toû*...).

e. Dittography: repetition of a letter or several letters or of one or several terms/words. In Acts 19:34, Codex Vaticanus twice repeats «Great is Artemis of the Ephesians!». In 1 Thess 2:7 some manuscripts read «we made ourselves kind» (*egenéthēmen ēpíoi*) whereas some better manuscripts (P⁶⁵ ℵr B...) read «we made ourselves children» (*egenéthēmen nēpíoi*). Even though this second reading is supported by good manuscripts, the first reading fits the context better and seems to be more original. The second reading is the result of a mistake due to the consonant *n* being written twice in succession.

f. Metathesis or transposition (e.g. in Jn 5:39 in the Bezae codex).

g. Assimilation to parallel passages (e.g. in Mt 19:17; cf. Metzger 49; cf. p. 409).

2. Intentional Changes

a. Changes in spelling and grammar (e.g. in Ap 1:4.6.15, etc.).

b. Corruption due to harmonisation. In many manuscripts at Lk 23:38 have a clause taken from Jn 19:20: «It was written in Hebrew, Latin and

Greek». Several manuscripts harmonise the short text of the «Lord's Prayer» according to Lk 11:2-4 with the longer text known from Mt 6:9-13. Frequently, quotations from the OT are extended or corrected to make them more faithful to the Septuagint text.

c. Addition of extra items. The oldest form of the text of Gal 6:17 preserved in P[46] B A etc., «I bear the mark of Jesus on my body» is expanded in various ways in many manuscripts: «(the mark) of the Lord Jesus», «... of Jesus the Christ», or «...of our Lord Jesus Christ»

d. Historical and geographical explanations (examples in Mk 1:2; 8:31; Heb 9:4, etc.).

e. Merged Readings. This is typical of late texts such as the Byzantine text. Many manuscripts juxtapose two alternative readings in Lk 24:53 «blessing» or «praising». In Acts 20:28, the two alternative readings «church of the Lord» and «church of God» are combined in the reading «church of the Lord and God».

f. Glosses. In Jn 5:34 the explanation of the movement of the water in the pool of Bethesda is surely due to later interpolation (cf. v. 7).

g. Changes for doctrinal reasons. The Church Fathers accused heretics of changing the text of the NT in order to make it fit their own doctrines better. This criticism is unfounded except in the case of Marcion and to a lesser degree Tatian. Marcion eliminated from the text of Luke any reference to the Jewish origin of Jesus and Tatian's *Diatessaron* is influenced by very extremist Encratic tendencies. It is also true that the orthodoxy of the Great Church tended to remove or alter such expressions which for any reason proved unacceptable, and to insert instead, in the text new elements with the purpose of supporting a particular doctrine, a liturgical practice or a moral custom.

The best representatives of the Alexandrian, Western and Caesarean texts preserve the clause (Mt 24:36 ‖ Mk 13:32) «About that day and hour no-one knows, neither the angels in heaven nor the Son...»; most of the manuscripts, instead (including those with a Byzantine text) suppress the words «neither the Son», given the doctrinal difficulty which this expression entails. In Lk 23:32 most of the manuscripts try to avoid the possibility of Jesus being considered like one of the criminals who accompanied him on the cross as could be implied from the oldest text attested by P[75] ℵ B, etc.: «Also other criminals, two with him, were led (out) to be crucified». With a simple change in the word order those manuscripts read: «Also two others, criminals, were led...».

II. CRITERIA AND METHODS FOR CHOOSING READINGS

The sources which have transmitted to us the text of the NT have been described (papyri, uncial and minuscule manuscripts, ancient versions and quotations from the Fathers) and the history of the transmission of the text and the history of research on it in modern times is known. Now, the theories and methods to be applied in the study of those sources and in modern critical editions of the NT text have to be studied.

New manuscript material is continually being discovered. The theories and methods also continue to be developed and refined. The discovery of new sources often requires established theories to be re-thought and give rise to new analytical methods more suited to the type of material discovered. It is also necessary to study afresh material known already for centuries to resolve old problems and to face others which continually arise.

Critical method studies the *criteria* to be used in the «selection» (*selectio*) of the reading which, among the different ones that exist, is closer to the original. This selection is made by following two types of criteria. Some refer to external factors and others to internal factors so we speak of external and internal criticism of the biblical text.

1. *External Criticism*

The following external factors affect the evaluation of a reading: 1) the greater or lesser *antiquity* of the manuscript in which the particular reading is found, 2) the smaller or large *number* of manuscripts which replicate this reading, 3) the better or worse *quality* of the manuscript shown in the care and trouble taken in copying, 4) the extent of geographical *spread* of the manuscript, and 5) the *documentation* which is more or less precise concerning the date, origin, character and especially genealogy of the manuscript or whether it belongs to a particular group of manuscripts or to a particular type of text.

One trend of modern criticism has shown a greater tendency to give primacy to external criticism, confident that the reconstruction of the initial phases of the history of the text makes it possible to identify the best manuscript or the type with the best text

This reconstruction assumes previous classification of the manuscripts into different groups and the identification of the oldest recensions to trace, then, the lines of development and to identify the primitive form of the text. This kind of study was begun by J. A. Bengel and developed by Westcott-Hort and Von Soden, and has crystallised into the separation of the four types of text mentioned above: Alexandrian, Western, Byzantine and Caesarean (the last only for the gospels).

The critical period which needs to be the subject of special research, comprises the first, two centuries of the textual history of the NT. Study of the papyri, especially of P^{45}, P^{46}, P^{66} and P^{75}, has opened such research to new possibilities.

In similar circumstances in principle more value must be given to the witness of a type of text of better quality than to another of inferior quality. Similarly, a reading supported by two or more groups is better than one supported by only one. Sometimes, however, one will have to opt for a reading represented by a single group of better quality against another reading attested by several groups of lesser quality.

2.   Internal Criticism

Other criteria of NT textual criticism concern internal aspects. They include the following: 1) when a reading fits in better with *the style and theological bias of the author and his work*, 2) when a reading *conforms to koiné Greek rather than to Attic Greek* (given the atticist movement which was imposed later), 3) suitability to *Semitic expressions,* and 4) to a lesser extent, *suitability to the context* or harmonisation with parallel passages of the NT or with quotations and passages from the OT. Other considerations have also to be taken into account such as the chronological priority of Mark's gospel, the Aramaic substrate in the case of the *logia* of Jesus or the possible influence of the primitive community in the formulation and transmission of a particular passage.

The three classic and more important criteria for internal criticism of texts are as follows (cf. p. 379):

a. The reading which accounts for the others is preferable. In the story of the rich young man, Mk 10:17-18 and Lk 18:18-19 both use the expression «*good* master» as well as in the reply by Jesus: «Why *do you call* me good? No-one is good except God». In the parallel passage, Mt 19:16-17, some manuscripts agree with Mk and Lk, while in others the text of the question is «Master, what *good thing* has to be done...?» and the answer *is* «*Why do you ask me about what is good? Only one* is good». To the question about which of the variants is the original, the reply will be that the reading agreeing with the parallels from Mk and Mt certainly derives from them, whereas the reading which differs from them is probably original.

Mt 19:16-17	Mk 10:17f./Lk 18:18f
–«Master,	–«Good Master,
what *good thing*	what
must be done...?»	must be done...?»
–«Why do you	–«Why do you
ask me about what	call me good?
is good? Only one	No-one is good
is good»	except God»

In Mk 6:47 the boat was said to be «in the middle of the lake». In the parallel (Mt 12:24) the manuscripts are divided, reading «in the middle of the lake» and «several stadia from land». If Mt had written a text like Mk, there is no reason for the change made. If, instead, the original reading in Mt was different from Mk, a copyist could have tried to harmonise it with Mk. The first reading has more probability of being original.

Such cases of harmonisation are common in the synoptic gospels, but they also occur in other texts. An example is Eph 1:7 and Col 1:14. The expression «in whom we have redemption *through his blood*, forgiveness of sins» of Eph has a very close parallel in the expression from Col attested by most of the manuscripts: «in whom we have redemption, forgiveness of sins». Some manuscripts of Col insert the expression *through his blood* which is peculiar to Eph.

b. The more difficult reading is preferable (lectio difficilior). The reading which at first seems to be more difficult to understand, although making good sense in the context, is more probable than another reading which makes the text easier or trite. In Jn 1:18 many good quality manuscripts have the variant «Only born God» instead of «Only born son». This reading, referring to Christ, is an easier reading and could at the same time be the result of harmonising with Jn 3:16.18 and 1 Jn 4:9. The discovery of papyri P[66] and P[75] provides external support for the more difficult reading «Only born God». However, there is always the doubt whether the author of the fourth gospel actually wrote «Only born God». It can be assumed that in the Alexandrian tradition there was confusion between the abbreviations for «God» and «son» ($\overline{\Theta C}$ / $\overline{YC}$).

c. The shorter reading is preferable (lectio brevior). A copyist tends to add words or explanatory phrases, whereas deliberate omission of part of the text is rare. Thus, in principle the shorter reading is preferable to a longer reading. In the parable of the «prodigal son» in Lk 15:18-19, some good quality manuscripts ($\aleph$B D 700, etc.) have the reading «treat me as one of your day labourers», which is not in the other manuscripts. This clause is certainly taken from v.19. It attempts to make the actual fulfilment by the son match all that he had thought to say to his father. The addition of this clause in some manuscripts can be explained better than its omission from others. However, this does not mean that the shorter reading is always and in principle the original. A reading can be shorter than another through haplography (cf. 1 Jn 2:23).

These criteria are not all applicable at the same time and in every case where there is a variant. In fact, some are mutually exclusive. A short reading could be one which does not match the author's style so well. A variant in a better manuscript could be the result of later harmonisation. These difficulties in forming safe and certain critical judgment often make textual criticism an art rather than an aseptic scientific operation.

3.   *Eclecticism*

In applying textual criticism some tension between external and internal criticism is inevitable. For example, codex B is considered the best manuscript and its Alexandrian text the best text type. Codex D is considered to be inferior, but it preserves readings from the Western text which was very widespread in early Christianity and, in the light of internal criticism, can occasionally be older than the Alexandrian text attested by B.

The combination of the two analytical models - external and internal criticism - can give rise to four different suppositions:

a. A reading attested by the best manuscripts is also endorsed by internal criticism.

This applies to the reading of Mt 5:47: «Do not the gentiles do as much?» attested by the best manuscripts (א B D, etc.) and by the text types Alexandrian, Western and Caesarean (the latter only in part). On the other hand, the variant «Do not the publicans do as much?» occurs in late manuscripts (K L W, etc.) and in the Byzantine type text; it is also the result of an obvious harmonisation with an identical expression in the preceding verse (v.46).

b. A reading attested by the best manuscript tradition is not confirmed by arguments of internal criticism.

The reading «he is like...» of Mt 7:24 is found in the Alexandrian text type and in most of the Caesarean and Western manuscripts (א BΘ, etc.). The alternative reading, «I will liken it to...» has only the support of the Byzantine text (C K L W, etc.). Internal criticism has no arguments in favour of one or the other, for the meaning hardly changes at all in either case. The manuscript tradition, however, favours the first reading.

c) A reading transmitted by manuscripts of inferior quality has, however, solid arguments from internal criticism in its favour.

In the reading «and do not look for glory *from God alone*», (Jn 5:44) the word «God» is not found in ancient manuscripts of the Alexandrian group (P⁶⁶ P⁷⁵ B, etc.). However, the context seems to require the inclusion of this word which could have disappeared in those manuscripts through haplography of the abbreviation Θ̄Ῡ in ΤΟΥΜΟΝΟΥΘ̄Ῡ.

*d. A reading is uncertain when *neither internal nor external criticism provide enough data and proofs* for making a decisive judgment for or against.*

In Mt 15:38, the readings «women and children» or «children and women» have documentary support of equal weight, perhaps the second more flimsy; this is very odd and therefore could have caused the second to be replaced by the first. However, it seems more cautious to incline to the former.

The tension between external and internal criticism makes it difficult on many occasions to make a definitive decision in favour of one reading or another. The cases which are most difficult to solve are those where א and B have different readings. However, more precise knowledge of the history of the NT text is necessary and more perfection in the methods and criteria for selecting variants.

In agreement with Burkit, against Horst, a modern movement connected especially with the name of G. D. Kilpatrick, grants grater importance to *stylistic and linguistic factors* and to factors related to work by copyists than to history and external documentary criticism. Within this perspective it is more relevant when a reading is attested by a manuscript, ancient or recent, or belongs to a primitive or late text type. What is decisive is the judgment about the value of the readings, a judgment which always has to be made in connection with the characteristics of the author and his work.

When the conclusion is reached that the original text could have been lost the last resort which the text critic can use is «*conjecture*», a resort more frequent and necessary in the edition of ancient classical texts but very much scorned in Old and New Testament criticism (Black). If internal criticism cannot avoid a certain measure of subjectivity, the danger is worse in conjectural criticism. This type can only legitimately be used in cases of proven necessity and when the proposed «conjecture» accounts not only for itself but also for all the false or secondary readings which have originated from it.

In the last fifty years the prevailing critical approach has shown *a tendency to a moderate eclecticism* with *general preference for the Alexandrian type* as is evident in the manuals by Nestle-Aland, Merk and Bover and in *The Greek New Testament* edition.

In the future it is necessary to refine and perfect the criteria for selecting textual variants. The methods for classifying groups of manuscripts have seen improvements over the last few years, but a definitive and well-founded theory of the history of the text is still missing. The manuscripts discovered in recent years have enriched the profusion of data available but advances in establishing analytical models and methods have not been developed to the same extent.

Study of the relationships among manuscripts has suffered on many occasions a certain lack in the database used, or inaccuracy in the control of such data and as a result, relative uncertainty in the results. The ideal, unattainable in practice, would be to compare each manuscript and all its variants with the other manuscripts and their variants to determine the exact place of each manuscript within the whole manuscript tradition. However, it is possible and also necessary to establish at least comparisons among a sufficiently wide and representative number of manuscripts, not just in connection with a specific text. These should always take into account the total number of variants, agreements and differences among the manuscripts under analysis.

Computer programs for analysing manuscripts are being developed for this purpose in Claremont (USA) and Münster (Germany). Once groups of manuscripts and the type of text they represent have been identified, the quality of the text of each type is determined. The best text will be the one which most often offers the best reading. By inspection (of a complete gospel, letter or the whole NT) a sufficient number of readings are selected from which are shown by internal evidence to correspond to the oldest and most original reading. Next, in each case the type or types of text this reading provides is checked. The result of this analysis shows that, generally, the Alexandrian type text is the most reliable, followed by the Caesarean, the Byzantine and the Western (at least apart from Acts).

However, it is to be hoped that in future NT textual criticism will pay more attention to *ancient* variants, wherever they come from (for example, from the Western text) and that this will be reflected in the manuals. Although the ancient variants may not be primitive or original (which is not always or even often the case) by their very existence and content they comprise an important witness for learning about the Christian communities of the first three centuries.

On the other hand, to try to form a *received* text which is also original, is to reconcile incompatible objectives. To try to create a *received* text remains somewhat arrogant and to find the original in disputed cases is utopian. One solution is to determine the existence of a majority text in a particular period (as did the Nestle edition before its revision) and to note in the apparatus the (selected) variants which are earlier than 300 CE (Epp).

Here follow various examples of eclectic, internal and external criticism.

1. *Mt 6:13.* After the «Lord's Prayer» the liturgy added the doxology «for yours is the kingdom, the power and the glory for ever». The Byzantine text, part of the Caesarean text and Alexandrian manuscripts have this version of the doxology in Mt 6:13. In this case there are not enough witnesses of external criticism; internal criticism, instead, considers this phrase to have been inserted here no doubt through the influence of the liturgy.

2. *Mk 1:1.* In the expression which begins this gospel, «Beginning of the gospel of Jesus Christ, Son of God», Codex Alexandrinus ℵ and part of the Caesarean tradition omit «Son of God». It might be thought that this omission has heretical implications. It is more likely, instead, that it is the result of a copying error caused by the similarity between the two final abbreviations of the sacred names $\overline{IY}$ $\overline{XY}$ $\overline{YY}$ $\overline{\Theta Y}$ («Jesus Christ Son of God»).

3. *Mk 9:29.* The sentence «This sort cannot go out by any means except by prayer» is expanded in most manuscripts by the addition «(of prayer) and fasting». The best representatives of the Alexandrian tradition (ℵ and B), Western and Caesarean, have resisted including what is in fact only an interpolation reflecting the importance given to the practice of fasting by the early Church.

4. *Mk 16:9-20.* The last pericope of the gospel, Mk 16:9-20, is omitted from the Alexandrian text (ℵ and B) and also unknown to Cyril of Alexandria. Some manuscripts with his text in one way or another reflect the doubts about its authenticity. Other manuscripts have a different and shorter text as the conclusion to the gospel. The fact remains that without this pericope Mark's gospel ends abruptly. However, the vocabulary and style of vv. 9-20 do not match the rest of the gospel and furthermore its connection with the preceding is extremely forced. Among the incongruities with the immediately preceding text is that in v. 8 the subject if Mary Magdalen whereas in v.9 it changes to Jesus; also Mary Magdalen is introduced afresh although already known from earlier references.

The best explanation is that during the transmission of the text the last leaf of the text was lost and with it the ending to the gospel. This was replaced by the text of another document, written perhaps in the first half of the 2nd century.

5. *Lk 23:34.* The reference to the words of Jesus on the cross, «and Jesus said: 'Father, forgive them, because they do not know what they are doing'» does no appear in the old witnesses (P^{75} B and others). This omission cannot be attributed to some copyists not so disposed to express forgiveness of the Jews, or convinced that the destruction of Jerusalem was proof that they had never been forgiven. Undoubtedly, this *logion* did not form part of the original text of the gospel. This does not mean that it was not an authentic saying of Jesus which very early on was included in the gospel text at precisely this place.

6. *Acts 8:37.* The Western text adds a whole confession of faith placed in the mouth of the Ethiopian official. For reasons of internal criticism, scholars usually consider this confession of faith as a secondary insertion.

7. *Acts 3:11.* Instead of the usual text «And as he was clutching Peter and John, all

the people came running in surprise towards them in the Gate...» the Western text reads: «When Peter and John were going outside, he went out with them, clutching them; surprised, they stopped in the gate...». This reading shows a more exact knowledge of the layout of the Temple than the common text.

8. *Jn 7:53-8:11*. The pericope of the adulterous woman is omitted by the Alexandrian text (P⁶⁶ P⁷⁵ ℵ B), part of the Caesarean and Western texts, some versions and quotations in the Fathers. In one way or another some manuscripts express doubts about the authenticity of this passage. Other manuscripts place the account after Lk 21:38, after Jn 7:36, at the end of Luke's gospel or at the end of John's. Before the 12th cent. no Father of the Greek Church comments on this passage. The first to do so notes that the best manuscripts leave it out. Internal criticism shows that intentional omission of this passage is not possible. The style and vocabulary used do not match those of the fourth gospel. It also breaks the continuity of the passages between which it is inserted (7:52 and 8:12ff.).

As a result, it cannot be said that this pericope genuinely belongs to the fourth gospel. Instead, it is an authentic element of oral tradition which was well known in other areas of the Western Church and could very well be fully historical and match real events. Perhaps because this account could be considered as unduly permissive, it was difficult to include it in a gospel and grant it the authority that would confer. However, the story is so typical of the way the real and historical Jesus of Nazareth would act that it was impossible to reject it or forget it completely.

BIBLIOGRAPHY

ALAND, K., *Synopsis quattuor evangeliorum: Locis parallelis evangeliorum apocryphorum et patrum adhibitis*, Stuttgart 1985¹³.

ALAND, K., *Kurzgefasste Liste der griechischen Handschriften des Neuen Testaments*, Berlin 1963.

ALAND, K. (ed.), *Die Alten Übersetzungen des Neuen Testaments, dir Kirchenväterzitate und Lektionare. Der gegenwärtige Stand ihrer Erforschung und ihre Bedeutung für die griechische Textgeschichte*, Berlin-New York 1972.

ALAND, K. - ALAND, B., *The Text of the New Testament. An Introduction to the Critical Editions and to the Theory and Practice of Modern Textual Criticism*, Gran Rapids-Leiden 1989 (translation of the 2nd revised German edition).

ALAND, B. - DELOBEL, J., *New Testament Textual Criticism, Exegesis, and Early Church History. A Discussion of Methods*, Kampen 1994.

ALAND, B. - DELOBEL, J., *Biblia Patristica. Index des citations et allusions bibliques dans la littérature patristique*, Centre d'Analyse et de Documentation Patristiques, 4 vols. y Supplément, Paris 1975-1982.

BIRDSALL, J.N., «The New Testament Text», *The Cambridge History of the Bible. From the Beginnings to Jerome*, eds. P.R. Ackroyd - C.F. Evans, Cambridge 1970, 308-376.

BIRDSALL, J.N., «The Recent History of the New Testament Textual Criticism (from Wescott and Horst, 1881, to the present)», *ANWR* II/26.1, ed. W. Haase, Berlin-New York 1992, 99-197.

BLACK, M., *An Aramaic Approach to the Gospels and Acts*, Oxford 1967.

BLACK, D.A., «Conjectural Emendation in the Gospel of Matthew», *NT* 31 (1989) 1-15.

BOISMARD, M.-E., «Critique textuelle et citations patristiques», *RB* 57 (1950) 388-408.

BOISMARD, M.-E. -LAMOUILLE, A., *Le texte occidental des Actes des Apôtres*, 2 vols., Paris 1984.

BOISMARD, M.-E. -LAMOUILLE, A., *Synopsis graece quattuor evangeliorum*, Louvain-Paris 1986.

CLARK, A.C., *The Acts of the Apostles*, Oxford 1933.

COLWELL, E.C., *Studies in Methodology in Textual Criticism of the New Testament*, Leiden 1969.

COMFORT, P.W., *Early Manuscripts and Modern Translation of the New Testament*, Wheaton, IL, 1990.

DUPLACY, J., *Où en est la critique textuelle du Nouveau Testament*, Paris 1959.

ELLIOTT, J.K., *A Bibliography of Greek New Testament Manuscripts*, Cambridge 1989.

ELLIOTT, J.K., *A Survey of Manuscripts Used in Editions of the Greek New Testament*, Leiden- ew York 1987.

EPP, E.J., «New Testament Textual Criticism. Past, Present, and Future: Reflections on the Alands' *Text of the New Testament*», *HTR* 82 (1989) 213-229.

EPP, E.J. - FEE, G.D. (eds.), *New Testament Textual Criticism. Its Significance for Exegesis, Essays in Honour of B.M. Metzger*, Oxford 1981.

FINEGAN, J. *Encountering New Testament Manuscripts. A Working Introduction to Textual Criticism*, Grand Rapids, MI, 1974.

FREDE, H.J., «Die Zitate des Neuen Testaments bei den lateinischen Kirchenväter», *Die Alten Übersetztungen des NT, Die Kirchenväter und Lektionare*, Berlin 1972, 436-454.

GREENLEE, J.H., *Introduction to New Testament Textual Criticism*, Gran Rapids MI 1964.

GREENSLADE, S.L. (ed.), *The Cambridge History of the Bible. The West from the Reformation to the Present Day*, Cambridge 1973.

KENYON, F.G., *The Story of the Bible*, New York 1937.

KENYON, F.G., *Handbook to the Textual Criticism of the New Testament*, London 1949².

KILPATRICK, G.D., *Essays in Memory of G.H.C. McGregor*, Oxford 1965, 189-206.

KILPATRICK, G.D., *The Principles and Practice of New Testament Textual Criticism*, ed. J.K. Elliot, Louvain 1990.

LAGRANGE M.-J., *Introduction à l'étude du Nouveau Testament. Critique textuelle*, II *La critique rationnelle*, Paris 1935.

MARTINI, C., *Il problema della recensionalità del codice B alla luce del papiro Bodmer XIV*, Rome 1966.

METZGER, B.M., *The Text of the New Testament, Its Transmission, Corruption and Restoration*, Oxford 1968².

METZGER, B.M., *Chapters in the History of New Testament Textual Criticism*, Leiden 1963.

METZGER, B.M., *The Early Versions of the New Testament. Their Origin, Transmission, and Limitations*, New York 1992³.

PASQUALI, G., *Storia della tradizione e critica del texto*, Florence 1952³.

SACCHI, P., *Alle origini del Nuovo Testamento*, Florence 1956.

VAGANAY, L. -AMPHOUX, C.B., *Initiation à la critique textuelle du Nouveau Testament*, Paris 1986.

VISONA, G., *Citazioni patristiche e critica testuale neotestamentaria. Il caso di Lc 12,49*, Rome 1990.

VÖÖBUS, A., *Early Versions of the New Testament*, Stockholm 1954.

3

Canonical Criticism.
The Text and the Canon

After studying questions connected with the canon and the text of the biblical books, it is necessary to consider the relationships between canon and text. In practice this means whether a «canonical text» existed and its relationship to what is called the «original text».

In the last few years, on the other hand, a theological movement which espouses «canonical exegesis» and a redirection of biblical exegesis and theology from the biblical canon has developed considerably and has a wide following, especially in North America. Here are described the direction of this movement and the critique it has received, restricting ourselves to questions connected with the canon, text and interpretation of the Bible.

I.   CANONICAL CRITICISM

After the Second World War, the North American intellectual and theological world was dominated by «The Biblical Theology Movement», whose aim was to establish a bridge connecting a fundamentalist view and academic study of the Bible. The movement was inspired by works of European authors such as W. Eichrodt (*Old Testament Theology* 1933), O. Cullmann (1946), G. von Rad (1957) and R. Bultmann (1953). Later, the «new hermeneutics» questioned the very foundations of the discipline and set off the crisis which «biblical theology» had entailed.

Childs attributed this crisis to lack of a canonical understanding of the Bible. Biblical theologies did not start from a direct understanding of the biblical texts but from preconceived patterns alien to the text of the Bible: «salvation history» in O. Cullmann, «understanding the self» in R. Bultmann, the «linguistic nature of being» in Ebeling and Fuchs, etc. Childs criticises the biblical theologies of von Rad, E. Wright and Zimmerli, saying that through historical criticism they establish a sort of canon within the canon, giving more priority to some biblical traditions than to others, mostly late. According to Childs, the canon forms the context from which it is possible to construct a real biblical theology and reclaim dimensions of the biblical texts, which have been forgotten by biblical criticism.

1. «Canonical criticism» *gives priority to the final or canonical form of the biblical books* (or of a collection of books) contrary to the privileged consideration granted in earlier periods to study of the earliest stages in the literary formation of the biblical books. The insertions and comments brought into the text in the final periods of its formation are not excrescences of late scholasticism and of some copyists who were not equal to the great texts they transmitted. Instead, they also have theological value and sometimes confer new value to what there was before.

The definitive and canonical form of the book of Amos confers on the prophet's message a perspective quite remote from the original meaning of the oracles of Amos. The collection of these oracles is now seen enriched with all the eschatological baggage typical of the interpretation of a later period (9:8-15). Childs acknowledges that first forms of the text could also enjoy some canonicity, since the authority granted to the collections of the prophet's oracles is what justifies and produces the reworking and reinterpretation of a later period.

«Canonical criticism» claims to be a further step in the development of modern criticism and goes beyond the study of sources, forms, traditions and redactions. Whereas that attempted to reconstruct the formative process of the biblical books, dissecting its text into small primitive units, this type of criticism focuses on large units of the text and the greater unit which comprises the whole Bible. The Bible is and means more than the whole and the sum of its parts.

2. «Canonical criticism» *takes account of the community* (Jewish or Christian) in which the texts of earlier periods acquired definitive and canonical form.

The Restoration period after the Exile was not a decadent phase dominated by ritualistic legalism (Wellhausen). This period was no less creative nor were its contributions to the history of biblical religion less important than those of earlier periods. Removal of the tension between Torah and Prophecy led to a new concept of prophecy and thus to a new post-prophetic period (Blenkinsopp). In this period, the authors of the books are no longer so important. Instead, it is the Israelite community which transmits these books, comments on them and uses them in the liturgy, in law and in the first synagogal institutions. The mediating function between Yahweh and the people of Israel which fell to the kings, prophets and priests in the monarchical period, now shifts largely to the community of the Israelites who can know the sacred texts directly through their interpretation. In this period, the Bible ceases to be the work of a few particular authors and becomes the book of a community and of a few readers and qualified interpreters.

Canonical criticism claims to be a necessary corrective to the course marked out by the Enlightenment, which removed the Bible from the closed confines of the churches and transferred it to the academic world of the universities. Canonical criticism tries to return the Bible to the living communities where it was born: post-exilic Judaism for the OT and early Christianity for the NT. The Bible has its own natural place (*Sitz im Leben*) in the believing community. It is not a source for reconstructing history. Its primordial function is canonical.

Thus, the Bible, that is to say, the set of biblical books collected into a canon, possesses two basic characteristics: the adaptability of its text to new contexts, meanings and re-readings, and the stability of the text itself, already surrounded by an aura of the sacred and the intangible (J.A. Sanders). Canonical criticism relinquishes the idea of canon as the *decision* of a synod or meeting of rabbis in favour of the idea of canon as a collection of canonical books by a formative *process*. This process reached boiling point in the 6th-5th cents. BCE, when the main lines and contents of the three great collections were determined: Torah, Prophets and Writings. In this way, emphasis on the *idea* of the canon tends to draw the *history* of the canon back to the earliest moments, long before the first lists of canonical books were drawn up.

II.   A CRITIQUE OF CANONICAL CRITICISM

The setting up of the canon involved the *creation of a global context* within which the Bible had to be interpreted from then on. And yet, it also entailed an absolute *decontextualisation* of the biblical texts. From the moment the canon was formed it was then considered that in itself every single text of the Bible was inspired rather than because of the inspiration of the author, of the book in which it occurs or of the whole of scripture. Each passage, each verse and even isolated phrases of the text could be quoted separately as proof material for settling a halakhic question in Judaism as witness («proof of prophecy») for defending the Christian faith.

The establishment of the canon entails the *loss of meaning of the literary form* peculiar to each biblical book. The books of the Bible came to be considered principally as inspired books. As a consequence, interpretations could be accepted which were remote from the first and original interpretation as established by the literary form chosen by the author.

The tendency of canonical criticism to give emphasis to the final stages of the formation of the Bible *does not correspond to the very dynamic of scripture*. The Bible places stress on the oldest traditions and on the founders, Moses and Jesus. The biblical books are always attributed to ancient authors, not to the redactors of recent periods. In Islam a similar trend is noticeable. All religious literature grants absolute priority to the earliest revelation, although it is certain that later developments can enrich and in fact do extend the reach of the primitive message. Simply think of the hermeneutic aphorism which says that the interpreter has to understand the work better than its author did (Gadamer).

Accordingly, liberal criticism, which has the basic aim of recovering «the original», has done no more than continue a trend of the Bible itself. The biblical message of «salvation in history» can do no less than leave the historical roots of revelation well entrenched. At root, Judaism and Christianity are historical religions. Without the first historical events - the deliverance from Egypt narrated in the Torah and the history of Jesus Christ told in the gospels - the rest of the Old and New Testament canon lacks meaning. Talmudic and patristic literature differ from biblical literature precisely because they are the work of compilers, commentators and later glossers and not of the founders and pioneers, or of their immediate followers like the OT prophets and the apostles and evangelists of the NT.

The Bible has always been read and recited in *short passages* and separate pericopes, not rapidly and all in one go like a modern novel. Isolated biblical sections are read in connection with the immediate context (the halakhic or moral application, homiletic preaching, theological proof, etc.) rather than in relation to the global context of scripture. Liturgy and private devotion use prayers and songs from the psalms in separate units or as small groups of psalms and not the complete psalter in succession.

The interpretation of a text in an older form than the one corresponding to the final and «canonical» redaction is perfectly legitimate and even necessary. In the case of a parable, for example, it is completely justifiable to isolate it as an object of interpretation and even of preaching. The text of a parable as defined by modern criticism, prescinding from the allegorical interpretation which the editors of the gospels included in the actual NT text. The «original» text detached by criticism could be uncertain in detail, but belongs to the original circumstances in which the parable was uttered which continues to be of interest and of theological value to a Christian.

If it can be stated that the oldest text is not necessarily better than the more recent and definitive text, it should not be thought that, on principle (canonical principle), the canonical text deserves more attention than the texts of earlier phases and periods. Late developments often lose the rawness and originality of the more primitive texts which preserve the freshness of the «actual words» of the prophets or of Jesus, or the power of the «actual deeds» fundamental to biblical revelation.

The canonisation process of the scriptures was prompted precisely by the growing feeling that genuine tradition was decaying with the passage of time through the continual insertions and changes introduced into the texts. The communities of the periods which gave almost definite form to the canon of the OT (2nd cent. BCE and even much earlier) and of the NT (2nd cent. CE) should not be made into referees of scripture, nor can there be a break in the development of the biblical tradition in the immediately preceding period.

The movement which defends canonical criticism makes it into a connection between scripture and theology. The other disciplines of biblical study then become ancillary disciplines which very often only distort the true canonical dimension of scripture. Among these disciplines, the furthest from «canonical criticism», and so held in the least esteem, is the «history of religion». However, it provides a large amount of data on ideas and religious symbols of the Persians, Greeks and others, that affected the biblical texts and thus tells us which interpretation a biblical book received in the Persian and Hellenistic periods. Study of the canonical texts alone does not allow us to know, for example, what interpretation the text of Nahum had in Qumran.

III. ORIGINAL TEXT AND CANONICAL TEXT

The problem posed by the relationship between the canonical text and the original text is particularly evident in the case of the book of Ben Sira. Until recently, this text was known only though the Greek version made by Ben Sira's own nephew (cf. p. 401). The translation tends to update the world of ideas reflected in the original Hebrew written years before. This barely gave space to belief in a resurrection, in agreement with the doctrine held later by the Sadducees. While only the Greek translation of this document was known, there was no problem at all. However, once a Hebrew text was known which is more genuine and closer to the original, inevitably the question arises: Which of the two texts is to be preferred? Is it the more authentic text, although it is less acceptable in terms of content, or the later text, although its teachings are more in line what seems to be the orthodox canon?

Similarly, the NT writers have been transmitted through three types of text: Alexandrian, Western and Byzantine. Which of the three text forms is canonical and what value and authority do variants of any one have? In the Byzantine period there was no single and monolithic text of the NT but instead different forms of the *Koiné* or Byzantine text, all equally authorised. The last twelve verses of the gospel of Mark (16:9-20) do not come from the same hand as the rest of the gospel. In spite of that, this passage, known already by Justin and Tatian in the 2nd cent., has to be considered as part of the canonical text of Mk. Even more extreme is the case of the intermediate ending of Mk found in some late Greek manuscripts and Latin, Syriac, Coptic, Armenian and Ethiopic versions (between vv. 8 and 9 or instead of vv. 9-20, cf. MS *k* of the OL). The churches which knew this text certainly considered it to be a canonical text, although it gives the impression of having an apocryphal origin, somewhat later than the apostolic period. More striking, perhaps, is the case of the Western text, which in Acts is 8.5% longer than the form of this book considered as «canonical».

Canonicity refers to books and not to a particular form or version of a book. The dominant situation in antiquity can be compared with the present, when very different translations were in circulation which included or omitted particular verses in certain books and had innumerable variants (end of Mk, Lk 22:43-44; Jn 7:53-8:11; Acts 8:37; etc.).

In Childs' opinion, the aim of textual criticism of the NT is to retrieve the best received text rather than the autograph text as it left the hands of an author. However, Childs does not define what the best received text is. On the other hand, no Church Father seems to have suggested that one form of the text was canonical and another not. More importantly, in Christianity the closure of the canon never led to the idea of a fixed text of the canonical books in the way that the Hebrew masoretic text was fixed for the OT.

As a result, the category «canonical» seems to have been broad enough to include variant readings which arose in the period when the apostolic tradition was still alive and was being transmitted partly orally and partly in writing. Others go further and include in the category of canonical text all existing variants, mistakes excepted, from the apostolic period to the Middle Ages (Parvis).

BIBLIOGRAPHY

BLENKINSOPP, J., *Prophecy and Canon. A Contribution to the Study of Jewish Origins*, Notre Dame-London 1977.

BOGAERT, P.-M., «Urtext, texte court et relecture: Jérémie xxxiii 14-26 TM et ses préparations», *Congress Volume. Louvain 1989*, Leiden 1991, 236-247.

CHILDS, B.S., *Biblical Theology in Crisis*, Philadelphia PA 1970.

CHILDS, B.S., *Old Testament Theology in a Canonical Context*, Philadelphia PA 1985.

CHILDS, B.S., *Introduction to the Old Testament as Scripture*, Philadelphia PA 1979.

CHILDS, B.S., *The New Testament as Canon: An Introduction*, Philadelphia PA 1985.

COATS, G.W.-LONG, B.O. (eds), *Canon and Authority*, Philadelphia PA 1977.

PARVIS, M.M., «The Goals of New Testament Textual Studies», *Studia Evangelica 6*, Berlin 1973, 393-407.

RENDTORFF, R., «Zur Bedeutung des Kanons für eine Theologie des Alten Testaments», *Wenn nicht jetzt, wann dann?*, ed. H.G. Geger *et al.*, Neukirchen-Vluyn 1983, 3-11.

SANDERS, J.A., *From Sacred Story to Sacred Text*, Philadelphia PA 1987.

TOV, E., «The original shape of the biblical text», *Congress Volume. Louvain 1989*, Leiden 1991, 345-359.

Chapter V

Hermeneutics.
Texts and Interpretations

«*Ein literarischer Text fordert Wiederholung des originalen Wortlauts, aber so, daß sie nicht auf ein ursprüngliches Sprechen zurückgreift, sondern auf ein neues, ideales Sprechen vorausblickt*»

«A literary text demands the original wording to be repeated, not however in order to go back to the original utterance, but in order to anticipate a new, ideal utterance»
(H.-G. Gadamer, «Text und Interpretation», *Hermeneutik II*, Gesammelte Werke 2, Tübingen 1986, 353).

Chapter V

Hermeneutics. Texts and Interpretations 423

I.   Introduction

The creative period of Jewish exegesis came before the Maccabaean revolt. Quite a number of the «corrections of the scribes» (*tiqqunê sōpĕrîm*) were the work of Sadducee scribes in the Hasmonaean period so that the pharisees already inherited a corrected text (Barthélemy; cf. pp. 281-282).

Several *factors* came into play in the birth and growth of biblical interpretation in the Persian and Hellenistic period:

1. The growth of the biblical collections ensured that later writings, especially those which make up wisdom and apocalyptic literature, had to include interpretation and reflection on the books and traditions of an earlier period. The apocryphal books continued this process of updating and rewriting the biblical texts.

2. Many passages in the biblical texts already presented difficulties to understand not to mention textual corruption, which was quite hard to interpret.

3. To enforce the laws and institutions of the Jewish people and to maintain their very identity and hope in the difficult conditions of the time, the old legal texts and historical traditions of Israel needed to be read and understood afresh.

4. The need to translate the sacred Hebrew texts into Aramaic, the language spoken in Palestine and in the Eastern Jewish diaspora, and into Greek, spoken by many Jews in the Western diaspora and even in Palestine, meant that the Hebrew text had to be interpreted and updated.

The *sources* for the study of Jewish hermeneutics are the OT, the Septuagint, apocryphal and pseudepigraphical literature, the writings from Qumran, the works of Hellenistic-Jewish writers (especially Philo of Alexandria and Flavius Josephus), the *targumim*, the Mishnah, Tosefta, Talmud, and the halakhic and haggadic Midrashim.

Interpretation was also known in ancient Near Eastern texts, in commentaries on texts which could form separate collections (G. Meier), or by means of glosses within the text, suitably marked to distinguish them from the actual text, or by means of interlinear glosses as known from 1QIs[a].

Once the history of the biblical text and the text nearest to the most original form of the text of each biblical book are known (parts III and IV), it is time to approach the field of hermeneutics and interpretation of the biblical texts. These two fields, history and criticism of the text and the history and criticism of interpretation are closely related. One example is enough to show how the text of a citation and its interpretation can affect each other. Jr 3:1 runs: «If a man dismisses his wife, she separates and marries another, will he return to her? Is this *land* not defiled?». The MT reading («*land*», hā'āreṣ) is replaced in the LXX and the Vulgate by another which fits the context better: «is this *woman* not defiled?». This passage quotes the law contained in Dt 24:1-4 which ends with the statement «you must not bring sin upon the land...». The fact that the passage in Jr is a quotation from Dt suggests that the MT reading, «the land» should be retained, as in the text quoted. This text cannot be examined only in the light of the methods of text criticism. The fact that this passage is a quotation is determinative in establishing the form of the text.

2

The Old Testament Interprets Itself

The Alexandrians could say that Homer is interpreted by Homer. It is no less true that the books of scripture interpret each other and that scripture is its own first interpreter. The last few years have seen great progress in studies on the interpretation of the OT as practised within the actual books of the OT and, in general, on Jewish and Christian exegesis of the OT. In the middle of this century, A. Robert could speak of the existence of an «anthological process» consisting of the re-use and modernisation of expressions or formulas from older biblical texts, resulting in a new text called «midrashic» (M. Delcor, A. Feuillet, B. Renaud, etc.). Later studies have refined the terminology a great deal as well as the classification of the genres and interpretative procedures of the OT (Fishbane).

There is no absolute divide between the final form of the text and later commentaries. From the beginning of biblical tradition, interpretation was an integral part of the text. The prophets were inspired by ancient traditions to interpret the events of their age. Their disciples did no more than continue this process of interpretation, creating and re-creating the text. The process of interpretation was to continue even after the text was established (Sanders).

Biblical literature, as well as all the Jewish and Christian literature generated by the Bible, are familiar more than any other with «intertextuality». The Bible has had a historical validity or a «historical potential» (*Wirkungsgeschichte*) greater than that of any other body of literature. Even patrology and early Christian literature are studied today more as an exegetical development of scripture than as independent theological works.

Although as yet in rudimentary form, the books of the OT already use interpretation procedures used later by rabbinic exegesis. These procedures are the *pěšāṭ* type, which attempt to explain difficulties of the biblical text, and the *děrāš* type, which tries to base in scripture legal regulations not considered in the Torah, or develop motifs of narrative and moral teaching contained in the biblical text. In the biblical texts, techniques of interpretation are used such as the rule *qal wā-ḥōmer*: Gn 44:8; Nm 12:14; Ex 6:12, etc. (cf. *Genesis Rabbah* 92,7).

Judaism is completely formed by the interpretation of scripture. Nothing is more important than the rabbinic representation of a God who studies and interprets his own Torah. This image expresses the conviction that revealed Law has to be the object of continual study and that its practical application has to be renewed continually to prevent it remaining a dead letter (BT, *Berakot* 8b, 63b and *'Abodah zarah* 3b).

I.   SCRIPTURE AND TRADITION

Pharisee Judaism had to establish a bridge between the revealed Torah and its interpretation as transmitted in tradition. Accordingly, it projected the origin of traditional interpretation back to the very moment of revelation on Sinai (Mishnah, *'Abot* 1,1). In this way the interpretation of the Bible became true revelation. Interpretation reveals new meanings of the sacred text which are no longer attained by direct revelation but through the labour of exegesis.

Among the most characteristic ideas of Judaism must be included the concept that revelation is not immediate and direct. It occurs always in connection with authorised tradition which transmits and interprets it. Tradition guarantees that revelation will be vigorous and understood at every historical moment. Revelation and traditional interpretation are related but quite distinct.

The relationship between scripture and exegesis can be considered from two different points of view: scripture is the basis of exegesis which in principle follows it, or conversely, scripture is itself an interpreted text and the essence of a whole tradition of interpretation.

The first point of view supposes that the creative process of scripture ended towards the close of the Persian period. From that time on the different methods and forms of biblical exegesis took shape. According to the second point of view, the Bible is the final precipitate of a long exegetical process. During the Persian period and even in a later period, scripture was open to every kind of interpolation and re-working.

After the canonisation of the biblical books, and once their interpretation had developed in the rabbinic schools, it was natural for the exegetical dimension of scripture to be forgotten. Scripture was considered more as the source of all interpretation than as a stream of interpretations. The character and pseudepigraphical processes of inner-biblical exegesis also help to conceal the exegetical nature of the Bible.

The biblical text was born already immersed in a current of oral traditions and has always been accompanied by a body of oral commentary (cf. p. 473). Oral tradition has not ceased to influence the interpretation of the biblical text and even how it was formed. A couple of examples will suffice. According to Dt 1:8, Daniel refused to drink wine. In the Bible there is no ban of any kind to justify Daniel refusing to drink wine (Dn 1:8). However, the Mishnah tractate *'Abodah zarah* 4,10, transmits the ban on drinking wine received from pagans, following an oral tradition possibly connected with Ex 34:15 where it is forbidden to eat food received from pagans. Similarly, Dn 6:11 alludes to the custom of praying in the direction of Jerusalem, an oral tradition included in the Tosefta, *Berakot* 3.

II. TEXT AND INTERPRETATION

There are many cases when a tradition contained in one book is found recast in another, frequently of a different literary form, in order to develop a law, teaching, counsel, etc. The prophetic text Jr 17:21-22, for example, is an exegetical recasting of the law given in Dt 5:12-14. Here, examples are given of the interpretation of legal texts in the prophetic texts and narrative texts connected with another legal text (Fishbane).

1. *Interpretation of legal texts in the prophets.* From the point of view of form, interpretation can be introduced by a citation formula and is a comparison of different biblical texts. Or else it need not be preceded by any introductory formula or may be only a comparison of texts.

– Comparison of texts preceded by an introductory formula.

Jer 3:1 is a good example: «Saying (*lēʾmōr*): 'If (*hēn*) a man dismisses his wife...*will she perhaps* (*hā-*) return to him again?...'. But you, who have fornicated with many men, can you return to me?». The formula «saying» (*lēʾmōr*) introduces the quotation from Dt 24:1-4, a text giving the law on polygamy. The comparison with this text is effected by the formula «If... perhaps?» (*hēn...hā-*) which expresses specific condition question The prophet then gives a judgment on the religious behaviour of the people of Israel, on the basis of the regulation cited above from civil law.

– Exegesis with neither comparison between texts nor introductory formula. Jr 5:21-24 is a commentary on the law in Dt 21:18-21. The prophet applies the saying in Dt on the rebellious son to the rebellious attitude of the whole people towards Yahweh. As in the previous example (Jr 3:1) a regulation from civil law is used to make a judgment about the moral and religious attitude of the people in relation to the Covenant provided by Yahweh.

2. *Interpretation of narrative traditions by means of legal texts.* The account of the creation of man in Gn 1:26-29 was used as a model to write the parallel account of Gn 9:1-7 on the rebirth of mankind after the flood. The differences between the two accounts only emphasise the parallelism between them. Gn 1:29 only permits vegetarian food: «I have given you every vegetable... and every tree.., you can use as food». Gn 9:3, instead, allows a diet of animal flesh: «Everything which moves and lives can be your food; and just as (I gave you) the green of vegetation I have given you everything». The expressions «can be food for you» (*lākem yihyeh leʾoklâ*) and «I have given you everything» (*nātattî lākem ʾēt kol-*) of Gn 1:29 are repeated exactly in Gn 9:3, but the phrase «all vegetation» (*kol-ʿēśeb*) is replaced by the words «everything which moves and lives» (*kol-remeś ʾašer hûʾ ḥay*).

The re-working of Gn 1 in Gn 9 assumes that vv. 4-6a(6b) have been inserted into Gn 9. The insertion is introduced by an expression common in legal texts: *'ak* («however», «on the contrary»). The inserted verses include the ban on consuming blood as given in the priestly lawcode (cf. Lv 17:10-12). The interpolation tries to justify authorising animal sacrifice so that their flesh can eaten. To kill a person, however, whether another person or an animal does so, incurs punishment. The reason given is that man has been created in the image of God (v.7, cf. Gn 1:27).

A grammatical analysis of the whole passage emphasises its syntactic inconsistency and proves that vv. 4-6a(6b) are in fact an interpolation. Vv. 1b and 5 show God speaking in the first person, v. 6b refers to God in the third person, and v. 7 reverts to direct speech.

III. THEOLOGICAL REWRITING

A book such as Deuteronomy can include earlier prophetic tradition (Zobel). Quite often the exegesis of a passage assumes that it has been completely rewritten theologically. For example, the harangue in Dt 31:4-8 on being courageous in battle is altered in Josh 1:5-9 to an exhortation to obey the Torah, which is indispensable for gaining victory in the holy war. The unconditional promise made to David of an eternal dynasty (2 Sm 7:12-16) is quoted in 1 Kgs 2:1-9, but there the promise is conditional on David's descendants keeping the Torah.

Among the many forms of theological re-working, *typological interpretation* is most conspicuous, later to be greatly elaborated in the NT and Christianity. Typological interpretation can be cosmic, historical or geographical in character, or be based on biblical characters.

The *cosmological typology* which stands out most is the one that elevates a cosmic event to a prototype of salvation history. The author known as Trito-Isaiah promises a new paradise world in which peace will reign even between wild animals (Is 65:17-25).

The *historical typology* which stands out most is the one developed in Josh 3-5. Three times the term *ka'ăšer*, «like...», expresses different historical equivalents: Joshua is portrayed as a new Moses; the crossing of the Jordan corresponds to the crossing of the Red Sea; the entry into Canaan occurs on the days of the Passover feast when the exodus from Egypt took place; the manifestation to Joshua corresponds to Yahweh's theophany to Moses (Josh 3:7; 4:14 and 4:23).

There are very important examples of *spatial typology*. According to 2 Chr 3:1, Solomon built «the Temple of Yahweh in Jerusalem *on Mount Moriah*», i.e., on the mountain on which Gn 22:2.14 places the sacrifice of Isaac. This equivalence has not the slightest historical or geographical validity, but no doubt is extremely evocative. The vision of the new Temple in Ez 47:1-2 combines various typologies referring to Eden, the tree of life and Mount Zion.

There are also many important *typologies based on biblical characters*. Noah appears as the new Adam in Gn 9:1-9. Joshua is the new Moses the deliverer (Josh 1), just as Elijah is the new Moses, witness of the new theophany at Horeb (1 Kgs 19).

IV. METHODS OF EXEGESIS IN THE OT

The two most common procedures of inner-biblical exegesis are the harmonisation of parallel passages and the insertion of isolated words or complete sentences.

1. *Harmonisation or interpretation by associating parallel passages.* Dt 15:12-18 interprets Ex 21:2-6 in the light of Lv 25:39-46. In principle, the regulation of Ex 21: «when you buy a Hebrew (*'ibrî*) slave he will serve for six years, but in the seventh he will go free», controlled the conditions under which a *ḥapiru* had to give his services to an Israelite owner. The text did not refer to a «Hebrew» or Israelite slave, as the term *ḥapiru* is usually understood in current translations, but to a non-Israelite (Harvey). Once this law was applied to a Hebrew or Israelite slave, the text of Ex seemed to contradict Lv 25:39-46, where it is laid down that an impoverished Israelite could freely put himself in the service of another Israelite, who had to treat him like a day labourer, not as a slave.

Dt 15:12 harmonises both texts, inserting elements from Lv into Ex: «If your fellow-Hebrew, man or woman, sells himself to you (as laid down in Lv) and serves you for six years, in the seventh you shall set him free from you (as laid down in Ex); then, when you set him free, you are not to let him go empty-handed. You shall load him liberally with presents...Do not regret setting him free, for because of the double wage of a day labourer (in line with the law of Lv) he has been serving you for six years (in line with the law of Ex)».

According to 2 Sm 7:2, Nathan forbids David to carry out his desire of building a temple to Yahweh. The book of Chronicles (1 Chr 17:1) tries to explain such a surprising ban. It justifies it from the fact that David was to blame for the death of Uriah (2 Sm 11:14-17) and of Saul's descendants (2 Sm 21:7-9). This explanation even appears in David's own mouth on two occasions: in the presence of Solomon (1 Chr 22:8) and before the assembly of the chiefs of Israel (1 Chr 28:3). Not without reason, the Chronicler has been considered to be a midrashist who re-writes and re-interprets the text of the historical books (J.M. Myers). However, the books of Chronicles are better considered as a work of history in its own right than as a simple commentary or exegesis on the sources it uses.

2. *Interpretation by inserting words or complete sentences.* Ps 18:7 is an interpolation of the type found often in the targumim which tries to avoid anthropomorphic expressions in reference to the deity (cf. p. 441). In the verse «He heard my voice from his Temple and my cry came *before him* into his ears», the expression «before him» (*lpnyw*) is an insertion. This gloss breaks the parallelism and metre of the verse. In addition, it is not attested in the

parallel text 2 Sm 22:7. The gloss tries to lessen the anthropomorphic effect of the reference to God's ears.

In the Bible there is already an evident tendency of rabbinic exegesis to expand on ideas and motifs of the biblical text. The parallel passages Ex 20:1 and Dt 5:16 add the promise of reward to those fulfilling the commandment to honour their parents; they will have a long life: «so that the days of your life may be many». The text of Dt also adds «and so that it may go well for you», so that the many years of whoever follows this commandment will also be happy years. The text of the LXX version goes even further, adding this gloss to the parallel text in Ex as well.

Ps 1:3 describes the happiness of the man who hates the company of sinners and delights in the Lord's Torah: «He is like a tree planted next to streams of water which produces fruit in its time and whose leaves do not wither». At the end of the verse are added the words: «in all that he does may he prosper». This gloss rationalises what is just expressed with a poetic image and also breaks the metre of the poem.

BIBLIOGRAPHY

DELCOR, M., «Les Sources du Deutéro-Zacharie et ses procédés d'emprunt», *RB* 59 (1952) 385-411.

DREYFUS, F., «L'actualisation à l'intérieur de la Bible», *RB* 83 (1976) 161-202.

DRIVER, G.R., «Glosses in the Hebrew Text of the Old Testament», *L'Ancien Testament et l'Orient*, Louvain 1957, 123-161.

FEUILLET, A., «Les Sources du Livre de Jonas», *RB* 54 (1947) 161-186.

FISHBANE, A., «Inner Biblical Exegesis: Types and Strategies of Interpretation in Ancient Israel», *Midrash and Literature*, eds. G.H. Hartman - S. Budick, New Haven - London 1986, 19-37.

FISHBANE, M., *Biblical Interpretation in Ancient Israel*, Oxford 1985.

GRECH, P., «Interprophetic Re-Interpretation and Old Testament Eschatology», *Augustinianum* 9 (1969) 235-265.

HARVEY, G.A.P., *The True Israel. Uses of the Names Jew, Hebrew and Israel in Ancient Jewish and Early Christian Literature*, Leiden 1996.

MEIER, G., «Kommentare aus dem Archiv der Tempelschule in Assur», *Archiv für Orientforschung* 12 (1937-39) 237-240.

MYERS, J.M., *II Chronicles*, Garden City NY 1965.

RENAUD, B., *Structure et attaches littéraires de Michée IV-V*, Paris 1964.

ROBERT, A., «Littéraires (genres)», *DBS* V (1957) 410-411.

SHINAN, A. -ZAKOVITCH., «Midrash on Scripture and Midrash within Scripture», *Scripta Hierosolymitana* 31 (1987) 257-277.

WEINGREEN, J., *From Bible to Mishna. The Continuity of Tradition*, Oxford 1959.

WILLI-PLEIN, I., *Urformen der Schriftexegese innerhalb des Alten Testaments*, Berlin-New York 1971.

ZOBEL, K., *Prophetie und Deuteronomium. Die Rezeption prophetischer Theologie durch das Deuteronomium*, Berlin-New York 1992.

3

The Interpretation of the Old Testament in the Greek Septuagint Version

Since it is a translation, the LXX is also a work of interpretation. The simple translation of the terms *tōhû wābōhū* (Gn 1:2 «empty and void» or «formless chaos» by *aóratos kaì akataskeùastos*, «invisible and disorganised» is a complete hellenisation of the biblical reference. Even more telling is the translation of the divine name *'ehyeh 'ăšer 'ehyeh* (Ex 3:14) by *egṓ eimi ho ṓn*, «I am the existing one» (cf. p. 320).

The LXX is *a work of Jewish exegesis*. As such it is comparable to a targum (cf. p. 000). This aspect, emphasised by Fränkel, Prijs, Seeligman, Gehman, Gooding, Koenig, Le Déaut, Harl, etc., is more obvious in some books than in others. It is more accentuated in the text of later recensions than in the original translation. It is evident in the use of Jewish hermeneutical principles, the tendency to wordiness, explanation by association with other passages, the explanation of names and places, the elimination of anthropomorphisms and anthropopathisms in references to God, etc. For example, the expression «they saw *God*» (Ex 24:10) is translated into Greek by «they saw *where the God* of Israel *stood*»; the expression «I shall no longer see *Yahweh* in the land of the living» (Is 38:11) becomes «I shall no longer see *Yahweh's salvation...*» in the Greek text.

However, it must be remembered that the presence of these targumic characteristics in the LXX version is much more restrained than in the actual Targums. The supposed tendency of the LXX to eliminate anthropomorphisms from the text, which C.T. Fritsch has tried to emphasise, has even been called into question by Orlinsky and Wittstruck. In Dt 32:10, speaking of the relations between Yahweh and his people, where the Hebrew text has the expression «like the apple of *his* eyes»; the Greek version omits the pronoun «his»: «like the apple of *an eye*» (*hōs kórē opthalmoû*). One should not see an anti-anthropomorphic theological tendency here, as Fritsch assumes, for one of the stylistic features of the LXX version of Dt is precisely the omission of possessive pronouns.

The *theological tendencies* of the Greek version are even clearer in *freer translation* such as Is or Pr. These are more like a Hellenistic Jewish midrash than a real translation from a Hebrew text into Greek. A typical example is the translation of Pr 24:28: «Do not be a witness against your neighbour without cause» as «Do not be a false witness» (*pseudḗs mártys*). There is no need to assume that the Greek translated the Hebrew word *amas* («with violence») instead of MT *ḥinnām* («for no reason») as BHS still continues to suggest (Orlinsky). All the translator has done is to interpret the word *ḥinnām* as meaning «false», as is done in *Midrash Rabbah* (Dt 3:12). The translation of the book of Proverbs provides many examples of inserted glosses. The LXX prefaces the text of 1:7 with a quotation taken from Ps 111:10: «The beginning of wisdom is the fear of Yahweh. Those who practise it enjoy sound judgment». The initial phrase of both texts is similar, which makes the association of the two passage easier.

Comparison of the LXX with other sources of Hellenistic Jewish and rabbinic literature can provide the necessary control when verifying possible interpretations of a theological nature which the translator could have inserted into the text. Jr 31:8 (LXX 38:8) runs: «Behold I will bring them from the land of the North..., among them [are] *the blind and the lame*» (*bām ʿiwwēr ûpissēaḥ*). The Greek version translates «Behold, I bring them from the North..., *on a Passover feast*». The discrepancy may be due to a different and possibly incorrect reading of the Hebrew text: *bᵉmôʾēd pesaḥ* (different word division and confusion of the letters *d* and *r*). This translation reflects the belief that the arrival of the Messiah had to occur «on a Passover feast», a belief also expressed in the Palestine targum (Ex 12:42) and common among Jews in the time of Jerome.

It should be noted that not every departure from the Hebrew text has to be regarded as indicating an interpretation by the translator or as reflecting a different Hebrew original (*Vorlage*). It is necessary to study each case while analysing parallel texts and the translation techniques used.

Before defining the Greek version of a particular book or passage as midrash, it is necessary to establish whether it is a midrashic interpretation made by the translator or a traditional interpretation, or even one still in progress which the translator does no more than reflect.

Properly speaking, midrash assumes the existence of a biblical text which is already established and «canonised». Given the various forms of interpretation of the biblical text (midrash, pesher, prophecy applied to the present, re-writing of narratives of biblical laws, etc.), it would be better if the term «midrash» were reserved for rabbinic midrash and did not include the different forms of biblical interpretation under the name «midrash», which otherwise becomes too generic and is no longer precise.

The LXX version used by the authors of NT has a decisive influence on their exegesis of the OT. For example, as «scriptural proof» of Christ's incarnation, Hb 10:5 uses the expression «you have opened my ears», from Ps 40:7. The author of the Letter to the Hebrews could not have found support in the MT since the reading there is: «you gave given me an open ear». Most of the quotations from the OT contained in the NT reproduce the text of the LXX in one form or another. Sometimes the quotation differs from the MT. This happens in Acts 14:17 which cites Am 9:12, where the LXX reads *ʾādām*, «man», against MT *^edôm*, «Edom». Elsewhere, the quotation of the NT agrees with some of the Greek versions, particularly the text of Theodotion, or instead differs from all text forms known to us (cf. p. 494).

The LXX version had enormous influence on the formulation of the Christian faith and on the language and literature of the Fathers (Harl), an aspect generally ignored by biblical scholars.

The «messianisms» are the touchstone of interpretation by the NT of the Greek version. The messianisms present in the LXX seem to be less common than was assumed to be the case in previous periods (Lust); the messianic movement found less of an echo in the Judaism of the diaspora than in the Palestine metropolis. However, the NT authors and Christian writers continued to find messianic echoes in many expressions of the LXX, which resulted in compilations of *Testimonia*.

BIBLIOGRAPHY

GARD, D.H., *The Exegetical Method of the Greek Translator of the Book of Job*, Philadelphia PA 1952.

GERLEMAN, G., *Studies in the Septuagint, I. The Book of Job*, Lund 1946.

GOODING, D.W., *Relics of Ancient Exegesis*, Cambridge 1976.

HARL, M., *La Bible d'Alexandrie. Traduction et annotation des libres de la Septante sous la direction de M. Harl*, Paris 1986-.

HARL, M., *La langue de Japhet. Quinze études sur la Septante et le grec des chrétiens*, Paris 1992.

HEATER, H. (JR.)., *A Septuagint Translation Technique in the Book of Job*, Washington DC 1982.

KOENIG, J., *L'Herméneutique analogique du Judaïsme Antique*, Leiden 1982.

LE DÉAUT, R., «La Septante, un targum?», *Études sur le judaïsme hellénistique*, eds. R. Kuntamann-J. Schlosser, Paris 1984, 147-196.

LUST, J., «Messianism and Septuagint», *Congress Volume-Salamanca 1983*, ed. J.A. Emerton, Leiden 1985, 192-207.

LUST, J, «Messianism and the Greek Version of Jeremiah», *VII Congress of the IOSCS Louvain 1989*, ed C. Cox, Atlanta GA 1991, 87-122.

ORLINSKY, H.M., «Studies in the Septuagint of Job», *HUCA* 28 (1957) 53-74, 29 (1958) 229- 271, 30 (1959) 153-167, 32 (1961) 239-268, 33 (1962) 119-151, 35 (1964) 57-88, 36 (1965) 37-47.

RÖSEL, M., *Übersetzung als Vollendung der Auslegung. Studien zur Genesis-Septuaginta*, Berlin-New York 1994.

SCHREINER, J., «Hermeneutische Leitlinien in der Septuaginta», *Die hermeneutische Frage in der Theologie*, eds. O. Loretz-W. Strolz, Freiburg 1968, 361-393.

SEELIGMANN, I., *The Septuagint Version of Isaiah*, Leiden 1948.

WITTSTRUCK, T., «The So-Called Anti-Anthropomorphisms in the Greek Text of Deuteronomy», *CBQ* 38 (1976) 29-34.

WITTSTRUCK, T., *The Greek Translators of Deuteronomy*, Yale 1972.

4

The Interpretation of the OT in the Aramaic Versions or Targumim

A targum lies at the border between two literary forms: translation and commentary. In this it differs from midrash. It can be said that targum is evolving towards midrash, which already considers the bible as a complete whole and is not tied to continuous translation of the biblical text. The Targums are the first links in the chain joining the interpretation contained in scripture with the various forms of Jewish interpretation of scripture.

The targumic version is an act of translation and interpretation which can take place in two ways: by inserting the paraphrase into a literal translation or by making the actual translation into a true paraphrase. In the first case it is easy to distinguish paraphrase from translation; in the second, both seem to be so intertwined that it is impossible to separate the translation text from the paraphrase. Examples of both procedures will give a better idea of the interplay of translation and interpretation which make up the targumic versions.

This chapter and its bibliography need to be completed by the chapter «Aramaic Versions of the Old Testament. The Targumim» (cf. pp. 324-332).

I.   TRANSLATION AND PARAPHRASE

According to Gn 2:15, in Eden man occupied himself by tilling the paradise garden: «Yahweh took man and placed him in the garden of Eden to till it and tend it». Targum *Neophyti* adds a couple of words which turn Adam into a wise student of the Torah: «..in order to work *in the Torah* and keep *its commandments*».

The targumist inserts the reference to the Torah on other important occasions. The biblical texts give no fixed time for the enmity between the serpent and the woman: «I will put enmity between you and the woman, and between your offspring and her offspring; she will strike your head while you shall try to strike her heel» (Gn 3:15). According to Targum *Neophyti*, the people overcome the serpent right up to the final victory, at the time when the Torah is studied and put into practice:

«I shall put enmity between you and the woman and between your offspring and her offspring and it will happen that when her sons keep the Torah and carry out the commandments, they will point to you and crush your head and kill you; but when they abandon the commandments of the Torah, you will point (to him) and wound him on his heel and make him ill; only that her son will take care, and you, serpent, will have no cure, for they will be ready to make peace in the future, on the day of the Messiah King».

A typical and very useful example of a translation followed by a lengthy paraphrase is found in the version of Gn 4:8 according to Targum Pseudo-Jonathan:

«And Cain said to his brother Abel: 'Come, let us both go out to the field'. *And it happened that, when they* both *went out to the field,* Cain began to speak and said to Abel: 'I see that the world has been created by love, but it is not governed by the fruit of good works, for there is preferential treatment in judgment. Why was your offering accepted with pleasure and my offering was not accepted with pleasure?'. Abel began to speak and said to Cain: 'The world has been created with love and is governed according to the fruit of good works and there is no preferential treatment in judgement. Since the fruits of my good works were better and earlier than yours, my offering was accepted with pleasure'. Cain answered and said to Abel: 'There is neither judgment nor judge and there is no other world, there is no granting of good wages to the just nor is there punishment for the wicked'. Abel answered and said to Cain: 'There is judgment and there is a judge and another world does exist; there is granting of good wages to the just and there is punishment for the wicked'. And on account of these words they were arguing *in the field. And Cain rose up against his brother, Abel, and* sank a stone in his forehead and *killed him»*.

The translator inserts a *complete* theological expansion which turns Abel into a proto-martyr and Cain into the prototype of an apostate persecutor of the just. It is quite possible that the expression «Come, let us go to the field» is not a «targumic» insert but the reading in an ancient Hebrew text. This reading, missing from the MT, has been preserved in many mediaeval Hebrew manuscripts and in the Samaritan Pentateuch, and is also reflected in the text of the LXX version and in the Peshitta and Vulgate.

II.   PARAPHRASE TRANSLATION

While being as faithful to the Hebrew text and as concise as possible, Targum Onqelos tries to give an explanation of the doctrinal and legal difficulties of the text. The version of Ex 23:19, «you must not eat meat together with milk», is a succinct summary of a whole exegetical process undergone by the ban on using milk for cooking meat to the ban on any mixture of meat products with milk products. This ban is one of the basic principles of rabbinic dietary law. Similarly, the phrase in Gn 4:24 «for Cain will be avenged seven times and Lamech seventy-seven» is translated in Onqelos as follows: «If seven generations were suspended for Cain, will not seventy-seven be for his son, Lamech?». The doctrine according to which God does not punish without offering a chance of repentance could hardly be expressed in fewer words; for a certain period the sentence remains suspended. All biblical exegesis, especially targumic exegesis, attempts to explain philological, stylistic or thematic difficulties of the biblical text, to harmonise possible contradictions between different passages, to mark the fulfilment of biblical prophecies, etc. For this the translator and interpreter (*meturgeman*) uses established principles of interpretation and translation techniques.

The classification that follows is by no means exhaustive.

1. *Explanation of difficult terms*. The explanation of difficult terms is always a challenge to every translator and interpreter. The original meaning in Akkadian of the term «Babel», «gate of god» was already completely unknown to the biblical authors. They explained it by using to a Hebrew verb which sounded vaguely similar: «Therefore it was called Babel because there Yahweh confused (*bālal*) the speech of the whole earth» (Gn 11:9). Onqelos expands this play on words, choosing the even more expressive Aramaic term *balbēl*. The Palestine targumim opted for a more common Aramaic term which develops the idea of the mix of languages (*'arbēḫ*, «to mix») although it causes the wordplay of previous interpretations to disappear.

A technique used for the interpretation of difficult terms is known as *noṭariqon* (cf. p. 480). It consists of dividing up a word into its components and then giving each of them a specific interpretation. For example, in the Palestine targumim, the term *'aḇrēk* in Gn 41:43, which is of Egyptian origin and probably means «to pay homage», is divided into two different words. These are *'āḇ*, («father») and *rēk*, («tender»), resulting in the translation and interpretation: «... father of the king, who is great in wisdom although tender in years».

2. *Double Versions*. The same word or phrase is translated by two words or phrases in collocation. In Gn 18:3, the term «favour», *hēn*, is translated in *Neophyti* by a pair of terms in common use: «grace and favour». In Gn 4:13 the term *(min)něšô'* («to bear») corresponds to two verbs in Targum Pseudo-Jonathan: «to tolerate» and «to pardon».

3. *Translation of anthropomorphisms*. The targumim do not provide a systematic and regular translation of anthropomorphic terms. The tendency to eliminate anthropomorphisms is evident in changes such as the alteration (mentioned above) of «son of God» (Gn 6:2) to «sons of the judges» or «sons of the nobles». The text of Gn 11:5 «Yahweh came down to *see* the city and the tower» is translated in *Neophyti* as follows: «And the glory of Yahweh's *Šekînâ* was shown to see the city and the tower which the sons of men built». Similarly, the expression «I shall stretch out *my hand* and wound the Egyptians» (Ex 3:20) is translated «And I shall send the plague of my punishments which will kill the Egyptians» in the same targum.

The *Tetragrammaton* is replaced by the expression *Šekînâ* («Glory») in contexts referring to a theophany or by the term *Memra* («Word») in contexts related to oracles and divine communications (Muñoz). To avoid anthropomorphic reference to God, other terms such as $Y^eq\bar{a}r$ («Glory») are used or circumlocutions such as $q^e\underline{d}am$-/$min\ q^e\underline{d}am$-, «before», or the divine passive construction. Of all these, only the term *Šekînâ* is used in rabbinic literature. Perhaps the fact that the Essenes and later the Christians made use of the other terms meant that the rabbis stopped using them.

4. *Modernisation.* In the same way that artists of the Middle Ages portrayed biblical characters and scenes with clothing, weapons and architectural motifs from their own mediaeval period, the targumists referred to places, peoples and institutions of past times of the biblical text contemporary. The Palestine targum brings up to date the geographical references of the «map of the nations» (Gn 10); after «the sons of Japhet were Gomer, Magog, Madai, Jawan, Tubal, Meshech and Tiras», the targum adds: «and the names of their provinces were: Phrygia, Germany, Media, Macedonia, Bithynia, Asia and Thrace» (cf. p. 326). The LXX Greek version follows the same procedure in Is 9:11 when it replaces the reference in the Hebrew text to Aramaeans and Philistines by a reference to Syrians and Greeks.

5. *Translation by Association. Neophyti* translates Ex 16:31 «and its taste like a pancake made with honey» by association with Nm 11:8: «its taste was like a bun of oil».

6. *Harmonisation.* The Genesis narratives portray Cain as a «tiller of the soil» (Gn 4:2) and Noah as a «man of the soil». Targum Pseudo-Jonathan harmonises the two readings, translating «man, tiller of the soil» in both cases.

7. *Different or contrasting meanings.* The targum version can give a passage a different meaning, even one opposite to the evident meaning of the text. This change of meaning is the result of adding or omitting a negative or inserting a question which implies a negative answer. The different targumic versions of Gn 4:14 «Behold you banish me from the face of this soil and I will have to hide myself from your presence», try to avoid any possible interpretation which would throw doubt on divine omniscience. The translation in *Neophyti* is «Behold you banish me today from upon the face of the earth, but I cannot hide before you. Cain will be an exile and a vagabond in the land and it will happen that whoever comes across him will kill him». The version in Pseudo-Jonathan is as follows: «Behold you banish me from the face of the earth, and is it possible for me to hide before you? And if I am wandering and exiled in the land, any innocent person who finds me will kill me».

8. *Symbolic Interpretation.* A symbol can be replaced by the object symbolised. This is the case when the term «seed» is substituted for «son» or the term «lion» for «king». Targum Onqelos changes the reference to a prostitute in Hos 1:2 into a reference to «a prophecy about the inhabitants of the errant city who continue to sin...».

BLOCH, R., «Midrash», *DBS* V (1975) 1263-1281.

HEINEMANN, I., *Darke ha-aggadah*, Jerusalem 1970 [Hebrew].

KLEIN, M.L., *Anthropomorphisms and Anthropopathisms in the Targumim of the Pentateuch*, Jerusalem 1982 [Hebrew].

LE DEAUT, R., *Targum du Pentateuque*, 5 vols., Paris 1978-1981.

MCNAMARA, M., *Targum and Testament. Aramaic Paraphrases of the Hebrew Bible: A Light on the New Testament*, Grand Rapids MI 1972.

MCNAMARA, M., *The New Testament and the Palestinian Targums to the Pentateuch*, Rome 1978.

MUÑOZ LEON, D., *Derás. Los caminos y sentidos de la Palabra divina en la escritura*, Madrid 1988.

PEREZ FERNANDEZ, M., *Tradiciones mesiánicas en el targum palestinense. Estudios exegéticos*, Jerusalem-Valencia 1981.

TAL, A., «L'exégèse samaritain à travers les manuscrits du targoum», *Études samaritaines. Pentateuque et Targum. Exégèse et philologie, chroniques*, eds. J.P. Tothschield-G.D. Sixdenier, Louvain-Paris 1988, 139-148.

5

The Interpretation of the OT in Apocryphal Literature. The Exegetical Character of Apocalyptic Literature

The fact that a book does not form part of the canon does not mean that in its own time it could not have an importance equal to or even greater than some canonical books. The importance of apocryphal literature, and of intertestamental literature in general, is based on the fact that this whole body of literature comprised *the indispensable channel for access to biblical sources.* The ancient Scriptures were meditated on and read through the world of ideas reflected in that literature. The interpretations included in the apocryphal books are often forced on the original and evident meaning ($p^e\check{s}\bar{a}t$) of the canonical texts. This is particularly significant in the use of OT texts in the NT. In Rom 5:12 «it was through one man that sin entered the world, and through sin death...» Paul does not refer directly to Gn 2-3, but goes through the traditions collected in the Book of Wisdom: «but through the devil's envy death came into the world» (Wis 2:24). The book of Genesis contains the canonical text, but the book of Wisdom provides the interpretation which is given new canonical value by Paul from the moment it becomes part of an NT text.

In the chapter on developments of canonical literature at the margin of the actual canon, reference was made to the various apocryphal writings which are real *«re-writings» of biblical texts* or contain exegetical expansions of them (cf. pp. 184-200). The following are exegetical expansions of the biblical books listed after them: Book of *Jubilees*, of Gn 1:1 - Ex 12:50; the *Martyrdom and Ascension of Isaiah*, of 1-2 Kgs (especially of 2 Kgs 21:16); *Joseph and Aseneth*, of Gn 37-50; the *Life of Adam and Eve*, of Gn 1-6; the *Biblical Antiquities (Pseudo-Philo)*, of Gn-2 Sm (Murphy); the *Lives of the Prophets*, of Kgs-Chr and Prophets; *Jacob's Ladder*, of Gn 28; *4 Baruch*, of Jr-2 Kgs-2 Chr-Ezra-Neh; *Jannes and Jambres*, of Ex 7-8; the *History of the Rechabites*, of Jr 35 and *Eldad and Modad*, of Nm 11:26-29. Similarly, Ps 151A (11QPs^a 151) is inspired by 1 Sm 16:1-11; 17:14 and 2 Sm 7:8. Ps 151B (11QPs^a 151) is inspired by 1 Sm 17:8-25. The *Prayer of Manasseh* gives what is presumed to be the text of the prayer mentioned in 2 Chr 33:11-13. *4Esdras* (3:1-2) uses the frame of the history of the destruction of Jerusalem by the Babylonians to refer to the destruction of the city by the Romans. The same happens in *2 Baruch* 6:1-2. *1 Enoch* 1-36 is an exegetical expansion of Gn 6:1-4. *2 Enoch* 71-72 describes the miraculous birth of Melchizedek. These chapters, like *11QMelchizedec*, expand on Gn 14:17-24 and are comparable to the oldest midrashim.

The OT is always the author's source of inspiration and at the same time offers the framework for the development of the new work. The exegetical expansions can be based on oral or written traditions which differ from the biblical texts.

In recent years, there has been an increase in the type of study which follows *the history of the tradition and interpretation of a passage, character, event or institution of the OT* as elaborated in post-biblical literature. For example, the account in Gn 12:10-20 involving Abraham, Sarah and the pharaoh is expanded in *Jubilees* 13:10-15, in the *Genesis Apocryphon* 20:21-34, in Philo's work *De Abrahamo* 19 (Loeb 6:49-53), in the works by Josephus, *The Jewish War* 5:379-382 (Loeb 3:319) and the *Jewish Antiquities* 1,8,1 (Loeb 4:81-83).

Innumerable examples could be given. The following are sufficient:
– Moses in Midian (Ex 2:15-25): Targum $Y^e r\hat{u}\check{s}alm\hat{\imath}$ I, Philo, *De Vita Moysis* 1:10-11 (Loeb 6:303-307); Josephus, *Jewish Antiquities* 2,11,1-2 (Loeb 4:277-279).
– Moses and Israel at the Red sea (Ex 14:21-31): *Pseudo-Philo* 10:2-6; *Jubilees* 48:12-14; Philo, *Moses* 1:32 (Loeb 6:367-369) and 2:45-46 (Loeb 6:573-577); Josephus, *Jewish Antiquities* 3,5,7-8 (Loeb 4:361-365).
– Elijah and the widow of Sarepta (1 Kgs 17:8-16): Josephus, *Jewish Antiquities* 8,13,2 (Loeb 5:745- 747).

Among the biblical characters or institutions studied in the manner mentioned above are, for example, Enoch (VanderKam), Noah (Chopineau, Fink, Lewis), Abraham (Lambrecht), Isaac (Yassif, Lerch), Melchizedek (Gianotto), Sodom and Gomorrah (Loader), Joseph (Kugel), Moses (Gager, Meeks), the Cloud (Luzárraga), the Ten Commandments (Segal), Elijah (Willems), Jeremiah (Wolff), Tobit (Gamberoni), etc.

The classifications made in terms of theological statute (canonical, apocryphal, patristic or rabbinic texts) are not suitable in a study of literary history. What is important is to be aware how a biblical character, motif or theme gives rise to countless intertextual expansions of every literary form. Study of the development of midrashic motifs is an exercise in «reverse engineering» (Kugel). Exegetical motifs generally start from a term or passage which presents some difficulty; only later did the midrashic elaboration stretch to different verses, often taken from very different contexts. The exegetical motifs migrate from one context to another, are combined with each other and influence each other. The first exegetical developments stem from problems of the biblical text which are rather simple or obvious. Later developments already focus on more complex and recherché matters. As a result, it is quite certain that in many cases where the biblical text presents a striking difficulty at first glance, earlier there had already been an exegetical elaboration of that passage (Gn 49:24 $r\bar{o}^{\,c}eh\ ^{\,}e\underline{b}en\ yi\acute{s}r\bar{a}^{\,}\bar{e}l$). Later rabbinic exegesis tends to establish connections between very different and separate texts which reflects the canonical status of the biblical texts and their resulting de-contextualisation (cf. p. 416). Before the 1st cent. CE, there already existed a whole body of midrashic explanations on problems of the biblical text, transmitted orally in the liturgical reading, translation and commentary of Scripture.

We will next focus attention on the apocalyptic perspective from which many of the works of apocryphal literature consider the books of the OT. Study of *apocalyptic literature* has in generally proceeded following very different interests from that represented by the *exegetical nature* of this form of literature, which consists largely in re-reading previous biblical literature according to apocalyptic models and ideas (Collins). The approach represented from the beginning of the 20th cent. by R. H. Charles has studied the literary history of the apocalyptic texts from its sources up to more recent insertions, in order to find in them references to theological, Jewish or Christian history and doctrine, of the different periods. This approach starts, in general, with a negative idea concerning everything connected with apocalyptic and loses sight of the mythological and cosmological elements peculiar to apocalypses (Rowley, Russell). The line of approach represented by H. Gunkel, instead, has attempted to recover the traditional material, also paying greater attention to the symbolic and allusive character of the apocalyptic imagination (Cross). It has also accepted the value of oral tradition in contrast to the one-sided concerns of the previous approach towards the written re-workings of the texts.

The exegetical nature of apocalyptic literature remains somewhat obscured by the presence of mythical elements which seem so alien to biblical tradition. Apocalyptic was influenced by eastern mythology and biblical tradition. Perhaps, therefore, this type of literature moves within the limits of the canon. It only succeeded in placing one solitary apocalyptic book within the canon, i.e., the book of Daniel, though not without having first made certain important changes to it (cf. pp. 178 and 400).

I.   ANCIENT JEWISH APOCALYPTIC

The influences of biblical tradition come from Zachariah's visions (chaps. 1-6), the Apocalypse of Is 24-27, Joel and Ez 38-39. Besides this line of tradition, which goes back to the biblical prophets and focuses on God's plan of history, apocalyptic also drinks from other biblical sources. Examples are the official cult of the Palace-Temple of Jerusalem which provides apocalyptic with symbols and images (Mowinckel, Cross) and the wisdom tradition, which it transmits without solving the problem of historical determinism and human responsibility (Hölscher, Von Rad).

Mesopotamian prototypes are easily recognisable in the character of Enoch. Like Enmeduranki, the seventh king before the flood according to some Mesopotamian lists, Enoch is the seventh patriarch before the flood (Gn 5:21-24). He reaches the age of 365 years, a clear reference to the solar year of 365 days; Enmeduranki was also connected with the sun-god Shamash. The motif of Enoch's translation to the heavens without undergoing death, follows the model of the hero Utnapishtim in stories of Mesopotamian origin about a universal flood (ANET, 95). Enoch's function as revealer of mysteries is parallel to Enmeduranki's function, the Sumerian king admitted to the divine assembly, where he is shown the mysteries, among which feature the heavenly tablets and techniques of divination. Enoch recounts «that which was revealed to me from the heavenly vision, that which I have learnt from the words of the holy angels, and understood from the heavenly tablets» (*Apocalypse of Weeks, 1 Enoch* 93:2). Enmeduranki was also considered to be the founder of the *barū*, the diviners' guild to whom methods of divination had been revealed (Kvanvig).

However, the Mesopotamian world of divination had very limited influence on the book of *1 Enoch*. Enoch does not use the divination techniques of the diviners (*barū*) such as the inspection of entrails or of oil floating on water. The only means of revelation used by Enoch is the dream, but this was not exactly typical of Mesopotamian diviners and has, instead, clear antecedents in biblical tradition, in the stories about Jacob and Joseph, for example. Similarly, astrology could have made the author of the Enochian traditions interested in the world of the stars; however, the author of *1 Enoch* does not resort to astrology to foretell the future. On the other hand, the ability to predict the future is a criterion of the veracity of a biblical prophet. However, the prophet is not a diviner. He disputes with the diviners and shows himself superior to them, for he counts on Yahweh's help (see the passages of Second Isaiah in Is 44:25-26 and 47:13).

The court legends in Dn 1-6 also originate in Babylonia. Daniel is brought up as a wise man in the Babylonian court (Dn 2) and, thanks to Yahweh's power, betters the Babylonian wise men in the interpretation of dreams and of mysterious writings.

The legends about Daniel and the traditions of Enoch, both of Babylonian origin, refer to a basic element of apocalyptic: the revelation of mysteries (*rāz*). Daniel receives revelation through the interpretation of dreams; Daniel's attention is focused on the history of successive empires (historical apocalypse). Enoch receives revelation by means of an ascent to the heavens and his interest is directed more to cosmology, astronomy and the solar calendar (cosmic apocalypse).

The most striking feature of these writings is the development of eschatological hope, here following a line of tradition originating in the biblical prophets. However, it is necessary to note that the writings of apocalyptic groups also showed a marked interest in legal or halakhic matters. According to the *Temple Scroll* and the *Halakhic Letter*, also known as *Miqṣat maʿāśē ha-Tôrâ*, the points of disagreement between the Qumran group and the mainstream Essenes, from whom that group separated, concern matters about the calendar (CD 3:14-15; 6:18-19), of primary interest in apocalyptic developments (*Jubilees*) and the correct order of feasts as well as the pre-scripts and regulations of purity relating to the Temple and regulations about tithes, impurity and marriage. The Essene world and the Qumran group in particular move between the worlds of halakhic interpretation and of apocalyptic revelation.

The formation and development of haggadic traditions in rabbinic Judaism later followed the same path as pseudepigraphical literature and biblical literature. This path consisted in the adaptation of old mythical representations of the religions of the ancient Near East or in the interpretation and literary expansion of biblical texts. The rabbinic interpretation of Gn 4:26 connects the beginning of idolatry with the person and generation of Enoch (*Genesis Rabbah* 23,6). Perhaps this interpretation preserves remnants of an old mythical tradition, independent of the tradition of the flood as punishment, which was about the influence of heavenly elements on human generations. The rabbis adapted this tradition to the case of Enoch's generation. This tradition is not attested in older sources and therefore it seems to be the product of rabbinic exegesis (Schäfer).

It should be noted that the return to mythological themes and motifs evident in apocalyptic literature also applies to wisdom literature and, later to gnostic literature. The sages and gnostics interpreted ancient Homeric or Mesopotamian mythology allegorically. Adam was presented as the First Man and the patriarchs as kings or sages, in terms of Hellenistic psychology and ethics. Sarah was turned into the character of mythological Wisdom, interpreted as the incarnation of that Virtue. God is equated with the Demiurge and at the same time interpreted as the cosmic principle of reason. The apocalypticists and the philosophers, Philo among them, lived in a world of interpreted myths. The first Christians did not refuse to use mythological language. Mythology and exegesis shape apocalyptic literature.

II. LATE JEWISH APOCALYPTIC

The classical works of apocalyptic (*1 Enoch*, *2 Enoch*, the NT Apocalypse, *4 Esdras* and *2 Baruch*) are all earlier than 150 CE. Charles assumed that apocalyptic disappeared around 100 CE to give way to rabbinic legalism. However, there is a whole body of apocalyptic Jewish literature which reaches to the mediaeval period: *Sēp̄er Zᵉrubbāḇel*, *Tᵉp̄illat Šimᶜōn ben Yōhai*, *Ništarôt Rašbî*, *Sēp̄er ʾEliyyāhu*, *Gᵉdullat Mōšeh*, *3 Enoch* (*Sēp̄er Hêḵālôt*), etc.

These works can be classified according to content or the characteristics of the literary form used. From the aspect of content, they can be descriptions of the end of time (*Sēp̄er Zᵉrubbāḇel*), of visions of the Throne[1] (*Maᶜāśê Merkāḇâ*; this is the central motif of *Hêḵālôt* literature, *Hêḵālôt Rabbati*, *Hêḵālôt Zutarti* and *3 Enoch*, works inspired by the vision of

---

1. With precedents in Qumran, cf. p. 194, and ramifications in Jewish-Christian literature, cf. p. 249, and in Gnosticism, cf. pp. 521-526.

Ezekiel), of literary expansions cosmological in character (*Maʿăśê Běrēšît*) or lastly, of journeys to heaven and hell (*Gᵉdullat Mōšeh*). All these works are in fact mixtures of very differing content. The four varieties mentioned appear already in classic apocalyptic and can also be found together in a single work, such as was the case of *1 Enoch*. All the motifs described refer to the domain of «secret», what is acquired through revelation.

With regard to the literary form, these works of apocalyptic content develop three forms known already through previous literature: apocalypse, midrash and treatise.

To the genre «apocalypse» or revelation of mysteries by supernatural means can be assigned works such as the *Prayer of Rashbi*, the *Sēp̄er ha-Rāzîm*, the *Narrative of R. Yᵉhōšuaʿ ben Lēwî*. The fact that these works attribute to characters of the Mishnaic period the pretence of having had access to new revelations is opposed to the rabbinic idea that prophecy had already ceased a long time before.

Works describing a revelation obtained by means of the midrash or interpretation of Scripture do not really belong to the genre of midrash strictly speaking. The best example is the work *Haggadat ha-Mašiaḥ*, a commentary on Nm 24:17-19 in the form of a biblical *lemma* followed by a commentary; the content is completely apocalyptic but its presentation follows a midrashic model. Another example is provided by the work *Maʿăśê Dāniʾel*, a sort of «re-writing» of the book of Daniel. These works, as well as *3 Enoch*, show the typical tendency of the post-biblical period to convert late apocalypses into midrashic works and to present it all in the form of exegesis of Scripture.

An example of a treatise is the work *Maʾămar ha-Gᵉʾullah*, «Treatise on Redemption».

Apocalyptic material can also be found in the form of *piyyuṭ*, in florilegia and quotations.

In late apocalyptic the question of genre is of minor importance. In this period content is more important than form. Accordingly, if attention is paid exclusively to the literary form there is a risk of rejecting apocalyptic material transmitted in the form of midrashim or treatises.

Most of the texts of late apocalyptic are post-Talmudic. Between 100 and 500 CE there seems to have been a complete lack of apocalyptic literature. Judaism of the Talmudic period does not seem to have shown the slightest interest in the world of apocalyptic. This poses a problem when explaining what could be the relationship between classical and late apocalyptic. Perhaps there was an indirect relationship, mediated by Christian apocalyptic; certainly it must more probably have been a direct line of continuity, kept hidden throughout the Talmudic period. According to Scholem, Talmudic apocalyptic is very much reduced, but is only the tip of the iceberg of a whole esoteric movement in the Talmudic period. The Mishnah was against apocalyptic, but at the close of the Talmudic period messianism was «rabbinised», as it were, which allowed the resurgence of apocalyptic movements. Christianity, instead, gave room to the development of the genre and of the symbols and ideas of apocalyptic. Eastern Christianity preserved the books of this genre better than Western Latin Christianity. The Church of Ethiopia has bequeathed to us the text of *Jubilees* and *Enoch*, the former refers to circumcision, a practice known in East Africa, so that the book of *Jubilees* was not out of place there.

BIBLIOGRAPHY (cf. pp. 204-207)

ALEXANDER, PH., «Late Hebrew Apocalyptic: A Preliminary Survey», *La fable apocryphe* I, Paris 1990, 197-218.

ALEXANDER, P.S., «Retelling the Old Testament», *It Is written: Scripture citing Scripture. Essays in Honour of B. Lindars*, eds. D.A. Carson-H.G.M. Williamson, Cambridge 1988, 99- 121.

BOGAERT, P.-M. -DEQUEKER, L. -JAGERSMA,H. -GUIGUI, A. -LAMBRECHT, J., *Abraham dans la Bible et dans la tradition juive*, Brussells 1977.

CHARLESWORTH, J.H. -EVANS, C.A. (eds.), *The Pseudepigrapha and Early Biblical Interpretation*, Sheffield 1993.

CHARLESWORTH, J.H., «The Pseudepigrapha as Biblical Exegesis», *Early Jewish and Christian Exegesis. Studies im Memory of W.H. Brownlee*, eds. C.A. Evans-W.F. Stinespring, Atlanta GA 1987, 139-152.

CHOPINEAU, J. et al., *Noe, l'homme universel*, Brussells 1978.

FINK, J., *Noe der Gerechte in der frühchristlichen Kunst*, Münster 1955.

COLLINS, J.J. - CHARLESWORTH, J.H.(eds.), *Mysteries and Revelations. Apocalyptic Studies since the Uppsala Colloquium*, Sheffield 1991.

GAMBERONI, J., *Die Auslegung des Buches Tobias in der griechisch-lateinischen Kirche der Antike und der Christenheit des Westens bis um 1600*, Munich 1969.

GAGER, J.G., *Moses in Greco-Roman Paganism*, Nashville TN 1972.

GIANOTTO, C., *Melchisedek e la sua tipologia. Tradizioni giudaiche, cristiane e gnostiche (sec. II a.C.-sec. III d.C.)*, Brescia 1984.

KAPLER, C. (ed.), *Apocalypses et voyages dans l'au-delà*, Paris 1987.

KVANVIG, HELGE S., *Roots of Apocalyptic. The Mesopotamian Background of the Enoch Figure and of the Son of Man*, Neukirchen-Vluyn 1988.

KUGEL, J.L., *In Potiphar's House. The Interpretative Life of Biblical Texts*, New York 1990.

LERCH, D., *Isaaks Opferung christlich gedeutet: Eine auslegungsgeschichtliche Untersuchung*, Tübingen 1950.

LEWIS, J.P., *A Study of the Interpretation of Noah and the Flood in Jewish and Christian Literature*, Leiden 1968.

LOADER, J.A., *A Tale of Two Cities. Sodom and Gomorrah in the Old Testament, early Jewish and early Christian Traditions*, Kampen 1990.

LUZARRAGA, J., *Las tradiciones de la Nube en la Biblia y en el judaísmo primitivo*, Rome 1973.

MEEKS, W.A., *The Prophet-King: Moses Traditions and the Johannine Christology*, Leiden 1967.

MASON, R., *Preaching the Tradition. Homily and Hermeneutics after the Exile*, Cambridge 1990.

MURPHY, F.J., *Pseudo-Philo. Rewriting the Bible*, Oxford 1993.

PUECH, É., *La croyance des esséniens en la vie future: immortalité, résurrection, vie éternelle? Histoire d'une croyance dans le judaïsme ancienne*, 2 vols., Paris 1993.

SCHÄFER, P., «Der Götzendienst des Enoch. Zur Bildung und Entwicklung aggadischer Traditionen im nachbiblischen Judentum», *Studien zur Geschichte und Theologie des rabbinischen Judentums*, Leiden 1978, 134-152.

SCHOLEM, G., *Major Trends in Jewish Mysticism*, Jerusalem 1967.

SEGAL, B.-Z., *The Ten Commandments in History and Tradition*, Jerusalem 1990.

THOMA, C. -WYSCHOGROD, M. (eds.), *Understanding Scripture. Explorations of Jewish and Christian Traditions of Interpretation*, New York 1987.

VANDERKAM, J.C., *Enoch. A Man for All Generations* (Studies on Personalities of the OT, Columbia 1995.

WILLEMS, G.F. (ed.), *Élie le prophète. Bible, tradition, iconographie*, Brussells 1985.

WOLFF, C., *Jeremia im Frühjudentum und Urchristentum*, Berlin 1967.

YASSIF, E., *The Sacrifice of Isaac. Studies in the Development of a Literary Tradition*, Jerusalem 1978.

6

The Interpretation of the OT in the Qumran Writings

Among the manuscripts of the Qumran community there are works of an exegetical kind, whose nature and only raison d'être is the interpretation of Scripture. In some cases, the interpretation is faithful to the letter of the text; in others, the interpretation is something added to its original meaning. In any case, these exegetical works imitate the expressions, compositional structures and literary forms of the biblical books: the *Community Rule* follows the model of the «Priestly Blessing» of Nm 6:24-26 in 2:2-10; the *Damascus Document* copies the structure and style of the book of Deuteronomy in its two sections, paraenetic introduction (CD 1-8:1-11) and central body of laws (CD 9-16).

In some cases, the biblical quotation follows a discussion on the theme of the quotation, in the form of a proof text or «scriptural proof». In others, the quotation precedes the commentary on the quoted text; the commentary can take the form of a pseudepigraphic writing, a pesher, an anthology or an explanation in midrashic style.

The genres of interpretation practised in the writings of the Qumran community are very mixed. The hermeneutical intention in some cases is to explain the biblical text and in others, to apply it to a new situation.

Biblical interpretation in Qumran represents the link connecting the interpretation of the Bible contained in the biblical books and the interpretation of the Bible developed in rabbinic literature.

I. THE AUTHORITY OF SCRIPTURAL INTERPRETATION AT QUMRAN

The principal activity of the members of the Qumran community was the study of Scripture. The community found its raison d'être in the interpretation of Scripture (Stendahl). This could apply to all Jews, but the interpretation of the «hidden mysteries» which the Scriptures contain was the fruit of a revelation reserved exclusively to the members of the Qumran community. They considered themselves as the true successors of Moses and the

Prophets and, therefore, very different and superior to the other Israelites. The Teacher of Righteousness, the founder of the Qumran Community, made himself out to be the authorised interpreter of the mysteries hidden in Scripture (1QpHab 2:1-9). The *Damascus Document*, the *Community Rule* and the *Temple Scroll* incorporate legal interpretations which claim to have the same authority as the canonical books. Whereas the *Damascus Document* interprets Scripture by direct reference to the biblical text, the *Temple Scroll* inserts interpretative elements into the text of the Torah, changing its interpretation into a new and true Torah (Wacholder). The chain connecting revelation and interpretation, which also links Moses, the prophets and the teachers of the Qumran community, confers on them enough authority to formulate new laws, comparable to those included in the Torah of Moses.

II. BIBLICAL TEXT AND INTERPRETATION

There are very many *implicit quotations* of the OT in the writings of the Qumran community. Even works which are not exegetical in character are completely permeated with biblical language (*Community Rule*, *Thanksgiving Hymns*, *War Scroll*, etc.). There are also very many *explicit quotations*, like the one in the Community Rule, 1QS 16-20, in reference to Is 2:22, and the *explicit allusion*, again in 1QS 6:13-23, to Lv 25:29-30.

In general, the interpreter respects the text meticulously, or its different textual forms. In many cases the biblical text followed in the Qumran commentaries depends on a variant known already from some other source, which indicates that all or nearly all the variants present in the commentaries testify to different recensions or textual traditions (Bruce, Dimant).

However, variants of an exegetical nature are also present. These can affect the grammar or syntax of a sentence, change of person, gender or number and the verb form; they can suppose an omission in the text or present different forms of paronomasia (metathesis, transposition of letters to form different words, *'al tiqre*, plays on words encouraged by the ambiguity of the consonantal Hebrew text, etc.). Some cases where it is believed a scribal error has been detected can be due instead to an intentional interpretation of the text transmitted in one translation or another. In Is 40:7-8, the text of 1QIsᵃ supports the short text of the LXX, which was assumed to be caused by homoioteleuton (Würthwein). However, it is just as likely that here the masoretic recension contains a gloss inserted deliberately through an exegetical process. In 1QIsᵃ, a corrector added the words which could have been interpolated in the MT, with the precise intention of making the text of 1QIsᵃ like the tradition represented by the MT (Brooke).

Qumran-style interpretation belongs to a very rich and varied textual tradition to which it attempts to be faithful. It is questionable whether the Qumran textual tradition and the corresponding exegesis reflect a variety of texts and interpretations, or whether, instead, they reflect a situation already dominated by an authorised line of tradition and exegesis, although it allowed certain textual variants and a variety of interpretations.

Sometimes the same text is found *copied* in a biblical manuscript and *commented on* in the form of a pesher or according to other genres of interpretation. For example, the book of Leviticus is found in one copy in the palaeo-Hebrew script (11QpalaeoLev[a]), appears translated into Aramaic in a targum (11QtgLev) and is commented on in the Hebrew legend of Melchizedek (11QMelq).

III. GENRES OF BIBLICAL INTERPRETATION AT QUMRAN

The genres of biblical interpretation used in Qumran are basically as follows: «re-writing», or midrashic or halakhic paraphrase, *pesher* interpretation, anthological interpretation through a selection of texts as «proof from Scripture» (*Testimonia*), and the interpretation of legal or doctrinal texts through association with others of similar theme. In addition, at Qumran there are genres of allegorical or typological interpretation.

1. «*Re-writing*», or *midrashic or halakhic paraphrase* can refer to long or short units of the biblical text.

The *Genesis Apocryphon* (1QapGen) is a narrative expansion of a whole biblical book (cf. p. 185). Biblical text and interpretation are combined to form a completely new text. For example, «But Yahweh afflicted pharaoh and his household with mighty plagues on account of Sarah, Abram's wife» (Gn 12:17) is re-written as follows: «And on that night the Most High sent a spirit of affliction, an evil spirit to afflict the two, him and his wife. He was afflicted and his whole house and he could not approach her and did not know her» (cf. pp. 445 and 457).

In a similar way, in the field of legal interpretation, the *Temple Scroll* claims to be a «new Torah»; it juxtaposes and associates different laws, harmonises some with others or inserts new legal interpretations. The text of columns 44-66 of the Scroll is a real *pastiche* made up of passages taken from Dt 12-23 (cf. p. 187).

2. The Hebrew term *pēšer*, «interpretation», denotes a type of *non-literal interpretation*. The term *pēšer* also denotes works of exegetical commentary (the *p^ešārîm*) which use this form of interpretation. The commentary can run verse by verse, or section by section. The *p^ešārîm* found at Qumran only comment on the prophetical books and a few psalms. The interpretation genre *pēšer* could also be used for the exegesis of books not belonging to the prophetic collection, although in fact no example at all has been preserved. The most important *p^ešārîm* are those concerning the books of Hab, Nah, Is, Hos and Ps 37 (cf. p. 201).

The most obvious formal characteristic of the *pēšer* is the use of this same word to introduce the commentary to the corresponding verse or lemma. The routine formulas include «its interpretation (*pēšer*) is...» or «the interpretation of the oracle refers to ...». An example taken from 1QpHab 7:3-8 is the following:

«And as for what he says: *So that the one who reads may run. Its interpretation concerns the* Teacher of Righteousness, to whom God has disclosed all the mysteries (*rāz*) of the words of his servants, the prophets: *For the vision will still continue for a time; the end will hasten and not fail: Its interpretation is* that the final age will be long and go beyond all that the prophets say, because the mysteries (*rāz*) of God are wonderful, etc.»

Lemma and interpretation can be related in different ways: without any textual connection to justify the relationship between them (1QM 11:6-7); repeating a key word of the lemma in the text of the interpretation (1QpHab 2:3-10) or altering a term which links the lemma with its interpretation. This last procedure supposes an alteration of the text of the lemma. It can be achieved through the technique known from rabbinic hermeneutic, which is to transpose the letters of a word in order to extract new meanings from the text. Such is the case in 1QpHab 2:5-6, where the letters of the lemma *ʿāmāl* («work») appear in a different order in the interpretation which follows, forming the word *maʿal* («transgression»). It is still surprising that such manipulations of the biblical text can be placed in the mouth of Yahweh, after the formula «as He said», as happens in the Damascus Document 7:14-15, in the quotation of Am 5:26-27 and 9:11.

The basic perspective of the Qumran *pēšer* is apocalyptic. This characteristic differentiates it from other genres of interpretation (cf. p. 475).

The interpretation of the OT typical of the Qumran *pešārîm* has elements in common with its interpretation in the NT. The *pēšer* corresponding to Is 54:11-12 describes the precious stones to be used in the rebuilding of Jerusalem, identifying them with members of the community in the manner of Ap 21:10-14 («twelve plinths... the twelve apostles of the Lamb»).

The Qumran community called itself «Israel», meaning that the history, promises and institutions of the OT had their fulfilment in their community, just as later the Christians also presented themselves as the «true Israel». 1QH 3:6-18 applies the prophecy of Immanuel to the Qumran community; 1QH 6:25-27; 7:8-9 does the same with the prophecy about the cornerstone of Is 28:16. These two prophecies are also used in the NT (cf. p.504).

It is worth noting that the interpretation of Qumran is not esoteric (contrary to Dupont-Sommer's opinion). It is neither a gnosis nor a secret teaching reserved only for initiates.

3. The *anthology genre of Testimonia* juxtaposes biblical passages referring to a single theme. The best representative of the genre is 4QTest, an anthology of messianic texts which nourish hope in the prophet of the last days and in the two expected Messiahs, one priestly and the other Davidic («the coming of a prophet and of the Messiahs of Aaron and Israel», *The Rule of the Community* 9:11). It combines different biblical texts referring to the

hoped-for prophet (Dt 5:28-29), the priest (Dt 33:8-11) and the king (Nm 24:15-17):

«I would raise up for them a Prophet from among their brothers, like you. I will place my words in his mouth and he will tell you all that I command them. If there is anyone who did not listen to my words, which the prophet will speak in my name, I myself will require a reckoning from him. And he uttered his message and said: Oracle of Balaam, son of Beor, and oracle of the man whose eye is perfect; oracle of him who listens to the words of God and has the knowledge of the Almighty, prostrate and with open eye. I see him, but not now; I perceive him, but he is not close. A star has risen from Jacob and a sceptre has arisen from Israel and it will break the temples of Moab and destroy all the sons of Sheth» (4QTest, *DSST*, 137).

These combinations of biblical texts are common in the *Rule of the Community*, in the *Hymns* and in the *War Scroll*. For example, 1QH 8:4-5 merges passages from Is 44:3; 49:10; 41:18-19. An example of a shorter type of anthology is the «phylactery», which generally reproduces passages from Ex 13:1-10.11-16 and Dt 6:4-9; 11:13-21, where it is said that the commandments should be like bindings on one's hand and like frontlets between one's eyes.

4. The *explanation of a text by association with others* of similar theme is particularly developed in the fields of halakhic and haggadic exegesis.

An example of halakhic interpretation may be the passage *Damascus Document* 4:20-52, concerning the monogamous nature of marriage, in which the texts Gn 1:27; 7:9 and Dt 17:17 are associated.

An example of haggadah could be the Hebrew legend of Melchizedek (11QMelq) which connects Is 61:1; Lv 25:13 and Dt 15:2 with the object of establishing a whole body of eschatological doctrine.

7. There are also cases of *allegorical interpretation* at Qumran. The *Damascus Document* (6:2-11) provides an example in which two biblical texts are associated, forming a single allegory:

«But God remembered the covenant of the very first, and from Aaron raised men of knowledge and from Israel wise men, and forced them to listen. And they dug the well: '*A well which the princes dug, which the nobles of the land delved with the staff*'. The well is the Law. And those who dug it are the converts of Israel, who left the land of Judah and lived in the land of Damascus, all of whom God called 'princes', for they sought him, and their renown has not been repudiated in anyone's mouth. And the staff is the interpreter of the law, of whom Isaiah said: 'He produces a tool for his labour'. And the nobles of the people are those who have arrived to dig the well with the staves that the sceptre decreed, to walk in them throughout the whole age of wickedness, and without which they will not obtain it, until there arises he who teaches justice at the end of days»

1QpHab 12:2-4, corresponding to Hab 2:17, interprets the term «Lebanon» allegorically as a symbol of the Council of the Qumran community. The root *lbn* («Lebanon») means «white» (*lābān*). The members of that council wore white at their meetings.

6. There are many examples of *typological interpretation* in the *Nahum Pēšer*: the term *kittîm* refers to the Romans, «Judah» to the members of the Qumran community, «Manasseh» to the Sadducees, «those looking for easy interpretations» to the Pharisees and «the lion» to Alexander Jannaeus, etc.

7. The Qumran writings also used *exegetical techniques practised in later rabbinic sources*. The *Damascus Document* (5:8-10) provides a case of *ribbûy*, a technique by which an element of a text is interpreted in an inclusive manner: a simple pronoun (*khm*) extends to women the law of incest which Lv 18:13 refers to men, without mentioning women. An example of *gᵉzērâ šāwâ* occurs in 11QTemp 52:133, of *diyyuq* in the *Damascus Document* 10:14-15, of *miʿûṭ* in 11QTemp 17:6-9, etc. (cf. p. 479).

IV. THE AIMS OF EXEGESIS AT QUMRAN

Jewish hermeneutics, especially at Qumran, had two objectives: *to explain* the biblical text in order to make it more understandable and intelligible («*pure exegesis*»), and *to apply* the biblical text to a new situation or to discover in it the answer to current questions which Scripture had not considered or even posed («*applied exegesis*»). Pure and applied exegesis can concern narratives (haggadic), legal texts (halakhic) and prophetic texts (Vermes). Only one example of each need be examined.

1.   *Explanation of Narrative, Legal or Prophetic Texts*

– Explanation of a *narrative* text: 1QapGen 19:14-24 is a midrashic expansion of Gn 12:10-20. The biblical account gives no explanation at all about how Abraham became aware that the Egyptians could eliminate him to take away his attractive wife. The author of the Genesis Apocryphon inserts a dream into the story, through which Abraham is warned to hide his wife. In this way five years pass during which the Egyptians respect his life until the moment when they notice that Abraham and Sarah are man and wife and the moment of danger is completely resolved for the patriarch.
– Explanation of a *legal* text: in Nm 30 it is established that a man's vow is valid on its own merits, whereas a woman's vow can be annulled by her father or husband. The *Damascus Document* (16:10-12) places limitations on this right. A father or husband can only annul those vows of a woman which she never should have made.
– Explanation of a *prophetic* text: the author of the Habakkuk Pesher (1QpHab 2:10-13) gives an eschatological expansion of Hab 1:6a: «For behold, I am raising up the Chaldaeans, that cruel and swift people». This passage is interpreted as announcing the arrival of the last conquering people, the Romans, called *kittîm*, «swift and powerful in battle, to slay many».

2. The Application of Narrative, Legal or Prophetic Texts

– Application of a *narrative* text: Habakkuk Pesher (12:3-4) interprets the words of the prophet, «For the violence done to Lebanon shall cover you», in terms which at first glance seem astonishing because of the strange connections they establish: «Because Lebanon (= the Temple) is the Council of the Community». A tradition known in Judaism equated the terms «Lebanon» and «Temple». On the other hand, the Qumran Community considered itself to be the true Temple. As a result, the text from the prophet Habakkuk could be interpreted as an announcement that the Qumran Community had been called to be the true Temple, which would replace the Temple of Jerusalem.

– Application of a *legal* text: in the inter-testamental period there was much discussion about the question whether the requirement of attention to elderly relatives was stronger than that of piety to God, or whether, instead the reverse held true (cf. the discussion in Mk 7:9-13 and Mt 15:3-6). The *Damascus Document* (16:14-15) finds an answer to this question in Mic 7:2: *one traps the others in his net*. The word *ḥērem*, «net» is interpreted as meaning «votive offering», which is also possible: «No-one shall consecrate the goods of his house to God, for as He said: *each one hunts his brother with a votive offering*».

– Application of a *prophetic* text: Hab 2:8b: «for (spilt) human blood and violence done to the land, to the city and to those who live in it» is applied in 1QpHab 9:8-12 to the «wicked priest, whom God delivered into the hands of his enemies for the iniquity he committed against the Teacher of Righteousness and the members of his community».

BIBLIOGRAPHY

BROOKE, G.J., *Exegesis at Qumran: 4QFlorilegium in its Jewish Context*, Sheffield 1985.

BROOKE, G.J., «The Biblical Texts in the Qumran Commentaries: Scribal Errors or Exegetical Variants?», *Early Jewish and Christian Exegesis, Studies in Memory of W.H. Brownlee*, eds. C.A. Evans-W.F. Stinespring, Atlanta GA 1987, 85-100

BRUCE, F.F., *Biblical Exegesis in the Qumran Texts*, Haag 1959.

BURROWS, F.F., *The Dead Sea Scrolls of St. Mark's Monastery*, I: *The Isaiah Manuscript and the Habakkuk-Commentary*, New Haven NJ 1950.

CAMPBELL, J.G., *The Use of Scripture in the Damascus Document 1-8, 19-20*, Berlin-New York 1995.

DIMANT, D., «Qumran Sectarian Literature», *Jewish Writings of the Second Temple Period*, ed. M.E. Stone, Assen-Philadelphia PA 1984, 483-550.

DIMANT, D., «Use and Interpretation of Mikra in the Apocrypha and Pseudepigrapha», *Mikra*, Assen/Maastricht-Philadelphia PA 1988, 379-419.

DUPONT-SOMMER, A., *Les Ecrits esséniens découverts près de la mer Morte*, Paris 1964³.

FISHBANE, M., *Biblical Interpretation in Ancient Israel*, Oxford 1985.

FISHBANE, M., «Use, Authority and Interpretation of Mikra at Qumran», *Mikra*, ed. M.J. Mulder, Philadelphia PA 1988, 339-377.

GABRION, H., «L'Interprétation de l'Écriture dans la littérature de Qumran», *Judentum: Allgemeines; Palästinisches Judentum, Principal: Religion*, ANRW II.19.ed. W. Haase, Berlin-New York 1979, 779-848.

GARCIA MARTÍNEZ, F., *Qumran and Apocalyptic Studies on the Aramaic Texts from Qumran*, Leiden 1992.

HARGAN, M.P., *Pesharim: Qumran Interpretations of Biblical Books*, Washington DC 1979.

PATTE, D., *Early Jewish Hermeneutic in Palestine*, Missoula, MT, 1975.

STENDAHL, K., *The School of St. Matthew and Its Use of the Old Testament*, Philadelphia PA 1968

VERMES, G., «Bible and Midrash: Early Old Testament Exegesis», *The Cambridge History of the Bible*, Vol. 1, Cambridge 1970, 199-231.

VERMES, G., «The Qumran Interpretation of Scripture in its Historical Setting», *Post-Biblical Jewish Studies*, Leiden 1975, 37-49.

7

The Interpretation of the OT in Hellenistic Jewish Literature. Philo of Alexandria and Flavius Josephus

The interpretation of the OT in Hellenistic Jewish literature can only be known by familiarity with that literature, its genres, aim and especially its biblical sources and the way it interprets them.

Not counting the LXX, Hellenistic Jewish literature is classified into three main genres: history, poetry and philosophy.

Conspicuous among the *historical writings* are the works of Josephus and two historical works of Philo, *Against Flaccus* and *Embassy to Gaius*. Jason of Cyrene wrote a history of the Maccabaean wars which the second book of Maccabees simply summarises. Alexander Polyhistor, Josephus, Clement of Alexandria and Eusebius preserve fragments of other historians, including Demetrius, Eupolemus, Artapanus and Cleodemos. The third book of Maccabees and the Letter of Aristeas are historical in form although in fact they are works of fiction.

The works of *poetry and drama* by Hellenistic Jewish writers are only known through quotations or allusions contained in works by Christian writers, especially Eusebius of Caesarea. They include an epic work on Jerusalem written by a poet called Philo, a long poem on Shechem composed by Theodotion and a work on Exodus written by the dramatist Ezekiel.

Among the *works of a philosophical nature*, the book of the *Wisdom of Solomon* is a reflection of the wisdom literature of Palestine, but it also exhibits the influence of Greek philosophy, Stoicism in particular. The fourth book of Maccabees, which praises the superiority of reason above the passions, also reveals Stoic influence. Clement of Alexandria testifies that Aristobulus, an Alexandrian Jew of the 2nd cent. BCE, used the allegorical method in his works about the Mosaic law (*Stromata* V, 14 and 97). The *Letter of Aristeas* also uses allegorical interpretation with the intention of justifying the dietary laws of Judaism (*Aristeas* 150-170).

I. HELLENISTIC JEWISH WRITERS

Now a review of the various Hellenistic Jewish authors can be made, noting the relationship of their works with biblical sources, of which they are often real interpretative elaborations. In general, the biblical text used is the LXX version.

The epic poet *Philo* (between 3rd and 2nd cents. BCE) sings the praises of Abraham, mentioning the Aqedah or the scene of the sacrifice of Isaac (vv. 8-10 of the first fragment). It provides haggadic elements with reference to giants. In the second fragment, Joseph is presented as governor of Egypt.

Theodotus (between 2nd and 1st cents. BCE) composed a poem, probably with the title *On the Jews*. Its language and metre were those of Greek epic. Its source of inspiration is basically Gn 34, with references also to Gn 17, on circumcision, and to Gn 27-33, on the events of Jacob's life. It also uses other post-biblical traditions.

Ezekiel (2nd cent. BCE), both a poet and a writer of tragedies, wrote a work of which the only remaining fragments are inspired by Ex 1-15, with Moses as the protagonist. The final act presents Moses and the Israelites in their long march through the desert at Elim (Ex 15:27). The content of the biblical narrative is dressed in the literary form of Greek tragedy. Ezekiel uses the text of a very old recension of the LXX, the nature of which is not yet defined.

Of the work of *Aristobulus* (2nd cent. BCE) only five fragments have been preserved. He is inspired by the books of Exodus, Deuteronomy, Genesis and Numbers. The first fragment deals with the astronomical circumstances associated with the feast of Passover when the sun and moon are in opposition. The second deals with the nature of God, resolving the biblical anthropomorphisms which scandalised the public cult of the time. In the third he states that some parts of the Law had been translated into Greek before the LXX version so as to be able to show that Plato and Pythagoras had done no more than drink from the sources of the Jewish Torah. The fourth fragment develops themes from the two preceding fragments and the fifth refers to the law of the Sabbath in terms taken from the cosmic order. The objective followed by Aristobulus is, ultimately, to complete an interpretation of the Torah, as is quite obvious from the title of the work by N. Walter, *Aristobulus, interpreter of the Torah* (*Der Thoraausleger Aristobulos*). The quotations from fragments 2 and 4 come from the text of the LXX. This version is also quoted in fragment 3.

The six fragments preserved of the chronographic work *Demetrius* (3rd cent. BCE) are connected in one way or another with texts from the OT. Basically, it uses the narratives of Genesis and Exodus as well as other data from later biblical history. Its intention is to establish a biblical chronology. The language and chronological system used correspond to those of the LXX version.

The exegete *Aristeas* (before 1st cent. BCE) reconstructs a life of Job from the Greek text of the book of that name. Aristeas deals with the patient figure of Job, leaving out Job as impatient and a sinner, and more characteristic of the canonical book of Job.

Eupolemos composed a work (definite date: 158/57), probably with the title *About the Kings of Judah*. In it he traced the history of Israel from Moses to Solomon, developing in greater detail what refers to the building of the Temple of Jerusalem, following the text of 1 Kgs 5-8 and 2 Chr 2-5. Eupolemos uses the text of Chronicles more than Kings. Undoubtedly it uses the text of the LXX, although he also shows that he knew Hebrew. The work ends with a calculation of the years elapsed from Adam and the Exodus up to the fifth year of the Seleucid king Demetrius (158/57 BCE). Eupolemos was certainly the ambassador sent by Judas Maccabaeus to Rome in 161 (1 Mc 8:17f and 2 Mac 4:11). As a descendant of a priestly family and son of another diplomat, John, the figure of Eupolemos combines in his person two cultural worlds, traditional Jewish and Hellenistic Greek. He certainly belonged to the group of those who at first rejoiced at the introduction of the Seleucid power.

Pseudo-Eupolemus (before the 1st cent. BCE) was probably a Samaritan of the 3rd cent. BCE. He portrays Abraham as an advocate of astrology. Abraham learned this science, created by Enoch, in Babylon and later taught it in Phoenicia and Egypt. The author does not balk at altering the biblical narrative, for example, by putting the narrative of Gn 14 before 12:10-20 to make it more obvious that astrology began in Babylon and reached Egypt through Phoenicia. Similarly, the dialogue between Abraham and the king of Sodom is changed into a dialogue of Abraham with the ambassadors of the Armenian kings who are alleged to have started the war referred to in Gn 14.

The novelist *Artapanus*, an Alexandrian of the 2nd cent. BCE, treats freely the biblical narratives of Gn 12:10-20, 37-50 and Ex 1:16. The three Jewish patriarchs are portrayed as founders of different branches of culture: Abraham taught the Jews astrology, Joseph, administration of land, and Moses, who has a longer history, established the Egyptian worship of animals as he is identified with Hermes. The literal agreements with the text of the LXX are noteworthy.

A whole series of ideas and concepts of *Judaism in the diaspora* could only be foreign to *traditional Palestinian Judaism*, which is centred on fulfilling the Torah. For the Jew of the Hellenistic diaspora the Pentateuch had become a body of laws based on a particular conception of divinity closer to philosophical reason than to the revelation on Sinai. This was evident in frequent references to the Logos and to concepts such as causality, fate, immortality, etc. The biblical commandments made the individual capable of triumphing over his passions, freeing the soul from the slavery of the body, so as to carry out the search for eternal life in the kingdom of the immaterial. This world of ideas is foreign to Palestinian Judaism, concerned more with observing the Torah. Only through serious allegorisation of the Pentateuch could the God of the bible be transformed into Reason pure and transcendental, completely spiritual and free of passions, the character of Moses be confused with a philosopher, a man of standing and a lawgiver, and the biblical patriarchs be changed into models of the laws of nature.

Another point of contrast between Hellenistic Jewish and Pharisaic Judaism concerns the concept of unwritten law, which for Philo is nothing less than the natural law, something very different from the rabbinic concept of oral law. Likewise, the pharisees refer to the collective tradition of the people of Israel, the only source of authority in Judaism; Hellenistic writers, instead, claim to be true individual «authors», moved only by their own tastes and ideas according to the individualistic spirit of the age.

A large part of Hellenistic Jewish literature had an *apologetic intent* of defence of Judaism, insisting therefore on the antiquity and glories of the history of Israel. Manetho, Lysimachus, Apion and other Greek writers were very critical of Judaism. Josephus felt obliged to quote them and refute them (*Contra Apion* 1,26; 2,1ff.). Latin authors such as Horace, Persius, Martial and Juvenal also made clear their derision of the Jews and Tacitus never stopped slandering them. However, the apologetic intent of Hellenistic Jewish literature never becomes missionary in tone. Its readers were not so much the gentiles as their own Jewish co-religionists, whose signs of identity it was necessary to reinforce, though still accepting the challenge of Hellenism.

Hellenistic Jewish literature consists largely in re-writing Jewish ancestral history as propaganda. The vision of history which Demetrius and Aristeas offer have features typical of the old deuteronomistic theology. The focus of interest shifts from insistence on fulfilment of the Law to glorification of the Jewish people and its ancestral heroes. A large and important segment of Hellenistic Judaism did not identify particularly with everything that the Law and rabbinic legislation meant. They were much more interested in the ancient stories of the people of Israel and its national heroes, in emulation of Greek, Babylonian and Egyptian history.

A series of works of Hellenistic Judaism exhibits a *certain tendency to Gnosticism* (cf. p. 523). «Salvation history» through Yahweh's intervention in the history of Israel and of other peoples gives way to «salvation through knowledge», gained through supernatural revelation granted only to the initiated. Concern for the Torah is subject to the desire for attaining full and true knowledge (gnosis). Circumcision and dietary laws lose importance. The signs of identity and of belonging to a Jewish community grow weak, lose clarity and become vague.

Lastly, mention can be made here of the *Hellenistic roots of certain features of Jewish hermeneutic* (cf. p. 479). These roots are found in Alexandrian philology and Stoic philosophy. A good example is provided by the interpretation based on etymological analysis of Hebrew terms. Starting with Heraclitus, the Greek philosophers reflected on the meaning and origin (*étyma*, «etymology») of proper names (*onómata*) in order to know the essence of things. In principle, these reflections never went beyond mere word plays between similar sounding words. Plato started a more rational and rigorous analysis of etymology (in *Cratylus*) which later was developed much more among Stoics. Appolodorus was the first Alexandrian grammarian to write a treatise on etymologies (*Perì etymologiôn*), undoubtedly influenced by his teacher, Diogenes the Stoic, from Babylon. Jewish hermeneutic developed the etymological interpretation and therefore inherits the traditions of interpretation of Babylon and Greece.

II. PHILO OF ALEXANDRIA

It is not easy to decide whether Philo is a philosopher who uses Scripture or an exegete of the bible who turns to philosophy.

As for the canon, it has been noted that basically Philo only cites the books of the Torah, but this not mean he did not know the other books (cf. p. 232). It has to be remembered that Hellenistic Judaism, especially Alexandrian Judaism, gave the person of Moses greater importance than he already had in the Judaism of Palestine. Philo portrays Moses as the true and only prophet and, at the same time, as a true philosopher. The prophets are the faithful disciples of Moses. Philo attempts to bring the teachings of Moses to the gentiles and at the same time to convince the Jews of the diaspora of the value of the Torah, which is above all the doctrines of the Greek philosophers.

For Philo, the bible, reduced essentially to the Pentateuch, is the great expression of religious humanism, raised to speculative mysticism. Philo's thought has an anti-historical character, evident particularly in his allegorical interpretation of the history of Israel. Similarly, the messianic idea has no role at all in Philo, although it is always present to some extent.

Philo uses various exegetical methods. Research on Philo has tended not to consider anything except *allegory*, understood from the viewpoint of the Greek world. At the beginning of modern research on Philo it was thought that Philonic allegory consisted basically in *applying Greek philosophy* to the Hebrew Pentateuch. It did not take into account the fact that Philo does real exegesis of the Pentateuch directly on the actual biblical text (Siegfried). Later it was realised that before Philo, allegory was already used in Judaism and that it had *its own Jewish character*istics such as paying more attention to ethical and religious interpretation than to matters of the physical world, the opposite to what Greek writers used to do (Stein).

Modern study on allegory in Philo goes in two different directions.

The first remains at the level of *philosophical matters* and of the logic which sets Philonic allegory in motion. Philo was a platonist educated in the technique of «dieretics», which enabled him to classify and organise reality in pyramidal structures, from the more universal to the more individual and specific (Christiansen). It moves in a dualist philosophical framework, with preference for the concepts of middle Platonism. It insists on divine transcendence and man's dependence on God, so that he would certainly prefer Platonism to Stoicism which showed itself as more inclined to immanentism.

The second approach lays more stress on the *religious and Jewish aspect* in Philonic interpretation. It does justice to the exegetical form which clothes Philo's works and the fact that Philonic allegory is always sparked off by biblical concepts or realities such as Wisdom or the Torah of Moses

(Nikiprowetzky). Allegory can take on various forms in Philo, with very different purposes in each case: the encomium, the anti-anthropomorphic allegory, the allegory attained through identification of characters, the allegorical development of a theme, etc.

Therefore, it is necessary to state that in Philo there is a merge of biblical Wisdom, which still retains mythological elements, and Platonic philosophy, which Philo transforms into a metaphor of a new Jewish Wisdom.

Philo's *exegetical works* are of two types:

1. *Allegorical commentaries* (*Loeb Classical Library*, vols. 1-5): treat passages from Genesis and Exodus, with references also to other books of the Law. These works interpret the text with great freedom in the manner of some commentaries by Greek philosophers. They focus interest on the figure of Moses the philosopher and not Moses the lawgiver. They do not consider the Torah as law since only the literal meaning can interpret the Torah as law and these commentaries use almost exclusively the allegorical method.

2. *On the Special Laws* (LCL vols. 7-8): they attempt to resolve specific questions concerning particular passages (*Questions and Answers on Genesis* and *Questions and Answers on Exodus*). They do not comprise real exegesis of the texts; rather, they are a systematic and logical explanation of them, using great freedom when grouping biblical themes and passages, sometimes adding lengthy digressions.

Philo also wrote other books not directly related to the bible (LCL vols. 9-10), although they too include biblical allusions. Later, the Alexandrian Fathers wrote exegetical works of these two types. Philo's work in fact was more widespread in Christianity than in Judaism.

The themes which Philo develops in his exegetical works are predominantly cosmological and anthropological or psychological. The Temple symbolises the World (*On the Special Laws* 1,66); the four colours of the high priest's vestments are a symbol of the four natural elements (*Moses* 2,88); Adam is a symbol of intelligence, Eve of sensitivity, and the animals of the passions (*Allegorical Interpretation* 2,8-9.24.35-38); Abraham's union with Sarah symbolises the union of intelligence and virtue (*On Abraham* 99), etc.

The same text can be given different allegorical interpretations. Jacob's ladder (Gn 28:12) denotes the air suspended between the sky and the earth as well as the soul set between sensitivity and intellect. Later, Christian exegesis would give many allegorical interpretations to a single biblical figure or narrative.

For Philo, Judaism provides the symbolic channel though which the soul and the mind of an individual can conquer bodily passions and reach spiritual freedom and immortality. The Greeks conceived the spiritual soul as captive in the material body which therefore was evil. A recurrent theme in Greek religion is the soul fleeing the bonds of bodily passions. For Philo, the Jewish laws, particularly observance of the Sabbath, circumcision and the dietary laws, once interpreted allegorically, reflect universal truths of the spirit. In this way the validity of Jewish practice is safeguarded while its spiritual meaning is enhanced.

III. FLAVIUS JOSEPHUS

Interest in recent years in the works of Josephus is evident in the recent publication of new editions, translations, bibliographical collections, a complete
concordance (Rengstorf), various monographs and an important joint work
(Feldman-Hata).

In particular, the problem of the biblical text used by Josephus has been
studied. Sometimes this is the Greek text, particularly the material corresponding to 1 Esdras, the additions to the book of Esther and the books of
Samuel where Josephus uses a proto-Lucianic text (Ulrich). Recently, Nodet
has provided proof for the use of the Hebrew text, against Schalit's thesis
that Josephus only used the Greek bible. The possibility cannot be excluded
that Josephus knew a Hebrew tradition which was independent of the MT
and the LXX, as seems to be indicated by the agreements with Pseudo-Philo
in data not found in either of the two known biblical texts. Josephus had a
«trilingual proficiency in the handling of the Hebrew, Greek and Aramaic
versions» (Feldman).

Special study has also been made of the way Josephus tries to resolve the
theological problems, contradictions and chronological incongruities of the
biblical text, as well as justifying the events narrated and making them more
likely, re-working Jewish tradition to make it suit rhetorical tastes and the
kinds of audience for whom the work was intended, the «Greek» or Roman
Greek and not only the Jews, his co-religionists.

Josephus promises his readers not to alter, add or omit anything from the
sacred text. However, he summarises, arranges or expands and dramatises
the biblical narratives. The first part of the *Antiquities*, which corresponds to
the period of biblical history up to the Exile, is a complete paraphrase of the
biblical text, larded with legendary material, particularly in books 1-5. This
comes from oral or written sources from midrashic traditions and has a parallel in other sources such as Artapanus, Demetrius, Eupolemos and Philo as
well as *Jubilees* and Pseudo-Philo. Josephus guarantees that the material
found in rabbinic sources is old. It is sufficient to follow up the many references given in the notes to the Loeb edition of the *Antiquities*. For example,
the information in *Pirqe of Rabbi Eliezer*, «(Cain) took Abel's corpse, made
a hole in the ground and buried it» has a parallel in *Antiquities* 1,54. There
are marked agreements between Josephus and Philo, for example, between
the prologue to *Antiquities* (1,1-21) and the introduction to Philo's *On the
Creation* (1.2-2.12). The two authors explain in the same way the fact that
the creation account precedes the account of the handing over of the Torah:
the sequence of the accounts is intended to prepare for obedience those who
were to receive the Torah. And there are also remarkable agreements in allegorical interpretation, such as the symbolic division of the Tabernacle into
three parts: earth, sea and sky (*C* 3, 181; Philo, *Quaestiones in Exodum*, 2,85;
De Vita Mosis, 2,18.88), or the description of the seven-branched candlestick
as a symbol of the seven planets (*Antiquities*, 3,182; Philo, *Quis Rerum Div-
inarum Heres*, 45,221-46,226; *Quaestiones in Exodum*, 2,73.75).

AMIR, Y., «Authority and Interpretation of Scripture in the Writings of Philo», *Mikra*, CRINT 2/1, Assen/Maastricht-Philadelphia PA 1988, 421-453.

ARNALDEZ, R., «La Bible de Philon d'Alexandrie», *Le mond grec ancien et la Bible, Bible de tous les temps* I, ed. C. Mondésert, Paris 1984, 37-54.

ATTRIDGE, H.W., *The Interpretation of Biblical History in the Antiquitates Judaicae of Flavius Josephus*, Missoula MT 1976.

BEGG, C., *Josephus' Account of the Early Divided Monarchy (AJ. 8:212-420). Rewriting the Bible*, Louvain 1993.

COHN, L.-WENDLAND, P., *Philonis alexandrini opera quae supersunt (editio maior)*, 7 vols., Berlin 1896-1930, reprinted in 1962.

COLLINS, J.J., *Between Athens and Jerusalem. Jewish Identity in the Hellenistic Diaspora*, New York 1986.

COLLINS, F.H. -WHITAKER, G.H., *Philo with an English Translation*, 10 vols. + 2 supplementary vols. Cambridge MA-London 1919-1962.

CHRISTIANSEN, I., *Die Technik der allegorischen Auslegungswissenschaft bei Philo von Alexandrien*, Tübingen 1969.

DANIÉLOU, J., *Philon d'Alexandrie*, Paris 1958.

FELDMAN, L.H. -HATA, G. (eds.), *Josephus, Judaism and Christianity*, Leiden 1987

FELDMAN, L.H., «Use, Authority and Exegesis of Mikra in the writings of Josephus», *Mikra*, CRINT 2/1, Assen/Maastricht-Philadelphia PA 1988, 455-518.

LEIMAN, S.Z., «Josephus and the Canon of the Bible», *Josephus, the Bible, and History*, eds. L.H. Feldman-G. Hata, Leiden 1989, 50-58.

KASHER, A., *The Jews in Hellenistic and Roman Egypt. The Struggle for Equal Rights*, Tübingen 1985.

MACK, B.L., «Philo Judaeus and Exegetical Traditions in Alexandria», *ANWR* II 21.1, 227-271.

MACK, B.L., «Exegetical Traditions in Alexandrian Judaism. A Program for the Analysis of Philonic Corpus», *Studia Philonica* 3 (1974-75) 71-112.

NIKIPROWETZKY, V., *Le commentaire de l'Écriture chez Philon d'Alexandrie*, Lille 1974.

NODET, E. *et al.*, *Les Antiquités Juives*, I, Paris 1990.

SIEGFRIED, C., *Philo von Alexandria als Ausleger des Alten Testaments*, Jena 1875.

SOWERS, S.G., *The Hermeneutics of Philo and Hebrews*, Richmond 1965.

STEIN, M., *Die Allegorische Exegese des Philo aus Alexandria*, Giessen 1929.

ULRICH, E., «Josephus' Biblical Text for the Books of Samuel», *Josephus, the Bible, and History*, eds. L.H. Feldman-G. Hata, Leiden 1989, 81-96.

WACHOLDER, B.Z., *Eupolemus: A Study of Judeo-Greek Literature*, Cincinnati, New York, Los Angeles, Jerusalem 1974.

WALTER, N., *Der Thoraausleger Aristobolos*, Berlin 1964.

WILLIAMSON, R., *Jews in the Hellenistic World. Philo*, Cambridge 1989.

WOLFSON, H.A., *Philo. Foundations of Religious Philosophy in Judaism, Christianity, and Islam*, 2 vols., Cambridge MA 1948.

8

Rabbinic Hermeneutics

The Judaism of the Second Temple period, and especially the form of Judaism shaped in the Qumran community, is based on three foundations: study and interpretation of the Torah, keeping the liturgical rules and messianic hope. Post-biblical Judaism was set up around the person of the rabbi, who was a combination of the earlier roles of sage, priest and messianic prophet. Study of the Torah and observance of the rules had to help speed up the coming of the Messiah. After the disaster of 70 CE, with the Temple destroyed and many of the messianic hopes departed, Judaism developed more along metahistorical lines, with the emphasis on the eternal and unchanging aspect of life, regulated by the Torah in accordance with rabbinic exegesis, and to a large extent it abandoned its previous path in the direction of a historical Messiah, which instead was developed within Christianity.

I.   HALAKHAH AND HAGGADAH

Judaism is based on hermeneutics, or the interpretation of Scripture. The basic concepts of this hermeneutic are those of *hālākâ* and *haggādâ*. Both have biblical roots; their earliest forms occur in the biblical books (cf. p. 431) and in Jewish literature of the second Temple period (cf. pp. 184-200).

Hālākâ , which is typical of literature of the Mishnaic period, extends biblical legislation. For example, it lists 39 types of work plus other types which were forbidden on the Sabbath day (Mishnah, *Šabbat*). *Hālākâ* tries to control every aspect of life, from dawn to dusk, from birth to death, even reaching beyond the Jewish people to all humankind by means of the so-called rules of Noah.

Just as the period when the biblical books were edited and biblical interpretation came into being corresponds to the Persian period and the start of the Hellenistic period (cf. p. 428), so *hālākâ* had its most important and decisive development in this same period. A typical example of the legislative activity of this period concerns the ban on marrying foreign women (cf. Neh 8 and 10).

The sources for the study of *hālākâ* are the same as for the study of biblical interpretation and of midrash. The LXX version, the deutero-canonical and apocryphal books and Hellenistic-Jewish literature itself contain pre-Mishnaic material. In addition to these sources there are others of a more practical kind, such as legal practices, casuistic disputes, customs, etc. Among the first sources linked more closely with Scripture, the LXX version is usually translated in agreement with tannaitic *hālākâ* (Ex 12:15; Lv 23:11; Dt 25:5; etc.) or with one of the opinions expressed among the rabbis (in Dt 21:12 it follows the opinion of R. Eliezer against R. Aqiba's), or also in opposition to the Mishnaic tradition (Ex 22:27). The book of Judith shows the *hālākâ* concerning circumcision of a proselyte (14:10) to be quite old. The first book of Maccabees shows the origins of the legislation which allowed the use of weapons on the Sabbath day (1 Mc 2:32.41; and contrast *Jubilees* 50:12). The *hālākâ* given in the book of *Jubilees* usually disagrees with pharisee *hālākâ*, for example in the laws concerning the Passover, it is even stricter than Šammai's, for example, forbidding under pain of death to load an animal, talk shop or fast on the Sabbath (49:13).

Many Mishnaic *hālākôt* date right back to the beginning of the Second Temple period. The law given in the Mishnah (*Šeqalim* 1-4) which requires every Jew to give half a shekel to the upkeep of worship in the Temple, has its earliest antecedents in Ex 30:11-16 which speaks of occasional tribute and a direct antecedent in Neh 10:33ff, where reference is already made to an annual tax (cf. Mt 17:24). The use of rabbinic sources for knowledge of pre-Mishnaic *hālākâ* present very considerable problems, which are even more aggravated when making use of them in connection with NT writings (cf. p. 494).

Haggādâ continues the narrative and wisdom tradition of the Bible. Haggadic midrash enjoyed less prestige than *hālākâ*. Unlike *hālākâ*, *haggādâ* lacked the slightest systematic arrangement and often fell into anthropomorphisms and anthropopathisms in referring to the divinity, always suspect for orthodox Judaism. However, M. Kadushim accepts *haggādâh* to be of value for its associative and a-logical character which sets in motion a whole set of concepts which refer to particular values (charity, worship, choice, etc.) even becoming what he calls a "mysticism of everyday life".

Hālākâ and *haggādâ* developed along parallel lines. According to common opinion, midrash was the frame for the development of *hālākâ* and is earlier than the form of *hālākâ* developed independently of Scripture. It can be asked in what period the midrashic type of *hālākôt* shifted to the creation of a *hālākâ* independent of Scripture. According to Lauterbach, this happened around 190 BCE or in Epstein's opinion, after the persecutions of Antiochus. However, there are no proofs that the formation of an oral Torah was in fact connected with Scripture. According to Urbach, *hālākâ* did not originate in midrash but in the administration of justice. It was not so much the business of the Sages as exegetes as of the Sages as judges in the courts.

The two routes by which *hālākâ* was created, through midrash and independently of Scripture, certainly developed at the same time and along parallel lines. The former was connected more with the world of Torah study, the latter with the world of legal practice, although it is quite certain that both spheres were closely related. The most important thing in all this is to acknowledge midrash as one source of the creation of *hālāḵâ*. Its function is not reduced to providing proofs from Scripture in favour of the law, still less did it consist merely of exegesis. To understand the development of ancient Judaism it is fundamental to accept this function of midrash as a source of *hālāḵâ*.

In any case, it is clear that independent *hālākhôt* gradually underwent «midrashization». A decisive contribution of the rabbinic movement after 70 CE was the biblical legalisation of *hālākhôt* which had arisen from custom and the courts. The «increasing influence of midrash» on *hālākhâ* is evident in the Mishnah: in later manuscripts there are biblical quotations not found in the first witnesses.

II. THE SCHOOLS OF HILLEL AND ŠAMMAI

Jewish, Babylonian and Alexandrian hermeneutics, Eastern or Western, Semitised or Hellenised, were all concentrated in a single individual, Hillel, in a period which turned out to be transient, ushering in a new era, and at a crossroads of peoples and languages: Palestine, bilingual in Aramaic and Greek (with Hebrew surviving in the synagogues and Latin with influence in the suburbs).

1. *The School of Hillel*

Hillel came to Jerusalem from Babylon. His teachers were the Alexandrians Šemayah and Abtalion. In Palestine he enjoyed a degree of acceptance among the Herodians, but he did not let himself be lured by messianic speculations or by the messianic provocations unleashed later among the zealots. Hillel lived in a period of transition and change. During the Herodian period the legal systems and judicial institutions were in crisis and lost much of their old coercive force.

Hillel promulgated rules and taught a doctrine based more on logic and *rational deduction* than on tradition and the *authorities*. Consulted in the case of a clash between the laws concerning the Passover and the observance of the Sabbath, Hillel devoted himself to the study of Scripture, but his questioners did not recognise the «arguments from Scripture» and did not accept his suggestion until he had referred to tradition and the teaching accepted by his teachers, Šemayah and Abtalion (JT *Pesaḥim* 6,1,33a).

Hillel established seven rules - or made use of them if they already existed - which governed every legal and exegetical interpretation of the biblical texts. For this he followed models and technical terms from Greek rhetoric. This use of Greek-style logic and hermeneutic methods introduced the principle of Socratic and Stoic realism into Hebrew law and thought, as well as the intellectual approach of questioning the most obvious. The play of question and answer became the road to knowledge and to know how to act in any situation, in a difficult blend of true gnosis and correct behaviour.

Hillel made it possible for the Torah to be tested by reason. The interpretation and application of the law in its literal meaning could sometimes be against the true spirit of the law, simply for example, because of a change in historical situation for which the law had been drawn up. Hillel, therefore, promulgated new decrees (*taqqānôt*), in each case responding to the demands of the moment. He did not worry about changing the letter of the law if necessary, as long as its meaning and original purpose were preserved.

The radicals, opposed to Hillel, could reproach him that by insisting on a rational interpretation of the Torah he was neglecting the need for an effectual fulfilment of the law. Hillel replied with the argument that his rational interpretation made it possible to retain the validity and application of the law to the new time and place of the diaspora. For these, instead, the laws from ancient times, intended for Israel, were ineffectual. Faced with new situations not envisaged in existing law, Hillel promulgated new *taqqānôt*, even in those cases where the new mandate was no longer based on a biblical *hālākâ*, for *hālākâ* had not evolved enough to found a new mandate within the old biblical legislation.

The school of Hillel accepted received tradition but equally it admitted and granted *juridical validity to practice*, without wondering whether the origin of an accepted custom could be foreign to the tradition of Israel. This symbiosis of tradition and modernity was possible thanks to a hermeneutical effort of interpreting the ancient legal texts of the Bible and bringing them up to date. Use or custom became *hālākâ* and was given a halo. This ensured that fulfilment of the law was within the reach of any Jew. The law did not become the privilege of the chosen and the perfect, which would have led to an elitist ethic remote from the Jewish people.

2. The School of Šammai

The School of Šammai accused Hillel of being modern since he accepted new rules (*hālākôt*) which he derived from Scripture. Šammai was known as a willing conservative, patriotic, opposed to foreign influences and so against proselytism amongst the pagans. However, in spite of the strict tendencies of his school, in one of every six cases where the Talmud reports on the differences between the two schools, the opinion of Šammai's followers is more open. In reality the attitude of the Šammai school shows a concern for retaining the basic principles and not only an absolute intransigence in the practical application of the law (A. Guttmann). According to Ginzberg, Šammai addressed the better off whereas Hillel was more concerned with the lower classes (Ginzberg). The differences between the two schools are certainly due to more varied and complex causes. In the theological field, Šammai's viewpoint was more theocentric, Hillel's more anthropocentric. In the area of relations with the gentiles, Šammai was more reactionary towards admitting proselytes, Hillel maintained a closer and more relationship towards them. The attitude of either towards women does not fit a simple opposition between strict and liberal. Contrary to Hillel's school, Šammai's acknowledges the rights of women more, defends their personal status and economic independence and gives credibility to their testimony in court.

III. THE SCHOOLS OF R. ISHMAEL AND R. AQIBA

Yochanan Ben Zakkay, the founder of the school of Yabneh, was a disciple of Hillel. He might perhaps be a grey figure, lacking his master's brilliance, but he is rightly considered the man who, after the national catastrophe of 70 CE, reorganised Judaism and made possible the «Restoration» of the institutions and life of the people of Israel. Opposed to political zealotry, loyal to Rome only to achieve his goals and independent of the power of the priestly class, Yochanan Ben Zakkay extended the legislation and interpretation of the old laws. This meant that the rules and interpretative trends of the Hillel school could become law and be applied to the new situation of the diaspora in which Jewish society had to live from then on. Yochanan Ben Zakkay accepted Hillel's process of *taqqānôṯ*, which enabled new laws to be created and the old laws of the Jerusalem Temple to be applied in a Sanhedrin now composed of lay-people, remote from Jerusalem.

In the 2nd cent. CE, Jewish hermeneutics flourished greatly. The schools of R. Ishmael and R. Aqiba represent two opposed movement (L. Finkelstein).

R. Ishmael based his hermeneutics on Hillel's fifth rule on «the general and the particular». R. Aqiba, instead, evolved the method of «inclusion and exclusion», which enabled him to give supreme importance to the most trivial details of the text, including accents, letters and particles. R. Ishmael's hermeneutics started from the principle that all doctrines or laws are expressed in human language so that their interpretation has to be ruled by the logic of reason. The meaning of a text cannot be forced at the expense of an atomised interpretation, applied to isolated words and letters, as the school of Aqiba did, even to the brink of any logic. For Hillel, the «promulgation» of new laws in terms of the demands of circumstance was more important than the «derivation» of other laws from Scriptural texts. Aqiba, however, gave preeminence to the «derivation» of laws from the sacred texts, hardly leaving room for pure *hālākâ* and the process of establishing new *taqqānôṯ*. Aqiba mixes the methods of *hālākâ* and *haggādâ* which Hillel carefully keeps distinct. After Aqiba, any oral tradition could be made legitimate from Scripture to the extent that it has been doubted whether Aqiba really accepted the existence of an oral Torah as separate from the Written one (Finkelstein). There was not yet the fear, expressed by Johanan Ben Zakkai, that a *hālākâ* without foundation in Scripture could remain forgotten.

The logical and reasoned interpretation of the school of R. Ishmael was provided with great critical, philological and historical precision. R. Aqiba, instead, closer to the Zealot movements and the mystical and apocalyptic trends of the time, gave free rein to a less exacting spirit, both in exegesis and in legal practice.

Although his journeys seem to have had no connection with Bar Kochba's revolt, Aqiba gave his approval to a messianic interpretation of that revolt. All the texts refer to the fact that Aqiba was executed in connection with the revolt, although the details given cannot be historical (P. Schäfer).

The school of Aqiba, continued by great masters such as Šim'on, Me'ir and Yehudah the Prince, had much more influence in the later history of Judaism, most especially in the compilation of the Mishnah. The name of Aqiba is cited 270 times against the 80 where his rival, R. Ishmael, is quoted.

As for the tradition of reading the biblical text, the two schools held different criteria. R. Ishmael did not allow any change at all to the consonantal text, but did in its pronunciation. R. Aqiba considered that the traditional pronunciation, which was not yet fixed by vowel signs, had the same value and the same unchangeable character as the consonantal text. R. Ishmael set no special meaning or value on the sequence in which the units of the biblical text appeared. According to R. Aqiba, however, the transmitted order was unchangeable and highly significant (BT *Sanhedrin* 4a-b; *Hullin* 72a; *Pesaim* 67b).

The schools of R. Ishmael and R. Aqiba developed two tendencies in Jewish hermeneutics which stem from Hillel: on the one hand, the search for freedom and reason in exegetical analysis, and on the other, obedience to the demands of the practical and legal order, as an antidote against a possible dissolving of Jewish being through assimilation to forms of pagan or Christian being.

Christianity, especially in its Pauline and Johannine forms, comes close in some degree to Essene movements, distancing itself from Hillelite pharisaism. The hermeneutics of Philo and Essene theology were more accepted by Christianity and rejected more in Judaism. From a very early stage, Christianity tended to set exact limits in doctrinal matters against the possible rise of heretical deviations. In practice, however, the need to adapt to very different cultural worlds forced it to accept a greater variety than existed in Judaism. Judaism, instead, though more liberal in doctrine, had to develop very precise rules of behaviour (*hālākâ*) to ensure the cohesion and survival of Jewish society.

IV. RABBINIC HERMENEUTICS AS DIALOGIC

The logic of Hillel hermeneutics was matched by a *dialogic style* which fostered and encouraged differences of opinion and viewpoint. 'Dialogic' is a term of particularly Jewish stamp (F. Rosenzweig, *Philosophie als Dialogik*; *Dialogik: Philosophie auf dem Boden der Neuzeit*, and M. Buber, *I and Thou*). Dialogic is the opposite of monologic. The former accepts and nourishes variety, the second excludes any method of understanding other than its own, in an attempt to reduce everything to one. The contrasting opinions of Hillel and Šammai could be considered as equally true and could be given equal approval by a voice from heaven: the «two opinions are the words of the living God» (вт ʿErubin 13b).

Rabbinic debate was always inconclusive and open to discussion. Even when a matter was settled by majority decision, it was still possible to teach a different opinion as long as it was defensible by rational argument. The discussion could be more important than the conclusions reached, since truth is always unattainable. Reason occupies a central position in rabbinic hermeneutics, although the sources of truth are not found in reason but in Scripture (Kraemer). Jewish theology, however, never crystallised into dogmas. At most, some basic statements about monotheism and the goodness of creation were formulated as a defence against Gnosticism.

The critical spirit of rabbinic exegesis did not shrink even from criticism of God himself, who is submitted to the interpretation by the rabbis of the divine Torah («My sons have beaten me», вт *Baba Meiʿa* 59b). This Talmudic passage testifies to the primacy granted to reason in Jewish hermeneutics. The sage is superior to the prophet and the ecstatic mystic. Tradition and revelation are two basic categories in Judaism (cf. p. 431). Tradition is elevated to the category of revelation which then even seems to be inferior to it. Tradition is transmitted by creating a new meaning and renewing the old meaning. This renewal (*ḥiddûš*) does not threaten the integrity of the text or assume the intrusion of something alien to the text, which is enriched thanks to its continual renewal. The written Torah submits to the needs and methods of interpretation peculiar to the oral Torah. «Oral law tries to speak about what written law says. But oral law says something more; it goes beyond the obvious meaning of the passage studied, without however forsaking the spirit of the overall meaning of Scripture» (Levinas, *L'Au-delà du verset*).

A very special characteristic of Jewish hermeneutics reflected in the Mishnah is a concern for collecting and keeping minority opinions which could not hope to have any regulatory force. This respect for the opinion of the minority expressed the conviction that in the application of law everything is questionable and nothing can become dogmatic. This mentality matches the legal and philosophical sensitivity of the Hellenistic world.

The structure of Jewish hermeneutics as dialogic set in motion a whole series of questions and objections. The real literary form of the halakhic midrashim is marked by its *dialogic (form)*.

In rabbinic dialectic, the relationship of «revelation-reason» takes on particular importance and, in rabbinic terms, is «biblical teaching» (*Talmud lomar*) - 'logic' (*din*). When human logic concludes to what the Bible says already, two positions are possible. Either a new meaning for the biblical text is sought, since teaching it would be superfluous or unnecessary, or counter-arguments are used to show the weakness of human logic, in order to make obvious the imperative need for the biblical text. The first approach is typical of Sifre Numbers (School of Ishmael), the second is typical of Sifra

(School of Aqiba). Both hermeneutical attitudes give rise to dazzling exegetical speeches.

A rabbi expounds the solution of a problem or a particular case and suggests a halakhic decision, which has its support in Scripture. Next, another rabbi puts forward objections and a general discussion begins, with arguments by some and counter-arguments by others. The debate ends with a majority decision which from that moment becomes a regulatory *Hālāḵâ*.

The dialogic style of the Mishnah and the Talmud could only lead to the development of some *compilation techniques* in museum fashion so that even the more obsolete opinions and rulings were included. The classification of laws was not systematic nor was it according to content. It resembled rather a sort of anthology of authors, sometimes choosing the weirdest interpretations, even though they were contrary to common opinion and established practice. This «principle of conservation» saved many *hālāḵôt* of the Šammai school from oblivion, as well as a large number of Sadducee traditions which had fallen into disuse after the destruction of the Temple.

Changes in circumstances and legal practice forced a method of exegesis to be developed which made possible hermeneutics to be «applied» to new laws and new conditions. On the other hand, the development of some exact methods of interpretation and of some «rules for the derivation» of laws from Scripture put a limit on a possible inconsistency in the interpretation of biblical laws and in the creation of new regulations derived from the old.

A fundamental difference separates Jewish from *Amoraite* and *Tannaitic* hermeneutics and from the hermeneutics of the Qumran Essenes and the first Christians. Among these the discussion opens with a question being set and concludes with a decision which ultimately has to be taken by the Teacher of Righteousness or by Rabbi Jesus. In Mishnaic literature instead, the discussion is resolved by a decision taken by the majority.

V. THE LITERARY FORMS OF RABBINIC INTERPRETATION: PĚŠAṬ, D^{E}RAŠ, PEŠER AND ALLEGORY

There are four main genres of interpretation in Jewish hermeneutics: *p^{e}šāṭ*, *pēšer*, *d^{e}raš* and allegory. The distinctions are very uncertain; even the Jewish interpreters were not necessarily aware of the differences among these four genres.

1. *Literal interpretation or* p^{e}šāṭ

Literal interpretation or *p^{e}šāṭ* was the most common interpretation especially in the application of legal texts to actual cases of litigation. At times it even suffered extreme literalism. Literal interpretation is less common in Talmudic than in midrashic literature. The literal interpretation was so evident and known that it not need to be included in a collection of laws. Philo himself, the greatest exponent of allegorical interpretation, and the Dead Sea Scrolls, where *pēšer* interpretation was typical, often also used literal exegesis.

Note that the term *pᵉšāṭ* is mediaeval and is not used as an exegetical term in the oldest rabbinic literature. At that time *kᵉ-mišmaʿô* was used, («according to its tradition or its meaning or its sound or its hearing»). In most cases, in the oldest midrashim, after citing the biblical text, a simple statement of its meaning or of its application is given. (For example, «this is said in order to exclude minors»). We can therefore class it as «stated exegesis» which is claimed to be obvious from text, context or tradition. This exegesis should not be confused with «philological» exegesis in the Middle Ages or the literal exegesis of Christian systematic disciplines. Since it is the obvious meaning of the text there is no need to consider it further here. The other meanings require more attention.

2.   *Pēšer interpretation*

Pēšer interpretation is typical of the exegetical writings from Qumran. According to this type of interpretation, the meaning of a biblical text is not the one which refers to the circumstances of the time when it was written but is instead the prophetic meaning received by the text in respect of the situation of the eschatological community (W. H. Brownlee, F. F. Bruce; cf. pp. 191 and 455). Examples of the genre *pēšer* can be found in passages of the *Hosea Pēšer* (2:8-12) and also in the gospel of Matthew (Mt 1:18-23; 2:1-6; 2:16-18; 3:1-13).

3.   *Dᵉraš and midrash*

a. Terminology. Until the beginning of the rabbinic period, the terms *dᵉraš* and midrash, from the same root *drš* («to examine, look for»), did not acquire the technical meaning of searching for the meaning of Scripture. These terms were applied to any kind of interpretation of Scripture, not necessarily as used in the midrashim.

Similarly, the awareness of the theoretical distinction between literal and midrashic interpretation is not attested until the beginning of the 4th cent. CE in the Babylonian Talmud. Interpretation by means of *dᵉraš*, consisting of the search for abstruse meanings of the text, was also the true literal interpretation of the text (A.G. Wright).

The term «midrash» can refer to three different things: the exegetical *process* by which a text is interpreted (*dᵉraš*), the actual *interpretation* of a particular verse or biblical passage using the midrashic method and the *compilation* of exegetical works brought together in collections called midrashim. Note, however, that the plural *midrashim* is completely unknown in the Mishnah, Tosephta, Talmud and halakhic Midrashim. The plural used in rabbinic literature is *midrašôt* («interpretations»); the expression *batê midrašôt* to denote centres of study, is very common. The plural form *midrašim* is a very late creation which seems to have part of the editorial process to denote compilations. Study of «comparative midrashic literature» can start from these compilations (Neusner) or from exegetical methods and actual interpretations of a particular passage (Kugel).

b. Definition. A clear and exact definition of «midrash» as exegetical process has to include three elements: midrash is a form of *exegesis* which starts with *Scripture* and is intended for the *Jewish community* (Porton). Rabbinic midrash has various features which distinguish it from other forms of Jewish interpretation.

Rabbinic texts comprise collections of separate texts the order and arrangement of which can be the work of one or more editors. Frequently, these separate commentaries, brought together in collections, refer to the same biblical passage and can be virtually identical, complementary or even contradictory to each other. Unlike other forms of midrash, rabbinic midrash is not usually anonymous; several expressions can be attributed to the same sage or rabbi. Rabbinic commentary can seem to be linked to a biblical unit or can form part of a dialogic, a narrative or a discourse. In other forms of midrash the commentary is linked with the biblical text commented on. Rabbinic midrash breaks up the text to a much greater extent than any other form of midrash with the exception of the targumim which, by their nature, discuss separately each and every element of the text. Frequently express reference is made to the particular type of exegesis used in a particular commentary.

c. The purpose of midrashic exegesis. Midrash can be used for very different purposes which can be known from the different styles employed.

One of these purposes is to connect newly-formed laws with passages from Scripture cited to support them. The purpose is for new usages to be more easily accepted by members of the Jewish community when guaranteed in one way or another by texts of Scripture (Weingreen). The connection between the new regulation and the corresponding passage from Scripture frequently seems to have been established at a late date, once the new law had already been accepted and could be included in the Mishnah. Midrash also had the purpose of solving problems and contradictions within Scripture (Vermes) and to keep the spirit of the Jewish community alive. Midrashic works seem to be intended for the public like synagogal sermons (J. Heinemann, A. G. Wright) although there are no proofs to show that they do in fact correspond to those sermons. The midrashim are too short to be sermons and in addition are too obscure and sophisticated to be intended for the general public. Possibly, many midrashic passages were intended exclusively for students of the schools. R. Tarfon, referring to Aqiba, gives a masterful definition of the basic objective of midrash: «You do research in order to agree with tradition» (Sifra, Nedebah 4:5). A parallel text in Numbers Sifre 75:2 runs: «Aqiba, doing his own research, succeeded in agreeing with the halakhah».

The whole of *Genesis Rabbah* is a complete example of a midrashic re-reading of the book of Genesis. It pays more attention to the message which can be drawn from the book for the present and future of Israel than to the actual story told in the book. Esau, Ishmael and Moab are turned into symbols of the Roman Empire, the last of the four empires whose fall was to precede the restoration of Israel (Persia, Media, Greece, Rome). Jacob's/Israel's brother, Esau, also becomes a symbol of Christianity, which considered itself as heir to the Jewish promises and also appropriated the legacy of the Roman Empire. Through Esau, midrash acknowledges the relationship linking Judaism with Christianity. Yet, at the same time it shows that Christianity, connected with the Roman Empire would end up ceding place to the sons of the blessing conferred on the Israelite descendants of Jacob. Examples of midrash occur especially in *Leviticus Rabbah, Sifre Numbers, Pesiqta of Rab Kahana* and in the Babylonian Talmud (*Sanhedrin* 90A).

This type of midrash, which evolved in rabbinic literature, is distinctly different from *periphrastic* midrash, typical of the targumim (e.g. *Neophtyi* Dt 29:9[MT 29:8]; Gn 2:15; 3:15; Dt 32:30, etc.) or of some books in the LXX version (e.g., LXX Pr 1:7 and Ex 22:8-9; cf. p. 439). The fundamental difference between midrash and targum is that midrash makes a careful distinction between biblical text and commentary, whereas targum is a paraphrase or «rewritten bible».

19th century critics paid no attention to the study of midrash since they considered it a worthless type of literature (Heinemann). Midrash has been the object of study in recent years from the aspect of the literary forms it uses (Wright) and the history of the formation of midrashic collections (Neusner).

Midrash reads Scripture as if things are not what they appear to be and the meaning of the texts is not only what is obvious and literal. Scripture has «seventy faces» and the aim of midrash is to discover the hidden meanings of the text. In this it is to some extent comparable to allegorical process and cabalistic investigation.

4. Allegory

Before the period of R. Judah the Prince, two groups of Palestinian pharisees, called *Dōršê Rᵉšûmôt* and *Dōršê Hāmûrôt,* used the allegorical method, although never overstepping certain marks (Lauterbach). The literary output of these groups was rejected later when a trend against allegorical exegesis became dominant in Judaism from the end of the 2nd cent. BCE. Some targumic texts give an allegorical interpretation of biblical legislation even though the application of this type of interpretation to legal texts was not authorised (Bonsirven).

The Jewish hermeneutic system developed by Hillel was based on Hellenistic models, including the allegorical method as well (Daube). The methods and terminology used by the Tannaites presume the influence of Greek rhetoricians (Lieberman). The exegetical principles, the style and the terminology of Hillel are comparable to authors such as Cicero (Daube). Sometimes the rabbis seem like Greek philosophers (Bickerman). Stoic, Epicurean, Platonic and Cynic elements can be seen in rabbinic midrash (Fischel; cf. p. 112).

However, the similarities with Alexandrian hermeneutics must not be exaggerated. A Jewish scribe did not necessarily depend on Greek philology but he was heir to a tradition with deep roots in the ancient Near East. The main difference between the Alexandrian philologists and Jewish scribes was that the scribes were interpreting a text they considered to be revealed by God himself and so required a listening attitude very different than for the texts of the Greeks (cf. p. 151).

VI. RULES AND METHODS OF INTERPRETATION

In Jewish hermeneutics there was a whole formative process both in terminology and in methods of expression. The gradual compilation of lists of rules of interpretation (*middôt*) emphasises this evolution: the first seven rules, attributed to Hillel, are made into thirteen by R. Ishmael and then thirty-two with R. Eliezer ben Joseph ha-Gelili (Zeitlin). The Alexandrian education of the teachers of Hillel, šemayah and Abtalion explains certain traits of rabbinic exegesis (Daube). The seven rules of Hillel are collected together in the treatise *'Abot of Rabbi Nathan* (37) and in the Tosefta, *Sanhedrin* (7,11). These rules are as follows (some examples are quoted throughout the book; cf. p. 499).

1. *Qal-wāḥōmer*: what applies in a less important case is valid in another more important one (argument from *a fortiori*).
2. *Gᵉzērâ šawâ*: identical words, used in different cases, apply in both (principle of verbal analogy).
3. *Binyan 'ab mikkātûb 'eḥad*: if the same phrase occurs in a certain number of passages, what refers to one applies to them all.
4. *Binyan 'ab miššênê kĕtûbîm*: formation of a principle by means of the relationship established between two texts.
5. *Kĕlāl ûpĕrāṭ*: law of the general and the particular. A general principle can be restricted if applied to a particular text; likewise, the particular can be generalised and become a general principle.
6. *Kāyôsē' bô bĕmāqôm 'aḥēr*: the difficulty of a text can be resolved by comparison with another text which has some similarity (not necessarily verbal) with it.
7. *Dābār hallāmēd mē'inyānô*: determining meaning from context.

Some of these rules are the simple application of logic and common sense. Others are open to greater misuse in exegesis (especially rules 2, 3, 4 and 6).

In the first half of the 2nd cent. CE, R. Ishmael extended the list of Hillel's rules to 13, so as to put a stop to the hermeneutic innovations of R. Aqiba. Further extension is attributed to R. Eliezer ben Yose ha-Gelili, probably between 130 and 160.

Hillel's rules led to the development of a atomised exegesis, which interpreted sentences, clauses, phrases and single words as completely independent of the literary context and historical circumstances mentioned in the text (G. F. Moore). In halakhic matters the reigning tradition prevented too arbitrary an application of the rules of interpretation. In matters of haggadah, however, excesses were very common since they did not entail danger to the practice of law. R. Eliezer's four last rules were probably the ones which gave rise to more fantastic and absurd interpretations. These four last rules concern the following: Gematria, which consisted of calculating the numerical value of letters; Noṭarikon, a procedure in which a word is divided into two or more parts and then each of them is explained as if it were a single word; the process called *Muqdām ûmeʾuḥār šehû baparāšiyyôt*, allowing it to be supposed that several passages refer to a later period than the period to which earlier passages refer (and vice versa; Strack-Stemberger).

As yet there has been no systematic classification of the methods of rabbinic exegesis in linguistic terms. This classification has to be synchronic before diachronic and should not be based on comparison with other types of interpretation method (Samley). The linguistic material for this classification goes from letters and morphemes up to sentences and longer units which are legal or narrative in content. There are quite a number of aspects which can bear meaning in a single letter: the form of the letter, the meaning of its name, its numerical value (*geᵐmatryāʾ*), its position in the alphabet, its acronymic value (*noṭariqon*), its phonetic value (*ʾal-tiqre*), etc.

Rabbinic interpretation does not give an explanation of pure signs but of signs as they occur in a specific text. The order and sequence of the letters, words or phrases can carry meaning. The position of the letters *ʾāleḏ* and *bêṯ* in the Torah gives cause for *Genesis Rabbah* (1:1) to account for the importance of these two letters in the alphabetic sequence. The sequence of the names Moses and Aaron serves in the Mekilta of R. Ishmael, *Pisaḥ* 1 (Ex 12:1 and 6:26-27) to explain that both are on a par. The criterion for deciding between two conflicting phrases is the order between them (Sifra, Lv 18:6-7, *keᵉlāl ûḏeᵉrṭ*). The Mekilta of R. Ishmael, *Baḥodeš* 5 (Ex 20:2) explains why the decalogue is found at the beginning of the Torah in Ex 20:2: the text of the decalogue is related to the foregoing sections which tell of God's good deeds to Israel. Relations of identity or contrast can be established between lexemes: *Genesis Rabbah* 1:1 gives a series of synonyms for the term *ʾāmôn* (Prov 8:30; Nm 11:12; Est 2:7; Neh 3:8); synonymy or use of a word in different contexts accounts for its meaning and invites midrashic interpretation.

In rabbinic exegesis the meaning is never immediate. The revealed word awaits an explanation to be understood. The commentary, therefore, is always necessary and exegesis forms part of a long tradition. The text has no existence outside the sounding-box of tradition. Being anchored in tradition does not mean submission to prejudices which limit freedom. It is to be ready to listen, to create a structure of expectation making the text approachable and intelligible. In modern thinking, daughter of the Enlightenment, inherited tradition connotes a tyrannical factor whereas for the rabbis it denotes something setting meaning free. The rabbinic interpretation of the term «heritage» in Dt 33:4 («Moses prescribed a Torah for us, *heritage* (*môrāšâ*) of the community of Jacob») is significant. The Babylonian Talmud (P 49b) reads *mēʾōrāšâ* «fiancée», «betrothed». Far from such insulting legalism, tradition remembers the love of a fiancée (Fishbane 76). Sifre, Dt 17:19, includes the saying: «The reading of the *Miqraʾ* leads to the Targum, the Targum to the Mishnah, the Mishnah to the Talmud and the Talmud to action».

Rabbinic methods of legal interpretation (*hālākâ*) and moral theological interpretation (*haggādâ*) correspond to mechanisms which control every procedure of interpretation. It has been possible to consider legal and theological hermeneutic as a model of what happens in every principle of interpretation (Gadamer; cf. p. 554). Every interpretation is an «application»: the application of a legal rule to a particular case in *hālākâ* and the application of a moral message, written or oral, to a new situation in *haggādâ*.

Jewish hermeneutics is a dialogic and makes a dialogic; it has the circular structure of question-and-answer. Dialogic between interpreters, who in principle disagree on the application of a legal text or the meaning of a religious text, leads to a juridical decision being made or the meaning of a religious text to be determined. However, the essence of the dialogic is rooted not just in the relationship established in discussion between interpreters but in the relationship, which is also a dialogic, which they try to establish with the text and what the text attempts to reveal: the eternal Torah and the divine will.

Often, non-Jewish scholars tend to reject rabbinic exegesis, considering it empty and worthless for understanding the text of the OT. However, it has to be acknowledged that the Mishnah and the Talmud preserve a great deal of material from oral tradition which goes back to the biblical period, although it must be emphasised that rabbinic interpretation is valuable in its own right.

Study of midrash has to begin with the Jewish context in which this type of interpretation originated and developed. Only after becoming acquainted with the methods, interpretations and collections of Midrash can study of the NT be approached from this perspective Often, NT scholars jump too quickly from midrashic interpretation to NT exegesis (cf. p. 495).

The oral Torah develops the systems of rules for purity and impurity contained in the written Torah, but it neither corrects nor contradicts it. The oral Torah does not consider as pure anything which the written Torah holds as impure. It confines itself to specifying which objects, places and actions are likely to produce impurity. A rabbi close to pharisaism, Jesus of Nazareth, could say quite rightly: «I have not come to abolish the (priestly) law. I did not come to abolish it but to fulfil it». The oral Torah is the culmination of the written Torah. The twofold Torah is the only complete Torah of Moses (Neusner).

VII. MEDIAEVAL JEWISH EXEGESIS: BETWEEN THE LITERAL MEANING AND MIDRASH

In order to know the history of the *biblical text* there is no other route except through the testimony of the mediaeval masoretes (cf. p. 272). Similarly, the *tradition of Jewish interpretation* of the Bible reaches us at the hand of the same masoretes and mediaeval Jewish philologists and exegetes. No attempt at all is being made here to describe Mediaeval Jewish exegesis. It is simply a matter of drawing attention to the importance of this link in the chain of tradition of Jewish interpretation. Enlightened modern criticism has usually accorded Mediaeval exegesis, whether Jewish or Christian, mostly scorn and neglect. It focuses its attention only on three aspects: 1) the relations between Karaism and the writings of the Qumran community emphasise the continuity that existed between the oldest exegesis and exegesis of the mediaeval period, 2) Mediaeval Jewish interpretation moves, as in earlier periods, between *pěšāṭ* and *děraš*, between philological and literal exegesis, which was more developed in Sephardi and philosophical and midrashic exegesis, dominant in Central European Judaism, 3) Jewish exegesis continued to influence Christian exegetes; this influence was always directed at granting greater weight to the literal and philological meaning of the biblical texts; some modern trends of study in non-Jewish circles today defend a return to contact with the sources of Jewish exegesis.

Mediaeval Jewish exegesis originated in the Islamic Arabic situation with *Sᵉ‘adiah Ga’on al-Fayyūmū* (882-942), whose biblical commentaries gave new life to literal exegesis in the context of polemics with karaism. This new exegesis spread over North Africa, especially in Qayrawan, reaching its zenith in Sephardi. Together with *literal exegesis* there was also development of movements focused on *philosophical and mystical exegesis*. The exegesis of *cabalistic theosophy* tried to uncover the mysteries of the divinity in Scripture, the hidden life of the divine according to his ten basic manifestations (the ten *Sᵉpîrôt*). Abraham Ibn ‘Ezra’ and Samuel ben Me’ir represent literal interpretation, Maimonides and Yosef Ibn Kaspi, philosophical and allegorical interpretation.

Talmudic literature has developed exegetical methods denoted by the term PaRDeS (= «paradise»), formed from the initial letters of the words for the *four meanings* of rabbinic hermeneutics: *Pᵉšāṭ* (literal and historical meaning), *Dᵉraš* (legal and ritual meaning), *Raz* (allegorical and philosophical meaning) and *Sôd* (symbolical and mystical meaning). Throughout the 6th-9th cents. CE, the *Gᵉōnîm* who directed the Talmudic academies of *Babylon* in Sura and Punbedita used these same methods. The interpretations established by these four paths or meanings were communicated to all the Jewish communities, even the most remote in Christian Europe. In this way a rich Gaonic literature grew up which took the form of a *Response* to questions posed by Jewish communities throughout the diaspora.

Arabic-speaking Jewish commentators, living in *Palestine* in the 10th cent., are of special interest since they are the contemporaries of the Tiberian masoretes.

The greatest representative of Palestinian rabbinism in this period is S^e‘a-diah Ga’on, already referred to. He was born in Egypt and after schooling in Alexandria and Jerusalem, moved to Baghdad where he soon became the highest authority in the academy there. S^e‘adiah Ga’on's exegesis is based on Arabic philology and philosophy and is marked by its development of the literal and midrashic meanings. His commentaries represent the Jewish or-thodoxy which later spread across Spain, North Africa and Western Europe. He wrote commentaries on the Pentateuch, Proverbs, Job and Isaiah. Frag-ments found in the Cairo Synagogue have provided new material, notably a commentary on Daniel.

1.   *Karaism and its Relationship to the Qumran Writings*

The golden age of Karaism was the 10th cent. CE. Karaite exegetes undertook intense research on matters of grammar and lexicography. They rejected the Talmudic tradition of rabbinism and so focused their research on the *study of «Scripture only»*, applying to Hebrew the progress made by Arab gram-marians and lexicographers in their study of the language of the Koran. In this period, Jacob ben Isaac al-Qirqisani published a sort of *summa*, *Kitâb al-Anwar wa-l-Maraqib*, and at the beginning of the 11th cent., Yusuf al-Bair published his treatise on theodicy, inspired by the Islamic mu‘tazilites, *Kitâb al-Muchtawi*.

The exegetes of Karaism include Yafet ben ’Eli (c. 920-c. 1010), who wrote commentaries on the whole Bible, except on Lamentations, Solomon ben Yeruhim, a contemporary of S^e‘adiah, whose commentaries on Psalms, Lamentations and Qoheleth have reached us, and Daniel al-Kumissi, whose complete commentary in Hebrew on the Minor Prophets and fragments of commentaries on the Pentateuch and the Psalms are known to us.

From the middle of the 19th cent. scholars had noticed some relationship between the *doctrines of the Zadokites* (the branch of the sons of Zadok from which come the members of the Qumran community) and the *teachings of the Karaites* (Geiger). The discovery in the Cairo Genizah of a copy of the Damascus Document confirmed the existence of this relationship. The rich and varied literature on Karaism available today sheds light on the literature of the Qumran sect and in turn Karaism is better known today, especially as regards its theological ideas, thanks to the discoveries at Qumran.

There are many important *connections between Qumran and Karaism*. The most important concerns their concept of Scripture.

The Karaites rejected the authority of oral tradition and proclaimed the principle of the *primacy of the written Law*. They developed exegetical methods based on philological analysis; they gave precise definitions of the terms found in the text and used different forms of reasoning, especially de-duction by analogy.

Other points of contact between the Qumran community and the Karaite community concern *apocalyptic hope in a Messiah* and certain *liturgical prac-tices*. The Zadokites, who were related to the Qumranites, followed a solar calendar with thirty-day months and celebrated the Feast of Pentecost on a Sunday, like the Karaites. As for *matrimonial law*, both Qumranites and Karaites forbade marriage with a paternal or maternal niece (a prohibition not found in the Bible) as well as a second marriage while the first wife was still alive. This strictness of the Zadokites and Karaites, opposed to the liberalism of rabbinic law, has been connected with the equally strict legislation of the early Christian Church. The legislation of the Christians is earlier than the more liberal regulation of rabbinism (Szyszman). There are also similarities between the burial rites of Qumran and the Karaites.

2. *Sephardic Jewish Exegesis*

The Jewish exegesis practised in Sephardi is marked by its *philological and literal stamp*, the result of contact with Arabic language and philology, although it continued to cultivate philosophical and symbolic exegesis. Rabbinic exegesis in Spain took its first steps towards the end of the 8th cent. The exilarch Natronai ben Zabinai, deposed by the Ga'onites of Baghdad in 771, sought refuge in Spain. The Talmudic school of Sephardi continued the tradition of the academies of Babylon and managed to exert enormous influence on the whole of Western Judaism. In Sephardi, the Jews contributed in a decisive way to the splendour of the culture of the caliphate of Cordoba. Use of Arabic enabled the Jews to improve themselves from knowledge of the philological and theological movements which flourished at the time in Islam. Study of the language and of Hebrew grammar reached its zenith in the 10th-12th cents., with masters such as Menahem ben Saruq († c. 960), Dunash ben Labraṭ (c. 920-980) and his disciple, Yehudah ben Ḥayyuy.

In the first half of the 11th cent., *Yonah ibn Yana*, known in Arabic as Abu al-Walid, first began to apply the advances in philology to exegetical study of the Bible. Ibn Yan followed an extremely critical method which did not resort to correcting the masoretic text where it did not follow the rules of grammar. This served to exclude him from the list of authorised exegetes. Basing literal interpretation on the philological method could lead to a rationalism which was unacceptable to mediaeval rabbis. In spite of this, the influence of this critical approach continued to affect later Jewish exegesis.

In the second half of the 11th cent., *Moses Ibn «Chiquitilla»* stated that the biblical prophecies refer to the period when the prophets lived and not to a future messianic age. Yehudah Ibn Bilʿam, his contemporary, also supported the use of the philological method in biblical exegesis with due respect for the text of masoretic tradition

The 12th and 13th cents. were the golden age of *philological exegesis in Sephardi. Abraham ibn 'Ezra'* (1089-1164), born in Tudela, was educated in Al-Andalus, travelled from Morocco to Egypt and returned to Toledo where he practised medicine and devoted himself to grammar and exegesis, astronomy and Neo-Platonist philosophy. In 1140, he suddenly left Toledo and led a vagrant's life in France and the Anglo-Norman kingdom until his death in poverty in 1164. In this period of his life he wrote an encyclopaedic work which influenced all the Jewish communities in Europe. For Ibn 'Ezra', the philological method and logical analysis are the only ways which allow the correct meaning to be drawn from the biblical texts. By this means and in opposition to traditional doctrine which attributed the authorship of the Pentateuch to Moses, Ibn 'Ezra' could state that some sections of the Torah, especially of Deuteronomy, were written at a later period and that the second part of the book of Isaiah (chaps. 40-66) is the work of another author, and thus he was ahead of modern exegetical theories about the existence of a Second Isaiah. Mediaeval exegesis anticipated many ideas of modern criticism (Sarnan). Ibn 'Ezra' achieved a synthesis between literal and allegorical exegesis even in his commentary on the Song of Songs, for which Jewish tradition required an allegorical interpretation.

In Sephardi, the *philosophical method* was also developed, so following a path already traced by the exegesis of S^{ec}adiah Ga'on, who had been influenced by Neo-Platonism. Exegetes of the school of Qayrawan, Hananel Bar Hušiel (c. 980-1056) and Nissim Bar Jacob (c. 990-1062), transmitted this knowledge to the commentators of Sephardi, Italy and the Franco-German world. *Rabbi Isaac of Fez*, known as Alfasi (c. 1013-1102), wrote a commentary on Talmudic jurisprudence using the Neo-Platonic method. *Solomon ibn Gabirol* (c. 1020-1057), better known as Avicebron, the author of *Fons Vitae*, developed the moral meaning of Scripture with the intention of proving it to be rational. This moralising trend of Jewish exegesis was developed by *Baḥya ibn Paqudah* in the 11th cent. and by *Yehudah ben Barzilay* of Barcelona at the beginning of the 12th cent.

R. Moses ben Maimon, known as *RaMBaM* or *Maimonides* (1135-1206), born in Cordoba and a contemporary of Ibn Rušd (Averroes), also from Cordoba, brought rabbinic exegesis to the zenith of its splendour, especially through his work *Mōrê n^{e}bōkîm* («Guide to the Perplexed») in which he emphasises the relationship between Revelation and Reason. According to Maimonides, the Bible contains the essentials of philosophical teachings so that philosophical interpretation is the best way to reinforce faith and to explain the true meaning of the Scriptures. This assumed developing symbolical interpretation together with literal exegesis, which earlier grammarians and exegetes had preferred to study. With Maimonides, Neo-Platonism, dominant till then, gave way to Aristotelianism.

Maimonides warns the reader of his *Guide to the Perplexed* that he intends to explain very obscure allegories about the prophetic books and to teach the distinction between the literal meaning and the esoteric meaning of the texts. Maimonides equated the first chapter of Genesis, *ma'āśê b^{e}rē'šît*, with physics and the first chapter of Ezekiel, *ma'āśê merkābâ*, with metaphysics.

The use of the methods of abstract reasoning and metaphysical interpretation could only lead to a dangerous slide to the borders of heresy. This applied especially since it was impossible to reconcile the Aristotelian doctrine on the eternity of matter with biblical teaching on creation (cf. p. 539). Maimonides felt obliged to accept the literal meaning of the Genesis accounts, explaining creation by the action of the *Logos* upon matter (*Physis*), but he also applied the metaphorical sense to those texts so as not to fall into an anthropomorphic interpretation of them. The 13th cent. witnesses bitter disputes between the Jewish communities on the orthodoxy of Maimonides' work.

3. *Jewish Exegesis in Mediaeval Europe*

Jewish exegesis in the other countries of Christian Europe was carried out in conditions very different to those in Islamic countries. The level of education of the population, including the Jews, was in general much lower. Up to the 9th cent., the dependence of the Jewish communities on the Babylonian academies was much greater. Deprived of contact with Arab culture and a philological education comparable to the exegetes of Sephardi, the only source of inspiration for the Ashkenazi exegetes comprised the Targum and Talmudic and Mishnaic texts for the interpretation of which they used the *homiletic meaning* to develop the literal meaning.

The most authoritative scholar of Ashkenazi Judaism was *Geršom of Metz* (c. 960-1028). In the first half of the 11th cent., Hananel Bar Hušiel of Qayrawan had very strong influence on European Judaism as a communicator of Gaonic literature in the West. In Italy, *Nathan of Rome* (c. 1035-1110) compiled the lexicographic work *Aruk*, an etymological dictionary of the Bible and the Talmud. In the 11th cent., *Menachem ben Helbo* brought Menachem ben Saruq's grammar (*Maberet*) to France and was the forerunner of the great French exegetical school.

The most outstanding representative of this school was *Rabbi Šelomoh ben Yiṣḥaq* or *Raši*, born in Troyes (1040-1106). Raši preferred the literal interpretation of texts, but, faithful to Ashkenazi and Gaonic traditions, he also developed the midrashic meaning, always concerned to vitalise the Jewish communities in the diaspora (Gelles). Raši formed a generation of followers who, unlike his predecessors, kept up a continual dialogic with Christian exegetes, especially with the «Victorines» of the Abbey of St. Victor in Paris, in this way taking an active part in the intellectual renaissance of the 12th cent. (cf. p. 546).

Samuel Ben Me'ir (*RašBaM*, 1085-1174), Raši's nephew, though not following his philological approach, notes the differences between the Hebrew Bible and the Mishnaic Bible, concluding that Talmudic texts could not be used to interpret the biblical text. *Yosef B^{e}kor Šor* of Orleans, a pupil of Rašbam, who used literal interpretation, developed especially the historical explanation of texts, and came close to interpretations like those of the Sephardi philosophy school, for example, in rational exegesis of the miracles in Gn 19 and Ex 9.

It is important to note that mediaeval exegesis could criticise exegesis by earlier rabbis. The *hālākâ* had a life independent of the exegesis which accompanied it and whose function was to establish the necessary link between the *hālākâ* and Scripture. The exegesis proposed by one rabbi might not please a later rabbi, who would suggest another in its stead. For example Raši rejected the tannaitic exegesis of Ex 23:2 (Mishnah, *Sanhedrin* 1,6).

Sephardi philological exegesis influenced the work of *David Qimchi* of Narbonne (*RaDaK*, 1160-1235) who translated into Hebrew the Arabic works of Spanish commentators and developed the study of Hebrew lexicography. Radak's commentaries include elements of polemic against Christian exegesis which were not present in Sephardi exegesis since it existed in the open society of the Muslim world and was not confined to the controversial atmosphere of Christian society. Keeping to the philological method, Radak rejects allegorical and mystical interpretations. He considers that the biblical prophecies should not have a messianic meaning conferred on them which they never had. In particular, he rejects the christological interpretation which some Christians give to Ps 110.

Together with literal and homiletic interpretation, predominant among exegetes in the 11th-12th cents, under the influence of Muslim mysticism and *kalam*, a sort of *allegorical interpretation* developed in these centuries, nourished by mystical tendencies and concerned with unveiling hidden meanings or secrets in Scripture. This mystical trend in exegesis was marked by the use of midrashic texts and by the homiletic character of its interpretations, stressing the moral value of the precepts and the perfection of life. The work of *Eliezer ben Samuel of Metz* (c. 1115-1198) follows this trend and Hasidic exegetes adopted his method in combination with their own allegorical method. *Yehudah Heḥasid* (c. 1150-1217) was the grand master of Ashkenazi mysticism and his disciple, *Eleazar Harokeab of Worms* (c. 1165-1230) was the greatest exegete of Ashkenazi pietism.

4. *The Influence of Jewish Exegesis on Christian Exegesis*

The influence of Jewish exegetes on the Christians, especially on Origen and Jerome, has always been in the direction of literal and philological interpretation. In the Middle Ages, Nicholas of Lyra (1270-1340) was influenced by Raši (Halperin). In the Renaissance, Sanctes Pagnini (1470-1536), François Watebled (†1547), better known as Vatable and the first Hebrew professor of Hebrew of the Collège Royale, Martin Bucer (1491-1551), Johannes Oekolmpad (1482-1531) and Sebastian Münster (1489-1552) made ample use of the rabbinic commentaries published shortly before in rabbinic bibles.

However, the Council of Trent (1545-1563) soon forced Catholics to restrict their attention virtually to study of the Vulgate only. On the other hand, Luther, in spite of preferring the Hebrew text, showed himself against rabbinic exegesis which he accused of being anti-Christian and of having perverted the meaning of the text by means of incorrect vocalisation of the Hebrew text. These factors ensured that, from the mid-16th century on, Christian exegetes ceased to keep in direct contact with Jewish sources and commentaries.

This alienation has continued until very recent times when several branches of exegesis have started a movement of «return to the rabbis»

(Barthélemy). For example, the authors of the «Tradition Oecuménique de la Bible» profess their proposal «to follow the masoretic text as closely as possible, explaining it by also using the work of the great Jewish exegetes of the Middle Ages: Raši, Ben 'Ezra', Qimchi, etc.» Similarly, the project of a textual commentary of the OT begun in 1969 by the Biblical Societies, basically under the direction of D. Barthélemy, very often uses grammars, dictionaries and commentaries by Jewish writers (cf. p. 385).

The contact of Christian scholars with Jewish sources, which had ceased suddenly in the mid-16th cent., has resumed in recent years. The same applies to mediaeval Arabic philology which in many cases was the basis for Jewish exegesis. Thus, the work *Hebraicae Institutiones* (1526) by Pagnini, a Christian, was based on Radaq's grammar *Miklol*, a Jew whose main source of inspiration was the *Kitāb al-Luma'* of Abu al-Walid Merwan ibn Ganah at the beginning of the 11th cent., who in turn had known the work of Yehudah Hayyug, *Kitāb al-Af'āl*. Similarly, Pagnini's *Thesaurus* is based on Radaq's dictionary *Sefer ha-Šorašim*, which in turn depends on Abu al-Walid's work *Kitāb al-Usul*, which was preceded by the *Kitāb Yami' al-Alfāz* of the 10th cent. Karaite David ben Abraham al-Fassi.

In the first period of the Renaissance, the trilinguist moved between Arabic, Hebrew and Latin, always in connection with Muslim, Jewish and Christian Spain, where these three languages had been in fruitful contact for some time. The line of advance then lay in philological analysis and literal commentary. However, the influence of Jewish exegesis on Christian exegesis cannot be disregarded as far as the spiritual meaning is concerned.

BIBLIOGRAPHY

BONSIRVEN, J., *Le judaïsme palestinien aux temps de Jésus-Christ: Sa théologie*, 2 vols., Paris 1934-35.

BREWER, J.D., *Techniques and Assumptions in Jewish Exegesis before 70 CE*, Tübingen 1992.

BRUCE, F.F., «The Earliest Old Testament Interpretation», *Oudtestamentische Studien* 17 (1927) 37-52.

DANBY, H., *The Mishnah*, Oxford 1933, reprinted in 1954.

DAUBE, D., «Rabbinic Methods of Interpretation and Hellenistic Rhetoric», *HUCA* 22 (1949) 239-264.

EPSTEIN, I. (ed.), *Hebrew-English Edition of the Babylonian Talmud*, London 1960-.

EPSTEIN, I. (ed.), *The Babylonian Talmud*, 35 vols., London 1935-52.

FINKELSTEIN, L., *Akiwa, Scholar, Saint and Martyr*, Philadelphia PA 1936.

FISCHEL, H., *Rabbinic Literature and Greco-Roman Philosophy*, Leiden 1973.

FREEDMAN, H. - SIMON, M. (eds.), *Midrash Rabah*, 10 vols., London-Bournemouth 1951.

GELLES, B.J., *Peshat and Derash in the Exegesis of Rashi*, Leiden 1981.

GINZBERG, L., *On Jewish Law and Lore*, New York 1977.

GUTTMANN, A., «Hillelites and Shammaites-A Clarification», *HUCA* 28 (1957) 115-126.

HALPERIN, H., *Rashi and the Christian Scholars*, Pittsburgh 1963.

HARTMAN, G.-H. -BUDICK, S. (eds.), *Midrash and Literature*, New York 1986.

HEINEMANN, I., *Darke ha-Aggadah*, Jerusalem 1954².

KADUSHIN, M., *The Rabbinic Mind*, New York 1972³.

KRAEMER, D., *The Mind of the Talmud*, Oxford 1990.

KUGEL, J., *Midrash and Literature: The Primacy of Documentary Discourse*, 1987.

LAUTERBACH, J.Z., *Rabbinic Essays*, Cincinnati KT 1951.

LAUTERBACH, J.Z., *Mkylt' drby Yšm'l: Mekilta de-Rabbi Ishmael*, 3 vols., Philadelphia PA 1933-1935, reprinted in 1976.

LEVINAS, E., *L'au-delà du verset. Lectures et discours talmudiques*, Paris 1982.

LIEBERMAN, S., *The Tosefta according to Codex Vienna*, 2 vols., New York 1955 and 1962.

MACCOBY, H., *Early Rabbinic Writings*, Cambridge 1988.

MOORE, G.F., *Judaism in the First Centuries of the Christian Era I*, Cambridge 1927.

NEUSNER, J. (ed.), *The Talmud of Babylonia: an American Translation*, Atlanta GA 1984-.

NEUSNER, J. (ed.), *The Talmud of the Land of Israel*, Chicago IL 1982-.

NEUSNER, J., *What is Midrash?*, Philadelphia PA 1987.

NEUSNER, J., *Introduction to Rabbinic Literature*, New York 1994.

NEUSNER, J., *Initiation to Midrash. A Teaching Book*, New York 1989.

PATTE, D., *Early Jewish Hermeneutic in Palestine*, Missoula MT 1975.

PORTON, D., «Defining Midrash», *The Study of Ancient Judaism* vol. I: *Mishnah, Midrash, Siddur*, ed. J. Neusner, New York 1981, 55-92.

SAFRAI, SH., «The Literature of the Sages. First Part: Oral Tora, Halakha, Mishna, Tosefta, Talmud, External Tractates», *CRINT* II-3, Assen - Philadelphia PA 1987.

SARNAN, M., «The Modern Study of the Bible in the Framework of Jewish Studies», *Proceedings of the Eight Wolrd Congress of Jewish Studies: Bible and Hebrew Language*, Jerusalem 1983, 19-27.

SCHÄFER, P., «R. Aqiva und Bar Kokhba», *Studien zur Geschichte und Theologie des rabbinischen Judentums*, Leiden 1978, 45-121.

STERN, D., *Parables in Midrash. Narrative and Exegesis in Rabbinic Literature*, Cambridge MA 1991.

STRACK, H.L. -STEMBERGER, P., *Einleitung in Talmud und Midrasch*, 7th ed., Munich 1982.

SZYSZMAN, S., *Le Karaïsme. Ses doctrines et son histoire*, Lausanne 1980.

URBACH, E.E., *The Sages. Their Concepts and Beliefs*, Jerusalem 1975.

WEINGREEN, J., «The Rabbinic Approach to the Study of the Old Testament», *Bulletin of the John Rylands Library* 33-34 (1951-52) 166-190.

WRIGHT, A., *The Literary Genre Midrash*, New York 1967.

9

Christian Hermeneutics

I. THE INTERPRETATION OF THE OLD TESTAMENT IN THE NEW

1. Introduction

According to the Jewish and Christian view, Scripture is neither self-sufficient nor can it be interpreted without the assistance of an accompanying tradition of interpretation. The moment Christianity was born, the written bible was transmitted together with a very large body of very differing oral and exegetical traditions. The interpretation of the OT by the NT belongs within this great tradition of the Judaism of the period. This means that to understand the exegesis of the early Christians it is first necessary to know the Jewish exegesis of that period.

Modern criticism as represented by the «history of literary forms» and the «history of religions school» (*Religionsgeschichte*) tended to see Christianity as a sort of syncretism, a precipitate of Jewish elements and various forms of paganism. It therefore tended to study the NT within the framework of the literature and institutions of the Hellenistic-Roman world rather than within Old Testament and Jewish tradition. However, the classical world does not provide much help in understanding how Christians read the Jewish scriptures. It is necessary to allow greater weight and value to the OT and Jewish substratum of the NT (J. Jeremias, B. Gerhardsson, M. Hengel, etc., especially Jewish scholars such as J. Klausner and H.J. Schoeps; cf. p. 31).

When the books of the NT were being written, the written and oral Torah had not reached its definitive form. The great liberties the NT takes with the OT fits in with this stage of Jewish history better than the later rabbinic period. The first Christians used the principles and methods of Jewish exegesis, with a single but a decisive difference: the «Christological» reading of the OT.

To understand the characteristics of Christian interpretation of the OT, attention must be paid to the following: *the formulae* used in the NT to introduce quotations from the OT, *the choice based on theme* of OT passages in the

NT (*Testimonia*), the basic *presuppositions* and *principles* of NT exegesis, and the *methods* of interpretation it follows.

A.   INTRODUCTORY FORMULAE TO OT QUOTATIONS

In disputes with his opponents, it seems that Jesus introduced OT quotations with the formula «*have you not read...?*». The gospels of Matthew and John, and only those two, use the formula «*so as to fulfil*» (*hína plērōthē̄*). The use of this formula is typical of Jewish Christians. Those coming from the Hellenistic world prefer to use the formula «*says the Lord*» (*phēsì Kýrios*) which in the OT is peculiar to prophetic announcements (Ap 1:8; 2:8.12.18; 3:1.7; Lk 11:49; Acts 21:11). An equivalent formula, *légei Kýrios*, occurs only in a quotation placed on Stephen's lips in Paul's Letter to the Romans (12:19).

Other expressions or formulae used in the NT correspond to Jewish exegetical use, especially in apocalyptic contexts.

The expression «*faithful is the word...*» *pistós ho lógos* (1 Tim 1:15; 2 Tim 2:11; cf. 1 Cor 1:9; 2 Thess 3:3; Ap 22:6) has its roots in the typical expression of apocalyptic Judaism: «Certain is the word which must happen (*nakon haddābār labô*) and true (*emet*) is the oracle» (1Q27 1,8).

The formula «*this/that is*», *hoûtos estin* (Rom 9:7-9; Acts 2:16ff.; cf. Mt 3:3; 11:10; Jn 6:31.50; Acts 4:11; Rom 10:6-8; Heb 7:5; 1Pt 1:24) is also found in an eschatological context and has its antecedents in *pēšer* interpretation (cf. 1QpHab 12:6ff.; CD 7:14f.; 4QFlor 1:11-14).

The use of the adversative «*however*» (*allá, de*) used to correct or shape the meaning of a quotation (Mt 5:12f.; Jn 13:18) corresponds to an exegetical technique of rabbinic Judaism (*Midraš to Psalms* 119:26).

B.   THE SELECTION OF OT PASSAGES BASED ON A THEME

The NT reads the OT selectively depending on both the themes and passages used.

The *Testimonia* juxtapose OT passages on a common topic. For example 1 Pt 2:6; Eph 2:20; Mt 21:42 and Acts 4:11 combine Is 28:16; Ps 118:22 and Is 8:14 to develop the theme of «Christ the Stone»:

«For it stands (written) in Scripture: *See, I am placing in Zion a precious (and) chosen foundation-stone; and he who believes will not remain ashamed* (Is 28:16). So that the honour is for you, the believers; instead, for those who do not believe, *the stone which the builders rejected has become the corner-stone* (Ps 118:22), *and a stone to trip over and a rock to stumble against* (Is 8:14); they stumble on it...»

Several copies of *Testimonia* have been found in Qumran; 4QTest is a compilation of Dt 5:28f.; 18:18f.; Nm 24:15ff; Dt 33:8-11:

«*I will raise a prophet for them from among their brothers, like you, and place my words in his mouth. And he will say to them all that I command. If anyone does not listen to my words which the prophets will speak in my name, I myself will hold him to account* (Dt 18:18-19). And he uttered his message and said: *Oracle of Balaam, son of Beor, and oracle of the man whose eye is open. The one who speaks hears the words of God and perceives the vision of the Almighty, prostrate and with open ears. I see him, but not now; I perceive him, but not close. A star will rise from Jacob and a sceptre will go up from Israel and it will shatter the temples of Moab and destroy all the sons of Sheth (Nm 24:15-17)...»*

Similarly, 4QFlor contains 2 Sm 7:10-14; Ps 1:1 and 2:1f.

It has been assumed that for disputes against the Jews the primitive Church had the use of a «Book of Testimonies» from which the biblical quotations contained in the NT were taken (J. R. Harris). According to Dodd, the quotations in the NT were instead made using large sections of OT texts and not just from isolated verses. These large sections, which make up the infrastructure of all Christian theology, can be grouped around three basic themes of Christian *kergyma*: apocalyptic and eschatology (Jl 2-3; Zc 9-14; Dn 7 and 12), the New Israel (Hos; Isa 6:1-9:7; 11:1-10; 40:1-11; Jr 31:3134; Hb 2:3f.) and the Servant of God or Suffering Just Man (Isa 42:1-44:5; 49:1-13; 50:4-11; 52:13-53:12; Pss 22; 3; 69; 118). Some specific texts were given a strong messianic meaning: Pss 2; 8; 110; Dt 18:15.18f.; 2Sm 7:14.

C.   PRINCIPLES OF NT INTERPRETATION OF THE OT

These principles can be reduced to four. They determine the specifically «Christian» nature of NT exegesis. although they also have antecedents in Jewish exegesis.

– *Eschatological Outlook.* Like apocalyptic Judaism, Jesus and the NT divide history into two periods: for a Jew the final period has not yet arrived; the Christian believes that it has already begun with the message of the saving action of Jesus the Christ. God's redemption takes place in history; the present generation finds itself at the gates of the final fulfilment of this salvation history.

– *Typological Appraisal of the* OT. NT typology is developed around two basic themes: creation (the «second Adam») and the covenant (the «new Exodus»). To Jesus in particular are applied the messianic figure of the king and of the persecuted just man, both present in the Psalter.

– *Principle of Corporate Personality.* In the OT an individual can represent all his or her relatives. This concept allows Paul to speak of the existence of all men «in Adam» or of the Israelites «in Adam». The result of Christological application of this principle is reference to the «body» or the «temple of Christ», i.e., all those believing in Christ.

– *Christocentrism.* The sayings (*logia*) of Jesus are sometimes similar to those of the rabbis in both content and form. However, Jesus has a very different basic approach to the OT from the rabbis. Jesus does not hesitate to criticise Scripture and interpret it in terms of his own doctrine and person. Quite often Jesus points out the fulfilment of Scripture in his own mission. The messianic interpretation of Scripture can also be found in the writings of the Qumran community, where passages from the prophets are interpreted with reference to the Teacher of Righteousness. However, what is new in Jesus' declaration is that the Kingdom of God is present and opens with his own mission. This Christocentric view was also to determine the approach of all later Christian exegesis.

D.   THE STUDY OF NT EXEGESIS OF THE OT: METHODOLOGY

NT exegesis of the OT uses all the methods of interpretation known in Judaism of the period: literal, *pesher*, midrashic and allegorical (cf. p. 475). It also uses genres such as the *Testimonia* (cf. p. 455) and the «homiletic preface». This genre, known among the rabbis as *yᵉlammᵉḏēnû rabbēnû* («what our master teaches us»), starts with an explanation of the text of the Pentateuch as read according to the lectionary, adds a second text used as an introduction to the discussion, sets out the appropriate commentary by means of new texts connected with the foregoing because of expressions they have in common, and lastly brings in a closing text, usually a repetition of the first, adding a final closing application. This genre occurs in Philo (*De Sacrificiis Abelis et Caini* 76-87) and in rabbinic literature (*Pesiqta Rabbati* 34,1). Jesus' discussions with Jewish rabbis often take on midrashic form. Mt 12:1-8 recounts a discussion about the law of the Sabbath; first it provides the topic of discussion and the question provoked by the biblical text quoted (Ex 20:10; 34:21); then it sets out a series of questions which can be opposed to the first question (making use of other biblical texts: 1 Sm 21:7; Nm 28:9), can be connected with the first question or with the biblical text cited in the beginning (through some shared , «sacrifice», «to do», «to eat»); it concludes, lastly, with an eschatological application through an *a fortiori* argument and the quotation of a fresh biblical text (Hos 6:6, «sacrifice»). This pattern follows the model of the rabbinic preface, with some changes, especially in an eschatological kind.

Midrashic interpretation of the NT differs from rabbinic interpretation in that the starting point is always a saying or deed from the life of Jesus. Rabbinic midrash, instead, begins with the biblical text. This always retains its supremacy over any historical event later than the biblical period, whatever its historical transcendence, because it will never be the eschatological salvation event which Israel is still hoping for. Rabbinic midrash attempts to uncover hidden meanings in the biblical text and not the meaning of a saving or eschatological event which in the history of Israel has not yet taken place.

Research on NT exegesis of the OT has to go though a whole series of stages, some of which still require enormous and difficult work.

The first stage consists of *determining which text or form of the text the author of a NT book had in front of him*, since the OT quotation does not always match the text of the LXX version. Resort to the argument that they tended to quote from memory cannot be used too much since this practice does not seem to have been as common as was once thought. Nor should too much be made of the assumption that Paul and the other NT authors remodelled the text of the OT in order to adapt it to the intended interpretation. It should not be forgotten that a biblical quotation lost all its value as «proof from Scripture» if the text quoted was made unrecognisable or its interpretation was arbitrary.

It is also necessary to analyse *the context from which the quotation is taken*. This does not mean pinpointing exact historical circumstances in which a biblical event took place or a prophet uttered his oracles or a narrator composed his stories. This concern, typical of modern criticism, did not particularly attract the attention of interpreters in ancient times; they knew, however, how to establish connections between a text and its context, although often they did it in a strange and currently incomprehensible way.

It is necessary to know the *meaning given by contemporary Jewish exegesis to the OT passages* cited in the NT. Study of the targumim as well as Mishnaic and Talmudic literature is very illuminating here (Vermes, Grelot, Le Déaut, McNamara, Forestell, Chilton). The discovery in Qumran of a targum on no less a book than Job has supported those who hold that the targumim preserve very old traditions. Against those defending the application of rabbinic texts to NT study (B. Gerhardsson) some deny this possibility and use other sources (M. Smith). The defenders of what is called the «history of religions school» object that rabbinic sources are much later than the NT and therefore cannot be used for the study of NT exegesis. The response is that the sources used by this very comparative school, particularly Mandaic and Gnostic literature, are just as late.

The warning against possible misuse of rabbinic sources has certainly to be taken into account. Yet it is still quite common for a particular interpretation by the NT of an OT passage to have parallels in a Jewish source of the period, such as a work of Philo and also to appear in a rabbinic commentary of a later period going back to sources different from the earlier sources and so representing an independent line of tradition. In reference to Gn 28:11.16 «He came to a certain *place*... Truly Yahweh is in this *place*», Philo comments that the «place» (*tópos*) mentioned can be understood as a place occupied by a body, the divine Logos and a name in reference to God himself (all the things are in Him instead of Him being in a place). It should be remembered that Philo is applying categories of Greek thought to the biblical text. However, the *Midrash on the Psalms* uses similar exegesis which shows that both Philo and the midrash transmit an interpretation known at least in the 1st cent. CE if not earlier.

It is also necessary *to reconstruct the history of the formation of rabbinic traditions, of the Mishnah and of the Talmud* as has been done with biblical sources and traditions for both the OT and the NT (Neusner). Within orthodox Judaism there can be great reluctance in accepting the application of historical-critical methods to rabbinic sources. Even among Christians there was the same reluctance with regard to the NT. To reconstruct a history of rabbinic traditions certainly has its risks, due both to the nature of these traditions and to the long period of formation and transmission they underwent, much longer than for the traditions collected in the NT.

The goal of students of rabbinic sources is to interpret correctly the Torah and *hālāḵâ*. They are less concerned with knowing the process of formation and transmission of the rabbinic texts. Those interested in the study of the origins of Christianity, on the other hand, wish to make use of rabbinic sources. They therefore need to know the period of their composition and to determine the facts that are of demonstrable antiquity and thus throw light on NT exegesis. In general, these facts are found more in the *haggādâ* than in the *hālākâ*.

2. Jesus and the Old Testament

In Jesus' interpretation of the OT there is something paradoxical because, on the one hand he does make use of current exegetical methods, yet on the other he states that the meaning of Scripture remains hidden, at least for many (Mt 13:9).

In the oldest gospel tradition, the idea was very much entrenched that Jesus considered the biblical prophecies to have been fulfilled in his person and his eschatological mission. The early Church did no more than develop and «theologise» this basic nucleus of the new Christian faith.

A. THE TEXT OF QUOTATIONS PLACED IN THE MOUTH OF JESUS

Most of the OT quotations attributed to Jesus in the gospels match the *text of the LXX*. In some cases the LXX text cited in the NT *is different from both the masoretic and the Aramaic text of known targums*. For example, Mk 7:7ff. and Mt 15:8f. quote Isa 29:13 in agreement with the LXX reading *mátēn*, «in vain (they worship me...)», which is very different from the masoretic and targumic reading: «the fear which holds me...». Similarly, Mt 21:16 cites Ps 8:3 in agreement with the LXX text, which here uses the term *aînon*, «praise» («from the mouth of little ones and children at the breast you prepared praise») whereas the MT speaks of ʿōz, «bulwark» («...you prepared a bulwark»).

At other times the text of the quotation placed in the mouth of Jesus *is different from all known texts*. The quotation of Is 61:1f. in Lk 4:18f. omits the hemistich «to bind up the broken-hearted» and adds instead «to set free the oppressed», an expression taken from Is 58:6.

In some cases the quotation attributed to Jesus *agrees with the masoretic Hebrew text* and differs from the Greek text of the LXX. For example, the quotation in Mt 11:10 «See, I sent my messenger before you, to prepare your path before you» (also Lk 7:27) combines Ml 3:1 and Is 40:3 and reproduces exactly the MT reading with the piʿel form *ûpinnâ*, translated *hos kataskeuásei* («who will prepare»), against the LXX reading *kaì epiblépsetai* («who will observe»), which translates the qal form. Probably the reading in the gospels reproduces the text of a collection of *Testimonia* in Hebrew (and/or Aramaic).

The interest provided by analysis of biblical quotations placed in the mouth of Jesus touches on a whole *range of issues*: the extent of bilingualism (or trilingualism) in the population of Palestine in the 1st cent. CE and among the disciples of Jesus, the state of textual fluidity in which the biblical text was transmitted in this period, the use of pesher interpretation which some-times implied the choice of a textual variant from among others and as a re-sult a judgment on matters of text criticism, and lastly, the possibility that there was a collection in Greek of the sayings of Jesus (in which the corre-sponding quotations from the OT were included) which was completed in the first moment of the formation of traditions transmitted by the evangelists.

The fact that the quotations placed in the mouth of Jesus reproduce a text closer to the LXX than to the masoretic Hebrew text may be due to the evan-gelists transmitting a collection of sayings of Jesus which was translated very early on from Aramaic (or Hebrew) into Greek and for the biblical quota-tions the LXX was used. However, the possibility cannot be excluded that Jesus himself sometimes chose one or other of the variant forms of the text then transmitted by manuscripts in use. The quotation mentioned above of Lk 4:18f, which has no parallel in any known text, could be the creation of Jesus himself.

B. THE EXEGETICAL METHODS USED IN QUOTATIONS BY JESUS

The quotations placed in the mouth of Jesus on some occasions presume lit-eral exegesis and on others midrashic interpretation. When interpretation concerned fundamental matters of a religious or moral nature, Jewish inter-pretation usually kept to *the letter of the text*. In disputes with the pharisees, for example, Jesus refers to the literal meaning of Ex 20:12: «Honour your father and your mother» and of 21:17: «Whoever curses his father or his mother will die» (Mk 7:10; Mt 15:4).

On the other hand, other quotations presuppose *midrashic exegesis*. The expression «how much more» (*pollō mâllon*), used several times, corre-sponds to Hillel's's first rule (*qal wāḥōmer*): «If you know how to give good presents... how much more (does) your Father...!» (Mt 7:11; Lk 11:13); «If the master of the house been called "Beelzebub", how much more his house-hold!» (Mt 10:25); «But if that is how God clothes the grass.. how much more will he clothe you!» (Lk 12:28).

Sometimes the pesher type of interpretation is used. This applies to Lk 4:16-21, already mentioned, where Jesus declares: «Today this scripture is fulfilled» (Is 61:1f.). The same type of interpretation is in force in the quo-tation in Mk 12:10f. (Mt 21:42; Lk 20:17) of Ps 118:22f.: «The stone which the builders rejected will become the cornerstone...». This quotation repro-duces exactly the Greek text of the psalm, which indicates the express inten-tion that the words of the psalm find their realisation in the person of Jesus.

Particularly interesting are two examples where there has been no hesita-tion in *altering the quoted text* so that Jesus could apply the prophecy to himself.

The first is in Mk 14:27 (Mt 26:31): «because it is written: 'I shall strike the shepherd and the sheep will scatter'» (Zach 13:7). This quotation slight-ly alters the LXX text: «Strike the shepherds and scatter the sheep».

The second example is Mt 11:10 (Lk 7:27): «He is the man of whom it is written: 'See, I sent my messenger before you, who will prepare *your* way before *you*» (a combination of Ml 3:1 and Is 40:3). The introductory formula is typical of pesher: «This/He is the one of whom it is written». Some slight changes in the text allow the prophecy to be applied to Jesus: Ml 3:1 MT, «..to prepare *the* way before *Me*»; Ml 3:1 LXX, «.. to *oversee* the path before *Me*»; Mt 11:10, «... may he prepare *your* path before *you*». However, the textual change could have originated in an already existing variant, transmitted in a collection of *Testimonia*.

The textual divergences in quotations of the OT by Jesus or the NT are to be considered as reflecting the textual fluidity in which the biblical text was transmitted in the period corresponding to the years of Christ's life and the formation of the gospel tradition.

Comparison of the sayings of Jesus and the Isaiah targum have led to the conclusion that Jesus knew the traditions transmitted by the targum which in this way became an important tool for studying the gospel texts (Chilton).

3.   *Paul and the OT*

The first Christians copied the way of interpreting the OT begun by Jesus. Jewish-Christian writers of the first period quote the OT with great freedom. They do not hesitate to shorten or alter the biblical text which they regard as something living transmitted within the tradition of Jewish interpretation. They also show the need for adapting the text of the OT to the new audience which now comprised Greek speakers and no longer only Aramaic-speaking Jews. They select and adapt the OT texts in terms especially of Christological interpretation which from then on governed Christian reading of the OT.

A.   ESCHATOLOGICAL AND CHRISTOLOGICAL INTERPRETATION

Paul develops an eschatological and Christological interpretation of the OT. In Paul's Christian experience, understanding of the Christ figure comes before Christological interpretation of Scripture. However, in his exegetical practice, Paul uses Scripture to explain the mystery revealed in Christ.

It is interesting to note that the exegesis of Jesus and of the disciples settled in Jerusalem seems to have a much closer relationship to the pesher type of interpretation practised by the Essenes of Qumran. Paul's exegesis, in contrast, provides more points of agreement with the type of exegesis practised later by pharisaic rabbinism. In the same way a certain opposition can be established between the eschatological emphasis which Jesus gives his preaching, as in the Essene movement, and the emphasis given by Paul to the theme of the Law in disputes with pharisee rabbinism.

However, these oppositions can detract from the character and doctrine of either side. It is not possible to establish an extreme opposition between the Essenes, tinged with apocalypticism, and the pharisees, marked by legalism. Neither are the characters of Jesus and Paul so opposed as some movements in modern criticism of the NT have given to suppose. Between Jesus and Paul there is continuity, though there is no doubt that the event of the crucifixion and later faith in the Resurrection determine a before, where the historical Jesus is, and an after, where Paul's preaching develops.

B.   THE TECHNIQUE OF PAULINE QUOTATIONS

More than half the quotations of the OT in the letters of Paul (not counting the pastoral letters) occur in the letter to the Romans. The rest are concentrated especially in the letters to the Corinthians and the Galatians. This is surely because these letters were directed to communities of Jewish origin who were able to understand the frequent biblical references of Paul's letters and in addition kept up lively disputes with their old co-religionists. On the other hand, the letters directed to communities of pagan origin, such as the Thessalonians, Colossians and Philippians, had no biblical quotations.

In most of his quotations, Paul cites the text of Scripture, allowing comparison of his text with the LXX and examination of the reasons for his changes. In a total of 93 quotations, Paul changes the text 52 times and on 37 occasions reproduces the text unchanged. In 4 cases no precise judgment can be formed.

In 30 of the 52 cases with changes in the text quoted, the alteration affects several aspects at the same time, sometimes making it difficult to recognise the OT text used in the Pauline quotation. 12 of these quotations are particularly important, for example, Ex 9:16 in Rom 9:17: «For Scripture says to Pharaoh: *Precisely for this did I raise you, to show in you my power and so that my name is announced in the whole earth*». The other quotations are as follows: Ex 34:34a (2 Cor 3:16); Dt 21:23c (Gal 3:13); 27:26 (Gal 3:10); 29:3 (Rom 11:8); 30:12-14 (Rom 10:6-8); 1 Kgs 19:10 (Rom 11:3); Ps 13;1-3 (Rom 3:10-13); Hos 2:25 (Rom 9:25); Is 28:11-12 (1 Cor 14:21); 52:5 (Rom 2:24); 59:7-8 (Rom 3:15-17). Among the changes inserted, clearly those concerning content predominate. Only in 15 quotations are the changes stylistic. On 13 occasions different OT passages are combined into a single quotation (Koch).

It is too easy to fall back on the explanation that Paul quoted from memory. It is precisely the quotations taken straight from a written text which are the ones with the greatest changes. This shows that the alterations are the result of intense exegetical activity. It can be assumed that the same applies to the other quotations.

In the period before the discoveries at Qumran it was thought that the textual variants provided by the Pauline quotations were due to adaptations made by Paul himself or by the Christian tradition he represented. However, Paul's quotations are somewhat more complex and a whole series of factors applies: Paul's interest in the Gentile world, the apostle's rabbinic formation, his knowledge of textual variants transmitted in manuscripts and the inclusion in his writings of texts marked by the genre of interpretation of the pesharim.

C.   PARALLELS TO THE PAULINE QUOTATIONS IN JEWISH WRITINGS
      OF THE PERIOD

The quotations from classical authors in Greek literature are free quotes. The specific quotations from the OT in Jewish-Hellenistic literature, however, reproduce the biblical text exactly (Aristobulus, 4 Maccabees and Philo). Rabbinic literature allows no freedom at all in quotations nor does it make combinations or blends of texts. Paul, though, quotes the OT very loosely.

Paul's liberties with the biblical text, however, are not comparable to what happens in writings such as the *Genesis Apocryphon*, *Jubilees*, *Biblical Antiquities* or the *Temple Scroll*. Unlike Paul, in these writings the author never tries to support or develop a statement of his own using a biblical quotation. Nor does Paul develop his interpretation of a text chosen previously, as does Philo or as happens in the pesharim. Rather than quoting or commenting on texts, Paul devises a new theological formulation from the ancient biblical traditions.

It is more appropriate to compare the Pauline quotations with those found in the *Damascus Document* (CD), the *Community Rule* (1QS) and in the *War Scrolls* (1QM), and at a different level, those in 4QTest, 4QFlor and the Pesharim. The closest analogy is provided by the *Damascus Document*, but Paul goes much further in combining texts and his exegesis therefore is less scholarly.

The discovery of the Qumran texts has enabled us to be aware that important ideas and conceptions which used to be attributed to Paul's genius and originality, have antecedents in Judaism of the Hellenistic period (300 BCE-200 CE). These are: insistence on all men having sinned (Rom 3:23; 1QH 1:22); man cannot gain God's forgiveness (Gal 2:16; 1QH 4:30); the Torah is a means to gain justification before God; only God can justify man; God predestined for salvation only those chosen by him; the importance of the Spirit; etc.

From available data it is not possible to state that Paul experienced the influence of the Essenes, although his words show obvious contacts with the Dead Sea Scrolls (Fitzmyer). It is more probable that Paul's followers, members of the Pauline school, such as those who composed the letter to the Ephesians, were directly influenced by the Essenes (Kuhn) or perhaps by Essene groups converted to Christianity.

D.   PAULINE EXEGESIS AND RABBINIC EXEGESIS

Pauline exegesis reflects well Paul's own rabbinic education. In his letters there are both literal and midrashic interpretations. Often the interpretation is governed by rabbinic rules of exegesis. Hillel's first rule, *qal-wāḥāmer*, is used in Rom 5:15-21: «For if for the wrongdoing of one all the rest died, all *the more (pollő mâllon)* God's grace...». The second rule, *gᵉzerâ šawâ* (analogy) is frequently used in cases where, to develop a particular argument, passages are brought in from many different contexts. The letter to the Romans has many developments of this kind. For example, Rom 3:10-18 links Pss 14:1-3; 5:9; 140:3; 10:7; Is 59:7f and Ps 36:1.

Another point of contact of Pauline exegesis with the exegesis of the rabbis concerns theme. 1 Cor 10:1-4 connects the crossing of the Red Sea with baptism and the meaning of the rock which followed the Israelites in the desert. The Pauline passage has to be read in the light of the rabbinic passages of the Babylonian Gemara (*Yebamot* 46a and *Keritot* 9a), which justify the baptism of proselytes by assuming that the Exodus supposes a baptism.

Most of Paul's quotations keep to the original meaning of the passage quoted. If he extends the meaning of the passage, he does so in accordance with principles already known through Jewish hermeneutics («corporate personality» and typology or «historical interrelationship») or in accordance with the demands of Christian hermeneutics («eschatological and messianic fulfilment» in Jesus Christ). In three cases, however, Paul's quotations do not take into account the original meaning of the text cited. The first two are Rom 10:6-8 and Gal 3:16 (the seed-descendance which is Christ). The third, Eph 4:8 («he gave gifts to men», *édōken dómata toîs anthrôpois*) is a quotation of Ps 68:19 which runs «you received presents in men». Paul changes the person of the verb («he» → «you») and also the actual verb («gave» → «received», MT *lqht*, LXX *élabes*) to agree with the idea developed in the passage which concerns the gifts granted by Christ (v. 11). However, this is not a definite case of an ad hoc creation of a variant. Perhaps Paul only followed a variant attested in the targum and the Syriac Peshitta version where the verb used is *ḥlq* («to give») instead of MT *lqḥ* («to receive»).

Paul makes more use of midrashic methods than of pesher or allegorical exegesis. This explains why Paul could have been classed among the Hillelites (J. Jeremias). However, on three occasions Paul applies the pesher method of interpretation in respect «of the revelation of a mystery kept secret for time eternal, but shown now» (Rom 16:25-27; similarly, Col 1:26ff.; Eph 3:1-11). Interpretations of an allegorical kind occur in 1 Cor 9:9f, where the allegorising is very restrained, and Gal 4:21-31, where instead the allegory on Sarah and Hagar is extensive

Perhaps it can be said that Pauline exegesis is rabbinic in form and Christocentric in content. In the Hebrew spoken by Paul the word *rō'š* means «beginning» and «head», which enables him to say that Christ is the beginning of creation and the head of his body, which is the Church (Col 1:15ff.).

E. PAULINE EXEGESIS AND PHILO

There are also points of contact between the exegesis of Paul and of Philo. Both depend on the exegetical tradition of the Hellenistic synagogue. Both operate in a pagan environment and make use of the methods of Geek rhetoric. On the other hand, Paul and Philo differ from rabbinic exegetical tradition in their general approach to exegesis. In Gal 3:16 Paul applies to Christ the promise given to Abraham and his «seed», who is Christ, thus deviating completely from the original meaning of the texts which mention «seed», *zera'*, *spérma* (Gn 12:7; 13:15; 15:18; etc.).

Comparison of the Pauline interpretation with contemporary Jewish exegesis highlights the bond linking Paul with the Judaism of the Greek diaspora, especially with the synagogues of Asia Minor and Syria. Several factors suggest connecting Paul with Hellenistic Judaism to counterbalance his closeness to rabbinic Judaism as noted under *d)*. These indications are: the use of allegory; the lack in Paul of literary forms typical of midrash; the presence, instead, of models from Hellenistic homilies; the restricted use of the seven rules; the lack of direct contact with Qumran and lastly, the cautious use of typological interpretation.

Paul establishes the model for Christian interpretation of the OT. This will continue to be Scripture, though no longer Letter, but Spirit, not Law but Grace. Christ is the end of the Law in the newness of the Spirit and not in the termination of the letter (Rom 7:6; 10:4).

4.   *The Old Testament in the Gospels*

There are more quotations of the OT in Mt and Jn than in Mk and Lk. The first two show more insistence on eschatological fulfilment. This confirms the opinion that the gospels of Mt and Jn are directed to Jewish-Christians or Jews or possibly to both at once. On the other hand, Mt's quotations generally show a Hebrew background, whereas in Mk and Lk (and in the narrative material both have in common with Mt) they are closer to the LXX. The quotation in Mt 2:23 «so that what the prophets said will be fulfilled: "He will be called a Nazarene"» does not match any known passage from the prophetical books and shows to what extent there are textual variants in Mt's quotations. Playing on the word *nāzîr*, the quotation sets up a typological relationship between Samson and Jesus and at the same time connects Jesus with his place of birth, Nazareth, from which Christians acquired the name by which they were known («Nazarenes/Nazarethans»).

a. The gospel of *Mark* is very sparing in explicit quotations from the OT. Only in 1:2f. are Ml 3:1 and Is 40:3 cited together, already accepted in Judaism as messianic. The expression «to prepare the way», common to both passages, gives rise to the combined quotation.

b. The gospel of *Matthew* uses the OT extensively, especially in the gospel of the infancy on the theme of the New Exodus and the New Moses. The gospel of Matthew is in many ways close to the way the rabbis viewed the OT. It includes the saying according to which not one *yôd* of the law would pass until everything was fulfilled (5:18). In the life and doctrine of Christ everything happens and everything is said «to fulfil» the saying by the prophets (1:23; 2:6.15.23; 27:9). Striking parallels have been noticed between the biblical quotations of Mt and the exegesis of the *Habakkuk Pesher* found in Qumran (Stendahl). However, Mt did not empty the prophetic text alluded to of its own meaning, whereas the *Habakkuk Pesher* allows the biblical text no other meaning than what concerns the present and eschatological situation (Bruce).

Mt's 11 biblical quotations have certainly to be considered as pesher-type interpretations. The quotation in Mt 1:23 of Is 7:14: «the virgin will conceive and bear a son and he shall be called Emmanuel» uses an impersonal subject and understands the name Emmanuel as a title. These are certainly not ad hoc creations for such changes have textual support in 1QIs^a (*wqr'*) (De Waard). The influence of the LXX is noticeable in the use of the term *parthénos* as a translation of Hebrew *'almâ* («girl»). The other quotations of this type occur in 2:15; 2:18; 2:23; 3:3; 4:15f.; 8:17; 12:18-21; 13:35; 21:5 and 27:9f. The readings given in these quotations in 1:23; 2:15; 2:18; 8:17 and 13:35 seems to correspond to variants in one of the branches of textual transmission. The readings in 3:3; 21:5 and 27:9f., however, seem to be related more to contemporary Jewish interpretations. Finally, the quotations in 4:15f.; 12:18-21 and 21:5 reflect interpretations of Christian origin. Study of these quotations brings into play as is easily seen, the problem of plurality in text transmission in the period before the unification of the consonantal Hebrew text, as well as the question of the extent of targumic interpretation and the influence of the LXX version on the text

The gospel of Matthew, like the Qumran pesharim, interprets biblical passages as prophecies of the present and future of the respective communities, Essene and Christian. Typical of the midrash practised in the Matthew school is its need to develop a whole biography of Jesus as a framework into which the quotations are inserted and the OT is interpreted in the light of the Christian event. The only example comparable with that kind of midrashic collection is the collection of narratives on Hillel's life compiled using quotations from Dt 15. In the development of Jewish midrash, the type of midrashic compilation, typical of the school of Matthew, seems to be a stage in the process from the large compilations of *Genesis Rabbah* and *Leviticus Rabbah* (Neusner). Early Christian literature is more like the literature of nascent Judaism than rabbinic Judaism. In the NT and «intertestamental» literature, the biblical quotation is re-worked within the new text. In the Mishnah and the Talmud, the biblical quotation is always separate from the commentary.

c. The gospel of *Luke* does not stop at connecting every saying or deed of Jesus with the OT as Matthew does, but frames the whole of the gospel between two global references to Scripture: «Today this scripture has been accomplished before you» (Lk 4:21) and the reproach to the disciples at Emmaus: «Oh ignorant and slow to believe in all that the prophets said! Did not the Messiah have to suffer this to enter his glory?» (Lk 24:25).

d. The fourth gospel, John's, is more subtle in its references to the OT. It often alludes to the OT from which it takes many of the themes it develops (Jn 1:14.17-18; 12:41). Following the calendar of Jewish feasts and the pilgrimages of Jesus to Jerusalem, the gospel of John tries to show that in Jesus the messianic hope of Israel is fulfilled and that what the Jewish rites symbolise actually happens. Jesus purifies the Temple at Easter (2:13ff.), arrives in pilgrimage at the Temple «on a feast of the Jews» (5:1ff.), on the feast of Tabernacles, he presents himself as the reality of what the feast means (7:2ff.) and in the second Easter returns to Jerusalem to carry out his redemptive mission (12:1ff.). Through typological interpretation, Jesus is presented as the true Temple (2:18-22), the anti-type of the bronze serpent (3:14f.), the true manna (6:30-58), the rock from which living water gushes (7:37-39), the eschatological Moses (ch. 6), the new Torah (ch. 1; 5:39-47; 14:6), the true paschal Lamb (1:29.36 and the passion narrative), etc.

The text of the seven editorial quotations of Jn does not diverge as much from known texts as do Mt's eleven quotations. The text is closer to the LXX. Jn's quotations follow the pesher model of interpretation, but not in such an evolved form as in Mt's quotations. These seven quotations occur in Jn 2:17 (Ps 69:9); 12:15 (Zach 9:9); 12:38 (Is 53:1); 12:40 (Is 6:9f.); 19:24 (Ps 22:18); 19:36 (Ps 34:20); 19:37 (Zach 12:10). The last one («They will look on the one they pierced») seems to be an ad hoc creation, because it is not easily explained as reflecting a textual variant or as the result of a paraphrase.

5.   *The Letter to the Hebrews*

The Letter to the Hebrews cannot be classed as an example of Hellenistic-Christian hermeneutic. Instead, it belongs within Jewish exegesis, although it still shows very distinctive features. There are 38 quotations corresponding to 27 OT passages, as well as several allusions and reminiscences of expressions from the LXX. The biblical text of those quotations is close to the Greek version attested by Codex Alexandrinus. Of the total of 38 quotations, 18 agree with the LXX and MT and 14 agree only with the LXX. No quotation in Heb follows the MT against the LXX and there are only 6 quotations, all from the Pentateuch, without any connection with the Greek version (1:6; 6:14; 9:20; 10:30a; 12:10; 13:5).

The quotations in Heb have been explained as free paraphrases of the corresponding biblical passages, as the result of using liturgical formulas or *Testimonia* of these passages, or as ad hoc creations of the author of the Letter. However, the agreements observed between Heb and the Dead Sea Scrolls indicate the possibility that these quotations knew variants of an LXX recension based on lost Hebrew texts. It is significant that both Heb 1:5 and 4QFlor repeat Ps 2 and 2 Sm 7:14, forming a sort of *Testimonia* on the messianic theme and that Heb 5-7 and 11QMelq show an equal interest in the eschatological person of Melchizedek.

Heb used a form of exegesis which attempts to examine a passage from scripture in the minutest detail. It represents the greatest attempt at typological analysis of the OT, looking for examples to support its doctrine on the meaning of Christ's sacrifice. For the author only Christocentric interpretation of scripture makes sense of the OT: the history of Israel has to be understood in the light of Christ's revelation (Heb 11).

6.   *Biblical Quotations in Other NT Writings*

The letters of James, Peter's two letters, the three by John, the letter of Jude and the Apocalypse have common features in their use of the OT. Nearly all the explicit quotations occur in James and 1 Pt. Ap provides several indirect allusions, but no exact quotation. The text of the quotations and even of the allusions is generally taken from the Greek version, as is easily seen in cases such as 1 Pt 2:9, quoting Ex 23:22. It is noteworthy that the letter of Jude (in vv. 14-15) quotes a non-canonical book (*1 Enoch* 1:9).

The genre of interpretation followed in these quotations is generally literal. The letters of Peter, especially the first, as well as the letter of Jude, also use pesher (cf. 1 Pt 1:10-12; 1:24f.). Here they differ from the letters of John and James and from the Apocalypse. 1 Pt 2:4-8 develops the theme of Christ «a living stone», combines images from the OT (also included in the writings of the Qumran community, 1QS 8:7f.; 1QH 6:26) and makes the appropriate Christological application of them, using a midrashic procedure of grouping together different OT passages (Ps 118:22; Is 28:16 and Is 8:14).

II. JEWISH-CHRISTIANITY AND THE INTERPRETATION OF THE OT

Study of the apocryphal literature of the NT and of the new texts found in Qumran as well as various archaeological finds in the place called *Dominus flevit* and in Mary's tomb in Jerusalem and elsewhere in Nazareth (Bagatti) have contributed to better knowledge of the Jewish-Christian branch of the early Church. This Jewish-Christian group was the channel through which many ideas, images and interpretations of the OT, typical of Judaism, passed to Christianity. It should not be forgotten, however, that Jewish-Christian tradition is largely obscure and that its very existence has been questioned (Neusner).

Christianity took its first steps in the Greek and Roman pagan world, but had its origin in the Hellenised Jewish world. The Church was born from Judaism by direct descendance. In its beginnings it was nothing more than a Jewish sect or religious group. The influence of the Greek and Roman world on the first Jews to become Christians could only be indirect, mediated through Hellenistic Judaism.

The order in which Judaism and Hellenist influenced early Christianity has often been inverted. Study in the past of the origins of Christianity emphasised Paul's activity throughout the Greek diaspora. In this way the conclusion was reached that Hellenism was found right at the start of Christian history. The Jewish elements to be found in Christianity did not belong to the first hour of Christianity but were the result of later Judaisation of Christianity. In this way, the Jewish roots of Christianity were completely forgotten, and, if not considered a syncretistic religion à la Gunkel, it was at least thought to be a product derived from Hellenism.

By establishing total antagonism between Judaism and Hellenism it was forgotten that at the turn of the age Judaism was already completely imbued with Hellenism. However, aware of the existence and vigour of a Hellenised Judaism, it is possible to explain better the texts of Paul and the fourth gospel. It is not necessary to resort to the influence of the pagan «Mysteries» on Paul, which raises more problems than it solves (cf. p. 31).

The question is more intense with regard to Christological doctrine and the theology of Paul's sacraments. These do not seem to find points of contact or antecedents in any Jewish movement of the period. In past years research has tended to make a separation between Paul and the Jewish world, and in parallel, between Paul and Jesus. Today, however, it is accepted that it is more in accordance with the facts to admit the Jewish and even rabbinic nature of Paul and his writings (Davies, Blank).

Study of Jewish-Christian exegesis begins precisely with analysis of traditions earlier than Paul, as included in his letters, as well as others contained in the other canonical and apocryphal writings. This leads to an analysis of the writings of the early Church Fathers, not forgetting information supplied by Jewish sources, especially those which refer to *minîm* or «heresies».

1.   *The Definition of «Jewish-Christianity»*

The first question to be asked in connection with «Jewish-Christianity» is to define this term exactly. Two definitions have been proposed, one too narrow, the other too wide.

Schoeps reduced Jewish-Christian to *Ebionism, an «unorthodox» movement of converted Jews*, which had remained midway between Judaism and unorthodox Christianity: they were Jews who acknowledged Christ as prophet and Messiah but did not go so far as to accept the divine sonship of Jesus.

Daniélou, instead, began with *categories of Jewish apocalyptic thought*, which were reflected in Christian works written up to the mid-2nd cent. CE. Schoeps had studied unorthodox Jewish-Christianity; Daniélou paid more attention to the forms of an orthodox Jewish-Christianity. His definition of Jewish-Christianity embraced «every version of Christianity and all Christian content derived from Judaism». It can also include, therefore, pagan converts to Christianity who were influenced by Jewish thought patterns. The criteria used by Daniélou to recognise this Jewish-Christianity are basically confession of Christ on one hand and Jewish structure of theology and life style on the other. In Daniélou's view attention to what is specific to Judaism and also to Jewish-Christianity remained very much in the background: observance of the Torah.

A *definition of Jewish-Christianity* has to include the following: early Christians, born Jews and speaking Aramaic, influenced by Hellenism but faithful to the practice of the law, with theological ideas as varied as in other Christian groups at the start of Christianity.

The group which the term Jewish-Christianity suits best is the Nazarene group. They were Christians of Jewish origin who continued to keep the Law. They kept their knowledge of Hebrew so that they read the OT and also, at least one gospel in Hebrew.

The origin of Nazarenes is earlier than the Ebionites so that they are not connected. Perhaps, towards the end of the 1st cent., there was a schism in Jewish-Christianity prompted by disagreements concerning Christological doctrine and how the community was governed. If Epiphanius and Jerome are to be believed, the Nazarene group survived up to the 4th cent., and certainly until the 3rd. They were not a large group. They covered the length of the Eastern Mediterranean coast, especially to the East of the Jordan Valley. Their roots were in Galilee and at first they had connections with Pella in the

Decapolis. There were Nazarene communities in Galilee and probably also in Jerusalem up to 135.

Jewish-Christianity should be considered as part of the many Jewish and Christian groups of the period. The Jewish-Christian groups may have been connected with various movements of Judaism: the Pharisee tendency which was dominant in Palestine; the apocalyptic and messianic tendencies, inclined towards zealotry, which had roots in Asia Minor; the Essene movements which were felt in Rome and are reflected in the *Shepherd of Hermas*; Essene groups of Alexandria who reached Palestine after 70 CE and were converts to Christianity, more inclined towards Ebionism than the Jewish-Christians of Rome and Syria; lastly, in Eastern Syria where Aramaic was spoken Jewish-Christian showed the influence of Jewish rabbinism (Goppelt).

a. Connection with the Christian Church. The Fathers of the 4th cent. could not in any way criticise Jewish-Christians over doctrinal matters. They could, however, in matters of Christian practice since the Nazarenes continued to follow the Law, circumcision and the Sabbath. These were «Judaising» signs which resulted in expulsion from the Church which, however, only happened very slowly for they never actually posed a threat to Christian orthodoxy.

Neither in origin or in nature was Jewish-Christianity Gnostic. However, it gradually became open to Gnostic influences up to the point that 2nd century Jewish-Christianity was very close to Gnostic movements which the Fathers considered as heretical. This assimilation speeded up the process of accusing the Jewish-Christians of heresy although the main motive for their rejection has already been noted: they continued to keep Jewish tradition and practices.

Gnosis influenced Jewish-Christianity or Jewish-Christian gnosis, but also in the reverse direction Jewish-Christianity influenced the evolution of Gnosis. Jewish-Christianity was the catalyst for conveying Jewish and Christian traditions to Gnosticism cf. p. 522).

b. Connection with the Jewish Synagogue. As for the Synagogue, exclusion of Jewish-Christianity was not so gradual as in the Church but took effect virtually from the end of the 1st cent. once the *birkat hamminîm* was formulated. It is possible that groups of Nazarenes still continued to take part in the life of the synagogues for some time during the first decades of the 2nd cent. No doubt contacts, some more polemical than others, persisted between Jews and Nazarenes, for they both lived in the same places. Three stages can be noted in the increasing rift between Jews and Jewish-Christians: the flight of the latter to Pella in the years of the Jewish War, the proclamation by the Jews of *birkat hamminîm* and lastly, the refusal of the Nazarenes to acknowledge and pledge support to Bar Kochba. By the middle of the 2nd cent. the rift was complete.

Disapproval was mutual. The Nazarenes did not accept the authority of the Pharisee movement which dominated Judaism after 70 CE. If they accused the Christian Church of no longer practising the Law, they also rejected the interpretations and *halakha* which the rabbinic pharisees developed from the Torah. Jewish rejection of the Nazarenes could be based on this restrictive view of the Law peculiar to Jewish-Christians. The main reason for the schism, however, was the Christological beliefs of the Nazarenes in which they went beyond the bounds of Judaism and strict monotheism. From Talmudic sources it can be deduced that they practised some evangelical proselytism among the Jews.

2. Sources for the Study of Jewish-Christianity

The sources for the study of Jewish-Christian doctrines have to be found principally in the traditions «of the presbyters» transmitted by Papias and Clement of Alexandria. The traditions of Papias are marked by a strong messianic and even Zealot element (since in Asia Minor Jewish nationalism remained more vigorous and could survive longer as tolerance there was greater). The traditions transmitted by Clement of Alexandria have a more millenarist tinge and seem much closer to Ebionism.

The indirect sources are represented by Christian writings of a later period. There are three groups: 1) the writings of the 2nd and 3rd cent. Fathers (Theophilus of Antioch, Justin, Irenaeus and Clement of Alexandria; with Origen the tradition loses its influence and prestige but Origen himself retains elements from Jewish-Christianity), 2) some late NT apocrypha (*Protogospel of St. James, Gospel of Nicomedus, Acts of Andrew and John*), and 3) old, Ebionite and Gnostic unorthodox literature.

To identify the works of the Jewish-Christian authors poses a whole series of methodological problems. It is first necessary to establish criteria for such an identification. The problem is especially acute in connection with the Jewish-Christian insertions into Jewish works as is the case in some apocryphal or pseudepigraphical writings of the OT: *Ascension of Isaiah, Testament of the Twelve Patriarchs, 2 Enoch*, the *Prayer of Joseph* and the *Sibylline Oracles* (books VI and VII). Once the Christian elements present in these works have been recognised, it is still necessary to know whether they are Christian insertions into Jewish works or whether they are Jewish-Christian works using Jewish sources and material.

Similar problems arise in respect of the label «Jewish-Christian» of some of the NT apocrypha (the *Gospel of Peter*, the *Gospel according to the Hebrews* or the *Gospel of the Nazarenes*, different from the *Gospel of the Ebionites*, the *Apocalypse of Peter* and the *Letter of the Twelve Apostles*) and writings of the subapostolic period such as the *Didache*, the *Odes of Solomon*, the *Letter of Barnabas*, the *Shepherd of Hermas*, the *Letters of Ignatius of Antioch* and the *Letter of Clement of Rome*.

3. The Ideas and Symbols of Jewish-Christianity

Jewish-Christian theology was basically Trinitarian which is quite surprising in such an early movement of Christianity which comes from monotheistic Judaism. They accepted the virgin birth and the divinity of Jesus. The Jewish-Christian had an embryonic doctrine on the Holy Spirit but no less evolved than in the Main Church at that time.

The themes, ideas and images typical of Jewish-Christian theology include the following: the resurrection seems to be equated with the ascension; the mystery of Christ is presented as a descent of the Beloved through the seven heavens inhabited by the angels down to hell where the just people of the OT reside, now saved by the Cross of Christ who ascends again to the heavens accompanied by the shining and life-giving Cross portrayed as a living thing; the mystery of the descent and the ascension represents the descent of the *divinity* beneath the angels and the lifting up of *humanity* above the angels; the Spirit (*rûaḥ* is feminine in Hebrew) is represented as a maternal principle; Trinitarian theology has an angelological structure; the Son is portrayed as the glorious angel, chief of the seven archangels, and the Holy Spirit in the form of Gabriel; the Word is called «the Name» and «the Beginning» or by other names connected with speculations on the book of Genesis; the upper heaven is called the *Ogdoad*, place of «rest»; the doctrine of the two spirits and various questions relating ro religious practice such as the dispute against blood sacrifice, the practice of praying three times a day, prayers of blessing, *maranatha*, etc.

4.   *Jewish-Christian Exegesis of the OT*

The Christological hymn included in the letter of Paul to the Philippians (2:6-11) certainly constituted an example of the expression of Christian faith in terms typical of early Jewish- Christianity: «He, in spite of his divine nature..., lowered himself, obeying even to death, death on the cross. Therefore God raised him above everything... so that every mouth declare that Jesus, the Messiah, is Lord, to the glory of God the Father». In this hymn are found the motifs of descent and exaltation, the Adamological hymn and the motif of the Messiah's enthronement.

The NT apocrypha exhibit characteristics peculiar to Jewish Haggadah, especially in respect of its use of the OT. The *History of Joseph the Carpenter* makes Joseph, the Just One, more an OT than an NT person. The *Didache* is a treatise in which Jewish-Christian halakhot are collected. The *Dialogue with Tryphon* of the apologist Justin gives a whole series of examples of OT exegesis based on Jewish models, on themes such as the creation, circumcision, the Sabbath, Enoch and Melchizedek, the theophany at Mambre. etc.

a. Testimonia. The most conspicuous feature of Jewish-Christian exegesis and the most prominent is use of the *Testimonia*, a genre which links together biblical quotations around a central topic and has Jewish antecedents (cf. p. 454). The most important examples are the *Testimonia* referring to the Cross. *Letter of Barnabas* 5:13 links together three OT quotations applied to Christ's Passion:

«It was necessary, in fact, for Him to suffer on wood for the prophet says about Him: "Free my soul from the sword" (Ps 22:21) and "he pierces my flesh with nails" (Ps 119:20), for "a band of evildoers has cornered me" (Ps 22:17).

The second quotation follows the text of the LXX, «nail my soul with your fear» against MT «my soul is consumed with longing». Later, Irenaeus (*Demonstration of apostolic teaching* 79) reproduces the same set of quotations but as if it were a single quotation and already without the possibility of seeing it as a composite text: «Free my soul from the sword and my body from nails, for a band of evildoers has cornered me».

Another example from the *Testimonia* on the Cross seems to be Jewish in origin:

«When one of you receives a bite he should turn to the serpent placed upon the *wood* (*xýlon*) and hope, having faith than even without life it can give life, and he will be all right» (*Letter of Barnabas* 12:7).

It is a paraphrase of Nm 21:8-9; reference to this text is achieved by means of a slight change to the text: the term «wood» (*xýlon*) replaces the LXX term «sign» (*sēmeîon*) while in turn alters the Hebrew term «standard», (*nēs*), in accordance with an interpretation found in Wis 16:1- 7: «symbol of salvation» (*sēmbolon sōtērías*). Another example associates Christ with Moses with his arms stretched out interceding for the Israelites:

«The Spirit spoke to the heart of Moses, inspiring him to make the form of a cross and of Him who had to suffer on it» (*Letter of Barnabas* 12:2).

This connection is also found in the *Sibylline Oracles* (VII 250-253) as well as in Justin, Irenaeus, Tertullian and Cyprian.

Justin collects various *Testimonia* concerning the tree in relation to the cross: the tree of life in paradise; Moses' stick which divides the waters of the Red Sea and makes water gush out in the desert; the rod of Jesse; the oak of Mambre; the wood of the ark; the rod of Elisha thrown into the Jordan and retrieved from the water, etc.

The *Gospel of Peter* has a passage where «the Cross of Glory» is connected with the glorification of Christ:

«And, as they were explaining what they had just seen, they again noticed three men coming out of the grave, two of whom used the third as a support, and a cross which went after them. And the head of the (first) two reached the sky while that of the person being led by them surpassed the skies. And they heard a voice coming from the skies which said «Have you preached to those who sleep?». And a reply was heard from the cross: "Yes"» (10:38-42).

Here are assembled different basic themes of Jewish-Christian theology: the descent from the cross to hell, the ascension and the voice from heaven. The cross which accompanies Christ to heaven is the same which will precede him when he comes «from the East» in the Parousia. With this idea is connected the custom of painting a cross on the Eastern wall of houses to pray towards the East seven times a day. Later, this connection between the cross and the East was forgotten and a cross was then painted on any wall without concern about direction. The apparition of a glorious cross is a common theme up to the 4th cent. The most transcendental event of this century was the apparition of a shining cross to the emperor Constantine on the Milvius Bridge in Rome.

b. Midrashic Paraphrase of the OT. Christian writings include paraphrases on OT texts which could derive from Jewish midrash. The *Letter of Barnabas* contains a series of quotations which could come from a Christian midrash on Lv and Nm (ch. 19, referring to «the red heifer»). Justin accuses the Jews of having expunged from the OT passages referring to Christianity; in fact, these were Christian insertions based on Jewish midrashic works as in the following passage attributed to *1 Ezra*:

«I wish to do what pleases you. For, from the commentaries which Ezra made on the law of Passover, they removed the following passage: 'And Ezra said to the people: "This Passover is our salvation and our refuge. If you reflect and think in your heart that we have to humiliate him on the cross and after that hope in Him, this place will never remain desolate, says the Lord of virtues. But if you do not believe him or listen to his preaching, you will be the laughingstock of the nations" '» (*Dialogue with Tryphon* 72,1)

Justin himself quotes a passage as if it were a text from the canonical book of Jeremiah although it really comes from a Christian midrash. It has the merit of being the oldest known Jewish-Christian text on the descent to hell:

«From the words of Jeremiah they also removed this passage: 'The Lord, the Holy God of Israel, remembered his dead, those who fell asleep in the heaped up earth; and he descended to them to tell them of his salvation'» (*Dialogue with Tryphon* 72,4).

5.   *The Bible in Disputes of the First Christians with the Jews*

Justin's debate with the Jew, Tryphon, and the relations between Jewish-Christianity and Jews led to raising the problem of the place of the bible in disputes between Jews and Christians. Relations between the two groups was marked by fierce rivalry, for each were in dispute over the territory for their missionary activity. The prevalent view is that from the crises of 70 and 135 CE Judaism closed itself off completely and abandoned any missionary activity. The withdrawal only happened very slowly and only under the pressure of unfavourable circumstances (M. Simon).

The existence of Jewish-Christian groups contributed to the formation of further groups of a syncretistic nature within the Church.

In the separation between Church and Synagogue Paul and Stephen played an important role. Paul declared the Torah to be null and void as did Stephen of the Temple. The band of Hellenists grouped around Stephen also ended up breaking its links with Judaism.

Another decisive factor in the separation of Church and Synagogue was the decree of the Council of Jerusalem. According to the decisions of this decree, the term Jewish-Christian has to be applied strictly to those Jewish converts to Christianity who demanded a Jewish observance beyond the demands accepted in the Council of Jerusalem.

Jews and Christians were thus in opposition from the beginning over a legacy which each considered their own, the *Tanak* or OT. The disputes revolved around the matters dealt with here: the extent of the canon, variants in the text, the method of interpretation and, above all, the actual exegesis of the more important passages of the OT which either side devised.

a) Jews and Christians exchanged accusations of changing or perverting *the* sacred *text.* Justin (*Dialogue* 71,2) reproached the Jews of having removed whole passages from the OT. In fact, these did appear in the Greek version used by Christians but were missing from the Hebrew text used by the Jews. However, these textual changes had nothing to do with disputes and evil-intentioned perversions by the Jews. Sometimes they really were interpolations inserted by the Christians into the text of the LXX version. Such was the case for the words «from upon the wood» which were added to Ps 95(95):10 after the clause «the Lord has ruled». this gloss allowed Christians to interpret the text of the psalm as a reference to Christ crucified.

The *Letter of Barnabas* provides another important example of how Christians did not hesitate to change the biblical text slightly to give it a Christian meaning. Several manuscripts of this letter reproduce the quotation of Isa 45:1 «(thus says the Lord) to my Anointed, Cyrus» (*tô Khristô mou Kýrō*) with a tiny variation: the addition of a subscript *iota* under the last letter. This variant changes the meaning significantly and allows the expression to refer to Christ: «(thus says the Lord) to Christ my Lord» (*tō Khristô mou Kýriō*).

In any dispute between Jews and Christians Is 7:14 always came up. Christians believed that the text of the Greek version contained a true prophecy of the virginal birth of Christ: «Behold, the virgin (*parthénos*) will conceive and give birth to a son». Tryphon, a Jew, responded to Justin saying that the meaning of the Hebrew word *'almâ* was not «virgin» but «girl» and that the Isaiah passage simply referred to king Hezekiah and not to a future Christian messiah.

b. Christian apologists tried to show that the prophetic texts could have a messianic *interpretation.* Justin interpreted Ps 100 as a messianic prophecy on Jesus of Nazareth (Justin, *Dialogue with Tryphon* 33,1; 57,1; 58,7). According to Justin, the Jewish rabbis deprived this text of any messianic meaning, making it refer exclusively to king Hezekiah. It is possible that the Jews knew a messianic interpretation of this psalm which they immediately played down in reaction to its use by Christians. A trace of this interpretation can be found in the Babylonian Talmud where it says that Hezekiah had been predestined to be the Messiah but became unworthy of that choice (BT *Sanhedrin* 94a).

It is uncertain whether the disputes between Christians and Jews took place face to face, in public debates or only on paper, by means of apologetic literature. Certainly there is no known Jewish work of anti-Christian polemic from the first centuries, nor have there reached us works of Jewish authors written in Greek later than the 2nd cent. CE. However, rabbinic literature has very many texts written in clear anti-Christian vein although they do not actually name the Christians. These seem to be included in the term *minîm* which refers to all those who by one path or another have deviated from synagogal orthodoxy.

Contrary to what is generally thought, Judaism did not close itself off completely after the two Jewish revolts. The withdrawal took placed slowly and not by choice but under the pressure of Christian propaganda and imperial authority after Constantine. It is quite possible that anti-Jewish Christian literature, which always based its arguments on passages from the Jewish scriptures, is not simply a literary fiction but was a real reflection of actual public debates between them (M. Simon).

BIBLIOGRAPHY

ARCHER, G.L. - CHIRICHIGNO, G., *Old Testament Quotations in the New Testament*, Chicago IL 1983.

BAGATTI, B., *L'Eglise de la Circoncision*, Jerusalem 1954.

BARTLETT, J.R., *Jews in the Hellenistic World. Josephus, Aristeas, The Sibylline Oracles, Eupolemus*, Cambridge 1985.

BLANK, J., *Paulus und Jesus*, Munich 1958.

BRUCE, F.F., *Biblical Exegesis in the Qumran Texts*, London 1950.

BRUCE, F.F., *This is That. The New Testament Development of Some Old Testament Themes*, Exeter 1958.

CHARLESWORTH, J.H. (ed.), *John and the Dead Sea Scrolls*, New York 1991.

CLINTON, B., *A Galilean Rabbi and his Bible. Jesus' own Interpretation of Isaiah*, London 1984.

DANIÉLOU, J., *Théologie du Judéo-christianisme*, Paris 1957.

DANIÉLOU, J., *Études d'exégèse judéo-chrétienne. Les Testimonia*, Paris 1955.

DAUBE, D., «Rabbinic Methods of Interpretation and Hellenistic Rhetoric», *HUCA* 22 (1949) 235-254.

DAVIES, W.D., «Reflections about the Use of the Old Testament in the New in its Historical Context», *JQR* 74 (1983) 105-135.

DODD, C.H., *According to the Scriptures. The Sub-Structure of New Testament Theology*, London 1953.

DOEVE, J.W., *Jewish Hermeneutics in the Synoptic Gospels and Acts*, Assen 1954.

EFIRD, J.M. (ed.), *The Use of the Old Testament in the New and Other Essays. Studies in Honor of W.F. Stinespring*, Durham NC 1972.

ELLIS, E.E., *Prophecy and Hermeneutic in Early Christianity. New Testament Essays*, Tübingen 1978.

ELLIS, E.E., *The Old Testament in Early Christianity*, Tübingen 1991.

ELLIS, E.E., «Biblical Interpretation in the New Testament Church», *Mikra*, CRINT 2/1, Assen/Maastricht-Philadelphia PA 1988, 591-725.

FITZMYER, J.A., «The Use of Explicit Old Testament Quotations in Qumran Literature and in the New Testament», *NTS* 7 (1950-51) 297-333.

FORESTELL, J.T., *Targumic Traditions and the New Testament*, Chico CA 1979.

FRANCE, R.T., *Jesus and the Old Testament. His Application of Old Testament Passages to Himself and his Mission*, London 1971.

FREED, E.D., *Old Testament Quotations in the Gospel of John*, Leiden 1955.

GERHARDSSON, B., *Memory and Manuscript*, Uppsala-Lund 1951.

GOPPELT, L., *Christentum und Judentum im ersten und zweiten Jahrhundert. Ein Aufriss der Urgeschichte der Kirche*, Gütersloh 1954.

GRELOT, P., *What are the Targums? Selected Texts*, Collegeville 1992.

HANSON, A.T., *The New Testament Interpretation of Scripture*, London 1980.

HARRIS, R., *Testimonies* I-II, Cambridge 1915 y 1920.

HÜBNER, H., *Vetus Testamentum in Novo. Synopsis Novi Testamenti et locorum citatorum vel allegatorum ex Vetere Testamento*, 2 vols., Göttingen 1991-.

JEREMIAS, J., «Paulus als Hillelit», *Neotestamentica et Semitica*, ed. E. Ellis-M. Willcox, Edinburgh 1959, 88-94.

JUEL, D., *Messianic Exegesis. Christological Interpretation of the Old Testament in Early Christianity*, Philadelphia PA 1988.

KAISER, W.C., *The Uses of the Old Testament in the New*, Chicago IL 1985.

KOCH, D.-A., *Die Schrift als Zeuge des Evangeliums. Untersuchungen zur Verwendung und zum Verständnis der Schrift bei Paulus*, Tübingen 1985.

KÖSTER, H., *Ancient Christian Gospels. Their History and Development*, Cambridge MA 1990.

LEANY, A.R.C., *The Jewish and Christian World 200 BC to AD 200*, Cambridge 1984.

LE DÉAUT, R., *La Nuit Pascale. Essai sur la signification de la Pâque juive à partir du Targum d'Exode XII 42*, Rome 1953.

LONGENECKER, R., *Biblical Exegesis in the Apostolic Period*, Grand Rapids MI 1975.

MCNAMARA, M., *The New Testament and the Palestinian Targum to the Pentateuch*, Rome 1955.

SCHOEPS, H.J., *Theologie und Geschichte des Judenchristentums*, Tübingen 1949.

SIMON, M., *Verus Israel*, Paris 1954.

SMITH, D.M. (JR.)., «The Use of the Old Testament in the New», *The Use of the Old Testament in the New and Other Essays*, ed. J.M. Efird, Durham 1972, 3-55.

STENDAHL, K., *The School of Matthew and its Use of the Old Testament*, Lund 1958.

STENDAHL, K. (ed.), *The Scrolls and the New Testament*, With a new Introduction by J.H. Charlesworth, New York 1992.

TOMSON, P.J., *Paul and the Jewish Law: Halakha in the Letters of the Apostle to the Gentiles*, Assen-Minneapolis 1990.

VERMES, G., *Scripture and Tradition in Judaism. Haggadic Studies*, Leiden 1973[2].

WAARD, J. DE, *A Comparative Study of the Old Testament Text in the Dead Sea Scrolls and in the New Testament*, Leiden 1955.

WENHAM, J.W., *Christ and the Bible*, London 1972.

WHITTAKER, M., *Jews and Christians: Graeco-Roman Views*, Cambridge 1984.

III. THE «BIBLE» IN THE 2ND CENTURY: THE HERMENEUTIC PROBLEM OF THE «OLD« TESTAMENT

1.   *History*

The 2nd cent. was the century of the formation of the collection of books which comprise the NT (cf. p. 237). At first, the Bible of the Christians was only the OT of the Jews, but very soon Christians felt the need to put down in writing the «acts and sayings» of Jesus. The account of the Passion was, it seems, the first element of tradition to be written down at a very early stage. Later, this account was extended by collections of sayings of Jesus which had first circulated in oral form.

It seems, however, that the impetus to form the collection of books which made up the «New Testament», did not only come from the gospels being put into writing, but rather from the edition of the Acts of the Apostles. This book unleashed great interest in the letters of Paul, so that towards the end of the 1st cent. CE, an initial collection of Pauline letters had already been formed, probably in Asia Minor. Somewhat later, Ignatius of Antioch shows that he knew the first letter to the Corinthians and the other Pauline letters, probably the gospel of John as well, and possibly those of Matthew and Luke.

In this period, however, *the sacred book of the Christians continued to be the* OT. Ignatius of Antioch felt obliged to confront some Christians who said they did not believe in what Scripture, i.e., the OT, said and did not accept its Christological interpretation (*Letter to the Philadelphians* 8,2; *Letter to the Magnesians* 8,2).

This situation began to change in the period when the most recent book to become part of the NT was written: the pseudonymous letter known as Second Peter which alludes «to the rest of the Scriptures» (3:16), referring to the Pauline letters, including the first letter to Timothy and probably to the gospel of Mark. At the beginning of the 2nd cent., the esteem for «Scripture» had lowered the standard of the OT enough for it to include the letters of Paul and probably also the gospels

From that moment on Christianity experienced a *double conflict*, at once internal and external: whether to accept or to reject the OT legacy, and whether to accept or reject the second *praeparatio evangelica*, the world of ideas and institutions of Greek and Roman culture which acted as a channel to express and extend the new faith. On the other hand, Jewish-Christian movements such as the Ebionites felt linked to the practice of the Law and the many institutions of the OT. Yet again, Greek Christians moved beyond discussions on actual religious practices, which posed the fundamental theological question of whether Christianity could and should remain within the frame of Judaism.

The first Council in the history of the Church, which took place in Jerusalem, had opted for a *compromise solution*, which would allow the co-existence of Christians from Judaism with those from Gentile Hellenism. It is not surprising that tensions persisted and that in the 2nd cent. a strong movement of rejection of the OT, headed by Marcion, ran through the whole Church. The Christian canon formed towards the end of the 2nd cent. CE, which supposes a new compromise solution and includes both collections of sacred books, is more testimony to the diversity of the Christian Church than a proof of its unity (cf. p. 254).

There still remained therefore the *problem of the relationship between «old» and «new»*, between the Jewish inheritance and Christian novelty. The

Christian Bible and even Christian orthodoxy would not be completely formed until this question had been resolved, towards the end of the 2nd cent.

A. CLEMENT OF ROME, IGNATIUS OF ANTIOCH AND THE *LETTER OF BARNABAS*

Clement of Rome maintained a degree of reserve towards the OT. The Letter of Clement to the Corinthians avoids interpreting the OT in Christological terms and, unlike Paul, does not even use typological interpretation. He uses the OT liberally, but almost always in its literal meaning, exhibiting also the influence of Greek culture as part of the Jewish-Christian background of the letter. Jewish-Christian circles at that time were more radical than Clement and went much further, even prohibiting any interpretation of the OT which was not strictly literal, and had therefore been superseded after the arrival of the new Christian economy of salvation (Hagner).

The first letter of Clement, towards the end of the 1st cent., shows that in this period the OT had already been so Christianised, even allegorical interpretation was no longer necessary, except for isolated elements in the text and for the purpose of edifying the faithful. This is how, for example, Rahab's scarlet thread (Josh 2 and 6) came to mean Christ's blood.

In the letters of *Ignatius of Antioch*, OT quotations are quite rare. There are fewer than ten and none comes from the books of the Torah. Ignatius seems to oppose Gospel and OT, following a trend of the time in certain Christian circles.

The *Letter of Barnabas*, instead, uses the OT liberally. The Jewish-Christian origin of this work is evident in its use of midrashic type exegesis. Its thought is akin to Paul and the Letter to the Hebrews, making Paul's attitude towards the OT even more radical. It uses allegorical interpretation in the matter of dietary laws or the number of Abraham's servants - 318 - which becomes a symbol of Jesus' name and of the cross. Symbolic interpretation of numbers had already been quite cultivated by the Jews and was a success particularly among Hellenised Jews. The 7 days of creation symbolised the 6,000 years the world had existed. The Sabbath was a symbol of the eschatological rest. In the apostolic and sub-apostolic period some of the more successful symbols in the history of Christian theology and art took shape: the sun, symbol of Christ; the moon and the ship, symbols of the Church; the sea, a symbol of the world, etc. (Rahner, Daniélou). Thus the *Letter of Barnabas*, never far from elements of Gnosticism, accepts the OT as meaningful only and exclusively in respect of the Christian gospel.

The application of allegory could lead to denying that biblical passages had any literal meaning and even that the OT had any meaning apart for the Christian meaning imposed on it. The process of Christians completely commandeering the OT took place throughout the 2nd cent. CE. The *Letter of Barnabas*, a Jewish-Christian writing from the beginning of the century, assumes that there has already been a complete separation of Synagogue and Church. For the author of the letter, the Scriptures of the Jews are starting to be more Christian than Jewish. Whereas the Letter to the Hebrews still allowed the biblical texts to have a literal meaning, the *Letter of Barnabas* denied this. Only allegorical interpretation is possible, by which circumcision means circumcision of the heart, for example, or unclean animals become evil men which whom no contact is possible. All the Christian truths, including the pre-existence of Christ, his death and his return at the end of time, were already prefigured in the OT.

B. THE CONTRAST BETWEEN JUSTIN AND MARCION

Marcion questioned radically the need and value for Christians to continue regarding the OT as sacred scripture. Marcion has been compared to Paul and there are reasons for this. However, Paul would have been horrified at the statements made by Marcion, who contrasted a just God with the Law and the God of the Jews with the good God of the Christians, the Father of Jesus Christ. Marcion practised literal exegesis of the OT so that he could stress how crude and antiquated its laws were. At the same time, he applied the critical method which poets used for studying the classics to the NT, going so far as to state that several NT passages were insertions. This led Tertullian to accuse Marcion in terms reminiscent of the critique sometimes made today of modern scholars: «(Marcion) was prepared to declare a passage as inserted rather than explain it» (*Adv. Marc.* 4,7).

Justin Martyr (†165), one of the first Christian apologists, made it possible for Christians to go on using the OT. Justin set out the arguments for justifying this use, although the channel for reaching it supposed a typological interpretation which inevitably forced the OT to some extent. Justin makes a less radical judgment of the OT than the *Letter of Barnabas*. For him, as for Paul and also for Barnabas, the Law is principally a *týpos* of the future, of Christ and the Church. Interpreting the OT literally, the Jews could not know its true meaning and did not know that the prophecies referred to Christ. Justin, like other Asiatic writers, did not have the requisite philological training and did not pay enough attention to the literal sense.

Justin was already stating what would later be the classical Christian doctrine on the OT. Unlike Marcion, he rejects the idea that Christian revelation is radically opposed to other revelations of God, to be found not only in the OT but also among Greek philosophers, who to some extent deserved the name Christian as well.

Following the footsteps of Paul and the author of Heb, Christians could accept the OT and incorporate it into their own world of ideas and religious experiences. However, this did not mean they stopped having difficulties. They also felt like rejecting a book which many considered at least strange and unworthy of philosophers, both for its literary style and the immoral or trivial content of most of its archaic legislation.

Justin already represents the view that would be traditional in the Church in which no tension at all is seen between OT and NT, for by then it had been completely Christianised (Prigent).

C. IRENAEUS OF LYONS AND GNOSTICISM

Prominent in the movement for rejecting the OT is the Gnostic *Valentine*, who does not hesitate to apply Jn 10:8 («all those who preceded me have been nothing but thieves and robbers») to the prophets. More restrained and systematic in his analysis is the Valentinian *Ptolemy*, author of the *Letter to Flora*, who divides the Pentateuch into three parts in descending order: one of divine origin, one of Mosaic origin and the last added later by the elders of the people. Laws such as those referring to revenge lead to evil and the ritual regulations have no meaning beyond the purely spiritual.

The Christian Church felt obliged to develop a theory concerning the relations between the OT and the NT for use not only in connection with the Jews, but against the world of the pagans and pagan converts who could be tempted by the Gnostic rejection of the OT. That was the task of *Irenaeus of Lyons* (c. 120/140-c. 200/203), who represents the line of tradition going back to the apostle John, through Polycarp of Smyrna. For Irenaeus, the revelation of God in the Law of the OT is valid, but it has been succeeded by a new revelation in Christ. The conception of the relationship between OT and NT developed by Irenaeus is more historical in character than those of his predecessors. He criticises his opponents, the Valentinians, for linking together some biblical passages in isolation from their contexts so as to prove their own speculations and theories. The same procedure was used by interpreters of Homer who combined passages from the *Iliad* and the *Odyssey* and ended up with a completely new story.

Irenaeus also criticised the Valentinians for explaining the clear by the obscure. If there is one thing obvious in the OT it is its monotheistic principle and not the Gnostic conjectures on the union of Eons. If the OT mentions ʾElohim, ʾEl-Šadday or Yahweh Ṣebaoth as one and the same God, the Gnostics interpreted these divine names as referring to different gods, all subordinate to the unknown God the Father.

In reaction to the arbitrary nature of Gnostic exegesis, Irenaeus shows no sensitivity at all to allegorical interpretation based on the symbolism of numbers and etymologies. Against the Jews Irenaeus tends to be a literalist in the Christological interpretation of the prophecies and an allegorist in the typological interpretation of the Law and history of Israel. However, against the Gnostics, Irenaeus uses the allegorical method to interpret the OT christologically and so be able to link the OT and NT against the division defended by the Gnostics (Orbe).

Irenaeus already sets up the principle of «exegesis within the Church» which will be further developed later in opposition to what can be called «exegesis in the cathedra». Exegesis has to be in agreement with the understanding of Scripture held by Church tradition (*regula fidei*). The interpretation does not have to be based only on rational criteria but has to take into account the doctrine and authority of tradition, which the Church transmits from apostolic times. This principle of interpretation is justified since the tradition of the Church is in some way earlier than its Scripture, created by the first apostles and their disciples.

2. Theological Development: the Unity of the Two Testaments

It has been possible to say without fear of exaggeration that the hermeneutic problem of the OT is *the* problem and not merely *a* problem of Christian theology (Gunneweg).

Christianity had very soon to ask the question whether the collection of OT writings should form part of the Christian canon or be excluded from it completely. The answer to this question, affirmative or negative, required in turn an answer as to what Christianity was and what, by excess or defect, went beyond or fell short of the limits of Christianity. Ultimately, it meant defining the framework within which Christian theology could work.

Many roads were followed, both to incorporate the OT into the Christian canon and to justify its rejection. This question, never fully resolved, has its origin in the OT itself. For extrinsic reasons it does not allow the adjective «old» to be added: its existence is before and independent of the other body of religious literature which called itself «*New* Testament», in opposition to the first. The Hebrew Bible or *Tanak,* as well as the LXX, used by Christians as the «Old Testament», are works by Jews for Jews, with their own independent frame of reference.

The hermeneutic problem of the Christian Bible, OT versus NT, derives from the fact that despite many points of contact between the old and the new, the old does not necessarily flow into the new and the new does not flow spontaneously from the old. Christian faith does not arise from the scriptures but from faith in the saving act made manifest in Christ, which has to be understood by turning to the old scriptures.

The fact that the so-called «Old» Testament had an existence before the «New» Testament and Christianity and was a separate entity, very soon made Christians ask the question whether the OT which by definition is pre-Christian is not therefore non-Christian. Or, in other words, whether the adjective «old» refers only to a temporal relationship or whether it also supposes a qualification of its intrinsic value with reference to an extrinsic criterion.

The inclusion of the OT within Christianity could not fail to influence both the understanding it had of itself and the formation of its institutions of worship and rule. The allegorical re-interpretation of the OT and the use of much of the Torah as the ethical and ritual norm of the new faith helped to give the Church a certain OT and Jewish aspect. The Church had accepted the Torah, yet kept in contact with the decadent Roman Empire, and so was gaining or regaining aspects of theocracy. The Law requires a sanctuary, an altar and daily sacrifices, and according to Heb the only valid sanctuary and the only valid sacrifice for a Christian are the sacrifice of Christ and the sanctuary in which Christ resides. In spite of this, sacrifice was to become exclusive to the priests and the cult would turn into a semblance and image of the OT cult. Christian baptism replaces Jewish circumcision, just as Sunday replaces the Sabbath but while the meaning certainly changes, a large part of the signs and ceremonial remains.

During the history of Christianity the question has been raised several times as to whether it should not have given up the collection of OT books, much as it gave up many OT institutions such as the Temple or circumcision. However, it is historical fact that mainstream Christianity not only did not reject the OT, it even incorporated it fully into its own canon of sacred books. Apologists and Christian theologians could not fail to ask themselves, therefore, what meaning the OT had in Christianity and how the OT had to be interpreted as a whole in relation to the NT.

Throughout the 2nd cent. and in fact throughout the whole history of Christianity, it gave very different and contradictory answers to these questions.

At first, the inclusion of the OT within the Christian canon did not have polemic significance against the Jews. Nor did it have an apologetic connotation, as if the value of the OT consisted in providing proofs favouring the NT. The OT had a more positive function for Christians; it was the channel of interpretation of the *event* of Christ's death and resurrection and of the *words (logia-děbārîm)* of Christ-Word; the OT provided the language, symbols and imagery, the literary forms (lamentations and hymns), the messianic titles, etc., to express that event and those words.

The inclusion of the OT within the Christian canon, achieved in opposition to very powerful counter-currents, such as Marcionism and Gnosticism, prevented early Christianity from fading into the world of mystery religions and a-historical mysticism or perhaps falling into a philosophy bereft of all reference to time. Marcion's radical Paulinism became a veritable attack on the OT roots of the Christian tradition. Gnostic dualism opposed God the Creator and God the Redeemer, the OT and NT respectively. Even in the less radical forms of Gnosticism, the OT Law had a position intermediate between God the Redeemer and evil.

A.   THE OT AS PROMISE AND PROPHECY OF THE NT

The Christian reclamation of the OT assumed, to a large extent, *leaving to one side the Jewish conception of the Tanak, basically considered as the Torah or Law.* Jesus himself quoted passages from books which are not part of the Torah, yet granted them legal force. For example, to justify his free approach to observance of the sabbath Jesus quotes 1 Sm 21:7 on the shewbread: «Have you not read what David did when he felt hungry and those [who went] with him? How he entered the house of God and they ate the shewbread» (Matt 12:3). Jesus was doing no more than follow the Jewish and rabbinic view which saw Scripture as Law and the prophets as interpreters of the Law. In Judaism the relationship between the Torah and the Prophets was a hermeneutic problem comparable, in some sense, to that supposed in Christianity in the OT-NT relationship. Ultimately, it is the problem of interpreting some obsolete laws which therefore needed an interpretation with an authority on a par with the Law itself to give them new legal force and validity. Jesus was different from the rabbis since when interpreting the laws he referred directly to the will of God, superior to the Law itself.

The Christian appropriation of the OT involved perceiving the OT less as Law and instead placing *emphasis on the understanding of the OT and the Pentateuch as promise and prophecy*. Already Paul himself had stated that *before* the whole Law Abraham believed in the promise (Rom 4). One of the earliest formulae of the Christian creed expresses this view of the OT: «Christ died... according to the Scriptures and arose...according to the Scriptures» (1 Cor 15:4). The oldest and most important narratives of Christianity, those referring to the death and resurrection of Christ, were modelled on the penitential psalms and the songs of the Suffering Servant. The understanding of the OT as prediction and promise corresponds to the structure of promise-fulfilment which characterises the whole OT and its very literary style, made of imperatives and narrative tenses (*wayyiqtol*) of the «command-fulfilment» type.

The gospel of Matthew, intended for the Jewish Christians of Antioch, places the emphasis on the OT Torah, and yet develops proof by prophecy. It even often quoted passages from the OT which in their original sense had no prophetic meaning at all or at least did not have the meaning attributed to them by the evangelist (cf. Mt 2:17f citing Jr 31:15). To this line of interpretation of the OT, under the structure promise/prophecy-fulfilment also belongs the process of attributing several OT titles to Jesus: «Messiah», «Anointed». «Son of Man», «Son of God», «Servant of Yahweh» and above all «Kyrios» (= Yahweh).

The best expression of the shift of Jewish emphasis on the Law to the Christian emphasis on prophecy is found in the change of order in which the books of the Hebrew Bible appear and in the Greek Bible just as it is transmitted between Christians. The centre of interest does not come at the beginning, in the Torah or Law, followed by the prophetic books and the Writings; instead it comes at the end: the books of the Prophets follow the Pentateuch and the Writings and precede the NT, of which they are the prophecy. This shift of the centre of interest had already begun in the gospel of Matthew, but was fully developed in the two works of Luke, the gospel which bears his name and the Acts of the Apostles. Christ appears in the «centre of time», preceded by Israel and the OT, whose witness points to Christ and the Church and followed by the Church (Conzelmann). Luke develops a concept of «salvation history» in which the OT fills the corresponding place in pre-history.

At the close of the process by which the OT was Christianised, Augustine classified the books of the OT by interpreting it all using categories of history and prophecy. This would have a decisive influence during the whole the mediaeval period through the *Institutiones* of Cassiodorus and the Pseudo-gelasian Decree. The OT books are classified as historical and prophetic (*De doctrina christiana* II,8,13).

The historical books form three groups: 1) the five books of the Pentateuch, followed by Joshua, Judges, Ruth, IV *Reges* and 2 Chronicles provide a continuous history (*historia quae sibimet annexa tempora continet atque ordinem rerum*), 2) the books of Job, Tobit, Esther and Judith which are unrelated either among themselves or with the previous group and lastly, 3) the books of Maccabees and Ezra.

The prophetic books are subdivided into two groups: 1) the book of Psalms attributed to David, and the three books of Proverbs, the Song of Songs and Qoheleth which are attributed to Solomon and are related to the books of Wisdom and Ecclesiasticus and 2) the book of the Twelve Minor Prophets and the four books of the great prophets (Isaiah, Jeremiah, Ezekiel and Daniel). The sum total of books is 44.

What is decisive in this classification is that the books of the Law are changed into historical books and the Writings into prophetic books.

B.   TYPOLOGICAL INTERPRETATION OF THE OT

Alongside the understanding of the OT as promise and prophecy of the NT there developed another understanding, derived from the first, which considers *the OT as a «type» of the NT*. The events, characters and institutions of the OT are changed into prefigurations of the NT. The first Adam is a type of the second Adam who is Christ. Typology combines a type and its antetype. Types prefigure something or someone, but their nature can only be seen in the light of the antetype, an event which has already happened or the person already revealed. The new becomes the hermeneutic key to the old.

There are very many typological correspondences between the OT and NT: baptism is the antetype of Noah's ark (Col 2:17; 1 Pt 3:21); manna is the type of the true eschatological bread which is Christ (Jn 6:31); Israel's wandering in the desert is the type of the Christian community (Heb 3:7-4:13), etc. The typological correspondences are not always explicit. For example, in Jn 19:14, the hour of the death of Jesus coincides with the hour of the sacrifice of the Passover lamb and in 1 Cor 5:7, Christ is portrayed as the sacrificed Passover lamb, which provides a kind of typological correspondence between the Passover lamb and Christ crucified. Typological interpretation has retained its importance and meaning up to the present (cf. p. 559, von Rad).

Once the Testaments had formed a unit within the same canon, two ways of interpreting the first Testament, the «Old» were possible: an *allegorical* line of interpretation, developed by the Alexandrian school, and *literal* interpretation, included within a typological interpretation and in terms of salvation history which was fully developed in the Antioch school.

IV.   GNOSTICISM AND GNOSTIC INTERPRETATION OF THE BIBLE

The first move in the study of Gnostic literature has to be to classify the works it comprises. Only in this way will it be possible to know which texts are of Christian-Gnostic origin, which were Christianised and which were expurgated of their original Christian elements.

The Nag Hammadi texts allow several principles of classification, with an inevitable degree of subjectivity (Tröger): 1) by literary form: dialogues, discourses of revelation, apocalypses, narratives, florilegia, collections of sayings, letters, prayers, etc., 2) by religious content: non-Christian writings, non-Christian with Christian elements, Christianised, Christian-Gnostic, Christian-Gnostic in dispute with the Grand Church and lastly, 3) by Gnostic school, such as the major movements of Valentinianism, Setianism and others.

Current research on Gnosis and the Gnostic library of Nag Hammadi centres on the analysing the concepts «Gnosis» and «Gnosticism», of «Christian Gnosis» and the relations between Gnosis and Judaism. All these matters are closely interrelated.

The Congress of Messina (1966) proposed a definition of «Gnosis» as «knowledge about divine mysteries restricted to an elite», and of «Gnosticism» as «groups of systems in the 2nd cent. CE» (later, therefore, than the birth of Christianity; Bianchi). These definitions have not succeeded in gaining the consensus of scholars. A wider definition, not so starkly phenomenological, has to take account of the non-Christian or pre-Christian elements of «Gnostic religion», restricting the concept of «Gnosticism» to the Gnostic movement as a whole in late antiquity. The whole setting was Gnosticism which was in the atmosphere at that time and so was very successful while the setting and the atmosphere were favourable.

1.   «Christian Gnosis» and «Jewish Gnosis»

a. Christian Gnosis. According to Harnack, Gnosticism was the result of an intense hellenisation or «globalisation» of Christianity. Current thinking, instead, favours the thesis that the origin and development of Gnosis were independent of Christianity. The discoveries at Nag Hammadi have put an end to the idea that when it started Gnosticism was a Christian heresy.

Gnosis and Christianity are irreconcilable. However, in its search for a superior form of knowledge and especially of a correct, that is, pneumatic interpretation of Scripture, Gnosis found in Christianity favourable terrain for expansion. Gnosticism was a new syncretistic type of religion which incorporated elements from Christianity, Judaism, Neo-Platonism, the Mystery Religions, etc.

The relationship between Gnosis and the NT poses the following dilemma: either Gnosis is earlier than the NT and is one its presuppositions or, instead, Gnosis arose after the NT and presupposes it. If the second option is chosen, the ideas and concepts of Gnostic character present in the NT turn out to be ideas and concepts original to the actual authors of the NT, especially of Paul and John. Today it is no longer possible to state that Gnosticism has nothing to offer the study of NT by being later. To give a clear explanation of Christian origins it has to be accepted that right from the start there was an exchange of ideas and symbols between Gnosticism and Christianity.

b. Jewish Gnosis. The fundamental question asked when speaking of Judaism and Gnosis is to know whether Gnosis has its roots in Judaism

(Friedländer, Quispel, Dahl, Betz, Pearson) or whether it arose outside the sphere of Jewish influence (Jonas, Van Unnik, Bianchi and the Messina group, Wilson, Maier).

This question brings into play many others which refer to the lines of development leading from Judaism to Gnosis; the relation between Gnosis and Jewish-Hellenism; the possibility that the strong anti-cosmic tendency, typical of Gnosticism, comes from Jewish circles which felt a deep distrust of the world and perhaps the scepticism of a Qoheleth; the role of apocalyptic in the development of Gnosis and the stumbling block of the whole matter: does the radically anti-cosmic attitude of Gnosis stem from a reaction within Judaism or did it come from outside Judaism and in opposition to it?

c. Arguments against the thesis of a Jewish origin of Gnosticism. Research on Gnosis does not usually make a big enough distinction between «biblical» and «Jewish». The Jewish element included in Gnostic writings is not really Jewish but biblical. Already before the birth of Christianity, the biblical element had extended far beyond the radius of Jewish influence. The Greek version of the OT had already been in existence for some time and was used by Christians right from the start. For this reason the mere use of the OT in Gnostic writings is not enough to assign Jewish origins to Gnosis. Christians who knew the LXX version and were influenced by Gnostic movements could easily make use of OT motifs for the literary development of their ideas and doctrines.

On the other hand, the use of the OT in Gnostic literature is very selective: certain texts and motifs predominate, especially those connected with the first chapters of Genesis and the monotheistic professions of faith. This makes more problematic the thesis which maintains the Jewish origin of Gnosis. As for the *Apocalypse of Adam* and the *Apocryphon of John*, it cannot be proposed that Adam and *Sophia* originate in Jewish Gnosis. The biblical elements and the post-biblical traditions are probably not «starting points» of Gnosis but «connection points» for the Gnostic development of biblical motifs in the manner of a relay race and not a long-distance race.

The thesis of the existence of a Jewish Gnosis is obliged to accept that this gnosis comprises a heresy within Judaism. This requires determining what is Jewish and what is heretical in Jewish Gnosis and what is the relationship between this Jewish Gnosis and Christianity with its own heresies. It is obvious that the Gnostic world shows a great interest in certain themes and texts of the OT, but the way it interprets them does not seem to be the work of Jewish authors, unless one speaks of marginal groups, in which case the qualifier «Jewish» loses all meaning.

The basic characteristic of Gnosticism, its radical aversion for the created cosmos, leads to an ascetic flight from the world or even to antinomism and libertinism. This anti-cosmic aspect has little to do with Judaism, with its biblical tradition rooted in the doctrine of a creator God and a «good» creation (Gn 1).

The explanation that Gnosticism arose from the reaction of a heretical Jewish movement as a protest movement within Judaism (Daniélou) has to face the fact that many of the statements which carry a marked anti-Jewish bias are not in fact directed against Judaism but against the Great Church, its interpretation of the OT and its Christological doctrine. On the other hand, anti-cosmicism is aimed not only at Judaism and the Christian Church but also revolts against the Greek understanding of the cosmos, its order and beauty.

The points of agreement between Gnosis and Jewish apocalyptic do not allow Essenism to be seen as a proto-Gnosis. Essenism is very far from Gnosis which is focused on self while Essenism is too tied to the Law which Gnosis detests. It is not possible to speak of pre-Gnosticism or proto-Gnosticism at Qumran or even in Philo.

Gnosis on its own, without its union with expanding Christianity, would not have had the success it did, nor would it have shown so much interest in the OT and Judaism. The Jewish element in the birth of Gnosis is indirect rather than direct and is very much affected by the Christian mission. Jewish-Christianity could act as a catalyst and intermediary between the Jewish and Christian traditions on the one hand and Gnosticism on the other (Strecker, Ménard).

To understand Gnosis and its origins it is necessary to start from a wider perspective which takes in the whole history of religions in antiquity on a global scale. Here belong Judaism, Hellenism, Christianity, Samaritanism, Platonism and the Greek world in general, including the syncretism of «late antiquity» in all its forms, not forgetting Egyptian, Persian and Mesopotamian influences.

Thus, more important that settling the problem about the origin of Gnosis is tracing the lines which could have led from Judaism to Gnosis but without attributing a Jewish origin to it. It is equally important to follow the trail leading from primitive Christianity to Gnosticism. From the Q source (the primitive source of the sayings or *logia* of Jesus), passing through Matthew and the *Didache* to the *Gospel of Thomas*, runs the same line of tradition in which the radical ethics of the source Q becomes the radical epistemology of the *Gospel of Thomas*. This is why Robinson speaks of a proto-Gnosticism and Koester considers the *Gospel of Thomas* as a sort of second edition of a «gospel of sayings» of Jesus.

2.   *Gnostic Interpretation of the OT*

The Gnostics rejected the God of the OT and so did not hesitate to invert completely the meaning of the OT texts, portraying as good what the OT considered as evil. The author of *The Testimony of Truth* (NHC IX 3,45ff) gives a positive value to the sin of Adam and Eve. Through the alleged offence they gained knowledge of their true being: a germ of spiritual nature, higher in category than an ignorant Demiurge, who tries to keep man and woman in ignorance.

Ptolemy's *Letter to Flora* attempts a middle road between the Catholic acceptance of the OT and Marcionite rejection of it. These Gnostics invoke two sources of inspiration: the Demi-urge and *Sophia*. The Demiurge inspires the literal meaning and psychic content of the text which is intended for psychic men; *Sophia* inspires the deeper, spiritual meaning, intended for Gnostics.

Whereas Marcion gave a strictly literal interpretation of both the OT and the NT, the Gnostics, instead set up a distinction between the two Testaments: they interpret the OT literally in order to emphasise the evil they find in it and interpret the NT through allegory so that the Gnostic doctrines become compatible with the canonical Christian texts. The Gnostics make wide use of allegorical interpretation. In orthodox circles, as represented by Irenaeus, this provoked a degree of mistrust in the allegorical method.

3. OT Traditions in Gnostic Literature

Gnostic texts contain a large amount of OT material: characters, names, narratives, quotations, paraphrases, motifs, etc. The texts used most are from Genesis but there is also material taken from the books of Kings, the Prophets and the Psalms.

Inserted in *The Testimony of Truth* (NHC IX,3) is a Gnostic midrash on the serpent which is at the same time a real targumic paraphrase of Gn 3:

«Then he [God] said, 'Let us cast him [out] of Paradise lest he take from the tree of life and eat and live for ever'. But of what sort is this God? First [he] maliciously refused Adam from eating of the tree of knowledge. And secondly he said, 'Adam, where are you?'. God does not have foreknowledge; (otherwise), would he not know from the beginning?... And he said, 'I am the jealous God; I will bring the sins of the fathers upon the children until three (and) four generations'. And he said, 'I will make their heart thick, and I will cause their mind to become blind,... that they might not know nor comprehend the things that are said'. But these things he has said to those who believe in him [and] serve him. And [in one] place Moses writes, '[He] made the devil a serpent...'. Also in the book which is called 'Exodus' it is written thus: 'He contended against the [magicians], when the place was full [of serpents]... Again it is written, 'He made a serpent of bronze (and) hung it upon a pole...'» (47-48).

The Gnostics' use of the OT could take on a variety of forms (Nagel): rejection of OT characters and events (NHC VII,2, *Second Treatise of the Great Seth*; NHC IX,3, *The Testimony of Truth*), interpretation in the opposite meaning (NHC II,4, *The Hypostasis of the Archons*; NHC II,5, *On the Origin of the World*), correction of the original meaning (NHC II,1; II,1; IV,1 and BG 8502,2, *The Apocryphon of John*), allegorical interpretation (*Pistis Sophia*) and etiological and typological interpretations (NHC I,5, *The Tripartite Tractate*; NHC I,3 and XII,2, *The Gospel of Truth*; NHC II,3, *The Gospel of Philip*; NHC II,6, *The Exegesis of the Soul*; *Pistis Sophia*).

These connections with Gnostic literature with Jewish literature and the OT in particular have supported the thesis of the Jewish origin of Gnosis. *The Apocalypse of Adam* (NHC V,5) and *The Apocryphon of John* are the most helpful of the Gnostic texts to support this thesis. The first work is of Jewish origin, and retains its Jewish characteristics without ever taking on the features of a Christian work. *The Apocryphon of John* is a Jewish Gnostic work, later Christianised in its final form. It has two sections: a revelation discourse and a commentary on Gn 1-6. It is also based on traditional Jewish interpretations of biblical texts and on Jewish apocryphal writings. It is in fact a Jewish work, «rewriting» the Bible, much like similar works such as *1 Enoch, Jubilees* or the *Genesis Apocryphon.*

According to this thesis, the authors of the first Gnostic texts were intellectual Jewish dissidents, open to Hellenistic syncretism. It is an unorthodox Judaism connected with Jewish wisdom traditions (Quispel), or it arose as a reaction to the loss of apocalyptic hope after the catastrophe of 70 CE (Grant). It should be stated that Christianity and Gnosticism are separate religions, both having roots in a third which is Judaism, and that at one point Christianity was about to be absorbed by Gnosticism (Pearson).

4.   *The Biblical Exegesis of the Manichees*

Introductions to the OT and NT do not usually take the slightest notice of Manichaean exegesis.

a. The OT and NT in Manichaean Exegesis. For the Manichees, Christ had completely abolished the OT, the Jewish testament as alien to Christianity. Unlike the prophets who preceded him (Zoroaster, Buddha and Jesus), Mani wrote his own works which were intelligible as they stood. The NT, instead, presents a whole problem of interpretation. For the Manichees, the NT does not enjoy the status of canonical Scripture. It is not a revealed book but a simple summary of the preaching of Jesus. All the texts transmitted in the NT present inconsistencies and anomalies due to the interference of numerous redactors (*scriptores*). As a result it is necessary to make a criticism of the NT texts in order to determine what is the authentic material to be attributed to Jesus of Paul, separating it from what later redactors added. Jesus is the interpreter *par excellence*, Paul is the interpreter of Jesus, Mani continued what Paul began and Adda is the true theologian of the Church.

b. Principles and Rules of Manichaean Exegesis. The critical and «modern» meaning revealed by Manichaean exegesis is surprising. Among the principles governing Manichaean exegesis the following can be mentioned: the Apostolic *writers* had their own aims and ideas which are reflected in the NT texts; to be of value, what is stated in a text has to rely on the testimony of a direct witness or has to be confirmed by another *author*; the social and literary context helps to determine the meaning of a difficult passage; the contradictions to be noted in a text may be due to changes in the author's thinking or insertions by later redactors; a narrative written in the third person is not likely to be the work of the author of the gospel; the presence of the same passage in different contexts is an indication that the text could have been reworked by *scriptores*; the historical context determines the meaning of a disputed passage, etc.

The Manichee NT contains only two parts: the Gospel and the Apostle, both in the singular. The Manichees only accepted one gospel and excluded books such as Acts. The Manichee NT does not depend on the Marcionite NT at the literary level, although it could have been a theological model with decisive influence on the formation of Mani's thought and on the acceptance of Christian scriptures by the Manichees. The Manichee gospel is completely independent of Tatian's.

The interest offered by Manichaean exegesis is based on the fact that it posed questions now hotly debated by modern criticism although the actual solutions proposed by the Manichees can seem very crude nowadays (Tardieu).

BIBLIOGRAPHY

BIANCHI, U. (ed.), «Le origini dello gnosticismo», *Colloquio di Messina 13-18 Aprile 1966*, Leiden 1967.

FELICI, S., *Esegesi e catechesi nei Padri (secc. II-IV)*, Rome 1993.

FRIEDLÄNDER, M., *Der vorchristliche jüdische Gnostizismus*, Göttingen 1989.

GRANT, R.M.., *Gnosticism and Early Christianity*, New York 1966².

HEDRICK, CH.W. -HODGSON, R., *Nag Hammadi Gnosticism, and Early Christianity. Fourteen Leading Scholars Discuss the Current Issues in Gnostic Studies*, Peabody MA 1986.

JONAS, H., *The Gnostic Religion. The Message of the Alien God and the Beginnings of Christianity*, Boston NY 1963².

KRAUSE, M. et al., *Nag Hammadi Studies*, Leiden 1971-.

LAYTON, B., *The Gnostic Scriptures*, Garden City NY 1987.

MAIER, J., «Jüdische Faktoren bei der Entstehung der Gnosis?», *Altes Testament-Frühjudentum-Gnosis. Neue Studien zu 'Gnosis und Bibel'*, ed. K.W. Tröger, Gütersloh-Berlin 1980, 239-258.

MÉNARD, J.-É., «Le judaïsme alexandrin et les gnoses», *Études sur le judaïsme hellénistique*, eds. R. Kuntamann-J. Schlosser, Paris 1984.

NAGEL, P., «Die Auslegung der Paradieserzählung in der Gnosis», *Altes Testament-Frühjudentum-Gnosis*, 1980, 49-70.

PEARSON, B.A., *Gnosticism, Judaism, and Egyptian Christianity*, Minneapolis MN 1990.

PEARSON, B.A., «Use, Authority and Exegesis of Mikra in Gnostic Literature», *Mikra*, CRINT 2.1, ed. M.J. Mulder, Assen/Maastricht-Philadelphia PA 1988, 635-652.

QUISPEL, G., «Jewish and Mandaean Gnosticism. Some Reflections on the Writing Brontē», *Les Textes de Nag Hammadi*, ed. J.E. Ménard, Leiden 1975, 82-122.

QUISPEL, *Gnosis als Weltreligion. Die Bedeutung der Gnosis in der Antike*, Zürich 1972.

ROBINSON, J.M., «On Bridging the Gulf from Q to the Gospel of Thomas», *Nag Hammadi Gnosticism, and Early Christianity*, 1986. 127-175.

ROBINSON, J.M., *The Nag Hammadi Library in English*, San Francisco-New York - Leiden 1977.

RUDOLPH, K., *Gnosis. The Nature and History of Gnosticism*, New York 1987.

SCHOLER, D.M., *Nag Hammadi Bibliography 1945-1969*, Leiden 1971; id., «Bibliographia Gnostica, Supplement», *NT* 13 (1971-).

STRECKER, «Judenchristentum und Gnosis», *Altes Testament-Frühjudentum-Gnosis*, 1980, 261-282.

TARDIEU, M., «Principes de l'exégèse manichéenne du Nouveau Testament», *Les règles de l'interprétation*, Paris 1988, 123-145.

TRÖGER, K.W., «Gnosis und Judentum», *Altes Testament-Frühjudentum-Gnosis*, 1980, 155-168.

VAN UNNIK, W.C., «Die jüdische Komponente in der Entstehung der Gnosis», *Gnosis und Gnostizismus*, ed. K. Rudolph, Darmstadt 1975, 476-494.

WILSON, R.MCL., *Gnosis and the New Testament*, Oxford 1968.

YAMAUCHI, E.M., *Pre-Christian Gnosticism: A Survey of the Proposed Evidences*, Grand Rapids MI 1973.

V.   EXEGESIS BETWEEN THE THIRD AND FIFTH CENTURIES. THE HERMENEUTIC PROBLEM OF BIBLICAL INTERPRETATION

Justin and Irenaeus made it possible for Christians to continue using the OT and knew it had to be esteemed even at the cost of Christianising it. Irenaeus also put great value on the authority of tradition and the Church for the interpretation of Scriptures. It is not yet full appreciated the freedom and the use of reason there was in the interpretation of Scripture during this initial period. This was to be the task of the Alexandrian and Antioch schools after the 3rd cent. *With the «problem of OT hermeneutics» resolved*, the problem posed by the OT itself, it was now more pressing *to resolve the «hermeneutic problem of biblical interpretation»* of the OT and NT. In resolving this problem, hermeneutics - Greek, Jewish or Christian - moved continually between the tendency to allegory and the inclination for the literal meaning.

I.   *History*

A.   THE ALEXANDRIAN SCHOOL: CLEMENT AND ORIGEN

Evidently, it is not possible to talk of an Alexandrian school as if it were an established institution or an organised group. Pantaenus, the school founder, Origen and Clement simply have in common an education in the same rich, cultural circle of Alexandria and follow the same line of interpretation of Scripture.

The precursor of the Christian School of Alexandria was *Philo* the Jew, who rejected the literal and obvious meaning of Scripture in cases where there were expressions unworthy of the divinity, or historical inaccuracies or any other difficulties. In such cases it was necessary to resort to the allegorical meaning and leave open the possibility of an interpretation allowing the many senses the text had. Philo's exegetical method, then, was basically apologetic: a correct interpretation of the Jewish Scriptures made them not unworthy of Greek philosophy. The allegorical method, Greek in origin, had its natural and original field of application in the interpretation of the Homeric myths. It was perfect for reconciling an ancient classical tradition, whether Homeric myth or antiquated biblical legislation, to a new situation and a new mentality.

Naturally, Christians used this process to interpret the «*Old* Testament» as well as for the interpretation of difficult and obscure passages from the gospels, such as the parables of Jesus. Some parables went through a whole process of allegory which, for example, allows a message of a parable originally aimed at the scribes opposed to Jesus to be applied to a new audience comprising Christian believers (J. Jeremias). Paul, who always has elements in common with Philo, uses the allegorical method when speaking of leaven as an image of impurity (1 Cor 10:4), or the rock of Moses as a spiritual rock which accompanies the Israelites. The allegorical view of the OT is explicit in Gal 4:21-3, when Paul expressly states that the text alluded to (Gn 16) has to be interpreted allegorically: the sons of Sarah and Hagar, Isaac and Ishmael respectively, represent those believing in Christ who inherit the salvation of the Israelites when they refuse to believe in him. Allegory has special emphasis in Heb which sets ups typological oppositions, such as Melchizedek-Christ.

Philonian allegory was basically vertical or anagogic: the literal meaning refers to the moral content and the worldly reality refers to heavenly. Christianity unfolded the temporal dimension of allegory: this becomes typology, considering everything connected with the OT as prefiguring the New Covenant.

Clement of Alexandria (c. 150-c. 215) used the allegorical method for a Christocentric interpretation of the OT as other Christian writers had done previously. Scripture as a whole, each one of its words and even each written sign speaks a mysterious language which has to be uncovered and is made up of symbols, allegories and metaphors. Scripture has therefore a whole range of meanings of every kind: literal and historical, moral and theological, prophetic and typological, philosophical and psychological and finally a mysterious meaning. The philosophical meaning is an inheritance from the Stoics. According to this meaning the tablets of the Law symbolise the universe, just as Sarah and Hagar symbolise true wisdom and pagan philosophy respectively. According to the mystic meaning, Lot's wife is a symbol of the attachment to earthly things which prevent the soul knowing the truth (Mortley).

Origen (c. 185-c. 254) is the chief representative of the thought and exegesis of the Alexandrian school. In Origen's view, Scripture sets out to reveal intellectual truths rather than narrate God's series of interventions in the course of history. Sometimes history does no more than hide the truth. Many biblical stories seem unbelievable, such as those about the first three days of creation, when the sun and the moon did not yet exist, or about a God who plants a garden and walks in it, about Cain who runs away from God's «face», etc. Similarly, it is not possible to take most OT legislation literally.

Origen rejected the literal meaning of the OT on the principle of rationality. The literal meaning is the one seized by more simple believers who are incapable of appreciating the meaning of metaphors, symbols and allegories, believing instead in the raw realism of the more improbable biblical stories.

For Origen, not all Scripture passages have a literal meaning; however, they all have a spiritual meaning, the only one which allows the mystery contained in Scripture to be perceived.

Origen did not set out precise rules of interpretation. He trusted in an exegete's intellectual ability and common sense more than in conventional opinion and popular tradition. He does not seem to be so inclined as Irenaeus and the Western Church in general to apply what would later be called the «rule of faith» as an exegetical maxim. Origen declares that without the allegorical method it is easy to make countless mistakes in interpretation. Deprived of strict controls, however, the allegorical method can lead to conclusions far removed from more sensible reason and from mere orthodoxy. One need only mention that the Gnostics were the most ardent followers of the allegorical method.

Against the criticism of Celsius or, later, of Porphyry, who condemned the immorality of countless minutiae in the Scriptures, or accused believers of believing without accounting for their faith, Origen tried to salvage the principle of rationality of faith and gain the intellectual respect of those pagan writers. It must be acknowledged that the critical and rational intention that inspired Origen is more decisive than the tool he used - the allegorical method - which was prone to great misrepresentation and misunderstandings. For Origen, the three meanings of the Scriptures (literal, moral and spiritual) correspond to the division of the real world into body, soul and spirit, and in turn correspond to interpretation in three stages: grammatico-historical, physical and allegorical. In practice, everything is reduced to the principle of opposition between the letter and the spirit, already to be found in Paul (2 Cor 3:6) (De Lubac, Daniélou, Hanson, Trigg).

B.   THE ANTIOCH SCHOOL: THEODORE OF MOPSUESTIA

Whenever Judaism has affected intellectual movements in the Christian Church, that influence has been transformed into a return by Christian exegesis to the literal and historical meaning of Scripture. The school of exegesis with the Syrian city of Antioch as its centre is a good example of that. The commentaries by Theophilus, the strict monotheism of Paul of Samosdata, the Greek recension of the OT attributed to Lucian, Dorothea's school of catechesis and the exegesis of Theodore of Mopsuestia (c. 350-428/29) are very largely patterned on Jewish teachers and models.

The Jewish community of this city was very influential, as it had been in the past. The Antiochenes were opposed to allegorical exegesis as developed by Philo and the Christians of Alexandria. Instead, they laid emphasis on the historical nature of biblical revelation which ought not to be broken up into symbols and allegories. The intellectual temperament of the Antiochenes was more Aristotelian than Platonic.

According to Antiochene exegesis. the biblical prophecies had a *twofold meaning*: *at once historical and messianic*. The Christocentric meaning of the prophecies was in the text, not something imposed on it through allegorical exegesis. *Theodore of Mopsuestia* classified some biblical prophecies as having a pure historical meaning and others which only had a messianic meaning. According to Theodore, Psalms 2, 8, 45 and 110 were marked by this messianic meaning. On the other hand, Ps 22 (21 in the LXX) only has an historical meaning; the messianic meaning is accidental. To anyone who argued from the title under which this psalm appears in the Greek version, «To the end» (*eis tò télos*) and points to a messianic interpretation, Theodore could answer, with sound critical sense, that the superscriptions of many psalms are not authentic.

According to Theodore of Mopsuestia, books containing no prophetic elements, either historical or messianic, and so with no more support than mere human wisdom, ought to be removed from the canon since they are not inspired books. In his view, this applies to the book of Job or to Chronicles, Ezra and Nehemiah. The same can be said of Song of Songs which neither Jews nor Christians used in their liturgy and Theodore compared to Pláto's *Symposium*. The cost of Theodore of Mopsuestia denying the inspired and canonical nature of these books was the order by the Second Council of Constantinople (553 CE) to burn his exegetical writings.

Thus the Antiochenes Diodorus of Tarsus (c. 330-c. 390), Theodore of Mopsuestia and John Chrysostom (c. 347-417) defended the literal and philological interpretation within the framework of salvation history. Of these, John Chrysostom, whose interpretations were one of the main sources of the *catenae*, became the one who made the exegesis of Antioch most widely known (Schäublin, Zaharopoulos).

C.   THE EXEGESIS OF THE CAPPADOCIANS

In the closing decades of the 4th cent., Cappadocia enjoyed a period of glory with three outstanding personalities. The exegesis of Basil (c. 330-379) is exclusively homiletic. Although revering Origen, his exegesis is more literal (Philokalia and Homilies on the Hexameron). Gregory of Nyssa (c. 329-c. 394) was a mystic, seeing a spiritual and moral meaning within the literal. He allegorises in *On the titles of the Psalms*, *Commentary on the Song of Songs* and *Life of Moses*. The last of these personalities was Gregory of Nazianzus. (c. 329-c. 389/390).

D.   EXEGESIS IN THE WEST: JEROME AND AUGUSTINE

The history of Western exegesis reflects the same comings and goings between East and West as in the history of the formation of the canon (cf. p. 233), of the transmission of the text and of translations into Latin (cf. pp. 349-357). The interrelationship of canon, text and exegesis is the key to understanding their history as a whole.

The Western Church, instead, concerned chiefly with practical theology and its legal organisation left little space to discussion of hermeneutical problems. The setting up of the canon of Scripture and of a rule of faith (*regula fidei*) as expressed in the Trinitarian creed and the financing of apostolic ministry of bishops entrusted with ensuring the orthodox of doctrine, led increasingly to a greater development of dogma, putting exegetical and hermeneutic problems into the background.

With Hippolytus of Rome (c. 170-c. 235), exegesis began to free itself from the shackles of debate and become more independent, and resulted in exegesis to a complete biblical book or to large parts of such a book (*Commentary on Daniel*, *Commentary on Song of Songs*). After Hippolytus, Christian writers were already using Latin in the West. Novatian contrasts the literalism of Jewish interpretation of the Law with spiritual interpretation, especially of certain dietary rules (*De cibis Iudaicis*). Cyprian (c. 200-c. 258) has transmitted collections of *Testimonia* in his *Testimonia ad Quirinum* and homilies commenting on biblical topics in a moralising or polemic way (*De centesima*, and *De montibus Sina et Sion*). Until the close of the 3rd cent., specifically exegetical works begin to appear, notably those by Victorinus of Pettau (*Commentary on the Apocalypse* and *De fabrica mundi*) and Reticius of Atun (*Commentary on Song of Songs*). The exegesis of these two writers has Asiatic elements such as millenarism and materialism and does not seem to have been influenced by Origen. The African Donatist Tyconius was the first to write a treatise on biblical hermeneutics, the *Liber regularum*, although it is not so general and systematic as the earlier work by Origen or the later one by Augustine. It simply sets out to provide keys for determining the hidden meaning of the text, a meaning which is always allegorical.

Ambrose promoted allegorical interpretation which emphasised the hidden meaning of the biblical text and so favouring the loss of interest in philological study of the Scriptures.

Even *Jerome*, closest to Antiochene exegesis and more inclined to endorse literal interpretation, was convinced that this led to heresy, so that the Christian interpreter had to delve into the true meaning of the biblical texts hidden behind the letters.

Jerome, straddling both East and West, changed from allegorical exegesis to literal and historical interpretation. He is the best example of the kind of influence which Jewish hermeneutics could have on Christian exegesis. The rabbis with whom he kept in contact influenced his intellectual conversion, which involved a complete change of direction towards the Hebrew language and the Hebrew text of the bible, to Greek translations by Jews and towards rabbinic methods of interpretation.

For *Augustine of Hippo* (354-430) the literal and spiritual meaning are equally valid (*signum et res*). The *regula fidei* determines which of the two meanings, literal or figurative, dominates in each case. This resort to the *regula fidei* poses the problem concerning the kind of relationships between biblical hermeneutics and dogma. Any progress of hermeneutics with respect to dogma results in a contradiction.

Just as reading of the Bible must come before any commentary on it, actual reading of patristic texts is more revealing than any introduction to them. A selection of texts which cannot be set out here is provided for reading.

1. *Irenaeus of Lyons, Adversus haereses*, III, Preface 1:1-4:2. In dispute with the 2nd

cent. Gnostics, Irenaeus insists on the apostolic nature of the NT writings and the public character of Church tradition transmitted from apostolic times (Irénée de Lyon, *Contre les Hérésies*, livre III, ed. F. Sagnard, Sources chrétiennes 34, Paris 1952, 94-118). Similarly, cf. Irenaeus, *Adversus haereses*, IV 26:1-4 (Irénée de Lyon, *Contre les Hérésies*, livre IV, ed. A. Rousseau, Sources chrétiennes 100, Paris 1965, 713-727)

2. *Tertullian, De Corona* 1-4. Tertullian emphasises the importance of oral tradition for resolving matters not dealt with in Scripture. He singles out especially the problem posed by interpreting the tradition received through the channel of written transmission (Corpus Christianorum. Series Latina 2, Turnholti 1954, 1039-45).

3. *Origen, On first principles* IV, 1:1-7; 2:1-9; 3:1-15. He sets out the allegorical method of interpretation, typical of the Alexandrian School (Origène, *Traité des principes*, Tome III (livres III et IV), eds., H. Crouzel-M. Simonetti, Sources chrétiennes 268, 256-399; similarly, GCS 22, 305-23).

4. *Dionysius of Alexandria, On Promises*, a work preserved by Eusebius of Caesarea in his *Church History* VII 24-25. Dionysius, bishop of Alexandria and shortly later than Origen, argues against those trying to draw millenarist conclusions from the Apocalypse. He shows great critical sense in the matter of authorship of the writings which make up the Johannine corpus (*Eusebius Werke* II: *Die Kirchengeschichte*, ed. E. Schwarz, GCS 9, Leipzig 1903, 684- 700).

5. *Theodore of Mopsuestia, Commentary on the Galatians* 4:22-31. Theodore provides a sample of Antiochene exegesis which is not so literal as commonly thought. In fact, it is strongly opposed to any form of spiritual interpretation which involves denying the historical meaning of the text (Theodore of Mopsuestia, *Commentary on the Epistles of St. Paul. Latin Version with Greek Fragments I*, ed. H. B. Swete, Cambridge 1880, reprinted in 1969).

6. *Augustine of Hippo, On Christian doctrine* II, i,1-v,9. Augustine discusses how ambiguities in the biblical text have to be interpreted in connecting biblical interpretation and Christian doctrine (*De Doctrina christiana*, Aurelii Augustini Opera Pars IV, 1, Corpus Christianorum. Series Latina 32, Turnholti 1962, 77-83).

7. *Ptolemy, Letter to Flora*. Passages concerning method of interpretation (3:8), insertions in the OT (4:1-4), Moses' additions (4:4-11), the Mishnah in the OT (4:11ff.) and the three elements of divine law (5:1-3) can be singled out (*Ptolemée: Lettre à Flora*, ed. G. Quispel, Sources chrétiennes, n. 24 bis, Paris 1966, 50-61).

8. *Diodorus of Tarsus, Commentary on the Psalms*, Prologue (*Diodori Tarsensis Commentarii in Psalmos. I. Commentarii in Psalmos I-L*, ed. J.-M. Olivier, Corpus Christianorum, Series Graeca VI, Turnholti 1980).

9. *Tyconius, Liber regularum*, 1-111. Tyconius sets out seven rules of interpretation (Tyconius, The Book of Rules of Tyconius, ed. F. C. Burkitt, Texts and Studies III,1, Cambridge 1894, 1-31).

2.   *Theological Developments: Between the Literal and the Allegorical*

Like Philo before them, the Fathers and theologians of the Church were obliged to fight on two fronts simultaneously: against exaggerated allegorism and against those opposed to allegory.

Extreme allegorism was what the Gnostics practised. By exaggerating the allegorical interpretation of the NT, they went so far as to deny the historical truth of the birth, life, crucifixion and resurrection of Jesus. The history of the gospels was made into pure allegory, just as the commandments of the law only had an allegorical meaning for the allegorists of Judaism.

The literalism against which the Fathers had to fight only affected some aspects of Scripture. Origen (*De Princ.* 4,2,1(8); Daniélou, *Origène*, 147-149) describes three classes of literalists: the Jews, who refused to interpret certain OT passages allegorically as prophecies on the coming of the Messiah; the Gnostics, who interpret literally the anthropomorphisms and anthropopathisms of the OT in order to emphasise to what extent the OT God is a lesser and evil god, and lastly, «simple» Christians, with no philosophical education, who envisage the God of the OT in the literal sense of the anthropomorphic expressions of the OT.

Therefore, both for Philo and for the Fathers of Christianity, some OT passages have to be interpreted only in an allegorical way, others only in the literal sense and others again in both the literal and the allegorical sense. The two types of interpretation alternate, with no precise rules. The danger to be aware of in every case was that of «wild» exegesis: anyone could claim to have received a divine revelation and, without the control of any exegetical rule whatever, could seize on any suitable interpretation of the text. St. Augustine was yet to face this kind of tendency (*De doctrina christiana, Prologus* 8).

Writers educated in Asia minor felt the tension between these two opposing tendencies even more acutely. On the one hand, the need to read the OT in Christological mode, contrary to the Jews and Gnostics, pushed them towards allegory. On the other hand, their historical, and at bottom even materialistic temperament, and the need to counteract the exaggerated allegorism of the Gnostics led them towards the letter of the text.

It cannot be said that Christians of Jewish origin preferred to use literal interpretation and Christians of pagan origin, allegorical. Both appear to be used in Jewish-Christian texts.

The actual setting of the interpretation of Scripture could determine or affect the kind of interpretation used. The two most common occasions were the homily, which tended to use allegory more, and commentary on texts, which favoured the literal meaning (not always though).

The homily could be on a specific biblical book or on the readings from the Christian lectionary. Here can be noted Origen's homilies on Numbers, Joshua and Jeremiah among other biblical books, the *Enarrationes* of Augustine on the Psalms, and the homilies of John Chrysostom on Genesis and of Gregory the Great on Ezekiel. In this homiletic literature «spiritual» exegesis is paramount. The biblical books are used as an *arsenal* for the moral edification of believers.

Commentaries on classical Greek texts were already well developed in the 1st century, especially in Alexandria. Philo was able, perhaps, to use existing commentaries. The oldest commentaries on the OT to reach us are all by Christian writers. We have the complete text of a commentary on the Song of Songs by Origen. The most prominent writers of commentaries among the Alexandrians were Didymus the Blind and Cyril of Alexandria and among the Syrians, Eusebius of Emesa, Apollinarus of Laodicaea, Theodore of Mopsuestia and Theodore of Cyrus (Guinot). Among the Latin commentators, Hilary of Poitiers stands out, as do Ambrosiaster, Jerome and Augustine. The proliferation of commentaries led to the formation of *Catenae* or extracts from the commentaries of various writers, arranged according to theme or biblical passage. Catechesis also provided a suitable setting for the practice of biblical interpretation.

When establishing a criterion to determine whether a passage has to be interpreted literally or not, the *regula fidei* (rule of faith) was used, together with a principle from reason: biblical passages which are totally contrary to reason are not to be interpreted literally. The rule of faith was the criterion of interpretation both for Scripture, the source of which is revelation, and for philosophy, based on reason. Philo and the Christian Fathers were aware of the idea of the subordination of philosophy to Scripture, symbolised allegorically by Hagar, the maidservant and Sarah, the mistress.

The differences between Philo and the Fathers are due to the different religious situations in Judaism and in Christianity. Among the Jews, there were apostates but no heretics. Among the Christians, there arose so many heresies that to get rid of them some people even considered it necessary to do away with philosophy, as it encouraged them.

Starting from the principle of the subordination of philosophy to Scripture, the Christian Fathers move between two trends: for some, pure faith in the doctrine of Scripture was enough and any resort to philosophy meant reduction in the value of scripture. For others, faith had more value if it was a rational faith and was able to account for itself (Simonetti).

VI. CLASSICAL CULTURE AND THE CHRISTIAN BIBLE

Besides the hermeneutic problem of accepting the OT by interpreting it afresh, Christianity also had to face the problem of *accepting Classical culture*. In line with its universalism Christianity tried to direct its message to the pagan world, without expecting it to forego completely its cultural and religious heritage.

1.   *Classical Education and Christian Education*

The synthesis made by Christianity of its double legacy - from the OT and from the Greeks and Romans - had its antecedents in the symbiosis between Judaism and Hellenism over the three centuries before Christianity appeared. Judaism then asked itself the questions posed by unavoidable contact with Greek culture, clearing the path later to be trodden by Christianity. In Alexandria, the translation of the LXX comprised the first attempt of fertilisation between the Hebrew Bible and Greek culture. In the intellectual climate of Alexandria, imbued first with Stoicism and then Neo-Platonism, Clement of Alexandria and Origen developed Christian thought in dialogue with the ancient culture.

The synthesis of Christianity and classical culture was in many ways the culmination of a cultural syncretism already quite widespread in the Greek and Roman world at the time that Christianity was expanding. This syncretism was most evident in the worship given to abstractions such as Concord and Peace, or to deterministic forces such as *Týkhē* and *Anágkē*.

The Christians did not create their own system of primary schools. Future pagan philosophers and future Christian bishops shared the same classrooms in their childhood. The fact that Christians were not particularly interested in creating their own educational network shows that they also had no great interest in moving away from the cultural legacy of Greece and Rome. Christian education depended principally on formation in the home, catechetical instruction and sermons in the churches.

Some Fathers, such as Jerome and Augustine, reacted against the pagan education they had received and adopted a reserved stance towards classical *paideia*. Others, instead, such as Justin, Athenagoras, Clement of Alexandria, Origen and Lactantius, were able to appreciate the legacy of the classical education they had received. The greatest enthusiasts for their classical education were Athanasius, Basil and Ambrose.

Too much emphasis on the values of a classical education could have a negative effect on other aspects of Christian culture. Ambrose, for instance, insisted in the need to learn Greek, but his complete ignorance of Hebrew and of the Jewish exegetical tradition did not worry him in the slightest. Only a few Christian writers, such as Origen and Jerome, tried to broaden their classical education and made a serious effort to gain a knowledge of Hebrew exegesis and perhaps even of Hebrew. Augustine, who hardly knew Greek, was disgusted with himself at being unable to answer the questions posed by Jerome who always relied on Hebrew sources.

Little by little and imperceptibly the Christian world ended up being split into two separate worlds: the East, with Greek and the West, with Hebrew. If they overlapped at all it was in completely forgetting Hebrew and the Jewish exegetical tradition.

A classical education could impede conversion to Christianity, for many of those educated in classical culture noticed with distaste the lack of elegance and style in the Jewish and Christian scriptures. Sinesius declared that he was prepared to be consecrated a bishop but on condition that he could continue philosophising in private, even though he would mythologise in public (Momigliano).

Literature which is not apologetic in character emphasises the mutual respect which pagan and Christian intellectuals had for each other. In his work *De viris illustribus*, Jerome gives a panegyric of both Christian and pagan writers. Similarly, Sulpicius Severus quotes Christian and pagan historians alike

To have adopted the radical approach of cultural terrorism and iconoclasm against pagan idols would have meant taking on the power of the Empire and the deified Emperor, and that would only have led to persecution and martyrdom. At the precise moment when the new faith had won over the Empire that the need for a compromise with pagan philosophy became more urgent, there was an attempt at mediating between biblical tradition and classical tradition. During the decline of the Empire, when the idea of religious universalism had also affected the pagan world, *Macrobius* established the corpus of books containing the revelation of all divine and human mysteries (400-420 CE). Macrobius' corpus included the works of Homer, Plato, Cicero and Virgil, so putting Latin writers on a par with Greek. Macrobius also revived the motif of poet-prophet, making the leading writers of the ancient world into inspired mediators who transmit the secrets of the divinity. A Christian contemporary of Macrobius, i.e. *Augustine* (354-430 CE), wrote the treatise *De doctrina christiana* (c. 427), into which he inserted the corpus of the great writers of antiquity, proposed by Macrobius, after the corpus of Christian Scripture. In this way, Virgil came to be accepted as a pagan prophet of the Christian Messiah.

However, it was not enough to have accepted the educational value of classicism as a second *Praeparatio evangelica*, on a par with the OT. It was also necessary to grant pedagogical value to the «liberal arts» of the pagans in the academic formation of a new Christian *intelligentsia*, with eyes fixed on the goal of a new Christian classicism. As models for a new Christian stylistic, Augustine used the pagans Cicero and Quintilian, the prophet Amos and the apostle Paul indiscriminately. His *De doctrina christiana* opened the way to a Christian encyclopedism, anticipating the mediaeval encyclopedism of Isidore of Seville, Rabano Mauro and others.

In the first centuries of Christianity, the attitudes of resistance against the Greek and Roman pagan world co-existed with acceptance of it. As late as 398, the 4th Council of Carthage forbade bishops to read books by pagans. However, this attitude did not prevail. In spite of the anti-intellectual movements active in Mediaeval Christianity, mediaeval culture helped to save ancient culture from oblivion and barbarism and was itself a continuation of ancient culture. Monotheism and the claim of religious universalism assumed a truly universal monotheism which required a fusion of biblical culture and classical culture.

Clement of Alexandria, Origen, Jerome and Augustine created a religion of learned men alongside the religion of the humble. According to a Muslim saying, the ink of learned men is more precious than the blood of martyrs. Christianity had many martyrs but would not have become a universal religion if several generations of savants had not succeeded the first generations of martyrs.

2.   *Greek Philosophy and the Christian Scriptures*

The Greeks were aware of their capacity for reasoning and were disgusted when they realised what irrational or foreign forces tried to dictate to them how they had to think or behave. It is equally true, however, that the Greek soul also harboured a mystical and even anti-rationalist tendency (Dodds). The meeting of Christianity and the Greek world, of the Christian Bible and Greek philosophy took place at this twofold level of reason and unreason.

Jaeger could say that Greek philosophy did not have a direct influence on the NT but only on subsequent generations. Today it is more accepted, however, that Paul knew the philosophical traditions of his time at first hand and not only through other Jews. He never stopped using them, although he was to reject pagan religion directly and use pagan philosophy with considerable reserve. The Christian Fathers also rejected pagan religion both in the early period of persecution and when they were able to change from persecuted to persecutors. However, as regards pagan philosophy, the Fathers soon changed their attitude. The first apologists tried to present the new religion as a doctrine which not only opposed pagan philosophy but was in fact the true philosophy.

An important element in this *change of attitude* was the conversion to Christianity of pagans with an education in Greek and Roman philosophy, from Aristides (131-161) to Clement of Alexandria (c. 185-211/15). Another important factor was the need to confront the criticisms of philosophers using the same weapons as them. Philosophy also proved to be very useful for confronting Gnostic heresies.

The Fathers tried to *harmonise Scriptures and philosophy*, aware of the opposition between them. They condemned the errors of many philosophical doctrines and drew attention to the disagreement among philosophers, clear proof of the futility of philosophy as an approach to truth. Scripture is divine in origin so that in it there cannot be more than the truth; philosophy is human in origin and is therefore a mix of truth and error.

In the eyes of the Greeks and also of many Jews, Christians could only appear to be terribly ignorant and very arrogant with it. Christians were ignorant of classical philosophy but came close to the Jews, having mastered the «*Old* Testament». But it is no less true that many Christians such as Clement of Alexandria, Origen, Jerome and Augustine considered that, besides the gifts of religious piety, a Christian should have secular knowledge of languages, history, philosophy, etc., of the time.

Christians debated between *two tendencies*. The first, represented by Irenaeus, feared that the availability of arguments from reason to settle matters not dealt with in Scripture would open the door to every kind of heresy. On the other hand, the movement represented by Origen, Gregory of Nazianzus, Cyril of Jerusalem and Basil considered it justified and necessary to reply with the means of reason to all the questions not resolved in Scripture or which remained obscure. The revelation contained in Scripture was teeming with mysteries and difficulties and sometimes even mistakes and inconsistencies. To this can be added the incorrectness of biblical language and its lack of elegance. On the other hand, the lack of precise demarcation between canonical and apocryphal could only feed the growth of new heresies.

Thus Greek philosophy, badly assimilated, and Scripture, badly understood were two continual sources of misunderstandings and new heresies. It is not surprising that Hippolytus, in his work *Philosophoúmena*, connects Greek philosophy with no fewer than 33 different heretical schools: Simon the Magician depends on Heraclitus, Valentine on Pythagoras and Plato, Basilides on Aristotle, Marcion on Empedocles, and so on.

The great challenges which Christianity had to face did not come from the more or less unorthodox movements that arose within it but from the philosophy of the Greeks. In particular, the challenges came from a cosmology opposed to the biblical doctrine of creation and providence, and an ethics which disputed territory with the biblical message of salvation. The theology of the Greeks, however, did not provide serious opposition to biblical theology but continued to provide the basic concepts used by Christian theology, leaving its mark of Platonism and Aristotelianism.

1. Plato coined the neologism «*theology*» to refer to the gods of traditional mythology. While the poets were concerned with the stories about the gods, scholars were busy in observing the movements of the stars, but did not take into consideration deities such as the gods of Olympus.

With Aristotle, theology became study of the cosmos, of immovable and immaterial causes and of the stars visible in the sky. In this way, academic theology brought a principle of reasoning into the world of the sacred universe and incorporated mythology or mythical theology within a global conception of the universe as that of a great Being.

The spread of Stoicism in the 2nd cent. BCE brought with it new ways of thinking. The divine *logos* now guaranteed the unity and divinity of the universe. Stoic philosophy developed astro-biology and also revived the theology of traditional religion, interpreting its gods as allegorical personifications of the forces of nature. The *ouranopolis*, the celestial city, was the common fatherland in which, supposedly, all men were equal, from emperor to slave. With Stoicism, the ethic of the ancient world reached it highest and most noble peak, an ethic which eventually formed part of Christian ethic or became its rival.

In the first half of the 3rd cent. CE, Neo-Platonism developed in Alexandria, represented chiefly by Plotinus (204-270 CE). According to Neo-Platonic doctrines, reality proceeds from the One, ineffable and absolute, and tends to reunite with him through ecstasy. Matter and intellect are only provisional supports in this ascent on the path of return to the divine origin; by a series of denials, the soul rises to the One. Neo-Platonism influenced Origen (185-254 CE), a contemporary of Plotinus and other Christian writers. To the perfection of moral life the wise Christian united perfection of theological knowledge, thus becoming a true «Gnostic».

2. At first, *Greek Cosmology* made no distinction between the origin and being of the gods and the origin and nature of the universe. Increasing rationalisation led the Greeks to develop cosmologies which were less and less animistic. For *Plato*'s Academy, the only way to resolve the aporia between the continuous flux of Heraclitus' Logos and the fixed permanence of Parmenides' Being was to accept a dualist cosmology: Being, the world without senses which opposes Non-Being, the material world. *Aristoteles* modified the cosmological concept of his teacher, not accepting the separate existence of Platonic Forms. Reality according to Aristotle only exists in objects of the senses as a combination of matter and form.

Later, the *Stoics* developed a cosmological system marked by materialistic pantheism: the world is a necessary condition for the divine to exist. Reason, for the Stoics, is not an epistemological tool, but the determinist or providential substance of the cosmos which relates and orders all the things in it. *Epicureanism* provides an atomistic conception of the cosmos, changed into an immense machine composed of innumerable interchangeable «seeds», the combinations of which explain the diversity and temporary nature of the universe. This mechanistic conception, typical of deterministic materialism, threatened the pagan gods and Christian Providence alike.

3. To these four cosmological systems correspond an equal number of conceptions of *ethics*. In his early writings, *Plato* followed the doctrine of his teacher, Socrates: virtue runs in tandem with knowledge and thus, moral evil is basically an error, an epistemological mistake. Later Plato developed a more pessimistic vision, in which man, in order to become similar to God, has to abandon earthly existence by means of contemplation. After death, the soul returns to its original purity which it enjoyed in a pre-existence. *Aristotle* shows greater confidence in human reason, capable of recognising what moral virtue consists of: the correct medium between two extreme ways of behaving. Man has to find the middle road, living wisely and sensibly.

Stoic cosmology equated divine reason with nature. As a result, man had the moral obligation to comply rationally and even cooperate in this fatalistic ordering of the universe. The *Epicureans* trusted only in sensation. Pleasure, which is only intellectual pleasure, is the channel of happiness of freedom from passion (*ataraxía*), and calm in the face of the anxiety caused by the superstitious fear of the gods and of death.

Of the philosophical systems developed by the Greeks, only two were susceptible to religious development of some kind: *Pythagorism*, with its idea of purification through the renunciation of earthly things and the practice of asceticism, and *Neoplatonism*, advocating an intellectual discipline whose ultimate aim was access to the divine world. These two systems remained faithful to the ideals of Greek rationalism and resistant to every Gnostic temptation. They could also easily lead to a kind of religious Shamanism.

Platonism was the more attractive form of thought for Christianity, but it did not therefore cease to instigate currents of thought considered unorthodox. Clement and Origen were the Christian thinkers who contributed most to making Plato the intellectual catalyst between Christianity and pagan classicism. Accepting the Platonic principle that knowledge is virtue and virtue knowledge, Clement and Origen became in some sense Christian Gnostics. Men of faith and thinkers in equal measure, they considered that a union with God entailed not only faith but a knowledge of the divine and of the mysteries of the universe. Origen considered himself more a doctor of Christianity than a presbyter of the Church. With Middle Platonism and Neoplatonism, Platonic philosophy became more mystical and religious, increasing even further its attraction to Christian thinkers.

The influence of *Stoicism* is evident in Christian writers such as Minucio Felix, Cyprian, Novatian, Gregory of Nyssa, Ambrose, etc. However, as Tertullian had already noted, Stoicism could also generate unorthodox movements, as well illustrated by the journey travelled by Pelagius. In some sense it can be said that with the passage of time, Stoic morality was super-imposed on the ideals of the Sermon on the Mount, leaving to them the utopian character which is their own.

The influence of *Aristotelianism* made itself felt in Christianity by the force of its logical capacity, emphasised particularly in the field of scientific methodology. The apologist Aristides used the Aristotelian argument of the movement to prove the existence of God, as would be done much later in the Middle Ages. However, the secular and scientific vision characteristic of Aristotelian thought could provide food for heresies and agnosticism, as happened with the Artemonites. Aristotle made happiness depend on physical well-being and external circumstances more than to the fulfilment of God's law and the doctrine of a provident God and retribution in life eternal. Until Thomas Aquinas, Christianity did not fully integrate Aristotelian thought into Christianity.

In the eagerness to make Greek philosophy compatible with the new biblical and Christian message, two lines of reasoning were used. Following a type of reasoning set in motion by Hellenistic Judaism, Christians could say that Homer and the Greek philosophers had made use of the OT sources which had now become Christian. In this way, an attempt was made to reply to the accusations levelled by pagan authors in the sense that Christian thought was nothing but plagiarism of classical sources. Another line of reasoning consisted in stating that Greek poets and philosophers had fulfilled the role of forerunners to Christian Revelation in the manner of OT prophets. This second view, more prepared to accept the value of the classics and the philosophers, played a very important role in the development of Western culture inasmuch as it allowed the fusion of Greek and Latin culture with Jewish and Christian culture.

By taking over the tradition of rational thought of the classics, Christianity also absorbed *the mystical experience of the Greek* of Platonic origin. This consisted in the initiation of the devotee in a process of identifying himself with the divinity. Mystical experience is of paramount importance in Jewish and Christian tradition, with its clearest manifestation the flourishing of Christian monks in Egypt and Pontus. In spite of the efforts of Christianity to absorb the rationality of the Greeks, to pagan eyes, even the less educated, the first Christians could appear more like credulous simpletons than as reasoning believers. In the early period and for many centuries it was not easy for Christianity to control fatalism, astrology, excessive asceticism, exaggerated belief in miracles, possessions by the devil, belief in dreams, etc.

The Christians used *Greek reason to explain the inconsistencies of the Scriptures*. They resorted to two types of explanation. The one used most, developed principally by Origen, consisted in accepting that far from restricting oneself to the letter of the text it was necessary to try and reach the deep mysteries hidden behind the letters. These truths are more worthy of God and the sacred, than what can be understood from the plain and obvious meaning of the texts. The second type of explanation states that the difficulty of Scripture was intentional: its aim was to obfuscate the minds of non-believers so that seeing they would not notice and hearing they would not listen. While it is true that Scripture could give rise to all sorts of heresies, it was just as true that Scripture denounced those same heretics who, like Marcion or Valentine, misunderstood it.

Origen boasted to Celsus that Christians had enough critical sense not to accept blindly what the texts appeared to say. The ordinary believer felt particularly bewildered by the existence of mistakes and variants in the sacred text and even more perplexed, if possible, by the corrections suggested by scholars. But the thorniest problem by far was to find the meaning of the texts. To give a rational solution to the problems posed by the difficulty of the texts, one had to resort to allegorical and typological explanation.

In cases where it was not possible to find a suitable reply in Scripture to a particular question, one turned to tradition, as Augustine had done, for example, to justify the custom of baptising babies. The growth of tradition gave theologians the chance to become active in the process of revelation. However, the fact that as yet there was no precise theological terminology accepted by everyone caused great confusion and presented further difficulty when deciding what the limits were between the orthodox and the unorthodox. Philosophical terms such as *homoúsios*, *hypóstasis*, or *substance* allowed some problems to be solved, although this also created new ones.

The similarity between pagan myths and rites and Christian beliefs and worship increased still further the perplexity of many Christians. The cult of martyrs and saints, the new Christian heroes, helped deal polytheism a hard blow. Dialogue with polytheism was out of the question, but meeting with pagan philosophy was even pursued and aspired to. Lactantius could consider Greek philosophy as no more than a continual source of heresies and problems for the Church. He also considered that its contradictory nature invalidated its possible use for explaining and defending the Christian faith. However, most of the Fathers, following Justin and Clement, considered Greek philosophy to be the most brilliant product of the human spirit; the reason of philosophers allowed access to certain truths of Revelation and provided tools for research into the meaning of Scripture.

Justin identified Christ with the eternal Logos who inspired Moses and the prophets and by whom, in turn the Greek philosophers were inspired. For Justin, Greek philosophy, divided into self-contradictory schools, was not in a condition to fulfil its purpose of leading men to God. Justin adopts an idea of Posidonius Apamea (*Protrepticus*), who said philosophy had been granted to men in primeval times but later ended up corrupted in the different schools. For Justin, Christianity is that original philosophy now found anew. Christianity is not, therefore, one more philosophy nor even the best philosophy among the others. It is the *only* philosophy, the primeval and original philosophy, philosophy restored (Droge).

By the year 200 there was such a degree of symbiosis between Christianity and paganism that Tertullian could show his fear of Christianity dissolving into a mixture of Platonism, Stoicism and Aristotelianism, the philosophical koiné of that period.

ALLENBACH, J., et al. (eds.), *Biblia patristica: Index des citations et allusions bibliques dans la littérature patristique*, 4 vols., Paris 1975-.

BENOIT, A. - PRIGENT, P., *La Bible et les Pères. Colloque de Strasbourg (1er-3 octobre 1969)*, Paris 1971.

BIANCHI, U., (ed.), *Le origini dello gnosticismo. Colloquio di Messina*, Leiden 1967.

BURROWS M.S. - ROREM, P., (eds.), *Biblical Hermeneutics in Historical Perspective*, Grand Rapids MI 1992.

DANIÉLOU, J., *Origène. Le Génie du Christianisme*, Paris 1948.

DANIÉLOU, J., *Les origines du Christianisme latin*, Paris 1978.

DANIÉLOU, J., *Message évangelique et culture hellénistique aux IIe et IIIe siècles*, Tournai 1961.

DROGE, A.J., *Homer or Jesus? Early Christian Interpretations of the History of Culture*, Tübingen 1989.

FROEHLICH, K., *Biblical Interpretation in the Early Church*, Philadelphia PA 1984.

GRANT, R.M., with TRACY, D., *A Short History of the Interpretation of the Bible*, 2nd Revised and Enlarged Edition, Philadelphia PA 1984.

GUINOT, J -N., *L'exégèse de Théodoret de Cyr*, Paris 1995.

HAGNER, D.A., *The Use of the Old and New Testament in Clement of Rome*, Leiden 1973.

HANSON, R.P.C., *Allegory and Event. A Study of the Sources and Significance of Origen's Interpretation of Scripture*, London 1959.

HANSON, A.T., *The Living Utterances of God. The New Testament Exegesis of the Old*, London 1983.

HATCH, E., *The Influence of Greek Ideas on Christianity*, New York 1957.

HORSLEY, G.H.R., *New Documents Illustrating Early Christianity*, 5 vols., North Ryde, Australia, 1981-1989.

JAEGER, W., *Early Christianity and Greek Religion*, Cambridge MA 1961.

KNOX, J., *Marcion and the New Testament*, Chicago 1942.

MARGERIE, B. DE, *Introduction à l'histoire de l'Exégèse*, 3 vols. Paris 1980-1983.

MOMIGLIANO, A., *The Conflict of Paganism and Christianity in the Fourth Century*, Oxford 1963.

MORTLEY, R., *Connaissance religieuse et herméneutique chez Clément d'Alexandrie*, Leiden 1973.

PELIKAN, J., *The Christian Tradition. A History of the Development of Doctrine*, 1. *The Emergence of the Catholic Tradition (100-600)*, Chicago-London 1971.

PELIKAN, J., *Christianity and Classical Culture. The Metamorphosis of Natural Theology in the Christian Encounter with Hellenism*, New Haven-London 1993.

PRIGENT, P., *Justin et l'Ancien Testament*, Paris 1964.

QUASTEN, J., *Patrology*, 3 vols., Westminter MD 1950, 1953, 1960.

RAHNER, H., *Griechische Mythen in christlicher Deutung*, Darmstadt 1957².

SCHÄUBLIN, C., *Untersuchungen zur Methode und Herkunft der antiochenischen Exegese*, Bonn 1974.

SCHOEDEL, W.-R., *Ignatius of Antioch*, Philadelphia PA 1985.

SIMONETTI, M., *Biblical Interpretation in the Early Church. An Historical Introduction to Patristic Exegesis*, Edinburgh 1994.

TORRANCE, TH.F., *Divine Meaning. Studies in Patristic Hermeneutics*, Edinburgh 1995.

TRIGG, J.W., *Origen. The Bible and Philosophy in the Third-century Church*, London 1983.

WELTIN, E.G., *Athens and Jerusalem. An Interpretative Essay on Christianity and Classical Culture*, Atlanta GA 1987.

WOLFSON, H.A., *The Philosophy of the Church Fathers*, vol. 1. *Faith, Trinity, Incarnation*, Cambridge MA 1956.

ZAHAROPOULOS, D.Z., *Theodore of Mopsuestia on the Bible. A Study of his Old Testament Exegesis*, New York 1989.

Modern Hermeneutics

The Jewish and Christian hermeneutic of the Talmudic and Patristics period and of mediaeval times corresponds to a *«pre-modern»* concept of the world as a «sacred cosmos» (Mircea Eliade) or a «symbolic universe» (P. Berger - Th. Luckmann): the revelation of the sacred in the space and time of secular experience creates a symbolic world, a global system of meaning. The subject, man or woman, is and feels part of the objective world with no awareness at all of an opposition between subject and object. A system of myths and rites, a metaphysical theology and a liturgy made up of symbols, explain and celebrate at the same time the origin, the being, the final destiny and regular rhythm of this present life. Myth and reality, word and thing, merge completely and as yet they have not been separated and challenged. The Bible has both a literal and a spiritual meaning which together determine an infinity of meanings, hidden in each expression, each word and even each letter of Scripture.

«Modern» hermeneutic corresponds to a world in which the «I», the thinking subject, and the physical and mathematical universe replace the sacred cosmos as the focal point. Epistemology, the theory of knowledge, replaces myth and metaphysics, explaining not just objective reality but only how it is possible to know the objective world. This puts a gulf between the thinking subject and the object. Critical rationalism of the Enlightenment ends up questioning the God of theologians and philosophers and the critical history of Romanticism puts an interdict on texts in which the revelation of the Bible is expressed

«Post-Modern» or *«Post-Critical»* hermeneutic is marked by a certain disenchantment with enlightened *conscience* and some glimpses of re-enchantment with the *world*. Post-modernism does not reject the values of modernity, rational criticism and freedom from dogma, but it accepts that enlightened criticism is not free from prejudice and its pretensions to objectivity are often no more than wishful thinking. The post-modern world is not the world of the ancient sacred cosmos but neither is it its simple negation or its dissolving in the world of the subjective conscience. It is a world created by language, made manifest in dialogue with the «other». Understanding takes

place through prior anticipations, through pre-understanding and pre-judice, through the hermeneutic circle of questions and answers (Heidegger). Understanding is not a monologue with objectivity but a dialogue with the subjectivity of the «other» or with the «other» expressed in the texts transmitted by tradition. Without it being possible to return to the pre-critical world of tradition which has become dogma, contemporary hermeneutic wishes to recover the mediating force of tradition and even the symbolising and imaginative meaning of allegory. Unlike enlightened hermeneutic, Post-modern thinking shows respect for openness to the divine and the sacred and especially to symbolic and religious language in general, typical of the post-modern era.

In this process of re-evaluation of tradition and of the interpretation of symbols and allegories, without however abandoning enlightened criticism of the texts of historical and religious tradition, lies the viewpoint of this book. It does not try a direct approach, supposedly free of presuppositions and prejudices, to the biblical texts of over two thousand years ago, but instead tries to emphasise the mediating role of Jewish and Christian tradition and of post-modern hermeneutic based on the play between literal and allegorical, in every attempt at complete understanding of the texts of the Bible.

To know and be aware of the presuppositions with which we, from our modern but post-critical period, approach the study of the pre-modern texts of classical and biblical tradition, it is necessary to know the history of modern hermeneutic. It originated with biblical exegesis, broke with biblical tradition and today returns to question yet again the value and meaning of the myths, symbols and archetypes, and in particular, those transmitted by classical and biblical tradition. Beyond the *method*, and the concern for scientific objectivity, hermeneutics raises the question of the *truth* of symbols and allegories which goes beyond what is accessible by means of that method and from study of the letter (Gadamer, *Truth and Method*).

I.   CHRISTIAN MEDIAEVAL EXEGESIS AND THE RENAISSANCE: THE RETURN TO THE ORIGINAL TEXTS OF THE CLASSICS AND THE BIBLE

It is a serious historical mistake to try and jump from the culture of classical pagan antiquity to the Renaissance of the 16th cent., as if nothing worth mentioning had taken place in all that time. The «Middle Ages» was not a transient and decadent period, like crossing a desert, which the term «Middle Ages» suggests, as erroneously thought in the Enlightenment of the 18th cent. Instead, it should be said that it is not possible to understand everything that happened after the so-called «Modern Period», both in the field of thought and in political and social activity up to Hegel and Marx, without considering the long history of the Jewish-Christian tradition which came before it. Mediaeval exegesis has been largely neglected, except for works such as those by H. De Lubac and Beryl Smalley.

To the historical mistake of ignoring Christian patristics and the Jewish Talmud corresponds another mistake, no less historical, made in Jewish and Christian tradition as well as in Islamic tradition. This happens when they close themselves to any influence of secular culture and try to deny the space and time of the culture of the century, signified especially in the culture of the Renaissance and the Enlightenment, but already represented in the Middle Ages by the thought of Abelard, Averroes or Maimonides. This attitude of withdrawal prevailed in Judaism up to the 18th cent., when Spinoza was condemned for attempting a compromise between Judaism and the spirit of the Lights. Only after Moses Mendelssohn (1729-1786) did Judaism begin a process of openness to anything modern. In Christianity, this openness also continued to provoke great crises, from the mediaeval period up to very recent years.

The exegetical tradition of the Middle Ages evolved particularly in allegorical or spiritual interpretation of the Scriptures, although literal interpretation continued with a real rebirth in the 13th cent. (De Lubac). In the Middle Ages, the philological and historical meaning tended to be forgotten in preference for allegorical speculations or systematic constructions.

The most striking feature of mediaeval hermeneutics, however, is not this preference for the spiritual meaning, but rather its fondness of *multiple meaning*. The text of Scripture is not univocal but invites endless meanings. Against the monism of meaning which tries to understand the single meaning of a text, in the Middle Ages there evolved a sort of exegetical polymorphism, best expressed in the theory that Scripture has four meanings, already formulated by John Cassian (c. 400):

Littera gesta docet, quod credas Allegoria:
Moralis quida agas; quod tendas Anagogia.
The Literal sense teaches past Events; your beliefs, Allegory;
The Moral meaning, your duty; your upward goal, Anagogy.

Even when the emphasis fell on the spiritual and mystical meaning, the principle remained that the spiritual meaning alone is valid when based on the literal meaning. This principle prevented anarchic whimsicality and loss of the true meaning of the biblical message.

In the Middle Ages, development of allegory as an exegetical tool and development of dogma as rule of faith, strengthened the idea of unity and harmony. This was typical of theological systematics and of the ordered life in that period, but it entailed the grave risk of losing the true meaning of Scripture. Once biblical interpretation was ruled by the *sensus fidei* and by dogma, it ceased to be the principal domain of philology and theology. The path of salvation passed through the sacraments and mystical contemplation, and even through more external religious experiences such as pilgrimages and the veneration of relics rather than through the interpretation and proclamation of the Word of Scripture. These could be reduced to a mere arsenal of «proofs from Scripture», to be used in theological disputes and definitions of dogma.

Christian interpretation of the OT in the patristic and mediaeval periods followed the tracks that had been left from the beginning by the NT writings. If a NT passage interpreted an event or character from the OT as prefiguring Christ, the mediaeval commentators considered that to be the true meaning of the corresponding OT text. The text of Hos 11:1 seems to be interpreted in Mt 2:15 as a prophecy of the return of Joseph with the child and his mother from exile in Egypt. Christian interpretation could not help considering that to be the meaning of the text from Hosea.

Modern criticism has drawn attention to the fact that this type of exegesis is only a Christian adaptation of the OT which in some way does justice to the real and pre-Christian meaning of the OT. This does not mean that the NT writers and Christian exegetes were unable to see the original meaning of the OT texts. Christians, however, never viewed the OT as something separate and self-sufficient, much as the Jews read the *Tanak* in connection with the Mishnah and Talmud.

Augustine and Duns Scotus Erigena (c. 810-877) directed reading and Christian interpretation of the Bible towards greater spirituality. Exegesis of the sacred texts is not merely research into the meaning of the words but a search for the meaning of life. By accepting multiple meanings, it was possible for more and more new meanings to be derived from Scripture. In the Middle Ages, the Bible was read not for philological reasons but in order to meditate on the sacred texts as a way of reaching the mystery of God and Christ's cross.

The mediaeval Christian read the Bible in the present and in the timelessness of the eternal Word. This makes mediaeval bible reading completely distinct from modern reading which, even in the case of theological reading, is always done in reference to the past, setting the text in its historical context. In modern times, even the four mediaeval meanings have been isolated from scripture, and each is considered separately, especially the historical meaning which was very remote from any spiritual meaning.

In the Middle Ages, they were not content with the immediate meaning of the text, which they found totally inadequate. What sets the interpretation in train is not something found in the actual text (a philological, historical or theological difficulty), but the unceasing comparison of one text with another in the search for the message revealed in them all.

To summarise, mediaeval exegesis tends to assume the existence of a meaning which differs from the literal meaning and values the spiritual meaning more. At all events, texts which appear to contradict Christian doctrine in any way can have no other meaning except the figurative.

Through Jerome's Latin *Vulgate* the Bible was present in the Middle Ages at all levels of society, from the stained glass of cathedrals to illuminated manuscripts, not to mention literature imbued with biblical reminiscences, and the *scriptoria* of monasteries. Devout reading (*lectio divina*) was the foundation of monastic contemplation and scholastic debate. Augustine had made the study of letters the beginning of biblical studies. In his footsteps, Isidore of Seville (c. 560-636), Duns Scotus Erigena (c. 810-877) and the Venerable Bede (672/73-735) were the great masters of the sacred page (*sacra pagina*). After the decadence of the Merovingian period, the Carolingian renaissance of Alcuin (†804) produced a greatly needed recension of the text of the Vulgate, followed by another, completed by bishop Theodulph of Orleans (†821; cf. p. 356).

The humanist movement had its origins in Italy in the 14th-15th cents. and later spread through other European countries. The Renaissance, a movement of return to the classics of Greek and Roman antiquity, was also a rebirth of patristics and a return to the first centuries of Christianity. Its aim was to revive theology through Scripture, under the influence of the *devotio moderna* («modern piety»). Erasmus considered himself a true successor to Jerome and Augustine. He also used allegory, particularly to bring out the ecclesiological meaning (Krüger).

The Renaissance proclaimed the return to the original languages and sources of ancient literature, both classical and biblical. The *Adnotationes ad Novum Testamentum* («Annotations to the NT») by Lorenzo Valla (1407-1457) was nothing but revolutionary. It tried to deal with the NT just like any secular work, placing it under the same rigorous examination of textual criticism. In his attempt at reaching a synthesis between classicism and Christianity, Erasmus insisted on the importance of philology and grammar in order to understand the literal meaning of Scripture, but at the same time accepted its spiritual and moral value, thus showing the concern that humanists had for anything touching the world of ethics.

For the men of the Renaissance, the prime objective was to prove the authenticity of the texts and, once they were suitably edited, to translate them from the original languages. This approach could not fail to question the Vulgate's authenticity in respect of the Hebrew and Greek texts of the OT and NT. The LXX version also had to give way to the Hebrew text. No other matter made so obvious the Renaissance spirit of «back to the sources». Interest in Greek and Hebrew texts, and later in oriental languages, which were gradually included in the polyglots, also brought about the renewal of biblical exegesis.

The humanists, as editors of texts and historians of ancient cultures, personified the ideal of the academic philologist as heir to the librarians of Alexandria. Lorenzo Valla as a pioneer (1407-1457) and later, in the 16th cent., the Estienne brothers in France, John Colet in Britain, Luis Vives in Spain, Johannes Reuchlin in Germany and Erasmus in the Netherlands created a whole network of cultural relations which produced the new Renaissance man. As well as editing, translating and commenting on ancient texts, compiling dictionaries, writing essays on grammar and rhetoric and studies on history and archaeology, the humanists declared above all the liberation of intelligence with regard to the ancient texts and the traditions they transmitted. This pretension to the independence of critical truth could not fail to arouse strong reaction as happened in the «case of Galileo». The first humanists, such as Valla, respected Christianity, yet were certain that the sacred texts would resist the proof of truth implied by applying the new philology.

At first, the Renaissance maintained friendly relations between Christian culture and the new culture, which attempted to return to the pagan classics. The first generations of the Renaissance were ecclesiastics, including popes and cardinals, who cultivated the classics much as they venerated the sacred scriptures. A Roman cardinal was aware that he had given up reciting his breviary for fear of ruining his Ciceronian Latin. The Reformation was the first blow against this cultural compromise between Christianity and the Renaissance, denouncing the spiritual corruption which that compromise entailed.

II. PIETISM AND THE ENLIGHTENMENT: SACRED AND PROFANE HERMENEUTICS

The Dutch Calvinist, Hugo Grotius (1583-1645) and Thomas Hobbes (1588-1679) were the first to favour the need for making religion subordinate to politics and to read Scripture in the same way as any other ordinary historical work.

In the *Tractatus theologico-politicus*, a study of the relationship between politics and religion, Baruch Spinoza (1632-1677) intended to establish the conditions for a possible peaceful social co-existence within a just State. The *Tractatus* also includes a full analysis of the laws governing historical criticism, free of theological prejudice. Spinoza made very advanced statements for his time: Moses was not the author of the Pentateuch since the biblical books are very late compilations; the biblical texts have been modified by insertions and copyists' errors; it is necessary to study the style and rhetoric of the biblical authors in order to understand the meaning of each, etc. Interpretation of the Bible had an important function in the thought of Hobbes, Spinoza, Locke and of scientists such as Boyle and Newton. In the 16th-18th cents., political thought always looked for its inspiration in the Bible. Later, the Bible lost importance in philosophical thought and political theory. Kant's ethical rationalism was the main force to shape modern thought.

The works of Hobbes and Spinoza only made limited forays into exegesis. Richard Simon (1638-1712) was the first person to appear as a scholar devoting his life to the philological and historical analysis of the Bible. R. Simon, however, was not «modern man». His critical boldness in epistemology went hand in hand with strict traditionalism in doctrinal matters though this did not save him from condemnation by the Church.

A series of great scholars, stemming mainly from Leipzig and Göttingen, studied philology in a golden age: J. M. Gesner (1691-1761), J. A. Ernesti (1707-1781), Ch. G. Heynes (1729-1812), etc. Augusto Wolf (1759-1824) stood out from them all and opened the path to enlightened philology and romantic understanding of the texts. This meant ceasing to be guided by aesthetic and moral presuppositions and focusing directly on study of the classical texts, placing them in the context of the ancient world, which also included the world of art, sport, music, philosophy, etc. The «study of antiquity» (*Altertumswissenschaft*) and the German classicism of Goethe, Schiller, Wilhelm von Humboldt, etc., owe much to the influence of Wolf and also to the new way of approaching ancient art proposed at that time by J. J. Winckelmann (1717-1768). The Reformation and the Counter-Reformation had slowed up this trend, an outcome of the Renaissance. Wolf showed that the character of blind Homer, transmitted by tradition, was an image superimposed on what, in fact, had been the work of several authors. The statement that Homer was not the «author» of the *Iliad* could not fail to put into question the Mosaic authorship of the Pentateuch.

The development of classical philology, now independent of faculties of theology, entailed gradual abandon of study of the NT and the LXX version, which in language and character could not be considered as classical texts. Study of the Hebrew OT was also gradually marginalised and assigned to Semitics. This led to the complete separation of philology and history from theology. Biblical studies ceased to receive the influence of many philological advances of the period or received them late. Once again, as in the time of Tertullian, the opposition between «Athens and Jerusalem» raised its head.

Enlightened rationalism tended to consider the original and true meaning of the biblical text to be the historical meaning. Theological interpretation is nothing more than a distortion or late re-working of that primary meaning. This way of thinking is very remote from what pagan Greeks as well as Christians and Jews held. The ancients were not so much concerned with historical accuracy nor so taken up with methodological issues. It was considered more important to immerse oneself in the current of tradition which connected the classics with their imitators and interpreters, or the sacred books with the community of believers, Jews or Christians. The classics inspired poets, historians and philosophers much as the sacred books inspired the religious life of synagogues and churches. For the ancients it was not important to derive *new* meanings from sacred or secular texts, but to discover *many* meanings which lay hidden from the beginning in the depth of the texts.

The true roots of «historical criticism» of the Bible do not go back, as is often supposed, to Luther and the Reformation. Nor did Descartes' philosophy have much influence on the development of biblical criticism. Even though up to Descartes, humanism focused its interest on philology and on textual criticism in particular, its basic concern continued to be directed to the doctrinal and moral content of the texts, with a fairly dogmatic viewpoint, both ahistorical and atemporal.

Only after the Enlightenment did reason, changed to historical reason by Romanticism, become a guiding principle in biblical criticism. The Enlightenment continued to take from the domain of morals the criteria and parameters to establish a positive or negative judgment on the content of the biblical texts. Nor did Pietism succeed in overcoming the conflict between a historical vision of the Bible and its value as source of these sources of faith. The Enlightenment did not develop a true historical view of the biblical texts. It was directed too much towards atemporal dimensions and values, although they were no longer orthodox but belonged to natural religion. The historical approach did not begin until the close of the 18th cent. and developed throughout the 19th cent., particularly in Germany.

Alongside critical reading of the Enlightenment at the close of the 18th cent. there emerged a way of reading the Bible typical of pietism, later to be one of the sources of romantic hermeneutics. Immersed in the atmosphere of the *Aufklärung*, pietism tended to merge with deism to form a kind of universal religion. Pietism reacted against the demands imposed by philology, which restricted itself to purely historical study of the biblical texts in order to achieve the most objective possible approach to them, thus eliminating any reference to the world of the interpreter. Scientific exegesis thus abandoned the hermeneutic requirement of a search for the whole truth of the texts, involving the individual and social world of the interpreter.

The discipline of hermeneutics had its beginnings in the Protestant principle of the Bible being sufficient on its own and needing to be explained from within. This entailed the rejection of any authority external to the Bible, whether the authority of the Church or the authority of tradition. However, this did not mean proclaiming the principle of the autonomy of reason in interpretation of the sacred texts. The first to use the term «hermeneutic» seems to have been Johann Conrad Dannhauerus (Dannhauer) in his work *Hermeneutica sacra sive methodus exponendarum sacrarum litterarum* (1654) and earlier in his *Idea boni interpretis* (1630).

The *Institutiones hermeneuticae sacrae* of Johann Jacob Rambach (1723) still reflect a certain compromise between pietism and the Enlightenment. In the 17th and 18th cents., in German, Dutch and British universities, sacred and profane philology still belonged to the same faculty. Later, Johann David Michaelis (1717-1791), Johann Salomo Semle (1725-1791) and Johann Jacob Griesbach (1745-1812) established the historical-philological approach of hermeneutics. The work of Johann August Ernesti (1707-1781), *Institutio interpretis Novi Testamenti* (1761), instead, was a landmark for the later romantic hermeneutics of Schleiermacher.

III. ROMANTIC HERMENEUTICS: EXPLAINING THE LETTER AND UNDERSTANDING THE SPIRIT

The Enlightenment demanded a measurable and external analysis of empirical data, prescinding from individual and collective subjectivity. Romanticism, instead, tried to recover for science the breadth and meaning of subjectivity.

Whereas Voltaire and Hume had produced a methodology of suspicion or antipathy, Herder (1744-1803) and Schleiermacher (1768-1834) developed, instead, a hermeneutics of sympathy and trust. Herder and Schleiermacher tried again to reconcile two great intellectual and spiritual movements of the 18th cent., Pietism and Enlightenment. They wished to do justice to objective science without sacrificing subjective conscience: the historicity of faith cannot be separated from its validity in the present. Herder applied the principles of «historicism» to the study of religion, and also the category of *Zeitgeist* («the spirit of the age») according to which each period has its was *élan vitale* and each people develops its own history. The popular and legendary poetry of the Hebrews is the spontaneous display of their spirituality and soul. Herder read the Bible, trying to grasp its latent spirit. For this he revived the category of myth. Human consciousness cannot do without mythological imagery, which, rooted in the very depths of human being, renews poetry and religious faith unceasingly.

The romantics felt the need to develop a «philology of the spirit» alongside the «philology of the letter». If the interpretation of the Enlightenment had begun to discover the historical events of the texts, romantic hermeneutics tried to uncover the radical historicity of every interpretation, including also the critical and rational interpretation of the Enlightenment. Rational truth, which attempts to replace religious dogma, is as historical and relative as dogma. For the romantics, hermeneutic understanding consists of the complete reconstruction of the ancient cultural horizon with which the interpreter tries to be in sympathy. The emblematic examples of romantic history were, therefore, the work of Sainte Beuve on Port-Royal and of Jakob Burckhard on the culture of the Renaissance in Italy.

The period of Reason and the Enlightenment «evidently» believed in the progressive evolution of humanity on the road to the goal of future fulfilment. The romantics replaced the pattern of eternal return with evolutionist belief. Intelligibility is not found at the end of time but at each moment in history, especially at its origins. Every period encloses within itself the secret of its own value which is enclosed in a pure state at the first moments. If the Enlightenment was cosmopolitan and egalitarian, Romanticism was individual, delighting in the exotic, especially the Oriental and glorified national differences, Germanic, Jewish etc., almost always upheld by biblical tradition.

In the Enlightenment, the philosopher could believe in the transparency of meaning and reduce reality to mathematical formulas. Romanticism discovered dark and mysterious areas in meaning. The undoubted progress of reason and science could not deny that human knowledge always starts from the unknown and ends up in the unknown. Reality is covered with a cloak of mystery. Positivism and Romanticism, forced to be bed-fellows, could only oppose each other openly. Romanticism considers the Cartesian rationalism of clear and separate ideas as a delusion. It tries, instead, to recover the sense of the sacred, of what is mysterious and secret. The conflict between them remains reflected in Ranke's famous words: «The historian simply wishes to show what really happened». This contrasts with Herder's famous statement that «the history of the world is a judgment on the world», meaning that the interpretation of history triumphs over the pure fact of historical events. Nietzsche was able to say later that there are no deeds, only interpretations.

According to romantic hermeneutics, it is necessary to determine an essential difference between exegesis, *the explanation* of the letter of the text, and hermeneutics, a discipline of overall *understanding* which involves both the object of research and the subjective researcher. To interpret a text means to apply its meaning to the present, to be able to relate it with its own time and the period of the interpreter.

Romantic hermeneutics shifts the problem of interpretation from external space, where historical criticism and philology are at work, to the internal sphere, the place of understanding, which involves the text and encases the interpreter. It tries to establish a communication theory in the full meaning of the term, a universal theory (Schleiermacher) which resolves the problems affecting any communication, oral or written alike, of a biblical text, a legal text a theatrical piece or a musical score.

Understanding comes from the whole (*Verstehen aus dem Ganzen*, F. Schlegel). Romantic hermeneutics contrasts critical atomism (which dismantles the object studied) with the «canon of totality» (*Kanon der Ganzheit*). The 18th cent. was ruled by a cosmopolitan and synchronic view of the human universe, in accordance with an ideal of simultaneity. Romanticism replaced this static view with one that was diachronic and dynamic: reality has infinite forms which cannot all be expressed at the same time and can only be approached through a historical perspective.

Understanding texts is more than the application of the rules of linguistics. To understand is to allow the written word to speak, giving it back its oral force, like music to a score. It implies listening rather than examining. The meaning does not exist in the written document but becomes and takes form in the passage from the letter of the text to its recreation in the reader's mind, who is supposed to share the genius of the author.

IV. POSTMODERN OR POST-CRITICAL HERMENEUTICS: THE RETURN OF TRADITION, SYMBOL AND ALLEGORY

Postmodern or postcritical hermeneutics starts from the work of M. Heidegger and, in actual fact, from his analysis of pre-understanding or anticipation of meaning. Hermeneutics studies the conditions for the possibility of understanding, which includes «application». Understanding of a legal text is not complete until it has been applied well to individual cases. Equally, understanding of a religious text is not complete until the interpreter brings it up to date and gives it life, applying it to new periods and circumstances. The Enlightenment, which assumed the existence of an objective understanding, free from all prejudice and detached from all reference to the present, could conceive a pure and objective understanding, divorced from any application.

Gadamer tries not only to recover the concept of application but also the concepts of «prejudice» and «tradition», all discredited by the Enlightenment. An interpretation completely free of prejudice is not possible and the attempt to overcome all prejudice is itself a prejudice. Pre-judice is a necessary presupposition which makes judgment possible. There are legitimate and necessary prejudices. Tradition supplies these presuppositions to understanding. Tradition, especially tradition which comes from the classics and the Bible, has the function of mediating between the past and the present. Historical understanding consists precisely in mediating between one and the other. Accordingly, there is no understanding free of prejudices or references to historical tradition, or unconcerned with its application to the present. To understand is not to remove prejudices, especially those of the past, but to differentiate between true prejudices and false prejudices. This it does by a circular process of questions and answers until it reaches the appropriate question which allows the true reply to be unveiled.

In criticism of Gadamer's hermeneutical questioning, it must be said that he presents a universal hermeneutic which is far beyond the control of scientific method. Gadamer has not developed a true methodological analysis, so that it has been possible to accuse his hermeneutic theory of pandering to methodological nihilism and, as a result, relativism or anarchism of interpretation (Betti). It can also be objected that he gives too much weight to tradition, considered as a critical stance which allows choice of valid prejudices and rejection of the false. Enlightenment, on the contrary, accused tradition of being no more than a source of prejudices preventing free and rational judgment. Gadamer criticises the hermeneutics of the Enlightenment of having opposed tradition and reason, and insists that the transmission of tradition requires an exercise of reason and of freedom no less valid than creative and innovative activity.

Gadamer projects two images of himself. On the one hand, the radical critic who as a scientific theorist, emphasises the bankruptcy of the methodology of enlightened thought, placating a movement of return to what is really important, to the *truth* («to the thing», *die Sache*) which is beyond *method*. On the other hand, he provides the image of the less critical romantic, facing the past, the pre-scientific world, the good times of the past and the traditions of yesteryear, which have to be saved from the attacks of enlightened reason. In this way Gadamer appears to be the Hegelian to tries to harmonise everything.

Ricoeur attempts a closer approach between hermeneutic theory and methodological development, between the understanding of the meaning and the explanation of the linguistic structure.

V. MODERN BIBLICAL CRITICISM: HISTORICAL-CRITICAL METHODS

The increasing awareness of method in 18th cent. Enlightenment and the rise of historical awareness in 19th century Romanticism also brought a flowering of philological, historical and literary studies. These studies were directed principally at determining the authorship, place and date, sources and original meaning of the classical and biblical writings, just when the study of textual criticism begun in the Renaissance was reaching maturity. Enlightened and Romantic criticism developed the «historical-critical» methods which were immediately applied in the field of biblical studies. After textual and literary criticism, there came in turn on the scene the methods of the history of forms or genres, of the history of tradition and of the redaction history.

1. In the second half of the 19th cent., *source criticism*, first applied to the Homeric epics, developed the theory of four sources or documents from which the Pentateuch had been formed (Yahwist, Elohist, Deuteronomist and Priestly) and the two-source theory of the synoptic gospels. Knowledge of the libraries of the ancient Near East and of immense epigraphic and manuscript material gave the impulse to critical work on the OT and NT texts, to the study of literature and biblical history and to the study of comparative religions («History of Religions School»).

2. At the start of the 20th cent., the *history of forms* began. Its aim was to analyse typical forms of literary expression, especially in the oral or pre-literary phase (legends, hymns, laments, curses, etc.). Form criticism claimed to be an improvement on source criticism: the Pentateuch and the synoptic gospels are not so much compilations of written sources as the precipitate of popular traditions, oral in origin and as vivid and varied as life itself. Analysis of literary forms also had the intention of finding their original setting and transmission.

The expression «history of forms» (*Formgeschichte*) was used for the first time in M. Dibelius, *Die Formgeschichte des Evangeliums* (1919). Form criticism of the NT reached its zenith in works by K. L. Schmidt, M. Dibelius and R. Bultmann (*History of synoptic tradition*). This movement, in fact, goes back to the work of Hermann Gunkel (1862-1932) on the history of the literary genres of the OT (*Gattungsgeschichte*). Gunkel developed this method in his study of the book of Genesis and the Psalms, creating a full classification of prose genres (myths, legends, sagas, historical narratives, etc.) and poetic genres (oracles, hymns, proverbs, etc.) in the Bible. Gunkel also wished to study the settings of the OT genres in the social and collective life of ancient Israel (*Sitz-im-Volksleben Israels*). In the NT, Dibelius tried to determine the church setting in which the gospel forms and traditions were born and developed (*Sitz-im-Leben der Kirche*). This setting was only determined by the need of the early church to have didactic and homiletic material available. C.H. Dodd and J. Jeremias tried to go back to studying the circumstances of the earlier period in the life of Jesus of Nazareth (*Sitz-im-Leben Jesu*), to which the oldest gospel traditions go back. This setting was one of eschatological hope in an imminent divine judgment and of Jesus' disputes with the pharisees.

Like living species, literary genres are born, grow and die. Therefore, form criticism attempted to write a true history of the literature of Israel and of early Christianity. However, this type of literary criticism often became pure formalism, detached from history.

3. After genre and form criticism there emerged *redaction criticism* (*Redaktionsgeschichte*) which also claimed to be both a corrective and a supplement to form criticism. This last approach broke up the synoptic gospels into very many separate literary forms (parables, miracle stories, *logia*, etc.), making the evangelists mere editors of existing collections. Redaction criticism aimed at studying, instead, the redactional frame into which the old traditions seem to be set. Its interest is focused not so much on the old traditions as in their use by the final redactor, who could quite rightly be called an «author». Redaction criticism tried to re-establish the synoptic evangelists, made out to be the first theologians of Christianity and the first exegetes of the early Christian tradition.

Other modern exegetical approaches also belong to the same school of evaluating the complete work, of the biblical «book», not only its earlier sources or traditions. «Rhetorical criticism» attempts to discover the structural models which shape a literary work and the rhetorical figures which make the whole a unit (parallelism, anaphora, inclusio, chiasmus, etc.; Muilenburg, Jackson-Kessler). «Canonical criticism» studies the biblical texts from the perspective of the whole canon (cf. p. 416). Other modern approaches to biblical study focus on semiotics and sociology (Gottwald, Meeks, Holmberg).

VI. CRITICAL EXEGESIS AND BIBLICAL THEOLOGY

Within modern biblical exegesis there is a degree of scepticism towards historical criticism and critical historical methods. The results never seem to be conclusive or as objective as supposed, and its field of vision is turned towards the biblical texts as they were before the Bible ever existed. Also, it seems to be very reductionist regarding what the Bible actually is and has been over time. In fact, historical criticism cannot attain the objectivity it was supposed to in the last century, but it is necessary to state clearly that it continues to be valid today and can by no means be given up. Critical and methodological thought leaves room for logical reasoning, allows analysis to be checked and ensures that the results are valid (Oeming). The attacks against the use of historical-critical methods often come from attitudes hostile to the achievements of modern criticism, if not from decidedly conservative or «fundamentalist» positions. These accept the methods and results of textual criticism much more than the results of literary criticism. They think that textual criticism helps to recover the original text of the biblical books, assuming that the textual variants never affect essential matters of Christian doctrine. The biblical originals were free of mistakes which only occurred in copying the manuscripts. They try to ignore the existence of a diversity of texts before or at the same as the formative period of the masoretic text.

In the Jewish world, conservative movements tend to consider the masoretic text as free from mistakes and corruption. The continual use of the masoretic text in the liturgy and in law guarantees its faithful transmission.

Known textual variants are very rare and any in mediaeval manuscripts have no value. The biblical manuscripts found in the caves of the Dead Sea are mixed and «vulgar» texts, the product of a very careless textual transmission. The Samaritan Pentateuch also is of much lower quality than the masoretic text. The text of the LXX is a translation which can never replace the text in the original Hebrew language and was transmitted very carelessly by Christian copyists. In any case, its variants reflect the exegetical anomalies of the Greek translators.

As for literary criticism, Jewish conservatism and Christian conservatism have very different concerns. The need for Christianity to establish a historical connection with Jesus of Nazareth and the first apostles has no equivalent in Judaism. There, the Bible is basically the Torah or Law, and so not affected so much by historical criticism. The discrepancies between the books of Kings and Chronicles are more a worry to fundamentalist Protestants than to the Jews. A Jew can always remain content with the explanation that the book of Chronicles is a midrash on Kings.

Among Catholic scholars, but less among Protestants, it is common to make a distinction between «exegesis» and «interpretation». This only makes more obvious the unresolved tension between the demands of rational criticism and the value of theological interpretation. Exegesis is the domain of the biblical scholar who explains the texts of the Bible using historical-critical methods. Interpretation is the distinctive domain of the theologian, who develops and applies the biblical message, or justifies the development of dogmatic tradition with proofs taken from scripture. In the patristic and mediaeval periods, interpretation was a gift rather than a science. This charismatic gift was a guarantee that the interpretation of the Christian exegete had been executed in compliance with the Spirit and in agreement with the Truth. The Christian interpreted the Bible perceiving himself to be a link in a long chain of Church tradition. The Christian interpreter had a duty towards rational truth but even more to the Church of which he was a part. Truth and Mystery were the same thing and not two dimensions in a state of tension, as would appear to the modern interpreter after the critique of the Enlightenment. The conflict of the enlightened conscience between religious mystery, reduced to dogma, and rational truth, between considering the Bible as the word of God or reducing it to a mere historical document, has as yet not found a solution. Recent calls to a «post-critical interpretation», to the transition from historical interpretation to «spiritual» interpretation (cf. Dierlinger, Smend, Reventlow) or the replacement of a hermeneutics of suspicion with a hermeneutics of agreement open to transcendence (Stuhlmacher 1977), do no more than emphasise further the deep unease in which biblical studies finds itself, divided between the demands of criticism and the search for theological meaning.

«Biblical theology», which enjoyed a period of splendour in the mid-20th century, finds itself towards the end of the century in a situation of crisis. The Enlightenment has considered biblical theology to be a historical and descriptive discipline (J.Ph. Gabler in the 18th cent.). Along the same lines and following *W. Wrede*, 19th century criticism has tended to equate biblical theology with the history of the religion of ancient Israel.

In the 20th cent., *W. Eichrodt* had already accepted OT theology as presupposing the history of Israel and of its religion. However, he stated that understanding the unifying structure formed by OT beliefs is specific to biblical theology, not forgetting its close connection with the NT.

G. von Rad followed the methodological approach of contemporary criticism but, as a theologian, tried to interpret the OT as a book of the Church, introducing Christ into the OT and defending, through typological interpretation, the Christian and ecclesiological nature of the OT.

Childs emphasises the contradiction of the Biblical Theology Movement which moves between critical history and theology conceived as confessional faith in a neo-orthodox manner. Childs does not reject historical criticism but neither does he allow it any theological relevance. The theologian does not need to read the text in its historical context; the text, in the canon as a whole, can be approached directly as the word of God. Not all critics accepted the imposition of the canon as the way to approach the biblical texts, nor did all theologians accept such a «de-historicisation» of the biblical and Christian message.

The real challenge of biblical theology lies not so much in constructing *a* biblical theology, from whatever perspective (Zimmerli) as in accepting the implications of historical criticism as the supposition or basis of *the* biblical theology. It is perfectly legitimate to try to go beyond a simple historical and phenomenological description of the thought and religion of Israel, not limited by the bounds to criticism set by Wrede. However, it is not legitimate to project a particular confession of faith and faith itself onto historical events as neo-orthodoxy tries to do (Collins). Theological *language* is intrinsic to biblical material and should not be marginalised on the altars of secular interpretation, but just as physics has its laws, history and time impose on the texts limited frames of reference within which they have to be interpreted. The Talmudists and the Fathers of the Church were able to view the Bible as a whole and to move from one text to another without barriers of time, genre, content, etc. The historian cannot permit himself such acrobatics and feels constrained to respect the limitations of time. The interpreter, halfway between historian and theologian, tries to preserve the «time gap» (Gadamer) and to save the gap between the event and its meaning, the figure and the prefigured, the symbol and the symbolised, the letter of the text and the spirit which overflows it. The departure from Egypt of a few Israelite clans was a blurred event lost in history; the «Exodus from Egypt» is not just another event in history but the starting point of the Yahwist creed and of the faith and history of the people of Israel.

The *defeat of the dualism between the critical view and the believer's vision* of the Bible can only be achieved by a hermeneutics which takes seriously that the *Word* contained in the Bible was and is a historical *word*, rooted in past history, very remote from today. The critical baggage collected by modern science from the Renaissance until today supposes a whole series of victories which modern awareness can no longer relinquish. It is, in fact, the only entrance to the historical witness of the prophets and evangelists. The concern for origins marking historical studies, points in the same direction as theology, which depends on the testimonies concerning the first founders, Moses and Jesus of Nazareth. The methods and tools of criticism can be misused and lead to error. Its neutral and scientific character can be perverted if they are used to weaken the generative force of meaning which the Bible has, imposing on it certain prior set limits in terms of ideological presuppositions or in virtue of reductionism of any kind. However, critical rationality cannot be relinquished, even to construct a biblical theology of any kind.

VII. JEWISH BIBLE, CHRISTIAN BIBLE

The touchstone of Christian hermeneutics is the relationship between «Old» and «New Testament», like the relationship between a written and an oral Torah in Judaism (cf. p. 222). Schleiermacher explained the relationship between OT and NT in terms of promise-fulfilment, separating rather than uniting the two Testaments. For Schleiermacher, Judaism is more distant from Christianity than other religions. Christianity is not really based on the OT. Schleiermacher did not actually say that it had to be abandoned, but he assumes that Christian doctrine does not need to take it into account (Smend). A. von Harnack, who wrote a key work on Marcion, was not far from Marcionism in considering the OT as being the witness of a «religion foreign» to Christianity. Harnack noted that much of the criticism directed against Christianity refers in fact to the OT, so that the OT has to be relegated to the realm of apocryphal literature. To reject the OT in the 2nd cent. was a mistake which the Church correctly opposed. To retain it in the 16th cent. was something which the Reformation could not avoid. However, to continue to retain it as a canonical document of 19th cent. Protestantism is nothing but the result, according to Harnack, of religious and ecclesiastical paralysis. Friedrich Delitzsch went even further in his rejection of the OT; his ideas continued to have an influence in his time. According to Bultmann, for Christians the OT is neither revelation nor God's word. It is useful merely as the channel of «pre-comprehension» (*Vorverständnis*) of the NT. As such, it is useful, therefore, but not necessary. The history of Israel is not the history of Christians. God was able to show his grace in that history, but it is not intended for Christians nor does it concern them. For Jepsen, the OT only exists as part of the Christian canon and thus has no intrinsic value.

The rehabilitation of biblical theology takes on a new challenge here. Both from a historical perspective and a theological perspective, the touchstone for constructing biblical theology lies in *accepting and understanding the fact that the Bible has had a twofold historical force* (*Wirkungsgeschichte*), one Jewish, the other Christian. Certainly, Christian theology cannot help thinking that from the viewpoint created by the historical appearance of Christ the Messiah, Christian interpretation of the OT is the only valid and true interpretation. It cannot cease to accept, however, that from the perspective of the OT itself, before Christianity appeared, the interpretation of the OT which it developed is not the only possible interpretation of the *Tanak* (Rendtorff, Koch). This acceptance can open up the possibility of a dialogue between Jews and Christians on common ground, the OT and biblical religion (Levenson).

Study of biblical literature in the universities has the object of understanding the OT itself and the history of its growth and interpretation, literal and allegorical, in Judaism and in Christianity. Biblical studies investigate the Hebrew and Greek bible and the history of its historical relevance (*Wirkungsgeschichte*) in Judaism and in Christianity. The philologist, the historian and the theologian study one or other aspect of this definition, but the historical connection between them should not be forgotten.

If the critical rationalism of the Enlightenment developed and perfected *methods* of *literal, philological and historical* interpretation, in an attempt to arrive at objective exegesis, free from prejudice, it is necessary for post-critical and post-modern hermeneutics to recover sensitivity for *symbol and allegory* (Gadamer, «*Rehabilitation of allegory*») as a channel for reaching the *truth* of the texts, especially biblical texts.

It has been stated that the body of Jewish laws collected in the Mishnah does not match the legislation or Halakhah then in force, in the Second Temple period, but represents the legislation to come into force when the Messiah was to arrive, when he would come to rebuild the Temple of Jerusalem (Wacholder). The NT claims to have started this messianic and happy kingdom already, ruled by the spirit of the Blessed. The sacred texts of the Jewish and Christian utopias still struggle to make the real world conform to the spirit and letter of the Torah of Moses and the New Testament of Jesus of Nazareth.

BIBLIOGRAPHY

BERGER, P. - LUCKMANN, TH., *The Social Construction of Reality. A Treatise in the Sociology of Knowledge*, New York 1966.
BETTI, E., *Die Hermeneutik als allgemeine Methodik des Geisteswissenschaften*, Milan 1955.
COLLINS, J.J., «Is a Critical Biblical Theology Possible?», *The Hebrew Bible and Its Interpreters*, eds. H. Propp - B. Halpern - D.N. Freedman, Winona Lake IN 1990, 1-17.
DODD, C.H., *The Parables of the Kingdom*, London 1935.
DIBELIUS, M., *Die Formgeschichte des Evangeliums*, Tübingen 1919.
DIERLINGER, H., «Der Übergang von der geschichtlichen zur geislichen Bibelauslegung in der christlichen Theologie», *Die historische-kritische Methode und die heutige Suche nach einem lebendigen Verständnis der Bibel*, Munich-Zurich 1985, 89-11.
EICHRODT, W., *Theology of the Old Testament*, 2 vols., London 1961 and 1967.
EVANS, G.R., *The Language and Logic of the Bible: The Earlier Middle Ages*, Cambridge 1984.

EVANS, G.R., *The Language and Logic of the Bible: The Road to Reformation*, Cambridge 1985.

GADAMER, H.-G., *Truth and Method*, New York 1975.

GOLDINGAY, J., *Models for Scripture*, Grand Rapids MI 1995.

GOTTWALD, N.K., *The Tribes of Yahweh. A Sociology of the Religion of Liberated Israel, 1250-1050 B.C.E..*, Maryknoll NY 1979.

HOLMBERG, B., *Sociology and the New Testament. An Appraisal*, Minneapolis MN 1990.

JACKSON, J.J. - KESSLER, M. (eds.), *Rethorical Criticism. Essays in Honor of M. Muilenburg*, Pittsburgh PA 1974.

JEANROND, W.G., *Theological Hermeneutics*, London 1994.

JEREMIAS, J., *The parables of Jesus*, revised edition, New York 1963.

KOCH, K., «Der doppelte Ausgang des Alten Testaments in Judentum und Christentum», *Altes Testament und Christlicher Glaube*, Jahrbuch für biblische Theologie 6 (1991) 215-332.

KRÜGER, F., *Humanistische Evangelienauslegung. Desiderius Erasmus von Rotterdam als Ausleger der Evangelien in seinen Paraphrasen*, Tübingen 1986.

LOURDAUX, W. VERHELST, D., *The Bible and Medieval Culture*, Louvain 1979.

LUBACH, H. DE, *Exégèse médiévale. Les quatres sens de l'Ecriture*, 2 vols, Paris 1956-1964.

MACQUARRIE, J., *Twentieth-Century Religious Thought*, London 1988.

MAIER, G., *Biblische Hermeneutik*, Wuppertal-Zurich 1991.

MUILENBERG, J., «Form Criticism and Beyond», *JBL* 88 (1969) 1-18.

MURPHY, R.E., *Medieval Exegesis of Wisdom Literature. Essays by Beryl Smalley*, Atlanta GA 1986.

OEMING, M., *Gesamtbiblische Theologie der Gegenwart. Das Verhältnis vom AT und NT in der hermeneutischen Diskussion seit Gerhard von Rad*, Stuttgart 1987.

RÄISÄNEN, HEIKKI., *Beyond New Testament Theology. A Story and a Programme*, Philadelphia PA 1990.

RENDTOTFF, R., «Zur Bedeutung des Kanons für eine Theologie des Alten Testaments», *Wenn nicht jetzt, wann dann?*, Fest. H.-J. Kraus, eds. H.G. Geger *et al.*, Neukirchen-Vluyn 1983, 3-11.

REVENTOLOW, H. GRAF, *The Authority of the Bible and the Rise of the Modern World*, Philadelphia PA 1985.

RICOEUR, P., *Essays on Biblical Interpretation*, ed. L.S. Mudge, Philadelphia PA 1980.

ROBINSON, J.M., *A New Quest of the Historical Jesus and Other Essays*, Philadelphia PA 1983.

SABOURIN, L., *The Bible and Christ. The Unity of the two Testaments*, New York 1980.

SMALLEY, B., *The Gospels in the Schools c. 1100 - c. 1280*, London - Ronceverte 1985.

SMALLEY, B., *The Study of the Bible in the Middle Ages*, Oxford 1952.

SMALLEY, B., cf. MURPHY, R.E., and cf. WALSH, K.

SMEND, R., «Schleiermacher Kritik am Alten Testament», *Epochen der Bibelkritik. Gesammelte Studien*, Band 3, Munich 1991, 128-144.

SMEND, R., «Nachkritische Schriftauslegung», *Die Mitte des Alten Testaments*, ed. R. Smend, Munich 1986, 212-232.

STEGMÜLLER, F., *Repertorium biblicum medii aevi*, 5 vols., Madrid 1940-1955.

STEINMETZ, D.C. (ed.), *The Bible in the Sixteenth Century*, Durham and London 1990.

Hermeneutics. Texts and Interpretations

THISELTON, A.C., *The Two Horizons. New Testament Hermeneutics and Philosophical Description with Special Reference to Heidegger, Bultmann, Gadamer, and Wittgenstein*, Exeter 1980.

VANHOOZER, K.T., *Biblical Narrative in the Philosophie of Paul Ricoeur. A Study in Hermeneutics and Theology*, Cambridge 1990.

VERNET, A. - GENEVOIS, A.-M., *La Bible au moyen âge. Bibliographie*, Paris 1989.

VON RAD, G., *Old Testament Theology*, London 1962 and 1965.

WACHOLDER, B.Z., *Messianism and Mishnah. Time and Place in Early Halakhah*, Cincinnati 1979.

WALSH, K. - WOOD, D., *The Bible in the Medieval World. Essays in Memory of Beryl Smalley*, Oxford 1985.

Abbreviations of Biblical Books
(with the Apocrypha)

Old Testament

Gn	Genesis
Ex	Exodus
Lv	Leviticus
Nm	Numeri
Dt	Deuteronomium
Josh	Joshua
Jgs	Judges
1-2 Sm	1-2 Samuel
1-2 Kgs	1-2 Kings
Is	Isaiah
Jr	Jeremiah
Ezek	Ezekiel
Hs	Hosea
Jl	Joel
Amos	
Obad	Obadiah
Jn	Jonah
Mic	Micah
Nah	Nahum
Hab	Habakkuk
Zeph	Zephaniah
Hag	Haggai
Zach	Zachariah
Mal	Malachi
Ps(s)	Psalms
Jb	Job
Pr	Proverbs
Ruth	
Cant	Song of Songs
Ecc or Qoh	Ecclesiastes or Qoheleth

New Testament

Gospels

Mt	The Gospel according to Matthew
Mk	The Gospel according to Mark
Lk	The Gospel according to Luke
Jn	The Gospel according to John

Acts	*Acts of the Apostles*

Epistles / Letters

Rom	Romans
1-2 Cor	1-2 Corinthians
Gal	Galatians
Eph	Ephesians
Php	Philippians
Col	Colossians
1-2 Thess	1-2 Thessalonians
1-2 Tim	1-2 Timothy
Tit	Titus
Phm	Philemon
Heb	Hebrews
James	James
1-2 Pt	1-2 Peter
1-3 Jn	1-3 John
Jud	Jude

Ap	*Apocalypse*

Index of Subjects

abdecaries 109
'Abot (Treatise) 14, 150, 393
accents, accentuation 95, 276, 278
Acts of the Apostles 246, 249
Alexandria 124, 128ff, 302
– School of 116, 137ff, 528
– text of the NT 339, 345, 413, 412
Alexandrian 96ff
– Period 96
– text of the NT 339ff
– philology 138ff
allegory, allegorical 137, 475, 478, 533, 554
alphabet 59, 83ff, 110, 139
– Canaanite 85
– Phoenician 85
anthropomorphism 441
Antioch, School of 530
apocalypse, apocalyptic, apocalyptical 72, 161, 178, 194, 226, 228, 483, 492
– Jewish 184, 446, 448
Apocalypses 247, 249
apocryphal 43, 174, 249ff
– books 209, 236ff
– gospel 43, 248, 507
– literature 444
Apostolic Fathers 247, 250
apostolic period 237
Aquiba, school of R. 472
Aquila 284, 309, 313, 315
Arabic 84, 125, 364
Aramaic 68ff, 324ff
– language 68ff, 74, 324ff, 439
– script 84, 103, 371
Aristarchus 140, 151

Aristoteles, Aristotelianism 125, 541ff
Armenian 362
Augustine of Hippo 350, 531ff
authority 153, 255, 383, 452
authors, 'classical' 138

Babylonian Period 157
2 Baruch 112, 194ff
Bel and the Dragon 182
Ben Sira (= Ecclesiasticus) 112, 121, 181, 401
Bible 128, 201, 510
– ancient versions 348
– Christian 560
– Gnostic interpretation of 521
– Greek 179
– Hebrew 78, 175
– in the 2nd century 513
– in the Persian, Greek, and Roman Periods 43ff
– Jewish 560
– reading 117
– Sadducee 219
– trilingual 74ff
– translation of 121ff
biblical
– criticism 555
– exegesis 526
– interpretation 528
– manuscripts 376
– origins 291
– text 265ff, 453ff
– theology 557
book, sacred 128 ff, 148ff, 513
books, apocryphal 236ff

books, canonical 236ff
– NT 237ff
Byzantine
– Period 112
– text of NT 345

canon, canons 43, 45, 148ff, 236ff,
242ff, 254ff, 416ff
– biblical 98ff, 156 ff, 208ff
– Essene 224
– Hellenistic Jewish 232
– OT 46, 233ff
– NT 46, 251ff
– Pharisee 222
– Qumran community 227
– of sacred books 148
– Sadducee 217
– Samaritan 211
– unsuccesful 242
canonical 43
– books175, 236ff
– criticism 416ff
– text 420
canonicity 153, 253
canonization 151
Cappadocians 531
changes, accidental 371
changes, intentional 374, 406
Chronicles 110, 175
Christian, Christians 309, 510
– Bible 535, 560
– education 535
– exegesis 487
– hermeneutics 490ff
– recensions 309
– scriptures 537
Christianity 30ff, 116, 125
– Jewish 504ff
christological 497
classical
– culture 535
– education 535
– literature 100
– philology 94, 551ff
classicism, biblical 133
classics, Greek 149
Clement of Alexandria 240, 528
Clement of Rome 250, 515
codex, codices 98 ff, 133, 240, 273
confusion of letters 371ff, 405ff

consonantal (text) 61, 279
Coptic 361
copying of manuscripts, copyists 91,
115, 140, 371
criticism 382
– canonical 416
– external 408
– internal 409
– literary 390
– modern biblical 555
– textual 379, 381, 387, 390, 405
culture, classical 535
cuneiform writing 81, 82, 95

Damascus Document (CD) 456ff
Daniel, Book of 174, 178, 400
Dead Sea 87ff
Dead Sea Scrolls 29, 91, 285ff, 376ff
derash 475, 476
Deuterocanonical books 71, 179
Diaspora, Hellenistic Jewish 229ff
– canon 232
Diatessaron 238ff, 358ff, 407
Didaché 240ff, 251
doublets 390

Ecclesiasticus cf. Ben Sira
eclectic (text), eclecticism 338, 410
editions 336
– duplicate or double 95, 383, 393ff
– modern 268, 336
– first printed 270
education 535
Egypt, Egyptian 82, 111, 149
Enlightenment 550ff
1 Enoch 112, 194ff
epigraphy 86ff, 387
eschatology, eschatological 169, 497
4 Esdras 156, 194ff
Essenism, Essene 153, 224ff
– canon 224
Esther (book of) 175, 182, 399
exegesis, exegetical 276, 321, 431, 444,
486
– at Qumran 457
– between the 3rd and 5th centuries 528
– Christian 487, 546
– critical 557
– in the West 531
– Jewish 482, 484, 486, 487

- pesher 476
- rabbinic 475ff
- rules and methods 479
- scriptural 452
interpretation of the OT
- Gnostic 524
- in Hellenistic Jewish Literature 460
- in the NT 490ff
- in Qumran writings 452
- and Jewish-Christianity 504ff
Irenaeus 240
Irenaeus of Lyons 517
Ishmael, school of R. 472
Islam 105
Israel 109 ff

Jeremiah 395
Jerome 353ff, 531
Jesus of Nazareth 74, 107
- and the OT 495
- quotations by 496
Jewish 209, 312
- apocalyptic 446, 448
- Bible 560
- Christianity 504, 505, 507
- elements in the NT 32
- exegesis 482ff, 484, 486, 487
- literature 210
- recensions 312
- writings 498
Jewish-Christian, Jewish-Christianity
504ff
- definition 504
- sources for the study of 507
- ideas and symbols 507
- exegesis of the OT 508
Job 122, 399
Jonah 175
Joseph and Aseneth 186, 245, 403
Josephus, Flavius 112, 162, 466ff
Jubilees 153, 169, 194ff, 228, 469
Judaism 10ff, 37, 115, 431, 510ff
- hellenising of 37ff
- Hellenistic 37ff, 229, 303, 460ff
- rabbinic/normative 105, 222ff
Judith, Book of 182
Justin 240, 516

kaige (recension) 164, 314, 381
karaism 483

koiné (language) 71ff, 114, 319

Lamentations, Book of 175
languages of the Bible 58ff, 121
language
- Aramaic 68ff, 121, 324ff
- Greek 71ff, 121ff
- Hebrew 59ff
- Latin 59ff
- sacred 58, 130
- Semitic 59ff
- Syriac 358ff
Latin 59ff, 349ff
Latin literature 100
lectio brevior 380
lectio difficilior 380
lectionaries 343
Letter of Barnabas 241, 245, 515
Letter of Jeremiah 180
Letter to the Hebrews 503
Letters of the Apostles 246
letters, shape of 103ff
lexical, lexicography 62ff, 75, 387
library 137, 286
linguistics 63
literacy 110
literal (meaning, exegesis) 482, 533
literature
- apocryphal 444
- early Christian 236ff, 243ff
- exegetical 201
- Gnostic 525
- Hellenistic Jewish 460ff
- parabiblical 169, 184
logia of Jesus 245, 409, 413
Lucian, Lucianic, protolucianic 310ff

Maccabees 181
Maccabaean Period 161
Manichee, Manichees 526
manuscript, manuscripts 272ff, 341, 343
- biblical 376
- copying of 94, 115ff.
- New Testament 340ff
- Septuagint 305
Masorah, masoretic (text) 272ff, 393ff,
495
Mesopotamia 81, 82, 111, 121
messianism, messianic 438, 511, 531
methodology 336, 370, 382ff, 407,

479ff, 493
midrash, midrashim, midrashic 201,
476, 482
minuscule 103, 343
Mishnah 121, 165, 431ff
modern editions 268, 336
modern research 266
modernisation 374

Nag Hammadi 236, 521
Near East 81ff
Nehemia 175
Neoplatonism 539
Neophyti (Targum) 326ff
New Testament
– Alexandrian text 339, 345, 413, 412
– ancient versions 348ff
– biblical quotations in NT writings
  503
– caesarean text of NT 347
– canonical books 237
– NT exegesis of the OT 493
– formation of the canon 251
– genres 242
– Greek text 333ff
– Greek and Jewish elements 32
– history of the text 263ff
– NT interpretation of the OT 492
– manuscripts 340
– neutral text of the NT 339, 413
– promise and prophesy of 519
– textual criticism 405ff
– versions 263ff
nomina sacra 413

Old Latin (Version) 310, 349ff, 379
Old Testament
– ancient versions 348ff
– as promise and prophesy of the NT
  519
– Greek version cf. Septuagint
– Aramaic versions 324ff, 439ff
– Christian canon 233
– exegesis 434, 508
– Hebrew text 268ff
– hermeneutic problem 513ff
– history of the text 263ff
– interpretation 436ff, 444, 452, 460,
  490
– in the gospels 501

– textual criticism 264, 370ff
– traditions in Gnostic literature 525
– versions 263ff, 344
– the problem of the OT 217, 252, 514,
  518
oral (transmission, tradition) 94ff
Origen 240, 311, 528

paideia 536
palaeography 86ff
paleo-Hebrew (scripture, scriptures)
90ff
Palestine 83
papyrus, papyri 89, 95, 101, 340
parallels 149ff
paraphrases, periphrastic 439, 440
parchment 89, 95
patristic 344
Paul, pauline 497ff,
– and the OT 497
– exegesis 499
Pentateuch 126, 211ff
– Samaritan 211, 297ff
– Targumim 326
– translation into Greek 302
Persia, Persian Period 43, 96, 210
peshat 475
pesher, pesharim 201, 475
Peshitta 359ff
Pharisees, Pharisee 222ff, 431
– canon 222
Philo of Alexandria 163, 230ff, 460,
464ff, 500, 528
philology 139ff
– Alexandrian 137ff
– comparative semitic 387
philosophy, Greek 76, 537ff
pietism 550
Platonism 540ff
prophets 201
prophetic 180
Prophetic Books 159, 329
Psalms 201

Qoheleth 177
Qumran 31, 97, 103, 194, 454
Qumran community 224ff
– origins 224
– character 224
– biblical canon 227

Torah 117ff, 158, 214, 222 ff
– oral 222
– written 222
tradition 431
translation 121ff, 302, 318, 439, 440
transmission 94ff
– oral 94, 104ff
– textual 94ff, 356, 371
– written 94ff
trilingual, trilingualism 8, 74

Ugaritic 388
uncials 86, 103, 341
unity of the two testaments 518

versions, ancient 348ff, 378
Vetus Latina cf. Old Latin (Version)
Vetus Syra 358
vocalic text 272
vocalisation 272ff, 278
volumen 96
Vulgate 336, 353, 379, 548

Wirkungsgeschichte 430, 561
Wisdom Literature 194
Wisdom of Solomon 174, 181, 452
writers 461
writing 80ff, 105ff, 111, 307, 341ff,
407ff
– alphabet 83
– cuneiform 81
– hieroglyphic 82
– materials
– parabiblical 194
– sacred 132
Writings 159, 330
– Jewish 498
– Latin 104
– Qumran 483

Zenodotus 151, 154

EASTERN SEMINARY LIBRARY
BS445.T6813 1998   128947
Trebolle Barr   The Jewish Bible and the C

3 0094 0004 9168 5

BS 445 .T6813 1998

Trebolle Barrera, Julio C.

The Jewish Bible and the
 Christian Bible

128947

The Library
Eastern Baptist Theological Seminary
6 Lancaster Avenue
Wynnewood, PA   19096